D1436191

THE BUILDINGS OF ENGLAND
EDITOR: NIKOLAUS PEVSNER
ASSISTANT EDITOR: JUDY NAIRN
BE38
WEST KENT AND THE WEALD
JOHN NEWMAN

*The publication of this volume has been made
possible by a grant from*
THE LEVERHULME TRUST
to cover all the necessary research work

THE BUILDINGS OF ENGLAND

West Kent and the Weald

BY

JOHN NEWMAN

★

PENGUIN BOOKS

Penguin Books Ltd, Harmondsworth, Middlesex, England
Penguin Books Inc., 7110 Ambassador Road, Baltimore, Md 21207, U.S.A.
Penguin Books Australia Ltd, Ringwood, Victoria, Australia

—

First published 1969

—

Copyright © John Newman, 1969

Made and printed in Great Britain
by William Clowes and Sons, Limited, London and Beccles
Gravure plates by Harrison & Sons Ltd
Set in Monotype Plantin

TO
MY PARENTS
who brought me up in Kent

CONTENTS

Map References

*

The numbers printed in italic type in the margin against the place names in the gazetteer of the book indicate the position of the place in question on the index map (pages 2–3), which is divided into sections by the 10-kilometre reference lines of the National Grid. The reference given here omits the two initial letters (formerly numbers) which in a full grid reference refer to the 100-kilometre squares into which the country is divided. The first two numbers indicate the *western* boundary, and the last two the *southern* boundary, of the 10-kilometre square in which the place in question is situated. For example Chislehurst (reference 4070) will be found in the 10-kilometre square bounded by grid lines 40 and 50 on the *west* and 70 and 80 on the *south*; Tenterden (reference 8030) in the square bounded by grid lines 80 and 90 on the *west* and 30 and 40 on the south.

The map contains all those places, whether towns, villages, or isolated buildings, which are the subject of separate entries in the text.

EDITOR'S FOREWORD

Mr Newman's two volumes on Kent are in my opinion the best of the whole series. He had several advantages over me. He is Kent-born and has spent most of his life in Kent, he did his own library preparation, and he travelled a little more at leisure than I usually do. But that is surely not all. I have nothing but admiration for his perspicacity and his talent for finding the mot juste. *Mr Newman, after completing his text, provided me with a list of the hundred best or most interesting places. I visited nearly all of them, reading his text as I went round. I found hardly anything to correct and little in the way of suggestions for adding material. Occasionally these will be found marked with my initials.*

AUTHOR'S FOREWORD

*First of all the scope of these two volumes must be explained. As
their names suggest, they do not cover one of them West Kent the
other East in the way Kentish Men and Men of Kent would understand. That division was tried to start with, but West Kent came
out much too slim, and East Kent much too weighty. The boundary
line eventually settled on takes the Medway towns and their
administrative dependencies into West Kent and the Weald. It
then follows the M2 for a short way, the A229, and so along the
A20 eastward from Maidstone to Hythe. Places along the A20 are
distributed to one volume or the other according to the position of
the church, churches N of the road taking their places into North
East and East Kent. So that is where Harrietsham will be found,
and Charing and Hythe. Maidstone, on the other hand, is in West
Kent and the Weald; and so are, for example, Bearsted, Lenham,
Ashford, and Sellindge. The line is inevitably somewhat arbitrary,
and I can only hope that users will not find it frustrating.*

*Still on boundaries, the normal practice of the series to follow the
most up-to-date county boundaries has been abandoned in order to
include in Kent the area that has since 1965 come under Greater
London. As the volumes on all the other Home Counties had been
published under the old dispensation, it seemed right to treat Kent in
the same way, and not reserve the new London boroughs of Bromley
and Bexley for the volume London III, which will not appear for
several years more.*

*I have done all the preparatory extracting of material for these
volumes, as well as writing them; and the list of those to whom I owe
a debt of gratitude is correspondingly long. In the first place Professor Nikolaus Pevsner's decision to give one of his drivers a chance
as an author has brought me, together with some misery, a great deal
of enjoyment. As a driver I could not help but learn much; and
Professor Pevsner has completed his role as unobtrusive mentor by
reading the typescript, taking it round with him to a hundred or so
of the juiciest places, and leaving much good advice in the margins.
This must not, however, be taken to imply that he is responsible for
more than a handful of the conclusions and comments here expressed.*

*Early on, Mr John Hopkins, Librarian of the Society of Anti-
quaries, generously provided a room during a whole year for me and*

my ever-growing piles of papers. I also want to thank Mr Nigel Gunnis for allowing me the privilege of working in the library of his brother, the late Mr Rupert Gunnis, who, sadly, died before he had had time to do more than promise to help me. These volumes are the poorer for not having had the benefit of Mr Gunnis's unrivalled knowledge of Kentish matters.

What I am not responsible for are the introductions and gazetteer entries on building materials, Prehistory, and Roman Kent. These have been in the usual hands, those respectively of Mr Alec Clifton-Taylor, Mr Derek Simpson, and Professor Barry Cunliffe. Their experience guarantees the standard of these parts.

I have also benefited from sources of information familiar to readers from previous volumes. The Ministry of Housing and Local Government's duplicated lists of buildings of architectural or historic interest (here abbreviated MHLG*) led me to many buildings I would otherwise never have known about. The same can be said of the National Monuments Record (*NMR*), rich in photographs of Kent buildings. Information on Victorian buildings is, as always, derived largely from unpublished sources. The late Mr H. S. Goodhart-Rendel's list of Victorian churches and their architects (abbreviated* GR*) still takes pride of place. Then there is Mr Peter Ferriday's Index of Restorations (*PF*), on permanent loan to* The Buildings of England*. The many facts and interesting details culled by Mr Geoffrey Spain from the Victorian technical journals (*GS*), and Sir Thomas Kendrick's Index of Stained Glass (*TK*), have also, through their kindness, been available to me. Mr A. C. Sewter sent a list of all the Morris glass in Kent, and Dr Paul Thompson a list of Butterfield's works there. In addition, Canon Bernard Wigan made a most generous, unsolicited offer to consult the parish papers held at the County Archive Office, Maidstone, and at Rochester for the Rochester Diocese. Much information on* C 19 *and* C 20 *restoration and fittings came to light, and whatever appears in the pages of* West Kent and the Weald *from that source is indicated by the initials* BW*.*

For timber-framed buildings, where help was most sorely needed, help of the most substantial kind has been given by Mr. E. W. Parkin and Mr S. E. Rigold, both of whom have allowed me to make use of their unpublished researches. A third expert in this field, Mr Kenneth Gravett, has read almost the whole text of both volumes and made many comments and improvements. Mr Nicholas Taylor has performed the same service with an eye to Victorian and later omissions. Conversation with Mr Taylor is always instructive, and my text has gained a good deal from what I have learnt in conversing with him. Some of the talk took place at Steventon, where Mr Emil Godfrey allowed us to go through the drawings of George Devey.

Local librarians have been a tower of strength. The heaviest barrage of questions was directed at Mr A. H. Watkins and his staff at Bromley (Local History Librarian, Miss E. Plincke), and at Mr R. G. Bird at Tunbridge Wells (Reference Librarian, Miss Jean Mauldon). Others who were particularly helpful were Mr John Walters of Broadstairs, Mrs Sylvia Corrall of Dover, Mr K. C. Sussams of Folkestone, Miss Anne Roper of Hythe, Mr G. E. Clarke of Margate, and Mr. B. C. Darbey of Ramsgate.

Many owners and custodians of houses and many incumbents have received me kindly and given valuable information. It is impossible to do more than thank them collectively, and point out that the description in these pages of private houses does not in any way imply that members of the public are admitted. Particular thanks however must be expressed to Mr L. R. A. Grove, Curator of Maidstone Museum, to Dr Felix Hull, the County Archivist, and to Dr William Urry, Canterbury Cathedral Librarian; to Mr Gerald Cobb, Mr H. M. Colvin, Mr C. R. Councer, Mr P. A. Faulkner, Mr John Harris, and Mr Harold Kalman for generously making available unpublished material, to Sir Kenneth and Lady Clark for giving every facility for solving the problems of Saltwood Castle, to Viscount De L'Isle of Penshurst Place, to Mr Edward Hollamby of Red House, Bexleyheath, to Mr Christopher Hussey of Scotney Castle, to Dr S. G. Brade-Birks, Rector of Godmersham, to the Rev. D. Ingram Hill for taking me to inaccessible places at Canterbury, to Mr Jonathan Coad for being my guide to Chatham Dockyard, to Professor G. Zarnecki for advice on Saxon and Norman sculpture, to Mr P. J. Tester for advice on tricky buildings in North West Kent, to Mr B. N. Nunns for help at Sidcup, to Mr A. D. Stoyel for help on churches round Otford, and to Mr H. E. Gough for help at Herne Bay.

The mass of correspondence was made possible by secretarial help given by Mrs Ingrid Wolfers, Mrs Ilse Ahmad, and, in particular, Mrs Mary Mouat. But the last and largest bouquet goes to my mother, who, with inexplicable enthusiasm and well nigh faultless accuracy, typed both volumes.

The gazetteers follow the normal conventions of the series. I have myself seen everything described. Brackets mark the exceptions to this general rule, where descriptions are based on information gained from some other source. Information ought to be as complete as space permits for churches prior to c. 1830, and for secular buildings up to that date of more than purely local interest. Moveable furnishings

*are not included in houses, but they are in churches. Exceptions to
the latter rule are plain fonts, altar tables, hatchments, chests,
chairs, bells, and poor boxes. Royal arms and coffin lids with foliate
crosses are mentioned occasionally, church plate of after 1830 only
rarely.*

*Victorian and later buildings are so numerous that a more rigorous
selection was inevitable; as usual, selection was dictated by architectural value or by significance otherwise in the light of architectural
history. Here too information was more erratic, so that also dictated
selection to some extent. Much that would have deserved a mention
must have escaped the net, especially in the parts of the county in
easy reach of London. For this reason, and because of the frailty of
human nature, prone to omission and error, readers are implored
to inform author or editor whenever they notice that something
important has been left out or that something that has gone in is
wrong.*

INTRODUCTION

PREHISTORY

BY DEREK SIMPSON

THE earliest evidence for human settlement in Kent is provided by hand-axes of Acheulean type from gravel deposits of the second interglacial period at Bowman's Lodge, Dartford Heath, Elham (E), and Cuxton, and of later date in the glacial period the human remains from Swanscombe. Apart from the rock shelters adjacent to Oldbury Hillfort, Ightham, none of these finds is associated with any form of settlement site and the same is true of artefacts of the succeeding Mesolithic period. Beneath The Chestnuts Neolithic barrow, Addington, was an extensive scatter of occupation debris and hearths associated with a Mesolithic flint industry; and surface scatters of flint-knapping debris and tools from other sites in the county (e.g., Holt Hill, Aylesford; Well Hill, Orpington) indicate the presence of similar temporary camps of hunters.

The first field monuments to survive in the county belong to the succeeding phase of early farming communities. The picture given by these monuments is a one-sided one, however, as the majority are sepulchral. Jullieberries Graves, Chilham (E), is the only example of an earthen long barrow in the county, a type which is better represented in the counties to the N and W. An important find from this site was a thin-butted flint axe of Scandinavian type, and similar axes occurred as stray finds at Ramsgate and Canterbury (both E). Similar Continental links have been suggested for a small group of five stone-built chambered tombs in the Medway region, although antecedents are also to be found for the form in South West England and Brittany. All these sites have been badly damaged in the past, and little remains of the oval or rectangular mounds which originally covered them (e.g., The Chestnuts, Addington; Kits Coty, Aylesford); documentary evidence indicates the presence of further tombs now completely destroyed. The only settlement sites of the period, at Grovehurst, Horsmonden, Milton Regis (E), and Wingham (E), are marked by circular or oval pits, probably serving as granaries, associated with round-based western Neolithic pottery, flint artefacts, and at Wingham an antler comb used in skin dressing. Elsewhere stray finds of flint and stone artefacts, including a ground stone axe from the axe factory of Tievebulliagh, Co. Antrim, found at Sittingbourne (E), complete the evidence for this phase of settlement, which probably did not begin until c.2500 B.C.

A cultural break in the prehistory of the region occurs after c.2000 B.C., when immigrants from the Rhineland settled in southern and eastern Britain. Twelve sites in Kent have produced burials associated with their characteristic drinking cups or Beakers. The barb and tang flint arrowheads which accompanied the later burials in The Chestnuts chambered tomb, Addington, must also belong to this group and probably too the jadeite axe from Canterbury (E), indicative of cross-channel trade. Where the circumstances of the burial have been recorded, the Beakers accompanied inhumation burials in pit graves unmarked by any covering mound. It is to the Early Bronze Age that one must therefore ascribe the majority of round barrows in the county, distributed largely on the chalk plateau of East Kent. Few have been excavated; a number may be of Roman or Saxon date. The most important Early Bronze Age grave groups (1650 to 1400 B.C.) are the incense cups from Tilmanstone (E) and Luddington Wood, Bekesbourne (E), segmented faience beads accompanying the cremation beneath the bowl barrow at Ringwould (E), a large bronze dagger, knife, and axe from a flat grave at Aylesford, and a bronze halberd from Faversham (E). All these objects are characteristic of the Wessex culture with its centre in Wiltshire and Dorset. The wealth of this culture, as attested by the richness of the grave goods, appears in part to have been based on the control of important trade routes between Ireland and the Continent, and the occurrence of decorated bronze axes of Irish type in Kent suggests that it was along this route that much of the trade with Northern and Central Europe passed. The evidence for this period is again provided largely by funerary monuments, although a possible settlement site may have existed on Broomwood Hill, St Paul's Cray. Towards the end of the period of the Wessex culture there appears to have been an actual population movement from South East England to the Low Countries, so the close similarity of pottery and other finds in the two areas suggests. Again Kent appears to have been one of the regions from which this migration took place; urns decorated with applied horseshoe shaped slips of clay as at Ringwould and Capel le Ferne (both E) find close parallels in

Holland. In the later Bronze Age continuing links with the Continent and with Ireland are marked by finds of gold bracelets and armlets (e.g. Aylesford, and Canterbury, E) and by continental forms such as razors (e.g. Ebbsfleet, Thanet, E), swords (Allhallows, Hoo), and other metalwork of Western European type. With one exception these objects occur as individual stray finds or as components in metalworkers' hoards (e.g. Marden, Saltwood, E, Sittingbourne, E). The exception is the hoard from Minnis Bay, Birchington (E), which came from one of a series of (? storage) pits containing pottery and occupation debris. This latter site is one of the very rare settlements of the period.

The introduction of iron tools and weapons in the C6 was not accompanied by any marked change in the economy of the period. It has been demonstrated elsewhere in Britain that the economic unit was the individual farmstead with its associated field systems, largely cereal-producing, the products stored in basket-lined silos in the farmsteads. This pattern was developed early in the Bronze Age and remained little altered until the Roman occupation. No complete Iron Age farmstead has been excavated in Kent, but sites such as Stone Castle Quarry at Greenhithe, Crayford, and Lullingstone, with disused grain storage pits containing Iron Age A and B pottery and artefacts, must belong to this category. Growing population pressure and land hunger, in association with the need to protect cattle, the symbol of wealth in Celtic society, gave rise to the construction of hillforts. Eleven examples are known in the county, the majority belonging to the C3 and C2 B.C.

At the beginning of the C1 Kent received its last wave of immigrants before the Roman conquest – the Belgae, from Northern France and Gaul. Technologically and socially more advanced than the indigenous Iron Age peoples, they had occupied almost the whole of South East England by the end of the C1 B.C. Among the innovations they introduced were coinage, wheel-turned pottery, and a more efficient form of traction plough enabling the heavier clay soils to be cultivated for the first time. Referring to the Belgae, and specifically to the group in Kent, Caesar states that they were the most civilized of the peoples of Britain. Again one knows little of the settlements of the Belgae in Kent, although farmsteads such as that at Crayford have produced wheel-turned pottery and Belgic occupation is attested beneath the Roman sites of Richborough and Reculver (both E). Hillfort building was not a general feature of Belgic strategy, although the earlier fortifications at Oldbury, Ightham, were remodelled and a broad flat-bottomed ditch constructed after the pattern of defensive Belgic sites in Northern France, while Bigbury, Harbledown (E), has produced a considerable quantity of Belgic metalwork suggesting continuing occupation. The cremation cemeteries of Aylesford, Swarling (Petham, E), and Deal (E) illustrate a further aspect of Belgic culture, and the imported brooches and bronze vessels of North Italian type emphasize the commercial advantage of control of the short sea route to the Continent.

Julius Caesar mentions four men in Kent who styled themselves kings during his campaigns of 55 and 54 B.C., and subsequent coin evidence shows that the area was ruled successively by Dubnovellaunus, who also ruled over the Trinovantes of Essex, Eppilus, the king of the Atrebates, whose centre of power lay to the N and W, and finally by the great Cunobelin, in whose reign the Catuvellauni overran much of South East England.

ROMAN KENT

BY BARRY CUNLIFFE

KENT was the first county of Britain to experience the force of the Roman armies, when in 55 and 54 B.C. Julius Caesar led his somewhat unsuccessful raids into, and rapidly out of, the hostile land. The warlike natives, treacherous tides, and internal politics preserved the country from further attack until, in A.D. 43, the armies, this time led by Aulus Plautius on behalf of the Emperor Claudius, once again rounded the Kentish coast to land on the sandy and unoccupied promontory of Richborough (E), where they proceeded to set up a supply base of some magnitude. There can be little doubt that the main disembarkation took place here, but the possibility of landings on a smaller scale elsewhere around the coast cannot be ruled out. From Richborough the army marched, largely unopposed, across East Kent to the Medway where, after a two-day battle, they successfully smashed the local resistance and were able to cross the Thames and halt temporarily before marching on Camulodunum. The centre of the war soon moved on, leaving Kent as a quiet backwater but for the Richborough supply base, and the military road – Watling Street – which linked it to London.

Civilian development began immediately. Two of the pre-Roman centres, Rochester (Durobrivae) and Canterbury

(Durovernum, E), both astride Watling Street on important river crossings, grew rapidly as market and administrative centres, but Rochester remained surprisingly small and was only 23 acres in extent when, in the late C2, it was enclosed by an earthen rampart and later a stone wall. The reason probably lay in its stifling nearness to London, only 28 miles away; nevertheless it would have functioned as an important posting station between Canterbury and the capital. Canterbury, on the other hand, developed into a densely packed town of more than 120 acres unhindered by the presence of walls until the late C3. With its marble-inlaid basilica, large theatre, regular streets, and fine town houses it was a typical flourishing cantonal capital. Indeed, it probably maintained its vigorous growth into the period of the Saxon settlement. Of the other settlements along Watling Street, Ospringe (E), Springhead near Gravesend, and Crayford, little is known except at Springhead, where excavations have uncovered an interesting religious complex. In all probability these settlements served as posting stations and trading centres: there is nothing incongruous in finding religious and commercial activities closely interwoven. Maidstone, too, originated as a Roman settlement on the road leading S from Rochester to Hastings and Lympne.

Two other minor towns of a rather different nature lay at the ports of Richborough and Dover (both E). Of these Richborough (Rutupiae) began as the most important. In about A.D. 85 the sprawling civilian growth, which sprang up after the army had moved out, was cleared away to make room for a huge triumphal monument, a quadrifrons, encased in marble and ornamented with bronze statuary, presumably commemorating the completion of the conquest of Britain. The late C1 and early C2 saw the growth of a substantial civilian settlement around the monument, with well-laid out streets, a masonry *mansio*, shops, and other buildings. For some reason, however, a steady decline seems to have set in some time about A.D. 150. The explanation may well lie in the gradual increase in the importance of Dover (Dubris) both as a naval base and as a port of entry, with its less silted harbour flanked by two magnificent lighthouses sited high on the neighbouring hills.

The countryside was densely settled. More than forty villas are at present known, most of them hugging the valleys of the Darent and Medway and the line of Watling Street. It is difficult to generalize about the style of building and date, but there is a distinctly local flavour about Kentish villas compared with those found elsewhere. Some, for example, were constructed in masonry at an unusually early date in the late C1 (cf. Eccles near Aylesford) and many were provided with underground cellars similar to those found on adjacent parts of the Continent. There are also structural and planning differences which give the impression of a distinct Kentish vernacular, deriving perhaps from a closeness to continental traditions. The same may also be said of burial, which in Kent and other areas of Eastern Britain sometimes took place below large barrows in the continental manner.

The close proximity of the Continent seems to have demanded a military presence in Kent from an early date. From the C2, if not before, the British Fleet (*Classis Britannica*) was based at Lympne, Dover (E), and possibly Richborough (E). Early in the C3 a new fort was built at Reculver (E), presumably to guard the approach to the Thames estuary, and by the middle of the century the Richborough monument was converted into a defended lookout post – part of an early-warning system to guard the shores against threat of pirate attack. By the mid 280s the situation had so deteriorated that new military measures had to be taken, resulting in the construction of two massive masonry forts at Richborough and Lympne replacing the earlier installations. It is possible that at this time the base at Dover was also rebuilt, but positive evidence is elusive.

All four bases, Lympne, Dover, Richborough, and Reculver, were probably interlinked by roads, making the deployment of troops both simple and rapid. The forts were also linked by roads to Canterbury, and it may be significant that it was at just this time that the town was enclosed by its first town wall. Whether it now functioned as a control centre for the forts remains unknown.

The great upheaval that followed the 'barbarian conspiracy' of 367 saw certain modifications to the Saxon shore fort system, resulting, in Kent, in the abandonment of the fort at Lympne possibly because of land-slipping. The last years of Dover and Reculver still remain to be examined in detail, but at Richborough, where military control seems to have remained to the end, there are signs of intensive occupation well into the C5. Indeed recent research work has demonstrated the presence of North Germanic mercenaries at Richborough and Canterbury, foreshadowing the Saxon settlements instigated by the sub-Roman leader Vortigern.

BUILDING MATERIALS

BY ALEC CLIFTON-TAYLOR

GEOLOGICALLY Kent belongs entirely to the Cretaceous system, apart from the extensive and still more recent Tertiary and Pleistocene clays and sands which stretch across most of North Kent from Cliffe Marshes on the Thames estuary to Sandwich Bay (E), including the whole of Sheppey. The county is by no means so deficient in building stones as Essex, Suffolk and Norfolk; yet the predominant impression left by the buildings of Kent is of rich, glowing reds, and these belong not to any of the stones but to the bricks and the tiles.

It can be said with confidence that Kent has produced some of the best brickwork ever made. Her Tudor bricks were already very good: e.g. Sissinghurst Castle. By the beginning of the C18 [45] they could be superb, as can be seen at Bradbourne, Larkfield. At this time rubbed and gauged bricks had become something of a Kentish speciality, and a considerable range of colour was available. The brickmaking materials were drawn from three different geological strata. From the alluvial clays and brick-earths of North Kent, particularly around Sittingbourne (E), Rainham and Faversham (E), and also at Crayford, next to Dartford, came good reds and also the yellow-brown stocks which are still made at Sittingbourne. From the Gault, a belt of stiff bluish clay overlying the Lower Greensand, came the 'white' (pale yellow) bricks of the Medway valley N of Maidstone, where the lime-content of the clay is sufficient to over-ride the usual reddening influence of iron. These are only worked now at Aylesford. From the brown and blue clays of the Weald, at many points along the SW portion of the county from Hythe to Edenbridge, came some of the loveliest bricks of all, the reds of Wealden Kent. A brickworks near Frittenden still produces hand-made, finely textured facing bricks and roofing tiles. But the soundest bricks often depend upon a combination of more than one kind of clay, and this Kent can also provide.

Kentish tilework is even more memorable: no English county, not even Sussex, can rival Kent in the profuse employment of tiles of superlative quality. Tiles were produced here by the Romans, and already in the reign of Edward III the Benedictine monks of Battle Abbey were sponsoring the manufacture of tiles at Wye near Ashford, while the Cistercian house at Boxley (E) N of Maidstone had its own tileyard close at hand. Both these

are on the Gault belt, but the Wealden and the Tertiary clays
were no less productive. Kentish tiled roofs sweep up in splendid
style, often to centrally placed brick chimneystacks which give
dignity even to quite small houses in the Wealden area, and on
one side of a house they may be carried down to within a few
feet of the ground to form what is delightfully known as a cat-
slide. Such roofs display vast areas of rippling red tiles that are
a source of unending pleasure.

Yet this is only half the story; for the Weald (of Kent, Sussex
and Surrey) is the region *par excellence* for tile-hanging. This
practice, so enjoyable aesthetically, was first introduced in the
latter part of the c17, and has been popular in Kent ever since.
Its original purpose was the practical one of providing additional
protection against the elements, usually for half-timbered houses
but sometimes for brick walls also. On timber-framed structures
all that was required was to fix laths across the closely spaced
vertical studs. Brick walls were sometimes provided with additional wooden battens to support the laths, but in other cases the
tiles were pegged, or later nailed, direct into the mortar courses.
Often just the upper storey or perhaps only the gable-end would
be tile-hung, these being the parts of the building most exposed
to the weather. 'The joints might be filled with mortar, but in
all the best examples they have been left open, to yield little
vertical shadows. There will also be horizontal shadows cast by
the overhangs, in addition to which every hand-made tile will be
slightly curved. Hence a good tile-hung wall is a creation of
infinite subtlety, an agglomeration of shallow and slightly irregular convexities, seemingly held in place, under the right
conditions of light, by a fine mesh of shadow. Colour, as always,
is of the greatest importance, and happily the Weald still abounds
in gorgeous terracottas, often with minute variations of tint and
gradations of density almost from tile to tile, some being a little
more orange, others a little more vermilion. Because these tiles
hang vertically, rainwater runs off them at once, and unlike
roof-tiles they do not remain damp for days and perhaps weeks
at a time. Lichens, mosses, seeds and root particles do not therefore adhere to wall-tiles as they often do to pitched roofs, and for
this reason they seem to be able to hold their richly glowing reds
to an incomparable degree. Elsewhere the colour may only be a
dark reddish-brown, but for tile-hanging a warm hue has almost
always been preferred.' (*The Pattern of English Building*, *p. 265*)

The quality of bricks and tiles in Kent is so good that fanciful
shapes were usually avoided: they would simply have been a

distraction. There are, it is true, a few scrolled brick gables of the familiar Dutch type in Thanet, while fish-scale and other more complicated shapes also appear from time to time in Kentish tile-hanging, but less often than in Surrey and Sussex, and usually they belong to the Victorian period. Roofing tiles themselves are almost always plain. Pantiles, so characteristic of the Netherlands and of all the east coast counties of England from Norfolk to Northumberland, are hardly ever seen in Kent.

Between 1784 and 1850, the period during which bricks were taxed, this was one of the counties which made most use of brick-tiles, which were not subject to the tax. These 'mathematical tiles', as they are often called, were produced, like the Kentish bricks, in various colours: red ones can be seen in Canterbury (E), Hythe (E) and Tenterden, yellow at Belmont near Faversham (E), dun-coloured at Chevening. So skilfully were they made that sometimes only an experienced eye can distinguish them from the true bricks which they were intended to resemble.

The geological strata of Kent run in approximately parallel bands, of varying width, from the Surrey border ESE to the Straits of Dover. Six of these strata can be distinguished, of which three, the clays of the Weald, the Gault and the Tertiary clays, have already been cited as providing the raw materials for bricks and tiles. The other three, alternating with these, have furnished Kent with most of her stone.

Of these three formations, the earliest are the sandstones from the Hastings beds along the county's SW fringe. Although these play a more significant role in neighbouring Sussex, they have made a delightful contribution to the Kentish scene, as for example at Scotney Castle. Among the most familiar of these stones is the variegated brown Calverley sandstone much in evidence at Tunbridge Wells, where it was quarried. For charm of colour and of texture (and they are also very attractive to lichens), these fine-grained Wealden sandstones, which were sometimes obtainable in blocks of formidable size, have no rivals among the building stones of south-eastern England. Their durability varies; they can be seen to specially good advantage on the gatehouse of Tonbridge Castle, while at Brasted Place near $\frac{24}{\&}$ Sevenoaks the sandstone, nicely varied in colour, is ashlared and 76 after nearly two hundred years the carved detail is still wonderfully crisp. Some of these sandstones are sufficiently fissile to yield roofing slates, similar to the famous Horsham slates of Sussex. A number of buildings in the Kentish Weald share in

the general air of strength and authority that characterizes almost
any building roofed with these massively beautiful slabs.

Moving northwards across the Wealden clays we reach the
Lower Greensand, a comparatively narrow but important band
along which occur some of Kent's major towns: Sevenoaks,
Maidstone, Ashford, and parts of Hythe (E) and Folkestone (E).
From the Lower Greensand comes the county's best known
stone, Kentish Rag or Ragstone, a limestone which was worked
by the Romans (e.g. for the walls of Londinium) and which
in the Middle Ages travelled well beyond the confines of Kent
itself. Although now used much more extensively for road-
metal than as a building material, the Ragstone quarries,
around Maidstone in particular, have been famous for centuries.
For all that, Kentish Rag is a building stone with very considerable limitations, both physically and aesthetically. Coarse-
textured and brittle, it is not at all easy to work, yet it also includes
sandy areas which may be decidedly soft. Dressed stone, and
even well squared blocks, are only obtainable with difficulty, and
the usual Ragstone masonry, as can be seen at Rochester Castle,
Old Soar at Plaxtol, Knole, and in many Kent churches, is
uncoursed, irregularly bonded and rubbly. Unfortunately,
especially in the London area, where it was a favourite building
stone for Victorian churches, the uneven surfaces of Ragstone
buildings are all too liable to harbour dirt, which does not add
to their attractiveness; but for want of anything better Kentish
Rag has played a useful and important part in the county's
building history, and sometimes it can be a real pleasure, as on
the remarkably well preserved Westgate at Canterbury (E).

The one stratum so far unmentioned, the Chalk of the North
Downs, stretching from Surrey to the cliffs of Dover and the
South Foreland, with an outlier in the Isle of Thanet, culminating
in the North Foreland, has not been much worked as a building
stone in Kent, although in certain places at the foot of the North
Downs it could have been. (A farm outbuilding at Allington,
near Hollingbourne, has chalk-stone walls with blocks 9 in.
square, probably early C19 and quite well preserved.) Nor was
pugged chalk walling, such as can frequently be seen in parts of
Wiltshire, Hampshire and Dorset, a Kentish practice. A few
chalk valleys have yielded calcareous tufa, that light, porous stone
sometimes employed in the Middle Ages for vault construction.
In Kent it was used for the quoins of a number of Norman
churches and for bonding flint walls. It can be well seen in the
C12 tower at Leeds, and in association with ragstone at East

Malling. But from our standpoint the principal importance of Kentish Chalk is as the source of flint.

Flint, which comes mainly from the upper layers of the Chalk formation, is fortunately not so all-pervasive a building material in Kent as in East Anglia, for, as has been shown, these builders had several more enjoyable alternatives. But the durability of flint – a silica which in itself is virtually indestructible: in a flint wall only the mortar is vulnerable – has always been a great attraction. This was recognized by the Romans, who made good use of it, and in all subsequent periods. Flint has been particularly in demand in the coastal towns, where the salty atmosphere can play havoc with brick as with other kinds of stone. The older parts of such places as Margate, Ramsgate, Sandwich, Deal, Dover and Folkestone (all E) have an abundance of flint buildings, including churches; at all these it could be obtained in the vicinity, if not actually on the site.

Flint-knapping – that is, fracturing the stones, and setting them into the wall with the split face showing – occurred comparatively early in Kent; and on the front of the C15 gatehouse of the former manor of Dent-de-Lion at Garlinge (E), close to Margate, knapped flints were laid in bands alternately with dull red and pale yellow bricks (one of the earliest instances, incidentally, of Kentish brickwork). Later, primarily in order to reduce the amount of mortar employed and so to strengthen the structure, the flints were not merely knapped but meticulously squared, a refinement of which many Late Georgian and Victorian examples can be seen in the Brighton area. Although more characteristic of Sussex, instances of this technique can be found here and there in Kent too, as at Sandwich (E).

A passing mention should perhaps be made of septaria, those curious concretions occurring on and off in the clays of the Thames basin and elsewhere. In Kent nodules of this soft crumbly stone can be seen in the church wall at Herne (E). Quite different, and much more attractive, are the *Paludina* limestones dug from the Wealden Clay, freshwater limestones consisting largely of snail and mollusc shells, of which the best-known is the so-called Bethersden marble. This stone is found in thin, somewhat irregularly shaped slabs never more than 7 in. thick; its great virtue is that, like Purbeck 'marble', it will take a fine polish, which however will not survive for long in the open air. Bethersden marble is therefore best seen indoors, providing as it did the material for slender shafts in many of Kent's churches, and for a number of tombs (Woodchurch, Chilham

(E), etc.). It was also in demand for secular work: e.g. the two handsome chimneypieces at Godinton. Externally it was at one time employed for paving, to which its slab-like nature is clearly well suited; it was used to good effect for the church path at Great Chart, and a good deal of it can still be seen on the field-paths around Bethersden. Its colour is sometimes brownish but usually grey, and somewhat mottled, owing to the abundance of fairly large shell fossils. There is another, harder variety of *Paludina* limestone, with small shells; this is well seen in the walls of the church at Staplehurst.

Kent has one important building stone not of local provenance: Caen stone from Normandy. This fine oolitic limestone was imported, principally for church building – and usually only for the finer portions: doorways, window frames and traceries, columns, corbels, copings and capitals, pinnacles, finials and gargoyles – not only under the Norman Kings but intermittently throughout the Middle Ages, and again in the Victorian period (when, however, Bath stone was still more in favour for dressings). Bell Harry, the central tower of Canterbury Cathedral (E), was built of bricks – nearly half a million of them – but was entirely faced with Caen stone, to which it owes much of its incomparable dignity and beauty.

Wood, principally oak, with some Spanish chestnut, still plays an important part in the overall picture of Kentish building materials, although not along the coast, where the climate is too exposed for much half-timbering. But in the interior of the county, especially in the Wealden area, timber-framed houses abound. There are indeed many more of them than a casual inspection might suggest, for in Kent a great deal of half-timbered construction was later masked. Some of it was completely plastered over: from quite an early date wattle and daub might be spread over the whole external face of a half-timbered house, and later, since Kent has plenty of good lime and sand, plastering presented no problem. In the Georgian age, and sometimes rather earlier, timber-framed houses in such delectable Wealden places as Tenterden, Cranbrook and Goudhurst might be covered or partly covered with hung tiles, while others, as at Biddenden, were weather-boarded. Yet others, as at Faversham (E), were refronted with brick. Thus a great deal of Kent's half-timbering is no longer instantly visible, although such features as jetties (overhanging upper storeys) soon leave us in no doubt what is underneath.

Where the timbers remain exposed the infilling is usually lath and plaster: but brick nogging, with the bricks arranged in herring-bone and other patterns, can be found from time to time. Normally the plaster is left plain, but pargeting (ornamental designs on the plaster, either in relief or incised), although less common than in Suffolk and Essex and less elaborate, is not rare in Kent.

Weather-boarding, usually from the C18 or early C19, occurs more often in the Weald of Kent than perhaps anywhere else in the country. The horizontal boards, chamfered along their lower edge, are nearly always painted white or cream, and look uncommonly well. Shingles can be seen on church spires in all parts of the county. Originally these were of cleft oak, but they need to be drastically restored, if not completely renewed, at least once every hundred years, and now for reasons of economy shingles of Canadian cedar are used instead. Only, I believe, on the octagonal turrets of the tower of Sissinghurst Castle can Wealden oak shingles still be seen: these date from 1958.

Thatch was once a very familiar roofing material here, as in so many other English counties. But so excellent and so readily available are the local tiles that to come upon a thatched roof in Kent now is something of an event.

THE BUILDINGS OF KENT

BY JOHN NEWMAN

KENT is tenth among English counties in order of size, and ninth in populousness; or rather that was the position in 1965, before the NW corner of the county was snipped off and given to Greater London. As has been explained in the Foreword, I am writing as if that had not happened. The county's position, between London and the Continent, has always been the most important thing about it. It explains why the metropolitan cathedral of England is in Kent, and why there are many more castles in Kent than in any other southern county. It must partly explain the constant prosperity through the centuries; and it is at any rate one reason why no-one who travels along the main roads through Kent from London to Dover or Folkestone will get a good impression of the county. Kentish scenery is not spectacular. There are no moors, no high hills, the North Downs can compare only in a few places, near Wye for example, and behind Folkestone, with the massive sweeps of the South Downs. Yet there is an extraordinary variety. To go from the well-clipped suburbia of Beckenham and Chislehurst just a few miles to the man-made cliffs of the Thames-side cement works is startling enough. The North Downs form the spine of the county, slipping down to the N by blanched and windy chalk uplands to the creeks and marshland of the Thames and Medway estuaries; and in the other direction dropping abruptly to the much lusher, undulating Weald, with its orchards and hopfields. Beyond the Weald lies Romney Marsh, flat and pullulating with sheep. Further E, where the downs are cut off by the sea, there are chalk cliffs, high and beetling by Folkestone and Dover, low and almost toy-like round the Isle of Thanet. But wherever one goes in Kent – some find it an annoyance, others find it endearing – a view free of buildings can hardly be had. Why is this so? Not just because so many people live in Kent. Historically three reasons can be put forward. First, almost all of Kent is good farming land. Secondly, the vast tracts of the county owned by the two great abbeys at Canterbury were at the Dissolution quickly given or sold to private individuals and not held in royal hands. The third and probably most important cause of all was

Gavelkind, the peculiar system of land-tenure in Kent, in operation already in the C II, whereby an estate was not inherited by the eldest son, but divided between all sons equally. Nor did the system, familiar in the Midlands, of open fields predominate; land was early enclosed and farmed privately. So in the Middle Ages, land not held by Christ Church or St Augustine's Abbey was owned in relatively small lots, and not in great estates. After 1535 the same forces broke up the monastic lands. Hence the multiplication of timber-framed farmhouses. Hence too the lack of great parks and the surprisingly small number of really big country houses. Even in the C 19 the same conditions prevailed. Mighty Victorian mansions rarely appear, mighty Victorian estate churches appear not at all. Prosperous agriculture kept industry, and with it big urban developments, at bay, except for the cement works along the Thames shore and the paper mills in the Medway valley.

ANGLO SAXON ARCHITECTURE means church architecture. It was to Canterbury that Augustine came in 597, sent by Pope Gregory the Great from Rome, to reform the Church in England. To convert the inhabitants was one aim, to build churches for them was another. Something remains of ten churches built by Augustine or his converts in Kent during the C7; and one, Bradwell, in Essex. That is an astonishing number, representing seven separate monastic foundations, and says a lot for the success of Augustine's mission. St Peter and St Paul, Canterbury (E),* the church of the abbey founded by Augustine outside the city walls in 597; St Andrew, Rochester, founded in 604; St Mary, Canterbury (E), c. 620; Lyminge (E), which was founded in 633; Minster-in-Sheppey (E), 664; Reculver (E), 669, all were connected with monastic foundations. But sadly, only Minster, and two undated churches, St Martin and St Pancras, both in Canterbury, keep walling to a sufficient height to impress the eye. Reculver, entire until 1809, is known from engravings. For the rest excavations have had to tell the tale.

The tale they tell is of surprising standardization of plan. The complete plan has been excavated at Reculver: rectangular nave, 24 ft wide, 37 ft 6 in. long, with entrances in the centre of the three outer walls; a chancel as wide as the nave, ending in an apse polygonal on its outer face, round inside, with a continuous clergy bench; porticus N and s overlapping the nave–chancel

* As this is an introduction to the whole of the county, places in the volume on North East and East Kent are here distinguished by (E) from those in West Kent and the Weald.

junction; and, most striking of all, a chancel screen of three arches, narrow, wide, narrow, on lofty, classically inspired stone columns.* The remains of St Pancras, Canterbury, show essentially the same plan, and the same tripartite chancel screen. Nave and porticus have been excavated at St Peter and St Paul, Canterbury, the apse at Rochester; so Reculver's plan, it seems certain, was imported with Augustine. Where was it imported from? Italy is one's first answer. But in Italy there is a dearth of churches of the C5 and C6 as small as the Kent ones. The form of the apse at Reculver is a standard Early Christian one. The apses of the C6 churches at Ravenna for example are like that. For the Reculver clergy bench the closest parallel is at Poreč (Parenzo) in Istria, across the water from Ravenna. The function of the porticus is not clear. At St Peter and St Paul, Canterbury, further porticus were added until all three sides of the nave were enclosed. That is explained by the church's purpose as a burial place outside the city walls. The same development at Reculver need not have the same explanation. All the early Kent churches conform to this plan, as far as one can tell, except Stone (E), which has a square-ended chancel, Richborough (E), and St Martin, Canterbury. At St Peter and St Paul and at St Mary, Canterbury, the chancel is quite lost; and the same is true of Minster-in-Sheppey, where the nave is unusually long (like the nave at Bradwell).

St Martin is a special case. According to Bede, Bertha, the Christian queen of Kent, worshipped there even before Augustine arrived. The church in its present state is clearly of two dates, both C7. The chancel is wholly of Roman brick, the nave of stone banded with brick courses. The question arises, is the present chancel the nave of Bertha's pre-Augustine church? It is only 15 ft wide, almost as minute as the Romano-British church at Silchester. This is a question without an answer; but it turns our attention to building materials. The earliest churches, i.e. the Canterbury ones, except the nave of St Martin, were built of nothing but thin Roman bricks, neatly laid; material and technique would not look out of place in C7 Milan or Ravenna. No doubt the bricks came from demolished Romano-British buildings. At Reculver the walling corresponds to what we find in buildings of the Roman occupation: bricks make thin bands only in the stone walls, and the same is true of Stone. At Minster, however, bricks are regularly used only for quoins and

* The columns were salvaged and now stand in the crypt of Canterbury Cathedral.

for turning the arched heads of windows. It looks as if an Italian method of construction was gradually forgotten as the generation of immigrant workmen died off. Two final points: first, as for detail, windows (Reculver, Minster) were splayed only on the inside, their heads turned in tile, the voussoirs radiating successfully; shallow buttresses mark angles. Secondly, the Canterbury churches show a preference for axial siting. At St Augustine's Abbey, the church of St Peter and St Paul had a second church, St Mary, built about twenty years later almost touching its E end. St Pancras is roughly in line, a good way to the E of these two; and recently a fourth church has been excavated (a C10 one admittedly) prolonging the line further W. At the cathedral, Augustine's Christ Church had a second church, dedicated to St John, and used for baptisms, burials, and trials, built in the C8 about 50 yds E of it.

So both to the close view and in bird's-eye these C7 churches present an appearance of orderliness and careful planning. The single relic of C7 Saxon SCULPTURE reveals similar virtues of intellectual control. This is the fragments* of the cross shaft which stood on a base in front of the central opening in the chancel screen at Reculver (E). The fragments show figures in moderately high relief, some in action, others standing in easy, relaxed poses. One fragment has interlace and a scroll of foliage, with half-length busts in the loops. Nothing else so supple, so classical, nothing that shows such understanding of the moving human figure, can be found in the art of C7 Europe. The figures on the contemporary Northumbrian crosses, Ruthwell and Bewcastle, look positively hieratic by comparison. This sculptural style, like C7 Kentish architecture, is, as far as one can tell, a relic in a remote corner of Europe of an art that prevailed in the eastern Mediterranean, in Syria and Egypt as well as in Italy, in the C4 and C5, but after that was in decline. Interlace can be found in Rome (*cancelli* in S. Clemente and S. Sabina, of the C5). Early Christian ivories make the comparison best, not only the great ivory throne of Maximian at Ravenna, but the little portable diptychs carved with sacred scenes; the famous Ascension diptych in Munich comes closest in iconography, the Andrews Diptych in the Victoria and Albert Museum goes well with the style. But the Reculver fragments are of stone, even though the carving has a delicate nervousness, not unlike the carving of an ivory. In stone nothing remotely comparable survives from the time before Charlemagne reawoke interest in

* Now kept in the crypt of Canterbury Cathedral (E).

antique art. Interlace and the hindquarters of a beast on a stone loose in the crypt of Rochester Cathedral; that is the only later piece of Saxon sculpture that can be mentioned. The sundial at Orpington is sculpture only in being carved with runes.

The church and cross at Reculver are indeed the last monumental remains of an era of civilized art in Kent. OTHER SAXON ARCHITECTURE in the county has nothing as homogeneous to show and little as impressive architecturally as the early churches. Still, the two major forms of church plan, aisled and cruciform, are both represented. Lydd was aisled. All that is left are three blocked arcade arches, a clerestory, and the springing of an apsidal chancel. A c7 date for it has been strongly argued, mainly because of the single-splayed window. The incompetent laying of its masonry may make it even earlier. Bearsted has but a single arch, with a through stone, and may possibly lay claim also to have been aisled. The cruciform church of St Mary in Castro, Dover (E), built *c*.1000, is by contrast truly memorable in scale and completeness, in spite of *Scott*'s unceremonious rescue of it from semi-ruin in 1860–2. It is the completest in the country of that typically Saxon kind of cross-shaped church where the tower stands on the ground, and choir and transepts open like rooms off it. One other great c11 Saxon building is known only from its crypt. That is the octagon Abbot Wulfric placed *c*.1050 between two of the c7 churches at St Augustine's, Canterbury, closely imitating William of Volpiano's octagon of Saint-Benigne at Dijon.

The only other sizeable building is the Late Saxon church at Lyminge (E). For the rest, there is a handful of village churches given away as pre-Conquest by one feature or another. At St Mary-in-Castro, Dover, are the only pilaster strips – round the tower arches. Double-splayed windows on the other hand are relatively common. Dover has them, and they occur at Stourmouth (E) and West Peckham (in the tower), and on a group of churches in the NW of the county, Darenth, Shorne, Swanscombe (tower), Wilmington, Wouldham. Northfleet, in the same area, has a good long-and-short quoin; St Mildred, Canterbury (E), a quoin with megaliths.

Instead of descending into the twilight of Saxo-Norman overlap,* i.e. the survival of Saxon modes after the arrival of the

* The main interest of which concerns towers used as chapels. A complete one with an apse survives at Godmersham (E). Similar towers at Bapchild (E) and West Kingsdown, and possibly Upper Hardres (E), have lost their apses. Orpington and Harrietsham (E) have piscinas that show that towers were similarly used in the c13 also.

Normans, we can make a fresh start at this point with the EARLY NORMAN style itself. In 1070 William of Normandy appointed Lanfranc to the see of Canterbury. Lanfranc was William's most trusted adviser, and had in 1063 been installed as first abbot of his new-founded abbey of Saint-Étienne at Caen. One of the new archbishop's first tasks was to rebuild Canterbury Cathedral. The new church was practically a replica of his abbey church at Caen; or rather a replica in plan, for it is only the plan – of transepts, nave of eight bays, and two W towers – that has left its mark. The NW tower survived until 1832. Britton's engravings show that it was massively austere, typically Early Norman, except in the later top stages. The cathedral is said to have been completed, with astonishing speed, in seven years.

We do not know how Lanfranc's choir was laid out. If it too followed Saint-Étienne, there will probably have been straight-ended aisles, and an apse projecting further E between them. That is the normal Romanesque staggered plan. The other characteristic Romanesque plan, to be found at Rouen Cathedral, begun before 1037, in which an apsidal ambulatory runs round the E end and apsidal chapels project from the curve, is represented at Canterbury at St Augustine's Abbey, where also the church was completely rebuilt in the last quarter of the CII. Work here began before 1073. A good deal of the crypt has been excavated, one of the earliest Norman crypts in the country. It was groin-vaulted and had two rows of circular piers down the centre, making four bays awkwardly narrow in span. At Rochester Cathedral is another early crypt, of Gundulf's new church begun in 1077 – or, to be more accurate, only the two W bays of it. Groin-vaults here too, and slender round piers, with capitals of the type with keeled corners that came before the invention of the block capital. Sir William St John Hope excavated the E end of Gundulf's cathedral, and found that it was square, with a central square-ended projection. That is not a Norman termination at all, but rather a Saxon one. Recently it has been shown that Malling Abbey, West Malling, another foundation associated with Gundulf, ended in the same way.

But what is without any doubt the most spectacular of these early crypts is back in Canterbury, the undercroft of Lanfranc's dormitory for the monks of Christ Church. Up to one hundred and fifty monks had to be accommodated; so the dormitory was vast, 148 ft by 78 ft, the undercroft twelve bays by six. It had groin-vaults, like the others, and the same sort of capitals as the

Rochester crypt; but the thick round piers are incised with bold patterns of lozenges, spirals, etc.

Lanfranc's huge establishment of monks at Canterbury has been mentioned. Much building went on for them in the C12, recorded in the drawing at Trinity College, Cambridge, made c.1160, of Prior Wibert's thoroughly expert drainage system. That layout, basically Lanfranc's, can still be traced today: an attempt to do that has been made in the gazetteer. Here only the highlights of the tour can be mentioned: the monumental infirmary hall, built c.1110–20; the lavatory tower in the infirmary cloisters, octagonal, and standing on an open rib-vaulted undercroft; the treasury, also on an undercroft, and itself vaulted with an octopartite rib-vault; and the Court Gateway and the great stone staircase to the guest hall beside it. All these must be mid-C12 in date. No other English precinct has Norman buildings so numerous, so entire, and of such variety.

Elsewhere in Kent MONASTIC BUILDINGS are scarce. At Rochester there is nothing but the E wall of the cloisters and the chapter house, built c.1120* and remodelled after a fire two decades later. Both cathedrals followed the Benedictine rule, as of course did all pre-C12 monasteries. The C7 foundation of St Augustine's, Canterbury (E), has been mentioned already, and so have Reculver and Minster-in-Sheppey (both E), which has no monastic remains beyond a C15 gatehouse. Minster-in-Thanet (E) was another, founded in 669. New sites were colonized by Benedictines in the C12. West Malling, founded from Rochester for nuns before 1106, keeps the W end of its church, and a walk 14 of the C13 cloister. Davington (E) was also for nuns, founded in 1153. The nave of its church, very austere except for the W doorway, survives. The great abbey founded by King Stephen and Matilda in the same year at Faversham (E), only a mile from Davington, is a total loss. In 1965, however, excavation revealed the plan of the church, tremendously big, with a choir of nine bays (where the royal founders were buried) as long as the nave. The most impressive C12 Benedictine building intact outside Canterbury is the refectory of St Martin's Priory, Dover (E), built at once on the foundation of the priory in 1139. Here once more it is the sheer size of it that impresses most. The guest hall here (now altered) cannot be earlier than c. 1180. The Augustinians are represented by Leeds, founded in 1119, by Lesnes Abbey, Belvedere, founded in 1178, by Combwell, Kilndown,

---

* By Bishop Ernulf. The W wall of the chapter house is diapered just like the wall of the N passage to the crypt Ernulf had, as prior, built at Canterbury.

late C12, and by Bilsington Priory, 1253. Only Lesnes has anything to show of its church, foundations with a straight E end and
straight-ended chapels in the transepts. That is remarkable, for it
is a pure Cistercian plan. The Cistercians themselves founded
only one house in Kent, which is not perhaps surprising considering that Kent was one of the most populous parts of the
country in the C12. The one house was at Boxley (E), founded in
1146. Nothing to speak of remains today. Finally, late in the C12,
came Monks Horton (E), which was Cluniac, and boasts a
richly carved W portal and a contemporary dormitory range; and
in 1192 the Premonstratensians settled at St Radegund's (E), on
the top of the Downs behind Dover, and at Langdon (E).
Nothing can be seen at Langdon Abbey. At St Radegund's is the
strange semi-fortified N tower of the church and bits of the
monastic buildings.

In the C13 the Friars arrived. In Kent, as in other counties,
little that is eloquent is left of their buildings. The Dominicans
built, with royal money, at Canterbury (E) from 1237, and the
Franciscans after 1224. At Aylesford in 1240 the Carmelites
founded their first English house, and a second in the county
two years later, at Lossenham, Newenden. The rare order of
Trinitarians had a house at Moatenden, Headcorn. Last of all,
as late as 1346, Dominican nuns were settled at Dartford.

To return to C12 NORMAN ARCHITECTURE. The first
building to break away from the blunt, massive, and somewhat
joyless style of Lanfranc and his disciples towards something
more festive was the choir of Canterbury Cathedral (E), started
before 1096 by Prior Ernulf, an enormously elaborated and
extended replacement of Lanfranc's choir. Ernulf built a second
pair of transepts, following the third church at Cluny in that, and
an apsidal E end with three chapels on the curve of the apse, but
aligned, as the English liked to align them, strictly to the E. The
plan that results is crazily complicated. Externally the walls have
bands of arcading, with carved capitals, and there is similar
arcading, painted perhaps originally, inside. The fire of 1174
gutted the interior, but the crypt escaped, in all its sumptuousness and new-found freedom of decoration. Instead of the strict
incised patterns of Lanfranc's dormitory undercroft, the crypt
piers seem twisted bodily, their capitals loaded with sculpture.
The sculpture itself makes a new paragraph. This one must
continue the survey of architecture. The only other major
Norman building in Kent is the nave of Rochester Cathedral.
Built in the mid C12 (we have no precise date), it is rather a tired

performance. The elevation is standard: arcade, gallery, with twin openings,* and clerestory (rebuilt in the C15). The piers in each bay have a different plan, but nothing is made of this hectic variety. The decoration is largely confined to zigzag. The W front of Rochester is the best part, a logical expression of the nave and lean-to aisles, punctuated by four turrets, and decorated in the favourite Anglo-Norman way with many tiers of arcading, and an unexpectedly rich W portal, of which more needs to be said in the sculpture paragraph. The W front of Malling Abbey, West Malling, is a version of this façade applied to an aisleless nave.

The C12 was as busy a time for building PARISH CHURCHES in Kent as for cathedral and monastic works. Early Norman churches are mostly small, an aisleless nave, plus a chancel usually narrower and lower than the nave, but sometimes built in one with it. A few have apsidal chancels, e.g. the ruined church of Maplestead, West Kingsdown, and the hospital chapels at Chatham and Harbledown (E), or apsidal sanctuaries, as at Sutton (E) and the chapel at Minster Court, Minster-in-Thanet (E). The tell-tale early material is tufa, a chalk deposit easily found and easily worked for dressings, which imported Caen stone soon put out of use. Tufa occurs at Leeds, founded it is said in 1137. At Leeds there is too a mighty tower arch with typical Early Norman forms: square responds with nook-shafts, soffit rolls, block capitals. Among parish churches only Smeeth (E) has the same character.

The grandest parish churches are in the eastern part of the county. St Margaret's at Cliffe (E), in its scale and completeness, takes the palm. Its aisled nave has a clerestory and arcades on lofty piers, alternating in plan between round and composite, both features of the greatest rarity in a C12 parish church.‡ The external arcading which the clerestory windows are set in (cf. Barfreston, E) suggests a date in the third quarter of the century. Earlier than that St Mary at Sandwich (E) had a clerestory to its aisled nave.§ New Romney, begun c. 1160, has arcades with 8 alternating supports, round and octagonal, and a low clerestory as well. The standard Norman arcade has round piers with scalloped capitals, and of course round arches, either plain, or with a soffit roll, or decorated with zigzag or billet. The longest

---

* But, very unusually, no gallery floor.

‡ St Margaret's at Cliffe has an astonishingly wide and high chancel arch. Similar, if smaller, ones are at Brabourne (E), Brook (E), and Walmer (E). Compare too the tower arches at St Clement at Sandwich (E).

§ So did the infirmary chapel in the precincts at Canterbury, c.1120.

such arcades are in Thanet: Margate (E), nine bays including the chancel, Broadstairs (E), five bays, and Minster-in-Thanet (E), five, not all of the same date.

Finally, a word or two needs to be said about chancels and about towers. Darenth has a two-storeyed chancel, or rather a two-storeyed sanctuary, its lower chamber groin-vaulted. Brabourne (E) was to have had a chancel vault. Darenth is very plain, Brabourne quite rich with carved decoration, very like the late C12 carving at Monks Horton Priory (E), to which Brabourne belonged. As for towers, the most unusual, without a doubt, is the W tower at Brook (E), as wide as the nave and with a first-floor chapel inside, i.e. a complete *Westwerk*, a standard form in Germany but of the utmost rarity in England. The tower at Sturry (E) is related to Brook's, but less large. There are only a few other W towers worth mentioning: St Mary's, Dover (E), and New Romney, both encrusted with blank arcading, the latter very tall, but not completed until *c.*1200; and the massive but completely plain tower at Leeds. The tower at Borden (E) approaches this in scale; and in St Mary at Chatham, there is the arch to what must have been quite a mighty W tower. At Reculver (E), at the very end of the century, a new W front was built into the Saxon church, complete with two W towers. The only other two-towered W façade is at Davington (E). Cruciform churches with central towers are Adisham (E), Northbourne (E), Sandwich, St Clement (E), richly arcaded outside, this one, and Ramsgate (E), also with external arcading. The rarer type, with a central tower but no transepts, is represented by the ruins of St James at Dover (E), and by Chislet (E). Towers on one side of the church, generally N of the nave, are quite normal in the C12.*

Smaller Norman churches often have no claim to notice except a richly carved doorway. The motifs are very standardized, mainly billet, embattling, sometimes rows of leaves, but after *c.*1120, zigzag above all. Zigzag is always useful for dating. The idea of turning it through ninety degrees so that the zigs point outwards seems to have occurred in the mid century. Only in the last quarter of the century was it undercut, e.g. to overlap a roll. That is how it is used by William of Sens at Canterbury from 1175. But NORMAN SCULPTURE is not just a matter of geometrical patterns. The capitals in Ernulf's crypt at Canterbury Cathedral, begun *c.*1096, demonstrate that for a start. The

---

* It should be put on record that Ospringe (E) had a round tower. It collapsed in 1695.

capitals (since they were carved *in situ*) need not have been carved as early as that. Comparison with datable manuscripts illuminated at Canterbury in fact puts them firmly in the 1120s, i.e. not long before the new choir was consecrated. Manuscript illumination too, not other sculpture, makes the best comparison with the splendidly spirited and sure design of these capitals, with beasts alone, beasts making music or fighting, jugglers, or just leaves or interlacing patterns of beaded bands, all brilliantly adapted to the semicircular fields a block capital provides for carving. The same sculptors worked on the external arcading of the new choir, and on the pier capitals in the infirmary chapel at Canterbury. The former is too restored, the latter too worn to make an impact like the crypt capitals. To follow the development of this style further one has to go to Reading, or Winchester (capitals from Hyde Abbey). In Kent nothing outside Canterbury compares with it.

The sculptured doorways in the cloisters at Rochester are too battered to tell one much. The dormitory doorway has one of the very few sculptured tympana in the county, the subject identifiable, just, as the sacrifice of Isaac. There is a second sculptured tympanum at Rochester, on the w doorway of the cathedral 11 itself. The subject here is Christ in Majesty with the symbols of the four evangelists, and the twelve Apostles on the lintel. It is clearly inspired from France, the closest comparison being with the w portal at Chartres. In quality Rochester is humble by French standards; in iconography it has the unprecedented complication that there are two column figures attached to the shafts of the doorway. These are not impressive as works of art either but the idea is again French, this time from the Île de France, where the abbey church of Saint-Denis was the first to have column figures on the w doorway (*c.*1140). Another column figure, quite small, was recently found at Minster-in-Sheppey (E), a figure too small for a doorway, so perhaps from the cloisters. An exquisite but yet tinier shaft, carved with figures of St Martial and a deacon, is re-used at Bobbing (E). Datable *c.*1190, it is the latest of the three. Roughly contemporary is the over-lifesize figure of Gundulf, from the w front of Rochester Cathedral. Christ in a mandorla was a favourite subject for tympana. Examples, crude and minute, are, *ex situ*, at Betteshanger (E) and Minster Court, Minster-in-Thanet (E). An unidentifiable figure of *c.* 1180 stands in the tympanum of the doorway to the Cellarer's Hall in the precincts at Canterbury (E). A large relief figure of a seated archbishop, also late C12, loose in the church at Godmersham (E), completes this list of undistinguished figure sculpture.

But so far no mention has been made of the most delightful late C12 carving in the county, on the church at Barfreston (E). No satisfactory explanation has yet been given why this little building, just a nave and a lower chancel, qualified for such a gorgeous array of sculpture. The S doorway is the outstanding piece, with Christ blessing in the tympanum, but no evangelist symbols. Medallions round the voussoirs bear tiny scenes, including probably part of a series of Labours of the Months. The style is brilliant in its small-scale elaboration and invention; details suggest a date not before c.1180. The S doorway at Patrixbourne (E) is clearly by the same workshop as Barfreston. The W doorway at St Margaret's at Cliffe (E) is conceived similarly, but by a rustic hand. The contemporary architectural sculpture on the W front of Monks Horton Priory (E) and at Brabourne (E) shows the same preference for busy little motifs as Barfreston and Patrixbourne.*

The chancel at Barfreston was before 1839 covered with C12 WALL PAINTINGS of fine quality; and even now this is the best century for wall paintings in the county. Canterbury (E) makes it so. The entire apse of the crypt chapel of St Gabriel in the cathedral has preserved its painted decoration, done about 1130. On the apse Christ is shown seated on a rainbow, surrounded by angels. It is an Apocalyptic vision; and on the soffit of the entrance is painted St John the Evangelist, seeing the vision. Scenes from the life of St John occupy the space to the l. and from the life of Christ the space to the r. In the chapel above, St Anselm's, there is a single scene preserved, or rather a single small but monumental figure, St Paul shaking off the viper at Malta. This must be a little later, say mid-C12, and is close in style and quality to illuminated manuscripts, in particular the Bury Bible at Corpus Christi College, Cambridge, completed before 1148. At Eastbridge Hospital, Canterbury, is a fine and unusually large late C12 figure of Christ in Majesty.

To return to sculpture, there are a few carved Norman FONTS. That at Darenth, tub-shaped, with figures and scenes under arcading, is the most ambitious; the Newenden font, carved with beasts on the square bowl, the most monumental. Swanscombe's must have equalled these before fire ruined it in 1902. The only

* The E window at both Barfreston and Patrixbourne is a wheel window, a feature of the utmost rarity and a stylistic connexion with North East France.

group is of lead fonts, and they are only a group in that they are all of lead. Brookland's has complete sets of Labours of the Months and Signs of the Zodiac, and may have been imported from North France. Anyway, it is unique in England. At Lower Halstow (E) there are figures under arcading, at Wichling (E) stylized leaves. All three date probably from the end of the century. For the rest, in Kent as everywhere else in England, the standard Norman font is a square bowl, with a row of arches sunk in each face, set on five round shafts. Many survive, too many to mention, some of them of Purbeck or local marble. Only at Oare (E), where the bowl rests on four heads, and Foots Cray (shafts with waterleaf capitals) are there memorable variations on the standard type. Apart from the fonts already mentioned, only a handful take another shape; Gillingham's is round and arcaded, the font at St Martin, Canterbury (E), round, extra big, and covered in geometrical patterns, and that at Harrietsham (E) (of Purbeck marble) has a bowl on a single stem, carved with zigzag.* The gabled funerary MONUMENT at Fordwich (E), with close-set arcading, can find a place at this point.

Perhaps no event in English history had such a cataclysmic effect on architecture as the Norman Conquest, but THE WORK OF WILLIAM OF SENS AND WILLIAM THE ENGLISHMAN AT CANTERBURY profoundly altered ecclesiastical architecture in South East England both structurally and in the matter of decoration. Fire gutted the choir of Canterbury Cathedral in 1174. The next year *William of Sens* was chosen to rebuild. Gervase's contemporary account chronicles the work year by year, beginning in 1175 with the W bays of the choir and reaching the E transepts by 1179; in which year William of Sens fell from the scaffolding and was unable to continue as master mason. His successor, *William the Englishman*, built, as a completely new structure, a prolongation far beyond the early C12 E end, the Trinity Chapel and the circular Corona, all upon a new crypt. So the Early Gothic style arrived in England. Both Williams built in a manner that was absolutely the latest thing in terms of the monumental church style of the Île de France in the 1170s and 80s; and English William was as French as William of Sens, as Professor Bony has proved. That it was an alien manner in England goes without saying; though one must remember

---

* Other Norman fittings can be consigned to a footnote. There are three PILLAR PISCINAS, at St Bartholomew's Chapel, Chatham, St Leonard, Deal (E), and St Augustine's Abbey, Canterbury (E; loose bowl only); and two DOORS with decorative iron hingework, at Hartley and Staplehurst, the latter very splendid. 12

always the contemporary, equally Early Gothic, abbeys of Yorkshire, Ripon and Roche, inspired by Cistercian Burgundy, and Wells in the West of England, begun soon after 1176. William of Sens certainly used Sens Cathedral as the basis of his elevation, but Professor Bony deduces by comparing details that he must have trained in the NE of the Île de France, the area bounded by Reims and Laon, by Arras and Valenciennes, i.e. considerably further N than Sens. William the Englishman on the other hand, by using detached responds in the Trinity Chapel aisles, and by the form of his triforium, shows that he came to Canterbury specifically from the Laon area.

What then are the essential features of this new style ? First of all, a great increase in height, both absolutely and in relation to width (which at Canterbury was of course fixed by the surviving walls of Ernulf's choir). Here the extra height is achieved in three ways: by making the arcade piers twelve feet higher than their predecessors, by making the arcade arches pointed not round, and by erecting a rib-vault over the choir, pointed in section. Greater height needs stronger, more efficient, support externally. William of Sens used the newly invented flying buttress as a means of taking some of the weight of the high vault down and out to the mighty Norman walls. In the Trinity Chapel and Corona, where the outer walls were all new, the weight, focused internally by ribs and piers, could have more concentrated support, in the form of deeply projecting buttresses, with quite a thin wall between them. The only structural feature which is purely Anglo-Norman and not French at all is the clerestory wall passage. The use of a three-storeyed not a four-storeyed elevation in the choir, and of a gallery, not a triforium, although that makes Canterbury like Sens, also makes Canterbury follow the normal Anglo-Norman cathedral system. The vaulting system however, sexpartite rib-vaults on piers of alternating form, is French not English. In the Trinity Chapel there is only room for a quadripartite vault, and the piers are round and coupled in depth, all of them, i.e. there is no alternation. That, the narrower span, and the raised crypt under the Trinity Chapel make William the Englishman's design happier, more taut and unified than the choir design, which looks what it is, experimental.

So much for the structure. The decoration is equally striking for its novelty in England. First of all there is the abundant Purbeck marble shafting. Detached shafts were something new; so were shafts so astonishingly long and slender as these. So

mouldings are deeper, more numerous and varied; Purbeck marble shafts are used to cluster round the quatrefoil piers, and rere-arches may be trefoiled. Billet and zigzag have disappeared, dogtooth reigns alone. A curious detail, the frieze of sunk roundels in the sanctuary, connects Hythe with Minster-in-Thanet and with the cloisters at Canterbury Cathedral. That suggests that the cathedral workshop was responsible for these two vaulted chancels, which is what we might expect.

The next stage is the stage when bar tracery made its first appearance, so that windows no longer needed to be lancets.* Bar tracery was evolved in France, and introduced to England at Westminster Abbey, begun in 1245. The church of Stone was built by masons from Westminster. It is not a large church, but inside it is designed with the greatest sophistication and adorned with luxuriant sculpture of the highest quality. The chancel is vaulted (the vault reconstructed by *Street* in 1860), and below the great geometrical windows runs shafted blank arcading. In the spandrels are delightful panels of stiff-leaf carved in high relief. Stiff-leaf capitals to the nave piers, which have the elaborate form of quatrefoil cores with Purbeck marble shafts in the angles. More foliage appears in unexpected places: in sunk quatrefoils above the chancel arch, and round the arch too dogtooth that has turned into foliage. This luxuriant style is represented elsewhere in Kent only in the splendid archbishop's doorway from the cloisters at Canterbury Cathedral into the N transept and in the cloisters at Malling Abbey, West Malling.

These major buildings do not by any means exhaust the pleasures that E.E. parish churches have to offer in Kent. Perhaps the finest that has not yet been mentioned is Woodchurch, with quite a mighty nave, related in style to the crypt passage at Hythe, and a sanctuary that emulates the loftiness of Hythe's. The sanctuary has shafted wall arcading as a dado below the windows, a form of decoration favoured in the south-east of the county, in several of the most memorable chancels, e.g. at Folkestone (E) and Cheriton (E), and, handsomest of all, in the N chapel at Alkham (E). Cooling has it also. A somewhat different sort of chancel arcading, rising the full height of the walls and enclosing lancets under the arches, can be found in several churches near the Medway estuary, at Stockbury (E), Rainham, Lower

* Plate tracery occurs only in the nave at Stone, and in two secular examples; one, of vast size, belonging to the Archbishop's Palace at Canterbury (E), built before 1243, the other to Squerryes Lodge, Westerham, a house with a first-floor hall.

Halstow (E), Sittingbourne (E), and Upchurch (E), and, an outlier
of the group, at Ash near Wrotham. At Cobham the chancel is
unusually large, with shafted lancets, impressive for its simple
spaciousness. The chapels of the Commanderies of the Knights
Hospitaller at Sutton-at-Hone (building in 1234) and Swingfield
(E) are similar in effect, and so is the much larger chapel of the
hospital (now St Peter's church) founded after 1244 at Maidstone,
and the chapel of St Bartholomew's Hospital, Sandwich (E),
founded in 1217.

To continue with parish churches: St Peter's Sandwich must
originally have been very impressive, with aisled nave and aisled
chancel, both with clerestories, and a central tower.* Appledore
had some, now very mutilated, arrangement of transepts with E
chapels. Complete, or nearly completely rebuilt, E.E. cruciform
churches are Cliffe, the finest of them, Faversham (E), the
largest, built as late as c.1301, Adisham (E), Ash (E), Ickham (E),
Littlebourne (E), and Teynham (E). This list should include
Chartham (E), under construction apparently in 1294, but, as we
shall see, Chartham must be considered as a Dec church.
Perhaps the clustered arcade piers at Wye (E) come from the
1290s too. Eastry (E) has a clerestoried nave, datable probably no
later than c.1230; Lydd is memorable for its length, Nonington
(E) for its just proportions. The list could be made to extend
much further, but there is space only to sum up the character-
istics of E.E. arcades. They have round piers, or occasionally
octagonal piers, and even more occasionally piers alternating
between round and octagonal; moulded capitals and bases, the
mouldings deeply sunk; and pointed arches with one or two
chamfers. Hollow chamfers are uncommon before the end of the
C13, though, as has been mentioned before, they can be found a
century earlier, in the Trinity Chapel crypt at Canterbury. The
way foliage capitals petered out after the 1180s has already been
described. Stiff-leaf proper is rare in Kent. All the important
examples have already been mentioned for one reason or another,
except the capitals on the tower arch at Westwell (E). The most
14memorable show of it is in the cloisters at Malling Abbey, West
Malling.

Far and away the commonest E.E. fittings are SEDILIA AND
PISCINAS. They are often grouped together, usually shafted,
with moulded arches, which may be round-headed,‡ trefoiled, or

* Hythe and Sandwich were both Cinque Ports. That accounts for the
grandeur of their churches.
‡ As late as the 1240s at St Peter, Maidstone.

just pointed. There are too many to give a list. Outstandingly sumptuous are the gabled and vaulted sedilia at Preston church, Faversham (E); but these cannot have been carved before *c*.1320, and with them we have arrived at the Dec style.*

But all this time ecclesiastical architecture has been running on far ahead of secular buildings. This is a good point to turn back to the C11 and say what there is to be said about CASTLES. Kent is rich in them, above all because of the nearness of the Continent. The earliest castles had no masonry walls, but consisted of a motte and bailey, that is to say a high, defensible earth mound, artificial or artificially heightened, and a wider enclosure beside it where temporary huts could be erected and cattle penned. Tonbridge Castle has an excellently preserved motte. There are others at Stockbury (E), Thurnham (E) (two), and at Newenden. Only after the Conquest were defences made stronger by masonry walls. Eynsford is a very complete example of the earliest kind of masonry castle, built *c*.1100. It is nothing but a low motte, roughly polygonal and *c*.200 ft at its greatest dimension across, surrounded by a high flint wall. Timber habitations leant against the inner face of the wall (and were provided with garderobes through it), and in the centre of the motte there stood, so excavations have established, a high timber watch tower. The Early Norman walling on the W side of the bailey at Rochester must have been part of something similar.

But at Rochester Archbishop Courbeuil soon built a magnificent keep. He began it in 1127, and built it 125 ft high to the 5 turret-tops, on a plan 70 ft square, palatial refuge and watchtower together, watching over the Medway crossing one way and the cathedral the other. No keep in England is higher, none better preserved. It is of course a tower keep, with the rooms piled one above another, and the hall up on the second storey. The arcade that divides the hall down the middle is in scale little smaller than the arcades of the nave of the cathedral. Sutton Valence has a small Norman tower keep, Canterbury (E) the lower parts of a large one. The early C12 St Leonard's Tower, West Malling, was clearly built for defence, but is not a 6 keep, as it was not designed to be lived in.‡ Possibly it was built

---

* There are only half-a-dozen E.E. FONTS in the county. Only one deserves special mention, and that must be very late: at Old Romney. Otherwise there are no C13 fittings, except what is left of the wooden CHOIR STALLS at Rochester Cathedral.

‡ Perhaps the same can be said of the small but massive tower at Stone Castle, Stone.

by Bishop Gundulf of Rochester, possibly in connexion with a chapel. Gundulf built the defensible tower that still stands, somewhat reduced in height, detached on the N side of Rochester Cathedral. His name is connected also with the (originally detached?) tower on the N side of Dartford church. St Radegund's Abbey (E), at the end of the century, had a N tower, which may also have been designed partly for defence.

But there are still two more tower keeps that have not yet been mentioned. Both were built by Henry II himself: Dover Castle (E) from 1168, Chilham (E) c.1171–4. Chilham is octagonal with square projections. The form may have been affected by the masonry of an earlier building that was incorporated into the forebuilding, but Henry showed his interest in polygonal keep-plans at Orford also, which is eighteen-sided. The angles of a polygon, being more than a r.-angle, are less liable to collapse if undermined than are the corners of a rectangle. Dover Castle however is historically far more important. Not only does it have the roomiest and most luxurious of all keeps, with walls so thick that whole suites of rooms are set within their depth, and two sumptuous chapels in the forebuilding; but, when the keep was finished in 1185, work went on, surrounding it with a turreted curtain wall, and the beginning of a second curtain wall, also with turrets. The notion of curtain walls was a novelty in Western Europe, brought back by the Crusaders who had seen the walls of Constantinople; and the notion of concentric defences was novel too. It remains to say that we know that Dover Castle cost over £7,000, a gigantic sum in the C12, and that the mason's name was *Mauricius*.

The next improvement in defensive design was to build projections round, not angled. The improvement was born of experience. In 1215 King John's troops undermined the SW turret of the keep at Rochester. When it came to be rebuilt in 1226 the turret's square plan was changed to round, which gave no angles vulnerable to undermining. John himself was responsible for continuing the curtain walls at Dover (E), and here, as early as 1204, the mural towers were built D-shaped. When, however, in the 1220s, new gateways, the Norfolk Towers and the Fitzwilliam Gate, were inserted, their rounded towers were built keeled, i.e. pointed at their foremost extremity. That looks like one of those rare examples in medieval castle building when intimidating appearance was preferred to the strongest defence. The Constable's Tower at Dover, also constructed in the 1220s, is a brilliantly sophisticated combination of gatehouse and residence, a successor to such gatehouse-keeps as Richmond in the North Riding of Yorkshire. The Constable must have been very confident in his castle's impregnability to have his dwelling in this exposed position. At Tonbridge Castle is another gate-24 house which is both spacious residence and the heaviest fortification of the castle. This was built in the early C14, and is a most impressive piece of architecture.

Tonbridge also had curtain walls with ranges of buildings against their inner side. This arrangement is found at Saltwood (E), probably a C13 building, with a great hall of c.1300 flaunting its great traceried windows above the walls, and at Allington, licensed in 1281. Much building went on in just these years at Leeds, a royal castle, but too much has been altered for one to say much of its defensive arrangements. Like Saltwood, Leeds stood in the middle of a moat as broad as a lake. Saltwood's moat is drained; at Leeds the moat very beautifully survives.

During the C14, haphazard planning gave way to a much more compact, regular, and standardized form. The curtain walls described a rectangle, with four big towers, one at each angle, the gatehouse in the centre of one side, and four ranges of rooms within the curtain, round a central courtyard. In the North of England, Bolton Castle, licensed in 1379, shows the type most fully; in the South, Bodiam, of six years later. In Kent it first appears at Westenhanger (E), after 1343. Queenborough (E), of 1361–77, long demolished, was remarkable in being round, but otherwise conformed to the type. Scotney, of c.1380, was quite a modest affair, and may have had a free-standing house within the curtain walls, not ranges attached to them.

The Duke of Bedford's scheme, after 1430, for enclosing Penshurst Place in a massive rectangular curtain wall with vast square towers at the angles and in the centres of the long sides would have been like Scotney on an immeasurably greater scale. Cooling, built for Sir John de Cobham in 1381–5, perhaps on a plan supplied by *Henry Yevele*, has the gatehouse set in the wall 35 of an outer courtyard to the E of the main moated castle. Hever Castle is a very interesting example of the way the Bodiam type 36 was soon adapted for a semi-fortified house. Hever was licensed in 1384. It is square, the walls of sandstone, with a gatehouse flush with the wall on the entrance side, and thin square corner turrets. The internal ranges are timber-framed. Wickham Court, West Wickham, begun after 1469, was similarly compact and similar in having internal timber-framing. But Wickham Court is built of brick, has octagonal corner turrets, and shows by its

projecting chimneybreasts and, even more, by the absence of a
gatehouse that its fortifiable aspect is largely a matter of form.
Should one connect this trend, discernible by the 1380s, as we
have seen, for castles to become less heavily fortified, with the
contrasting increase in the FORTIFICATION OF TOWNS?
Suffice it to say that the monumental Westgate of Canterbury
dates from 1375-81, and what is left of the town walls of Canterbury and Rochester from the C14. The fine series of C14 stone
38 BRIDGES over the river Medway, at Yalding, Teston, West
Farleigh, Aylesford, and the mighty, but long-demolished bridge
of 1387 at Rochester also suggest an increasing pride in community endeavour.

So much for Kent's medieval castles. The county is just as
rich in unfortified domestic buildings, even from the C12 and
C13. Kent was no border county, unsafe unless one lived in a
fortified house. In Canterbury there is nothing above ground of
the C12 town which Dr Urry has recently rediscovered so fully
from documents, but the undercrofts of half-a-dozen C12 and
C13 stone houses have survived. At West Malling there is the
shell of a Norman town house, with a hall on the first floor.
Excavation at Eynsford Castle has established that the house
built in the mid C12 within the C11 walls had a first-floor hall as
well. Chilham Castle (E) is built on part of an unfortified stone
house that may be as early as the C11. The ruins of Walmer
Court (E) are Norman too, of a semi-fortified house it seems.

There is more left of Norman communal buildings than of
private houses. Not only are there the monastic ranges at
Canterbury (E), in the infirmary cloister, at Horton Priory,
Monks Horton (E), and Minster-in-Thanet (E), a grange, i.e. the
farming headquarters, of St Augustine's Abbey, Canterbury, all
three built to a standard design, but there are several hospitals
and halls for pilgrims as well. Lanfranc at the end of the C11
founded two hospitals, one dedicated to St John outside the North
Gate of Canterbury, the other, for lepers, at Harbledown, a
discreet couple of miles from the city. At Harbledown (E) the
lepers lived in wooden houses. Nothing is left of the houses, and
the original church has been enlarged; but the springing of its
apse survives. At St John's Hospital, Canterbury (E), much more
remains, enough to allow one to speak with surprising completeness about Lanfranc's provisions. A hall can be traced (only its N
end stands) c. 26 ft wide by c. 150 ft long, and a chapel with two
parallel naves, rebuilt c. 1200, placed at r. angles to the hall, at
the centre of one of the long sides, so that men and women could

use both hall and chapel without ever mixing. The small isolated C11 building is identified as a mortuary.

Two C12 halls for pilgrims or other visitors to Canterbury remain. The North Hall by the gateway into the cathedral precinct is a mid-C12 building. Eastbridge Hospital is in the centre of the city, built c.1190. Both have halls with one aisle, standing on a vaulted undercroft. Little is left of the North Hall except the extraordinarily majestic staircase up to it; Eastbridge Hospital, converted into almshouses, remains entire, with a C14 chapel beside the street, across the head of the hall, and timber-framed dwelling houses at the far end. The C13 Maison Dieu at Dover (E), a communal hall for pilgrims to and from the Continent, had a chapel attached to its E end, like monastic infirmaries. Nothing significant of that is visible now, but only an early C14 addition: the splendidly spacious S aisle, a whole hall in itself, on an undercroft, with a SW tower, and noble four-light side windows.

Halls on the first floor were a feature of private houses also in the C13. The vaulted undercroft of what must have been a$_{23}$ splendid one is left at Nettlestead Place. Luddesdown Court is much more modest, but has a memorable stone fireplace with a lintel on moulded corbels; and Squerryes Lodge, Westerham, is recognizable by its upper doorway, finely moulded, and a plate-traceried window. At Temple Manor, Strood, hall and undercroft are complete, the only domestic survival from the houses of the Knights in the county.* There is a small, very complete, hall-house of this type at Ickham (E), another at Hoad Farm, Acrise (E), and fragments of others in Sandwich (E). By c.1300 first-floor halls were obsolete.

Ground-floor halls open to the roof on the other hand were due for a much longer run of popularity. By the mid C14 a complete standardized house-plan had emerged, in which an open hall was flanked at one end by service rooms, and by private rooms for the owner at the other. The main doorway into the house, at the service end of the hall, led into a passage, commonly known as the screens passage, because it was separated from the hall proper by a wooden screen, and from the other side of which doorways opened into the service rooms, kitchen, pantry, and buttery. A second doorway led out of the far end of the screens

---

* The houses at Sutton at Hone and Swingfield (E) have been mentioned already, for their C13 chapels. The Knights Hospitaller had a preceptory at West Peckham in the C14. On Western Heights, Dover (E), a Templars' church has been excavated, small, but with a round nave, as usual with the Templars.

passage. This solar–hall–service plan is universal throughout the country during the later Middle Ages; in Kent it can be found on the largest scale and on the smallest. Convenient and economical of space, the most important thing about it architecturally is that it was an asymmetrical layout. This is, as we have seen, a contrast to fortified houses, which were at this time, in the early C14, tending towards symmetry of plan. A preference for symmetry on aesthetic grounds was, it need hardly be said, a Renaissance preference. What tortures of reconciliation that involved in the C16 we shall see in due course.

25   Penshurst Place is probably the grandest and most perfectly preserved example of this type of unfortified house in the country. It was built from 1341 for Sir John de Pulteney, a London draper and merchant, who was four times Lord Mayor. The hall itself
26 at Penshurst is very large, and keeps not only its original collar-beam and crown-post roof, but even the tiled floor and central hearth in the hall. The screens passage was entered through a two-storeyed porch on the N side; the solar, on a vaulted undercroft, is at first-floor level, approached up a spacious flight of stone steps. The workmanship throughout is first-rate, but not showy.

37   At Knole a century later the plan is essentially the same, in spite of the fact that here, in an archbishop's palace on the grandest scale, there is a complete quadrangle with a gate-tower in front of the hall and a back court behind. The solar is developed into a whole state suite ending in a chapel at the far SE corner of the back court, and the kitchen is so large that it is set within one of the ranges of the back court. The great scale of Knole is of course a sign of the secular power of the Archbishop of Canterbury in the C15. Archbishop Bourchier was its builder, c.1456–64. A mile or two away, at Otford, Archbishop Warham between 1503 and 1518 built a second quadrangular palace, hardly smaller. Of this not much remains. Of earlier episcopal palaces there are the ruins at Charing (E) of the Archbishop of Canterbury's, mostly early C14, and the tiny fragments, mid-C13, of the Bishop of Rochester's palace at Halling. Of the C16 Archbishop's Palace at Bekesbourne (E) barely anything is left, of Ford at Hoath (E) nothing. The only seriously fortified archiepiscopal residence was Saltwood Castle (E), where Archbishop Courtenay (1381–96) built the great gatehouse.

At the other end of the scale from Penshurst and Knole are the timber-framed yeomen's houses, but it is not yet time to discuss them. For the present a few words remain to be said about the

prehistory of the Penshurst type of layout, which can be traced
very fully in Kent in moderate-sized stone houses. The earliest
relevant house is Court Lodge, Great Chart, which is of the
C13, with a ground-floor hall. Its plan needs further investigation. At Old Soar, Plaxtol, datable c.1290, the solar end is all
that is left; but that includes not only a first-floor solar, but a
chapel opening from one of its corners, and a spacious garderobe
off another. That is rather a messy plan. Nurstead Court, of
c.1320, on the other hand is so compact that service rooms, hall,
and two-storeyed solar end stood under a single roof. Only half
the house now remains, but the whole thing is recorded, including the fact that there was a free-standing kitchen. Nurstead's
hall was, however, aisled, with timber piers. The C14 part of 27
Hoad Farm, Acrise (E), has a similar over-all roof, and so does
Court Lodge, Mersham, where the solar is on the first floor above 28
the kitchen. Contemporary with these are the first examples of
the plan as it came to be standardized. They are Ightham Mote
and, somewhat smaller, the Old Rectory, Southfleet, and Battel
Hall, Leeds.*

So we have reached the early C14 again, and it is time to study
the DECORATED STYLE and see how it manifests itself in Kent.
The place to start this time is not Canterbury, although we shall
be back there soon, but Chartham (E). In 1294 the vicar of
Chartham was engaged in building works at the church. The
whole cruciform church is of one build, but the chancel is the
sumptuous part, and it is natural to assume that this was the part
for which the vicar took special responsibility. The glory of the
chancel is the window tracery, which is to a decidedly post-
geometrical pattern. There are quatrefoils, but they are subcusped, and the main cusps are split open. Straight bars or spurs
extend from the back of these split cusps. There is nothing in the
way of a reverse curve, i.e. no ogees, but the orderly geometrical
shapes are distorted in fanciful ways to create a richer range of
patterns. The result at Chartham is perhaps more curious than
beautiful. Inside, a further fancy, the window hood-moulds are
linked, and jump up between the windows in little bottomless
trefoils. Split-cusped tracery never caught on as tracery with
ogees did. Admittedly it can be found as far away as Whitby
Abbey in the North Riding, but to call it Kentish, as people
generally do, is not unreasonable. Split cusps appear first on a
monument in Rochester Cathedral, to Bishop de Bradfield, who 18

* Remembered especially for its extraordinarily elaborate stone laver just 29
inside the main door.

died in 1283. At the other end of the time scale, the great window inserted in St Anselm's Chapel, Canterbury Cathedral (E), in 1336 has split-cusped tracery, with ogees as well. Other examples are the choir screens at Canterbury Cathedral of 1304-5, the chancel windows at Cliffe, and isolated windows at Bobbing (E), Ulcombe, Kenardington, and St Mary Cray. The heart-shrine at Brabourne (E) has split cusps too. The other Chartham peculiarity, the bottomless trefoils, appears again immediately after 1300, on the gatehouse at St Augustine's Abbey, Canterbury (E). Similarly, after 1301, the sedilia at Faversham (E) have sex-foiled openings, the lowest lobe missing.

In following both details we are led back to Canterbury. What in the way of new architecture had Canterbury to show at this time? Nothing major, just as in the county as a whole; but enough to show that at Canterbury a workshop was active with a markedly individual and advanced style. The stone screens, built in 1304-5 to enclose the choir of the cathedral on three sides, show the style most clearly. The screen is closed below, dotted with four-petalled flowers, pierced as arcading above, with even, two-light openings, under a straight top frieze, with a row of pierced trefoils and a row of battlements. The N and S doorways are not made an excuse for any contrast. The stone stalls in the chapter house, rebuilt in 1304, are handled in a precisely similar way, clearly and soberly, with no lively silhouette, no ambiguity of surface, no forms seen one behind another, nothing indeed that we usually associate with that luxuriant style we call Dec; rather, it foreshadows the Perp style that first appears fully-grown at Gloucester in the 1330s, but was heralded by St Stephen's Chapel, Westminster, begun in 1292. St Stephen's Chapel had wall panelling exceptionally close in handling to the choir screens at Canterbury.

The great gateway at St Augustine's Abbey, built between 1300 and 1309, represents the style in a full-scale structure. One notices the designer's penchant for wall-panelling here too, but there are ogees, and the way the lofty octagonal angle turrets have their profiles eaten into by gabled niches half-way up is characteristically Dec. The internal vaulting is supported on what were once very finely carved caryatid figures.* One has a salutary reminder of the relative positions and values of a great ecclesiastic

---

* Such caryatids found favour in Kent in the C14. A splendidly preserved pair support the chancel arch at Westbere (E), and the roof principals in the halls at Ightham Mote, Battel Hall, Leeds, and Penshurst Place rest on caryatids. At Penshurst the figures are of wood and very large.

and a great secular lord at this time if one contrasts this gate-tower, little more than an opulent piece of display, with the contemporary gate-tower of Tonbridge Castle, where first-class 24 masons were employed and built something mightily defensible. If on the other hand one wants to point to something purely in the spirit of the early C14, then one must point to the chapter room doorway at Rochester Cathedral, with its ripe abundance of sculpture; or to the playfully intricate sedilia at Preston Church, Faversham (E). Or one must point to monuments, and the time to do that has not yet arrived.*

Parish church building continued busily in the late C13 and C14, particularly in adding aisles. To find a C14 arcade of octagonal piers and double-chamfered arches is a standard experience. Aisles added right to the E end of the chancel, giving three E gables of equal or nearly equal size, was a favourite development. New Romney, with its splendid reticulated tracery, 21 is perhaps the best example. Upchurch (E) and Lynsted (E) are others. It became standardized in town churches, e.g. Holy Cross, Canterbury (E), of c.1380. Complete new churches are rare, except in the Weald, where the forests were cut down and permanent villages settled only as late as this. And here only Smarden, with its fantastically wide, aisleless nave, was not remodelled in the next century. Chartham (E) c.1294 has already been mentioned. It is cruciform without provision for a central tower. Barham (E) was built on the same plan at a similar date.‡ Early C14 transepts are at Yalding and Boughton Aluph (E) (after 1329). At Wingham (E) chancel and transepts were built in connexion with the founding in 1282 of a college of chantry priests. The transepts have the remarkable feature of shallow E projections, lit by big windows, probably to give extra altar room for the priests. At Adisham (E) and Ickham (E) similar transept chapels were built, in imitation of Wingham. Just occasionally a C14 parish-church mason departed from the beaten track by a flight of the imagination. The nobly broad and lofty chancel of Hawkhurst of c.1360 is one example. The same mason worked elsewhere in the neighbourhood. His must be the aisled tower at Sandhurst and the enlarged chancel at Rolvenden,

* Though the delightful sculpture on Archbishop Meopham's monument set up in Canterbury Cathedral c.1336 must be mentioned, for its little reliefs of evangelists and seated monks are very close to the doctors on the Rochester doorway.

‡ Bishopsbourne (E) near by is clearly by the Barham mason, but in plan an aisled nave and chancel, without a chancel arch.

both of them bold and unhackneyed in their handling of space. The towers at Herne (E) and St Nicholas at Wade (E) in the NE of the county are a pair, datable c.1330. Both are placed over the W bay of an aisle and are vaulted inside. Wave-moulded arches, sculptured corbels, and the splendid traceried windows give them a sumptuousness which no other early C14 building has in Kent.* These towers are faced with knapped, squared flints, the most up-to-date and expensive material in the early C14 for the non-stone parts of the county. At Sittingbourne (E), for example, this is the material used throughout, in the early C14 parts of
22 Cliffe, and at Higham, and in the C15 tower of St Nicholas, Strood, these knapped, squared flints and ragstone blocks make a pattern of black and white bands. Flushwork, so popular in East Anglia in the C15, but first found (Erpingham Gate, Norwich) c.1300, was never attempted in Kent.

But the most vivid Dec delights are in small things, and first of all in window tracery. Flowing tracery of the sort associated with Lincolnshire and the North East Midlands is hardly known in Kent. Windows at Sutton-at-Hone, the E window at St Nicholas at Wade (E), and one window in the N transept at Rochester Cathedral are about the only examples. Mouchettes do turn up, but only in the simplest compositions, and in the very delightful triangular window in the nave gable at Sheldwich (E); a rare place for a window of any sort in this part of the country. We have already seen a Kentish attempt to enliven the rigours of geometrical tracery, at Chartham. Geometrical tracery of the purest kind still occurs at Meopham, consecrated as late as 1325. Cusped intersecting tracery is the commonest early C14 kind, and the fine windows at Herne (E) are nothing more than that with little trefoils and quatrefoils tucked into available corners. Other major windows are content with a single big feature, e.g. a star at Hawkhurst, a spoked circle at Thurnham (E). At the other extreme of whimsical complication come the windows at East Sutton. There is nothing else quite like them. The SEDILIA at Preston church, Faversham (E), have been mentioned already. Other vaulted sedilia of the C14 are at Cliffe, Woodnesborough
30 (E), and a superb set of c.1380 at Cobham.

STONE SCULPTURE of the C14, other than monuments, has partly been dealt with. There is not much more. Naturalistic foliage on capitals of the S arcade at Marden, humpy, post-naturalistic leaves on the chancel arcades at Upchurch (E), the

---

* At Birchington (E) a third such tower was planned.

tower arches at Stone, and the sedilia at Warehorne just about exhaust the list, except for the exquisite figure of God, from a reredos perhaps, at Southfleet, and the late C14 fragments of figures at Cobham, these too of first-rate quality. The standard of C14 sculpture was consistently high, as monuments confirm. In the C15 quality drops sharply; so it is ironical that the only major figure-sculpture that survives as a whole, the statues of kings on the pulpitum in Canterbury Cathedral (E), were made c.1420, and are dull and lifeless, as C14 figures hardly ever are. The unusual carved tympanum at Bridge (E) is Late Perp and very humble as a work of art.

All too little, here as throughout the country, is left of the colour that decorated churches, in the C13 and C14 above all. The structure itself was coloured, as the broad zigzag bands on the piers at Cliffe, or the Archbishop's doorway in the cloisters at Canterbury (E) still show; and monuments too, demonstrated by the splendidly preserved colour on the effigy of Bishop John de Sheppey in Rochester Cathedral. And by means of wall paintings and stained glass it was possible to leave no surface uncoloured. Those in Canterbury Cathedral have been mentioned already. There, even the floor was made multicoloured in front of Thomas Becket's shrine, by the pavement of opus alexandrinum laid down c.1220, with roundels of the Labours of the Months and Signs of the Zodiac. Similar C13 roundels appear in the wall paintings at Brook (E), which is perhaps now the best place in Kent for catching an idea of the effect of WALL PAINTINGS in a medieval church. The N wall at Capel also has a pretty complete coverage, this too of the C13, and so do the transepts at Cliffe. Finest in quality, though very faded, are the figures under canopies at Stone; the product surely, like the church, of a royal workshop. Best preserved is the Wheel of Fortune at Rochester Cathedral, and the pier at Faversham (E) painted after 1301 with scenes from the life of the Virgin. The large figures at Bishopsbourne (E), also of c.1300, must have been fine things once. Better preserved is the figure of St Michael at Lenham. As far as iconography is concerned, it is worth making a comparison between the C12 Christ in Majesty at Eastbridge Hospital, Canterbury, the C13 figure of Christ at Fawkham, and the two C14 representations of the Trinity, at Boughton Aluph (E) and on the wood tester of the Black Prince's monument, c.1376, in Canterbury Cathedral (E).

Of STAINED GLASS, apart from the glass in Canterbury Cathedral, even less is preserved. But glass does not fade like wall paintings, so the glass that has survived, and not been restored away, makes a more immediate impact. There is quite a lot of Dec glass scattered through many churches, and once again it is a constant joy to find how sensitive and deft C14 artists were in even the most unlikely places. Chartham (E) has the fullest display, in all the chancel windows, much restored in 1881; grisaille with sparing colour, mainly in the foliage borders. It is fascinating to watch how as glazing proceeded from E to W, from *c*.1294 over it may be fifteen years, the bud-like leaves of the earliest windows burst out into precisely accurate hop and passion flower. But, to digress for a moment, NATURALISTIC FOLIAGE was beginning to displace stiff-leaf well before the 1290s. In Kent it makes its earliest appearance on two monuments in Rochester Cathedral, of Bishop de St Martin † 1274, and Bishop de Merton, whose death occurred three years later. Other good stained-glass borders of naturalistic plants are at Bobbing (E), Bishopsbourne (E), and, especially, Harbledown (E) with its Canterbury bells. The other complete window is at Selling (E), datable 1299–1307. Here too colour is kept for the small figures in the centre of each light and for armorial bearings, and not allowed to dominate the whole window in the early C13 way. Small but enjoyable panels, mostly single figures in tracery lights, are at Brookland, West Kingsdown, Leigh, Upchurch (E), Willesborough, Stowting (E), Fordwich (E), Graveney (E), Upper Hardres (E), Ditton, and Lullingstone. Interesting fragments of the glass at Mersham are datable *c*.1396. The Mersham window

32 incidentally is an excellent example of the way tracery was designed for the glass it was to take. The result at Mersham is very bizarre.

C15 glass is, generally speaking, much less good. The only major window is that in the NW transept at Canterbury Cathedral (E), executed by the royal glazier between 1465 and 1482. Nettlestead is the only parish church where the whole original glazing can still be reconstructed. Otherwise the best are a Coronation of the Virgin at Wormshill (E), and figures in St Edward the Confessor's Chapel, Canterbury Cathedral, and at Kemsing. There is early C16 glass at Cranbrook (*c*.1514), Lullingstone, and West Wickham.*

To return to architecture, and to pass from what is arguably proto-Perp to the PERPENDICULAR STYLE in all its glory,

---

* And worthwhile C17 and C18 Swiss and German glass at Patrixbourne (E), Temple Ewell (E), and Mereworth.

there is no more glorious Early Perp building in England than the nave of Canterbury Cathedral (E). Archbishop Sudbury called for subscriptions to rebuild the C11 nave in 1378, but work got properly under way only after the election of Prior Chillenden in 1391. It was complete by 1405. The transepts were rebuilt more slowly, the N not entirely vaulted until after 1468, but to a design that departs from the nave system only in trivial details. The design of the nave was, almost certainly, *Henry Yevele*'s. As at Winchester, where too the nave was being rebuilt during these years, the Norman fabric conditioned the plan and the great girth of the piers. So a dominant W–E vista down the nave was inevitable, and all diagonal views into the aisles were blocked. The presence of the aisles is mainly felt by the floods of light that enter through the lofty arches of the arcades from the equally lofty aisle windows. So the nave becomes a hall filled by light, one does not quite know how. This hall-like character is stressed by the great super-arches that in each bay enclose arcade, blank-panelled triforium, and clerestory in a single unit, and by the dense lierne-vault that presses the space down from above. It was a very English thing to make capital of structural limitations in this way, so that the new nave becomes in its way a re-interpretation of the old one, exploiting the possibilities inherent in its structure. We know that Yevele was sensitive to past styles, for his completion of the nave of Westminster Abbey is astonishingly faithful to the C13 work. Canterbury of course is not the same as that, for it is thoroughly Perp, not in any way a pastiche. Its virtues too are Perp virtues, sober serenity and calm. Nothing is forced, and that makes it, not an exciting, but a moving building to be in.

The other modifications of the ground plan of the cathedral are chapels added in the C15.* St Michael's Chapel off the SW transept, *c.*1420–8, has a lierne-vault; but the Lady Chapel built as its partner E of the NW transept has the first large-scale fan-vault in eastern England. It was built by Prior Goldstone (1449–68); so the little fan-vault in Henry IV's Chantry is an earlier fan-vault in the cathedral, for Henry died in 1413, his widow in 1437, and the altar in the chapel was consecrated in 1439. Another significant change is made in this chapel, for the vault is four-centred in section, i.e. flattened. This is not however the first sign of a preference for depressed arches, a preference which was to become almost universal in Late Perp times. The chapel at

* The Black Prince's Chantry, after 1363, and the chapel of Our Lady of the Undercroft (1370s) were merely inserted into the fabric of the C12 crypt.

Horne's Place, Appledore, has windows with depressed ogee heads, and the date of licensing the chapel was 1366. A fan-vault was also planned for the Lady Chapel at Rochester Cathedral. The last important monastic building in the county, the Christ Church Gateway into the precinct at Canterbury (E) of c.1517–22, returns to lierne vaulting. In its broad proportions, however (contrast the great gateway of St Augustine's Abbey, two hundred years earlier), and its somewhat vapid sense of display the Christ Church Gateway is characteristic of the last decades of monastic architecture.

As for parish churches, the spate of new building continued undiminished through the C15 up to the time of the Reformation. But, as in the C14, few entirely new churches were erected. It was rather a matter of enlargement, by throwing out, or more often widening existing, chapels and aisles, and rebuilding naves, or more rarely chancels, larger. The two characteristic additions are nave clerestories and W towers. Towers will deserve a paragraph to themselves.

New Perp churches are few enough to list. Holy Cross, Canterbury (E), built c.1380, Kingsnorth, and Headcorn are late C14, and Queenborough (E), that royal foundation of extraordinary meagreness, went up in 1366–8. The most ambitious
31 new church is Maidstone, begun in 1395, with its chancel aisles that were going to be vaulted, and its lofty, handsome arcades. Mention Eastchurch (E) of 1431, Hernhill (E), Nettlestead, Nurstead, St Nicholas, Rochester (1423), and Stone-in-Oxney (1464), and the list of new Perp churches is complete; except for
43 Smallhythe, a chapel of Tenterden, built in 1516–17 of brick, with stepped end-gables.

Several churches came to be much enlarged when they were made collegiate. The late C14 was the great period for endowing COLLEGES. The grand new church at Maidstone was built because Archbishop Courtenay had in 1395 been granted permission to found a college. Collegiate buildings, completed by 1398, gatehouse, and residential range, but not the hall, survive s of the church. At Cobham the college was founded in 1362. The church did not need enlarging, but the college buildings survive *in toto*. They comprise three ranges of living quarters round a quadrangle, with the hall on the s side. Bredgar (E), founded in 1382, was a minor affair. The college buildings form a single range. A college was founded by Archbishop Kempe at Wye (E) to restore the worship of God there, 'by the augmentation of the number of God's ministers'. This, too, built between 1432 and

1448, has a hall and ranges round a quadrangle. At Wye the church was thoroughly remodelled, on a cruciform plan. Only the nave is left now. Finally, the cruciform rebuilding of Ashford *c.*1475–83 was connected with Sir John Fogge's plan, ultimately thwarted, to make the church collegiate.

So we can pass on to Perp TOWERS. Once again Canterbury Cathedral (E) possesses the outstanding ones, the SW tower of 1424–34 by *Thomas Mapilton*, and *John Wastell*'s magnificent Bell Harry tower over the crossing, perhaps the finest of all Late Perp towers. Bell Harry was built *c.*1495–*c.*1503. Crossing towers are rare. The only others are at Ashford, Ash (E), Boughton Aluph (E), and Folkestone (E), all but the first with independent stair-turrets, not a felicitous way of handling a crossing tower. But such a stair-turret is natural enough in a W tower, and that is where the overwhelming majority of Perp towers were placed. A rough count produces eighty-two such towers, plus two NW ones, Wouldham and Eythorne (E), and two SW, Snodland and Maidstone. Harrietsham (E) even got a Perp W tower, though it had a N tower already. In studying these towers one feels overwhelmingly the standardization that medieval churches ran to. It is not a matter, as in Somerset or East Anglia, of many variations on recognizable themes; for the Kent towers eschew the embellishments – pinnacles, pierced parapets, decorated bands, and panelling – which make such variations possible. The situation is as, for example, in Devon; there are just two basic types, one with diagonally projecting buttresses, the other with pairs of buttresses at the angles, each set at 90 degrees to its fellow. Generally there is a projecting stair-turret at one corner, generally octagonal, and rising higher than the main body of the tower. Early C14 towers, as at Meopham, Rolvenden, Herne (E), and St Nicholas at Wade (E), or indeed Minster-in-Thanet (E) before 1200, have buttresses set back from the angles. The new type, with deeper buttresses, stepping in by deep set-offs, and not necessarily carried as high as the top parapet, appears already in its characteristic form soon after 1395 at Maidstone. The first datable tower with diagonal buttresses is Addington of 1400–3. A number of towers can be roughly dated by bequests for building them. On that evidence the busiest time for tower building was the early C16. Money was left to the tower at Chilham (E) as late as 1534, for the W door in the Charing (E) tower in 1537. One or two dragged on long after the Reformation; Aldington for instance, left unfinished after 1547, and the ambitious tower at Stoke, abandoned after 1541 a quarter done.

Big, simple towers are generally the most satisfying – Chilham
(E) say, or Goodnestone near Wingham (E) – not the most self-
conscious ones, such as Egerton, Charing (E), or Biddenden,
which, with their numerous string-courses and set-offs on the
buttresses, seem somehow fussy and debased. Bearsted has
animals on the parapet in place of pinnacles. Only Tenterden
33 transcends the type to become something really memorable. But
Tenterden is on an exceptional scale; and in that is matched by
two untypical towers, Lydd and Ashford. Lydd was built in
1442–6 by *Thomas Stanley*, one of the masons working on the
SW tower of Canterbury Cathedral. It is vaulted internally,* and
crowned by small pinnacles. Ashford also is pinnacled,‡ but on
the other hand, with its polygonal buttresses, is related to
Wastell's crossing tower at Canterbury.

Medieval SPIRES in Kent are without exception of timber.
New Romney admittedly has the stump of a stone spire, but that
is all. The timber spires are generally short and stocky, with
broaches and a covering of shingles. The recessed spike so
common in Hertfordshire turns up once or twice, e.g. at
Wingham (E). The spires of Bexley, Upchurch (E), and Willes-
34 borough (and the detached belfry at Brookland), probably all C15
in date, are built up of overlapping polygonal cones, which
makes an odd outline.

As with towers, so with LATER MEDIEVAL FITTINGS, Kent
has plenty to show, but little that is really outstanding. The com-
40 pletest ensemble is the chapel at Ightham Mote, fitted up after
1506. The finest single item is unquestionably the C14 LECTERN
at Detling (E). It probably came from Boxley Abbey. Swanscombe and Lenham have simpler, C15 lecterns. Higham boasts
the only indisputable medieval PULPIT, this too C14, and a
DOOR made by the same carpenter.§ As for REREDOSES, the
fragments at Cobham have been mentioned. That at Minster-in-
Sheppey (E), again C14, is also a wreck.‖

C14 FONTS are rare, and decorated with nothing more than
tracery patterns, e.g. Sandhurst, Hythe (E). Only Otham has
sculpture, corbels supporting the bowl. From *c.*1400 onwards
fonts are more frequent, but more standardized, octagonal on an

* Like Folkestone (E), Maidstone, Gillingham, and Eythorne (E).

‡ The only other towers with pinnacles (much thicker and in fact rather
clumsy) are at Penshurst and Chiddingstone.

§ Bromley also has a C14 door.

‖ Much the best C14 reredos was at Sutton Valence, but this is now in the
Victoria and Albert Museum. An early C14 painted reredos, from a Dominican
foundation, is at Battel Hall, Leeds.

octagonal stem, with shields and roses alternately on the faces of the bowl, as Herne (E) and St Clement, Sandwich (E), both datable to the first decade of the C15, show. The font at St Stephen, Canterbury (E), is dated as late as 1591, that at Queenborough (E), with a relief of the castle, 1610. The Perp type is little changed in both. Farningham has carvings, not good, of the Seven Sacraments, and so is one of only two Seven Sacrament fonts outside East Anglia.* Southfleet and Staple (E) have similar, crude sculpture, of miscellaneous subjects. As for font covers, the tallest, with doors, are both early C16, at East Malling and Newington (E), even with unobtrusive Renaissance details.

The commonest C15 and early C16 fitting is the ROOD SCREEN. There are fragments of C14 screens, some of them parclose rather than rood screens, at Allhallows, Cliffe, Newington near Sittingbourne (E), Northfleet (especially delightful), Stansted, and Ulcombe. Perp screens are too numerous for all to be listed, and anyway they run to standardization. The way this came about is documented at St Stephen, Canterbury (E), where in 1519 *Michael Bonversall* contracted to make a screen copied from the screen at Holy Cross, Canterbury. Fragments of both show that he faithfully carried out the contract. Fragments are generally all that any church has left. Only at Shoreham does the vaulted coving under the rood remain. In one or two other churches the screen extends the whole width. Those at Eastchurch (E) and Leeds have the greatest width to span. Screens went on being put up in churches to the very last moment before roods were banned. There are Renaissance details on the screen at Boughton under Blean (E), and the Brenchley screen is dated 1536. Over the rood the roof was sometimes decorated especially lavishly. Such a celure is left only at Rainham, in the sanctuary at St Mildred, Canterbury (E), and, in an odd position, halfway down the nave, at Yalding.

Next a word on STALLS is needed. Stalls with MISERICORDS were not confined by any means to collegiate churches like Cobham, Wingham (E), and Maidstone; about a dozen others have them, including Ashford, which was planned to become collegiate. The best set of carved misericords is, far and away, that at Faversham (E). Probably they came to the parish church when the abbey was demolished after 1536.‡

Finally the C15 COPE at East Langdon (E) needs to be noted,

* Nettlecombe, Somerset, is the other.

‡ The stalls at Barming, with fantastic stall ends carved with Samson and the lion etc., are German, probably c.1300.

and PRE-REFORMATION PLATE; and that need not detain us long. Nothing has survived except a late C12 chalice and paten at Canterbury Cathedral (E), a copper-gilt chalice, mid-C13, at Bredhurst (E), and two early C16 silver patens at Walmer (E) and Cliffe.

And so to PRE-REFORMATION MONUMENTS. Here pride of place must be given to BRASSES. There are more monumental brasses in Kent than in any other single county. They can be found in over one hundred and fifty churches. Furthermore Cobham has the largest collection of brasses anywhere, sixteen in all. As the series ranges from the second decade of the C14 to 1529, Cobham is an excellent place for tracing the history of brasses, the gradual deterioration in technique during those two-and-a-half centuries, and the smaller and smaller sizes that were favoured in the C15, as the brass slipped lower down the social scale as a means of commemorating the dead. But at Cobham neither the highest nor the lowest achievements by the makers of brasses can be found. No more need be said about the lowest achievements. As for the highest, the brass at Chartham (E) † 1306, may stand for that. It represents a bareheaded knight, his legs crossed, one arm reaching to draw his sword – the very pose favoured on contemporary stone monuments of knights. The Chartham brass is the earliest in the county, the fourth earliest in England, thirty years later than the oldest of all, at Stoke d'Abernon, Surrey. The earliest brass at Cobham is of a lady. In the handful of other early C14 brasses priests predominate: at Woodchurch † 1333, Horsmonden, after 1338, and Kemsing † 1347. The brasses at Minster-in-Sheppey (E) of c.1330–5 are of foreign workmanship, but cut out of the plate in the way universal in England, but not usual on the Continent. The charming little brass at East Wickham commemorates civilians. That introduces all the possible types. Nothing further can be given except two lists, of specially fine brasses and of curiosities. First the fine ones: Mereworth, knight † 1366; Northfleet, priest † 1375; Ashford, lady † 1375; Sheldwich (E), knight and lady † 1394; Seal, knight † 1395; Dartford, c.1402; Upper Hardres (E), a splendid bracket brass, a very rare type, † 1405; Stone by Dartford, priest † 1408; Otterden (E), knight † 1408; Addington, knight and lady † 1409; Lydd, priest † 1420; Bobbing (E), two knights c.1420; Brabourne (E), knight † 1433; Erith, civilian † 1435; Graveney (E), civilian † 1436; Preston, Faversham (E), knight and lady † 1442;* Ulcombe, knight † 1470;

P. 220

P. 587

---

* The scale and sureness of the figure at Crundale (E) † 1466 justifies including it here, though it is not a brass but an incised alabaster slab.

Ashford, knight † 1490; Hever, knight † 1538. The brass at East ^{P.}
Sutton, † 1629, signed by *Edward Marshall*, is a freak in its ³¹⁰
excellence at such a late date. All these are full-length figures.
Half-lengths, especially half-length priests, are normal. In the
C15, however, a few symbolic brasses occur. The shroud brass at
Sheldwich (E), † 1431, is the earliest, and after that the heart with
inscribed scrolls at Margate (E) † 1433. Also at Margate is a
skeleton brass, † 1466. Then comes the Saltwood (E) brass,
† 1496, of an angel holding a heart. Much later is the brass plate
at Leigh, c.1580, emphasizing the resurrection of the body, a
doctrine associated generally with the C17. Last in this little list
of oddities is the series of forgeries laid down at Pluckley by Sir
Edward Dering c.1628–35. But one may as well include here
stone monuments with iconographical oddities. There are three of
them: first the haunting C13 coffin slab at Penshurst, carved with [19]
a relief of a woman, her head frontal, her bust in profile, pinned
down by a foliate cross; and second two priests apparently
carved as if in their lidless coffins, that at Lenham identified as
commemorating a priest who died in 1327, that at Bridge (E) to
one who died in 1512.

The brasses in Canterbury Cathedral (E) are known only by
the indents in which they were laid; but when it comes to
MEDIEVAL STONE MONUMENTS even a national survey would
have to include several that are in the cathedral. The earliest,
said to be to Archbishop Walter † 1205, of Purbeck marble, has
no figure, but a gabled top, with heads projecting in relief from
quatrefoils. The monument at Rochester to Bishop de Glanville
† 1214 is a plainer version of it. The shrine of Thomas Becket,
set up in the Trinity Chapel in 1220, but destroyed at the
Reformation, must have been something like this, if the representations of it in the stained glass of the chapel are anything to
go by. One shrine does survive, a mid-C14 one at Newington,
near Sittingbourne (E); and two heart-shrines, at Brabourne (E)
and Leybourne. Purbeck marble was the normal material for
carving monuments from in the C13. The difficulty with which it
is worked made the development of fully three-dimensional
effigies slower than it might otherwise have been. Kent has no
specially early effigy, and those that are earliest in style, i.e. least
raised up into the round, are unfortunately not dated. These are a
bishop in the S choir aisle at Rochester Cathedral, a knight in St
Bartholomew's Hospital chapel, Sandwich (E), and just the head
of a priest at Detling (E). The effigies of Bishops de St Martin [20]
(† 1274) and de Merton († 1277) mark a distinct advance, the

figures fully in the round, hand raised to bless, with elaborate canopies over their heads; and indeed, as has already been noted, they are advanced in another way, for the canopies have some of the earliest naturalistic leaves to be found anywhere. Bishop Ingoldsthorpe's monument, also at Rochester (date of death 1291), is a less good version of these. It is not a sign of a falling off in invention in the 1290s, for the monument of Archbishop Peckham † 1292 at Canterbury (E) is novel in several ways. In the first place the effigy is of wood, covered originally with gesso and coloured; that is to say it must have been infinitely more realistic than any carved in Purbeck marble. Secondly, the figure is set under an arch and upon a high base, against the side of which stand little weepers; and thirdly, ogees can be found in the details, perhaps here earlier than anywhere else. Ogees of course were to have a spectacular career; but the monument itself seems to have been the model for the famous series at Westminster Abbey, starting with Edmund Crouchback's. Weepers also appear on the mid-C14 monument at Folkestone (E). This is of a knight. Another knight of about this time is at St Peter, Sandwich (E). They both are recumbent, with straight legs. The earlier, more animated pose with crossed legs can be found in monuments at Lydd, Shorne, and Penshurst. The Penshurst monument is of Purbeck marble; the legs are broken off but originally crossed surely, so lively is his sword-drawing posture. The others are carved in freestone, and so is by far the outstanding monument of this type, that to Sir Robert de Shurland of c.1320 at Minster-in-Sheppey. Sir Robert, legs crossed, turns as if to rise from a drugged sleep. At his feet stands a small page.*

Later in the C14 the quieter, straight-legged pose prevailed. The change in conception can be demonstrated by contrasting the Minster knight with the monuments at Ickham (E) of c. 1340, and Ightham of c.1374; or, best of all, with the Black Prince's monument in Canterbury Cathedral (E). The Prince died in 1376, and his monument was set up in accordance with the detailed directions in his will. The figure, of gilt brass, lies on a high tomb-chest under a wooden tester painted with the Trinity. Encased in full armour, legs rigidly outstretched, hands joined in prayer, the figure is little more than a symbol of a knight.

The Black Prince's monument belongs to the grandest kind, that stands free and can be viewed from both sides. In those conditions the canopy above the monument can play a very impor-

---

* As in the contemporary monument in Exeter Cathedral.

tant part. Such monuments in Kent are practically confined to
Canterbury Cathedral, for Bishop Sheppey's monument at
Rochester (date of death 1360), already mentioned for its excellently preserved colour, has lost all but a few pieces of its
luxuriantly sculptured canopy; and the splendid tomb of John
Wotton, of c.1417, at Maidstone, is splendid mainly because it
has on its reverse side the magniloquently canopied sedilia. The
Canterbury Cathedral series starts with Archbishop Meopham's
monument, erected c.1336 as a screen across the mouth of St
Anselm's Chapel. It has no effigy, and its small-scale sculpture
has already been praised. It achieves its effect by colour contrast,
between black Purbeck marble and white freestone. The next of
these archiepiscopal monuments makes similar play with colour,
this time between Purbeck marble and alabaster. This, the
monument of Archbishop Stratford, who died in 1348, has one
of the very earliest known alabaster effigies. The alabaster workers
never reached a higher standard than in the figure of Stratford,
a beautifully robed, hollow-cheeked ascetic. At Canterbury one
can appreciate the decline in later alabaster figures well enough,
e.g. in that of Archbishop Courtenay † 1396, and even in the
early C15 royal effigies of Henry IV and Joan of Navarre (dates of
death 1413 and 1437).

Perp monuments are altogether not of great interest. Quite the
most enjoyable is that of Archbishop Kempe † 1454 at Canterbury, with its original and entirely delightful wooden canopy.
For the rest, the most notable monuments are all very late. In
Canterbury Cathedral only one need be mentioned, the wall-
monument to Archbishop Warham, who died in 1532, with its
colossal and fussily elaborate canopy. Equally spectacular is the
Peche monument at Lullingstone († 1522), with a first-rate 41
effigy unexpectedly relegated to basement level. The small type
of wall-monument with a tomb-chest and a panelled back-plate,
standard in many parts of the country, turns up at St Dunstan,
Canterbury (E) († 1524 and † 1533), in Bethersden marble, at
Penshurst, at Otford, at Stone in 1526–7, and at Faversham (E),
made in 1534 by *Alen* of Bearsted. None of these, for all the late
dates, shows any knowledge of Renaissance details. Only at
Goudhurst, on the stone reliefs dated 1537 that belong with the
wooden Culpeper effigies, does there seem in the poses of the
figures to be a trace of evidence that Italianate art was known in
Kent at this time.

Altogether the COMING OF THE RENAISSANCE to Kent is
stealthy. First in point of time are the pilasters that flank the

doorways on the Christ Church Gateway at Canterbury (E). The gateway is dated 1517, but was not completed until 1522. The pilasters are stuck on quite incongruously as an afterthought, among a riot of Late Perp niches and panelling. Unfortunately, since they have been quite renewed in the 1930s in artificial stone, it cannot now be proved whether they were in fact an afterthought. The question is of more interest than it might seem, for the pilasters are decorated with candelabra of Italian Quattrocento type just like the pilasters on the window mullions at Layer Marney, Essex, which are terracotta, and date from c.1520. The other earliest structural uses of such details are all in terracotta, at Sutton Place, Surrey, after 1521 and in a series of buildings in Suffolk, near Old Shrubland Park. Such forms in stone and as early as c.1522 place the Christ Church Gateway in a category by itself.

For the rest it is a matter of carpentry. The rood screen at Boughton under Blean (E) and the font covers at Newington near Sittingbourne (E) and East Malling have been mentioned already. Quite a lot of Early Renaissance panelling, with profile heads in relief, is scattered about in houses in mid-Kent. The most splendid roomful, at Boughton Court, Boughton Malherbe, datable before 1529, has gone to America. What remains to be seen is at Faversham (E), that in the Guildhall datable before 1533, at Hadlow, at Godinton, in two houses at Great Chart (Court Lodge and Singleton Manor), at Chilston Park, Boughton Malherbe, and at Cogan's House, Canterbury (E). The painted Royal Arms of Edward VI at Westerham completes this list, for it has unobtrusive S-shaped scrolls of Renaissance extraction.

It would be truer to say that the C16 in Kent, at any rate all but the last quarter of it, is remarkable for the contented acceptance of old forms, than that new ones were eagerly embraced. Only in building materials was there a decisive change of allegiance. Before the C16 BRICK was rarely used. In England the use of bricks was rediscovered in the C13. Little Wenham Hall, Suffolk, of c.1270–80 is the earliest English building where the walls are all brick. As for Kent, the bricks used at Allington Castle for window reveals may be C13. They are a pale pink. C14 examples are window reveals at Grench Manor, Gillingham, c.1380, and the vaults at Horne's Place, Appledore, after 1381, a C15 one (before 1445) the Dent-de-Lion gate-tower at Garlinge (E), where bricks and knapped flints make a pattern of alternate stripes. Equally successful pattern-making, checks of red brick and flint, is at Tonford Manor, Thanington

(E), c.1449. Pale yellow bricks were a Thanet speciality, made from mud not brick earth, best seen at Sandwich (E), e.g. at the top of Fisher Gate (1571) and in Manwood Court of c.1580. The ruined church of Midley, Old Romney, was built almost wholly of similar bricks, probably c.1500.*

The earliest building of any consequence walled entirely in brick, with stone dressings, is Wickham Court, West Wickham, after 1469. Compared with, say, East Anglia, that is not an early date; while the mid-C16 gate-tower of Lullingstone Castle is the first large-scale building to be of brick throughout, with cut brick for details, a stage already reached at Tattershall Castle, at Caister, at Herstmonceux and Faulkbourne in the 1440s. But after 1500 brick quite suddenly became the most prestigious of materials to build in. Hampton Court is the classic example of that, but in Kent the contrast between Knole, the Archbishop's Palace built in the 1450s of ragstone, and Otford, the Archbishop's Palace begun after 1503 in brick, is telling enough. But Bell Harry, the great crossing tower of Canterbury Cathedral, of course is ashlar outside, even if it is lined with brick inside. The other great early C16 brick courtyard house in Kent was Shurland at Eastchurch (E), probably complete by 1532, where only the shell of the entrance range stands. Even less is left of the one built in 1541-4 for the king himself on the site of Dartford Priory. That however was brick also. At Knole, on the other hand, which had become royal property, an outer court, the Green Court, added in the 1540s, was built of ragstone, not brick. The earliest part of Boughton Place, Boughton Malherbe, c.1519-29, 44 and Hall Place, Bexley, begun after 1534, confirm that sizeable houses were still being put up in local ragstone, or rather in flint and ragstone at Hall Place. Boughton Monchelsea Place was ragstone-built in the 1560s, but then the most prolific ragstone quarries in the county are at Boughton Monchelsea. Among the most enjoyable early C16 brickwork is the entrance range and terraced garden layout of Roydon Hall, East Peckham.‡ The house itself has been too heavily restored to give much visual enjoyment now, but it is dated 1535. It had stepped gables, a favourite C16 form, that lent itself of course to being built in brick. Smallhythe church, of 1516-17, has stepped gables; so has 43 the entrance gateway, sole survivor of the Roper mansion at Canterbury (E), and the surviving part of Whorns Place, Cuxton; so

* Also at New Romney, dated as late as 1676.
‡ The brick garden pavilions at Hales Place, Tenterden, must be of the second half of the C16, for one has ill-proportioned classical columns.

has Brunger Farm, Tenterden. Old St Alban's Court, Nonington
(E), has them, and a datestone of 1556, Bax Farm, Tonge (E), has
them in association with the date 1567. As late as 1570–80 Sir
Roger Manwood's two charitable buildings, both of brick, have
stepped gables, his almshouses at St Stephen's, Canterbury (E)
and his school, Manwood Court, Sandwich (E). The stepped
gable at Ford Place, Wrotham, dates from the last decade of the
C16.

The C16 was the century when TIMBER was used most
prolifically in South East England. The standard early C16 type
of timber-framed house, built by the typical prosperous small
farmer, occurs literally thousands of times in Kent. But in
general the earliest use of timber was for ROOFS. Here, as in all
timber construction, standardization was the rule. In Kent
standardization is very little relieved by variations on the basic
themes. There is nothing that begins to be comparable with the
great timber church roofs of East Anglia. In Kent, as in the rest
of South East England, the principal trusses almost invariably
consist of tiebeams from the wall-plate on one side of the building
to the wall-plate on the other, and crown-posts strutted in four
directions, standing on the tiebeams. Crown-posts differ from
king-posts in not rising to a ridge-piece, but to a longitudinal
beam below the roof ridge. Crown-post roofs are almost as
universal in churches as in smaller domestic buildings. The
earliest datable ones are, not surprisingly, ecclesiastical. Stiff-
leaf carved on the wall-plates proves the late C13 date of the s
chapel roof at Newington near Sittingbourne (E). It has other
early features: straight, not cambered, tiebeams, and struts two
ways not four. The earliest fully developed crown-post roof that
can be dated is in the chapel at Salmestone Grange, Margate (E),
consecrated in 1326. There are crown-posts in the great hall roof
26 at Penshurst Place, after 1341, a roof so wide that the posts stand
on collar-beams instead of tiebeams on the wall-plates. In other
large domestic halls arched braces spanned the width more
comfortably. Arched braces occur at Ightham Mote, Battel Hall
at Leeds, Yaldham Manor, Wrotham, and the Old Rectory,
Horsmonden; and occasionally in churches, e.g. at Graveney (E),
Headcorn, and Cudham. Hammerbeams are unknown, except in
a barn at Westenhanger (E), unless hammerbeams are concealed
in the roof of the s chapel at Borden (E). The C15 type of roof,
common in East Anglia and the West Country, of low pitch,
panelled, and with carved angels against the ridge piece, occurs
twice, at Eastchurch (E) c.1431, and at St Clement, Sandwich (E).

One or two houses have an aisled hall with timber piers. Nurstead Place has been mentioned already. One pair of splendid round piers is left carrying a timber arch, on which a short crown-post stands. Naturalistic leaves on the pier capitals give the date: early C14. Also Dec is the single-aisled hall at Electric House, New Romney. In both of them the timber structure is set within stone outer walls. When we come on to houses in which the structure is altogether of timber, we find that the normal plan is of the type which has already been described as the commonest of all late medieval house plans, at all levels of society above the humblest – the level we are concerned with here being that of yeoman farmer – a hall in the centre, open to the roof, screened from a passage at one end, with the service rooms beyond it, and with a private living room, or solar, beyond the other end of the hall. The whole ensemble is set under a single roof, hipped at both ends. The fact that the hall was open to the roof, but the kitchen and solar each had bedrooms above, making two-storeyed ends, gave the exterior a characteristic arrangement. The two-storeyed parts have the upper storey jettied out, on the projecting ends of its floor beams. The jetty could be in two or even three directions, but it always projects towards the front. So the upper part of the hall seems recessed, and across the centre of the house the roof eaves have to be carried on braces, not on the wall of the hall. This type has been christened the Wealden house, and it is well known that it occurs far more abundantly in Kent than anywhere else. In fact, to repeat it again, in Kent it is *the* timber-framed house structure. 'Wealden' however is slightly misleading, for the thickest concentration is not in the Weald, but to the NE, near the ragstone hills E of Maidstone. It has only recently been discovered that Wealden houses occur far beyond South East England: examples have for instance been identified in Coventry. As for the period of the Wealden house's popularity, the earliest datable ones belong to the later C14, as at Larkfield, where the wooden window tracery gives the date away. Wide spacing of the upright struts generally means an early date, close studding is not in general use before c.1480. The hall at Wye College (E) of c.1445 is the earliest datable example of close studding. Many of the handsomest Wealden houses are datable, by details such as mouldings, to c.1520. Pattenden, Goudhurst, can stand as the exemplar. Old Bell Farm, Harrietsham (E), survives in an unusually complete state. The superb house built as the parsonage at Headcorn[42] can be dated after 1516. By c.1550 the open hall, with a central hearth, was felt to be out of date, and the Wealden house's days were over. Brick hearths and chimneybreasts were built and floors inserted across the open halls. Open halls in Wealden houses now are probably without exception C20 restorations. The restorer has put the clock back at e.g. Old Hall, Sundridge; Synyards, Otham; Mill House, Benenden, to mention three at random.

Before we leave the subject of the Wealden house a word is needed about its antecedents. Aisled timber houses are known, with the aisle posts set within partition walls, e.g. at Fairfield Cottages, Eastry (E). Hamden, Smarden, has crucks in the main truss as well, the only proper base crucks to have been discovered in Kent. Crucks standing at first-floor level turn up at Frogholt, Newington, near Hythe (E) and at Burnt House, Yalding. Upper crucks involved a jetty; but the immediate precursors of the Wealden type are houses with the plan developed but not the single-hipped roof. Lower Newlands, Teynham (E), and a house at Sheldwich (E) show this type most clearly. Wardes at Otham, a C14 house, has an overall hipped roof, but kitchen and solar above one another at one end (cf. the stone version of this plan at Mersham already mentioned).

The Wealden house was designed to stand free, as a farm house. But such houses can be found in towns; St Radegund's Club, Canterbury (E), is an example. Town houses, where space was restricted, naturally grew upwards, to gables, as the group of Chequers Inn and Cobley's shop at Tonbridge shows, and Arden's House, Faversham (E), of c.1538–40, or to a second continuous overhang, as along Strand Street, Sandwich (E), and the great hostels along Mercery Lane, Canterbury (E). The C14 timber-framed courtyard house in the Market Square, Faversham (E), is the greatest possible rarity.

As for churches, timber has occasionally other structural uses besides roofs. There are for instance several TIMBER PORCHES of which the Perp one at Shoreham is the most ambitious. TIMBER TOWERS are popularly associated with Essex. Kent has one at High Halden, which Mr Rigold believes to be as early as the C13. Before 1847 there was another at Monks Horton (E). The 34 detached belfry at Brookland, already mentioned, is the most enjoyable thing of this kind, an octagon growing up in three overlapping stages, all generated from four mighty upright posts. It is c.60 ft high, the lowest stage C13, the rest C15. Benenden's detached belfry, destroyed in 1672, was reliably said to have been no less than 132 ft high.

The last few pages have plunged deep into vernacular building. But conservatism in the C16, the topic from which these pages took off, can be illustrated just as well by the most ambitious MID SIXTEENTH CENTURY HOUSES; for from this point onwards of course domestic architecture replaces ecclesiastical at the summit of architectural ambition. The flamboyantly lofty brick gate-tower at Sissinghurst Castle is the best example. A 45 gate-tower for display not defence as early as the first decade of the C14 is the Fyndon Gate at St Augustine's Abbey, Canterbury (E). Then in the mid C15 there is Dent-de-Lion, Garlinge (E), still with arrow-slits, i.e. vestigial defences, and, in the mid C16, Lullingstone. Christ Church Gateway, Canterbury (E), is purely for show; and so, to go outside Kent, are such sensational pieces as the gate-towers at Oxburgh Hall in the 1480s, and Layer Marney Towers c.1520. At Roydon Hall, East Peckham (1535), the gate-tower has dwindled to be little more than projecting polygonal turrets each side of an arch in a broad, low entrance range. Yet after that, instead of the gate-tower dwindling away altogether, we come to Sissinghurst and its crazily high tower, 45 and the date of that can hardly be before 1560. The evidence for this dating is the Tuscan pilasters and entablatures that frame the semicircular entrance arch and the window above, on the inner side of the tower. Such sober classicism was introduced to England at Old Somerset House, after 1547. Sir Richard Baker inherited Sissinghurst in 1558. The extension of Boughton Place, Boughton Malherbe, has windows of classical proportions 44 at a precociously early date, for an upstairs fireplace here is inscribed with the date 1553. The doorway at Boughton Place, flanked by well carved, if excessively tapering, Corinthian pilasters, should probably be associated with this date. Both Boughton and Sissinghurst mix their pilasters with moulded, four-centred, i.e. Gothic not classical, arches. The source of this Somerset House kind of classicism was probably France. Sissinghurst Castle had a French plan too (as Hasted's engraving bears witness, for the house itself has long gone) – the plan that was invented at Bury (begun in 1511) in which the house stood round three sides of a courtyard, and a wall or loggia, with the gate-tower in the middle, bounded the fourth.

Artistically the highest achievements of this classicism in the mid century are in EARLY ELIZABETHAN MONUMENTS. There are four in particular, all free-standing tomb-chests with re-cumbent effigies, which is to say that there is nothing revolutionary about their conception. The alabaster monument to Sir

Thomas Cheyne † 1558 at Minster-in-Sheppey (E) has pilasters and splendidly carved shields of arms, in strapwork surrounds, very early for strapwork anywhere in England. It had been invented only a quarter of a century earlier by Rosso Fiorentino in the Galerie François Ier at Fontainebleau. The Shrewsbury monument at Erith, date of death 1568, has strapwork too, and egg-and-dart borders and Doric columns attached at the angles of the tomb-chest as well. The monument to Sir Thomas Moyle † 1560 at Eastwell (E) has Doric pilasters and entablature. The
46 finest of the four is without a doubt the Brooke monument of 1561 at Cobham. This has, on the sides of the tomb-chest, Ionic columns and kneeling sons and daughters in front of shell-headed niches. Such an arrangement connects it with the Norfolk tomb at Framlingham, 1554. The wall-monument († 1571) at Tudeley has Ionic columns too, but they are by no means so finely proportioned.

In England in the last quarter of the C16, the wall and gate-tower were abolished, which produced a U-shaped plan, with far-projecting wings. The most splendid ELIZABETHAN
47 MANSIONS in the county had this plan. Cobham Hall was begun c.1580. When work stopped in 1603 the wings, terminating in rectangular turrets at their outside angles, were complete, but not the hall range that was to link them together. One wing ending in a turret, part probably of such a house, is left at Otterden Place (E); and the same amount of Ford Place, Wrotham, where the dates 1582 and 1605, not certainly authentic, occur. Major in scale, brick with stone dressings, all three seem to have been austerely sparing in decoration. Ford Place has perhaps the earliest shaped gables in Kent, and Cobham has just one piece of magnificence, the stone porch to
48 the chapel, dated 1594, built up with coupled columns, Tuscan below, Ionic above, into a full-scale frontispiece. In its assurance and bravura, it is an exceptionally fine piece. What England could produce in the way of frontispieces with superimposed columns at this time is very fairly demonstrated by the one at Ightham Court, its thin little columns set wide apart. The date on it is 1575. Another is at Lynsted Park (E), c.1599. The very Serlian forecourt gateway at Brenchley Manor is dated 1592.

The typical Elizabethan brick house is more compact in plan than these, an E, with a projecting porch in the centre and short projecting wings. Chillington Manor, Maidstone (now Maidstone Museum), dated 1561, is the earliest and completest example; Hollingbourne Manor (E) exemplifies it best, though

These parts then were left uncovered, and so must have been houses with brick-nogging between the timbers, but in towns in the C17 façades might be covered with plaster, and moulded decoration applied, which is to say that they might be pargetted. The earliest PARGETTING is the best, the house in Bank Street, 53 Maidstone dated 1611,* though a much more spectacular pargetted house in Maidstone is known from early photographs, and the Queen Elizabeth Guest Chamber, Canterbury (E), which is quite ambitious too, is not dated. The pargetting in Week Street, Maidstone, dated 1680, is much feebler. That in West Street, Faversham (E), is dated as late as 1697, but the same tradition of covering a house with coarse, eye-catching designs is carried on into the C18, with vegetable patterns painted on plaster at Calico House, Newnham (E), where one can read the date 1712.

This chronicle of the survival of Jacobean modes has taken us a good seventy years past a crucial point in the history of English domestic architecture, which for convenience can be called the REACTION TO INIGO JONES. Jones was the first Englishman to understand the theoretical assumptions that lay behind Italian Renaissance architecture. He had been to Italy before 1600, and went a second time, with the virtuoso Earl of Arundel, in 1613–15, more particularly to study architecture, especially the architecture of Palladio. Then in a series of buildings, the Banqueting House in Whitehall, the Queen's House, Greenwich, and probably a house for Prince Charles at Newmarket, all designed by 1619, he demonstrated his new creed. Gone are Jacobean projections and recessions, and lively gabled skylines, gone are mullioned and transomed windows. In place of all this exciting, undisciplined bustle Jones offered simplicity itself, a building a rectangle in plan, a rectangle in elevation, crowned by a balustrade (Banqueting House, Whitehall; Queen's House, Greenwich) or a hipped roof with dormers (Newmarket). Windows took on a rectangular, upright Italianate shape, with wooden casements. What made these buildings architecture was the relationship by their proportions of the parts to one another; and what made them art was Jones's sensibility in choosing his proportions. Kent

* This house presents a problem. Can the windows, with the transom arched up in the middle, be as early as 1611 ? Generally such windows (cf. e.g. Sparrowe's House, Ipswich) are assigned to the 1670s. In stone, it is true, they can be found at Charlton Park, Wiltshire, c.1607–18, but that is in stone. However, the earlier date seems to be proved by a complete set of such windows, surely original, at Valence House, Sutton Valence, of 1598.

is probably the most interesting county of all in which to pursue
56 these ideals. Chevening, built for Lord Dacre before 1630, is
governed by them. Its hipped roof and brick walls, seven bays
by five, two-and-a-half storeys high, have since the late c18 been
hidden behind a skin of stucco and fireproof bricks; but the
plan, the rooms two-deep within the rectangle, i.e. what became
standardized as the double-pile plan, survives. Such discipline at
such an early date makes one believe Dacre family tradition,
that *Inigo Jones* himself had a hand in the design of Chevening.

Chevening was imitated in the neighbourhood at once, at
St Clere, Kemsing, built for a Parliament man, Sir John Sedley.
His new chapel in the house was consecrated in 1633. St Clere
has the double-pile plan, the hipped roof and chimneystacks
paraded in a row in the middle of it; and originally it had casement windows (changed to sashes in the c18) in flat eared frames,
of brick, rendered. Yet most oddly, at the corners of the entrance
front of St Clere are octagonal turrets, a Jacobean idea that would
have been anathema to Jones. The new idiom soon became
naturalized in the county. The list of later hipped-roofed brick
houses begins with Bridge Place (E) after 1638. Only a fragment of
Bridge is left, but it is known to have been a square, two-storeyed,
of nine bays, built round a small central courtyard. It has superimposed pilasters finely executed in cut and moulded brick.
58 Hall Place, Bexley, grew a hipped-roofed addition *c.*1649-53,
round three sides of a courtyard. Here are stone quoins, oval end
windows, sunk segmental arches over the lower windows, all
details which had quite a long life of popularity ahead of them.
The staircase tower projecting into the courtyard exploits these
motifs with bizarre consequences. Yotes Court, Mereworth, has
an H-plan and gables at the back and is dated 1656 and 1658.
Only at Groombridge Place, after 1654, does this type of house
regain the poise that had been reached at Chevening. What
makes Groombridge such a lovable house is its siting within a
moat and the fact that it is perfectly preserved, even with one or
two of its original casement windows. What makes it distinguished is its loggia of Ionic columns across the centre of the
entrance front, the loggia which hides the fact that the front door
is off centre, and leads into a passage at one end of the hall, i.e.
that the plan is still the medieval one, discarded, we have seen, at
Somerhill already in 1611. There is nothing in Kent that raises
the new type of house to the heights of sophistication that
Pratt's Coleshill inhabited. But at Cobham Hall, the centre
block was built at last in 1662. It lost its hipped roof in the early

C19, but originally only the centre three of the nine bays rose to a third storey, above the four giant Corinthian pilasters and the entablature they carry. These are refined and classical in a way few could manage at that date; only, say, Hugh May at Eltham Lodge, of 1663-4. Mr Colvin has found in the building accounts the names of Mr Jarman and Mr Mills. Were they the two well-known architect-masons *Edward Jarman* and *Peter Mills*? Bromley College of 1670, its giant pedimented portal in a rusticated surround, is more typical of the City of London masons' style of the time. From the 1680s Kent can show several fine hipped-roofed houses, with brickwork more expert than ever before, but with all the signs that a standard model has been attained. Owletts, Cobham, is dated 1684; Red House, Sevenoaks, 1686; and the largest of them all, Squerries Court, Westerham, was built before the latter date. The Guildhall, Rochester, of 1687 comes in here.

The C17 was the golden era of cut and moulded brickwork; the golden decade was the 1630s. No county has anything that compares with the virtuosity and braggadocio of Broome Park's cut and moulded brickwork. Broome (E) was begun in 1635 and completed three years later, for Sir Basil Dixwell, a man of no more than local distinction. In plan (an H), in its mullioned and transomed windows, and above all in its fantastic skyline of tall chimneystacks and shaped and pedimented gables, it is thoroughly Jacobean in spirit. Yet it may be that the source that inspired it lies on the Continent, no less than Inigo Jones's did. Pedimented gables are generally called, and will here be called, Dutch gables, but it may turn out that the ancestors of Broome lay not in Holland, but in Belgium and North East France. What needs emphasizing about the Broome gables is that they are altogether made of brick, even the deep scrolls from which they spring, and that the pediments are split open by other pediments pushing their way upwards. Broome also has pilasters, brick of course, giant ones, that take up an alternating rhythm by their relationship with the gables above. The way the rhythm changes from façade to façade is subtly worked out, and an added subtlety is that the pilaster capitals merge with the entablature in a way that suggests that the designer of Broome had handled giant pilasters often enough before. All the same, to repeat it, Broome is a unique feat in England: both the gables and the pilasters are in a class on their own.

Shaped gables and Dutch gables, on the other hand, make plenty of appearances in Kent. To take shaped ones first, the

37 Earl of Dorset added them all round Knole in 1605. The shape of
these is produced from segments of circles, a semicircle at the
top, then a step and a quadrant at the bottom. At Knole the
gable crests are tweaked up to take an obelisk or a heraldic beast;
however, the simple shape which has been called a 'compass
gable' satisfied most people. Ford Place, Wrotham, has them,
perhaps even a little earlier than Knole. A fully surviving array of
compass gables is at Godinton of 1628. Charlton Court, East
51 Sutton, of 1612 substitutes S-curves for the quadrants. As for
Dutch gables, Broome has the earliest. Only the Richard's
Charity, Goodnestone by Wingham (E), before 1672, and an
undated cottage at Wingham (E), copy the Broome gables.
Maison Dieu House, Dover (E), has the less complicated sort
first found at Kew Palace in 1631, and tapering pilasters between
the upper windows. But at Dover the date is as late as 1665.
Dutch and shaped gable ends are a special feature of North East
Kent, i.e. of Thanet and the mainland near by. A few have dates:
Hoath (E), 1659; Ickham (E), 1663; Worth (E), 1675; Ash (E),
1691; Sarre (E), 1691; Broadstairs (E), 1710; and latest of all a
cottage at Combe, Ash (E), dated 1723. All these are of brick or
brick and flint.

The other mid-C17 motif that needs charting is the pilaster.
Giant pilasters are nowhere used to more spectacular effect than
at Lees Court (E), marching across its long, low façade (thirteen
bays, but only two storeys). Date and architect are not known,
for one does not know how to interpret the date 1652 that Hasted
gives. Conceivable that was the date of completion. The old
attribution to Inigo Jones cannot stand, for in his known
buildings giant pilasters never occur; and he would hardly have
designed Lees Court's licentious Ionic capitals, with bloated
swags from volute to volute. The interiors, destroyed c.1913,
were just what a City of London designer would have made of
the Jonesian interior style. The unfinished ashlar façades at
Scotney Castle, probably of the 1630s, were similar to Lees in
their great scale and in their slightly gauche interpretation of
Jonesian motifs, e.g. the raised flat window surrounds, with
ears and radiating voussoirs. Syndale House, Ospringe (E), a few
miles from Lees Court, recently demolished, had giant pilasters
and was built c.1652. Another house of the 1650s with giant
pilasters, this too no longer extant, was Bayhall, Pembury. All
these were of stone or plastered brick, the carving carried out in
stone.

In brick, the only other giant pilasters in the county are at

Restoration House, Rochester, jostled by much else, and, a very rustic version, at Boughton Manor, Boughton Aluph (E). There is no date for either. Commoner are superimposed pilasters, or pilasters only across the upper storey. The best, Bridge Place (E) and Maison Dieu House, Dover (E), have been mentioned already. The date 1627 at Wallet's Court, Westcliffe (E), can hardly refer to the puny pilasters there. They must be several decades later. Superimposed orders come at the Well House, Goodnestone near Wingham (E), a sort of countrified version of the Whitehall Banqueting House; but the alternating rhythm of wide and narrow bays suggests that influence from Broome is being exerted here. The same can be said even of Vicarage House, Wingham (E), dated as late as 1697. This has upper pilasters, and so has an undated house at Paramour Street, Westmarsh (E).

Of POST-JACOBEAN SEVENTEENTH CENTURY INTERIORS not much need be said. The most important, at Lees Court (E), have gone, but the plaster ceiling of the 1660s in the hall at Cobham Hall Inigo Jones himself would have been pleased to acknowledge. The Godinton interiors, strictly post-Jacobean, have already been described. That leaves nothing but the painted room at Old Wilsley, Cranbrook, of *c.*1680, and three plaster ceilings of the same period, at Owletts, Cobham, of 1684, Groombridge Place, and the church of King Charles the Martyr, Tunbridge Wells. All three are characteristic of plaster-work of the period, with big wreaths of boldly modelled fruit and flowers. The plasterers at Tunbridge Wells were *John Wetherel* 59 (1678) for one half, *Henry Doogood* (1690) for the other. Both used the same design, but Doogood was demonstrably the more talented plasterer.

The history of post-Reformation domestic architecture has been a history of reactions to successive waves of classicism. POST REFORMATION CHURCHES are quite another story. Here Gothic reigned practically unchallenged, and if it died, as in the end it did, that was through inanition, not by the assaults of classicism. In Elizabeth's reign ecclesiastically there is just a blank. But when in 1625 an anti-Catholic built a new church at Groom- 55 bridge, he built in Gothic; and when in 1649 a Parliament man built a new church at Plaxtol he built in Gothic. Plaxtol is very much altered, but some windows with typical cuspless C17 tracery survive. Groombridge is just a brick chapel, with buttresses (they are rusticated, however, one notes) and Late Perp windows. Groombridge should be compared with the N chapel at Hollingbourne (E) of *c.*1638, and the extension of the S chapel at Tunstall (E) dated 1655. The N aisle at Ightham of c.1639, also brick, has windows of two pointed lights. Curiously enough, the slightly earlier C17 ecclesiastical buildings show more irritation with tradition. Chiddingstone, remodelled in 1625–9, introduces, as does Groombridge, a classically round-headed arch to the porch; at Hothfield, the arcade piers, of before 1624, can be interpreted as a sort of foliated Doric – at any rate they are not 54 traditional; and the piers at St Nicholas, Rochester, are classical without a doubt. St Nicholas was rebuilt after a fire in 1624. The arches of the new arcade are pointed and wave-moulded, but the piers that support them are whole-hearted, monumental Tuscan columns. Finally, two towers need to be mentioned, that mix Classical and Gothic in just this undiscriminating way, at Ringwould (E) in 1628 and Goudhurst in 1638–40. The Goudhurst tower was the work of *Edmund Kinsman*, *James Holmes*, and *John Young*. Kinsman is known to have worked in the City of London, so it is no surprise that the square-topped W window, rising higher in the centre, is identical with the windows of St Katherine Cree, built in the City of London in 1631.

CHURCH FITTINGS tell the same story, of total inactivity in the later C16, and pride resumed after about 1620. The single dated Elizabethan fitting is the HOURGLASS STAND at Leigh.* Hourglasses of course were for timing sermons, so it makes sense that the standard new C17 fitting was a PULPIT. The earliest dated pulpit is at St Nicholas at Wade (E), 1615. The best, highly carved, and with its tester preserved, is Lenham's, of 1622. Others with dates are at Hever (1621 on the tester), Cowden, 1628, Lamberhurst, 1630, Sevenoaks, 1635, and North Cray, 1637. Compare any of these with the pulpit at Meopham, made for St Margaret, Westminster, in 1686, and the dramatic improvement in wood-carving effected by the vast amount of practice provided in the post-fire churches and Livery Halls in the City is easy to demonstrate. Woodwork of a quality nearly as high is in the stalls by *Roger Davis* in Canterbury Cathedral (E), of 1676 and 1682, and the Royal Arms of James II at West Malling. At Tunbridge Wells are a few bits of woodwork from a City Church, Wren's St Antholin.

FONTS stay octagonal, and, on the whole, what mouldings they have are Perp. That is the case at Queenborough (E), given in 1610, which is to be remembered for its crude relief of Queen-

---

* Others, undated, are at Cowden and East Langdon (E). The hourglass stand at Cliffe is dated 1636.

borough Castle, its cannon in position. Also octagonal, but easier to recognize as Jacobean, are the fonts at Maidstone, Chiddingstone (1628), and Groombridge (c.1625). When after Charles II's restoration fonts were ordered to be replaced in churches, they too stayed faithful to the old shape, or rather reduced it to its barest essentials. Marden has one dated 1662, and a tall cover with doors. The rest are in a group in the eastern extremity of the county: Nonington (E) 1662, Ripple (E) and St Margaret's at Cliffe (E) 1663, and Walmer (E) 1664. The two exceptions to this rule are the sumptuous black and white marble font and cover at Canterbury Cathedral (E) given in 1639, and the crude lead one at Eythorne (E) of 1628.

To complete the roll of C17 fittings one can mention the FAMILY PEW at West Peckham, the PARCLOSE SCREEN set up in 1635 at Pluckley, with Tuscan balusters, the brass LECTERN at Canterbury Cathedral (E), made in 1663 by *William Borroughs*, and the earliest CHANDELIER of many in Kent, at Lynsted (E), dated 1686. Not exactly a fitting, but best mentioned here, is the ROOF PAINTING at Queenborough (E), of 1695, with puffy clouds, an angel, and putti.

If fittings have little to offer, ELIZABETHAN AND STUART MONUMENTS in Kent have very much. Viewed in a national context, they are quite as representative and have quite as many memorable peaks as domestic architecture. The earliest ones, at Cobham, Eastwell (E), Erith, and Minster-in-Sheppey (E), have been discussed already. The position of the Cobham monument, in the middle of the chancel, blocking the view from the altar, suggests that those who erected it felt a new pride and self-confidence in their family. Proud and self-confident, without a doubt, are the monuments of the next half century. They are large, and highly coloured, and where there is a figure, he or she generally does not lie in the old way, hands folded in prayer, but is clearly alive, kneeling or reclining on one side. The first monument to express this new ethos is that of Dean Wotton † 1567, in Canterbury Cathedral (E). He kneels, almost life-size, before a prayer desk, which stands in front of a sort of reredos, framed by first-rate Corinthian columns. By the last decade of the C16 columns have become the normal accompaniment of figures, framing them and supporting a pediment or coffered arch on a wall-monument, supporting a canopy over the grandest free-standing monuments. This last kind is naturally not common, and also not unnaturally the figures under the canopy are recumbent and do not kneel. The earliest, at Lullingstone, date of death 1581, is rather bad; and the monument erected at Chevening before 1611 is not much better. The monument at Eastwell (E), however, of the mid 1620s, now deprived of its canopy, is by a first-rate sculptor. Before that date indeed the standard of these monuments, for all their showiness, rarely rises high. A list of the most gorgeous would include the series at Ashford, those at West Malling († 1624) and Wateringbury (1628), the colossal monument at Mereworth, set up as late as 1639, and the colossal-seeming monument at Hinxhill (E) (1632). The reclining effigies of knights at Southfleet († 1605) and Swanscombe († 1609) are better than most. Monuments with kneeling figures are, generally speaking, the smallest, cheapest, and least interesting. Exceptions are the Hales monument at Canterbury Cathedral (E), of after 1596, with its narrative reliefs, and one or two late examples, where the kneeling figures turn outwards in a more or less lively pose. This happens first at Birchington (E), date of death 1618, then at Linton († 1627), and then again at Yalding, after 1656. These admittedly are signs of life among the boring, hectoring display, but they are hardly more than a flicker compared with the work of two sculptors who have not yet been mentioned. These two, Epiphanius Evesham and Nicholas Stone, changed the course of monumental design in England almost as decisively as Inigo Jones changed the course of English architecture. Evesham took the hackneyed formulas and charged them with emotion; Stone, who had trained under Hendrik de Keyser in Amsterdam and learnt the far more varied traditions of the Continent, invented many new formulas. *Epiphanius Evesham* is fully represented in Kent. His first signed works are two trifling tablets of *c.* 1595, at Hythe (E) and Mersham. His monument at Boughton under Blean (E) to Thomas Hawkins † 1617 is the earliest one that matters. It has conventionally recumbent figures, but in two respects it is new: first the alabaster is not coloured, and was clearly not intended to be; and secondly the children carved in little on the sides of the tomb-chest do not kneel in the usual disciplined, unemotional way, but stand or kneel in groups, the girls in tears. Five years later Lord Teynham died and for him Evesham set up at Lynsted (E) a standing monument framed by side columns. Lord Teynham lies, his eyes open but unseeing. Behind him his widow kneels erect, her face full of grief, but reining her emotion in. Below, their sons and daughters mourn among the objects of their delight, hawks and lap-dogs. The third monument of the group is unsigned. It is at Otterden (E) to

Sir Justinian Lewin, who died in 1620. Sir Justinian left but one daughter, so Evesham, for surely the sculptor must be he, boldly placed both mother and daughter on the same register. Again the armoured man lies, here clearly dead, and his wife, kneeling at a lower level, raises her eyes to gaze into his face, while the little girl clings to her in a frenzy of grief. By the standards of Italy in these years this display of emotion would seem very tepid; but in England it is unprecedentedly Baroque.

None of the most exciting monuments of *Nicholas Stone* is in Kent. The one at Wingham (E) of 1624 is quite conventional, and so is that at Mersham, of 1626. A hanging monument at Wingham, also c.1624, and its twin at Elmsted (E), date of death 1622, with robed angels in a twisting pose to l. and r. of the inscription plate, though not known to be Stone's, depend on his ideas. Stone's monument at Boughton Monchelsea is almost totally destroyed; which leaves three that deserve more extended comment. One, to Sir Heneage Finch, at Eastwell (E), made in 1632, has a waist-length bust, one of his finest pieces of sculpture. But it is not anything new, for such busts were by tradition reserved for scholars and lawyers. Sir Roger Manwood's monument († 1592) at St Stephen, Canterbury (E), has such a bust, and a very lifelike skeleton as well. Stone's little black and white marble monument of 1626 to Orlando Gibbons, the King's Musician, in Canterbury Cathedral (E) is a translation of the type into up-to-date Low Countries language, with an exquisite shoulder-length bust on a pedestal. The other scholar monument in the cathedral is unattributed and a completely original conceit. Dean Boys † 1625 is shown seated, looking up from his desk, in a book-lined study, into which the usual columned wall-monument has been transformed. Stone's monument at Chilham (E) of 1631–2 is symbolical, as he loved to be. It consists of an Ionic column, 11 ft high, with an urn on top, and seated figures around, of the four Cardinal Virtues, sadly feebly carved. By it Sir Dudley Digges honoured his dead wife, as the book of Genesis says that Jacob honoured Rachel.

Other early C 17 sculptors identifiable as carving monuments in the county are *Maximilian Colt*, who at Otham († 1620) introduces an important new motif, busts in roundels* on a columned wall-monument; *John & Matthias Christmas*, with a tiny monument with kneeling figures at St Nicholas, Rochester; and *Edward Marshall*. Marshall was a popularizer, not an inventor.

---

* The earliest bust in a roundel is much earlier, c.1587, at Boughton Malherbe, conceived like a miniature.

He popularized black and white marble instead of alabaster and black touch, e.g. in his beautifully positioned monument to Elizabeth Culpeper † 1638 at Hollingbourne (E). Her effigy, recumbent on a tomb-chest, is otherwise old-fashioned. A new, and short-lived, fashion of the 1630s, begun by Stone's monument of Dr John Donne in St Paul's Cathedral, was for a standing figure in a shroud. Marshall's Astley monument at
60 Maidstone, ‡ 1639, runs to four shrouded figures, revealed by open doors with inscriptions on them (or are they rather the lids of tombs thrown up as the Astleys rise in their shrouds at the Last Trump ?).* He also took up Colt's device of busts in roundels, and gave it a personal formulation. Marshall's busts are waist-length, set in deep, garlanded ovals. He signs an outstanding one at Ightham († 1641), with angels and allegorical figures as well as an eloquent bust of a strong-minded old lady. Busts, like shrouded figures, could come several at a time. At Addington († 1651) there are two on one monument, at Birchington (E) (1651) as many as six. At Brenchley, a nice touch, the half-
61 length busts, he and she, link arms and clasp hands affectionately. The date of death here is 1652. To finish the list of Marshall's signed works in the county, there is a tablet at St Mary Magdalene, Canterbury (E), and, if the signature Edward Marshall refers to this Edward Marshall, he signs the most splendid C17 brass in Kent, and arguably in all England, at East Sutton, date of death 1629.

Some of the most memorable mid-C17 monuments have no figures at all. Dean Fotherby † 1619 is commemorated in Canterbury Cathedral (E) by an alabaster tomb-chest, its sides coated with a gruesome array of skulls, bones, and rib-cages. The dismantled monument at Boughton Malherbe († 1663), with a black marble pyramid and three white marble lions, must have been extraordinarily impressive. This colour contrast is the *raison d'être* of *John and Henry Stone*'s monument set up in 1653 at Maidstone, a black slab on four stout white balusters: but by far the finest thing in this vein is the Oxinden monument at Wingham (E), of 1682. A completely original conception, with black ox-heads at the corners of the base, and four mourning putti round a lofty obelisk down which fruit and flowers cascade, it is also a virtuoso piece of sculpture. It is in fact very Dutch in

---

* The monument at Ospringe (E), † 1631, with a recumbent effigy in a shroud, may also be by *Marshall*. There is a similar, less good, monument at Boughton Aluph (E), the date of death also 1631.

spirit; and it is most likely that the sculptor was the Dutch émigré, *Arnold Quellin*.*

If the Oxinden monument is a climax in LATER STUART MONUMENTS, it is not the largest that the county can boast of. The prize for size is shared between the monument at Aylesford, almost certainly by *Nost*, of Sir John Banks † 1699 and his wife 62 and son, showing off in semi-Roman garb, and the colossal allegorical structure crowded into a tiny chapel at Waldershare (E), the *magnum opus* of *Thomas Green* of Camberwell – death date 1712. Altogether this was a period of liberation in monumental design. If there were busts they might be draped *all'antica*, as e.g. at Elmstone (E) † 1671; monuments with figures could dispense with canopies, and have figures standing free, as e.g. the seated, armoured Tufton († 1670), and his standing, periwigged relative († 1679), both at Rainham. The monument at Groombridge to Philip Packer († 1686), showing the dead man seated, his head lolling to one side, must be one of *John Bushnell*'s peculiar inventions.‡

So much for realism: allegory is represented again by the Plot monument († 1671) at Borden (E), with a figure of St Michael trampling the Devil. The excellence of the workmanship which sculptors could now achieve is best seen perhaps in virtuoso cartouches, as e.g. at Chislehurst († 1682), at Otterden (E) († 1702), and Beckenham († 1718). To take the story on to the end of the Stuart period, one may single out the monuments with half-length busts, at Hunton (1711) and at Goudhurst († 1702), the latter of exceptional quality; and two slightly peculiar conceptions, the monument of 1704 at Penshurst, by *William Stanton & William Woodman*, where two dancing angels balance a large urn, and the monument at Northfleet († 1709) probably by *Edward Stanton*, with two uncomfortably agitated kneeling figures.

The dates of houses and monuments mentioned show that the Civil War and the Commonwealth period did not cause much slackening in activity in Kent. But the Restoration of Charles II revived the arts without a doubt, and raised most crafts to a new level. The new level reached in carpentry and plasterwork has

---

* The monument seems to have caused a sensation in East Kent, for close copies of it are at Canterbury (E) now under the tower, which is all that is left of the church of St Mary Magdalene (†1691), and at Barham (E) as late as 1750.

‡ The contorted pose of the bust of Charles II on Delangle House, Chartham (E), also suggests Bushnell.

been remarked on already, and in following the career of the
hipped-roofed house we have reached well beyond the Restoration. But a paragraph on EARLY EIGHTEENTH CENTURY
BRICKWORK is needed to do justice to the bricklayer's craft. It
has to be put this way, because Kent by c.1700 had become
surprisingly provincial; busily provincial, maybe, but provincial
all the same. London architects simply were not employed,
unless one accepts the possibility that *Talman* provided designs
for Waldershare Park (E), built for Sir Henry Furnese c. 1705–12,
in brick with a stone frontispiece of Corinthian pilasters and
stone window surrounds that might be understandable as the
centrepiece of the E front of Hampton Court, reinterpreted by
the designer of Drayton. *Hawksmoor* probably designed the
monumental and very Baroque Archbishop's Throne, carved by
Grinling Gibbons and presented to Canterbury Cathedral (E) in
1704. Sir John Vanbrugh's name is coupled with the style
adopted by the Board of Ordnance for military and naval
63 buildings in the early C18. The gatehouse at Chatham (1720), the
castellated officers' quarters there (1729), and the barrack block
at Upnor are early and typical examples of the style. There is no
evidence that Vanbrugh personally contributed any designs to
the board, though undoubtedly he invented the idiom, powerfully
monumental even on the smallest scale, e.g. for his own house at
Blackheath, by taking motifs from medieval castles, round
turrets, battlements, and corbel tables, and having them executed
in brick with plenty of unrelieved walling. Wateringbury Place of
1707, with pilasters and an attic storey above the entablature, is a
version of Winde's Buckingham House, London. The sources of
a house like Finchcocks, dated 1725, are harder to pin down. Its
emphasis on height, and the illusionism of its convex quadrant
links between main block and wings, making them seem to project more boldly than they really do, establish Finchcocks as the
best Baroque house in the county. But there is neither the
strength nor the subtlety here that, say, Archer would have
shown. The central pediment is very awkward, unsupported and
allowing the façade to climb on up above it. The pilasters too, of
two different heights, have not been given much thought. Finchcocks has plenty of charm, but it is a provincial charm, the charm
of a local man's major work that has turned out unexpectedly
well. Who the local man was, we cannot say; but another work of
his is Matfield House, dated 1728. Here the same pilasters appear
carrying a bit of entablature with one triglyph on it, and the
same windows, segment-headed, and in the projecting bays

round-headed. The façade of Matfield is an excellent example of Kentish brickwork, the bricks of two colours, brown and russet, used to clarify the design. Where specially fine jointing is needed, e.g. on window heads, the bricks are rubbed to touch each other flush. The apogee of this type of brickwork is Bradbourne, Larkfield, completed c.1713–15. Here at least four colours of brick are used, and there are decorative rubbed-brick panels as well. Bradbourne has pilaster strips, a central brick pediment, and extremely long windows, an early c18 fashion. Milgate Park, Bearsted, is a less ornate version of the Bradbourne design. Close in style, but with a top parapet and no pediment, are West Farleigh Hall of 1719, and Went House, West Malling. Another group of houses, these ones E of Canterbury, based on a single pattern can be identified. Bourne Park, Bishopsbourne (E), after 1701, is the grandest version of this pattern, for it is thirteen bays wide and five deep, with a five-bay central pediment. This very broad, low pediment, with three little windows in it, and a hipped roof, are the hallmarks of the group. Goodnestone Park, Goodnestone near Wingham (E), was a nine-bay version, built c.1704, but has been heightened. Barham House (E), undated, is nine bays wide also, and the façade is intact. Kenfield Hall, Petham (E), Stourmouth House (E), and the Vicarage, Wingham (E), as late as 1760, complete the group.

Westwell, Tenterden, dated 1711, stands apart from these all-brick houses in having sandstone dressings. They make it one of the nicest of all the houses of this period. Occasionally brick was exploited in other ways than for textural and colour variations. Window lintels might be cut into frilly patterns, as e.g. at the Corn Exchange, Rochester, of 1706. The windows of the Corn Exchange also have elaborate projecting brick keystones, a notion that was taken up and played for all it was worth on a spectacularly bizarre cottage at Bredgar (E) dated 1719.

Inside such houses as these, one will be surprised not to find a spacious timber staircase, with turned, twisted, and fluted balusters, and carved tread-ends. The finest as a piece of carpentry is at Bradbourne, Larkfield: but the most dramatically disposed are those at West Farleigh Hall and at Ferox Hall, Tonbridge, rising out of two-storeyed halls, and the circular, unsupported staircase at Chevening, designed by *Nicholas Dubois* c.1721.

If the Baroque style of Hawksmoor and Vanbrugh barely touched Kent, the style that succeeded it made a heavy mark. One of the major achievements of PALLADIANISM is in the county,

67 Mereworth Castle, 'covered', i.e. roofed, in 1723. The architect of Mereworth was *Colen Campbell*, who in 1715 had focused the discontent felt with the architecture of Wren and even more of Vanbrugh, Hawksmoor, and Archer, in the introduction to Volume I of *Vitruvius Britannicus*. Campbell 'entered the lists', as he put it, with his two heroes, Palladio and Inigo Jones. Mereworth was Campbell's most fulsome act of homage to Palladio, for it is a copy of the Villa Rotonda built on a knoll outside Vicenza.* Campbell's patron was Captain John Fane, later to be Earl of Westmorland. The site was not a hill-top one, but moated and in a valley. Thus the function of Palladio's villa, as a belvedere with a deep portico facing each point of the compass, Campbell misunderstood. Two of Campbell's porticos cannot be reached externally by steps. Internally, too, although he kept the circular central room open to the dome, he did away with Palladio's carefully integrated, symmetrical plan, to get in a long gallery across the full width of the house at the back. Visually the two most important changes are first the increased size of Campbell's villa, and secondly his lead-covered dome, much more Baroque in shape than the low tiled one built by Palladio.

66 The interiors give a fuller display of Campbell's taste than any of his other surviving houses. The circular central hall, or salon, has plasterwork busts and allegorical figures over the pedimented doorcases, and a Jonesian upper balcony; the coved ceiling of the gallery was executed by the Venetian painter *Francesco Sleter*, in the pale and subtle colours of the contemporary, not the C16, style of the Veneto. The other members of the Palladian triumvirate, Lord Burlington and William Kent, did not build anything in the county; although *Burlington*'s designs for the school and almshouses at Sevenoaks clearly influenced the buildings put up, in local ragstone, in 1724–32. *James Gibbs*, not strictly a Palladian, may be mentioned here for the Great Room which he added to Fairlawne for Lord Barnard, *c*.1720.

Second-generation Palladianism could not be better illustrated than by Godmersham Park (E), of 1732, plain outside, but with sumptuous plasterwork in the hall and dining room; or by the splendid Belvedere in Waldershare Park (E), of 1725–7. *Roger Morris* built Combe Bank, Sundridge, *c*.1726–7(?). Here it is the 68 exterior which is more worth-while – square, with four corner towers under pyramid roofs, a close imitation of Lord Burlington's Tottenham Park, Wiltshire, of 1721. It has been greatly

* Foots Cray Place, another copy of the Villa Rotonda, built *c*.1756, was burnt down in 1950.

added to, for to start with it was little more than a villa. Two
excellent later villas are *Sir Robert Taylor*'s Danson Park,
Bexleyheath, of *c.*1759–62, with a tight top-lit oval staircase in the
centre; and *Robert Adam*'s Brasted Place, built as late as 1784–5, 76
for Dr Turton, George III's physician. Brasted is a true villa,
but un-Palladian in its asymmetrical layout of rooms off a small
staircase-hall.* The porticos, back and front, splendidly carved
in local sandstone, have the full Adam savour. Adam's other
house in Kent, Mersham-le-Hatch, Mersham, was an early one,
begun in 1762. In fact it was his very first completely new house,
and what is surprising about it is that in spite of his four-year stay
in Rome, Adam was content to turn back at Mersham-le-Hatch
to a Palladian formula which he had employed even before he left
Scotland. Only the three-storey bow on the N front has a more
personal distinction. The interiors at Mersham-le-Hatch are also
not outstanding. The hall chimneypieces are Adamized versions of
Kentian ones; the drawing-room ceiling, designed in 1772, the
only one in his mature style. One of the first architects to take up
the Adam style, and give it a certain personal inflection, was
Thomas Leverton. His, almost certainly, is the house built at
Bromley in 1777–80 for Peter Thellusson, now Quernmore
School. No original interiors are left here, except the back stairs.

Kent is altogether poor in EIGHTEENTH CENTURY IN-
TERIORS, beyond those already mentioned. Decorative painting
is almost non-existent. The *Thornhill* paintings on the staircase
at the Admiral's House, Chatham Dockyard, are said to have
come from H.M.S. Royal Sovereign, built in 1701; there are
crude staircase paintings at Milgate Park, Bearsted, of *c.*1710; the
very pretty ceiling painting at Yotes Court, Mereworth, belongs
to the 1740s. Still essentially Baroque are the large inset paintings
at Danson Park, Bexleyheath, of *c.*1766. The interiors, with
columned and pedimented doorcases, at Kenward, Yalding, after
1749, may justly be called Palladian. The pretty plasterwork of
1756 in the hall at Sprivers, Horsmonden, is, in its modest way,
Rococo. *James Wyatt* remodelled the double entrance hall at
Cobham Hall, in 1773–4, in an Adam style; and it was probably
he who created the superb gilt Music Room there out of the 77
two-storeyed C17 hall. The Saloon at Broome Park (E) of 1778 is
his too, and is the best Adam-style interior in the county.

Wyatt's outstanding achievement in the county was his

---

* But it must also be stressed that the internal plan of Combe Bank is not
symmetrical either.

4—W.K.W.

78 mausoleum in the park at Cobham Hall, designed in 1783. It is
an essay in pure French neo-classicism. A mausoleum is a more
serious affair than a garden building, but its function is partly the
same, to be seen from a distance in the park; so this is the para-
graph for GARDEN BUILDINGS AND FOLLIES. The Belvedere at
Waldershare (E) has been remarked on already, but the full-scale
Triumphal Arch, at the head of the valley at Mereworth, has not.
The park at Godmersham (E) has two little c18 temples. Further
than that however it is hardly worth going. The numerous
Gothic follies strewn around at Kingsgate (E) in the 1760s by
Lord Holland are mostly gone or altered out of recognition.
There are castellated cottages at Sidcup and Newington by
Hythe (E), and a Gothic birdhouse, of c.1761, at Knole; but the
two memorably foolish follies may both belong to the c19. The
Waterloo Tower at Quex Park, Birchington (E), with its lofty
cast-iron spire, designed on the model of Beazley's spire of
Faversham church, was set up in 1819 to house a peal of bells;
and the shell-lined grotto tunnelled into the chalk at Margate (E)
may well be as late as that. The virtuoso shellwork at Mereworth
Castle is however mid-c18.

From Gothic follies to other GEORGIAN CASTELLATED AND
GOTHIC BUILDINGS. Here too, as in almost everything associated with the Georgian landowner and his estate, Kent was not
a pioneering county. Ordnance castellation at Chatham has been
touched on. Possibly even earlier than that are the battlements on
the façade of Sharsted Court, Newnham (E), refaced in 1711.
The castellated window-bow on The Cedars, Tenterden, is in a
similar spirit. The India House, Margate (E), datable 1767, has
battlements too. Sidcup Place is said to have been designed in
1743, with tiny square rooms projecting at the angles, in imitation of a fort. Later additions still just let one see how this could
be. The first house to have monastic, not military, overtones was
the mansion built over one wall of the cloisters at Malling Abbey,
West Malling, after 1740. That, then, was a matter of keeping in
keeping, which explains its Gothicism at such an early date.
Gothic did not begin to gain popularity as a style for houses
rather than for features, ruined or otherwise, in a park, until
Horace Walpole had shown the way at Strawberry Hill. Wyatt's
Lee Priory, Littlebourne (E), acknowledged by Walpole as a
'child of Strawberry', has, sadly, been demolished; so the county
has no major c18 Gothic house at all. Wood Street House,
Bapchild (E), of c.1776, which goes no further than an ogee-
headed window and door, hardly counts. The Gleanings,

Rochester, classical towards the road, Gothic to the river, and rendered both ways, can hardly be earlier than 1800.

The characteristic LATE GEORGIAN HOUSE is severely plain, with no mouldings or only subtly refined ones, little liveliness of grouping, and columns on the whole confined to a giant portico or portico-like feature. *Adam*'s Brasted Place, already discussed, falls into this category. The most delightful villa of the late C18, Clare House, East Malling, of 1793, is by a lesser man, *Michael Searles*, who did the Paragon, Blackheath, and had a passion for colonnades. A colonnade runs round the big bow at Clare House. Howletts, Bekesbourne (E), after 1787, by *John Leach*, is another villa, with a splendid portico. Sundridge Park, Bromley, of *c.*1799, which both *Nash* and *Humphry Repton* claimed to have 79 designed, during the period of their uneasy collaboration, has three giant Corinthian porticos, one attached, another encircling a bow. It is built on a trapezoidal plan, so that the entrance front is asymmetrical, and the house makes best sense from the s, where the ground falls away to Repton's landscaped park. This attempt to make a classical house picturesque is not entirely happy. Nash made the synthesis more successfully on a small scale three years later at Cronkhill, Shropshire. This, the first Italianate villa, was immediately imitated in Kent, where *Robert Lugar* built Dunstall Priory, Shoreham, in 1806, prominently featuring a stout round tower, but alas without Nash's sense of picturesque grouping.

Other big names appear, but not to offer their more interesting works. *Soane* did some fine stables at Lees Court (E) in 1786; but his only house, Ringwould House (E) of 1813, is small and routine. *S. P. Cockerell*'s Pierremont House, Broadstairs (E), is ingeniously planned but otherwise undistinguished. *Samuel Wyatt* was the architect probably of Belmont (E), of 1787–92, certainly of Court Lodge, Wrotham, of 1801–2, a minor work. *Charles Beazley* did Hollingbourne House (*c.*1798–9) and Ospringe House (1799) (both E), the latter with stumpy Greek Doric columns to the porch. The mightiest of all these houses, and the most characteristic in its meticulous austerity, is *Daniel Alexander*'s Mote Park, Maidstone, begun in 1793. Alexander was better known for his prisons; so that brings us to LATE GEORGIAN PUBLIC BUILDINGS.

Alexander himself was responsible for Maidstone Prison (1810–17), *George Byfield* in 1808 for Prison and Sessions House at Canterbury (E). The Shire Hall, in front of Maidstone 83 Prison, is perhaps the finest public building in this vein. *Sir*

Robert Smirke built it in 1824, one of his best efforts in the astylar cubic manner which was his form of neo-classical reduction to essentials. The young *C. R. Cockerell* similarly started from first principles in his Lady Boswell's School, Sevenoaks, of 1818. It was a sign of the times that architects could specialize in public buildings, and make a name throughout the country in their profession. In the C18 TOWN HALLS, such as Maidstone's of 1764, Queenborough's (E) of 1793, Hythe's (E) of 1794, were local jobs. So was Deal (E) Town Hall of 1803. To confront these, not perhaps with Smirke's Shire Hall, but with *Amon Henry Wilds*'s Town Hall of 1836 at Gravesend, with its monumental Greek Doric portico, is to demonstrate the new concern for civic magnificence felt in the early C19. TOWN PLANNING tells the same story. Ramsgate was laid out as a seaside resort, with Cecil Square and Hawley Square, joined by a street, from 1769 onwards, a modest reflection of what had been going on in London for nearly a century. Canterbury (E) got its public park at Dane John in 1790. But the 1820s and 30s are the period of planned development of towns. Ramsgate (E) was growing with terraces and crescents in the second decade of the C19, *A. H. Wilds* planned Milton to the E of Gravesend *c*.1820, *H. E. Kendall* planned Rosherville, Northfleet, to the W of Gravesend, *c*.1835. Herne Bay (E) was laid out on an almost virgin site in the 1830s. The Radnor Estate at Folkestone (E) was started in the 1840s. Architecturally these are not much; but *Philip Hardwick*'s Waterloo Crescent, Dover (E), of 1834 is splendid in itself and excellently related to the harbour. All these were, or hoped to be, fashionable waterside resorts... even Gravesend. *Decimus Burton*'s
81 Calverley Park at Tunbridge Wells, begun *c*.1828, was made possible by the attraction of the mineral springs. But instead of the town-house out of town which was *de rigueur* by the seaside, Burton had to create a semi-rural world for permanent residents. True, he had his crescent, but for the most part Calverley Park looks to Nash's Regent's Park for inspiration, with its villas embowered each in its own garden, overlooking a communal landscaped slope.

   MILITARY STRUCTURES deserve a paragraph at this point. Brompton Barracks, Gillingham, of 1804 enclose a parade ground with buildings any town square would have been proud of. The
82 Vanbrughian castle air returns as late as 1812 at Fort Clarence, Rochester. Fort Clarence was a belated defence against Napoleon. The Military Canal across Romney Marsh and the Martello Towers of 1806, at Folkestone (E), Dymchurch, etc., were also

constructed after the real Napoleonic threat had passed. But the really serious defences against French invasion were begun as early as 1793. These were the mighty emplacements on the Western Heights, at Dover (E), with a Citadel and Drop Redoubt completed by 1814, according to the defensive theories of the C17 military engineer Vauban. If necessary, 4,000 soldiers could have been hidden in the hill, the last impregnable stronghold of the British Army. At the same time the medieval walls of Dover Castle were mutilated to take a complementary battery of guns.

Secular building has been racing ahead of ecclesiastical; so it is necessary to break off here and consider Georgian churches, their fittings and monuments. The list is, by the standards of other counties, not particularly impressive, and is yet further evidence of the shortage of big landed families in the county. Among EIGHTEENTH CENTURY CHURCHES Mereworth is the exception 69 that proves the rule. In 1744 the Earl of Westmorland pulled down the medieval church, which stood close by his twenty-year-old castle, and built a new one half a mile away. The nobleman made his gesture with panache. The new building, of local sandstone, has a body inspired by Inigo Jones's St Paul's, Covent Garden, with its deep wooden eaves, and a landmark of a steeple, which is a version of Gibbs's at St Martin-in-the-Fields. The massive semicircular portico completes this cosmopolitan farrago. The interior is by contrast remarkably single-minded, a barrel-vaulted nave and narrow flat-roofed aisles, separated by close-set Doric columns carrying an entablature, not arches. Simple ratios determine the width of nave and aisles and the spacing of the columns. Nothing as deeply neo-classical as this interior had been built in England at this date, except Lord Burlington's Assembly Rooms at York.

The only C18 church in the county that can be named in the same breath as Mereworth is Faversham (E), where the nave was rebuilt in a noble, masculine idiom by *George Dance Sen.* Tuscan columns carry an entablature and a clerestory with lunette windows. Equal in quality, but quite different in style, is the extremely sophisticated version of Wren's Gothic steeple of St Dunstan-in-the-East which *Charles Beazley* placed on the tower of Faversham in 1799.

For the rest local men were employed, *Samuel Simmons* to build St George, Deal (E), in 1706–16,* *Charles Sloane* in 1731 at Gravesend. Otterden (E), built in 1753–9, a mere box, was

* *John James* gave advice to Simmons, but it seems to have been on minor matters.

probably designed by the rector, *Granville Wheler*. Teston, of 1736, is anonymous and nothing special; Chart Sutton of 1779–81 is by *Henry Holland* and also nothing special, a feeble attempt at Gothic. Both are greatly altered.

NONCONFORMIST CHAPELS are more enjoyable than these, because less self-conscious. Several Unitarian Chapels have survived with their C18 aura unimpaired – Bessels Green for example, built in 1716, Maidstone of 1736, and Tenterden of 1746. Two early C19 chapels are polygonal, at a time when greater interest was being taken in, one can hardly say liturgical, but acoustic requirements. They are *Thomas Read*'s Unitarian Chapel of 1819–20 at Dover (E), and the Providence Chapel of 1828 at Cranbrook.

C18 FITTINGS in Anglican churches are few and far between. Brass chandeliers are the most common, and very handsome they generally are. But they are so standardized that nothing further needs saying. Apart from these, nothing sticks in the mind, except the Archbishop's Throne at Canterbury Cathedral (E), mentioned already because *Hawksmoor* probably designed it; the 71 equally magnificent pulpit at Trottiscliffe, designed in 1775 by *Henry Keene* for Westminster Abbey; and the undated lectern at St Paul's Cray. There are a few plain marble fonts, e.g. at Ash (E), 1726, and Mereworth, *c.*1746; a reredos or two, e.g. one at Crundale (E), 1704, and another, quite grand, but unimaginative, at Teston, *c.*1736. *R. Bridge*'s organ case at Faversham (E) of 1754 is another typical piece of Georgian joinery. Few churches contain complete sets of Georgian fittings, and those that do have no more than a rustic charm. The best are on Romney Marsh: Fairfield, for example, and Old Romney. The church interiors most completely innocent of Victorian restorations are Badlesmere (E) and Stelling (E). Lullingstone has pretty plasterwork and a screen loft added before 1738, and stained glass of 1754 by *William Peckitt* of York.

GEORGIAN MONUMENTS are markedly less plentiful than Stuart ones, and there is little of the highest quality, although most of the big names can be found. As it had been in Charles II's reign, when Quellin and Gibbons set new standards to wood and stone carvers, so under George I immigrant sculptors, Michael Rysbrack, Peter Scheemakers, and Louis François Roubiliac, led the way. Rysbrack, born in Antwerp, arrived in England about 1720. James Gibbs took him up for a time, and it is probable that the big monument to Lord Barnard at Shipbourne, executed to *Gibbs*'s design before 1723, is *Rysbrack*'s work. The mood is elegiac, no longer the pompous one of say the Nost at Aylesford, but design and execution are both somewhat limp. Similar in scale, but much finer, is Rysbrack's monument to Sarah Young at Chartham (E), dated 1751. The subtly integrated group, her husband standing in a toga, she seated, looking up at him, and a putto extinguishing a torch, is both lively and dignified. Rysbrack's other monuments are minor ones: at Canterbury Cathedral (E) (1752), Chislehurst († 1760), and three tablets at Hollingbourne (E) after 1725, 1738, and c.1764. To compare the Young monument with *Peter Scheemakers*'s grandest Romanizing monument in Kent, to Sir Christopher Powell † 1742 at Boughton Monchelsea, is, like almost any comparison between the two sculptors, very much in Rysbrack's favour. Scheemakers's monument at Betteshanger (E), on the other hand, date of death 1740, shows him at his very best. Sarcophagus, pyramid, and bust are ingredients used frequently enough, but the colour contrast of the marbles and the splendid relief of ships in full sail lift this monument out of the ordinary.* Scheemakers signs a monument at Benenden, of 1750, with a bust. It is possible that the fine unsigned monument set up after 1735 at Hougham (E) is also by him. Here the bust is in Carolean dress, commemorating a man who had died in 1658; and one remembers that Scheemakers's fame rested on his costume statue of Shakespeare (1740). *Roubiliac*, the youngest and most original of the three sculptors, appears in a minor capacity only, as the author of a small wall-monument at Tonbridge († 1753).

The first English-born sculptor to match the virtuosity of the continentals was *Sir Henry Cheere*. Born in 1703, i.e. two years before Roubiliac, he formed his style on the small, crisp, curvaceous shapes of the French sculptor, though his monuments never approached Roubiliac's in ease and inventiveness. His major monument in Kent, to Charles Polhill † 1755 at Otford, shows that very well. Colour and textural contrasts are excellently handled, but the standing figure in a toga, with seated allegorical females on either side, is quite uninspired. Cheere's other monument at Otford († 1754) has an excellently lively bust; but the whole family of busts on monuments at Shoreham – dates of death 1725, 1739, 1746, 1751 – does him less credit. Several other monuments in the county are by Cheere or in his

---

* Such naval reliefs figure on the Narborough monument at Knowlton (E) († 1707), probably by *Gibbons*, and, most delicious of all, on an unattributed tablet at Chislehurst († 1749).

manner, but are unsigned. Far and away the finest, finer than
72 any of the signed ones, is at Shadoxhurst († 1760).

Busts are the stock in trade of *Sir Robert Taylor* too, as
monuments at Womenswold (E) of *c.*1739 and *c.*1752 show. A
monument at St Nicholas, Rochester, † 1759, with a lively un-
conventional putto, is also by Taylor, and unusually good.
Thomas Adye's monument at Beckenham, date of death 1737,
makes use of putti quite freshly too.

A parenthetical paragraph suffices to call attention to the
three Gothick monuments. The first, strikingly early, is the
70 whole wall at Lullingstone encrusted in playfully vegetable
arcading (date of death 1738). Then, in 1758, comes *Richard
Bentley*'s more antiquarian but no less incorrect monument at
Linton. The charming anonymous concoction at Detling (E),
† 1778, is no further advanced.

At the end of the century allegory won an outright victory over
portraiture, classicism over realism. *William Tyler*'s fine monument at Eastry (E), date of death 1777, is decisively more
classical in the draperies than anything we have yet seen, and the
female figure is as much allegorical as a portrait. The *Flaxman* at
Lydd shows a woman and her baby carried by angels heavenward on clouds. Commemorating a death in 1781, it is Flaxman's
earliest known monument. Unfortunately nothing very significant can be found among Flaxman's later work in Kent. There
is a tablet in Rochester Cathedral († 1798), one at Beckenham
(† 1800), and a third, *c.*1806, in Canterbury Cathedral (E). The
monument at Throwley (E) († 1814) has a relief of a dead soldier
lifted by Victory. *John Bacon Sen.* carved the monument at
Eastry (E) to Captain John Harvey † 1794, in which, characteristically, an angel of victory hovers over the relief representing
the sea battle of 'The Glorious First of June'. The monument to
Lady Henniker in Rochester Cathedral († 1792) is more magniloquent. *Thomas Banks* designed the allegorical figures here, of
73 Truth and Time: a vividly Baroque, not neo-classical, figure this
last. Both the figures are made of Coade stone. It was *Bacon* who
popularized that most boring of all allegorical figures, the mourning
female leaning on an urn. From his own hand is the female at
St Mildred, Canterbury (E), date of death 1789. Nothing need be
said of the numerous other versions from other hands that were
produced in the following forty years or so.

In the first years of the C19 more specifically Christian
symbolism began to come back into favour. Hence *John Bacon
Jun.*'s elaborate piece at Rochester Cathedral in memory of Lord

Henniker (1806) has, not Truth and Time, but a girl holding a nest with a pelican in her piety.

It was Flaxman who brought allegory and portraiture together, by portraying typical mothers and children, or typical mourners, in contemporary, not classicizing, dress. *Sir Francis Chantrey* exploited Flaxman's invention with unfailing resource. In Kent there are mourning families at Chilham (E) (1822) and Chisle-hurst (1823), and the monument at Chevening (1827), with a sleeping woman, a baby at her breast, to commemorate Lady Frederica Stanhope, who had died in childbirth. Immediacy, not grace, was Chantrey's strong point. Even his allegorical mourners (as e.g. at North Cray, 1821, and Erith, 1826) are more substantial than the general run. Chantrey's only other monuments in the county are at Seal, a set of Grecian tablets, one with a relief portrait, done in 1832.

The Stanhope monument was followed by *E. H. Baily*'s monuments at Linton. That to Viscount Brome († 1835) shows 75 the youth sitting up in his bed of fever; the figure of Countess Cornwallis († 1840) lies on her couch tossing in sleep. Finally *Lawrence Macdonald*'s monument of 1850 at Eastwell (E) shows Lady Winchelsea reclining on a day bed reading a book; and that is really not the same conception at all. There are Grecian overtones in all three, just as in the overwhelming majority of monuments, of whatever size or pretension, in this period. Smaller monuments, and tablets, are a disappointment. Hardly anything sticks in the mind, except *William Behnes*'s tablet, with its crisp and evocative economy, at Holy Trinity, Tunbridge 74 Wells († 1833), *Carew*'s, with a bust, at Sevenoaks († 1825), and the unexpected Baroque-revival tablet of 1833 at Chidding-stone.

MONUMENTS OF THE VICTORIAN AGE start appropriately with, in its first year, the overscaled figure of Lady De L'Isle holding a Bible, by *Theed* at Penshurst, and the accurate Gothic of the wall-monument at Chilham (E) by *John Brine & Sons*. Chilham also has *Alexander Munro*'s child group, of 1858, Victorian sentimentality at its sickliest. It was Pugin's († 1852) own monument at St Augustine, Ramsgate (E), that reintroduced the medievalizing effigy, recumbent on a tomb-chest. A whole series in Canterbury Cathedral pick up the motif; and as late as 1889 *Hamo Thorneycroft*'s relief at Cranbrook is a memorial to an artist conceived very much like Pugin's, except of course for the attendant putto.

So much for C19 monuments; but we are still not ready to

consider Victorian architecture. The first third of the C19 was an uneasy period for architects, who had to satisfy their clients' craving for STYLEMONGERING. Few could maintain a high standard, whatever the style they tackled, as can easily be demonstrated by following a career or two. *Decimus Burton*'s is the career most fully illustrated in the county. His Calverley Park at Tunbridge Wells has been discussed already. The mildly Italianate style of the villas is derived from Nash and Barry. Calverley was developed for John Ward, who had already in 1823 employed Burton, then only twenty-four, to build him Holwood, 80a substantial country house. Holwood is splendidly Grecian, using the austere Ionic of the Ilyssus temple: the best thing of its kind in Kent. Burton's first church, Holy Trinity, Tunbridge Wells, of 1827–9, is just as substantial, but Gothic, and his ignorance of the style lets him down ludicrously. His other churches, St Peter, Southborough, of 1830–1 and Riverhead of 1831, are humbler, and so easier to accept. In 1829 Burton switched to Tudor, for the additions to his father's house at Mabledon; Holmewood, Langton Green, 1827, is in a sort of sub-Grecian. Thereafter Burton turned to a weird hybrid Tudoresque, of an elephantine playfulness which is really unexpected as early as 1831, the year when Burrswood, Groombridge, was begun, and 1832–3, the date of Bentham Hill, Southborough.

Picturesque Tudor is handled by *Salvin* with a finesse which is altogether different at Scotney Castle, begun in 1837, overlooking a slope quarried and planted strictly in accordance with Picturesque principles.

H. E. Kendall is our next specimen. He completed a proudly dignified Commissioners' church at Ramsgate (E), St George, begun in 1824 to *H. Hemsley*'s design, with a w tower modelled on Boston Stump. Yet Kendall's design of 1838 for Chiddingstone Castle is castellated, and completely uninteresting.

G. L. Taylor on the other hand built two unimpressive churches at Sheerness (E), c.1835, one in a wretched lancet style, the other classical and better; and then c.1838–40 he went to 86town with the spectacular Gothic tower, modelled on Fonthill, which he added to Hadlow Castle.

In Kent however the fullest illustration of this theme is the work of a local firm, founded by *John Whichcord Sen.* of Maidstone. He built Holy Trinity in 1826–8 in the dull classical style used by *Sir Robert Smirke* at Strood in 1812 and St John, Chatham, in 1821–2. By 1839, at St Stephen, Maidstone, *Whichcord* had gone Gothic. His Royal Insurance Offices of

1827, in the High Street, are designed like an Italian palazzo. His magniloquent Oakwood Hospital of 1830 is classical, his West Kent General Hospital of 1832, Italianate. His son, in the partnership *Whichcord & Ashpitel*, carried on, with a Jacobean Ophthalmic Hospital and Italianate Public Baths.

The JACOBEAN REVIVAL had begun very early in Kent. Earliest of all are the large additions by the *Reptons* to Elizabethan Cobham Hall, remarkably faithful to what was already there. The dates 1812 and 1818 occur on the exterior; but what reveals the accuracy of their observation best is the strapwork plaster ceiling dated 1817. The additions to Godinton, an exact match with the red brick and shaped gables of the house of 1628, were made early in the C19. Such sympathy for existing buildings was the prerequisite for a real revival of the style. The first Jacobean-style house built *de novo* was *J. B. Papworth*'s St Julian's, Underriver, of 1818–20. It has shaped gables, but in the projecting window-bays there is Perp tracery. Could Knole near by have suggested this mixture to Papworth? The final stage of a style's acceptance is reached when an architect will choose to graft it on to an existing house in another style. That happens in Kent before 1832 at Lamorbey Park, Sidcup, where *John Shaw Sen.* garnished a plain Georgian house with mullions and transoms to the windows and strapwork panels and cresting. As for the Italianate style, there is nothing to compete with the transformation in sandstone wrought for Viscount Beresford to Bedgebury Park, Kilndown, in 1836.

None of this however is more than playing about with styles. The shift to historicism came in the 1830s, whereby accuracy of details and mouldings at last began to mean more than plausibility at a distance or vague evocativeness. It was the passionate conviction of Pugin that won the battle. In *Contrasts* (1834) he attacked across the whole field, from cathedral to bank to water fountain. Yet for him Gothic was not just a style, but the true and Christian form of architecture; so naturally what mattered most was that Gothic churches should be built. *Pugin*'s second house was in Kent, at Ramsgate (E), and the church of St Augustine which he began there in 1845 is the pearl of VICTORIAN CHURCHES in the county, the only one of Pugin's buildings that satisfied his almost impossibly high standards. Pugin's love and conviction sing out in the strangely intricate interior, full of his beloved screens and glowing with the splendid glass made by *Hardman*. Pugin's house, The Grange, w of the church, and the terrace of houses to the E are, in their blunt shapes and harsh materials, much more typically Victorian.*

It is wrong to think that Pugin was the first to insist on period accuracy and a close study of genuine medieval churches. Thomas Rickman, inventor of the terms E.E., Dec, and Perp, has a better claim to that honour. *Rickman* in partnership with *R. C. Hussey* rebuilt Goodnestone, near Wingham (E), in 1839, with a chancel copied, surely, from some medieval Midlands church. Hussey alone rebuilt Frittenden in 1848 in a similar spirit. *Rickman & Hutchinson*'s Lower Hardres (E) of 1831–2, if nothing much to look at, is memorable as a sincere attempt to do a humble village church. It errs mainly in being too big. So does *Sir G. G. Scott*'s early church at Ramsgate (E) of 1846–7, which is also based on severe E.E. models; and the same can be said of *P. C. Hardwick*'s church at Collier Street of 1849. *R. C. Carpenter*'s Christ Church, Gravesend (1854–6), is the climax of this particular type, although it is Dec. Carpenter was a real artist, and the favourite architect besides of A. J. B. Beresford Hope, one of the founder members of the Cambridge Camden Society and most vocal of the Ecclesiologists. *Carpenter, Willement,* and *Butterfield* all contributed to the Ecclesiological showpiece that Beresford Hope made of the chancel at Kilndown (1840–5).‡

It was Butterfield whom Beresford Hope's patronage launched, for when the latter bought the ruins of St Augustine's Abbey, Canterbury (E), in 1844 and founded a college for training Anglican missionaries there, *Butterfield* was his architect. His chapel, cloisters, and library (like a great hall) recreate a medieval world, without recourse to medieval planning. Butterfield is well represented in Kent altogether, with a farouche ragstone school of 1844, at East Farleigh, one of his first works, and the excellently direct church at Langley of 1853–5, grouped with a school. The chancel tiling at Langley is a characteristic piece of polychromy. In his later years constructional polychromy took a vicelike grip on him, as the grinding contrasts of colour and texture show on his School House, King's School, Rochester, of 1878.

So much for the High Church architects. The other end of the

* *Thomas Willement*'s re-instatement of the nave and cloisters at Davington Priory (E) in exactly these years makes a house-cum-church very like Pugin's. Davington, like The Grange, has lost much of its interior decoration, but enough of both is left to show the bold forms, bright colours, heraldry, and texts favoured by them both.

‡ More surprisingly, Beresford Hope got *Carpenter* to design him a French pavilion roof in 1854 for his mansion at Bedgebury Park, Kilndown.

Anglican scale, where the sermon was still the *clou* of the service and robed choirs were not heard, is perfectly illustrated by *Ewan Christian*'s first church, Hildenborough, of 1843–4. Its short 87 transepts and lowering timber roof, like an upturned boat, are both functional and internally of startling power, if less wilful than E. B. Lamb's more famous solutions of this problem. The only other Kent church of Christian's which is as effective is St Peter, Rochester, of 1858–60. That, with its exciting outline and multicoloured material, is decidedly High Victorian. *R. L. Roumieu*'s St Mark, Tunbridge Wells, of 1864 is a knockout in the same mood.

The mid-Victorian decades have better things to offer than this. The peak of achievement is perhaps the noble and very carefully thought-out Early French Gothic church at Bexley-88 heath by a little known architect, *W. Knight* of Nottingham, who won a competition in 1869, and built the church between 1872 and 1877. Nothing on the other hand is more characteristic than the drastic remodelling in a powerful Late Norman style of Bicknor (E) church in 1859–61 by *Bodley*.* Several other leading church architects appear in a good light in the 1860s and 1870s. *Street*'s St Andrew, Gravesend, of 1872 is tiny but good. The R.C. church of 1863 at Sheerness (E) shows *E. W. Pugin* at his best, resourceful and impressive. The same can be said of *Sir A. W. Blomfield*'s early church of St Mary, Strood, of 1868–9. *St Aubyn*'s big church at Erith (1874) impresses too, but is not remarkable for its resourcefulness. *Burges*'s church at Murston (E) of 1873–4 is Burges all over, with its rotund E apse and its colossal W rose window, in spite of his re-using the genuine Late Norman arcade. *Clutton*, who had been Burges's collaborator in the Lille Cathedral design, also appears, as architect in 1862–3 of the cheap but powerful St Michael, Chatham, and in 1874 of the pretty Frenchy mortuary chapel intended for Louis Napoleon's body at Chislehurst. Only *James Brooks* however would be ready to admit that his churches in Kent fairly illustrate the quality and range that he was capable of. The favourite style of Brooks's early maturity, a personal version of E.E., with mighty round piers and elemental tracery, is there, very satisfyingly, at the church of the

---

* Neo-Norman found almost no favour in Kent. From the 1840s, the period when the style was most popular, there are only Christ Church, Tunbridge Wells, of 1836–41, a dreadful affair by *R. Palmer Browne*, and *J. Wilson*'s equally dreadful Baptist Chapel of 1840 at Ramsgate (E). 1853 is the date of both *Salvin*'s Betteshanger (E) and *A. D. Gough*'s St Paul, Chatham.

Annunciation, Chislehurst, of 1863–70, broad and luminous in the nave, dark and lofty in the chancel; and at All Saints, Gravesend, of 1868–71, which is tighter and more dramatic inside. His St Peter and St Paul, Dover (E), however, is very late, of 1893, and quite different. It is E.E., cruciform and spectacularly upstanding outside. The interior has passage aisles and an unbroken sweep of space from W to E, a typical Late Victorian solution but rarely handled with such grandeur as this.

LATE VICTORIAN CHURCHES are an easily recognized group. Apart from Brooks's, there is one by *Leonard Stokes* at Folkestone (E), a most thoroughgoing application of the passage-aisles-and-wagon-roof formula. *Micklethwaite & Somers Clarke*, in their St Saviour, Folkestone (E), of 1891–2, attempt no more inside, in spite of a W front of staggering uppishness. *Norman Shaw* at All Saints, Swanscombe, of 1894 is good. Although the church is unfinished, Shaw designed all the fittings, and they are good too. *J. F. Bentley* did Chiddingstone Causeway, his only church for Protestants, in 1897, deriving it closely from the Shaw church at Bedford Park. The story continues after Queen Victoria's death, and it is the same story, with *Caröe*'s fine church at Dartford, Christ Church of 1909, and even to 1916, the date of 89 *Temple Moore*'s very personal and wilful St Augustine, Gillingham. *Caröe*'s other major church, St Bartholomew, Herne Bay (E), of 1913 is also very personal, indeed feverishly novel, as Caröe liked to be.

VICTORIAN CHURCH FURNISHINGS do not need much comment, as the historically most important, Beresford Hope's in the chancel at Kilndown, and the artistically most satisfying, in *Pugin*'s St Augustine, Ramsgate (E), have been referred to already. Other Ecclesiological ensembles are at Boughton Malherbe, 1848–50, i.e. early; and Frinsted (E), 1870. As a complete contrast *F. C. Eden*'s fastidious furnishing of Elham (E) *c.*1908–17 in several Renaissance styles may be mentioned. STAINED GLASS on the other hand was of course inserted almost everywhere. Much good glass in Kent was blown out by bombs in the Second World War, but by no means all. *Morris & Co.* made the best Victorian glass without a doubt. Speldhurst and Langton Green both have good collections of it. *Burne-Jones* designed much of it; and in the Congregational Church at Maidstone, oddly enough, is Burne-Jones's very first panel of stained glass, made for him by *Powell*'s *c.*1857. It is delightful. Of Morris's followers *Holiday* has a good early window at Westerham of 1864, and another at Blean (E) of 1866, and the less well-known *G. H. Cook* one at

Crockham Hill in 1906, *Baillie Scott* at Sevenoaks in 1908, *H. Thackeray Turner* at Margate (E) in 1910, and the young *Charles Holden*, who did Sutton Valence School in 1910–14.

The whole Devey–Shaw–Arts-and-Crafts tradition, as should now be abundantly clear, is in essence conservative, ignoring technical advances just as, for the most part, it ignored changing social conditions. To trace the ACCEPTANCE OF NEW MATERIALS after *c.*1800 we must look in other directions. CAST IRON had been developed for structural use in Coalbrookdale, Shropshire, as early as the 1770s, and there the first iron bridge went up. The cast-iron spire on the Waterloo Tower, Birchington (E), completed in 1819, shows that forty years later the material was still something of a curiosity. When it was used in a supporting role cast iron had to be disguised, e.g. as Gothic piers in the arcades of St John the Evangelist, Gravesend, in 1834, as Greek Doric columns to support the pier at Gravesend of 1842, and as Gothic arcading in the iron-framed façade of a shop in Maidstone High Street, put up by *Ashpitel & Whichcord c.*1855. But Paxton's Crystal Palace had in 1851 changed all that. There, in a mighty exhibition hall in Hyde Park, cast iron had been frankly exposed for what it was. The forerunners of the Crystal Palace were greenhouses; but naval engineers had during the 1840s developed independently straightforward cast-iron framed structures. The earliest, at Chatham Dockyard, slips constructed in 1845–7, are the finest and most advanced, using nothing but I-section horizontal and vertical girders. They were designed by *Col. G. T. Greene* in the 1850s. He designed a slip at Chatham in 1852; but the most splendid structure of all is the four-storeyed Boat Store at Sheerness (E) of 1859.

From that the jump to MODERN ARCHITECTURE is easy to make. In terms of materials it is a jump from cast iron to reinforced concrete. Reinforced concrete was developed in France by Hennebique in the 1880s, but in England was not in significant use until after 1900. Few engineering firms specialized in handling it, and no architect would have dreamt of showing it. The Erith oil works then, of 1913–17, are epoch-making in England. The young Danish firm of *Christiani & Nielsen* handled the concrete, but, according to Mr Nicholas Taylor's researches, it was *S. Rowland Pierce* who was responsible for the frank display of concrete surfaces in the twenty-four massive cylindrical silos and the warehouses that link them to the riverside. The rough-shuttered pilotis at the base of the silos are an astonishing fore-[95] cast of Le Corbusier.

Meanwhile, on the Continent, concrete and glass architecture was hardening into a style. The INTERNATIONAL MODERN STYLE found its way to England just before 1930. *Colin Lucas*'s house for himself at Platt dates from 1933, just before he joined the famous partnership of Connell, Ward & Lucas. The only other building in the style in Kent that is worth mentioning is *Godfrey Samuel*'s very Corbusian By-the-Links, Bromley, of 1935. Just as uncompromisingly modern, but less fashion-conscious, are *C. G. Kemp*'s pithead buildings for East Kent mines, notably at Northbourne (E), in 1934, and *David Pleydell-Bouverie*'s airport building at Ramsgate (E) of the same year and his Amusement Park (1938) on the beach at Folkestone (E). 96 Finally, just before the war, *Gropius* himself designed Wood House, Shipbourne, with his partner *Maxwell Fry*.* Wood House is weatherboarded, a sign that at last the prospect of exposed concrete was becoming less dazzling. Before leaving the subject of concrete though, space must be found to mention the Christian Scientist Church at Tunbridge Wells of 1931, by *Cecil Burns*, a local architect, who here copied Auguste Perret, with his concrete tracery and semicircular plan, more fruitfully than anyone else ever did in England. It is sad that in becoming a clinic, the church has lost almost all that made it Perret-like. Burns's Kent and Sussex Hospital, of 1934, also at Tunbridge Wells, is also Perret-style, see the strict symmetry, exposed concrete beams, and columnar loggia.

So to the POST-WAR PERIOD, and a return to social concern. The chances offered by the bombing of Canterbury (E) were not adequately taken; indeed the fate of the whole city centre is in the balance as this is being written. So nothing there qualifies for this survey but two imaginative shops by *Robert Paine & Partners*, especially David Greig's of 1952–4. Two other good solutions to the problems which this very understudied type of building offers are the recent shop by the same architects at Maidstone and *Bertram Carter*'s shop at Bromley, of 1954–7.

As for CHURCHES, the two that should be mentioned are at opposite poles, the new nuns' church at Malling Abbey, West Malling, by *Robert Maguire & Keith Murray*, completed in 1966, and a church and community centre for a suburb of Gillingham, St Matthew, Wigmore, of 1963–5 by *Peter Bosanquet & Partners*. Both, in accordance with the Liturgical Movement of the 1960s,

---

* *Fry* had designed the village at Kemsley (E) in 1925–6 for workers in the Bowater Paper Mills. Its Beaux-Arts plan and Queen Anne prettiness show what a turnabout Fry had to make before becoming Gropius's partner.

are planned to encourage the greatest possible participation in the service by the congregation. The only furnishings of note are two very recent STAINED GLASS windows, one at Marden by *Patrick Reyntiens*, and the sincere and tender window designed for Tudeley by *Marc Chagall*.   99

In PUBLIC BUILDINGS there is plenty to commend. Post-war schools are some of them outstandingly good, thanks to the policy of the County Architect's Department to call in outside firms for individual jobs. Best of all perhaps is the Sir William Nottidge School at Whitstable (E) of 1952, by *Yorke, Rosenberg & Mardall*; but *Elie Mayorcas*'s Gordon (Westcourt) School of 1958–9 at Gravesend is unusually elegant, and so is the Girls' Grammar School at Sittingbourne (E), built in 1957 by *Charles Pike & Partners*. The Spastics' School of 1961–3 at Dene Park is 97 another admirable job. This is by the *Architects' Co-Partnership*. Recent hospitals too seem to be setting a high standard, to judge by the new buildings at St Mary's Hospital, Sidcup, and the first stage of *Gollins, Melvin & Ward*'s rebuilding of Sevenoaks Hospital. The paragraph can end with a miscellany of memorabilia: the sports hall and hostel at the National Recreation Centre, Crystal Palace, completed in 1964 by the *L.C.C. Architect's Department*; the lighthouse of 1959–60 at Dungeness by *Ronald* 98 *Ward & Partners*; and *Louis Erdi*'s novelty number, the Dover Stage Hotel on the harbour front at Dover (E), built in 1956–7.

When it comes to domestic architecture, good individual houses can be found, for example *Leslie Gooday*'s ingenious Bosphorus House, Sevenoaks, of *c.*1961–2, and excellent small houses by *Powell & Moya* at Toys Hill, and by *Gerald Beech* at Broadstairs (E). The house built at Lympne in 1964 by *Sir Hugh Casson* is on a scale few these days can match. But much more important are the signs that architects and their clients are concerned with housing the commuters and the council house occupiers in environments that enhance their lives. That is why one applauds the little estate at Bridge (E) by *Leonard Manasseh & Partners*, the much bigger estate of 1959–61 by the *L.C.C. Architect's Department* on the outskirts of Edenbridge, and *James C. Williams*'s sensitive piece of urban renewal, The Dene, at Hythe (E). That is why the new barracks, anything but barracklike, of 1963–6 by *Tripe & Wakeham* at Chattenden deserve a cheer, and the Invicta Park Barracks at Maidstone, too, built in 1962–5 by the *Directorate of Works War Office*, first under *Ralph Iredale* and then under *Sir Donald Gibson*.

The latest developments give the greatest cause of all for hope.

In 1965 permission was given to build a whole new village, of two thousand houses, at New Ash Green, to the design of *Eric Lyons & Partners*. What has been built to date, and the published plans, are both extremely promising. Most recently of all the Greater London County Council has begun Thamesmead, which will transform the dreary Erith marshes into a whole new town for 60,000 people designed by the *G.L.C. Architect's Department*, intersected by lakes and canals and the marsh drained to become fields and parkland.

FURTHER READING

William Lambarde's *Perambulation of Kent*, published in 1576, is the earliest of all county histories. The county history proper however is Edward Hasted's, a mine of information, published first in a four-volume folio edition in 1778–90, and again, much revised, as ten quarto volumes from 1797 to 1801. For churches there is Sir Stephen Glynne's *The Churches of Kent*, 1872, especially useful for its many descriptions, the first as early as 1829, of churches before Victorian restoration. The drawings of churches by Henry Petrie, taken *c*.1806–10, are another valuable early source of information. The drawings themselves are lost, but a set of photographs of them is in Maidstone Museum. Later books on the subject are Dr Francis Grayling's two volumes of 1913, and V. J. Torr's *Kent Churches* of 1951, more selective, but fuller than Grayling on the chosen churches and fittings. For Canterbury Cathedral of course there is Professor Robert Willis's splendid monograph of 1845. In 1869 he published an equally exhaustive account of the Monastic Buildings at Canterbury. For Rochester Cathedral and Precincts Sir William St John Hope's monograph (1900) did the same service. For secular buildings there is nothing as exhaustive: the numerous articles in *Country Life* are the most useful source; and Arthur Oswald's *Country Houses of Kent* (1933). The magazine of the county archaeological society, *Archaeologia Cantiana*, has plenty of useful articles on secular and ecclesiastical buildings alike (concerning the latter, G. M. Livett and F. Elliston-Erwood are the names to look for); and so does vol. LXXXVI of the *Archaeological Journal*. What is missing however is anything from the Royal Commission on Historical Monuments and anything beyond the first three volumes for the county (on Roman remains and the history of monastic houses) of the *Victoria County History*. *Archaeologia Cantiana* vols 25-8 cover Church Plate. For the rest, books dealing with one type of object throughout the country have to be consulted, e.g. Tristram's on medieval wall paintings, Nelson's on medieval stained glass, Aymer Vallance's on church screens, Mill Stephenson's on brasses, and many others too numerous to mention.

*

ADDINGTON

ST MARGARET. On the summit of a wooded hillock. The tower
is quite a beacon from the s. It is a w tower, joined to the pre-
existing nave by short pieces of walling. Perp, with diagonal
buttresses and a big polygonal SE turret. Hasted quotes an
inscription, which is now lost, recording 'goodly building' in
1400–3. The church is Early Norman in its walling, see the
herringbone masonry high on the s side, and all four original
quoins. Nave and chancel without a division. The ghost of a
big round arch in the s wall is revealed inside as not Norman.
Dec N window. N porch with a pretty c16 bargeboard.
Gabled chapels, originally a pair, the N rebuilt in 1858. A will
of 1463 refers to one as 'de novo constructa'. The arches to
them look older than that. AUMBRY in the s chapel. Also a
boarded and painted wagon roof. c14 chancel arch. – HELM.
Said to be early c17. – PLATE. Cup and Paten Cover, 1664;
Paten, 1718; Flagon, 1721. – BRASSES. Richard Charlis
† 1378. Top half of a knight originally c. 34 in. long. – William
Snayth † 1409. Fine brass of a knight and a lady under a
double canopy. 36 in. figures. – Armoured figure, c.1415. At
present hidden by the bells. – Armoured figure, c.1445. 18 in.
– Thomas Chaworth, after 1446. Priest, also hidden. –
Robert Watton † 1470. Man in fancy plate armour, and his
wife. 28 in. long. – MONUMENT. William Watton † 1651.
Large and complex wall-monument, incorporating numerous
inscriptions, and two fine relief busts in ovals. Alabaster and
black touch, with marble side columns. Open segmental pediment and another within it, on an armorial panel. Four pairs
of clasping hands up the spine of the monument.

ADDINGTON MANOR, by *P.C.Hardwick*, has been demolished.

THE CHESTNUTS, ¼ m. w of N. This is a small megalithic
chamber flanked by a straight façade of five stones, and
originally set at the E end of a barrow some 50 ft long and 64 ft

in greatest breadth. Excavations revealed primary inhumation burials accompanied by Western Neolithic pottery in the chamber. Much of this material was removed and thrown into the forecourt area, to make room for cremation burials accompanied by Late Neolithic pottery and flint arrowheads. Sealed by the mound and extending over an area of several acres around it there are traces of Mesolithic flint knapping, hearths, and occupation.

CHAMBERED TOMB, 50 yds NW. The site consists of a ruined burial chamber of eight stones at the NE end, originally covered by a mound 200 ft long orientated NE–SW, traces of which survive at the NE end. Most of the mound was destoyed in the construction of the park road which cuts through it.

0030

ALDINGTON

ST MARTIN. Fine big W tower, under construction c.1507–47 (evidence of wills). Canopied niches and cusped quatrefoils for shields around the W window, as well as the usual diagonal buttresses, taken practically to the top. Octagonal NE turret. Impressively lofty tower arch. Top-storey window lights arched but not cusped, confirmation that the work was dragging on to the mid C16. The crowning battlements came only in 1911. Saxo–Norman evidence in nave and chancel, to be sought on the N side, first the tall, narrow doorway to the nave, secondly the blocked chancel window made without dressing the stones or directing the voussoirs accurately. Original NE chancel quoin, again not of dressed stones, evidence that the chancel has been lengthened. That happened in the C13, see the remains of two E lancets, left each side of a big Perp window. Late in the same century came a gabled S chapel, and a lean-to S aisle (later heightened, not widened). The SW vestry or treasury, which looks late, has extremely thick walls, and an early window inside. Mr Elliston Erwood took it to be the stump of an C11 tower. Aisle and chapel arcades with a round pier, double-chamfered arches, and octagonal respond capitals. The same details on the chancel arch, and the W arch to the chapel. Corbel heads on them both, and a naturalistic leaf or two on the former. Three C14 SEDILIA and priest's door as a group, without room for a piscina. Cusped ogee arches. Embattled top. Rudely carved spandrels. – STALLS. Complete set in the chancel, with

splendid poppy-heads, and MISERICORDS. – ROOD
SCREEN. About 1490. Parts of the base only, either side of the
chancel arch. – PULPIT. Made up, with a large relief of a
pelican in her piety. – PANELLING. In the s chapel. Dated
1617. Not indigenous to the church. – FONT COVER. Mid
C17. Gothic-classical compromise. – STAINED GLASS.
Medieval pieces higgledy-piggledy in two N windows. –
PLATE. Cup and Paten Cover, 1662. – MONUMENTS. John
Weddeot, 1475. 19 in. brasses. Inscription misplaced. – John
Blechynden † 1607. Tablet inscribed with Latin hexameters.

COURT LODGE. Originally a manor house of the Archbishops
of Canterbury. C19 w front, but behind that the walls of what
seems to be a chapel of the late C14. Outlines (visible inside)
of two N, two S, and an E window. The tracery pattern can be
reconstructed from the remains of a s window, three daggers
over two cinquefoiled lights. Another C14 window in the s
wall of the modern house, in a plane forward of the rest.

RUFFIN'S HILL, ¼ m. SW. Two-thirds of a C16 brick house.
Two-storeyed s porch, red brick diapered blue. Four-centred
porch arch, hood-moulded window above, with one mullion
and one transom. More English bonding in the E wall, and a
chimneybreast; the rest refaced in the C18. The original
extent of the one-storeyed hall can be traced inside by the
close-set, boldly moulded ceiling beams.

(STONELEES. C16 half-timbered house, very long, with a continuous overhang. Closely set uprights. C17 oriel at the r. end.
NMR)

ALLHALLOWS

ALL SAINTS. The w end of the nave is the earliest part – earlier
that is than the latest C12, the date of the s arcade. Both
arcades have required existing walls to be thinned down.
Reset in the SW respond a tiny piece of Saxon interlace. The
s aisle has the combination characteristic of c.1190 in this
northernmost promontory of Kent (cf. Stoke, Grain), but unusual elsewhere in the county: unmoulded pointed arches
on piers that are still Norman in form. Piers octagonal in this
instance, with square abaci. The capitals are reduced to
pieces of what looks like fluting – a cackhanded attempt at a
scallop capital. Nailhead beading on one. W lancet in the s
aisle. N arcade of the early C13. Round piers and heavily
moulded capitals. Two slight chamfers on the arches. Blocked
C14 E arch in the N aisle. C14 chancel arch of two sunk waves

dying into the imposts. The chancel itself virtually of *Christian*'s restoration of 1886–91. There is no chancel s window, only a blocked doorway. The vicarage is said to have been attached to this side of the chancel. It was demolished in 1842. Perp work in the nave clerestory and the remodelling, without widening, of the aisles, the s doorway abnormally richly moulded. Bequest of 1472 'to the werkes of the body of the church'. – FONT. Plain Norman tub, just like the base of a pier. – CHANCEL SCREEN. C14, with pairs of square-headed lights. – PULPIT. C17 type, with a small tester. Yet the fineness of the mouldings makes a late C18 date more probable. – MONUMENT. Thomas Coppinger. Parts of a monument erected in 1587, with a small brass of a kneeling man in armour.

7050 ## ALLINGTON

ST LAURENCE. A C19 rebuilding. The only old parts are the N doorway and the outer arch of the porch-tower, which are E.E. Yet the low, thick tower, with its shingled spire, and the short church, nave and chancel not distinguished outside, make a medieval-looking group. Lancets. – PLATE. Cup, 1595 by *I.H.*; Paten Cover, 1726 by *Gabriel Sleath*.

ALLINGTON CASTLE. In 1281 Stephen de Penchester and his wife were granted a licence to embattle their manor house at Allington. Today, the battlements are all Sir Martin Conway's, who in 1905 found a ruin, and by 1929 had, with *W.D. Caröe* as architect, built anew what had gone, in a tactful, scholarly manner, but adapting as he went to make the castle a usable home. That was the second remodelling. The first was Sir Henry Wyatt's in the early C16. Wyatt built the straight two-storeyed range that divides the courtyard into two unequal parts, with a long gallery on the upper floor. Also C16 in date is the picturesque half-timbered and gabled conglomeration tucked into the SE corner of the curtain wall.

What remains when these additions have been subtracted mentally is a castle typical of the Edwardian plan of the late C13, but without the least sense of symmetry. It is moated, built of ragstone, a curtain wall punctuated by a gatehouse near the NW corner and by broad, D-shaped wall-towers at intervals and not always at the corners. The most impressive is SOLOMON'S TOWER, at the SW angle, with a subsidiary lobe containing a staircase. The SE tower keeps its C17 tiled cap, hipped in the outward direction. Garderobe shoot at the bottom. One originally trefoiled window-light in the W wall, some slit windows here and there, larger windows of the C16 and C20, but no feature that gives more explicit evidence about the building history, not even significant variation in the wall construction. This is perplexing, because the peculiar appearance of the NW angle, square without a tower, with a break forward in the wall W of it and heavy buttressing, suggests that an earlier building is incorporated at this point. There is documentary evidence of an earth castle thrown up at Allington in Stephen's reign and destroyed in 1174-5, and of an unfortified manor house before Penchester got his licence. Whether it is part of the latter that we see here cannot now be established.

So to the GATEHOUSE, architecturally the most coherent part of the castle. A ruined BARBICAN stands directly before it, on the bank of the moat. The gatehouse itself is a puny affair, projecting but little forward of the curtain wall, with two round turrets. Arch moulded with a mere chamfer. There was a drawbridge, and a portcullis. From the machicoulis upwards all is C20.

Internally there are two ranges of early buildings. Against the W curtain the so-called PENCHESTER LODGINGS do indeed seem to be the earliest part. Caen stone dressings. Two-storeyed straight flights of steps lead up to a square turret and so to upper rooms. Lancets light the lower rooms, and their heads are turned in pale yellow brick. Brickwork before 1300 is a great rarity. On the E side of the main courtyard lies the HALL and its appurtenances. Here the dressings are of ragstone. This too goes back to the late C13, as the three service doorways show, with sharply pointed two-centred heads and a chamfer. So the kitchen and buttery lay S of the hall. One lancet in the S wall of the kitchen (now refectory). The two-storeyed hall PORCH however is C15. Hall doorway with continuous mouldings, convex, step, and hollow chamfer. The hall itself had disappeared by Sir Martin Conway's time, so the present hall, with its long transomed lancets, and the range that continues round to the gatehouse, is all *Caröe*'s work, inventing not copying.

There must also have been buildings against the S curtain wall. The wall-tower here contains a colossal fireplace.

In 1951 Allington Castle was bought by the Carmelites. In the room W of the gatehouse some C15 STAINED GLASS has been inserted, including a donor figure. Also some SCULP-

TURE, especially a fine Madonna fashioned from a trunk of black bog oak by *Clare Sheridan*.

By the stone farm buildings NW of the castle, a round stone DOVECOTE. Remains of another.

ANERLEY
3070

ST PAUL, Hamlet Road. 1865, by *Bassett Keeling & Tyre*, at a cost of £6,000 (GS). It was enough money to give the architects a riotous time. Outside they concentrated on the W front, with polygonal NW vestry and SW tower, spire and staircase tourelle. Lushly hideous plate-traceried windows. The church behind a minimum stock-brick job. Broad nave, narrow aisles, short chancel through a weird tripartite chancel arch. Piers of cast iron. Busy stencilled patterns over everything. All is perverse, ugly, and scorns period precedent.

ORCHARD LODGE, Anerley Road. Some lodge. Three-storeyed front, thirty-seven bays long, with wings nine bays deep. Red brick and brown brick. Built in 1849 by *Charles Lee* as the North Surrey District School. Some school.

APPLEDORE
9020

ST PETER AND ST PAUL. E.E., largely reconstructed after a French raid in 1380. Of the early C13 the stubby W tower with clasping buttresses and quatrefoil belfry windows erratically punched in it. (The tower doorway was inserted in 1510 and bears the arms of Archbishop Warham.) Of the same date or a little later the N transept chapel and its miniature sanctuary, better appreciated from the inside, where one can see a blocked W lancet and the sanctuary arch on shafts with stiff-leaf foliage.* This is an unusually complex scheme for a parish church, and it is sad that more of it has not survived. The church belonged to St Martin's Priory, Dover. The post-1380 work is messy. The nave and N aisle were thrown into one and the S arcade rebuilt on ugly piers. Timber chancel arch. Holy water STOUP beside the tower arch, with a triple head. In the S aisle various large Perp windows. One with an ogee head was 'made' by Robert Clerke c.1480. Nave crown-post roof on tiebeams with pierced spandrels. – SCREENS across the full width of the church, those to N and S probably

---

* Outside, puddingstone quoins. Puddingstone also at the base of the S aisle E quoin. This gives the full width of the C13 E end and shows that it was not regular.

c.1380, the rood screen later. Altogether the interior seems very full of timber. – FONT. Perp. – LITANY DESK incorporating some panels with flowing tracery. – STAINED GLASS. s chapel. Two heraldic roundels, but the rest modern pastiche by a local artist, *G.W.Humphrey*. – PLATE. Cup, 1562; Paten Cover, 1577; Almsdish, 1791. – MONUMENT. Low tomb-chest in the s chapel, under a depressed multi-cusped arch with heads in quatrefoils in the spandrels. Late C14.

The village street is a good shape, wide with mown grass in front of the houses, and widening further by the church only to be abruptly cut off by three houses barring the way to the s. The houses at the s end present the usual pleasing mixture of brick, tile, timber, and plaster. One might single out the SWAN HOTEL, a little N of the church, C18 brick, the central arched window forcing its way through the eaves under a little pediment; and the heavily timbered front of SWAN HOUSE opposite. At the far end on the r. POPLAR HALL has a characteristic late C18 Kentish front. Red brick. The side windows in canted bays carried the full height of the house. The pattern comes in two or, more impressively as here, three storeys.

(UNION SMOCK MILL. Nothing left but the octagonal brick base, dated 1791. NMR)

HORNE'S PLACE, 1 m. N. A fine farmhouse, obviously enclosing a medieval timber-framed house, it hides its treasure behind it. This is a domestic chapel, built by William Horne and licensed for divine service in 1366. The chapel is short and high (i.e. 22 ft long and 23 ft high), of well squared ragstone blocks. The s and w walls are rebuilt more roughly incorporating plenty of small yellow bricks. William Horne's house was attacked by Wat Tyler in 1381. Tunnel-vaulted undercroft, its vault turned entirely in these bricks. The chapel itself is an exquisite little building and the details are of the utmost refinement, far above the level of the parish churches round about. Large Perp E window. One N and one s window with pretty cusped tracery under ogee arches depressed as far as they will go, and an outline of the rere-arches inside that is even more mannered. Panelled roof with moulded arched braces on stone corbels. The catherine wheels on the corbels suggest the chapel's dedication. There was a w gallery (see the joist sockets) and a N doorway below it into the house.

BARROW, ½ m. N. A mutilated round barrow which may have supported a windmill.

ASH

3½ m. N of Wrotham

ST PETER AND ST PAUL. A handsome church, sympathetically restored by *Sir T. G. Jackson* in 1901–3. Flint walls of
course, but unusually much colour in the dressings. Mostly
ragstone, but the S aisle and porch dressed with a glowing
sandstone. Brick SE turret to the tower. The plastered and
whitewashed interior is equally attractive. Of a C13 church the
W tower and chancel remain. E window of 1863. The internal
treatment of the chancel is with two large blank arches of
different designs to N and S. Lancets are set within the E
arch on each side. Early Perp chancel arch. The nave was completely rebuilt contemporarily with a N aisle reaching halfway
along the chancel. Dec aisle E window, of three pointed lights
under a segmental head, with the usual Kentish combination
of ogee forms and spherical triangles. Standard but well
proportioned arcades, octagonal piers and arches with two
hollow chamfers. Boldly carved crown-post roof. In 1472 a
bequest was made 'reparacioni navis'. That may date the S
porch and the widening of the S aisle. – FONT. Presumably
Perp. Sunk rectangular panels on the stem. – STAINED GLASS.
Quarries and borders, much restored, in the N aisle E window.
– PLATE. Cup, 1565; Paten, 1713. – MONUMENTS. Richard
Galon † 1465. Half-length priest. Brass a foot long. – Dr
Maxfield. Small late C16 hanging monument. Poor kneeling
figures, but the alabaster foliage panels are of a purity worthy
of Quattrocento Italy. – Thomas and Sophia Lambard. A
pair of large, exceedingly restrained tablets by *John Bacon Jun.*,
1813.

Church and Manor stand side by side, looking across a field at the
straggling houses of the village. ASH MANOR, of red brick,
bears the recut date 1637. Plain symmetrical front of three
storeys and three bays, with broad segment-headed windows
and a three-storeyed gabled porch. The parapet quirks up in
little gables over the side windows.

SOUTH ASH MANOR, 1 m. SW. An impressive half-timbered
N front, a long recessed centre between slightly jettied ends.
The two-storeyed porch is clearly later, perhaps as late as
*c.*1600, with its braces forming decorative patterns of squares
and hollow-sided lozenges. The wooden caryatid figures beside the door do not belong. (Elizabethan painted decoration
in the dining room. MHLG)

A rectangular ROMAN BUILDING, measuring 104 by 53 ft, lies
½ m. NW. Its plan suggests that it began as a basilican structure
but was later modified to include baths.

ASHDEN HOUSE see LYMPNE

ASHENDEN see SMALLHYTHE

ASHFORD

ST MARY. The substantial central tower, 120 ft high, plays
cat and mouse among the buildings of the town. Occasionally
it appears full length, looking a little top heavy, with its
thick octagonal buttress-turrets, and its plain, bold set-back
pinnacles. The church itself spreads, even sprawls around it,
the result of numerous enlargements. Church and tower both
of crumbly ragstone. The history is this. The earliest visible
part is the W wall of the S transept, with a blocked and mutilated Dec window. So already by the mid C14 there was a
church with transepts. During the next hundred years or so
the E half grew to its present size, a chancel with three-bay
aisles, and transepts also with E aisles. All the piers are round
with octagonal caps, a slightly abnormal form, but the details
differ in each part and show that the aisles were built one after
the other and not in a single campaign. The major campaign
however, c.1475–83, rebuilt the central tower and the nave,
through Sir John Fogge's enterprise. According to Leland
Fogge intended to make the church collegiate, but Edward
IV's death (in 1483) put an end to his plans. It is hard to
believe that he planned to rebuild the E parts too, which
already gave ample accommodation for a college of chantry
priests; but the tower responds towards the chancel and transepts do require higher arcades than the present ones, so
that the arches to N, S, and E limp down awkwardly. It seems
then that Fogge's ambition was not yet satisfied. As architecture however the nave is unimpressive, and still continues the
round piers and octagonal capitals of the earlier work. The
tower too, only recasing the old one, blocks all vistas through
the church. At the same time no doubt new windows were
inserted. Deep external reveals. The E and W windows, both
renewed, of notable size, of five lights with a transom and
panel tracery in two tiers. C19 enlargements: the aisles

widened in 1827, to give extra space for galleries; the nave lengthened by one bay in 1860 (and even then the gallery was replaced by *Clarke*, whom the *Ecclesiologist* usually considered a safe man). – SCULPTURE. Outside, below the E window, a small, very mutilated seated figure, the remains of a Trinity ?* – FONT. Perp. On a boldly concave-sided stem. Quatrefoils on the eight faces, enclosing roses and shields alternately. – STALLS. The back row each side and the return stalls, sixteen in all, have MISERICORDS, mostly of foliage, but including a pelican in her piety, and swine eating acorns. – PULPIT. Presented in 1897. Designed by *Pearson*. – CHANCEL SCREEN. 1919, by *Caröe*, in a Comperish Perp. – ROYAL ARMS. Dated 1660. – ARMOUR. Sir John Fogge's very large tilting-helmet. – STAINED GLASS. Armorial window in the S transept, 1834 by *Willement*. – Kaleidoscopic W window, c.1862 by *Lavers*. – E window, 1882 by *Lavers & Co*. Quite different and much less enjoyable. – PLATE. Early C17 Cup by *C.B.*; Cup of 1632; Flagons, 1710, a pair by *John Bodington*; Almsdish, 1780 by *Daniel Smith & Robert Sharp;* three Patens by *H.B.*, 1784. – MONUMENTS. Quite a number, as one would expect. First the brasses: Head of a priest, c.1320. – Elizabeth, Countess of Atholl, † 1375. Fine and very large, the figure 56 in. long. Unhappily the canopy is almost all gone and so are her arms. – Sir John Fogge † 1490. This was also of high quality. The large tomb-chest stands in the most honourable place, N of the high altar. Elaborate quatrefoils on the sides, and niches between them (these now filled with modern plasticiny statuettes). Of the brasses only Sir John's head is left, resting on a helmet with florid mantling. On the N side another brass, an angel holding an inscription. – Two small children, what remains of the brass to Thomas Fogg † 1512. – In the S transept, no fewer than three large standing wall-monuments of alabaster. The Late Elizabethan and Jacobean pattern is of large figures under a coffered arch, with side columns carrying a heavy top hamper that includes a coat of arms. Kneeling children, and sometimes wives, at the bottom. – Thomas Smythe † 1591. Reclining effigies. He, with eyes open, has an open book in his hands. That is to say, he is no longer resigned to death in the medieval way. – Sir John Smythe † 1609. Kneeling figures. – Sir Richard Smythe

* There was an 'Image of the Holy Trinity' somewhere outside the church, for in 1478 and 1512 people asked to be buried in the churchyard before it.

† 1628. Better carved than the other two. Reclining figure in armour, and at the top decidedly Mannerist angels reclining on the sides of a scrolly open pediment. The original iron railings in front of all three monuments.

CHRIST CHURCH, Beaver Road. 1867. Quite large, and sturdily E.E. without any fuss. Ragstone. Clerestoried nave. *H. J. Austin* was the architect. He had won the job in 1865, while still an assistant in Scott's office. Later, as Austin of Paley & Austin of Lancaster, he did many first-rate churches in the north-western counties. – PLATE. Paten, 1835 by *Paul Storr*.

Ashford was first of all a market town. Secondly it became a railway junction, and in 1851 a new town was laid out to the s by *Samuel Beazley*, especially for the employees in the loco-motive works.* Plans for a second great increase in population, overspill from London this time, were shelved in 1967. So the centre of Ashford still keeps its pre-railway market-town character.

One naturally begins in the CHURCHYARD, where houses hem the church in on every side. They are a good varied collection requiring little individual comment. The GRAMMAR SCHOOL, in the middle of the w side, bears dates 1635 and 1636. Red brick. Simple rectangle, with a large end-gable on kneelers. Brick hood-mould over the large segment-headed window. In the SE corner, a small courtyard, formed by a plain C18 red-brick block and a close-studded half-timbered house, with, at the l. end, the jambs of a medieval stone door-way. This is THE COLLEGE. The Vicarage was built on this site in the reign of Edward IV, and the Vicar still lives here.

Leaving the churchyard on its N side one enters a tangle of tiny streets that stand on the site of the market. At the heart of the tangle, No. 4 MIDDLE ROW has an overhang and gables in two directions. At the top of one gable 1659 is carved. No. 1, facing on to the High Street, has pargetting with geo-metrical patterns, C17 work, redone in more modern materials. No. 54 High Street, immediately opposite, was once the finest C17 house in the town, built late in the century. Stucco grooved to look like masonry. The roof overhangs to the s and w on splendidly large carved brackets. At the waist the house is severed by a brutal shop-front. From this point downwards the HIGH STREET widens out, but nothing more need be noticed until it narrows again and becomes EAST HILL.

* Beazley's station has been replaced by a good modern building, 1963–7, architect *H. Pittaway*, with the booking hall on a bridge over the lines.

Here, on the l., the first sign of C18 prosperity, with the tall seven-bay front of the COUNTY HOTEL. Red brick with a tile-hung top-storey and parapet. Doorcase on Tuscan half-columns. More tall red-brick houses of the early C18, on the other side of the road, Nos. 89 and 91. Here a short detour needs to be made down STATION ROAD, where Tannery Lane on the l. leads to WHIST HOUSE, a nice red-brick and hipped-roof house dated 1707. S of the house, intriguing C19 TANNERY buildings. EAST HILL was Ashford's posh quarter. There are several large detached late C18 and early C19 houses, butting straight on to the road. They are mainly notable for plainness. BROOKE PLACE, on the l., after 1798,* yellow brick, three wide bays. Porch on paired Doric columns. NIGHTINGALE HOUSE faces it. This is a little earlier, of dark red brick, enlivened with white string-courses and key-stones. Three storeys and five bays, the end bays set back and made subordinate. Lower down on the same side BRIDGE HOUSE, the earliest of the three, with a slightly projecting centre bay and sunk panels below the windows. The full stop in this direction however is the FLOUR MILLS, early C19, overshadowed by a taller block with a tower, loudly announc-ing the date 1901. (But Kelly says the mills were built in 1890.)

But there is still a little more to see in other directions. So back to Middle Row and N into NORTH STREET. Here, first of all, on the l., a half-timbered front, overhanging twice and dated 1671 in the gable. Otherwise it differs in no way from timber town houses of a hundred years earlier. There-after the other side of the road needs watching, for two mid-Georgian houses with porches on Ionic columns. First comes No. 22, red brick, c.1770, with sunk panels below the first-floor windows; then NORTH STREET HALL, three bays and two tall storeys. Yellow brick, and the Ionic capitals of the more refined type that came in only after c.1770.

It remains to return once more to the High Street to pick up two last items in the w half of the town. w of Middle Row and isolated in the middle of the road is the MARKET HOUSE (now shops), noted as a 'good modern edifice' in 1808. Stuccoed and painted grey. Meagre pediments in three directions. The bowed end with columns on the upper level added in the C20. Finally, at the far end of NEW STREET,

* As the present house cannot be the one Hasted notes as built before 1757.

the happiest surprise in the town, the NATIONAL SCHOOL of 1841, a charming Italianate group in red brick and sandstone, a two-storeyed pavilion with short wings each side leading to single-storey pavilions set forward. Broadly but not at all coarsely detailed. *Alexander Apsley* of Ashford designed it. *See* p. 643

ASHURST 5030

ST MARTIN OF TOURS. Pretty W bellcote, weatherboarded and painted white. Nave and lower chancel of sandstone rubble. S porch, dated 1621, but still with a four-centred arch (rebuilt). One ogee trefoiled lancet in the S wall of the nave looks genuine and gives a Dec date.* Otherwise nothing escaped the touch of *H. W. Curzon*, who went to work in 1865 (PF). (Or was *Ferrey* the culprit? *Home Counties Magazine*) Inside, wrapped round the NE corner, an arched recess, hardly usable as an Easter Sepulchre (Grayling's suggestion). – FONT. C13. On five shafts, the square bowl arcaded and rounded at the corners. – PLATE. Cup, 1623; Paten, 1728.

ASHURST PARK, 1¼ m. E. A large Early Victorian mansion of greyish sandstone. Quite a handsome composition, a three-storey centre of five bays between lower balustraded wings that come forward a little and are canted. A loggia on Tuscan columns links the wings across the centre. All the details debased. No architect's name seems to be known.‡

CHAFFORD PARK, ½ m. NE. No more than a farmhouse. But the C18 brick front displays two large white-painted medallions with heads in high relief. The heads are of women, turned abruptly to one side. They wear antique costume and are named SARA and IEKRETIA. Do they come from the Elizabethan mansion of the Rivers family, which was pulled down in 1743? To the NW a fine long range of farm buildings, C16 brick at the top end, continuing down the hill as a weatherboarded barn, all under one roof.

AYLESFORD 7050

ST PETER. Sizeable unbuttressed W tower of rubble ragstone. Norman except for the Perp top stage. Three original windows in the W and S walls, four in the N. Ragstone church of

---

* And Petrie's drawing shows a Dec E window in the chancel.
‡ Mr R. G. Bird tells me that Ashurst Park appears in a guide to Tunbridge Wells of 1840. It is not mentioned in the previous edition of 1834.

nave and N aisle of a width as great; chancel and N chapel continuing the aisle, but with a lower roof. Rood-loft stair turret to the SE of the nave. There are various renewed Dec windows, and two original ones in the N aisle. S porch of 1852. Is the S doorway accurately copied? The wind-blown stiff-leaf would be evidence of late C13 activity. Altogether the restorer of 1878 was pretty heavy-handed – he spent £3,500 (PF). Late Dec arcade and W arch of the N chapel. Perp nave arcade of five bays, with a section of four shafts and four hollows, and two-centred arches. It must replace an earlier arcade of the same length. – BENCH. One old poppy-head in the chancel. – ROYAL ARMS. Carved and coloured. They are the arms of William and Mary, and dated 1689. – HELMS. Two in the chancel. Two more, plus swords, in the N chapel. – PLATE Cup and Paten Cover, 1627; Flagon, 1711; Paten and Almsdish, 1724. – MONUMENTS. John Cosyngton † 1426. Brass. Figures of a knight and a lady 29 in. long. – (Palimpsest brass in the vestry dated 1545.) – Sir Thomas Colepeper † 1604. Tomb-chest with reclining effigies. Small kneeling children below. Mainly remarkable because the colouring of the figures is apparently original with no touching up. – Sir John Banks † 1699. A stupendous pile of marble, rising to the roof. Sir John, in wig, cravat, and semi-Roman dress, stands in an elegant pose by an urn on a tall pedestal. On the other side his wife, robed as a Roman matron, leans pensively on the pedestal. Below, their son, Caleb, reclines on his elbow, in Roman armour and wig. Backcloth held by flying putti, side pilasters, wide arching cornice and, at the very top, a garlanded cartouche of arms. Flowery Latin inscription. Everything indeed that could set a suitable seal on the career of a successful *nouveau riche*. The sculptor, on grounds of style, was *John Nost*. – Sir Paul Rycaut † 1700. Modest tablet flanked by Ionic columns. The account of his career in exotic climes outruns the space provided.

THE FRIARS, ½ m. W. Aylesford in the South and Hulne in the North were the first two English houses of the Carmelites or Whitefriars. They were founded in 1240 or 1241. In 1247 the European General Chapter of the Order was held at Aylesford. After the Reformation the church was pulled down and two ranges of the cloisters were turned into a dwelling house. This was gutted in 1930, and in 1949 the Carmelites returned.

The buildings were arranged compactly, N of and at an oblique angle to the River Medway. No recognizable feature remains from the C13. Approaching from the landward side one arrives first at a two-storeyed gatehouse, with four-centred inner and outer arches. Cross-slits low down either side of the outer arch show that fortification was not omitted. Late C16 windows, mullioned and with one transom. A small round-headed doorway with an architrave-cornice on dentils has John Sedley's initials and the date 1590 in the spandrels. Excavation in the 1930s and in 1959 found traces of the C13 chancel and the enlarged church, rebuilt from 1348, which was 154 ft long. It had the normal plan of a friars' church, an aisleless nave and a chancel separated by two cross-walls. The outlines of the walls are marked in white on the pavement. Of the cloisters, S of the church, the S and W walks remain, with the residential ranges behind them. Moulded Perp arches, shafted inside. There was never any tracery. Sir Walter Redesdale bequeathed money in 1451 'for the new work of the cloister'. The walling with the windows over the walks is modern. The refectory lay on the upper floor of the S range. Its pulpit was in the projection in the S wall. The inner arch, steps, and the window to the r. of it are the only original features. The kitchen occupied the junction of the two ranges, on the ground floor. Wide stone fireplace and the rere-arches of two W windows. Next to it, in the S range, the Prior's Hall, with a trefoiled aumbry at the N end. The C15 doorway into the SW corner of the Prior's Hall may not be in its original position. At the N end of the W range a simple C18 block, and W of it the blocked C15 gateway into the Curia, or service court. The Curia is extremely pretty, with ranges round three sides, of ragstone on the ground floor and plastered above, with large dormers with decorated bargeboards. All this however must be post-Reformation. Stone doors and windows like the 1590 doorway in the gatehouse. The stone building incorporated in the SE corner, backing on to the very river bank, was originally free-standing. It may have been the guest house. Two C15 doorways and two trefoiled single-light windows.

The returned Carmelites employed *Adrian Gilbert Scott* for their new church, begun in 1958. It lies E of the medieval church, on the site of which the congregation sits for open-air services. Open SANCTUARY, from which arcaded loggias lead to free-standing CHAPELS to E, N, and S. It sounds much more interesting architecturally than it is. – ALTAR and CERAMICS in the chapels by *Adam Kossowski*. – WOOD SCULPTURE by *Philip Lindsey Clark*.

The church stands on a mound above the village. The best view is from the bridge, where it appears behind the eight even brick gables of a row of cottages. The BRIDGE itself is the first of the series of medieval bridges over the Medway and is built of ragstone. It is probably C14 and has an exceptionally wide central arch, the result of later alteration. Two refuges each side of the road project on buttresses like pulpits. The tight village street starts at once to the l., N of the bridge. Rows of brick cottages on both sides, and, at the end on the l., the CHEQUERS INN, a long plastered front overhanging at two levels. The upper overhang rests on brackets and there are two timber oriels under it. Small gables with pendants. To the r. of the bridge, the GEORGE INN also overhangs to the street. Only two-storeyed, and the black-and-white timbering a faking of 1714, as a large date proclaims. That is a remarkable date for such a thing.

ALMSHOUSES. The Hospital of the Holy Trinity, founded in 1605 by John Sedley. Seven bays, plus two at the l. end added in 1892. A simple range, one-storeyed with half-dormers in irregularly spaced gables. Four-centred doorways. Ragstone, galletted. Restored in 1842. A triangle (the symbol of the Trinity) and 'DEO UNI' in a circle.

NATIONAL SCHOOL, ¼ m. S. 1853 by E. W. Stephens of Maidstone. Ragstone and stock brick. Big white bargeboards, and a half-timbered oriel at the r. end.

STATION, ½ m. SW. Tudor. Looking rather startled, with its tall chimneys. Is this by Stephens too? 1856.

PRESTON HALL (now a Chest Hospital), ½ m. S. Built for Edward Ladd Betts, the partner of Sir Morton Peto in his building and entrepreneurial activities. Peto had built a sumptuous Jacobean mansion at Somerleyton in 1844, with John Thomas as his architect. Betts in 1850 followed suit and employed Thomas to rebuild Preston Hall in the Jacobean style. The mansion that resulted could hardly be drearier. The materials, rock-faced ragstone and ashlar that seems to have been coloured artificially a greyish-yellow, are repellent in the extreme. The main house is symmetrical on the entrance (S) and on the garden side, with on the former a porte-cochère and central tower between complex shaped gables, and three bays running up the full height of the latter, the centre one of gargantuan size. On this side too a weedy tower on the r. and a weedy turret with a cupola on the l. Long lower service wing to the W and a stable range at r. angles to it. The original garden layout partly remains, with a big fountain carved by *Thomas* in 1851. Of course Thomas was primarily a sculptor (Prince Albert's favourite, no less), and so it is not surprising that the only part of the house with a spark of vitality is a bearded head carved on the keystone of the front door.

KITS COTY, 1½ m. NE. This megalithic burial chamber consists of three uprights and a massive capstone. The chamber was originally covered by a long barrow which existed and was recorded in the C18 as almost 200 ft long. The chamber lay at the SE end of the mound.

LOWER KITS COTY, 500 yds S. This is a jumbled and half-buried group of nineteen or twenty sarsen stones (the Countless Stones) which represent the remains of a megalithic tomb destroyed in the C17.

THE COFFIN STONE, N of Tottington Spring-head. This large recumbent stone, 14 ft long, formed, in the C19, one of a pair, beside which were found a number of inhumation burials. The stone probably marks the site of a megalithic tomb.

WHITE HORSE STONE, 1½ m. NE, in the angle of the Pilgrims' Road and the Rochester–Maidstone road. This single standing stone 8 ft high may mark the site of a former megalithic tomb.

MESOLITHIC SETTLEMENT, 1 m. SW, on Holt Hill. Over the whole of the hill is a surface scatter of flint waste, side and end scrapers, and blades indicating temporary occupation by Mesolithic hunters.

At Eccles, 1 m. N, is the site of an interesting and important ROMAN VILLA still undergoing excavation. Provisionally five phases have been recognized. In the first a ditch of Claudian date ran across the site. Later (55–65), a building, possibly a granary, was put up. Between 65 and 100 a set of elaborate baths were erected incorporating a detached circular *laconicum*. Later, in period IV (100–150), the baths were greatly extended to incorporate at least four heated rooms and a cold plunge. Finally (150–290) extensions and simplifications brought the number of heated rooms to seven and replaced the cold plunge with a swimming bath 44 ft long.

BADSELL MANOR FARM *see* CAPEL

BARHAM COURT *see* TESTON

BARMING

ST MARGARET. The W tower with its needle spire is a fine sight
from the road, in a clump of tall churchyard trees, an island
among a sea of orchards. The tower is Perp, battlemented, but
unbuttressed, with a SE turret, and accompanies a Norman
rectangle of a church. A triangle of E windows, and evidence
of another in the original W wall. C15 chancel arch, and C19
differentiation of roof levels. Stone S porch. N aisle of 1850, by
Hakewill. Simple sanctuary decoration, stencilling and a relief
over the altar, by *Comper*, 1898.* – STALLS. The bench ends
are very enjoyable. There are poppyheads to start with; but
the four with figure carving are something quite out of the
ordinary. The three major ones, Samson and the lion,
17   Christ in limbo, and St Michael slaying the Devil, are a good
7 ft high; and there is a fourth, lower one, the Bull of St Luke,
which must have been one of four intermediate stall ends.
They are free-standing pierced sculpture, not mere reliefs, and
the big ones are not on the stall ends but above, like the wing
of a wing-chair. The style is very wild. Note St Michael's
exaggerated wings, the twisting tail of the dragon, the crinkly
draperies, and the alarming foliage. The style is also hard to
date; but the stall ends must in fact be German, *c.*1300, on
the grounds of their similarity to ones in Germany itself, e.g.
in three churches in Cologne, St Severin, St Aposteln, and
St Gereon. – PLATE. Cup, 1639; Paten and Flagon, 1812.

BARMING PLACE, ⅝ m. NE. Swagger mid-Georgian house dated
1768. The show front faces W, three storeys and five bays, of
red brick laid as headers throughout. Stone rusticated quoins,
cornice and balustrading in the parapet. White keystones to the
windows. Porch with a broken pediment and Tuscan columns.
Segmental window-heads, the centre window larger and
elliptical-headed, with a lunette window above. Low flanking
blocks, contemporary with the house, but looking like an
afterthought. Brick with stone doorcases, and, further out,
pedimented stone screens. The E front has three windows to
the show front's five, and is of ragstone dressed with brick.

BARNS CRAY *see* CRAYFORD

BASING MANOR *see* COWDEN

BASSETT'S FARM *see* COWDEN

* I owe the details of the C19 work to Canon Bernard Wigan.

BATTEL HALL *see* LEEDS

BAYHALL *see* PEMBURY

BAYHAM   6030

BAYHAM ABBEY. The real, the medieval, abbey is over the border in Sussex. In 1870–2 *David Brandon* built a Jacobean mansion on the hill for Marquess Camden. The symmetrical front of local sandstone has two shaped gables and looks down one way over a lake and to the monastic ruins in the other direction. *Brandon* also built the CHURCH in the park. 1870. Sandstone. E.E., with SE tower and spirelet. Disused at the time of writing.

BEARSTED   8050

HOLY CROSS. Three beasts crouch on the parapet of the W tower. The present ones are restorations – the originals were 'very worn' already in Hasted's day. Otherwise it is a normal Perp tower, quite large, with diagonal buttresses and a SE turret. The church, of ragstone, is considerably restored (C19 s porch and vestry re-using an old window), but its history can be unravelled. Apart from the tower the only Perp modifications were lengthening the chancel a little and re-building two piers of the arcade taller and slenderer and throwing an ill-assorted lot of arches over them. Rood-loft turret on the s side. The arcade, of a continuous four-bay N aisle and chapel, was built originally in the early C14. Half-round responds and one round pier. Dec tracery in the aisle. Note the NE window, two ogee lights with a pointed trefoil between them, producing a concave-sided arch with a flat top. C13 evidence in the nave and chancel: one lancet in the s wall of each, trefoiled SEDILE, PISCINA with shoulders and a square top. The origin of the nave can be pushed back yet further. Part of the stonework of the s wall looks early. Inside however the springing of an unchamfered arch at the W end of the N wall. Was the arch round or pointed? Whichever it was, *c.*1200 is absolutely the latest possible date for the arcade it implies. The throughstone in the arch however is a Saxon feature. Was this the arch to a porticus? Or could Bearsted have been that rarity, an aisled Saxon church? Painted consecration cross on the jamb. – STAINED GLASS. N chapel E window 1875 by *O'Connor & Taylor*. Terrible. – MONU-MENT. Susanna Cage † 1634. Hanging monument, unusual in that the figures kneeling by a prayer-desk are brasses (18 in. high). Remarkable too for being signed, by *I.C.*

The church, up a lane, is no part of the village proper, round four sides of a large green. A half-timbered house on the N side of the green, another on the S side, but nothing that needs comment.

BARTY HOUSE, Sutton Street. Early C18. The porch later, with untapering Greek Doric columns.

MILGATE, ¾ m. SE. The house has a splendid Earliest Georgian W front. The date of its erection seems not to be known, but it is a slightly reduced version of Bradbourne, Larkfield, of 1713–15, and must surely be by the same designer. Brown brick with warm red dressings. Seven bays, the centre three brought forward slightly under a pediment. In the pediment a large oval window. Sunk panels in the parapet and under all windows. The windows themselves exceedingly tall, with keystones of brick. The only other enrichment is a broad rubbed-brick frame round the central window and the excellent doorcase, with fluted Corinthian pilasters, and, instead of a pediment, a flat hood above a finely carved panel of foliage. From the N it is very clear that this front was added to an earlier house, again two-storeyed, but considerably less high. The oldest element however is in the SE corner, a colossal brick chimneybreast, with diapering, by which one dates it to the C16. Hasted calls the house 'considerably improved and augmented' by Sir Thomas Fludd, who bought the estate early in Elizabeth's reign. Apart from the chimneybreast however, all that is externally visible is of the late C17, red brick and blue headers and a cornice with carved modillions, which the window frames interrupt. The E front falls into five symmetrical bays plus two more. Hipped roof. This casing, six bays by seven, must hide a courtyard house. Early Georgian staircase sweeping round in a single flight. One fluted and two different twisted balusters to the tread.*

BECKENHAM

3060

The churches of Beckenham are a thoroughly pedestrian lot. Even to mention some of them is to give them undue prominence.

ST GEORGE. A humble medieval village church was replaced in

---

* Miss Pauline Plummer reports PAINTINGS on the staircase ceiling and upper walls, à la Verrio or Laguerre, but disappointingly crude. The sight of them suggests to Mr Croft-Murray that *Lanscroon* was the painter.

1885–7 by the present confident town church, by *W. Gibbs Bartleet*, of Beckenham. Tower completed 1902–3. The placing certainly is good, with the pinnacled s w tower closing the top of the High Street. Ragstone, with generous buff ashlar dressings. Dec. w narthex with a big rose window over it. Clerestoried nave and aisles, transepts, and canted apse to the chancel, also with pinnacles. All the proportions rather broad and low, the chancel especially broad. – STAINED GLASS. Apse windows and two under the tower, 1963–6 by *Thomas Freeth*. – PLATE. Paten, 1633 by *R. W.*; Flagon and Almsdish of 1711; Almsdish, 1734; two Cups by *S. W.*, 1812. – MONUMENTS. Saved from the old church. None is a major work, but together they make an unusually fine collection of consistently good quality. Sir Humphrey Style † 1552. What remains of the tomb-chest and cresting is altogether Perp, without any Renaissance elements yet. Brasses of kneeling figures, 13 in. high, unusually well executed. Sir Humphrey is armoured and wears a tabard. – Margaret Damsell † 1563. A 23 in. brass, again very good and animated for its date. – James Burdett † 1710 (N aisle). Cartouche with lively mantling. – Peter Burrell † 1718 (N transept). Another cartouche, outstandingly well done. The edges of the cartouche are fantastically curled and undercut, and round it dangle luscious but tightly controlled bunches of flowers. – Hugo Raymond † 1737 (s aisle). By *Thomas Adye*. Hanging monument. Plain black pyramid on a plain black base, to show off the two vivacious white putti unveiling a medallion. Adye repeated the design at Bengeo, Herts. – Peter Burrell † 1756 (s transept). The only failure in the series. Large hanging monument in various veined marbles. In front of a pyramid with an oval medallion bust, a putto, much too small, stands disconsolately leaning on a large urn. – Stephen Holland † 1768. Again a pyramid on a hanging tablet. But note the yellow marble favoured in the mid century, and the tight, refined, up-to-date details. – Richard Acland (N transept). The monument must have been put up after his wife's death in 1771. A heavily draped woman, her hands clasped, stands by a heavily draped urn. – Amy Burrell, 1790 (s transept). Hanging monument, large but detailed with delightful delicacy, by *John Hickey*. On the sarcophagus, a relief of an old man and a woman with a baby doing homage to a languid woman by a tree. What is the subject of this scene? – Frances Hoare † 1800 (N transept). By *Flaxman*, 1801. Grecian tablet, notably severe by comparison with the earlier monuments. Mourning members of her family, contemporarily dressed, in relief on either side of the inscription. – Catherine Vansittart † 1810 (s transept). Another large hanging monument, this time with a profile medallion on a draped altar. By *Chantrey?* asked Gunnis. – William, Lord Auckland, † 1814 (s transept). Grecian tablet with a profile medallion in very low relief. Carved in 1849 by *Henry Weekes* (Gunnis). – Jemima Wilson † 1865. Still in the pre-Chantrey tradition, with its female wreathing an urn with flowers. Signed by *Gaffin*, and poorly carved.

LYCH GATE. Most of the timbers are old. A plain piece of late medieval joinery. In the churchyard, plenty of good c18 HEADSTONES.

ST BARNABAS, Oakhill Road. By *A. Stenning & H. Hall*, 1878 or 1884. Red brick. E.E. Brooksian, with its tall proportions, nave and apsidal chancel under one roof, and the mighty block capitals to the nave piers. The interior not however as taut and bare as Brooks could have made it. Enlarged 1912, 1933.

CHRIST CHURCH, Fairfield Road. 1876 by *Blashill & Hayward*. E.E. Stock brick, even the spire. Reconstructed with new roofs after bombing, by *Charles Sykes*.

The SCHOOL of 1901, by *Hooper*, and the SUNDAY SCHOOL of 1877, on the corner of the High Street, also of stock brick and of no interest except that, though similar at first sight, in every detail each is characteristic of its date.

ST EDMUND (R.C.), Village Way. By *J. O'Hanlon Hughes*. Consecrated in 1937. The only memorable church in the borough. Pale brown brick. Tall, much-windowed tower, with a curious pyramidal top of green copper. The dramatic thing is that this tower stands at the E end, over the chancel, which is thus top-lit. Wide pointed tunnel vault in the nave, swooping down over the passage aisles. Unfortunately, not content with his effect, the architect stuck spindly ribs over it. This and other fussinesses spoil what would otherwise be worthy of Sir Giles Scott himself.

ST JAMES, St James's Avenue, Elmers End. The original church, of 1879–88 by *A. R. Stenning*, is hidden by the pretty Perp building of 1934 by *G. Sworder Powell*, which doubled its size. Symmetrical s elevation to the road, with two wide gables and low flanking porches on the slant. Arcade of exceedingly wide four-centred arches. – REREDOS. Painting of the Resurrection by *A. K. Lawrence*, 1955.

ST MICHAEL AND ALL ANGELS, Ravenscroft Road. 1955–6

by *W.H.Hobday & F.J.Maynard*. Neo-Byzantine, of all
things.

ST PAUL, Brackley Road. By *Smith & Williams*, 1872 (GR).
Dec. Ragstone. – FONT. White marble. A shell held by a life-
size kneeling angel. Date of death 1912, very late for such a
Victorian and embarrassing piece. That is one's immediate
reaction; yet of course it is a copy of *Thorwaldsen*'s font,
carved in Rome in 1823.

HOLY TRINITY, Lennard Road. 1878 by *E.F.Clarke* (GR). The
stunted pyramid-spire was added in 1883. Ragstone. Geometrical tracery.

BAPTIST CHURCH, Elm Road. 1889 by *Appleton & E.W.
Mountford*. Yellow and red brick and stone. Saddleback tower
with a spirelet on it.

CONGREGATIONAL CHURCH, Crescent Road. 1887–8 by
J.W.&R.F.Beaumont. Rock-faced ragstone. Dec. Decidedly
ambitious.

METHODIST CHURCH, Bromley Road. 1887, by *James Weir*.
Ragstone. Perp.

All three Nonconformist churches are identically planned,
with a prominent tower and spire l. of the entrance front,
wide, shallow transepts, and a school set across the further end.

TOWN HALL, Church Avenue. 1931–2 by *Lanchester & Lodge*.
Toned down considerably in execution, compared with the
published design. Tall central tower, with aedicules in all four
directions high up and an octagonal top stage. Mauvish-
brown brick and mauvish-grey brick.

PUBLIC HALL, Bromley Road. 1883, and unusually fresh for its
date. The architect was *George Vigers*. Red and yellow brick.
Tall roof with perky dormers in two rows and a lantern.
Angle tourelles with lead caps. Semi-octagonal pilaster strips
between the windows. Striped arches at the bottom. A loggia
has been added. All done with the liveliness and freedom that
mark the nineties rather than the eighties of the last century.

CATOR PARK SECONDARY SCHOOL, Lennard Road. Neo-
Wren with a Neo-Vanbrugh centrepiece. 1913–14 by *Wilfrid
H.Robinson*.

ALEXANDRA COUNTY PRIMARY SCHOOL, Cator Road.
1952–3 by *Elie Mayorcas*.

RAWLINS ALMSHOUSES, Bromley Road. In a corner of St
George's churchyard. 1694, reconstructed in 1881. Of the
humblest. One-storeyed plus dormers. Deep coved cornice
with sunk patterns in the plaster.

TELEPHONE EXCHANGE, Kelsey Park Road. A gaunt Office of Works design of *c.* 1925, surprisingly effective (Nicholas Taylor).

OFFICES AND SHOPS, Albemarle Road. 1965–7 by *Derek Stephenson & Partners*. A typically thunderous affair, four-storeyed, with a castellated cresting of rectangular dormers at the top. Facing of grey aggregate panels, in accordance with the taste of the mid 1960s.

COPER'S COPE HOUSE, Southend Road, is the only remaining pre-C19 building in the modern borough of any architectural pretension. The handsome early C18 front has even quoins and a pediment over the centre bay on giant pilasters. Brown and red brick. Rusticated pilasters to the doorcase, and a triangular pediment on a triglyph frieze. In the C19 the house was doubled in depth and given shaped end-gables.

The transformation of the village surrounded by mansions in their small parks into a residential suburb of London began in SOUTHEND ROAD, with large Italianate houses of *c.*1850. Just beyond are the Lodges of Beckenham Place. (For Beckenham Place itself, *see The Buildings of England: London except the Cities of London and Westminster.*) E of this, and N of Bromley Road, lies the CATOR ESTATE, laid out *c.*1864 and still with many of its original houses. Tall and yellow, with tentative polychromy, they are rather earnest and stodgy.

For light relief one should go to WICKHAM ROAD, where Nos. 70–74, by *Francis Hooper*, 1897, express the tile-hung Norman Shaw style at its wittiest. The teasing conflict between symmetry and asymmetry on Nos. 70 and 72 is exceedingly cleverly done. No. 76 is also by *Hooper*, *c.*1905, more relaxed but also less personal, in fact even more like early Norman Shaw.* Wickham Road ends with a roundabout and an amusing cross-section of Beckenham's history. On the l. BURRELL COTTAGE, a demure C18 three-bay house, in brown brick; on the far side the SOUTH LODGE of Eden Park, a crisp white Regency job; and on the r., the servant of suburban Beckenham, PARK LANGLEY GARAGE, in a rampant 'Road to Mandalay' style of *c.*1925.

Finally, working back further E, Nos. 124–8 BROMLEY ROAD is a semi-detached pair of houses of 1884, very early but already very assured work of *Ernest Newton*. ST CHRIST-

---

* Chichester Lodge, one of Shaw's own early houses, of 1869, was in Wickham Road. It has been demolished. (No. 34 Wickham Road appears to be by *Hooper*, and so does No. 11, Court Down Road. Nicholas Taylor)

opher's School stands opposite. Early Georgian house, disfigured by a projecting addition on the ground floor. Five bays and three storeys. Brown brick and fine red brick. Spacious staircase, with one turned and two twisted balusters to the tread. Of the new housing for which the Victorian mansions are making way all over Beckenham only one group deserves the highest praise. That is *Eric Lyons*'s WEST OAK, The Avenue, of 1960, reached from Bromley Road via Downsbridge Road. Short two-storeyed terraces. How well sited they are among the trees, and how strongly designed, comes out very clearly by comparison with MORLEY COURT, next door, perfectly adequate work by *Fitzroy Robinson & Partners*, 1965–6.

See p. 643

THE BEDEWELL see EGERTON

BEDGEBURY PARK see KILNDOWN

BELVEDERE

4070

ALL SAINTS, Nuxley Road. 1853–61 by *W. G. & E. Habershon.** w tower and shingled spire. Nave and low aisles. Colossally deep transepts. Shortish chancel. That is to say, definitely not in accordance with ecclesiological ideals. Careful Dec tracery and careful knapped flint walling. The interior looks less eccentric, as the nave arcades carry straight past the transepts. Galleries in the transepts, with curvaceous balcony fronts of cast-iron foliage, part naturalistic, part palmettes.

ST AUGUSTINE, Gilbert Road. Designed in 1910 by *C. Hodgson Fowler*,‡ consecrated in 1916. Red-brick Romanesque, better inside than out. The w front finished off in 1961.

LESNES ABBEY, New Road. Richard de Lucy laid the foundation stone of the Augustinian abbey on 11 June 1178. The abbey was suppressed by Wolsey as early as 1524, and the buildings razed. Sir Alfred Clapham excavated the site in 1909–13, but the remains were only laid bare after a second campaign in the mid 1950s. They now lie lonely and diagrammatic in a great expanse of mown grass running up to Abbey Wood at the s.

The foundations do indeed provide a useful diagram from which to learn the layout of monastic buildings. The church consisted of aisled nave, transepts with three square-ended

---

* The church was built as a proprietary chapel for Sir Culling Eardley Eardley but after much litigation consecrated within the Church of England.
‡ But the Rev. W. P. Hockenhull names *Temple Moore* as the designer.

E chapels, and aisleless chancel, which is not a normal Augustinian plan but a Cistercian one. The nave had eight bays and was 132 ft long. The bases of several shafts remain, with leaf spurs of the undercurling kind called 'waterleaf', a trademark of c.1180. As the design of the church shows no development from E to W, this is dated waterleaf of 1178. Pilaster buttresses and clasping buttresses. Lady Chapel E of the s transept. It was under construction in 1371. The diagonal buttresses at once single it out as later than the rest. The monastic buildings lay on the Thamesward side of the church, as considerations of drainage dictated. On the E side of the cloisters was the rectangular chapter house, with more of the 1178 shaft bases at the doorway.* N of this lay the dormitory on an undercroft, with the rere-dorter at its N end. The refectory, on the N side of the cloisters, can be recognized by the steps up to the pulpit, lit from two lancets. The kitchen lay NW of the refectory, with a narrow serving-hatch through the wall. The W range was rebuilt, encroaching a little on the area of the cloisters. At its s end the only complete feature to survive, a doorway with an odd wide stopped chamfer outlined by a roll. Clapham thought it C14. A separate infirmary block NE of the chapter house has not been re-excavated. A few C13 TILES in a transept chapel.

ROYAL ALFRED HOME FOR AGED SEAMEN, Upper Park Road. 1957–9 by *Gollins, Melvin & Ward*. Long four-storeyed block facing E and W with a short central projection at the back. Curtain walling, the spandrel panels the palest of blues. Single-storey ranges snaking out at front and back. In design and colour a little insipid perhaps for the old salts.

Before 1957 the seamen occupied the eponymous Belvedere, the house built for Sir Sampson Gideon c.1775 by *James Stuart*, author of *The Antiquities of Athens*. There was little about it that was Grecian.

POWER STATION, Erith Marshes. One of *Farmer & Dark*'s crisp no-nonsense jobs, 1957–60. The two chimneys have an especially elegant, soaring shape. The turbine-house as severely rectangular as possible.

8030

BENENDEN

ST GEORGE. Pale sandstone. Perp, large and handsome, if a bit short on character. Struck by lightning in 1672, patched

---

* Capitals excavated from the Chapter House have crocket capitals, just like those e.g. on the gallery of Canterbury Cathedral choir.

up, and restored to glory by *David Brandon* in 1862. The
nicest thing is the vault of the two-storeyed N porch, eight ribs
and a salamander on the boss. Another two-storeyed porch on
the S side. W tower, and a higher battlemented turret with a
big plain pinnacle. Nave and battlemented aisles continued
past most of the chancel. The windows all renewed except
two in the S aisle and two in the chancel. The E window copies
Rolvenden's. Brandon completely rebuilt the interior in a
conscientious locally-correct Perp, a smug replacement of the
semi-classical C17 work.* – MONUMENTS. Sir John Norris,
hanging monument with a bust by *P. Scheemakers*, 1750. –
Thomas Hallett Hodges † 1801. Standing wall-monument.
An urn-bearing sarcophagus before a truncated pyramid.

BENENDEN SCHOOL. Built as Hemsted for Viscount (later
Earl of) Cranbrook by *David Brandon*, 1859. It cost £18,544
(GS). The old Hemsted had been a large Elizabethan house,
and Brandon provided a successor as Elizabethan as the real
thing. Red brick and sandstone. Symmetrical N and S fronts
with large mullioned-and-transomed windows, small gables,
and battlements. On the S side the window-bays rise the full
height of the house, linked to each other by a loggia *à la*
Hardwick. Brandon at Benenden was determinedly archaeological, and only the lower service wing reaching out to the l.
gives the game away at a distance. Internally however the plan
is 'medievalized classical' in Professor Kerr's phrase, i.e. hall
and staircase separated by a double row of columns between
them instead of a screens passage. Kerr was also happy to find
that 'even the position of the Vegetable-Store is a point of
merit'. Recent additions for the school 1961–5 by *T.E.
Heysham*. To have made them neo-Georgian cannot be justified on any ground, one would think. Lord Cranbrook employed a second architect, a far less pedantic one than Brandon.
He was *George Devey*, and the SOUTH LODGE to the park
could be his.

The village also is largely the creation of Lord Cranbrook. The
church, at the top of an expansive slope of mown grass, looks
across to a row of tile-hung cottages, one of them labelled
'1609 Edmund Gibbon Founder of this School'. The red-

---

* Another casualty of the 1672 storm was the detached timber belfry. The
churchwardens' accounts at the time noted that it was *c.*134 ft high. If it
really was, it must have been an extraordinary object, more than twice as high
as the belfry at Brookland. It was octagonal, of three stages, and stood on nine
posts as opposed to Brookland's four.

brick and sandstone PRIMARY SCHOOL was built by *Devey* in 1861. There are mullioned windows and a central gable with a semi-classical cartouche. The open porch at the lower end starts in stone at the bottom and turns via a brick bit to a half-timbered turret with a tiled cap. But the most skittish detail of all is the minute bell-turret perched on a buttress. This little building is every bit as sophisticated as Norman Shaw was to be, and Shaw first built in this style six years later.

VILLAGE HALL. 1908, also playful with its big scrolly brick gables in three directions. But the stone doorcase is very correct.

Pompous WAR MEMORIAL down the road to the E.

BENENDEN CHEST HOSPITAL, East End. It is at once obvious what these wide-spreading, sun-catching ranges among the pine trees are. The Garland Wing, E of Jackson Way, built in 1906–7 by *A. William West*, had a long, two-storeyed front to the S, bent slightly thrice into a widely-splayed U. For its date it was a remarkably unaffected building; but continuous balconies added in 1961 by *Riches & Blythin* make it now look all of the latter date. W of Jackson Way, the Lister Wing, of 1937, is also long, two-storeyed, and with balconies. Brown brick, and rounded characteristically at the ends. By *Sir John Burnet, Tait & Lorne.* Good, but not so relaxed – as so often with the self-conscious 1930s. Extensions to the Lister Wing, 1953 by *Oswald Pearce.* Staff Centre etc. of 1963 by *Riches & Blythin.**

Until the C19 Benenden was a typical Wealden parish, without a nucleus but liberally scattered with yeomen's farmhouses. Many good ones still remain hidden away among the wooded hillocks. The typical Wealden house of about 1500, with its closely set uprights, a recessed centre between jettied-out ends, and a big hipped roof carried across the centre on braces, can be found three times over, in PYMPNE MANOR, 2 m. NE, OLD PAPER MILL, 1¾ m. SW, and MILL HOUSE, 1½ m. W of S. They are as like as three peas. All much restored, and the latter two with the halls opened out to the rafters and the crownposts showing.

Dilapidated WINDMILL at Beacon Hill, on the road to Rolvenden.

BENOVER *see* YALDING

* These facts were kindly provided by Mr T. Barnett.

BENTHAM HILL see SOUTHBOROUGH

BERENGRAVE see RAINHAM

BESSELS GREEN

5050

A few houses round a sloping triangular green, the best of them the early C19 BESSEL'S HOUSE, built for Dr Epps, the homoeopathic doctor. Yellow brick. Two-storeyed, with one-storeyed stone-faced wings. The windows in two bows. Behind it, the C18 BAPTIST CHAPEL, of brick painted, distinguishable from its manse only by the big, round-headed windows.

On the A25, 200 yds E, UNITARIAN CHAPEL, of 1716, in a churchyard full of tombstones. The chapel, of red and blue chequer brick with segment-headed side windows with casements, is appended to the S to a two-storeyed house. An avenue of limes leads to the door. The scene is complete, an embodiment of the gentle, familial spirit of C18 Nonconformity.

BETHERSDEN

9040

One of the nicest, most unselfconscious villages in these parts. The street is short but indubitably a street, although the houses stand behind gardens and rarely touch each other. The church is at the W end, above the road.

ST MARGARET. Quite large, and Perp throughout, though not built to a consistent design. Ragstone. Good typical W tower, with angle buttresses reaching high up. On the stair-turret a scrolly wrought-iron weathervane. Battlemented aisles continued as chancel chapels. Much of the tracery was harshly renewed in 1873, and a misleading Dec E window introduced. Doorway to the S chapel, and next to it, rood-stair turret with a large and very moronic head corbel. Stone S porch, with a Perp stoup on the angle.* Open airy interior, largely because the nave piers are so tall and the arches so wide and high. In form it is standard work of the C14 – so, as often, the complete Perp exterior is misleading. Wide chancel arch, resting at the S on a grotesque bearded head. Arches to the chancel chapels of different dates, the S arch probably early C16. – REREDOS. Early C19. Lord's Prayer, Creed, etc., set under shafted cinquefoiled arches with good crockets. – STALLS. Perp traceried panels built into the fronts. – ARMOUR. Helm in the

* The floor is of Bethersden marble slabs.

N chapel. – STAINED GLASS. C15. Canopies in three S windows. – PLATE. Flagon, 1631; Paten, 1726; Cup and Paten Cover, 1765. – MONUMENTS. William Lovelace † 1459. 22 in. brass. – Thomas Lovelace † 1591. Brass of low quality, 17½ in. long. Palimpsest. – Sir George Choute † 1721. Fine architectural tablet curved to fit across a corner. Relief of bay branches and a pair of scales at the bottom (behind the organ). – Thomas Wilmott † 1769. Rustic Rococo cartouche. – George Witherden † 1778. Rococo cartouche, of almost the same design, but carved with a Londoner's finesse. – Samuel Witherden † 1779. Adamish, but clearly by the same hand as the last, see the characteristic gaping cherubs.

WHISTON, ⅓ m. SW. Built as the vicarage by Jonathan Whiston in 1676.* Pale red brick with random grey headers. Two storeys divided by a raised brick string-course. Five bays.

THE THORN, ¼ m. E. c.1700. Two storeys, five bays, large hipped roof. Red brick with sunk panels of blue headers below the upper windows. Late C18 doorcase. Inside, a contemporary staircase with two twisted balusters per step, and a Bethersden marble chimneypiece. The marble is in character little different from Purbeck, and often, as here, a pale brownish grey.

4070

BEXLEY

ST MARY. C13 flint church, heavily restored in 1882–3 by *Champneys*.‡ Shingled spire, octagonal in the top half, pyramidal below, on a cornice with brackets; basically medieval, that is, touched up in the C18. Lancets low down in the W tower, one S lancet in the nave, one S, one N in the chancel, with a few old stones left in them to convince us of their genuineness. Wide, gabled N aisle continued as a chapel. There is a lancet here too. Has the aisle been widened then since the C13 ? Perhaps not, for the E bay, clearly later than the rest by the tighter packed flints, has an early C14 window in it. On the other hand an internal string-course, wholly renewed, goes round W, N, and E walls. E.E. N doorway also. E.E. S doorway. S porch of 1882. Nave arcade of four bays, round piers, arches with one large and one small chamfer. The E bay is wider than the rest, and there is no chancel arch. No doubt the

* The fact is recorded on a tablet in the N aisle of the church.
‡ The round-headed arch over the S doorway suggests that Norman walling is incorporated.

nave E pier had to be rebuilt when the rood loft was introduced. The rood-loft turret* is on the S side, projecting internally, with a crocketed conical cap. Perhaps too the strangely
splayed N arch in the chancel is an amalgamation of two, done
at the same time. Three SEDILIA, stepping up towards
the E, with continuous mouldings that look C15 rather
than anything else. – (FONT. The bowl is dated 1684, and is on
a medieval stem.) – CHANCEL SCREEN. By *Champneys*
(BW). Elaborate in itself, with a loft, and incorporating a
chapel screen, stalls, and pulpit. – PLATE. Almsdishes, 1635
and ? 1638; Cup, 1751. – MONUMENTS. Thomas Sparrow
† 1513. Brass of a civilian, 13 in. long. – Sir John Champeneis,
c.1590. Hanging monument with small kneeling figures between Corinthian columns. Entablature and three achievements on top. – Anne Bishope † 1674. Nice cartouche, of
London standard. – Sir Robert Austen, 1687. Standing
marble monument without figures. Vivacious architecture
however; twisted composite columns, scrolly top pediment
with two cartouches between the points, inscription in an
oval frame. – Lady Mary Cosein. Tablet of c.1700, with the
inscription written on a cloth held up by two frolicking putti.
– John Styleman † 1734. The monument, a large hanging one
with cartouches of arms pinned to a pyramid, was erected after
1750 by *J. Annis.*

ST JOHN, Park Hill Road. By *G. Low*, 1881–2. Clerestoried
nave, lower chancel, canted at the end, NE tower and stone
spire towards the road. Ragstone. 'Style "Early French" not
very strongly defined', was Mr Goodhart-Rendel's diagnosis.
Bare, lifeless interior, in spite of stencilling all over the walls
and roof of the lofty chancel.

BEXLEY HOSPITAL. At the SW corner of Dartford Heath and,
strictly speaking, in the borough of Dartford. The hospital
buildings are themselves of no interest, but the battlemented
WATER TOWER is quite a landmark. Stock brick. Remarkable
CHAPEL of 1899 by *George T. Hine*: remarkable because it is
neo-Georgian.

The church lies E of, and across the River Cray from, the short
winding HIGH STREET. On the church side of the river one
or two late C18 houses, the best HIGH STREET HOUSE of
1761, beside the church. On the far side, a row of recent shops
on the l., by *S.F. Everson & D.F. Searles*. Nothing special,

* Reconstructed in 1883.

but their yellow brick and white weatherboarding help to enliven what is otherwise a bit of a dark alleyway. On the r. Nos. 57–9, late C17, with a hipped projecting centre. Dull red brick. Then, on the same side, the STYLEMAN ALMS-HOUSES, dated 1755, a two-storey row of twelve, with a central broken pediment. Raised brick band between the storeys, but no further ornament. Finally, on the l., as the street broadens out into suburban roads, a gauche little ragstone CONGREGATIONAL CHAPEL, as late as 1890, by *G.Baines*. The spire an overgrown pinnacle.

58 HALL PLACE, 1½ m. E of N. It is a delightful surprise to come upon the house, chequered grey and white in front, healthy red brick behind, with its demure walled garden towards the road and its splendid early C18 wrought-iron GATES.* The colours immediately establish the two periods; on the S side of the C16 house a back court was built in the middle of the C17. Sir John Champeneis, Lord Mayor of London in 1534, bought the estate three years later, and the fact that a great deal of medieval carved fragments is incorporated in the walling of the present house suggests that he soon rebuilt, using the materials so plentifully supplied by the recently dissolved monasteries. Not much later, but probably after his son, Justinian, had succeeded in 1556, the N front was adapted to make it as nearly symmetrical as possible. Thus from the road one sees the hall, with long wings coming forward on either side. As left by Sir John there was only one bay window lighting the hall, the r. one, of two–four–two lights with two transoms, the lights arched. The solar wing projected as far N as it does today, but two-storeyed for only a short way, continued by a low chapel and a narrower wing N of that. Evidence for this arrangement is in the upper half of a straight quoin half way along the W wall.‡ Chapel E window of three trefoiled lights under a segmental head. The service wing, E of the hall, projected northwards, but was lengthened to make it as long as the W wing. Quoins mark its original length on both sides. The most telling item of the remodelling was the duplication of the hall bay window, which of course made nonsense of the original arrangement of the hall, with its upper and lower ends in the traditional way. Modern central doorway, re-

* Attributed to *Thomas Robinson*.
‡ This and other modifications are confirmed by the internal dressings of the walls, chalk in the earlier work, brick in the later, discovered by Mr P. J. Tester during alterations in the mid 1950s but now hidden.

placing a C17 one. On the W side all the larger windows are modern; the solar however did originally have a bay window, and the turret is a rebuild of an old one. Four projections on the E wall, the S one the buttery chimneybreast, the other three communicating with the exceptionally spacious kitchen and the rooms over it. The centre of the three not a chimneybreast but a garderobe turret. Mr Tester assigns all these to the second phase, and also the chequered facing with rough flints and chalk ashlar. To complete the account of the C16 house, the internal features that belong to it are two openings above the S doorway to the hall, which Mr Tester assumes to have led from the hall gallery into a two-storeyed S porch, demolished to make way for the C17 additions. Several medieval and Jacobean fireplaces have been brought in.

In its way the C17 work is equally interesting. It forms three sides of a quadrangle on the S side, two-storeyed, in red brick still largely in English bonding, with a deep hipped roof on a wooden bracket cornice. Pedimented dormers. Rusticated stone quoins and a stone string-course. Vertical laces of stone break the E front into a rhythm of 2, 7, 2. The upper windows are altered, but the wooden cross windows survive below, set under sunk semicircular arches with stone blocks at the base and apex of the arch. That is a typical mid-C17 detail. Similar treatment of the S front, ten bays, with a big centre doorcase, a triangular pediment on carved brackets and big ears to the door surround, another mid-C17 trick. Less regular W front, with two sets of oval windows on both levels. Inside the courtyard the lower windows are set in blank arcading, and the N side is almost filled by a splendid four-storeyed staircase tower (reconstructed in 1968). It is square, the outer angles chamfered for most of their height, and the irregular fenestration following the flights of the steps. Circular window in the middle at the top, blank ovals below it. The main windows however adapt the form of the external ones, so that the sunk arch is flattened and the keystone balances a horizontal stone bar on it, a distinctly Dutch motif. Pyramid roof growing into a picturesque two-storeyed turret with a cupola. The staircase has big bulbous balusters and ball finials on the newels. The baluster shape is repeated as a sunk pattern on the newel-post, an odd idea. In an upper room in the SW corner of the old house a fine plaster ceiling clearly of the same mid-C17 date, with big oval wreaths, in enriched rectangular frames, but distinctly Jacobean-looking foliage growing from the waists of naked figures on the sloping side parts. Sir Robert Austen bought the house *c*.1640 from the last Champeneis. The finishing touches to his building were being made a decade later: bell dated 1649, spit-rack dated 1651, 1653 found inscribed on the head of the staircase turret.*

Red-brick BARN SE of the house. It may be C16 or C17.

Hall Place is now municipally owned. The grounds run down to the river in an extremely pleasing way.

4070   BEXLEYHEATH

88 CHRIST CHURCH. 1872–7 by *William Knight* of Nottingham, who had won a competition judged by Burges in 1869. The church is so grand, with such noble, soaring proportions, that one grasps at any facts that will give substance to the enigmatic Mr Knight. The materials are ragstone dressed with ashlar, and slate roofs; the plan cruciform with the central steeple, alas, barely begun. The transepts as high as the nave, the chancel not quite so high, ending in a canted apse. The style is Early French Gothic, interpreted with great freedom and originality, and makes effective use of plate tracery in the W window and the nave clerestory. Fine rose window in each transept. Internally the nave, with arcades of four wide arches on short round piers, yields to the glory of the chancel, to which the crossing space belongs, and its exceptionally lofty arches. Well-managed shafts and string-courses high up however binding all together. Interesting detailing of the crossing arch corbels. Apse arcading of elemental Norman forms that must have appealed to Burges. Only the spindly timber roofs do not satisfy – that and the total absence of worthy fittings to match the scale of the building.

TRINITY BAPTIST CHAPEL, Broadway. 1868 by *Habershon & Pite*. Classical.

DANSON PARK, 1 m. w. A crystalline villa, built *c*.1759–62 for Alderman Boyd by *Sir Robert Taylor*, and set in a park landscaped *c*.1761 by *Capability Brown*. The park now looks a little bare, with its second-generation trees, and large, rather uncompromising lake. The park boundary too is now marked by all-too-visible semi-detacheds. The house consists of a *piano nobile* and half-storey above a rusticated stone basement, the walls rendered, the roofs low and slated. It has five windows

* Dates reported *in litteris* by Mr Tester.

on each side, but is not a square, so although the centre three are in a canted bay on the S front and at the sides, the former looks spacious, the latter taut. The entrance is on the N side, up a grand flight of steps to a balcony as wide as the projecting, pedimented centre. Doorcase with attached Corinthian columns. The internal planning allows for a three-bay hall in the centre of the N front, rooms running the full width of the E and W fronts, with bowed projections, and an octagonal room in the centre of the S front. That leaves the core of the house for the staircase, which is elliptical, in a tight, funnel-like, top-lit well, with eight Ionic columns below the dome. Elegant wrought-iron balustrade. The decoration of the three main rooms was completed, probably c.1770, by *Chambers*, with exquisite marble fireplaces, and a reticent palmette frieze and enriched ceiling in the octagonal room.* The W room has contemporary bookcases set into the walls and an ORGAN dated 1766. The Saloon is decorated with fine inset paintings of gods and goddesses, to be associated with Taylor rather than ^{See} Chambers. Are they by *Andrea Casali*? See p. 643

Ashlar STABLES NW of the house, designed with the same lucidity.

RED HOUSE, Red House Lane. 'More a poem than a house . . . ⁹⁰ but an admirable place to live in too.' That was Dante Gabriel Rossetti's verdict on the newly completed home of his friend, William Morris. The plan that Morris should have a house built for him in the country and that *Philip Webb* should design it, had been hatched during a trip to France the two took with Charles Faulkner, rowing down the Seine and visiting medieval cathedrals, in the summer of 1858. The contract was signed in April 1859, and late in the summer of the following year Morris and his bride moved in. Rossetti was not the sort of person to view Red House objectively, but his contradictory remark reflects the difficulty one finds in making a cool assessment of it as a work of architecture. One's first thought is of the imagination and boyish enthusiasm of Morris himself, Morris who wanted a house 'very medieval in spirit', who lived here with such zest for five short years. How relevant are Morris the designer and Morris the inhabitant? Then there is the fame of Red House, the status accorded it already by Lethaby as a pioneering building in which the

* Mr John Harris has identified a drawing by Chambers in the Soane Museum as for the octagonal room, and found his design for the Saloon chimneypiece in the Metropolitan Museum, New York.

revival of styles of the past was first abandoned, so that it
became the first link in the chain that led to Gropius and
modern architecture. But the recent researches of Mr Brandon-
Jones and Dr Thompson have proved that Red House has
been put in a false position: that the first product of Webb's
independent practice leant heavily on the style of his master,
G. E. Street, and even more on that of Butterfield. On the other
hand Morris himself thought of it as being 'in the style of the
thirteenth century'. Finally it takes a considerable effort,
surrounded by a sea of suburban semi-detacheds, to remember that Morris and his friends, arriving from London at
Abbey Wood station, had three miles to drive through the
North Kent countryside before they reached his home in its
orchard of apple and cherry trees.

What then do we see, as we turn in past the high garden
wall through the heavy wooden gates? A house, substantial
but not large, built of deep red brick (laid in English bond),
with steeply pitched roofs covered with red tiles. Some of the
gables are half-hipped, and there are half-hipped dormers
too. The tall chimneystacks, at strategic points, taper by
means of sloping set-offs now and then. The windows vary
greatly in size and proportions, but they are all segment-
headed and sashed, a Georgian shape, that is to say, not a
Gothic one. Every one of these motifs had already occurred
in parsonages and cottages by Butterfield, e.g. at Baldersby,
in the North Riding, c.1855. One characteristic detail Webb
took from Street, the pointed tympanum, either set back or
merely outlined by a relieving arch. That too comes from
unpretentious buildings, like schools, where Gothic forms were
reduced to the greatest simplicity. What Webb did, and it was
indeed a revolutionary step to take, was to make use of this
easy, informal, pared-down style in a gentleman's country
house.* Webb also subscribed to the principle that roofs and
windows should express the character of the rooms within.
To appreciate the elevations then prior knowledge of the plan
is needed. The house is two-storeyed and L-shaped. The
rooms on both floors face N and W, with passages running
round the S and E fronts, i.e. round the inner sides of the arms
of the L. The staircase projects at the junction of the two arms.

* Butterfield certainly held more hierarchical views on architectural
propriety. His Milton Ernest, Bedfordshire, a house comparable in size to
Red House, is equipped with plenty of external shafting and window tracery.

The two major rooms lie on the upper floor of the N arm, the drawing room at the W end, and Morris's study at the E.

The N front is the entrance front. The two-storeyed porch projects nearly in the centre, with a very sharp gable and a pair of windows under a pointed arch. The entrance arch repeats the shape. To the l. two windows under a hipped dormer, and then a strong, high chimneystack. To the r., a single window below, a trio above, lighting the drawing room. Thus the front is quite asymmetrical, the gables building up from l. to r., the chimneystack weighting down the l. end. The shapes all push upwards, yet the big expanses of plain wall low down give the house its solid, comfortable look. And is it too fanciful to imagine the deep eaves projected like guy ropes, tethering the roofs to the ground? Fancy certainly begins to blossom on the W side. Again, near the l. end, a chimney-stack, this one of towering height, and next to it the strangest oriel, on a stem that steps out brick by brick to the full width, nearly shaving off the corner of a downstairs window on the way. The oriel windows show by their shape that they too light the drawing room. Quieter r. half, kitchen windows below, a pair of big half-dormers for bedrooms, and a long slope down to the back yard at the S end. It is typical that the upper half of the front is the more strongly characterized. Webb's contract drawings have 'roses', 'white jasmine', 'passion flower', 'bergamot' scribbled against the walls here.

From the SE, looking into the angle of the two wings, the view is far more picturesque, and the grouping apparently random. The house forms two sides of a courtyard focused on a well-head and its conical cap like a witch's hat. In Morris's time it really was a courtyard, for there were wattle fences on the S and E sides.* But this is the back of the house and Webb could relax, not bother about aligning the roof levels, let the varied fenestration create its own interest: the bulls-eye windows of the upper corridor, the long wide main-stairs windows, the long narrow one for the back stairs, and little slits for larder and pantry. The pyramidal staircase roof with its pretty lead capping, half louvre, half flèche, is enough to draw everything together to a climax. Morris's study is the only important room to look out this way. The study's E window consists of a bulls-eye over two sashes, made to read as plate tracery by the pointed blank arch that encloses them.

* Later, too, Morris proposed to complete the courtyard with ranges, as a home for the Burne-Joneses.

So we come round again at the front door. Above it a text: DOMINUS CUSTODIET EXITUM TUUM ET INTROITUM TUUM, just as Pugin would have had it, but in letters that belong to no known medieval alphabet.* From the far end of the spacious hall rises the main staircase, a solid piece of joinery, with tall newels that end in gawky pinnacles, and its structure frankly revealed on the undersides of the treads. The upstairs corridors run off at different levels, each through an exposed brick arch. One also notices the way the wooden window frames and door lintels are made very visible. But most remarkable of all is the decoration of the staircase vault. The flat top is painted with trios of dashes in two directions, but the concave sides have a stylized pattern in blue and green, of fans linked by loops into diagonal trails. It is highly effective and further removed from nature than any Morris pattern in other media. The design is pricked on the plaster, and week-end guests were expected to help with its execution. In fact the decoration of the whole house was the work of *Morris* and his friends, and the birth of the Morris firm in 1861 was the result of their experience here. Almost all of what they did in the rooms has alas been swept away, and the staircase is now the only ensemble.

The drawing room however, on the first floor, was originally the pièce de résistance. The ceiling, open to the roof, was covered with floral designs, and *Burne-Jones* began painting the walls with scenes from the medieval romance of Sir Degrevaunt. These remain, on the S wall, and surprisingly amateurish they are too. In the centre of the S wall the vast settle brought from Morris's first studio, in Red Lion Square, with a loft added by Webb, to do double duty as a minstrels' gallery and a way into the roof. Today however the noble
91 brick fireplace, with its grand hood reaching the full height of the wall, is the most memorable feature. It is an astonishingly free piece: not a period detail, barely a moulding. Above it the inevitable motto: ARS LONGA VITA BREVIS. Brick fireplaces in other rooms, notably the hall and dining room, but nothing on a comparable scale. In the dining room another massive home-made piece of furniture, a chest with three gables. In the hall a cupboard, painted with scenes from the Nibelungenlied by *Burne-Jones*. Stained glass in the lower corridor, two

* No doubt Webb designed them, as he later designed the characteristic lettering on Morris glass.

small experimental figures by *Morris*, and quarries with comical birds and bushes by *Burne-Jones*.

BICKLEY

ST GEORGE. 1863–5 by *F. Barnes* (GR). Dec in a costly manner. Ragstone. Clerestoried nave, transepts, canted apse to the chancel. W tower and spire redolent of St Mary, Oxford. (The spire was rebuilt by *Newton* in 1905–6.) Cruelly hideous and inappropriate arcades. The interior has recently, under the direction of the Vicar, Canon *Hugh Glaisyer*, been turned from light to very mysteriously dark by blocking all the chancel windows, the clerestory, and all but single lights of the aisle windows. – MONUMENT. The Wythes family. Large canopied tomb-chest with side pieces, in a straightforward Perp style. 1871 by *Butterfield*.

In 1780 John Wells built himself BICKLEY HALL (to the design, it seems, of *Robert Mylne*). The house has only recently been demolished, but building on the park began as early as 1861, hence the date of the church. What makes Bickley architecturally interesting falls midway between the 1860s and the 1960s. This is an unusually representative group of wealthy suburban houses that plot the progress of that sad period in English domestic architecture when the freedom that had been won by Norman Shaw, abandoned in a nostalgic yearning for the C18, was buckled into the neo-Georgian straitjacket. One of the prime bucklers was *Ernest Newton*, who lived in Bickley and began his career in Shaw's office.

BEECHCROFT, Bickley Park Road, of 1885, is one of his first houses. The vocabulary, tile-hanging above red brick, and a half-timbered gable jutting forward in the centre, is Shaw's. The desire for symmetry, and the closed outline of the hipped roof, are not. Newton admits a playful detail or two, but the house is noticeably crisp and spare. WESTWOOD, Bird in Hand Lane, comes next. Also by *Newton*, 1891. The same ingredients, with the same windows, rectangular but of any convenient proportion. Big off-centre chimneybreast. SUFFOLK HOUSE, at the corner of Pines Road, is also clearly Newton's, at about the same date. By 1902, however, to judge by LITTLE ORCHARD, Page Heath Lane, Newton has almost made the transition. All is Georgian vernacular, including the pair of canted window bays; all, that is, except the long staircase window, pushing the porch over to the left.

As late as 1909 however the battle was not won, as two houses
in Wells Road by *Quennell* demonstrate. DENBRIDGE
HOUSE, for himself, is still gabled and quite informally
grouped. LINDEN OAK on the other hand is in a Queen
Anne style, with big brick quoins, though not tidied into
strict regularity. *Quennell* faces up to pure style-copying in
1913. The evidence: DEERWOOD in Woodland Road.
ENGLEFIELD, opposite, is by him too; 1912, and very weak
with its silly patterns in the gables. Arts and Crafts fanciful-
ness with no longer any sense of purpose. Intermingled with
the Quennell houses, in Woodland Road and St George's
Road, several much fussier houses, c.1911–13, all obviously
by the same hand, writing the very same tale.

Finally three houses in Chislehurst Road. BICKLEY COURT,
c.1905–7, is again by *Newton*. L-shaped neo-Georgian not
entirely regularized, with canted window-bays at the back.
CROSS HAND and AMAPOLA, however, are both of 1927–8,
the former neo-Georgian, the latter still like an early Lutyens
design in its playfulness.

BULLERS WOOD, off St Nicholas Lane. *Newton*'s first major
house, of 1889, famous for having been decorated internally by
Morris & Co. In fact it was only a remodelling of an earlier
house, which is left partly showing at the SE corner. The
entrance front faces W and a projecting wing at the l. had to be
incorporated. Newton achieved this by throwing out three
more projections further r., a generous window bay, a porch,
and a bay-cum-chimneybreast. He then tied them together
with a deep white egg-and-dart cornice, through which no
gable breaks. Big wide windows, stone-mullioned below,
wood above. The emphasis on the horizontals is very strong,
and such overt Georgianisms as the cornice remarkable in
1889. Perhaps they are not hard to explain – that was the year
in which Shaw, Newton's master, was rebuilding Bryanston.
Even so the façade does not quite come together as a whole,
and that is the measure of the architect's immaturity. Narrow
N side, three-storeyed, as the land falls, with a single bay the
full height. On the E side a typical sheer chimneybreast at the
l. end. The rest quite informally grouped and somewhat altered.
Throughout the details are fresh and original, especially the
treatment of the porch, with a flat far-projecting hood, and
continuous glazing above it between long wooden brackets.
The interior has lost all its original Morris wallpapers and
hangings, but the drawing room ceiling remains, beamed, and

stencilled by *Morris* himself with a scarlet pimpernel pattern in delicate buff, green, and pink, The white woodwork however is the right colour, and one is struck by the spaciousness of Newton's planning. The setting is still superb, a steep wooded hillside plunging down below the formal terrace. The STABLES, by the entrance, are *Newton's*, 1884. In the same year he built a cottage at the foot of the hill, now BULLERS WOOD COTTAGE, reached from Bullers Wood Drive.

BIDBOROUGH

5040

ST LAWRENCE. Superbly sited on the brow of a narrow spur, with views to E and W. Cottages on a lower level ring it round to W and S. The church is small and built of sandstone. Nave and chancel Norman in origin, see one N window in the latter and the reset S doorway, a Perp one surrounded by an unmoulded arch on tall shafts, the capitals with two scallops, the bases perhaps once with spurs. Narrow two-bay N aisle thrown out in the C13. Arches with a slight chamfer. Perp W tower, of very big blocks of masonry, but quite humble, ending in a squat shingled spire. S aisle 1876–7 by *Christian*. One Dec, one Perp window reset in it, as well as the doorway. The chancel largely rebuilt at the same time, with a new chancel arch. Early Perp E window. – STAINED GLASS. A lot of very late glass by *Morris & Co.*: 1909–25. – The E window of the S aisle is a *Burne-Jones* design of 1891, the two-light window there, Generosity and Love, to designs of *Burne-Jones* of 1880 and 1882.* – PLATE. Cup, Paten, and Paten Cover, all 1658. – MONUMENT in the churchyard, N of the chancel. Mary, Countess of Darnley, † 1803, by *Sir R. Westmacott*. Sarcophagus with scrolls at the ends and putto heads, with half-spread wings.

WYATTS, Rectory Drive. Built after 1788, as the Rectory, 'after a design of Mr *Wyatt*'s' (Hasted). Nothing special. The entrance front added to, the W front of five bays, the centre three in a bow. Painted brick.

THE GRANGE, 200 yds SW. Long, close-studded front, facing N, with a continuous overhang, and a gable at the road end. Impressive at a distance, but a close look reveals that nine-tenths of the timbers are modern.

* According to information received from Mr A. C. Sewter.
6—W.K.W.

BIDDENDEN

ALL SAINTS. From the E the church appears Perp, a jumble of gables rising to a climax in the boldly battlemented W tower. The history is jumbled too and must be traced inside first. The starting point perhaps is the enigmatic pieces of walling on either side of the chancel arch; E responds of earlier arcades, it may be. The church reached its present size *c.*1300, and of that date there remain the Geometrical N window in the chancel, the fine PISCINA and SEDILIA, on grouped attached shafts, a reset doorway in the N aisle, and the nave arcades, four bays on slender round piers. The N arcade is taller, has less boldly projecting capitals, and may, but need not, be by a little the later. The E arches of both arcades were later widened to take the rood loft. C14 chancel arch, with early C19 windows in the gable above. Later C14 the two-bay arcades to the chancel chapels – concave-sided octagonal piers. Crown-post roof in the nave. The rest of the story is the usual one, of Perp enlargement by widening aisles and enlarging windows. The exterior tells it all. The N aisle basically Dec; see two windows near the W end, characteristically Kentish with their concave-sided hexagons at the top of the tracery. Low NE vestry. In the S wall the rectangular projection is for the rood loft stairs. Stone S porch (N.B.: its E window is shafted inside). Bequest of 1463 for one S window, and *c.*1510 for a new aisle (H. Sands). What was the W doorway in the S aisle for? Its beautiful head-corbels suggest that it was an important one.

Finally we come to the W tower, with which goes a slight lengthening of the S aisle. Scale, design, and material – small blocks of greyish paludina – all suggest a comparison with Tenterden. The window system is the same, with a large four-lighter over the (battlemented) W doorway and paired windows at the top: the latter look like early C16 work at the earliest. Biddenden otherwise suffers by the comparison, especially in its gauche outline, first narrowing too much and then ending in top-heavy battlements. Angle buttresses. Polygonal N stair-turret. – FONT. C13. Octagonal bowl of local marble with two sunk pointed arches on each face. The shafts of the base new. – PULPIT. Jacobean on a C20 base. – PLATE. Paten Cover, 1560, the earliest piece of Elizabethan plate to survive in the county; Cup, 1561; Flagon, 1592, covered in strapwork and foliage; Almsdish, 1761. – BRASSES.

Margaret Goldwell † 1499, a 13½ in. figure between her two husbands. Engraved c.1520. – John Mayne † 1566, in armour, 10½ in., set in the back of the altar tomb of Walter Mayne † 1541. – Thomas Fleet † 1572, fragments of a civilian, interesting because it is a palimpsest brass. On the back are bits of fine Flemish brasses of c.1360 and c.1520–30. The earlier work includes the hem of a priest's vestments and two evangelist symbols in a border. – The next three brasses, of civilians with their wives, are disconcerting. The men, 20 in. long, face their 17 in. long wives, two or three identical wives to each husband: cocks and their hens. They are: William Boddindam † 1584 and two. – Richard Allarde † 1593 and three. – John Eurenden † 1598 and two. – Josiah Seyliard † 1609, a 20 in. civilian between his two wives. – Bernard Randolphe † 1628, small reclining figures. – William Randolphe † 1641, 21 in. civilian. – MONUMENT. Black and white marble tablet to Herbert Randolph, with Corinthian side pilasters, ostentatiously signed by *Francis Grigs*, FECIT ANNO 1645.

The village street is very short and very perfect, at first sight perhaps seeming perfect to the verge of phoniness, too like a poster advertising the homely Home Counties. But all is genuine, even the long half-timbered range bending round the SE corner, with C17 oriels under the eaves.* All, that is, except the shop-windows of the Tuck Shop. Just out of sight of the street are three grander houses. To the S HENDON HALL is on the r., early C18 red brick, with a GAZEBO on the garden wall, brick and a tiled pyramid roof. BIDDENDEN PLACE faces this, again red brick and probably early C18, with a big hipped roof. The windows are slightly irregular, evidence that an earlier house is encased. From the earlier house come the datestone of 1624 and the bargeboards on the dormers. Just N of the street THE OLD CLOTH HALL, a long half-timbered range, tile-hung to the S and with various gables. It is obviously a composite building, mostly of the C16. The E gable, with two overhangs, dated 1672, was the final addition. Clothworkers occupied it as workshops.

The timber-framed houses scattered through the parish are unusually fine and varied. The following, to take them in clockwise order starting at the SW, need a special word.

---

* Mr Gravett draws attention to the original casement windows with ingenious fasteners.

CASTWISELL (or CASTWEAZEL) MANOR. Two storeys. Closely set uprights, continuous overhang. Half-hipped roof. Perhaps mid C16, if a comparison with Standen (see below) is valid. It is a lovely sight across a pond beside an ash tree.

WORSENDEN. Like the last, but all hung with glowing orange tiles and with the bressumer painted white. Nicely placed among its farm buildings.

LASHENDEN, 1½ m. N. Close-studded, and again a continuous overhang. Gable at the l. end with two overhangs and oriels under them.

On the main road NE of Lashenden is a good modern building, the hatchery of STERLING POULTRY PRODUCTS. 1960, by *Jenkins & D.R.Gosby*

STANDEN, 1¼ m. NE. A compact front, two-storeyed and jettied across the whole of it. The upper part is decorated with curved braces making chains of hollow-sided lozenges, some wide and some narrow. Splendid brick chimneystack at the l. end. Text over the door. (More texts inside, and 1578 on a fireplace. Igglesden)

VANE COURT, 1½ m. NE. This is the only house in Biddenden of the Wealden type. Four bays, the end ones overhanging. Curved braces carry the roof-eaves across the centre two. This arrangement, and the wide spacing of the uprights, were normal in the middle of the C15. Hipped roof of outsize proportions.

WEAVERS' COURT (alias THE COT), ¾ m. NE. As long as Vane Court, but later, i.e. mid C16 judging by the many close-set uprights and the continuous overhang, showing that the hall was never open to the roof, but one-storeyed from the start. The oriel windows will have been inserted later still.

4050

BIGGIN HILL

Chaotic sprawling housing spattered all over the side of a long, steep-sided valley, a place to make the most ardent free-enterpriser admit the virtues of planning; though New Addington, next door, is unfortunately no advertisement for the latter. The shacks of the first pioneers have largely given way to cosy suburban houses and gardens. Visit the next valley westwards, over the Surrey border, to see what glorious country this once was.

ST MARK. Built in 1957–9 with materials from the demolished Victorian church of All Saints, North Peckham, and designed by *Sir Giles Gilbert Scott, Son & Partner*. Yellow brick without, red brick within. Detached, slightly tapering, NW campanile with pretty cresting. Very free neo-Gothic church, its design governed by the need to re-use the old nave roof. All the windows are engraved by the vicar, the Rev. *V. Symons*, copying woodcuts from the early C15 German Biblia Pauperum. – PLATE and ALTAR CROSS. Also by Mr *Symons*.

NORHEADS FARM, ⅝ m. W. Straightforward red-brick farmhouse, dated 1715. Five bays, two storeys, and a big hipped roof.

The AERODROME, famed from the early days of the Second World War, is to the N. The most conspicuous building is the neo-Georgian OFFICERS' MESS, 1930, like a large country house.

BILSINGTON

ST PETER AND ST PAUL. As prettily placed as its neighbour Bonnington, on the edge of Romney Marsh, but not so pretty to look at. Less picturesque bell accommodation, more attention from C19 restorers (*Joseph Clarke* in particular, in 1883). Stone. Small. Stump of an unbuttressed Perp W tower, with the Sidney arms and the date 1590. What significance should one give to that? Lancets in the chancel, Dec two-lighters in the nave. C12 walling however, see a blocked Norman window in the nave. A blocked lancet too. – FONT. Rustic Perp. – STAINED GLASS. Trinity and Virgin and Child in the heads of the nave N windows; *c*.1400. Faded, but nothing rustic about the quality. – PLATE. Cup and Paten Cover, 1630.

MONUMENT, ¼ m. W. Stone obelisk on a podium, in memory of Sir William Cosway, M.P. for Kent, who fell off a stage coach here in 1835, and was killed. *G. Cooper* of Canterbury fecit. Struck by lightning recently. Must it be pulled down?

BILSINGTON PRIORY, ¾ m. N. Even the site of the church is unknown of the priory founded in 1253 for Augustinian Canons by the Provost of Beverley. What does survive is the complete domestic block, perhaps the infirmary hall, much restored by *Micklethwaite* in 1906. He had good evidence for what he did, but he destroyed the texture and history of the building by his operations. The hall itself, on an undercroft, has characteristic mid-C13 plate-traceried windows, two lights with a central shaft, and a quatrefoil pierced above them. Internal seats on the sills. Elsewhere only rectangular or shouldered slit windows. Three-storeyed rectangular building SE of the hall, continued, two-storeyed, further S. Three-storeyed tower-like structure in the angle between this and the hall. Original spiral staircase to the top storey of both, but no other unrestored feature internally worth comment.

₆₀₆₀

BIRLING

ALL SAINTS. Perp W tower. Diagonal buttresses; SE turret; battlements. Nave and gabled aisles of the early C14. Standard four-bay arcades. Trefoiled lancets, and a pair of them ogeed in the S aisle. One two-light N window. The chancel is a C16 rebuilding, the windows eccentrically distributed. Only the SW one has cusping of the lights. Six-light E window. The chancel is notably wide but does without a chancel arch. Its present appearance is largely due to a refitting c.1828 in a minimal Gothic style by the Nevill family. The cast-iron lid of their vault is prominent. – FONT COVER. Wood, tier upon tier, carved 'by several ladies', and given in 1853. – BENCH ENDS. Two fine poppyheads. – STAINED GLASS. E window. Typical of the 1840s. – ARMOUR. Two C16 tilting helms with Jacobean crests. – PLATE. Cup, 1617; Cup, c.1685; Flagon (really a tankard), 1697. – BRASS. Walter Mylys † 1522. Large (35½ in.) but bad figure of a civilian.

The church is excellently placed above the village, which consists mostly of Nevill estate houses, unattractive in themselves, but compactly grouped.

BIRLING PLACE, ¾ m. NW. Confused red-brick house of various dates, made regular to the S with a five-bay front of c.1800. Fine square-headed window, of six lights with four-centred arches, i.e. c.1500, reset in the W wall. On this side early brickwork, and a stone string-course above the upper windows. The house stands within a stone perimeter wall, which describes roughly a circle. In it, towards the E, a stone arch matching the Perp window. Simpler medieval stone arch towards the W.

BISHOP'S FARM see BOUGHTON MONCHELSEA

₀₀₃₀

BONNINGTON

ST RUMWOLD. An exceedingly rare dedication.* The church sits like a plump little grey hen by the bank of the Royal Military Canal. Of stone. Norman chancel. Nave rebuilt

---

* St Rumwold, son of the king of Mercia, cried 'Christianus sum' as he was born and died three days later.

their mouths chamfered, grouped in pairs to make a cause-way over the several streams of the River Beult.

BOURNE PLACE see EAST PECKHAM

BOW HILL HOUSE see YALDING

BOY COURT see ULCOMBE

BOYS HALL see WILLESBOROUGH

BRADBOURNE see LARKFIELD

BRASTED

4050

ST MARTIN. N of the village, facing the Downs. Much but-tressed w tower. One reaches the w doorway through the middle of a buttress, under a little pointed and ribbed tunnel-vault. The doorway is C14, and leads into a church of 1864–5, by *Waterhouse*. Local sandstone, snail-crept. The old founda-tions were used, so there are deep transepts. The s arcade in-corporates the original short round piers, early C13, and double-chamfered arches. Other anomalies, such as the reti-culated tracery in the N transept facing geometrical tracery in the s, suggest that Waterhouse was following old lines. All his own are the half-dormer aisle windows and some extra-ordinary and original cuspless tracery. – PLATE. Cup, 1565 by *I.C.*; Paten Cover, probably 1565; another old Paten; Flagon, 1793 or 1813. – MONUMENTS. In the tower: Dorothy Berisford † 1613. Severe tomb-chest with just a little geo-metrical decoration.– Margarita Seyliard † 1615. Simple tablet. – In the N transept: Robert Heath † 1649. Alabaster reclining figures, he robed as a judge. They look *c.*1600. Nor do they fit the black and white marble chest with its back plate. *Thomas Stanton* agreed to make a monument in 1664, and only charged £60.* – John Turton † 1806. Heavily Grecian tablet, with Doric columns beside the inscription and a sarco-phagus. On the latter books and serpent-entwined staff. Turton was George III's doctor. By *Sir R. Westmacott*. – Mary Turton † 1810, also by *Westmacott*. Relief of a classically robed man leaning pensively on an altar 'To Gratitude'. – H. Avray Tipping † 1933, author of *English Homes*. Pastiche of a C17 tablet. The squared-up lettering hard to read.

* Discovery made by the late Rupert Gunnis and unpublished.

BRASTED PLACE. Built for Dr Turton in 1784–5 by *Robert Adam*. A villa, of beautiful Tunbridge Wells sandstone ashlar, grey streaked with yellow and brown. On this scale Adam's exquisitely refined detail shows to its very best advantage. The detail is of course Etruscan, but the villa form is still thoroughly Palladian. Five-bay entrance front, the centre three under a pediment. Porch with coupled Tuscan columns. The garden front is of only three wide bays, but more richly treated, with coupled giant Ionic angle pilasters and a deep portico on two pairs of elongated Ionic columns. The roof was heightened in 1871, and the extensive service wing thrown out to the w. The service wing also has alien French-pavilion roofs and a funny clock turret. Of the Adamesque interiors all that can certainly be assigned to Adam is the overdoor and the severely noble white marble chimneypiece in the SE room. The plan however, has remained unchanged and is of remarkable and prophetic informality, the staircase and the three main rooms on the ground floor leading off a narrow vestibule without any imposed symmetry.*

THE PHILIPPINES, Brasted Chart. In a wood. Built in 1834, and already coarsely, i.e. post-classically, detailed, with much balustrading. Two big bows on the N front; the s front dominated by an octagonal lantern.

Far too many vehicles roar down the village street, but it is a good one none the less, with unusually few bogus intrusions. The street is not quite straight and varies in width, at one point opening out into a little green. At the w end Church Road comes in, and ALMS ROW COTTAGES start the village here on the s side. Various half-timbered houses are embedded in the row, among them one whole Wealden house with recessed centre and jettied ends. On the l. the self-consciously pretty VILLAGE HALL of 1900, then nothing for a bit until on the r. VILLAGE HOUSE, an early C18 brick front, next to the fake timbering of CHARTSIDE HOUSE. On the N side the cottages become continuous. Opposite, by the green, the climax of the walk, RECTORY LODGE, early C18, blue and red brick, and THE WHITE HOUSE, a fine late C17 box, brick painted white, with a big hipped roof and a shell hood over the door. N of the green, DURTNELLS' new offices, 1966, are an attempt to do a Wealden house again in C20 terms.

* According to Miss S. Blutman's researches on late C18 country-house planning.

By *Prudence Durtnell*. Vertical struts, overhang, recessed centre are all there; but the scale is wrong – that is the basic incongruity. *E.T.Hall*'s blowsily half-timbered WHITE HART INN of 1885 is much less earnest. And so the street ends at the modest entrance to Brasted Place, and the LODGE of Combe Bank (for which *see* Sundridge). The lodge may well be mid-C18. Canted ashlar end to the road. Bracketed eaves.

BRATTLES GRANGE *see* BRENCHLEY

BRENCHLEY

6040

ALL SAINTS. A sandstone church, handsome at a distance, especially the W tower with a concave-sided cap on the turret and a big weathervane; less satisfactory at a close inspection. First, the tower turns out to rise by short, jerky stages at the top. Perp windows there, but a C14 W doorway. Ample support from the angle buttresses. Secondly, *Clarke*'s restoration of 1849 involved rebuilding the chancel, and new windows in the transepts, and he irritatingly introduced split-cusped tracery throughout. Deep C14 N porch, of stone, the outer arch remarkably large. Nave and aisles dating from the C13. W lancet in the S aisle. Arcades of four bays, short round piers with moulded caps, those on the N slightly the more elaborated. Double-chamfered arches. The tower encroaches at the W end. A little later transepts were thrown out to N and S, without affecting the arcades. PISCINA in the E wall of each, neither ogeed, the sole remaining old features. In the SE corner of the N transept a thickening of the wall perplexingly stop-chamfered as an impost. Near by, a piece of C13 string-course. Perp nave clerestory and fine crown-post roof. Pierced tie-beam spandrels. Celure over the E bay, honouring the rood, by being boarded and painted blue. Modern repeating pattern in yellow and white. Original carved wood bosses. The width of the chancel arch is original and also, so it seems, the unusual width of the chancel itself, as there is a stump of old masonry in the S wall. SEDILIA apparently preserved at the rebuilding, two shafted blank arches on the dropped sill of the SE window, with an odd trefoiled moulding. PISCINA to match. – ROOD SCREEN. The lower part only, linenfold panelling finely carved, blank tracery at the two tiers. In one panel the tracery is intertwining branches. (The screen bears the date 1536.) The linenfold panelling on the front of the W gallery may also be old. – STAINED GLASS. E window, 1910 by *Dearle* of *Morris & Co*. Pale and poor. – PLATE. Two Cups, *c*.1629; Flagon and two Patens, 1775 by *Charles Wright*(?). – MONUMENTS. Thomas Robertes † 1517. 18½ in. brasses of a civilian and three wives. – 17 in. brasses, *c*.1540, of a civilian and his wife. – Elizabeth Fane † 1596 (not 1566, as the inscription wrongly has it). Tablet with a surround typical of the late C16. – John Courthop † 1649. Tablet with a surround typical of the mid C17. – Walter Roberts † 1652. Alabaster hanging monument, with touches of black. An elegantly dressed couple, revealed half-length in a strapwork frame, as if at a window with curtains knotted back. Arms linked, they touch hands fastidiously and half look at one another. Sensitively carved for the mid C17. – William Courthop † 1772. Hanging monument with a broken pediment. Marble of several colours. – Stephen Hooker † 1775. By *Wilton*, after 1788. Tall, slender hanging monument of white marble, detailed with exceeding refinement. – Francis Storr † 1888. In a mid C17 style surround, that looks tame beside the real thing.

The centre of the village is tiny, a matter of single houses, not groups, round a tree in a triangle of grass. The church on the S side, down a path lined by huge clipped yews. At the top of the path, OLD VICARAGE, a comfortable tile-hung cottage with an overhang, the vertical tiles painted white. The timber-framing of the BUTCHER'S SHOP on the E side is exposed, close studs and a continuous overhang. Another white house to the N, a late C18 front, of wood blocks cut to look like rusticated stone. The most spectacular item is the OLD PALACE, in the NW corner, a long range, half-timbered above the overhang. A nearer view however reveals its phoniness. Barely a timber is old. The gables added *c*.1890. In a perverse way one prefers the alien red and yellow brick of THE BULL, an ugly pub of *c*.1870 across the road.

The street continues westwards with a few nice cottages. Soon it widens out again. Here, on the l., another restored half-timbered house. This, THE OLD WORKHOUSE, is probably of the early C17, cf. Marle Place below. Porch on posts, with an oriel window on the upper level. MONCKTONS, opposite, was built in 1739. Its character, however, is of the early C19. Seven bays, two storeys. Rendered walls. Deep eaves and low slate roof. Handsome Doric porch. Bow on the S end, carried on columns.

BRENCHLEY MANOR (Old Parsonage), ⅓ m. NW. C16 half-timbered house of impressive size. Two-storeyed, with an overhang continued round the E and S fronts. Closely spaced uprights, the timbering now rather too tidied up. (Panelling dated 1573. Linenfold, with a frieze of foliage scrolls. Early C18 staircase with slim turned balusters and carved tread-ends. NMR)

S of the house low brick forecourt walls, and, most re-markable, a large sandstone GATEWAY, dated 1592, of a Serlian classicism. Round archway. Fluted and banded Doric pilasters with a somewhat shallow triglyph frieze. Small pediment and stubby finials composed of scrolls back to back.

MARLE PLACE, 1¼ m. S. Again half-timbered, but hung with

Brenchley, Marle Place, 1619

C19 tiles. Dated 1619 on the porch gable. Characteristically for that date, the house is almost square, with two gables in each direction, a centrally placed N porch with an oriel win-dow, and a grand central chimneystack, of four octagonal shafts with star tops, linked to a square core. The N windows in two-storey canted bays l. and r. of the porch, mullioned-and-transomed, one, three, one lights.

BRATTLES GRANGE, 1 m. W of s. Typical C16 half-timbered house, with a continuous overhang, restored and extended to l. and r. by *Albert C. Freeman* in 1903.

BRENZETT

ST EANSWITH.* The church lies prettily up a short lane couched against tall trees. Behind stretches the open marsh. Basically Norman, as one can see in the chancel. Herringbone masonry low down in the s wall, and a blocked priest's door with a barely pointed head. The chancel arch has zigzag rolls up the jambs, tucked in as if they were nook-shafts. The arch is new. Have the jambs also been reset more widely apart? In the C13 the chancel threw out a N chapel (of shaly brown slabs) and the nave a narrow N aisle, entirely without N windows. One can see why aisles were so often widened later. Finally in the early C14 the W end was flanked by dark, narrow aisles one bay long. Was this connected with the erection of the shingled W spirelet, supported (on six posts) within the space of the nave? The church is over-restored. One s window with mildly unwarrantable Dec tracery is dated 1826. Of the same time probably the W doorway and the windows with Y-tracery. The more plausible Dec windows and the horrible boarding inside date from 1876. – REREDOS. In the N chapel; C18. Creed, Ten Commandments, and Lord's Prayer are given a more architectural frame than is usual in Marsh churches. Cornice with plain modillions and a small broken pediment. – The SOUNDING BOARD of a pulpit, used as a table. – TEXT BOARDS. Four in the N aisle. Black and oval with gold lettering, typical of Romney Marsh. – STAINED GLASS. E window 1874. Signed by *Lavers, Barraud & Westlake*. – PLATE. Cup, 1715; Paten Cover, 1715, by *William Gibson*. – MONUMENT. John Fagge † 1639 and his son, John Fagge † 1646. Erected after the latter date. Alabaster effigies broadly but sensitively carved, on a large, plain tomb-chest. One is recumbent, the other in armour lies behind, propped, not too uncomfortably, on his elbow: a decidedly old-fashioned pattern for *c*.1650.

BRISHING COURT see BOUGHTON MONCHELSEA

BROADFIELD see PLAXTOL

BROAD FORD see HORSMONDEN

* An early Kentish saint.

BROADWATER DOWN see TUNBRIDGE WELLS, p. 556

BROMLEY

4060

CHURCHES

St Peter and St Paul. Bombing in 1941 left a tower without a church. The tower is a good example of the Kentish type. Flint. Diagonal buttresses, N turret, octagonal at the top. The new church, 1948–57 by *J. Harold Gibbons*, takes its cue from it, in materials, in scale, and in being Gothic. The relation of church to tower no longer as before. Apsidal chapel E of the tower, and N of the nave. Nave and chancel under one roof. Short, high N transept, given all the architectural emphasis. The freedom with Gothic motifs is imitated from Sir Giles Scott, but the gusto has gone out of it and so has every trace of finesse. – FONT. Norman, on a modern base that does not fit. Square marble bowl, with four shallow sunk arches per side. – DOOR. In the tower. Probably C14. A strip of blank tracery across it with quatrefoils between ogee archlets. –PLATE. Cup and Cover, 1791; Paten, 1796; Paten, 1801; Cup and Cover, 1807; Flagon, 1817; Spoon of doubtful date. – BRASS. Richard Thornhill † 1600. 35 in. figures. Damaged.

St Andrew, Burnt Ash Lane. 1929 by *Sir Charles Nicholson*. Really very poor. N aisle not yet built.

St John the Evangelist, Park Road. 1879–80. By *George Truefitt*, who put much thought into the rebarbative design. The church lies along the road, aisled nave and apsidal chancel under a single colossal roof. S transept not projecting but carried up in a gable that develops on the E side to include a stunted octagonal spirelet. Obtrusive plate tracery. The W end done in the same take-it-or-leave-it spirit – four lancets stretched to improbable lengths between two far-projecting buttresses. The S aisle calmly continues as a lean-to against one of them. Greek cross plan to the aisle piers. The interior badly proportioned and further spoilt by whitewash and appallingly brash STAINED GLASS in the N transept window, 1951 by *Francis Spear*.

St Luke, Bromley Common. By *Arthur Cawston*, 1886–90. The top of the tower and the spire only completed in 1910. E.E. Red brick, with dressings of stone and yellow brick. Continuous nave and chancel. Low aisles. NW steeple. Externally it seems thoroughly conventional. Spacious interior unbroken from W to E, solid and convincing. Stone arcades, brick arches, but the way the stone continues some way above the capitals is very characteristic of the date.

A short way along Southlands Road, St Luke's Institute, 1891, an early work by *Ernest Newton*. Yellow brick. The end towards the road a dexterous play with geometrical shapes. Especially neat the contriving of the porches, white triangles in profile that continue the line of the roof. More ordinary side elevation with buttresses between big segmental windows.

St Mark, Westmoreland Road. Of *Evelyn Hellicar*'s church of 1897–8 the almost detached NW tower and the arcades remain. Reconstruction (after bombing) in 1953 by *David Nye & Partners* to *T.W.G.Grant*'s design. Parabolic transverse arches support the nave roof, and conflict uneasily with Hellicar's Late Perp shapes.

St Mary Plaistow. Nave 1863–4 by *Waring & Blake*. Chancel added 1881, by *W.R.Mallett*. s transept and narthex 1891. N transept 1899–1900 by *Wadmore, Wadmore & Mallett*. Aisles never achieved, nor the intended SW tower. The view from the road is as confusing as the history. It takes a moment to realize that this is the s side, with a fanciful porch to the s transept. Flint, banded with Bath stone. Dec tracery. The chancel walls and roof painted in 1890, painted ORGAN CASE, ALTAR, and REREDOS (in a C15 Flemish style), all somewhat amateurishly executed, but, with the E window by *Ward & Hughes* (or should one say in spite of it?), a rich ensemble. The contrast with the wide, bare nave and transepts is extremely painful.

Holy Trinity, Bromley Common. 1839 with a W tower of 1842. By *Thomas Hopper*. Still pre-archaeological, and lacking in architectural ambition. Flint, especially black on the tower. Windows with sandstone surrounds and cuspless wooden tracery. In 1884 *C.Pemberton Leach* did his best to make it more acceptable, by replacing much of the tracery with Dec designs in Bath stone (note the characteristic change from a local to a non-local stone) and by adding a stunted apse. – MONUMENT. George Norman † 1855. Signed *T.Gaffin*. Mourning soldier either side of a gravestone.

Baptist Church, Widmore Road. Cheap Early Christian. 1864 by *R.H.Moore*.

Presbyterian Church, Upper Park Road. 1895 by *John C.T.Murray*. Red brick and stone. Mainly E.E. It has a rather good steeple in the usual Nonconformist position, l.

of the entrance front. Plain brick tower with a transparent bell stage; stone broach spire ringed once by crisp lucarnes.

PUBLIC BUILDINGS

TOWN HALL. In two independent parts, at r. angles to one another. The earlier half, in Tweedy Road, 1906 by *R. Frank Atkinson*, the later, in Widmore Road, by *C. Cowles Voysey*, completed in 1939. The contrast between them is most instructive. Both of red brick with stone dressings; both two-storeyed, consisting of a long centre and narrow, barely projecting wings. Atkinson is neo-Wren, Cowles Voysey is neo-Georgian. Atkinson's stone enrichment overdone in a typically Edwardian way. Circular domed porch, big broken pediment. Cupola. Cowles Voysey confines the stone to a plinth and a reticent centrepiece. What gives his design distinction is the subtle subordination of the wings by a slight reduction in the size of the windows, and the deftly placed chimney-stacks. His is the greater discipline without any doubt.

TECHNICAL COLLEGE AND RAVENSBOURNE COLLEGE OF ART AND DESIGN, Bromley Common. 1957–62 by *George, Trew, Dunn*.* Two colleges in one building, a long six-storey slab on a sloping site at r. angles to the main road. Detached hall block on the N, workshops by the road and at the lower end. Basically simple, the part at the top end (built first) more straightforwardly designed, but the Brutalist creed of the moment required angular workshop skylights and various protruding concrete pieces, e.g. the sloping under-sides of staircases and large lintels on the littlest windows.

BOYS GRAMMAR SCHOOL, Hayes Lane. Designed in 1908 by *H. P. Burke Downing*, and completed in 1911. Main block with wings. Red brick and stone. The neo-Wren style handled with considerable panache. At the r. end a pretty little rough-cast CARETAKER'S HOUSE. Hall of 1933 at the back, also Wren-style.

PUBLIC LIBRARY. *See* p. 185.

PERAMBULATION

Bromley's existence as a market town at a fashionable distance from London was challenged by the arrival of the railway in 1858. The population in 1861 was 5,505. By 1871 it had almost

---

* Begun under the firm's former name, *Pite Son & Fairweather*.

doubled, and continued to increase at the rate of about five thousand per decade until 1914. By then the town had become an outer suburb, a status which it retains today. What survives from pre-railway Bromley is a number of isolated buildings, mostly tucked away and not readily found, and the shape of the market square, on which all roads converge.

The starting place then is the MARKET SQUARE. The square itself is filled up by a miserable half-timbered block of 1933, by *T.P.Bennett & Son*. The only reason for dwelling in the square is DUNN'S shop, on the E side, by *Bertram Carter*, 1954–7, set back from the street line to make a much needed breathing space. Off-centre picture window on the first floor. The interior fascinatingly intricate, with subtle shifts in levels, made possible because a temporary building of 1948 was enclosed by the new shop. At the NW corner of the square one C18 brick front. Adjoining, but in the HIGH STREET, a much taller group, the ROYAL BELL HOTEL, MARTIN'S BANK, and No. 181, designed as a group by *Newton* in 1898. The three parts are clearly distinguished from each other, the first with panels of pargetted strapwork, then with Newton's favourite lead-covered bows, and the last part rising up to Tudor gables. Altogether it is a fine design. Original decoration in the hall, including a characteristic chimneypiece, and in the main first-floor room. Staircase with brass and alabaster balustrade. Newton clearly hoped that this would be the beginning of a grander High Street, but no further efforts have been made to replace the mean cottage shops on the E side. The w side mostly a no less mean rebuilding of the 1890s.

At the end of the High Street, on the r., the red brick walls of BROMLEY COLLEGE. Stone gatepiers with bishop's mitres for finials, and fine wrought-iron gates dated 1666. The college is what was more often called a hospital, i.e. almshouses, founded by John Warner, Bishop of Rochester, under whose will of 1666 a college was to be built for 'twenty poore widowes (of orthodoxe & loyall clergymen)'. The land was not acquired until 1669, and an Act authorizing building passed in 1670. The college forms a quadrangle, presenting a long front to the road, with the treasurer's (l.) and chaplain's (r.) houses as moderately projecting wings. The widows were spaciously housed, with two rooms on the ground floor, two bedrooms, and a semi-basement kitchen. Each was expected to be attended by one resident servant and, if possible, by a spinster daughter. The building is of red brick, with raised bands between the storeys. Hipped roof. Grand stone central entrance arch, reaching right up to the eaves. Big curved pediment with the bishop's arms, supported on Tuscan half columns. Triangular porch canopies in the wings, flanked by little bulls-eye windows with little round-headed windows on the upper level. This is the sort of architecture popularly associated with the name of Sir Christopher Wren. But that is to place its origin considerably too late, for the style had developed even before the Civil War, and became the speciality of the masons and bricklayers of the City of London both before, and even after, the Great Fire. The College is memorable as one of the largest, one of the soberest, and one of the earlier examples to survive. A paved walk within the quadrangle sheltered by a lean-to roof on correctly proportioned Tuscan columns of stone. A second quadrangle, similar in design, but with wood columns, added in 1794–1805 for twenty more widows. CHAPEL in the range between the two quadrangles, red brick with diapering. Dec windows. By *Waring & Blake*, 1863. Complete set of glass of that date by *O'Connor*.* Was it the same architects who propped up the external walls of the entire college with red-brick buttresses?

SHEPPARD'S COLLEGE is an isolated building to the NE in a Tudor style, erected in 1840, to house five spinsters made homeless by their mothers' deaths.

A route through the N and E parts of Bromley is best begun by leaving the Market Square along WEST STREET. This continues as COLLEGE ROAD. Nothing to report, except, at the change-over, PRIMARY SCHOOL, by *St Aubyn*, 1854–5, enlarged 1870; and the *Owen Luder Partnership*'s nine-storey OFFICE BLOCK in Sherman Road, behind Bromley North Station. Lift, staircases, etc. separated and stressed in towers at one end à la Kahn. Completed 1968. No more stops before LONDON LANE, the turning on the l. after St Mary's Church. Halfway along it a notice on the right announces QUERNMORE SECONDARY SCHOOL. It comes as a shock to find that the school is in reality a splendid late C18 house in excellent condition, with no utilitarian additions obtruding on the entrance (W) side. The house was built as Plaistow Lodge for the fabulously wealthy Peter Thellusson, the intricacies of whose will caused so much litigation that an Act had to be passed to pre-

---

* PLATE. Cup, 1784; Paten and Almsdish, 1797.

vent anyone else from making another like it. He bought the estate in 1777. His architect is not known but the style of the house points to *Thomas Leverton*.* Yellow stock-brick block five bays by three and two-and-a-half storeys high. Rusticated ground floor of Portland stone. Pediment over the centre three bays on pilasters with finely carved, idiosyncratically designed, Composite capitals. Pedimented first-floor windows, the central one Venetian. Two-storeyed wings, curving forward slightly, link the main block to pedimented pavilions, which each have just one very large Venetian window with a panelled tympanum. Statues in niches and *Coade* stone panels. Exquisite detailing throughout. Early C19 stone porch with Greek Doric columns and entablature. The E side unenriched brick, with the central three windows of the main block in a wide bow. No recognizable internal features except the back stairs, with metal balustrading characteristic of Leverton.

The continuation of London Lane w of College Road is PLAISTOW LANE. Just beyond Sundridge Park Station, THE GABLES, a good early house by *Ernest Newton*; the gables tile-hung of course. In LODGE LANE, a turning to the l. off this, just before the entrance to Sundridge Park, two houses of the International Style of the 1930s, evidence, if any is needed, that any style at all can be handled well or badly, lightly or heavily. The candidate for the derogatory epithets is STILLNESS, 1934 by *Gilbert Booth*. Better by far the last house in the road, BY THE LINKS, by *Godfrey Samuel*, 1935. The entrance side the favourite Corbusian combination of a long horizontal slit window over a recessed ground storey carried on pilotis; the garden side generously glazed and quite without mannerisms of any sort.

By the Links because Sundridge Park is now a golf-course. That it is an unusually umbrageous golf-course is due to the fact that the park was landscaped by *Repton*.

79 SUNDRIDGE PARK, the house which the landscape setting was to show off, still stands on its shallow s-facing slope with Elmstead Wood rising behind. It is a large, rambling mansion, with three giant porticoes, and stuccoed a dazzling white. The building history is not completely clear, which is unfortunate, as the house has a highly remarkable, not to say revolutionary, plan. Repton was first consulted by E. G. Lind, but, when in 1796 Sir Claude Scott bought the estate, his services continued to be

* Leverton exhibited in 1780 a design for a 'gentleman's seat' in Kent 'now building'.

of two pointed lights, and must be part of the 'rebuilding' for which *Thomas White* received £890 in 1790. (One on the N keeps its great wooden shutters.)

What is clear is that Brookland escaped the attentions of the Victorian restorer. So much eccentricity could not otherwise have gone unscathed. The interior is equally gratifying, but much more unified. One now sees that the church was built steadily from E to W. The chancel is a good, typical mid C13 ensemble. Large N and S lancets with shafted rere-arches and traces of an E triplet, PISCINA and two stepped SEDILIA with continuous mouldings. There is no chancel arch, and the nave arcades begin without a break, the S (seven bays) starting one bay further E than the N. Octagonal piers, moulded capitals, those at the E of Bethersden marble, arches double-chamfered and with continuous hood-moulds to nave and S aisle. The design of capitals and bases develops, or rather degenerates, twice towards the W, and the W end can hardly have been reached before the early C14. Both arcades lean out rakishly, and the N arcade was early strengthened by two internal flying buttresses. Crown-post roofs in nave and S aisle. – WALL PAINTING. E end of S aisle. C15. The upper parts of four figures, three in armour and a bishop on the r., represent the murder of Thomas Becket. – FONT. Lead. Norman. It is cylindrical, only 16 in. high, and has the Signs of the Zodiac and Labours of the Months in two rows under arcading, little vignettes of considerable charm if not high artistic merit. The former are labelled in Latin, the latter in Norman French. The subjects are as follows:

January	Aquarius	Janus feasting
February	Pisces	A man sitting by the fire
March	Aries (entitled Capricornus)	Vine pruning
April	Taurus	A woman holding two plants
May	Gemini	Hawking
June	Cancer	Scything
July	Leo	Haymaking
August	Virgo	Harvesting
September	Libra	Threshing
October	Scorpio	Treading grapes
November	Sagittarius	Knocking down acorns for a pig
December	Capricornus	Killing the pig

The lead is laid in ten vertical strips each containing two Signs and two Labours, so the symbols for March to October are repeated. (The old calendar began in March.) Below the rim rope and zigzag mouldings, in which are set three small C13 plaques of the Resurrection, inserted to support the hinges of the font-cover. In Britain the font is unique, but one very like it is at Saint Évroult-de-Montfort in Normandy. Dr Zarnecki thinks both were made in North France c.1200. Manuscript illuminations provide the clue.

The other fittings are all minor in themselves, but an important part of the unrestored ensemble. – PULPIT. C18 two-decker. – BENCHES. Three at the back of the N aisle. Late medieval, with simple rectangular ends. – BOX PEWS. A set, c.1738. – Various C18 RAILS, with sturdy twisted balusters. – A curiosity is the TITHE PEN at the W end of the S aisle. Also the SCALES, dated 1795, of the Hundred of Alloes Bridge (the WEIGHTS AND MEASURES too), said to be the only hundred set in existence. – Yet another curiosity is the GRAVESIDE SHELTER, to keep the minister dry during funerals. – STAINED GLASS. C14 canopies in the N aisle E window, of exquisite refinement. Worth a really close look. – PLATE. Elizabethan (?) Paten Cover; Cup, 1689; Paten, 1719; Flagon, 1725. – MONUMENTS. Brass to Thomas Leddes † 1503, a 13½ in. figure of a priest. – Also an unexpected number of C18 tablets, and several very fine black ledger slabs, of the C17.

8050

BROOMFIELD

ST MARGARET. A tiny blocked Norman N window fixes the date of the nave walls. A renewed lancet also in the nave N wall, and an original Perp window. Small Perp W tower, without buttresses. Standard Perp tower arch. Similar chancel arch. All else belongs to *G.M.Hills*'s restoration of 1879. He removed all trace of the chancel of 1749, except its date tablet. – PLATE. Paten, 1631.

Broomfield can hardly boast that it is a village, but the knot of houses on the road that climbs up W of the church out of the lush valley of the River Len can't have changed much since the C18. ROSE FARM makes the best group, the farmhouse, just two-thirds of a C15 Wealden house, the half-timbering plastered over, a barn lower down, with the roof slope passing down each side of the carriage entrance, and some cowl-less oasts at the back. More self-conscious, but equally charming, further down the hill, BARRACK COTTAGES, C18, symmetrical or nearly so, three plus one plus three bays. Ragstone, with red-brick angle strips and centre bays. Brick surrounds to the windows, which have round heads and big, white keystones.

BUDD'S FARM see WITTERSHAM

BURHAM 7060

ST MARY. The old church, beside the Medway, was deserted as the village moved to higher ground at the foot of the chalk Downs. It was rescued from dereliction in 1956. One Norman s window and another (blocked) N window in the nave. C13 chancel with a N chapel. Rude C13 nave arcades. Square piers and pointed single-chamfered arches. Perp W tower, with a W window that looks Dec rather than Perp. Diagonal buttresses panelled with knapped flint squares on the outer faces. Finally, as the drift to the hills began, chapel and aisles were demolished, leaving the church little larger than it was in the Norman beginning. – FONT. Norman. Square bowl with four arches on each side. – BENCHES. The backs pierced with rows of trefoils. Two poppyheads. – PLATE. Cup, 1795.

ST MARY. Reality was faced in 1881, and E.W. Stephens built a new church in the village. It looks like a town church, and not a very attractive one, with its central tower and short transepts. Short chancel. Clerestoried nave. Early Dec. Ragstone laid like crazy-paving. Better proportions inside, where one finds that the tower stands over the chancel, and the E projection is merely the sanctuary.

Near Burham Court Farm is a rectangular ROMAN VILLA. It measured 34 by 60 ft, and at one end it contained a channelled hypocaust with wall flues.

About 50 yds E of the Medway an underground VAULTED CHAMBER was discovered. It was rectangular, 40 by 19 ft, and originally 12 ft high, with walls 2 ft wide towards the base thickening to 3 ft near the springing of the vault. The inner faces were of dressed chalk blocks decorated with broaching. Light was provided by a shaft cut into the middle of a transverse groin. In the s wall were three arched niches and in the opposite wall was the 11 ft high arched entrance leading to a zigzag passage. Some have suggested that the chamber was a Mithraeum, but it is more likely to be a cellar, though nothing is known of the villa to which it would have belonged.

1030

BURMARSH

ALL SAINTS. The church has a curious hump-backed outline.
Perp w tower hugely buttressed. Very short nave, its roof
hidden behind battlements. Chancel with high-pitched roof.
The walls are of a small aisleless Norman church. One N
window remains in the chancel, and the nave S doorway, with
the usual shafts with scallop capitals, round the arch a roll,
zigzag, and billet, and at the apex a crude head baring its teeth.
The C13 tower arch shows that the present tower had a predecessor. The roofs were all renewed in the restoration of
1878. The crown-post roof in the chancel is prettily stencilled.
No fittings survive beyond one TEXT BOARD and a PITCH
PIPE. – PLATE. Cup and Cover, 1630.

BURRSWOOD *see* GROOMBRIDGE

BUSTON *see* HUNTON

CALEHILL HOUSE *see* LITTLE CHART

CAMER COURT *see* MEOPHAM

6040

CAPEL

ST THOMAS OF CANTERBURY. Basically Norman, a nave and
a lower chancel. One small N window in the nave demonstrates
the date. The walls rendered, except the nave S wall, which
has been rebuilt, with one early C16 window at the W end.
Shortish battlemented W tower with a tiled pyramid top, all
probably reconstructed after a fire in 1639. A pair of barbed
and ogeed lancets suggests a C14 origin for the tower. Happily
rustic and unaffected interior, with a w door like a farmhouse
door, and another as the priest's door in the chancel. Tower
arch and chancel arch of the same C14 or C15 date. Striking
crown-post roof. Much more striking, however, once one's
eyes get attuned, the WALL PAINTINGS covering the E
two-thirds of the nave N wall. Narrative scenes in two tiers,
dated by Professor Tristram *c.*1230–50. He identifies the
scenes as follows:

Upper tier (partly destroyed)   Death and Burial of the Virgin
Lower tier   Christ's Entry into Jerusalem
                                  Last Supper
                                  Betrayal
                                  Christ appearing to Mary
                                     Magdalene

On the splays of the C12 win-
dow   Cain slaying Abel★
                                    Conviction of Cain by God

At the E end of the wall, a bit of a large C16 figure. – ALTAR
RAILS. Dated 1682. Handsome turned balusters.‡ – PLATE.
Cup of 1565.

BADSELL MANOR FARM, 1¼ m. E. The house stands at the SE
corner of a moat, and its own SE corner is a fragment of a late
C15 or early C16 house. Sloping sandstone plinth rising from
the water, brickwork with diapering. Brick chimneybreast
and two tall polygonal brick stacks. The arched windowlights in the E wall seem all C19.

CAPEL MANOR see HORSMONDEN

CASTLE TOLL see NEWENDEN

CHAFFORD PARK see ASHURST

CHALK   6070

ST MARY. Loathsomely contorted grotesques disport on the
Perp W porch above and below an image-niche. Porch and
unbuttressed W tower are additions to a possibly Early Norman church – see the herringbone lay of the flints in the S
wall of the chancel. Late C12 N aisle to nave and chancel.
Sharply pointed arches and large, square, angle-shafted piers,
crude but typical Transitional work. Much renewed late C13
lancets in the chancel; only a few stones of the E triplet are old.
The gabled aisle windows may be to the original pattern of
c.1300. A C13 S aisle has been destroyed, and the arcade left
embedded in the wall. Low-side window in the chancel. Simple
C13 PISCINA with a shelf; C13 SEDILE. In the N aisle two
cusped arches of different dates.

CHAPEL FARM see LENHAM

CHARLTON COURT see EAST SUTTON

CHART SUTTON   8040

ST MICHAEL. Of locally quarried ragstone, used in the C14
to build the W tower; in 1779–82 by *Henry Holland* for the

★ The same subject occurs, also on a window splay, at West Kingsdown.
Was there some special significance in the position?
‡ The name of the man who carved them is known, so the Rev. F. A.
Forbes tells me. He was *Michael Davis*.

nave; and in 1897 for the chancel. Holland's half-hearted efforts at a Gothic style have been almost all improved away. One W lancet is left, and a blocked four-centred S doorway below a quatrefoil window. The tower has a tall arch on semi-octagonal responds, shallow angle-buttresses, and a W window with a subcusped quatrefoil over two ogee cinquefoiled lights, favourite forms of the second quarter of the C14. – PLATE. Cup of 1569, and Elizabethan Paten Cover; Paten, 1728 by *Edward Cornock*; Flagon and Almsdish, 1729 by *Richard Bayley*.

CHART PLACE. Built in 1708 by Sir Christopher Desbouverie, a two-storeyed house, seven windows wide, the r. three more close-set than the rest. Gabled roof. Spoilt in the mid C19, with grey rendering. Top balustrade and Greek Doric porch are additions a little earlier than that.

FARMHOUSE and GRANARY, built as a pair NE of the house, probably c.1708. Red and grey chequer brick. Shaped end-gables. (A similar BARN further E.)

4050

CHARTWELL
2 m. S of Westerham

Sir Winston Churchill's home, as everybody knows, in a lovely position on the hillside. The house was almost completely rebuilt for him in 1923 by *Philip Tilden* in dull red brick and an odd undecided style. Two-storeyed entrance front with an C18 stone doorcase, very large and splendid and out of place. The garden front is twice as tall and has stepped gables.

7060

CHATHAM

The fame and fortune of Chatham depend, as they always have done since the C16, on the dockyards. The medieval church stands on the hillside above the dock area, but growth of the town has always been governed by the urge to join this village nucleus with the suburbs of Rochester across a mile or more round the S side of a hairpin bend taken by the river Medway. This has not been easy to effect; for the reverse slope of the North Downs descends to the Medway in a series of steep-sided valleys that run from S to N, so that the pattern has been carved against the grain of the hills. As a result Chatham tends to fall apart in the middle. If only one could clear everything away and start again, knowing that there are 47,000 inhabitants to build for, there would be a wonderfully varied site; but as it is the houses go on spilling southwards up the valleys and the town centre gradually dies off, blighted by cars and parks to put them on. The glimpses between the buildings, of the Medway from all angles, and of Downland in unexpected places, are almost always better than the buildings themselves.*

CHURCHES

ST MARY, Dock Road. Rebuilt by *Sir A. Blomfield & Sons*. Chancel 1884-7, free-standing SW tower 1897, clerestoried nave 1901-3. W baptistery. Built of rock-faced ragstone, large, but architecturally neutral. Norman jambs worked into two W doorways. The medieval church had been replaced in 1788 (and the sumptuous late C13 sedilia found then disgracefully destroyed). Inside, however, one finds a complete Norman W end. The doorways, enriched with zigzag internally, stand l. and r. of a wide tower arch. Only the jambs of this are old. They have shafts, one set forward and two set back. Bottom of a newel staircase in the SW corner. One inner pilaster buttress with nook-shafts, in the S wall. The S doorway was a magnificent Transitional piece. Three major and four minor jamb-shafts each side, with crocket capitals. Leaf sprigs and dogtooth between them. Round arch with keeled mouldings, which once bordered broad bands of carving, now, alas, broken away. – FONT. A genuine C14 piece? – REREDOS. Triptych by *Clayton & Bell*. – ORGAN. 1795, by *Samuel Green*. – ROYAL ARMS, of Queen Anne. Small. Carved in relief. – STAINED GLASS. E window 1891 by *Kempe*. – PLATE. Patens, a pair by *R.M.*, 1629; Flagon, 1635 by *J.B.*; two Cups, 1636 by *W.D.*; Flagon, 1735; Flagon, 1742 by *Gurney & Cooke*. – MONUMENTS. Reinold Bailey (?), 1622. Two sizeable kneeling figures from a wall-monument. – Several draped cartouches, with putto heads and skulls, commemorating naval men or members of their families. Dates of death between 1698 and 1755. – Sarah Proby. 1794 by *James Paine*. Handsome Grecian tablet.

CHRIST CHURCH, Luton Road. 1884 by *E.R.Robson*, better known as the architect of the London Board Schools. Here, as there, he is, in a modest way, pleasingly independent-minded. Wide nave with narrow aisles hardly discernible outside. Shallow transepts doubly gabled. The broad space

---

* Plans for the redevelopment of the town centre over the next five years have recently been announced.

from W to E has a decidedly Late Victorian feel, especially as the large W window copies the E one. Dec window tracery freely rendered. Tower and copper spire reared on the porch in 1926. Robson had intended an exhibitionist SE tower and spire. – *Kempe* enriched the chancel with STAINED GLASS in 1890–1 and a REREDOS and other fittings in 1896 (PF).

ST JOHN THE DIVINE, Railway Street. 1821–2 by *Smirke*. Ragstone box, dully classical. The S front towards the street made symmetrical by slightly projecting end bays. Small square tower over the W front. Apse by *G. M. Hills*, 1863, in a sort of Quattrocento style. – STAINED GLASS. E window signed by *Alexander Gibbs*, 1868. Bad.

ST MICHAEL THE ARCHANGEL (R.C.), Hills Terrace. A cheap* but very powerful nave by *Clutton*, 1862–3, and a weak chancel by *Walters*. Stock brick banded with black. The W front just a huge wheel window, and a double doorway under a completely un-Gothic flat hood, flanked by two buttresses. Bold and noble nave arcades, round piers paired in depth in the Early French style Clutton loved. Nave and aisles under a single roof-gable. – FONT. Seated figures in niches overwhelmed by crocketed gables and colonnettes with lushly blooming capitals.

ST PAUL. By *A. D. Gough*, 1853–5. Ragstone. Not small. Neo-Norman in style, with a great deal of shafting and zigzag, especially on the SW doorway. 'Thoroughly mean and rather pretentious', as Mr Goodhart-Rendel justly sums up. Neo-Norman SCHOOL and neo-Norman VERGER'S HOUSE, besides.

PUBLIC BUILDINGS

TOWN HALL, Military Road. 1898–9 by *George E. Bond*. An expression of civic pride in the newly formed borough; but how lamely the Renaissance motifs are handled, how ill adapted to the scale and to the awkward island site! Tall tower with a green dome. Loggia above the entrance at one corner. Ashlar.

CROWN HOUSE, Brook. Borough Offices. 1964 by *E. H. Banks*. Quite a good four-storey slab, with a concrete screen on top. Symmetrical.

POLICE STATION, Brook. Completed 1964. By *E. T. Ashley-Smith*, the County Architect.

POST OFFICE, Railway Street. 1901–2 by the *Surveyor to the*

* The estimate quoted in *The Builder* was for a mere £1,695.

Office of Works. In a firmly handled Arts and Crafts style. Red brick and stone. Typical low tower, and gable, breaking through the cornice. Cleverly, the triple gable of Scotts Warehouse next door is made to read as the completion of the composition.

MEDWAY COLLEGE OF TECHNOLOGY, Horsted Way. Low, spreading group, the earlier part, *c.*1951, at the back, of dull red brick, the later, similar in proportions but, typically, more assertive, with lime-green panels below the windows and an alternating rhythm of mullions. This is by *E. T. Ashley-Smith*, the County Architect, 1956–63.

New buildings for the college, further N, on a splendid high-lying site off City Way, are at the time of writing in process of erection. Designs by *Robert Matthew, Johnson-Marshall & Partners*. Curtain-walled point-block, and lower buildings vertically boarded.

ST BARTHOLOMEW'S HOSPITAL CHAPEL, High Street. The chapel of the hospital, founded outside the East Gate by a monk of Rochester, Hugh de Trottescliffe, 1124. It consists of nave, chancel, and apsidal sanctuary, with a contemporary chapel N of the chancel. Flint. Greatly restored by *Scott*, who added a N aisle and S vestry and reconstructed the nave. Three original S windows here, even so, two with timber lintels; and a blocked arch, perhaps to the hospital buildings. C13 SEDILE in the r. jamb of the sanctuary arch. – PILLAR PISCINA in the vestry.

SIR JOHN HAWKINS'S HOSPITAL, High Street. The almshouses for decayed mariners, founded in 1592, were rebuilt, in red brick, in 1789–90 round a tiny quadrangle open to the street. Two-storeyed terraces flank the Council Room, with its two round-headed windows and a round-headed doorway, under a broken pediment. A large pump with a lamp on it takes up the centre of the courtyard.

WESTMINSTER BANK, at the corner of High Street and Railway Street. 1903 by *W. Campbell Jones*. Arts and Crafts style, in Portland ashlar. Low dome at the corner, and two irregular gables starting the ascent up the hill. An appropriate companion for the Post Office.

NAVAL WAR MEMORIAL, Great Lines. Conspicuous columnar object by *Lorimer*, 1920–4, to which, after the Second World War, *Sir Edward Maufe* added quadrant walls and diminutive pedimented pavilions. – SCULPTURE. Massive, lifeless figures of soldiers by *William McMillan* and *Sir Charles Wheeler*.

FACTORY, for Elliott-Automation, $1\frac{1}{2}$ m. s, off Maidstone Road. Begun in 1961 by *Yorke, Rosenberg & Mardall*, and not yet completed. Five-storeyed, faced with white tiles, the windows continuous round the whole buildings. Three square tower-blocks, the centre one lying back to the s, linked to the others by glazed staircases. As one expects with these architects, the whole group is impressively grandly scaled.

PERAMBULATION

All that can be recommended is a walk along NEW ROAD, a high-level route cut parallel with the High Street c.1794. The E half, wide and straight, is quite impressively urban, dominated by GIBRALTAR PLACE, a three-storeyed red-brick terrace of fourteen houses, over a high basement. Central pediment with the date, 1794. Extended in 1812. w of the bridge over Railway Street, the road becomes more bitty. On the N side, a five-storeyed block, with balconies, built in the early 1950s, jauntily bowed towards the w to view the great loop of the Medway. At the far end, beyond the hospital and really in Rochester, early C19 stock brick TERRACES.

BARRACKS. See Gillingham: Brompton, p. 280.

DOCKYARD*

The first record of the Navy anchoring in the Medway is in 1547, when 13s. 4d. was paid for the 'hier of storehouses'. Soon 'Jillyngham Water' became a regular anchorage, so that in 1596 Lambarde could write: 'No Towne, nor Citie, is there (I dare say) in this whole Shire, comparable in right value with this one fleete.' Chatham was considered a safer anchorage than Portsmouth, the other harbour of the king's ships. The first ship which is known to have been built at Chatham was launched in 1585. Philipot in 1659 speaks of the 'Arsenals, Store-houses and Ship-docks erected by the late K. Charles', and in spite of the disastrous and humiliating firing of the fleet by the Dutch in 1667, as it lay off Chatham, the Medway continued as the main anchorage of the British fleet. The dockyards were laid out anew in 1685, and the first twenty years of the C18 saw a complete new set of administrative buildings and storehouses. These, still the nucleus of the Dockyard, greatly impressed Defoe in 1720:

* I have to thank Mr Jonathan Coad for being my guide in the dockyard, and for showing me the results of his researches undertaken for the Ministry of Public Building and Works. A number of the facts given below I owe to him.

'The buildings here are indeed like the ships themselves, surprisingly large, and in the several kinds beautiful. The warehouses, or rather streets of warehouses, and store houses for
laying up the naval treasures are the largest in dimension, and the
most in number that are anywhere to be seen in the world.'

Normally the Dockyard is entirely closed to members of the
public. Nevertheless, a tour is here described from the Main
Gate northwards along the main thoroughfare with occasional
branchings-off to the E, following the chronological development of the dockyard, as the promontory and St Mary's
Island were gradually reclaimed and built on through the C19.
In 1746 the dockyard covered 61 acres, by 1772 had increased
only to 68. St Mary's Island, bought in 1855, added 173 acres,
and by 1885 500 acres were enclosed and there were 10,000
ft of wharfage. The present size is less than that; for in
1958 the Admiralty sold the thin strip along the river at the S
end, the site of the Gunwharf and the Royal Marines Barracks.
From Chatham DOCK ROAD runs N to the MAIN GATE, set in a 63
high protective brick wall put round the dockyard in 1718–20.
The Main Gate is dated 1720 on its inner face. Towards the
outside world it presents a Vanbrughian appearance, sham-
ming fortification, with its massive square towers l. and r. of
the entrance arch, the turret-like chimneystacks at their
angles, and the small, blank windows, bulls-eyes over pairs of
round-headeds. In the centre an immense coloured relief
of the Royal Arms. This is not contemporary, but dated 1812,
and signed *Coade & Sealy*, i.e. it is of Coade stone. Inside,
the towers are seen to house lodges, with windows at three
levels. In the bushes l. of the gate a BELL MAST, very tall and
strong, surrounded by a pretty little circular pavilion on
Tuscan columns, c.1820, an amusing combination. In line
ahead from the gate, the yellow brick DOCKYARD CHURCH,
1808–11. The usual minimal classical affair, almost square,
with galleries, as workmanlike as any storehouse. Venetian
N (ritual E) window.
SW of the Main Gate, parallel with the river, three immensely
long C18 brick buildings. Nearest the river, the STOREHOUSES,
in two parts, the N of 1796, the S of 1783. Both four-storeyed,
now and then rising to five. Remarkable not only for size, but
for keeping all their original tackle, hoists, internal timber
safe areas, etc. Next to the E, the ROPERY, of 1785, three-
storeyed, one hundred bays and 1,140 ft long. The interior

of the ground floor is a truly amazing sight, open from end to end. What is more, ropes are still made here in the traditional way. Some of the machinery dates back to 1806. The upper floors similarly have no internal partitions. E again, the late C18 HEMP STORE, SPINNING ROOM, and TARRING HOUSE, all concerned with rope-making, the first two both of two tall storeys, with pilaster strips.

N of the church lies the C18 administrative and residential centre. The *clou* is the ADMIRAL'S HOUSE (Medway House), built in 1703. Plum-coloured brick. Seven bays by five. Three storeys and a hipped roof on a cornice with deep, carved brackets. Fine staircase with three slim twisted balusters per tread, and a ceiling, painted by *Thornhill*, that depicts Neptune crowning Mars. Tradition has it that the painting was intended for the Great Cabin of H.M.S. Royal Sovereign, built in 1701. Additions to the S, including a BILLIARD ROOM, decorated *c.*1790. The house stands in an extensive walled garden. The other officers were only a little less nobly housed. For them the three-storeyed OFFICERS' TERRACE was erected in 1727-9, further NE. Twelve houses in all, two brought forward each end and two more in the middle. These are four windows wide, the rest three. Deep Doric porches. Battlements, of idiosyncratic shape, justified by the associations they conjure up. Once more the spirit is Vanbrugh's. Service road at the back, mews and a garden for each house beyond that. The long three-storeyed block S of the mews was built in 1734 as the SAIL LOFT. Given an ugly coat of rendering in the C19, it is interesting for its construction with the top floor slung from the roof structure. On the floor below, where the sails were finished off, the original benches and lockers of the sail-makers survive. Humble PAY OFFICE linking again with the Admiral's House, said to have been built in 1808, but looking Early Georgian. N of the Admiral's House, the yellow brick MAIN OFFICES, 1813, with a pedimented centre and bowed ends, built originally as a mold loft. The next building, now NAVAL STORE DEPARTMENT, had a similar original purpose. Clock of 1802 in a turret in the centre. The building was erected in 1722. E of this SAW MILLS, a composite building apparently of one period, built by *Marc Brunel* in 1813-14. Stock brick. Originally partly open on colonnades. Internally constructed with iron columns and beams supporting a stone slab floor, an early example of iron-framing in southern England.

The next important buildings are the SLIPS (now Boat Stores). Until 1966 there were two timber slip sheds. The S one, of 1813, was burnt down in that year, which leaves only No. 3 SLIP, dating from as late as 1837. Massive, close-set posts, in two rows, meeting in a U at the landward end, support the steep roof with its vast eaves, on raking struts. In 1845–7 SLIPS 4, 5, and 6 were constructed, and roofed with a cast-iron structure, by Messrs *Baker*.* They make a fascinating contrast with the timber slip shed, of so few years earlier, especially as none has walls, so that each opens into the next without any visual impediment. The iron framing is strikingly slender, even frail; upright columns, with curved braces bridging alternate wide and narrow spans, and subsidiary straight braces. It is an important landmark in constructional history; but one notices that the braces spring from vestigial Tuscan capitals, a hint of architectural grammar, such as the timber shed does not bother with. SLIP No. 7, immediately beyond, marks another advance in technique. This was designed in 1852 by Col. *G. T. Greene*. Built in 1853–5. It is much higher than the others, again with a gabled roof, but constructed without any curved members at all. In fact the uprights and horizontal girders throughout are of standard I section. Nave and aisles construction, just as in the timber shed, but far higher, lighter, and bridging a far wider span. Well handled glazing of the end wall. Greene's idiom, which was to find its most splendid expression at Sheerness, is already fully developed here.

E of the slips, various low timber-framed structures, among them the old MAST HOUSE, clad with weatherboarding or iron plates, and built already by the 1760s. Further N, beside the docks, FITTING SHOP, erected in 1874,‡ and BOILER SHOP No. 1 of 1876, more impressively large iron-framed sheds similar to Greene's in structure, but just a little fussier in the bracing. Finally, two brick PUMPING STATIONS, that of 1873 arcaded, with a tower at the N end, the brickwork red and yellow with plenty of extrovert notching. The 1902 station, by contrast, returns to the utilitarian brick style of the 1820s.

A postscript is enough for the other early C20 buildings, which lie away to the NE, immediately inside the dockyard

---

* Professor A. W. Skempton kindly provided these facts and information on the other iron-framed dockyard structures.

‡ But, according to Professor Skempton, probably first set up at Woolwich in 1860.

gates at the N end of Dock Road. ST GEORGE'S CHURCH,
1905–6. Red brick. (Typical Late Victorian interior. Passage
aisles and a lofty clerestory.) COMMODORE'S HOUSE, 1903,
large, with a cupola; ROYAL NAVAL BARRACKS, 1901. Handsome GATEPIERS and RAILINGS, with Arts-and-Crafts overtones. The *Civil-Engineer-in-Chief's Department of the
Admiralty* was responsible for everything.

7070   CHATTENDEN

1½ m. NE of Frindsbury

BARRACKS, for the Royal School of Military Engineering.
1963–6 by *Tripe & Wakeham*. A complete environment,
excellently sited and of excellently workmanlike design.
Small CHURCH near the road, SE of the main buildings. The
teaching blocks, TACTICAL SCHOOL, DEMONSTRATION
HALL, and FIELD ENGINEERING SCHOOL, low, but massive,
of a purplish-brown brick. Further NE, OFFICERS' HOUSING,
yellow brick below, red tile-hanging above, and white
weatherboarded cornices. Separately sited to the N, OTHER
RANKS' HOUSING, of the same materials, but three-storeyed
flats and terraces, not detached houses, the inevitable military
hierarchy.

BOMB DISPOSAL SCHOOL, Lodge Hill. By *Barron & Smith*.
Rectangular block, the top half glazed and the roof-line zigzagging syncopatedly.

4060   CHELSFIELD

Church and COURT LODGE stand alone, severed from the
village by the Orpington bypass. Suburbia has so far been held
off, just.

ST MARTIN OF TOURS. Early Norman nave and chancel.
Herringbone laying of the flints in the chancel S wall and the
nave N wall. S windows visible inside (the N lancet also in
origin Norman, its sill lowered). Soon afterwards a great
lengthening of the nave took place (see the N wall), and of this
the W triplet partly survives. The E wall of the chancel was rebuilt early in the C13, with three tall lancets – internal shafts
with shaft-rings. Also C13 the brief S aisle and the N tower.
Traces of a NE annexe, i.e. the E doorway in the tower and the
faint mark of a gable above it. The squint and barred window
in the chancel must have opened into it. Perp S porch with C18

battlements. *E. Nash*'s restoration in 1857 replaced the chancel arch, and rebuilt the NE annexe as a vestry. – ALTAR RAILS. Stumpy turned balusters. – PLATE. Cup and Cover, 1639; Paten, 1715. – MONUMENTS. Robert de Brun, rector, † 1417, in a recess on the N side of the chancel, coped tomb-chest of local marble, with the indents of a small Crucifixus, St Mary, and St John. In a charming way the tomb of 1668 on the opposite side of the chancel is made a pair to it, minus the brasses. – 15 in. brass of a priest, *c*.1400. – Brasses also in the chancel to William Robroke, priest, † 1420, a lady, *c*.1480, and Alicia Bray † 1510, each a foot and a half long. – Peter Collet † 1607. Hanging monument, with small kneeling figures better done than usual. Two babes propped up at the sides. – Peter Heyman, a third babe, has his own inscription. – Brass Crosby † 1793. Adamish tablet, with two small mourning figures high up.

CHEVENING

4050

ST BOTOLPH. Well scaled, battlemented Perp w tower, begun after 1518. Local ragstone. Diagonal buttresses and octagonal NE turret. Tower arch with continuous mouldings. It is an addition to a C13 building of rubble stone and flint. One lancet in the s wall of the nave. E of this a three-bay arcade with round piers and double-chamfered arches. No N aisle, but three early C13 blocked arches in the nave N wall. But was there ever a N aisle? The outer arch chamfer is continuous, which suggests that the arcading never opened into an aisle.* In the s aisle two PISCINAS, each with two tomb recesses to the W. s chapel (Stanhope) basically C13, nearly matching the s aisle. Contract of 1584 for making the roof. C19 N vestry. s porch remodelled in 1858. Heavy restoration of 1869 and 1902 outside, in which all the windows, Perp square-headed, were renewed. – FONT. Perp. Octagonal. Buttressed stem. Encircled quatrefoils on the bowl. – PULPIT. Jacobean. Simple and renovated a good deal. – ARMOUR. Late C17 set in the s chapel. – PLATE. Cup 1660 by *P.B.* – MONUMENTS. John Lennard † 1590. Tomb-chest with alabaster effigies of a knight and lady lying on a mat. They are better carved than many – his head must surely be a

---

* Canon Scott-Robertson (*A.C.* XVI) recorded that the lancet was, before the C19 restoration, set under one of these arches. This is the arrangement common in C13 chancels (cf. Ash, Lower Halstow (E), Rainham), but not usual in any other part of a church.

portrait. – Griffin Lloyd † 1596. 27½ in. brasses, and eight
small children. – Ann Herrys † 1613. Hanging alabaster
monument. Kneeling figure, in ruff and farthingale, with two
tiny children behind her. So far nothing special. But large
angels, l. and r., flamboyantly pull back the curtains of a
canopy, a motif that had occurred rarely by that date. –
Sampson Lennard † 1615. Erected by his wife, Lady Dacre
in her own right, before 1611. High tomb-chest with obelisks
at the angles and coffered canopy-arch. Reclining figures, and
kneeling children below. Not particularly good quality. –
Robert Cranmer † 1619. Hanging monument with kneeling
figures, entirely ordinary. – 1st and 2nd Earls Stanhope.
Tablet erected after 1786. Typical of the date, with its small
relief of a disconsolate female by an urn. – Lady Frederica
Stanhope. Signed by *Chantrey*, 1827, and the sculptor's favourite figure. Lady Frederica had died in childbirth, so
Chantrey showed her on a couch asleep in a loose nightgown
with her baby contentedly sleeping at her breast, a touching
piece of wish-fulfilment.

Opposite the church, very attractive red-brick ESTATE COT-
TAGES of the C18 and C19, making one side of a little street.
One is C17, a brick refacing of a timber-framed structure.
Cartouche of moulded brick, carved door-canopy brackets.
The character of the brickwork, the glowing red bricks laid
for the most part in English bond, should be remembered
when the big house is considered. Behind them, the high park
wall of the big house.

CHEVENING PARK. The house stands in a magnificent park,
below the wooded escarpment of the North Downs. It is not
an attractive house to look at, a flat-roofed seven-bay block of
three and a half storeys, organized in spite of its height by
stumpy Ionic pilasters across the centre three bays into a
Palladian formula. The facing materials are grey-buff fireproof mathematical tiles, and, on the attic, stucco. The entrance front faces N, and on this side the drabness of the main
block is offset by concave quadrant corridors to l. and r. which
lead to early C18 red-brick service blocks, two-storeyed with
hipped roofs and bulls-eye dormers. The forecourt is enclosed
by contemporary wrought-iron railings with splendid gates
in three directions. All this is the work of the Earls Stanhope.
General James Stanhope, the 1st Earl, bought Chevening in
1715 and by 1717 improvements were in hand. *Thomas Fort*,
of the Office of Works, seems to have been architect. His then

CASTLE. High Street House, the Streatfeild seat, a sizeable late C17 hipped-roofed house, was inflated into a sandstone castellated mansion early in the C19 and dubbed 'castle'. This was done in two stages, the first c.1808–9, the second in the 1830s, to the design of *Henry Kendall*, exhibited in 1838 when work had already been going on for three years or more.* Gatehouse feature on the E, and on the S side. Symmetrical N front, three-storeyed. Windows with hoodmoulds. Altogether it is a stodgy building; but of historical interest as one of the very few examples of the castellated revival in Kent. The best feature is the buttressed garden wall curving away to the SW, to a Gothic stone ORANGERY.

CHIDDINGSTONE CAUSEWAY   5040

ST LUKE. 1897–8 by *J. F. Bentley*. The church was paid for by the Hills family and Sargent, the portrait painter, recommended Bentley to them; it was his only building for Protestants, a village church, but by no means in the Kentish vernacular. Broad and stocky N tower, broad nave and chancel with balancing organ chamber and family pew. No aisles. Wide-jointed Bath stone ashlar meticulously laid. Freely Dec details. The windows and buttresses placed with fastidious whimsy: see e.g. the ogeed lancets in the tower, or the way the S wall of the nave is treated. Seven-light E and W windows, expressing the form of the wagon roofs.‡

Of the FITTINGS *Bentley* designed the stone-and-tile sanctuary PAVEMENT, the ALTAR RAILS, and the FONT, a sturdy and uncompromising piece, of alabaster and Cipollino marble from Euboea, octagonal with tulip-shaped bowl and an absurdly shallow basin. As in the church itself, form and use are far apart. – STAINED GLASS. The smouldering E window, 1906 by *von Glehn*, dominates too insistently. German Expressionist in its purplish-blues and orange-browns and in the thick, confusing leads. The Crucifixion scene however seems to be derived direct from a C16 Italian model. Sanctuary S window also by *von Glehn*.

CHILSTON PARK *see* BOUGHTON MALHERBE

* As Mr Denys E. Bower kindly explains. Inside there survives the refined mid-C18 staircase with fluted balusters. Also late C16 panelling in a room in the SE corner, and C16 heraldic GLASS in the hall and on the staircase.

‡ Derived from Norman Shaw's Latimer Road church, is Mr Nicholas Taylor's comment.

CHISLEHURST

CHURCHES

ST NICHOLAS. C15 church, of rough flints, enlarged and partly rebuilt in the C19. The tower stands over the W bay of the N aisle, and bears a tall shingled spire, quite a landmark. The windows in tower and aisle segment-headed, of two lights. Four-bay arcade, besides the tower bay, on piers quatrefoil in plan. Arches with two chamfers, tower arch with three. Probably this C15 work was undertaken by the rector of 1446–82, whose monument stands in the founder's position on the N side of the chancel. No more of it is left. The W wall of the nave however is old, and in the gable a small blocked window rudely turned in flint may be Saxon.* In 1849 the chancel was practically rebuilt by *Ferrey*. Old PISCINA. There were lancets before the rebuilding. He also added the S aisle (with the Perp S doorway reset), copying the Perp N windows but modifying the arcade to make it approach more nearly the style of the late C13. The spire rebuilt by *Wollaston*, after a fire in 1857, a little higher than before. The chancel lengthened eastwards, with a fancy E wall, by *Bodley & Garner*, 1896. – FONT. Norman. The usual square arcaded bowl on five shafts (three renewed). – SCREENS. Chancel screen and screens in the N chapel. Basically genuine Perp. – ORGAN CASE. 1888. – REREDOS. 1896, by *Bodley & Garner*. Alabaster. – Of the same year the fine red and white SANCTUARY PAVEMENT by *Farmer & Brindley*. – STAINED GLASS. Sanctuary windows 1896 by *Burlison & Grylls*. – S aisle W window, 1894, one S window, 1900, by *Kempe*. – MONUMENTS. Alan Porter † 1482. 9 in. brass. Half-effigy of a priest. – Sir Edmond Walsingham † 1549. Early C15 tomb-chest, the side panels with tracery of considerable complexity. In 1581 a backpiece was added with an inscription to Sir Edmond. Corinthian colonnettes and embryonic strapwork. Another inscription added in 1630. The whole repainted. – Sir Richard Betenson † 1679. Big black and white marble tablet with side scrolls and three cartouches attached to the top pediment. Mid-C17 in feeling. The odd thing is the Tuscan pilaster that supports it, flanked by palm-scrolls. This must be addition at the death of Lady Betenson in 1681. – Sir Philip Warwick † 1682. Large and outstandingly elegant cartouche carved with great finesse.

---

* The seemingly C12 corbel on a fat face, in the N chapel, looks ungenuine.

Putto-heads and a skull among the scrolls. The scrolls themselves have a peculiar tendency to assume the shape of half-
spread wings. – Thomas Farrington † 1694. Another good
cartouche, but not in the same class. Note the wreathed skull
at the bottom, and the bravura of its carving. – Thomas
Farrington † 1712. A third cartouche. Putto-heads again
around the knotted drapery. – Roland Tryon † 1720. Hanging
monument, with at the top a medallion bust, and on the cornice over the tablet an urn and two reclining cherubs. Rather
flabbily executed. – Sir Edward Bettenson † 1733. Large
hanging monument, with more marble than ideas. Signed by
Thomas Easton. – Lord Thomas Bertie † 1749. Hanging
monument with trophies of arms at the top, and an urn. What
makes it memorable is the relief at the bottom, an exquisitely
carved representation of a naval battle, the ships riding on
waves as stylized as rocaille work. The monument is not
signed, but Cheere would have been proud to have done it. –
Roger Townshend † 1760. Tablet by *Rysbrack*. – Sir Richard
Adams † 1774. Large tablet in the Adam taste. – Lord Robert
Bertie † 1782. Large tablet. – 1st Viscount Sydney † 1800.
Exceedingly large tablet. – William Selwyn † 1817. Signed
by *Chantrey*, 1823. Very large hanging monument. A young
man stands, two young women sit pensively by a tomb.
Chantrey eschews realism, for all the contemporary dress, yet
he makes one accept that these really are Mr Selwyn's children
and no generalized mourners. – 2nd Viscount Sydney. 1845 by
W. Brown of London. Allegorical female too small for the
substructure. – Earl Sydney † 1890. Reclining effigy in
Garter robes, by *Sir E. Boehm*, completed by *Alfred Gilbert*.

ANNUNCIATION, High Street. A fine, masculine church by
James Brooks, 1868–70, the ragstone exposed inside as well as
out, just as in his church at Perry Street, Northfleet (*see* p.
420). The simple system of a high clerestoried nave and chancel nearly as high, both with low aisles, is treated in Brooks's
usual emphatic manner, exposing problems, not smoothing
them away. Most surprising of all, not to say wilful, the mighty
SE tower is set diagonally to the church, just touching the S
chapel at one corner. Tower and chapel however are an afterthought of 1885. The tower, left incomplete, was weakly
finished off in 1930 by *E. J. May*. The W front of the church,
towards the street, has a tremendous wheel window, its forms
– all circles, nineteen of them – blunt and elemental. The
clerestory windows of the nave however match it in scale –

each a circle over two lancets. One or two strange happenings on the N side, the single flying buttress to support the chancel arch and the vestry chimney sticking out of the chancel roof. Big E window with the simplest bar tracery. The nave is full of light from the large windows high up, and the broad space satisfyingly held in by the tight curves of the roof principals. Short and thick round arcade piers (four bays) with Brooks's favourite stylized leaf capitals. The chancel is dim and lofty, a most effective contrast, heightened admittedly by the screen and wall paintings. – FONT. No doubt by *Brooks*. – PULPIT. His probably too. – CHANCEL SCREEN and LOFT. Only the base is of 1877, with figures of the apostles by *Westlake*. The rest is post-1918 in Comper's manner. – REREDOS. Vast. Designed by *Brooks*, executed in 1877 by *Westlake*. Gabled centre. Tiers of roundels l. and r. – WALL PAINTINGS. 1882 and 1892, by *Westlake*. – MOSAIC. Above the chancel arch. By *Salviati*, 1890. Designed by *Westlake*. – STAINED GLASS. E window and W window, 1870 by *Hardman*, apparently to *Brooks*'s design.

ST MARY HALL. Across the road. Also by *Brooks*, 1878. Simple gabled rectangle, with an annexe. But it is constructed in a, for that date, surprising manner, timber-framed, the square panels filled with red brick-nogging in interchanging patterns. The windows, true to the method, occupy unnogged panels under the eaves.

CHRIST CHURCH, Lubbock Road. 1871–2, by *Habershon & Pite*. A big church, with a conspicuous SW tower. Ragstone. Geometrical tracery. Long clerestoried nave, transepts and a canted E apse. Internally the transepts are unstressed, so the nave has seven bays altogether and the chancel seems quite remarkably small. It need hardly be said that, in spite of the revival of ritual in the C19, churches to serve the needs of Evangelical Anglican services went on being built. – STAINED GLASS. All in the E parts by *E.Frampton*, 1897 etc. It is extremely poor. One N window by *Kempe*, 1906.

ST JOHN THE BAPTIST, Mill Place. 1886 by *E.Crutchloe*. No longer used as a church.

ST MARY (R.C.), Hawkwood Lane. 1854. The architect of this simple ragstone building was *W.W.Wardell*.* PRIEST'S HOUSE on the N side. In 1874 however *Clutton* added a mortuary chapel to the s. It was ordered by the Empress Eugénie for the body of Louis Napoleon, the home of whose exile had

---

* Information received from Mr D. Evinson.

since 1870 been Camden Place (*see* below), although in the
end he was buried in a far grander setting at Farnborough,
Hants. Ashlar. The chapel's roof is sharply gabled, but rises
behind a rich pierced parapet; an arrangement that echoes the
chapel in the Château at Amboise. Internally there is a stone
rib-vault on wall-shafts with naturalistic leaf capitals. Clever
Cluttonian detail. – SCULPTURE. Christ in the Tomb. In a N
recess. – MONUMENT. The Prince Imperial † 1879. He lies
recumbent, fully armed.

METHODIST CHURCH, Prince Imperial Road. 1868–70. Ragstone. E.E. style, not cheaply, but somewhat baldly realized.

PERAMBULATION

Chislehurst is no ordinary suburb. This is because of its relationship to its common. Whereas most commons lie to one side of
their towns, here the common is the very heart of the place.
Chislehurst is blessed by the arrangement, and even the present
demolition of big old houses to put half-a-dozen in the place of
one does not seem to be destroying the leafy spaciousness.

St Nicholas's church is the obvious place to start, for it stands at
the common's edge. From the W of the churchyard one can
see quite a number of buildings more or less hidden among
the trees, all of the C19 and most of them rather ugly. Turning
first to the S, in MORLEY ROAD, a pretty pair of cottages,
No. 2 MORLEY COTTAGES and WHIN COTTAGE, part of a
larger scheme designed in 1878 by *George & Peto*. They introduce the *leitmotif* of late C19 Chislehurst houses, wide tiled
and half-timbered gables over red-brick walls. Immediately S,
in HAWKWOOD LANE, the R.C. church on the r., and on the
l. the new buildings of the GIRLS' TECHNICAL SCHOOL,
1960 and 1967 by *E. T. Ashley-Smith*, the County Architect.
The last house before a lovely shaft of unspoilt hillside is
COOPERS, a plain brick house of the late C18, three bays in
the centre, with lower wings. It seems all of one date, although
the front is yellow brick, the back red. At the back canted bays
flanking the centre. The interiors however are of *c.*1750, and
the staircase has two turned balusters per step and richly
carved tread-ends. So it is a matter of recasing, it seems.

Back to the church, and now E, down MANOR PARK ROAD.
Here is the MANOR HOUSE, basically a gabled half-timbered
house, with a two-storeyed porch; but now roughcast and
greatly added to. In MANOR PARK an early house by *Sir*

Aston Webb, COOKHAM DENE, *c.*1882. He uses the Norman Shaw idiom but has nothing much to say in it. Back in the main road, ST PAUL'S CRAY ROAD, one should turn l. Here almost at once the best C18 house in Chislehurst, CHESIL HOUSE. Red brick. Only three bays and two storeys, yet all the windows have arched centres making them into simplified Venetian windows. Plain parapet with a centre pediment growing up through it. Lunette window in the pediment. Porch on fluted Ionic columns, with a broken pediment. A date *c.*1770 would seem appropriate. Later addition at the r. BULL LANE runs NE, nearly opposite. Here comes EASDENS, an unusually confidently handled house of the early C20. The main shape is a familiar one, a low block with a deep gable-ended roof and a wide nearly central gable. Colossal chimney-breasts at each end. Shell-hood on brackets over the front door. The architect, surprisingly, was *Sir Aston Webb*, who built it as a church hall. Where Holbrook Lane joins the A222, quite a nice group of houses in the George–Newton vein, Nos 1–5 SHEPHERDS GREEN.

FARRINGTONS SCHOOL lies s of the A222. Symmetrical group, rendered neo-Georgian houses of 1911 and 1925, with the brick hall between. The hall has pilaster strips and a little cupola. The CHAPEL is of 1935. Brick. Cruciform, with a short octagonal crossing tower. Romanesque in style. All but the earliest building by *Crickmer & Foxley*. Farther on down Perry Street, WESTERN MOTOR WORKS has a high-spirited new showroom, 1966–7 by *Oliver E. Steer*.

In the other direction, i.e. further w, on the N side of the main road, SUNNYMEAD (Bromley Borough Education Department), dated 1875 on a rainwater head. It is a typical High Victorian medium-sized house, the sort of thing the Shaw style was to supersede very quickly after 1875. Red brick with black brick bands. Stone round the windows, with shafts and foliage capitals in a few places. Polychrome tympana above the windows. Gables and beefy bargeboards. Even a detail like the shape of the sash-frames of the windows is worth noting. N of this, in KEMNAL ROAD, a house on a larger scale. This is *David Brandon*'s FOXBURY, built in 1875–6 for H. J. Tiarks. Stone. Jacobean; i.e. with pierced strapwork parapets and a shaped gable over the porch. Low tower with a copper dome at the r. of the entrance front, where the service wing begins to branch out at the r. All in all a poor effort.

The High Street lies at the NW corner of the common, but has no building of interest in it, apart from the Annunciation Church and Hall (see above). In MEAD ROAD, however, which lies a short way to the E, GOLDEN MEAD, by *Sir Ernest George*, *c.*1887. Several other houses in the road look as if they are by him too. They all have a simple shape, usually with one large gable, and red-brick walls are hung for their top half with tile. Rectangular windows of various proportions. Moderately emphasized chimneystacks. Indeed it is a style stripped of practically all period and vernacular reminiscences.

The last area to be explored lies on the W side of the common. CAMDEN PLACE, off Prince Imperial Road (now Chislehurst Golf Club House). The main block, facing E, of red and yellow brick, seven bays wide, three storeys high, was built shortly before 1717 by Robert Weston. Giant pilaster strips mark bays 1, 4, and 7. In the 1860s this relatively plain edifice was decked with a one-storey pavilion l. and r., with a centrepiece displaying a big clock with sculpture round, and with a skyline of stone balustrades. The S façade, however, of austere brown brick, is clearly late C18, ending towards the W in a two-storeyed bow. What makes one eager to see inside is the knowledge* that this range is the work of *George Dance Jun.* Dance was employed, to remodel the whole house, so it seems, by the 1st Earl Camden, the Lord Chief Justice, in the 1780s. In 1788 a room, apparently called 'the School of Athens', was completed. Another room was called 'Sir James's Grecian Room'.‡ Neither, unfortunately, can be identified, and what is left today is neither Raphaelesque nor Grecian. The Breakfast Room, r. of the front door, has an exquisite plaster ceiling, close in feeling to Adam, but easily distinguishable from Adam's style. The l. pavilion, which was built by Dance, and merely cased in the 1860s, contains a remarkable Egyptian chimneypiece of polished pink granite. Could this be by Dance? The S range consisted of a suite of contrasting rooms, first an octagonal vestibule, now swallowed up by a broad corridor, then a bow-ended library, with primitivist pilasters (a remodelling of 1807 apparently, also by *Dance*), and finally a big, bow-ended drawing room, with, lining the bow, Ionic columns that carry spheres. The inset wall paintings in both rooms must be Victorian. All this then is disappointingly bitty; so the great spectacle of the house is

---

* Which I owe to the generosity of Mr Harold Kalman, who has identified the drawings in the Soane Museum.

‡ Quoted by Mr Kalman from letters in the Kent Record office.

the dining room in the r. pavilion, lined with fine c18 *boiseries* from a Bourbon hunting lodge.

Camden Place was bought in 1890 by William Willett Jun., the builder who had principally championed the cause of 'Pont Street Dutch' in Kensington and Hampstead, and who after moving his own house (*see* below) to Chislehurst, invented daylight saving. He developed the Camden Place estate in two groups for high-class medium-sized commuter residences, and, apart from the first few in Camden Park Road, *Ernest Newton* was his architect. This individualistic suburbia reveals the full range of Newton's talent before he sided with the neo-Georgians. The range is conspicuously wide, far wider than is generally supposed. One can generalize, all the same, and say that Newton uses red brick with a tile-hung top part, and proportions comfortably broad and low, with two storeys and dormers, a hipped roof, and gables for calculated effects. CEDARS, of 1893, Willett's own house opposite the entrance to Camden Place, states his case characteristically at the outset, with a sheer chimneybreast l. of the front door. The arched door-hood on columns is a special Newton favourite. One window bay, with a flat top not a gable, at the front, the back, and the side of the house. Typical too is the garden wall. The next three houses, also of 1893–4, are the ones not by Newton, but in 1910 *Newton* made a big, immediately recognizable, addition to the second, AVONHURST. Then comes *Newton's* DERWENT HOUSE, building in 1899, with a pair of tile-hung gables in the centre of the front. Stone porch and complex window over it, in the r. bay. Dramatic chimneybreast on the downhill end. BONCHESTER HOUSE, of 1898, next door, is more broken up, with a roughcast bay coming forward on the r. It has a vertically boarded gable, not one of Newton's strong points, and a bow window under a lead dome. The next house, ELM BANK, is the smallest, but altogether too full of fun and games. Hipped l. half of the roof, gabled r. half, with a complex chimneybreast between them. Superimposed on the chimneybreast is a projecting bay, the front-door half slipping off it. One reaches the door up a flight of steps that spread out diagonally. The dormer window like a half-closed eye is as dotty as the lunette in the bottom l. hand corner of the façade. Finally, more sober, FAIRACRE, L-shaped. The porch bay has a chequered brick-and-stone top part, and the doorway continues the rhythm of an arched loggia at the r. end. It is a first breath of the Georgian revival.

At the bottom of the hill, in LUBBOCK ROAD, are Willett's
enormous STABLES, built before 1908 (now a mixture of cottages and garages), one of *Newton*'s happiest and most relaxed
works. On the same side of the road are Nos 41–45, cottages
clearly by *Newton*, as are Nos. 23–27 LOWER CAMDEN
ROAD, opposite.*

The second, later, group of *Newton* houses is on the other side
of Camden Place, in THE WILDERNESS. On the right are
MOORLANDS, *c.*1907, with the usual prominent chimneystack and a circular bay window (the house has recently been
greatly extended in diluted Newton style), and THE BRAKE,
this time with a Georgianizing porch and a weakly half-
timbered gable. The Brake is late, *c.*1916. Opposite is PARK-
MORE, also late, larger and more formal, in purplish brick
with red-brick dressings and white plastered coving. The segmental doorway is banded in stripes *à la* Lutyens. Good
details include the three tall brick windows at ground level to
the r., the pargetting in the gable over the door, and some
pretty leaded 'gutterstrades'. The best house is COPLEY
DENE, *c.*1909, next door, worthy of Lutyens in its masterly 94
handling of asymmetry. The entrance wing, with a square
roughcast porch and a polygonal roughcast bay, three little
dormers and two big chimneys, is balanced at r. angles by a
big hipped-roofed wing with a projecting triple chimneystack.
HOLNE CHASE is quieter, with a central polygonal bay set in
a roughcast gable. It was built *c.*1914.‡

Two final grace notes. Off YESTER ROAD, overlooking the Newton houses in Camden Park Road, GREATWOOD, one of the
lamentably few good new developments in Chislehurst. Short
staggered three-storeyed terraces on the hillside. Charcoal
brickwork, white balconies and cornice. Further w, in Grange
Drive, BABINGTON HOUSE SCHOOL, red brick, Jacobean.
1879 by *Jarvis*. Of interest to specialists only.

CLARE HOUSE *see* EAST MALLING

CLIFFE   7070

ST HELEN. A major parish church, basically of the C13 but remodelled in the C14. The work of both periods is of the

---

* The potency of Newton's style, even after the Second World War, can
be demonstrated to anyone who continues along to the end of Lubbock Road
and back up the hill to Camden Place.

‡ Mr Nicholas Taylor has been my guide to Ernest Newton and his
patron, and has kindly contributed several pieces of the text.

greatest variety and interest. If only the pleasure were not dimmed by the thorough restorations – in 1853 by *Austin* (chancel), 1864 by *St Aubyn* (tower and transepts), and 1884 by *Romaine-Walker & Tanner* (PF). The E.E. church was cruciform, as the deep transepts show outside. Long lancets, the N and S triplets not genuine. C13 W tower, with clasping buttresses. Perp top stage, modern battlements and staircase projection. No W doorway. The Dec alterations are distinguishable from afar, by the black and white banded walls, knapped flints, and ragstone. The aisles were considerably widened, with a two-storey S porch, the chancel completely rebuilt in a characteristic early C14 way, quite long, quite lofty, but quite narrow. Three fine two-light windows to N and S between strong, simple buttresses. The tracery deserves study. Three different designs, all having a bulbous form that grows from the central mullion mouchettes haphazardly packed into the spaces. A quatrefoil in the bulb of the easternmost window with split cusps and linking bars, the typical features of 'Kentish tracery'. This and the multiple cusping are both quirks of early C14 work connectable with Christ Church, Canterbury. The connexion at Cliffe is that the manor and advowson belonged to the Prior of Christ Church. The E window of the chancel must be ignored: it was designed in 1884. Traces of a demolished N vestry. Internal hood-moulds to the windows, on excellent head corbels. Vaulted SEDILIA and PISCINA integral with the chancel fabric. Ogee arches with crockets, finials, and pinnacles. Foliage in the spandrels. Considerably restored, but even so one of the most luscious pieces of Dec carving in the county.

The lavishness of the E.E. church was also something more than normal, and of that the exterior has given no hint. In the first place the tower is vaulted and the lancets of the ground stage placed within large blank arches. No mouldings however beyond a simple chamfer. Tower arch abaci in the form of a roll carried on as a string-course. Nave arcades of five bays. Shortish circular piers with unelaborately moulded capitals and bases. Wide arches with two slight chamfers. Everything points to a date little if anything after 1200. The pointed arch from N aisle to N transept however, *c.*1190 at the latest, is an alteration of the time when the nave was built. The nave piers boldly painted with thick red zigzags, a distinctly Norman and not E.E. embellishment. Masonry lines in the spandrels, and a repeating fleur-de-lys motif round the arches. Clerestory lancets, above a slight set-off, probably added in the C14, when the aisles were widened. In the transepts the E.E. style is in full flower. They open off the E bay of the nave. The system is full-scale shafted wall-arcading, two bays to the E and two narrower bays to the W, enclosing the lancets. Many minor differences between the two transepts. The S is the more coherent design, but plainer in detail than the N. It is not really possible to say which is the earlier. Trefoiled PISCINAS in both transepts, that in the N the centre of the E side, so that the shaft of the blank arcading stops short on a corbel to which adhere two rows of trefoiled leaves. Upper angle of a stone REREDOS immediately W of this corbel. – WALL PAINTINGS, on the E wall of both transepts, part of the original scheme of decoration. N transept: scenes illustrating the martyrdom of St Edmund. S transept: scenes and figures incoherently under one of the arches, including Christ in Majesty at the top but not in the centre. Sparse trails of leafage on the wall above, perhaps as late as c.1300. – SCREENS. Tower screen, c.1370. The lights grouped in threes with intersecting mullions, and pretty tracery. – Rood screen. The base is late C15, with blank tracery in the panels. It is *in situ*, see the rood-loft doorway. – TIE BEAM, on pierced spandrels, acting as a strainer at the E end of the nave. It was needed because there was never a chancel arch. – STALLS. Three each side are old, the misericords uncarved. Small heads on the arm-rests. – PULPIT. Early C17. Arcaded, and somewhat richer than the usual run of such pulpits. – HOUR-GLASS BRACKET. Wrought iron. Dated 1636. – STAINED GLASS. C14 glass, greatly restored, in the tracery of two chancel windows on the S side, together with a few later bits. – PLATE. Paten, c.1520, silver-gilt: central sunk sexfoil enamelled with the Trinity; Cup, 1668 by *W.G.*; Patens, 1735, a pair by *Joseph Sanders*; Flagon (really a tankard), 1735 by *R.L.* – MONUMENTS. Late C14 tomb recess on the N side of the sanctuary. Cusped and subcusped arch. Embattled top and a row of small lion heads and leaves below it. – Thomas Faunce † 1609. 25 in. brass of civilians. – Bonham Faunce † 1652. 26 in. brass of civilians.

(MANOR FARM, West Street. Close-studded Elizabethan house, with a continuous overhang, and fine integral brick chimney-stacks. NMR)

QUICKRILLS, 100 yards S. Late C17 five-bay house in two parallel ranges. Dull red brick. Door-hood on carved brackets.

THE RECTORY, 1m. s. A large medieval stone house, so altered
in the C19 that nothing original but walling is left. The present
medievalizing windows do not constitute reliable evidence. A
writer in 1883 thought he could discern the plan of a large hall
with a solar at the E end. By this account the service wing to
the w had been demolished. The remaining walls, on the
other hand, suggest some more complicated arrangement.

6060

COBHAM

ST MARY MAGDALENE. The memorable part of the church is
the chancel, very wide, but nobly proportioned in itself, and
housing a fabulous collection of brasses (see below). It is of
the middle of the C13, and makes austere architecture, with
tall lancets, five a side and three E ones, of even length. Internally they are shafted; the E shafts, of Purbeck marble, are
linked by a continuous hood-mould and rest on a string-
course. Contemporary DOUBLE PISCINA *ex situ*, including
dogtooth in the trefoiled arch mouldings. It was displaced in
30 the late C14 by a PISCINA of outstanding elaboration, with a
panelled back and a triple canopy. Three canopied SEDILIA
of the same date. S doorway to a ruined annexe (a vestry?),
or rather to a passage w of it. Archaeologically the strangest
feature is the remains of a spiral staircase in the SE corner,
access, to judge by the complex corbel, to a loft. A loft over
the reredos is not known elsewhere in England, but occurs in
several places in France. The way it avoids the C13 string-
course suggests that it is an original feature. One more archaeological note to complete the account of the chancel: in
the SW corner part of a blocked arch, of the latest C12, i.e.
pointed, but unmoulded and on plain imposts. Its unexpected
position suggests that it was the entry to a chancel chapel, not
the chancel arch itself. Higher up, a fragmentary opening, with
part of a jamb made of Roman tiles. That would be Saxon
evidence: but can it be taken seriously? Four-bay aisled nave,
C13, but not matching the scale of the chancel and probably
later in the century. Round piers, arches with two hollow
chamfers (except the w arch of the N arcade). The N arcade
the earlier, and its central pier an odd man out. Aisles of the
original width; at least the piscina in the S aisle looks C13. In
1362 however Sir John de Cobham founded a college in the
church. The chancel was of course already of collegiate proportions. But he added a lean w tower, in ragstone, a contrast

with the flint walling elsewhere, and continued the aisles one bay w to clasp it.* New aisle windows at the same time. Two-storeyed N porch, vaulted below. Perp nave clerestory. Chancel arch by *Scott*, who restored the church in 1860. – FONT. C13. Octagonal bowl on shafts. – SCREEN. In the N and S tower arches. Partly old. Vallance, noticing the crowded lights of the richest piece, thought it might be from a pulpitum. – STALLS. In the chancel. Those on the S side contain old work. – TILES. Quite a lot with patterns, in various parts of the chancel. – STAINED GLASS. E window by *Lavers & Barraud*, c.1863. – ARMOUR. Four tilting helms, two dated as early as the first quarter of the C15. – SCULPTURE. In the vestry. Fragments of first-rate quality, five small headless figures, and three larger female heads, all c.1370. – PLATE. Cup and Paten Cover, 1634 by *I.B.*; Set, the gift of Sir Joseph Williamson, 1678 by *R.M.* – COFFIN SLABS. Three in the chancel, one especially fine, with stiff-leaf tufts at the head and the foot of the cross. – BRASSES. Nowhere in the country is there such a large and coherent group of brasses as at Cobham. The main series is arranged in two rows across the chancel. It commemorates members of the de Cobham and Brooke families, Lords of the Manor. The remainder, scattered in various places in the church, and much more insignificant, are of Masters of Cobham College. Restorations in 1839 and 1865–6 have left them in a deceptively pristine-looking state, but few details of the figures had to be renewed. The main series is best described row by row, starting at the r. of the E row. – Joan de Cobham, c.1310–20. By some way the earliest, a very substantial (65 in.) figure under a flimsy canopy with no ogee detail in it. – Thomas de Cobham † 1367. – John, 3rd Lord Cobham, † 1408. He was the founder of the college, and holds a church. Otherwise the two are a pair, the figures 59 in. long, and were probably laid down c.1370. Lord Cobham's brass is not quite finished. They are not of first-rate quality. – Margaret de Cobham † 1395. 58 in. figure. Virgin and Child at the apex of the canopy. – Maude de Cobham † 1380. 61 in. figure. – Margaret de Cobham † 1375. 59 in. figure. – John, 2nd Lord Cobham † 1354. 56 in., but with a modern head. The canopies of these three are almost identical, but the figure of Lord Cobham is close to the other two

---

* This lengthening must be post-1370, as the application in that year to build the college was for buildings 'equal in extent with the length of the church' – and the college extends only as far W as the flint bays of the aisles.

Cobham, brass to Sir Nicholas Hawberk † 1407

knights. It is quite possible that the 3rd Lord Cobham laid down all six. – John Sprotte † 1498. 18 in. priest. Poor. – Rauf de Cobham † 1402. 13½ in. demi-figure in armour, holding the inscription plate. – Sir Thomas Brooke † 1529. Figures under canopies, attempting to keep in scale, but the figures only 36 in. long. Plenty of fussy hatched shading. – Sir Reginald Braybrok † 1405. – Joan, Lady Cobham, † 1433. – Sir Nicholas Hawberk † 1407. These three go together, for Sir Reginald and Sir Nicholas were two of Lady Cobham's husbands. The brasses of the men are especially fine, as works of art the best in the church. They are figures c. 58 in. long, their little sons on pedestals at their feet, the canopies enriched with tabernacles of the Trinity etc. The brass of their widow is smaller, 49 in. long, without a canopy, with crudely engraved groups of children. – Lady Margaret Broke † 1506. 36 in. figure under a double canopy, her husband missing. The earliest of the large brasses to show a decisive drop in quality. – Reginald de Cobham † 1402 (N aisle). 23½ in. figure of a priest on a bracket. His head new. – William Tannere † 1418 (chancel). Demi-figure of a priest, 18 in. long. – John Gladwyn † 1450 (nave). 24 in. figure of a priest. – MONU-MENTS. Robert Holte † 1503. Outside, at the NE corner of the N aisle. Exceedingly worn demi-figure holding an inscription (still legible c.1800, but not now). – Sir George Brooke, 9th Lord Cobham. Large alabaster and touch tomb-chest with[46] reclining effigies, erected in 1561 and placed with extraordinary arrogance in the centre of the chancel almost within the sanctuary. But what gives it special interest is the beauty and purity of the classical detail at this early date. Small kneeling figures of ten sons and four daughters round the sides of the monument, in front of shell-headed recesses and between Ionic columns, fluted by means of black inlay. Triglyph frieze, heretically, below the bases of the columns. Well carved effigies. Like the brasses, more restored than it looks. A beam fell and shattered it in the C18, and it was only pieced together again in 1840 and again in 1865. – Small wall-monument, c.1600, in the N aisle. Figures of two women and six children huddled together at their prayers.

THE COLLEGE. In 1362 Sir John de Cobham founded a college consisting of a master and four priests, to say masses for the souls of his ancestors. Application to erect college buildings on the S side of the church was made in 1370. Under the will of the 10th Lord Cobham, they were adapted in 1598 as twenty almshouses; and so they remain to this day, calm and humble, the perfect place, one would think, to live one's last years. The C14 college was built round two quadrangles, close to the s side of the church, leaving just enough room for a processional path. The complete E arch over the path and springers of two more. The masonry is of squared ragstone blocks, or flint in inconspicuous places. The windows rectangular, of one or two lights, chamfered. One E window however of three cinquefoiled lights. Modern chimneystacks, but not less effective for that, as seen from the w. The hall lies on the s side, lit by two s windows, traceried, over two cinquefoiled lights with a transom. The s court is almost totally ruined. In its SE corner however a wide fireplace with a depressed stone arch is enough to show that the kitchen lay here. Trace of a second fireplace as wide. The round-headed doorway near it in the s wall has above it the Cobham arms and an inscription of 1598, under a heavy triangular pediment. So the new college abandoned the former kitchen. Inside the main quadrangle one sees walls of 1598. Mr P. J. Tester's excavation of 1962 revealed that the E and W ranges were reconstructed narrower, and the N range probably built from scratch. Doorways with pointed arches and rectangular windows, exactly like the C14 work. The s wall was masked by a pentice – that is why it is built of flint. One C14 window here high up. Both original doorways to the hall screens passage are *in situ*. The hall has its original roof, with arched braces on stone corbels, tie-beams and crown-posts, and wind-braces for length-wise stability. C15 fireplace and hood, clumsily by-passing one of the corbels. Bracket on a head-corbel against the s wall. Mr Tester's suggestion is that a candle placed on it gave light for someone to read by at meals.

The College lies over the ridge of the hill, hidden by the church from the village. But the church itself is well placed to be the visual focus of the street, set above the sloping churchyard at its W end. NE of the churchyard, STONE HOUSE, originally the college school-house. One recognizes the same rectangular upper windows on the W side, and below them a two-centred arched doorway. No other medieval features – the brick traceried windows and the bargeboards with their curlicues cannot be earlier than the C19. The LEATHER BOTTLE INN opposite, of Dickensian fame, now exposes its half timbering, most of which is modern. It started off as a modest cottage on the street. Nicer, because less conscious of their looks, the brick cottages w of it. Further w, MEADOW HOUSE lies a long way back behind a field. May the field never be built on. Meadow House was built in 1770, in dark red brick, a two-storeyed centre of five bays, with low pavilions in line with it. The pavilions have large but simplified Venetian windows and pedimental gables. At the roadside, the MEADOW ROOM, 1898, a village hall characteristic of the sophisticated charm of the period. Battered brick buttresses that are quite unnecessary, and alternating high and low windows. In BATTLE STREET, a big, handsome group of OASTS, with early C19 details; and NE of it, disgracefully insensitive new houses.

All this is visible from the churchyard; so now turn, or retrace your steps, to the E, into the short, tight street. Nothing to comment on here, nor yet when the houses fall back. Only the pretentious SCHOOL of 1874, on the l., COUNCIL HOUSING on the r., and, beyond it, recent intruders. Two houses especially have a sickeningly chi-chi, 'look at me, aren't I daring,' air about them. Cobham is permanently damaged by them. Yet if it has been decided to allow expensive new houses in the village, why not encourage something really daring? Or at any rate, well designed. Why should Cobham be denied what New Ash Green, created out of nothing, can have, or what the War Office can provide at Chattenden? Finally, on the l., MILL FARM HOUSE, a glowing red-brick cottage dated 1712 on a cut brick panel with a scrolly pediment, and, facing the lime avenue of Cobham Hall, ROSE COTTAGE, a wide-eyed Gothick cottage.

COBHAM HALL. Cobham Hall is a splendid mansion, splendid in scale, and set in a *Repton* landscape of splendid maturity.*
It contains much that is architecturally interesting and at least two parts of memorable beauty. As a structure however it is a good deal more complicated than it looks.

EXTERIOR. The house is in essence Late Elizabethan, built of a rosy red brick, with stone dressings. The present entrance is on the N, but until the early C19 it was on the W side, and that is the show front. It has two far-projecting wings, ending with strong turrets attached to the outer angles; a motif favoured in Early Elizabethan years, e.g. at Melford Hall, Suffolk. A second pair of turrets in a somewhat equivocal position beyond the inner ends of the wings. The centre block, linking the wings, is clearly later, and a map of 1641 shows the

* So mature in fact that from the house one is not aware that the park has been drastically shorn to the N, W, and E.

wings standing like two separate houses. How did this come about? William, 10th Lord Cobham, began building c.1580. Holinshed calls it 'the statelie augmenting of his house', so, as was natural enough, the wings were additions to an existing building. Dates on the house and items in the accounts trace the course of the augmentation. The s wing is dated on the s porch 1584. It was roofed in 1587. Lord Cobham imported 200 tons of Caen stone in 1591, and the porch of the N wing, which was no doubt what the stone turned into, has on it the date 1594. This wing was roofed in the same year, but the turrets were not leaded until 1601. The wings were complete by the next year, but in 1603 the 11th Lord Cobham, as a result of the plot to put Lady Arabella Stuart on the throne, forfeited his title and estates, and work on the house stopped for sixty years.

47   The s wing then was the first to be built, and established the character of the whole. Its s front is almost symmetrical, two-storeyed, of fifteen bays, of which the fourth, eighth, and twelfth form rectangular projections. The upper windows have mullions and two transoms, the lower have been sashed. Continuous string-courses above the windows at both levels. Plain parapet. The vertical stresses are the turrets, which, starting square but soon becoming octagonal, rise to four storeys, with ogee lead caps, closing the ends of the façade firmly, and the pairs of tall octagonal brick chimneystacks, rising from slightly projecting breasts from the lower string-course. Their spacing, in the rhythm 1, 2, 2, 1, is very telling. The whole front, in spite of slight irregularities of the fenestration, in spite of the weak central doorway, has a grave and serious beauty. No other part of the building achieves an equally sustained architectural effect. The s wing ends at the w in a two-storeyed canted bay and a shaped gable with three finials. The N side contains the main entrance to the wing. The round entrance arch framed by squat Tuscan attached columns and a heavy entablature. Above it an oriel window on brackets and a big egg-and-dart frieze. The parapet rises here to take in a dormer window. Top pediment with scrolls up the sides, set on S-scrolls, making a sort of Dutch gable. Big, evenly distributed windows, with three mullions, the upper ones with two transoms, the lower with two. Three l. of the entrance answer those to the r., plus two more at the r. end separated by two chimneybreasts.

The N wing repeats the s as exactly as possible. But as it

contained the chapel on the ground floor and a long gallery above, there are on the s side two canted window-bays and, between them, a sumptuous but extraordinarily incongruous stone porch, of 1591–4. Paired columns on two levels, en- 48 riched Ionic above Tuscan. Tall bases and entablatures, breaking forward over the columns. At parapet level, antae support bulgy baskets of fruit, and between them the splendid achievement of the 10th Lord Cobham. Severe triangular top pediment on an attic. The inscription DEO OPT MAXI marks it as the entry to the chapel.* In its classicism it far outstrips the tentative details elsewhere; indeed, it has few rivals in England for its date. The bay at the w end of the N wing is of the early C19, and so is the gable above it.

The centre block was built for the 6th Duke of Lennox and Richmond, who inherited the house in 1661. The 4th Duke had in 1649 obtained a design for a completely new house on a palatial scale from *John Webb*, but his nephew merely supplied the missing centre. Who was his architect was unknown until Mr Colvin's discovery of recent payments, in connexion with the building, to 'Mr Jarman' and 'Mr Mills Surveyor' Thus he concluded that the block was designed by *Peter Mills*, one of the leading mason-architects in the City. Traditionally work began in 1662 (the date on the front is bogus); work on the interior was paid for in 1672. The front was two-storeyed. The attic was added in 1768–70 by *Sir William Chambers* and given elizabethanizing trim by the *Reptons*. Originally there was a hipped roof and dormers, with an attic only in the centre. The 1662 front however remains. Four Corinthian pilasters, the centre two more widely spaced, and an entablature. Big central stone doorcase, with Tuscan columns and half-pilasters beside them, and an open seg-mental pediment springing from too far in. The front is nine windows wide, the centre three more widely spaced. Window surrounds with architraves, of Jonesian purity. Did Chambers insert them perhaps, in place of something coarser?

Externally the most important alterations to the house were made by *Humphry & J. A. Repton*, 1800–20. The entrance was transferred to the N front. This involved building a corri-dor out to the N, with an arch in the centre acting as a *porte-cochère*, and a raised walk above it to the terraced garden. The N side of the N wing was pepped up with added window-bays

* NP points out that the inscription was added later, and suggests that the porch was intended as the central feature of the then unbuilt centre block.

(one dated 1812) and bits of strapwork. The frills which were
added in other places have already been mentioned. The
Reptons also made a tiresome habit of putting bogus dates
about the place.

The service court, formed by extensions eastwards of the
N and S wings, was also tudorized by the *Reptons*. Clock-turret
in the E block dated 1818. But the court was formed, it seems,
by *Chambers*. Rainwater heads dated 1770. Part of the N range
may be genuinely of *c.*1600, but it is hard to separate the
Elizabethan parts from those that imitate them; for the whole
court is very carefully made to conform, in height and materials,
even to the extent of using old bricks, laying them in English
bonding and giving the windows mullions and transoms. The
windows however have incorrect mouldings and are of Portland stone. The zigzag diapering of the N range must also be
over-zealous antiquarianism of the 1770s. One doorway on the
S of the S range seems to be a real C16 piece. Over it is an inscription with the date 1789. The W range, i.e. the back of the
centre block, got a two-storeyed addition – a corridor and
picture-gallery – in 1771–3. The Elizabethan chimneystacks
above may be of the same date. At the NE corner a tower with
a corbelled-out parapet, and a round-headed stone window
surround that looks oddly Vanbrughian.

INTERIOR. The strange history of the building makes for an
inconsequential layout of the rooms. One enters on the N side
into the CORRIDOR added in 1801. This, like all the Repton
interiors, is weakly Gothic, i.e. has a depressed pointed rib-
vault of plaster. From the corridor turn to the r. into the N
wing. First comes the stone STAIRCASE in a spacious square
well. This appears to be all early C19, with its Gothic screen
and coarse wrought-iron balustrade. Arms of the Duke of
Lennox in the ceiling: another Repton attempt to mislead?
The room on the ground floor where the public enters has a
large chimneypiece, the first of the series of original chimneypieces, two of which *Giles de Witt* contracted to provide in
1601. This one is dated 1587. In the large room next to the
staircase the next chimneypiece. It is decidedly peculiar. At
the sides half figures of old men support colossal bulging
baskets of fruit, with more fruit and a cabbage poised on a
bunch of plume-like leaves. The half-figures grow out of big
termini pillars. In the centre of the overmantel stands a nearly
naked female figure, in front of a large black rectangular slab
engraved with a country scene of thatched half-timbered

houses. Similar engraving on the fireplace lintel of Moses striking water from the rock. Marble niches at the E and W ends of the room. Are they C17 work? W of this the Gothic CHAPEL, by the *Reptons*. In it another alabaster chimneypiece. Note the two parrots pecking at the swags of fruit.

The LONG GALLERY occupies most of the upper floor of the N wing. It was remodelled c.1806–9 with vestibules at the ends. In them minor C18 chimneypieces. In the gallery itself two major Elizabethan ones. The first, with bulgy Corinthian columns and bulgy termini caryatid figures and a big coat of arms, is dated 1599. The second is chaster, almost all of pale mottled marble of several hues, and with an overmantel relief of the three Fates. Between them a smaller bearded man holding a scroll. Again flat landscape behind. Small allegorical figures between the termini. Absurdly, the inner pair of these termini projects further than the outer. Here the State Coach of the Earls of Darnley is kept. The end room in the wing, the so-called QUEEN ELIZABETH ROOM, has another chimneypiece, also with a relief in the overmantel, representing Peace triumphant over War, as a solid female seated on a pile of armour. The 'Elizabethan' plaster ceiling with its date 1599 is too flat and delicately detailed to be genuine, and indeed was designed by *J. A. Repton* in 1817 – a notable effort, even so, for the date.

The N half of the original centre block is wholly occupied by the stupendous GILT HALL. The gilded plaster ceiling[77] was executed in 1672. In 1779 it became a music room and the organ was installed, and presumably the N and S galleries, on yellow scagliola marble columns, are of that date. The walls however were not decorated until 1791–3, when *Wyatt* lined the lower half with white veined marble and carried the order round as paired pilasters with an entablature. The pilasters were made for £301 by *Bartoli*. The plaster enrichment of the upper walls continues the rhythm upwards, by means of alternately wide and narrow panels, the former with drops of musical instruments, the latter with cameo medallions. The exquisiteness of it all, the careful separation of part from part, so that no flowing rhythm can build up, is typically neo-classical, and a striking contrast with the robust garlands and arabesques of the ceiling. The coved cornice, however, also of the late C18, decorated with gilt swags, cleverly bridges the gap between the styles, and indeed one accepts the room as a whole. Fine white marble fireplace, by *R. Westmacott*, 1778, with large-scale figures of a youth playing a flute and a maiden playing a tambourine. Relief copied from Guido Reni's 'Aurora' in the Casino Rospigliosi in Rome. Contemporary plumed chandelier.

The VESTIBULE next to the Gilt Hall, in the centre of the block, was formed by *Wyatt* in 1773-4, and leads straight into the back corridor added at the same time. He divided the deep, narrow space into two parts: a square, and behind it, through a screen opening in the centre with a marble segmental arch on Ionic columns, a more than semicircular recess. In the latter an exquisite marble chimneypiece, with putti on the frieze. Side niches. In them pairs of figures rather too small and perhaps not what was originally intended – the bases do not fit.* Plasterwork in an Adam style in both parts. The next room to the S is the LIBRARY, formed in 1817-20 by *G. S. Repton*. In the LOBBY at the S end of the block another marble fireplace, a pair to the one in the vestibule. On the first floor two rooms with plasterwork by *Wyatt*. In one C18 Chinese wallpaper, and in the other a fireplace by *Vardy*, 1773.

In the S wing, a fine STAIRCASE of *c.*1672. The balusters grow from foliage bulbs and end in four-way Ionic capitals. (The VESTIBULE in the centre of the wing, with plasterwork, is by *Chambers*. John Harris)

GROUNDS. *Humphry Repton* made a Red Book for Cobham Hall in 1790. In executing his plans, as we have seen, he diverted the drive to the N side. This was to allow formal gardens before the W front. Two *Coade* stone vases remain to mark where they were. The present gardens with flower-beds on the S side also represent the sort of thing Repton wanted. The landscaped park began only a little distance from the house, so that it should no longer be 'exposed to the cattle on every side'. As for the four radiating lime avenues, he cut three of them down. The one that he left runs south-westwards towards the village, and is now very old and dishevelled.

78   MAUSOLEUM, ¾ m. SE of the house. Best reached from the road that runs E as the continuation of the village street. It is a long way, but one is rewarded by a distant view of the Hall, like a little town buried among the trees. Nobody except Lord Carlisle at Castle Howard had a more magnificent mausoleum than the 3rd Earl of Darnley. *Wyatt* designed it in 1783, but in the event it was not used. Today it stands in the middle of

---

* But an identical chimneypiece is at Ickworth, Suffolk.

a wood, in lamentable condition. It is built of Portland stone, a powerful and sombre building in spite of the crisp, delicate detailing which was Wyatt's natural language. He based himself on Neufforge or French Grand Prix designs. The main body is a square with chamfered corners. A Doric order and entablature run right round it, two recessed columns against each face and two columns projecting against the chamfered angles. Sarcophagi on the projections, and above the recessed columns segmental lunette windows within sunk segmental arches struck from a different centre, an ambivalent motif. The mausoleum is crowned by a completely plain pyramid. The rusticated basement is masked by a deep ditch. Steps on the E side lead down to it, where in a circular chamber under a stone saucer dome there are thirty-two deep slots for coffins. At the W side, in a recess, stands a stone table, prepared for the 3rd Earl's own coffin. The circular chapel, on the main storey, has a circular coffered dome balanced on the heads of the lunettes. Round the walls pairs of attached composite columns, their red marble facings now mostly pulled off, support a deeply projecting entablature decorated with slim, weightless swags. The spacing of the columns reflects the external shape, which is indeed repeated inside the walls behind them, but with a remarkable variation: the four main sides are convex, in a vertiginous counter-rhythm to the entablature. Pedimented reredos like an altarpiece in an Italian church.

LODGE, ½ m. N of the house, beside the A2. By *J. A. Repton.* Elizabethan.

In Cobham Park is a small ROMAN VILLA sited on a low ridge. In its original phase it consisted of a strip of five rooms with a front corridor. Later rooms were added to the W, and later still what may be a bath block was attached to the E end. A large outbuilding was found near by.

OWLETTS, ⅓ m. NW. Built in 1684 for Bonham Hayes. Five bays by three, two storeys under a generous hipped roof. Two large, symmetrically placed chimneystacks and a deep moulded brick string-course give it distinction. So do the alterations of *c.*1700, one-bay wings coming forward at each end, and a panelled parapet instead of the original eaves. At the back the centre bays project a little, with three large windows and round ones above, to light the staircase. Various low additions on this side. Late C18 doorcase, attached to a modern porch added by *Sir Herbert Baker,* who lived here. Staircase with stout twisted balusters and a plaster ceiling dated 1684. Two big circular wreaths of foliage and flowers, and hardly any unenriched space around them. The screen of Ionic columns by *Baker*.

At SOLE STREET, 1 m. SW, SOLE STREET HOUSE, a plain late C18 red brick house; and YEOMAN'S HOUSE, a half-timbered Wealden house, restored by *Baker*, not, as happens so often, by putting back all the missing timbers, but by allowing the varied materials, dark uprights, white plaster, brick-nogging, and a bit of weatherboard, to tell against each other.

COLDBRIDGE FARM *see* BOUGHTON MALHERBE

7040   COLLIER STREET

ST MARGARET. 1847–9 by *P.C.Hardwick*. Solid and serious, E.E. in style. Ragstone. Nave and N aisle, lower chancel, S porch-tower with a tall shingled spire. The chancel windows shafted inside and out. Spacious, but plain and undemonstrative interior. The village-church character is only betrayed by a certain excess of optimism in the scale.

COMBE BANK *see* SUNDRIDGE

COMBWELL *see* KILNDOWN

7070   COOLING

ST JAMES. A small but complete C14 ragstone church, as it appears from the outside. The window tracery all cemented but correctly representing what was there. The nave windows pure Dec, but those in the chancel with vertical bars above the lights, a Perp alteration. The stop-chamfered NE and SE buttresses are a nice touch. The W tower characteristically banded with knapped flint at the bottom and the W window an early C14 design (cusped intersecting tracery), but the short buttresses diagonally set, not normal before the second half of the C15. The surprise inside is the lower part of the chancel walls. Six arches N and S, on marble shafts springing from marble benches, unfortunately all over-restored. The S arches run straight on with three trefoiled SEDILIA, and a fine double PISCINA, shafted trefoiled and with a big trefoil pierced in the spandrel. So the chancel was originally built *c.*1260. Tiny S vestry, its walls inside decorated with thousands of cockle-shells. – FONT. C13. Of the Purbeck type. The square bowl on five circular shafts. Five trefoiled arches sunk slightly into each side. The E face with a cross in the centre, on a stepped base and with two discs above and below each arm. – PULPIT. C18. Of the simplest. – BENCHES. Six with crude fleurs-de-lys for poppyheads. – PLATE. Cup, 1683; Paten, 1683 by *G.S.* – BRASS. Feyth Brook † 1508. 18 in. figure. Bad.

COOLING CASTLE. John de Cobham obtained a licence to fortify his manor house at Cooling in 1381. French raiders had sailed up the Thames two years before and demonstrated how feebly defended was this approach to London. So Cobham's interest in the matter was not merely a personal one, and he recorded his altruism in building a castle on the North Kent marshes by attaching a copper tablet to the outer gatehouse, like a deed with a pendant seal. It reads as follows:

> Knouwyth that beth and schul be
> That I am mad in help of the cuntre
> In knowyng of whyche thyng
> Thys is chartre and wytnessyng.

Today it needs a considerable effort to take the castle seriously. It stands low and unimposing beside the road just w of the church, separated from the river by two or three miles of flat and innocent meadows. Within the gatehouse a modern, absurdly suburban-looking, house. Yet a considerable amount remains from the C14, enough to allow one to appreciate the complete layout. Some of the building accounts also survive. They show that work went on at least until 1385. *Henry Yevele* was paid on various occasions for measuring work done. *Thomas Crump*, a local mason from Maidstone, was entirely responsible for building the outer gateway. This gateway is 35 perfectly preserved. Short, semicircular-fronted flanking towers with boldly projecting rings of machicolations and battlements. The towers are entirely open towards the inside. Arrow slits of the exclamation-mark type, as they are in other parts of the castle as well. No windows. It admits one to the extreme SW corner of the outer ward. Remains of circular turrets at the other corners. The inner ward stands quite independently on the w side, originally moated and reached from the outer ward only by a drawbridge. Rectangular enclosure, with round angle-turrets originally machicolated (see one machicouli on the NW turret) and a turreted gateway not quite in the centre of the E wall. Postern doorway at the N end of the W wall. The living quarters were probably in ranges along the inner sides of all four walls in the regular manner of Bodiam (licensed 1377). Cooling has never been excavated. Corbels for floor joists on the S wall. In the NE corner a three-bay vaulted undercroft, with quadripartite vaults and chamfered ribs on short wall-shafts. It supported the Great Chamber. The wall at this point is externally patterned with knapped flint and stone chequers. Garderobe beside the S turret of the gatehouse. A circular staircase in the S corner leads down to a room at the lowest level, within the angle-turret. Light comes in from the S by three slit windows with curving jambs which make it impossible to see out (or shoot in).

Within the outer ward a fine BARN.

COOLING COURT, ½ m. S. Dated 1700. Red and blue bricks in a chequer pattern. Five bays, the centre one very narrow. Several windows blocked, giving it a one-eyed look. A perfect setting, however, with a pond, a willow tree, and green, green grass.

LODGE HILL, 1¼ m. S. On the highest point for many miles, overlooking both the Thames and the Medway. Built c.1760, of dark red brick. Three-bay block with wings set back slightly. The centre plain, the wings with a lunette window over a Venetian window. Two-storeyed throughout. Plain top parapet. At the time of writing uninhabited and the setting for bomb disposal practice.

CORNER FARM see LANGLEY

COURSEHORN see CRANBROOK

COURT AT STREET see LYMPNE

COWDEN

ST MARY MAGDALENE. W steeple riding the roof ridge. The tall, tapering belfry stage carries a pyramid roof, out of which grows the slim spire. The whole thing shingled and resting on six massive posts, with arched braces in both directions, within the late C13 W end of the nave (see one trefoiled lancet to N and S). S porch Perp. N aisle of 1837, re-using old windows. The chancel is essentially Dec, with one original N window, of two ogee lights under a square head. PISCINA, cinquefoiled, under a crocketed arch. Two other Perp PISCINAS at the W end of the chancel, i.e. for altars immediately W of the rood screen. Crown-post roof in the nave, and deep moulded wall-plates in nave and chancel. – PULPIT, with a hexagonal sounding-board. Dated 1628. A good, bold piece, out of the usual run of early C17 pulpits. On it a contemporary HOURGLASS STAND, on a modern bracket. – FONT. Perp. Octagonal, with the usual encircled quatrefoils. Much retooled. – STAINED GLASS. Seven small grisaille panels, greatly decayed, based on engravings by *Lucas van Leyden*. – Cast-iron SLAB to John Bottinge † 1622. In the C17 Cowden was a famous centre of the Wealden ironworking industry. In the churchyard (N of the chancel) two more slabs, 1726 and 1730.

The short village street, seen from the E, starts with the long white CROWN INN on the r., and on the l. the half-timbered front of a Wealden hall, whose history can be easily traced: first the blocking of the recessed centre when a floor was put across the open hall, and then the underpinning of the overhangs with brick. Round the corner the street continues more narrowly, closed at the end, where the road turns sharply again.

Cowden is unusually rich in timber-framed farmhouses. The following are the best:

WAYSTRODE MANOR, ½ m. N of W. An impressive display of closely set studs. Recessed centre between three-storeyed gables, the l. one higher, the r. one with an elaborate bargeboard.

BASING MANOR, 2 m. W. L-shaped. Tile-hung. (Jacobean panelling in an upstairs room. Under it a black-letter inscription has been found. *A.C.*, XXI, p. 103.)

CRIPPENDEN MANOR, 1½ m. NW. Tile-hung. Gabled only to the E. The original entrance front faces W. Built in 1607, says an inscription in the hall. Hall overmantel with fluted columns; and a splendid screen entirely formed of small panels decorated with a strapwork pattern round sunk saltire crosses. Two arched openings between Ionic columns.

BASSETT'S FARM, 2 m. NE. Towards the road a tall gable with oriels of one, three, one lights tucked below each overhang. Early C17 (cf. Springhill, Fordcombe, of 1622).

COXHEATH see LINTON

CRANBROOK

ST DUNSTAN. The church takes second place to the windmill
as the town's most prominent landmark. The W tower not
especially grand (though its deep-set W doorway is) and
decidedly too short for the high, wide, clerestoried nave. The
large clock in the S wall of the tower has a fine face with a
figure of Time within the open scrolly pediment, a modern
copy of the original figure kept in the church; c.1700. Tower
and church are Perp, of yellow sandstone. Battlemented aisles
continued as chancel chapels. The chancel projects by one
bay. The windows to a dull, uniform design. As often,
however, the ghost of an earlier church can be discerned:
rough walling in the N aisle, and a length of late C13 string-
course inside; narrow C14 chancel arch; S porch also C14,
with a rib-vault and good central boss with a head among
foliage. (C15 doorway and timber framework across the outer
arch of the porch, an unusual survival.) Thus the nave had
already reached almost its present dimensions before 1400.*
The N chapel clearly, the S chapel less clearly, not built in
one with the aisles. Priest's door in the S chapel, a rich C14
piece with diagonal buttresses and a frieze of delicate little
mouchettes. Reset. The chancel may also be earlier than its
Perp appearance suggests, see the apex of a richly moulded arch
high in the E gable. Bequests give rough dates for the remodelling. Two were made already in 1473 and 1477 for a new
Lady Chapel, and in 1479 and 1480 for the 'new work in the
north part'. By 1500 the nave was not yet begun, but a
bequest of 1501 'to the repair of the gable for the steeple'
may mark the start of work on the tower. In 1522 and 1524
the nave was under way, when gifts came in to 'the new
making of the middle ile'. The arcade design is a stereotype
but effective for all that. Six bays, with compound piers of
four shafts and four double-waves, and wide four-centred
arches also double-waved. The large clerestory windows
framed by a horizontal moulding and the vertical shafts that
reach down to demi-angels over the piers and up to demi-
angels on the roof corbels. Most of the S arcade collapsed in
1727 and was rebuilt in 1863 by *Slater*, who also provided a
new nave roof. The chancel restored by *Christian* at the same
time. At the W end four huge and splendid wooden BOSSES,

* Almost, because the inner ends of the porch ribs were cut short when
the S aisle was widened.

three with green men, the fourth a bird among foliage. The still naturalistic leaves date them c.1300. – ALTAR RAILS. Early C18, with slender twisted balusters. – PULPIT. Disused. C18, with marquetry panels, as also on the large sounding-board, now turned into a table. – CHANDELIER. Brass. Bought secondhand in 1736. A splendid specimen. – FONTS. The steps in the s aisle lead to a font for total immersion, built in 1725, and, it is said, used only twice. – More normal, the font of 1852, Perp, but unusually nicely done, especially the flying tracery at the base of the bowl. – LECTERN. c.1866. Brass. – ROYAL ARMS. Given in 1756. Finely carved arms of George II. – HELMS. Three of the Roberts family in the chancel. – In the s chapel the TABARD and two BANDEROLES of Sir Thomas Roberts, who died in 1706. – STAINED GLASS. One window in the N aisle is completely glazed with early C16 glass. The numerous shields of arms suggest that the glass was made for Sir Richard Guilford † 1508. Scenes of St George and other saints. On style the figure scenes are clearly work of the Flemish glass-painters already working in London before 1500. Mr Councer adduces evidence that the glass was made after 1514. – Chancel N and s windows c.1858-9 by O'Connor. – Three windows in the s aisle by Kempe, 1902. – PLATE. All gilt. Cup and Paten Cover, 1628; Flagon, 1722 by N.G.; Cup and Paten Cover, 1729 by G.S.; three Almsdishes by I.E., 1730. – MONUMENTS. Brass of a civilian, c.1520, 19 in. long, with a chrysom child and the merchant's mark, T.S. – Sir Thomas Roberts † 1627. 15 in. brass of a kneeling civilian. – Richard Fletcher † 1585. Small tablet in an alabaster surround. Notice the skull. – William Rookeherste, alias dictus Roberts, 1599. Similar, slightly larger tablet. – The Roberts family, 1740 by Joseph Pickford (Gunnis). White marble standing monument with a broken pediment and splendid long drops of oak-leaves, which frame, not an inscription, but the family tree showing forty-four persons in eleven generations. The C18 passion for pedigrees was a major reason for erecting monuments – few show it as blatantly as this. – The Baker family, erected 1736. A bulky obelisk on a bulky sarcophagus on a bulky base. The inscription begins, 'Near this Pile of Marble...'. – Thomas Webster, R.A., † 1886. Marble relief of Webster lying in his painter's smock holding his paintbrushes. Big putto with wreaths at his head and feet. A curious mixture of naturalism and allegory. By Hamo Thorneycroft, 1889. – Boyd and Claud Alexander.

Designed as a pendant to the above. Profile medallions and a dreamy figure of Africa in the lowest low relief, characteristic of its date: 1913. By *W. Robert Colton*.

COUNCIL OFFICES, High Street. By *Denis Clarke-Hall* and *K. Barnes*. Completed in 1964. Single-storeyed. Towards the road a blank wall of red patterned brick with a long concrete canopy. Behind, the U-shaped Council Chamber bows out into a tiny courtyard.

COURT HOUSE, behind the Council Offices, in Wheatfield Drive. 1964–6 by *E. T. Ashley-Smith*, the County Architect. Top-lit hall and low flanking blocks. Not so freshly thought out as the Council Offices.

CRANBROOK SCHOOL. The school was founded in 1576 by Simon Lynch. The present buildings are of the C18, C19, and C20 and make a most attractive group by the SE corner of the churchyard, in red brick of various hues. The boldest element is SCHOOL HOUSE, 1727–9,* seven bays and three storeys with a deep white cornice and plain parapet. One-storey loggia on Tuscan columns across the three recessed centre bays. Segment-headed windows, the central two blank. To the r. and behind, the centre of the group, *T. G. Jackson's* BIG SCHOOL of 1883–4 is a hotter red, but otherwise by far the more charming and accommodating building. Three wide projecting bays between four narrow receding ones, tall and steep roof and a pretty cupola. Plenty of vivacious cut and moulded brick enrichment. Next, a utilitarian Neo-Georgian block of 1927, and, peeping out in the r. corner, the LIBRARY, built as the Schoolroom in 1859 by *Martin Bulmer*. On the other side of the road only beefy CROWDEN HOUSE, 1877.

PERAMBULATION. Emerging from the churchyard at the far end from the school, one sees the High Street stretching broad and straight up the hill, and, to the l., Stone Street quickly curving out of sight round a corner. The latter, with its various surprises, makes the more rewarding walk. First then up the HIGH STREET, where the l. is the side to watch at the beginning, though there is scant reward for the watcher in the yellow brick CONGREGATIONAL CHURCH of 1857, with a Dec front and a mean wooden clerestory; or the plain late C18 CLERMONT. LLOYDS BANK, exciting at first sight, is almost totally

_____
* Mr A. L. Congreve kindly told me of accounts, which give the name of the architect, *John Feildhouse*, and the cost, £800.

C20 half-timbering.* Higher up on the r. the CRAMP INSTITUTE of 1807, typical of its date; windows under tall sunk arches and a pedimental gable across the façade. Salmon brick. It faces THE STUDIO, a Wealden hall-house, its l. end later replaced by a three-storeyed gable. Original cusped barge-boards to the gable. A little further up, also facing each other, the last houses to note. On the l. WEBSTER HOUSE, a three-storey, very red brick Early Georgian house of five bays. C19 bay-windows have been added, and the whole thing looks more mid-C19 than mid-C18, except for the doorcase, with fluted Doric pilasters and triglyph frieze. SHEPHERDS is nicer, an early C18 front, also five bays, but only two storeys. Giant angle pilaster-strips. Parapet. Pinkish-grey and red brick. Notice the window-heads cut into frills, consistently for once over the whole façade. The Council Offices (see above) are a little way further up. Back down the High Street, where the VESTRY HALL of 1859 makes an effective end to the view with its big polygonal bay.

In STONE STREET the tile-hung GEORGE HOTEL extends along the r. side. Sturdy late C17 staircase inside, with turned balusters. The structure of the building however is C15. As one rounds the corner, suddenly the windmill appears in the distance majestically riding above the houses. At this point, however, down an alley to the r. is a building that can easily be missed. Yet the PROVIDENCE CHAPEL, of 1828, is one of Cranbrook's memorable buildings, a seven-sided front faced with timber grooved to look like stone and supported on square Tuscan piers. Five large round-headed windows in the centre. The interior has the usual galleries on three sides. Where the street plunges down into a little valley WATERLOO ROAD runs away to the l. with humble weatherboarded cottages and, just in sight, the towering redness of Crowden House (see Cranbrook School, above). The PARTICULAR BAPTIST CHAPEL of 1787, at the bottom of the hill, here called ST DAVID'S BRIDGE, is as humble as any cottage, weatherboarded and marked out as something special only by its round-headed windows and the solitary gravestone in front. HILL HOUSE, on the r. near the hilltop, provides another surprise, among a sea of C19 tile-hanging a sumptuous early C18 doorcase, large, with excellently carved Corinthian

---

* Mr Gravett observes that the structure is genuine inside, with a crown-post roof, unusually reinforced with side purlins.

capitals and a froth of foliage within the broken segmental pediment.

And now at last UNION MILL has been reached, and one can see why it dominates the town. It is a full-scale smock-mill set on a brick base almost as tall as itself, the whole thing 72 ft high altogether. A prominent tablet gives the first miller, the date of building, and the builder: Henry Dobell, 1814, and *Humphrey*. The mill is also notable for still being in full working order, and working, what is more, though not by wind. Black base and black spines to the sails, otherwise all white and weatherboarded. The usual boat-shaped cap, fantail and gallery. RAMMELLS HOUSE, opposite, has a front towards the road by *Ernest Newton*, 1883, his earliest work, and already quite distinguished with its alternating strips of brick and roughcast, and its sheer window-bay. Big addition of the 1930s at the l.

Further out, in the hamlets strung along the A229, are several more items. The most rewarding house is no doubt OLD WILSLEY, at Wilsley Green, of two parallel half-timbered ranges joined by a modern N wing. The main range facing the road is extremely attractive, the timbers hidden by a warm ochre rendering. It seems to have been originally a large but typical C15 hall-house of the Wealden kind, with a two-bay centre and the ends jettied out on the upper floor. To this house large bargeboarded gables have been added, bay-windows under the overhangs, and a two-storeyed bay-window in the centre. Inside the hall the service screen partly survives with two doorways. (Crown-post in the room above, from the time when the hall was open to the roof.) The SW room has an early C17 stone fireplace, panelling, and a frieze with carved brackets. But what makes Old Wilsley something special is the room in the NW corner, lined with large-fielded panelling of the late C17, which is entirely painted. Marbled mouldings. In each panel of the dado a hound, and, on the door, the hare they are chasing. The main panels have New Testament scenes, with, on the doors, the Destruction of Sodom and of Nineveh. As paintings they are not very brilliant, but the artist seems to have had by him an early C16 model, engravings perhaps, either Netherlandish or German.

Immediately s of Old Wilsley, the entrance to GREAT SWIFTS, a neo-Georgian house of *c*.1935 by *Geddes Hyslop*. (Inside are several brought-in pieces: an early C18 staircase from Tangier House, Taunton; some unusually fine panelling with gadrooned mouldings from Ashley Park, Walton-on-Thames; a Rococo chimneypiece from a house at Blackheath. *Country Life*, November 1939, p. 524)

At GODDARD'S GREEN, ¾ m. sw, the eponymous house has a fine long half-timbered frontage, partly overhanging in the centre, and with two balancing gables at the ends, each with a canted bay rising from ground to gable. Closely set uprights on the upper storey. C17 casement windows; modern imitation doorway. Brick chimneybreasts each with three star-shaped stacks. At the back the roof runs down in a tremendous sweep. (A stone fireplace inside is dated 1634 – and that would be a reasonable date for the gabled additions.)

Further sw, HARTLEY HOUSE, built by *Whichcord Sen.* in 1839–41 as a workhouse. Grey sandstone ashlar. Symmetrical. Central entrance arch with a four-centred shape. Pedimental gable.

OLD CLOTH HALL, 1 m. s of E. A U-shaped building, one third modern, half-timbered, but with the lower storey rebuilt in brick.

COURSEHORN, 1¼ m. s of E. C18 farmhouse built round an earlier house. (Inside, fine Tudor ceilings and a stone fireplace also of the C16. *A.C.*, XLVII, p. 244.)

GLASSENBURY, 2 m. w. In a small, heavily-wooded park, the moated house of the Roberts family, originally built, says Hasted, *c.*1473. The s front is apparently C18, two storeys, nine bays, the centre five under an exceedingly wide broken pediment. Brick with sandstone quoins and a banded central chimneystack. Otherwise the exterior is an uneloquent jumble. (The hall has panelling dated 1571. Igglesden)

CRAYFORD

ST PAULINUS. This is a puzzle church. Not that a superficial look at the exterior rouses any suspicions. There is a nave with a Perp w tower and a N aisle as wide as the nave, a chancel with battlemented s chapel, and lean-to N chapel. All the windows are renewed (by *J.Clarke** in 1862), but one on the s side of the nave was Norman. The E window can be ignored, the others represent what was there before. Much of the flint walling has also been re-laid. The NW quoin however has not been tampered with, and in it are many blocks of tufa, with a characteristically pitted surface, a readily quarried chalk

---

* As Mr Geoffrey Spain kindly points out.

deposit exploited by the Normans as a building stone. The lowest courses of a blocked doorway in the w wall of the N aisle are further evidence that the church is Norman in its bones. But this means that nave and aisle are both Norman, and together they are too wide for that to be probable; and there is a straight joint in the centre of the w wall, which means that either the nave or the aisle was once an aisleless nave. Considering the position of the blocked doorway, it must be the present N aisle which formed the original church.

That is as far as the outside can help, and a first view of the interior adds confusion to confusion. One can hardly any longer speak about 'nave' and 'aisle', but rather of two naves, for the single arcade runs down the very middle of the church and dies into the wall above the apex of the chancel arch. The complete set of Norman windows has left its mark inside, four in the N wall and four in the s. Half of them must have been reset, and, as we have seen, the evidence outside suggests that it is the N windows that are in their original places. This is confirmed by the outline of three round-headed windows in the E wall of the N nave – so the E, N, and w walls of the Norman church can be identified. That it originally had a chancel narrower than the nave and the chancel N wall later rebuilt in line with the nave's when a new chancel was built further E cannot be proved, as no NE quoin of the nave can be seen, though that is the natural assumption. One s window gives an early C14 date for the chancel. Also a few stones of the three canopied SEDILIA. All else is Perp: chancel arch, arches to N and s chapels, and the arcade of four and a half arches on piers with four shafts in the main directions and hollows between. Square-headed Perp windows. The w tower was under construction in 1406 by *John Wells* 'cementarius'. It is stone, with diagonal buttresses and a w window that looks earlier than the rest. So the essentials of the remodelling are Perp, but the chancel aligned on the original s wall of the Norman church is Dec. Intermediate stages in the history must be missing. Probably the Norman building threw out a s aisle and s chapel, in which the s windows were reset. If this aisle and chapel were unusually wide, a new chancel further E might have been aligned on the arcade to allow a view of the high altar from all parts. This plan was perpetuated when the arcade was rebuilt. Roofs dated 1630. – PULPIT. Also *c.*1630. Hexagonal, with tapering angle pilasters. – ALTAR TABLE. Designed by *James Brooks* and painted with figures of the four evangelists; *c.*1895. It was made to match the REREDOS now in the S chapel. – PLATE. Cup, 1634; Flagon, 1637 by *P.C.*; Paten, 1738 by *I.R.*; Paten (really a Salver), 1740 by *John Tuite* (?); Processional Cross, brass, captured in 1868 at Magdala, Abyssinia. Probably C18. – MONUMENTS. – Blaunche Marlar. Small hanging monument with a kneeling figure; *c.*1600. – William Draper † 1650 and Mary † 1652. Large standing monument of black and white marble. They lie stiffly on their sides propped upon an elbow, the lady above and behind her husband. Small kneeling children, a boy at the l. and a girl at the r., and a tiny swaddled infant almost at ground level. Big double back-plate like a reredos, with an open segmental pediment on Corinthian columns. Gunnis saw *Thomas Stanton*'s hand in it. – Robert Mansel † 1723. Large plain standing monument of grey-veined marble. – Margaret Collins † 1732. Leathery cartouche with two putto heads. The inscription ends with the verse:

> Adam thus blest
> (as by his Eve was crost)
> Had surely kept
> the Paradise he lost.

– Elizabeth Shovel, widow of Admiral Sir Cloudesley, † 1732. Large and grand hanging monument. Putti hold a canopy over a black obelisk which stands on a sarcophagus balanced on a putto's head. – Henry Tucker † 1851. Remarkable as a pastiche of a late C17 tablet. That was a period usually ignored by the mid-Victorians. The putto is too innocent, the wreath of flowers too tight and square to be quite convincing. – Several more nice tablets in the nave.

IRON AGE SETTLEMENT, just to the W of the church. The settlement was discovered during building operations and appeared to consist of a series of storage pits and gulleys (possibly hut foundations) containing Iron Age A, B, and C pottery.

BARNS CRAY, ½ m. E, was laid out from 1914 onwards as a garden village to house workers employed by Vickers to make ammunition. Designs of 1919 for extensions, by *J. Gordon Allen*.

CRIPPENDEN MANOR *see* COWDEN
CROCKENHILL

ALL SOULS. 1851 by *E. Nash*. Ragstone, E.E. – STAINED GLASS. E window 1853 by *Holland* of Warwick (TK).

4050

CROCKHAM HILL

HOLY TRINITY. Built, of local sandstone, in 1842 by Charles
Warde of Squerryes. The architect, whoever he was, did
it in Perp. Almost unbuttressed W tower. Nave and lower
chancel. Much vigorous cusping of the tracery. The builder
was a Mr *Horseman.* – SCREEN, incorporating the PULPIT, a
weedy Gimsonish affair by *Lord Ferrers.* – MONUMENT.
Octavia Hill, co-founder of the National Trust, † 1912. Recumbent figure of a little old lady in a shawl. Not particularly
well carved, but heartfelt. By *Dora Abbott.*

Crockham Hill is a promontory of the sandstone ridge, and
superb views over the Weald can be had from it. The views
were discovered in the 1880s, and a number of wealthy men
built mansions to catch them.

KENT HATCH, ¾ m. NW. By *Mervyn Macartney,* c.1882. Norman-Shavian, with many half-timbered gables.

HEATH HOUSE, at the top of the village. Tall. In the same style.

LEWINS, ¼ m. SW. By *J. M. Brydon,* 1876. A third house in the
Shaw style, this time designed around a broad tower. Not one
of these houses begins to show the master's sureness of touch,
for all that they ape his manner.

At FROGHOLE, ½ m. NE, two slightly later sandstone houses:
HIGH QUARRY, of 1905, and further E ACREMEAD, a long,
ambitious house by *Smith & Brewer,* 1906, its N and S fronts
both symmetrical, the former with three small weatherboarded gables in the centre, smacking of Philip Webb's
Standen, the latter sheer on a falling slope.

HILLFORT, 1 m. N. This is a roughly triangular fort of 11 acres
defended on the E and W by a single bank and ditch and on the
S, where the approach is more gentle, by two lines of ramparts.
An entrance occurs on the SE.

CROFTON *see* ORPINGTON

3070

CRYSTAL PALACE

The Crystal Palace was burnt down in 1936. Of the grand terraced gardens in the Barry manner laid out by *Paxton* on the
hillside, there is nothing now to be seen but a few Italianate
arcades. The sculpture has all been carted away except a
gigantic head of Paxton set starkly on a pedestal (signed by
W. F. Woodington, sculptor of the Lion Brewery lion, and

dated 1869). By the lake at the foot of the hill however the STATUES of prehistoric monsters still disport themselves. They are of bronze, realistically painted, and lifesize. The iguanodon was large enough for twenty-one gentlemen to dine in its half-completed body. The statues were suggested by Professor D. T. Ansted and made in 1854 by *B. Waterhouse Hawkins* under the direction of *Professor R. Owen*. A recent addition to the herd is the GORILLA by *David Gwynne*, 1961. For the rest, C19 recreation has given way to C20 recreation. The NATIONAL RECREATION CENTRE, covering the lower slopes, *c*.1956–64 by the *L.C.C. Architect's Department*, is devoted to sport. The STADIUM has sickle-shaped seating on the N side. Further E is the SPORTS HALL, a vast rectangular building, concrete-framed and with a gently zigzagging roof that results from its construction, cantilevered out from a central spine. Internally this divides the space lengthwise down the middle. On the l. the main training area, on the r. three swimming pools. Practice rooms and squash courts are cleverly slipped in under the tiered seating. The interior is very impressive, not least because there has been no attempt to impress, no contrived effects.

To the N, the HOSTEL, an isolated eleven-storey point block, planned as six hexagons round an open hexagonal well. The eye cannot analyse the complicated shape. Clad with vertical cedar boarding. Similar boarding on the STAFF HOUSES, which with their black brickwork and uncompromising butterfly roofs are extraordinarily effective. They and the hostel provide an exotic foil to the saneness of the rest.

CUDHAM 4050

ST PETER AND ST PAUL. Flint churches are not easy to restore without spoiling their looks, and Cudham is no exception. Yet the restorations of 1846 and 1891–2 (by *Christian*) were kinder than many round here. (The worst part is the renewal of all the Dec windows.) An interesting history can still be traced. It starts in the nave, which is Saxo-Norman, i.e. Saxon in its high, narrow proportions, Early Norman by the one small S and one small N window. Of the C13 the chancel (two N lancets are partly original) and the S tower. Chancel and tower arches similar in details, and curiously interlocked via an inner tower buttress chamfered off to become part of the chancel arch. In the C14 the nave grew a short N aisle and the chancel a S chapel: clasping buttresses to both, an extraordinary motif to find as late as this, unless they are evidence of earlier enlargement. The Dec arcades are replacements. Low-side window at the W end of the aisle. PISCINAS in chancel, S chapel, and aisle, all in the E walls, another anomaly. In the NW corner of the chancel a corbel is half buried in the wall. What does it signify? Nave roof with moulded arch braces. In 1487 20 shillings were left 'to ye makyng of the church roffe'. – FONT. Perp. Shields in quatrefoils on the eight faces. – STAINED GLASS. One S window in the nave, 1897 by *Kempe*. – MONUMENT. Perp panelled tomb-chest in the chancel. Above its E end a canopied niche. – BRASS of Alys Waleys † 1503, 20 in. long.

CUXTON

7060

ST MICHAEL. On a hillside above the Medway. Norman nave and chancel of flint, see on the N side the window in the chancel and all three original tufa quoins. Perp additions at both ends: an extra bay to the chancel, and the unbuttressed W tower. S chapel. All windows Perp. C19 additions on both sides: S aisle and widening of the chapel, N porch and sundry buttresses, all of stone spotted with flint like currant pudding. Chancel arch widened probably in the C15. Wide arch S of it to the rood-loft stairs. Of the restoration of 1860–8 the tower arch and the gauche hammerbeam roof. S arcade on round piers. – SCREEN. Across the tower arch. Perp. – WALL PAINTING. C13 leaf trail on the splays of the early window, and a crude head at the top. – PLATE. Cup, 1618; Paten Cover, 1618 by *I.I.* – MONUMENT. Ann Harley † 1603 (behind the organ). Large hanging monument. Corinthian columns. Obelisks and top achievement. Strapwork enclosing a panel with verses, from which dangle fruit and symbols of death.

WHORN'S PLACE. C16 brick gateway with a moulded arch of four-centred shape. The late C15 house of Sir William Whorne and the grandiose Tudor stables which lay beyond it have gone, and the present house is formed from an outbuilding. It is also of brick and of the C16, with a gable to the N and to the S, and, towards the road, a crowstepped gable with the Leveson arms. Two-storey projection towards the river. C19 porch.

At UPPER BUSH, a hamlet ¾ m. E, a well restored Wealden house.

MEDWAY BRIDGE, taking the M2 over the river to bypass the Medway Towns. Concrete. The roadway is carried out over the marshy ground on close-set posts and lintels, but leaps lightly over the river on a half, a whole, and a half elliptical arch, cantilevered from the slim piers. The central span is as much as 500 ft. *Freeman, Fox & Partners* were the consulting engineers.

DANSON PARK see BEXLEYHEATH

DARENTH

5070

St Margaret. Archaeologically the church is important, but visually it is rather charmless. Flint. Nave with s aisle, chancel and separate sanctuary, c13 sw tower. The nave is the earliest part. The tile quoins and the double-splayed window over the N doorway, with its outer splay of Roman tiles, are typical of Late Saxon work, that is to say of the late c10 or the c11. The Saxon chancel has gone, but the square-ended Early Norman sanctuary, i.e. the E bay of the chancel, remains. It is of two storeys. The sanctuary proper is low and has three small stepped E windows and a groined vault. The chamber above it is now sealed up, and was originally lit by two windows in the E wall. The chancel is also Norman, and to it, late in the c12, a s chapel was added. The chapel is now destroyed, leaving only the arcade with square, many-scalloped capitals and pointed arches – not the usual Transitional combination in Kent,* though quite normal both in Hampshire and West Sussex. The s arcade is a c14 extension of a one-bay c13 chapel (N.B.: the capital of the W respond has been reset and its base adapted for the octagonal pier). Crude head corbels, probably of the later date. – FONT. Norman. Large and tub-shaped. Dated c.1140 by Dr Zarnecki. Round the bowl under an arcade of eight arches is a characteristically incoherent variety of subjects. They are, reading clockwise from the E: baptism by immersion; a bearded man grappling with a dragon; a rampant lion; a gryphon; Sagittarius; King David; a fantastic beast; a crowned man holding a flabellum. – PULPIT. c18. Square, with a bowed front. – ALTAR RAILS. Early c18. Twisted balusters. – PLATE. Flagon, 1627, by *W.S.*; Almsdish, 1681.

The church's companions are early c19: MILL HOUSE, to the E, a white box covered by a pedimented roof; and two gothick LODGES to the w.

* Except on the Grain promontory.

DARENTH HOSPITAL, 1¼ m. NE. Kelly gives the following information: built in 1876–88 as a lunatic asylum, by *C. & A.
Harston* of London, at a cost of £454,000. One of the largest
asylums ever built: it has a frontage nearly half a mile long.
Yet even so, for that money the architecture is dismally mean.
The site of a large and interesting ROMAN VILLA covering about
3 acres lies on the E bank of the river Darent, ¼ m. S of the
church. Although totally excavated last century, there is still
some doubt about the functions and relative sequence of its
individual parts, but basically there are three units: a main
house with basilican buildings on two sides, defining a central
courtyard or garden. The house originated as a strip of rooms,
divided by timber partitions, with corridors at both the front
and back. At r. angles lay a basilican building, later divided by
masonry partitions and floored with tesserae; in one end a
hypocaust had been inserted – more likely to heat a corn-
drying oven than to provide comfort. The other basilican
structure retained its 'industrial' style throughout, with what
is thought to have been a fulling works added to one end. The
main bath suite lay between this and the house. In the centre
of the walled courtyard an elongated tank was found with a
cistern at one end. From its axial position and finish it was
probably an ornamental garden feature. Outside the garden
on the same axis was the well, contained within a well-house.

DARTFORD

5070

HOLY TRINITY. The large, composite, over-restored building
one would expect, part flint and part ragstone, smoked to a
uniform blackness. The state of the exterior can be attributed
to *A. W. Blomfield*, 1862–3. One would have preferred it if he
had left something of *Mylne*'s extensive brick modifications
of 1792–3. It was Mylne who first lopped off the SW corner
for road widening. The grand E window of *c*.1333 however
had been mutilated in 1783, and Blomfield's E window does
not copy it. S porch, 1846 by *Edward Cresy*. The N side of the
church must be considered first. The N tower is Norman, with
clasping buttresses, the NW one enlarged to contain a staircase.
The fourth stage Perp. E.E. chapel built against its E wall.
Late C14 aisle built against its W wall. Windows on the
ground stage on three sides, and a S doorway (of tufa), confirm
that from the first it stood on the N side of the Norman church.
Yet the present N wall of the chancel ignores the tower and
indeed is not built in one with it. In this wall two simple blank

black weatherboarding. Thus the materials distinguish the use of each building. It is also apparent to the eye that the whole design has grown out of the requirements of spastics – hence the wide corridors and colossal windows, hence the concrete chutes as fire-escapes. Only the assembly-hall skylights, six sharp inverted Vs, are there for their own sake.

DITTON 7050

St Peter ad Vincula. Small Norman church. Since 1860, when *Scott* removed the chancel arch, the only original feature has been a N doorway into the chancel (now hidden inside the vestry). Herringbone masonry however and another, blocked, doorway S of the chancel, and typical tufa dressings. Low, plain, unbuttressed but Perp W tower. A nice pair of original early C14 windows flood the E half of the nave with light. – STAINED GLASS. In the N Dec window, contemporary glass, leaf borders, and, in the mouchettes at the top, a pair of angels swinging big censers above their heads. – LEAD PLATE. Early C19 vernacular art from the roof – a shakily drawn three-masted schooner. – PLATE. Cup, 1689; Paten, 1698. – MONUMENTS. Rowland Shakerley † 1576. Only the feet of his brass, and the inscription 'made by a young gentlewoman as an argument of her unseperable good meaning towards hym'. – Richard Brewer † 1672. Nearly top-quality tablet, with a scrolly open pediment, side scrolls, and swags, erected after 1691.

DODE see LUDDESDOWN

DORTON HOUSE see SEAL

DOWER HOUSE see PEMBURY

DOWLE STREET see PLUCKLEY

DOWNE 4060

St Mary the Virgin. Flint. Nave and chancel under one roof. W tower E.E. with a shingled spire. One renewed lancet in the S wall of the nave, otherwise all windows Late Perp. The church over-restored in 1879 by *Daniel Bell* (BW). Two vertical breaks in the S wall suggest it had a history, now beyond recall. – MONUMENTS. Brasses to a civilian and wife, c.1400. Small. – Thomas Petle, c.1420. Tiny. – Jacob Verzelini, the famous Venetian glass-maker, † 1606, and wife. Large and fussy brasses.

The centre of Downe has a proper villagey feel. A timber-framed house of the Wealden sort, WALNUT TREE COTTAGES, opposite the church; but the main ingredient is the hard, unaccommodating flint cottages that one finds scattered all over the chalk uplands behind this part of the North Downs. One or two outlying houses, however, are in a softer mode:

ORANGE COURT, ½ m. E of N. The fronts of farmhouse and outbuilding diapered with alternating red and grey triangles of brick and flint.

DOWNE COURT, ⅜ m. E of S. A red-brick front of three bays. Dated 1690, but not yet achieving symmetry.

In Luxted Road on the r., first PETLEYS, early C18, flint and red brick relieved by a white doorway and cornice; then, further on, DOWNE HOUSE, the large, irregular, gaunt home of Charles Darwin.

DUKE'S PLACE see WEST PECKHAM

0010

DUNGENESS

The shingle bank at Dungeness is four miles deep and still increasing. The first lighthouse was built in 1615, when '1000 persons . . . perished there for want of light' each year. There are now two LIGHTHOUSES and the base of a third, made into a circular house. It is the base of *Samuel Wyatt*'s tower of 1792. Beside it the brick tower of 1904, painted black. Strongly battered sides and white window reveals showing an immense thickness of wall. A little further E stands the excellent new lighthouse, 1959–60 by *Ronald Ward & Partners*. Other materials, other shapes, but happily the same functional tradition. Chunky spiralling staircase ramp, slim tower banded black and white. The tower is built up of prestressed concrete rings; so it does not need to taper. Through the rows of holes below the lamp platform the fog-horn blows. Trinity House keeps all three buildings immaculately shipshape, shaming the scruffy shacks that surround them and sprawl for miles northwards up the coast.

NUCLEAR POWER STATION 'A'. 1960–5. Architect *Maurice H.J. Bebb*. Two tall Reactor Buildings, with the Switchgear Building to the N and the Turbine House on the seaward side. Aesthetically a disappointment. Large but not overwhelming, tidy but not sleek. The symmetry is positively Palladian – central *corps-de-logis* and low wings to l. and r. as seen from the lighthouses. Even more disturbing is the clutter of wires and pylons all around: and most destructive of all are the lines of vast pylons striding insensitively across Romney Marsh. The Marsh scenery is so precious that the cables ought to have been laid across it underground, whatever the extra expense.

POWER STATION 'B', planned to be the most powerful nuclear power station in the world, is being designed by *Howard Lobb & Partners*.

DUNSTALL PRIORY *see* SHOREHAM

DUNTON GREEN 5050

ST JOHN THE EVANGELIST. 1889–90 by *M. T. Potter* of Sevenoaks. Humble red-brick nave and lower chancel. Carefully textured brickwork inside too. The nave has arcades pushed right against, but just not touching, the walls. Yet it seems that aisles were not envisaged.

BROUGHTON HOUSE. The remarkable one-storeyed LODGE is opposite the church. White brick. Square pyramidal roof and central chimneystack. The plan however is not so simple. The side to the road is convex, the other sides recessed between diagonal corner projections, that give the roof its chamfered corners.

The house itself, also of white brick, *c.*1830, is much less spirited. Five bays by three. Two storeys. Portland stone for the paired Ionic columns of the porch, the plain top cornice, and the window surrounds, the lower ones with prim triangular pediments. It is all very precise and undemonstrative. The Victorian era might be centuries away.

DYMCHURCH 1020

ST PETER AND ST PAUL. Norman with an enlargement of 1821. The chancel windows have slightly pointed heads, but the S doorway is purely Norman. It has shafts with scalloped capitals, a thick roll and zigzag round the arch. The interior fills out the picture. The W doorway, hidden within the tower, and the ample chancel arch repeat the same motifs. In 1821 the nave was greatly widened northwards and covered by a wide, sparsely timbered roof characteristic of that date. At the same time the little tower was slipped in between the deep W buttresses. In the S wall, near the chancel arch, a shallow C13 recess, decorated on its back wall with a masonry

pattern and traces of scrolls. What was it for? A sedile to a
nave altar? – WEST GALLERY. Probably of 1821. – FONT. A
plain but curious piece, circular bowl on an octagonal shaft
on a base consisting of a fat roll resting on four fins. C13, or
C15, or could it be of the 1660s? – PLATE. Cup, dated 1732.
The centre of Romney Marsh administration was at Dymchurch
and NEW HALL, immediately s of the church, contains the
Court Room of the Lords of the Level, with simple C18 seating and Royal Arms of 1739. The building was newly erected
in Lambarde's time, but nothing earlier than the C18 can now
be seen. Otherwise Dymchurch cannot offer much.
The single long street runs directly below the sea wall for
two-thirds of its length without once getting a glimpse of the
sea. At the s end are two MARTELLO TOWERS (a third is a
little further N), part of a whole series built in 1806 as gun-
posts against a possible Napoleonic invasion. On the other
side of the road, sporting a glazed belvedere, is the SILVER
WAVES HOLIDAY CAMP, in the commercial version
of the international style of the 1930s. The architect was
Edwin A. Jackson. It is gaunt enough in its present state of
neglect, but at least it does not indulge in any of the modernistic touches which were generally thought to give the style a
mass appeal. Everywhere in and around the town there has
been much recent bungalow building, all of it nondescript
except the lively skyline of SYCAMORE CLOSE, opposite the
church; by *David Bristow,* 1965.

EASTBRIDGE see NEWCHURCH

EAST FARLEIGH

7050

ST MARY. Norman tower (see one w window) with shingled
spire, aisled nave and chancel of *c.*1300, plus a s chapel (i.e.
the chapel 'newly built' in 1411?). Heavy-handed restoration
has left it all unattractive and unreliable. The nave arcades
were rebuilt in 1891 in an alien form and, even more alienly,
in Bath stone, by *J.L.Pearson.* The renewed tower arch, unmoulded on the simplest imposts, on the other hand, must
copy the Norman one. Perp chancel arch. The arch between
the s aisle and s chapel looks C14, on a corbel formed into half
a grimacing man; yet Petrie's drawing of 1806 shows no s
aisle; so arch and corbel must be reset. Reset too must be the
w window of the aisle, of *c.*1300, four lights with Y tracery
and three circles in the top parts. Large cusped ogee arch
over a recess in the s chapel; and another, with a depressed

arch and cusps doubled in depth, in the chancel. Two-storeyed Perp s porch. – PLATE. Cup, two Patens, and Flagon, 1796 by *R.H. & D.H.* – MONUMENT. Agnes Wilberforce † 1834, by *Samuel Joseph*. Relief of a heartbroken family by an urn raised on a high pedestal.

SCHOOL. An early work by *Butterfield*, 1846, and of ragstone, i.e. a local material, and without any polychromy yet. But already the school rises aggressively high, firmly pushing the church, behind and below it, into the background. Towards the road, a large jagged gable and a large geometrical window. Round the corner a similar smaller gable and on both floors lancets in threes. The modest MASTER'S HOUSE (1855 by *J.Clarke*) nestles up under its SW side. *The Ecclesiologist* praised the 'happy avoidance of any mere chapel effect', and commented: 'We fully expect to see a characteristic style arise for our church schools'. So it did, but, fortunately for children, one may feel, it was Street's style, e.g. Inkpen, which was imitated, and not this, which looks in fact surprisingly ecclesiastical.

BRIDGE over the river Medway. C14. Jervoise calls it the finest medieval bridge in South England. Ragstone, of five arches springing almost from water level, each having a pointed tunnel vault with four chamfered ribs. Bold triangular cutwaters. Altogether a powerful piece of functional design. Is the kink in the middle of the bridge also functionally desirable ?*

GALLANTS MANOR, ½ m. SW. Two blocks set corner-to-corner. That towards the road is timber-framed on a stone ground storey with the pointed arch of a blocked doorway in its S wall; the other is all of stone and inside it there are four pointed chamfered arches in line, arranged 1 + 2 + 1. They clearly led from screens passage to service wing. (Four doorways is one more than usual.) The house deserves more thorough investigation.

EAST MALLING 7050

ST JAMES. Quite a successful shape inside and out. Ragstone. It seems a complete Late Perp building, from the tall w tower to the battlemented and clerestoreyed chancel. Nave also with battlements and clerestory, and aisles that end well short of the w end. But this is to see only the trimmings. The tower

* NP suggests that it may just be that the bridge was begun from both banks simultaneously, to meet, not on a single axis, in the middle.

must once have had no buttresses. One Norman window N, and one (blocked) S. Early materials, tile and tufa, re-used in the chancel, but the blocked N and S windows all C14 or later. (The top-lighting of the chancel is cancelled out by the huge modern Perp-style E window.) The nave arcades agree in having an E arch and then two more W of a short piece of wall. Standard piers and responds, the moulding of the E ones early C14. So there must have been transepts at first, the S one lengthened into an aisle almost at once, the N only after a century or more. Original N transept N and E windows, a characteristic early C14 pattern, embellishing three sharply pointed arches under a segmental head. – FONT COVER. Early C16, with doors. Conical cap of pierced tracery. Also a pierced cresting repeating a pattern of birds fiercely attacking fruit that has a positively Viking spirit. – PANELLING of the sanctuary. Early C17. – STAINED GLASS. In the heads of the N aisle windows contemporary with the tracery. Coronation of the Virgin in the W window. – PLATE. Cup and Paten, 1609, by *F. G.*; Paten, 1706; Flagon and Almsdish, 1728. – MONUMENTS. Thomas Selby † 1479. Brass with 26 in. figures, she with a butterfly headdress. – Richard Adams † 1522. 25½ in. brass of a priest. – Richard Mannyng † 1611. Alabaster hanging monument, with a waist-length figure, as in a pulpit, his hand on a skull. – Thomas Twisden † 1683. Large tablet. – Jane Sympson † 1690. Large tablet, with a scrolly pediment, side-scrolls, and swags at the foot, a handsome pattern typical of the period (cf. e.g. tablets at Ditton and All Saints, Maidstone). – Jane Twisden and others. Large tablet. 1779 must be the significant death date. – Sir John Twisden † 1810. Hanging monument by *Thomas Assiter* of Maidstone, with a Baconian woman leaning upon an urn.

East Malling village still has its points. CHURCH STREET for instance, blocked at the end by yew trees and the church, but starting with a jumbly group that has caught up in it a half-timbered Wealden house. Half-way down, COURT LODGE, an early C18 hipped-roofed box, red and blue brick with a pedimented doorcase. The constricted HIGH STREET, unpicturesque (except to the traveller passing in the train), climbs southwards up an incline. On the l. the neat, white early C19 VICARAGE.

A population explosion is taking place elsewhere in the parish, and has brought with it two worthwhile schools: BLACKLANDS PRIMARY SCHOOL, Mill Street, by *E. T. Ashley-*

Smith, 1960 and 1964, and further N CLARE SECONDARY SCHOOL, off Beech Road, 1957 by *Read & McDermott.* The housing they serve could certainly be worse, but grows on the 'fill-up-the-next-field' principle which can only produce uneasy appendages to the old community. Worse still, here it is a park, Clare House park, that is being obliterated.

CLARE HOUSE, ¾ m. NW. A charming neo-classical villa built in 1793 for John Larking, banker and timber merchant, by *Michael Searles.* Two-storeyed, rendered a pinkish white. Windows cut into the walls without surrounds. Heavy projecting slate roofs. Yet the outline of the house is extremely lively. From the S one sees a five-bay box, bowing forward in the centre three bays, which are encircled by a one-storey colonnade of coupled Tuscan columns.* Behind, to l. and r., short wings ending polygonally. Above, a low dome on a drum like a concave-sided lozenge with chamfered corners, a complex shape produced by the chimneystacks hidden in it. The veranda that shades the rooms over the colonnade, not intended by Searles, clouds the pellucid geometrical design.

The elevation expresses the remarkable geometry of the plan, a circular central hall, with one big room leading off it in each direction, a circular library to the S, to the E the dining room, like an elongated octagon, and the drawing room, an oval, to the W. Entrance vestibule and a lobby fitted into the odd corners of the square. Delightful staircase in the hall, swinging up to a first-floor balcony. Wrought-iron balustrade. The decoration inside, as out, is reduced to the minimum, just palmette plaster friezes, and marble chimneypieces. The most remarkable of these is in the library, charcoal-coloured, with columns of a Soanian primitiveness. Bedrooms on the first floor the same size and shapes as the ground-floor rooms. The same plan in the cellars, the same in the attics. Office wing on the N side, later widened.

The house stands in the remains of a small but delightful park. It would be a tragedy if any more of it were lopped off. The whole point of a crisp white house like this is that it stands amid the natural verdure of trees and sloping pastures.

PARIS HOUSE, The Rocks, ¼ m. SE. A highly peculiar early C18 front, two-storeyed, of red brick.‡ Five bays between big

---

* Colonnades were a Searles speciality, as in his Paragons at Blackheath and New Kent Road.

‡ Described as newly done in an indenture of 1714, according to Mr W. G. Burton's information.

symmetrical ragstone chimneybreasts that project from the façade. Panelled parapet below, not in front of, a hipped roof. Brick round the corner to the l., stone to the r. Yet it seems all to have been built in one go.

At WELL STREET, a scattered hamlet ½ m. SW, THE BARRACKS, a sizeable C16 half-timbered house, not restored. Carved bargeboard on the gable at the r. end.

₆₀₄₀   EAST PECKHAM

ST MICHAEL. The village has moved away to the valley to be near the river Medway, 2 m. S, leaving the church on the hill at the edge of a wood. It does not grace its romantic setting, with a W tower smothered in Roman cement and the large, regular Perp S windows all mechanically renewed by *Clarke* c.1857 (PF). They light the S aisle and chapel that goes right to the E end, and was made yet brighter by Late Perp E and SE windows. Ragstone walling. Ragstone S porch, also Perp. But there is plenty of evidence left of earlier periods. One Norman window in the chancel. A lancet high on the N side of the tower. It was in the years before and after 1300 that the church expanded to its present size. Four-bay aisle arcade on round piers, with a chamfer and a hollow-chamfer arch moulding, and a hood-mould. A single building campaign produced it, yet the capitals are all slightly different. Chancel arch on corbels, and two-bay arcade to the chapel, with an octagonal pier and side-pieces to the responds, mouldings similar to those in the nave arcade, but a bolder, more undercut hood-mould. The tower arch belongs to the same period. Crown-post trusses on moulded tiebeams, in nave and aisle. Corbel in the N wall of the chancel, bearing the base of a statue that did not originally belong to it. Oak PEWS by *Clarke*, 1863. – STAINED GLASS. Two old canopy-tops in a S aisle window. E window of the S chapel by *O'Connor*, 1857 (TK). – MONUMENTS. Brass, c.1525, of a civilian and his wife. 16½ in. figures. – Several large tablets, typical of their various dates. – Elizabeth Goldinge † 1595. – Roger Twysden, 1611. – Elizabeth Twysden † 1655. Circular cartouche. – Twysden family, 1689. Double tablet, under an open pediment.

Rustic HEADSTONES in the churchyard, mostly of the C18.

HOLY TRINITY. The church of the village, built in 1842 by *Whichcord & Walker*. Nave and polygonal apse. Lancets. W buttressing mass and a bell-gable on it.

ROYDON HALL, ⅓ m. SE of St Michael's church. According to an inscription over the entrance doorway the house was built in 1535. It is roughly square, but the brickwork of the N (entrance) and E fronts is wholly of 1870, and so are all the windows. The latter have eliminated Sir William Twysden's sashes of c.1680. Some of his brickwork remains on the S front. That leaves only the W side to witness to the character of the C16 work. Brick laid in English bond. Two storeys rising to three: even, crowstepped gables, each with a small window in it, of brick with a brick mullion. Below the gables runs a string-course on moulded brick corbels consisting of tiny trefoiled arches. The sheer chimneybreasts upset the symmetry of the front and cut across two of the gables as they sprout into elaborate star-topped stacks. The N front does contain two old features. The deeply projecting central porch has a round-headed stone entrance arch, which can be little if anything earlier than 1600, flanked as it is by Tuscan half-columns on high bases carrying an entablature. Chimneybreast on the r. side of the porch, a most peculiar place; and another in the wall further r. Both have star-topped brick stacks.

Internally, nothing can be ascribed to the 1530s. Elizabethan panelling in the E room, and a chimneypiece with bunches of fruit on the lintel and a cartouche framed in strapwork. The NE room has fine walnut panelling. At the remodelling in 1870 a staircase was made to fill the centre of the house, on the site, doubtless, of a small internal courtyard.

Before the N front stand the lower parts of an entrance range, wholly of the C16 and wholly symmetrical. As in the house, brick with cut and moulded details. Low, four-centred archway in the centre, fat octagonal turrets at the ends. In between, on each side a triangular projection and a polygonal one taking a fireplace. So although now no more than a wall exists between the turrets, there was originally a range of rooms here. Walls return to the house E and W, perhaps not the original arrangement.

C16 garden TERRACES E of the house, that at the highest level enclosed by the original brick walls. The back wall ends N and S in octagonal turrets, the S turret enlarged by a polygonal appendage into a sort of lodge-like summer house.

LITTLE ROYDON. Square, hipped-roofed house of c.1700. N front six bays wide, the others irregular.

At HALE STREET, 1¼ m. SE, an unrestored half-timbered Wealden house. Two-centred doorway.

BOURNE PLACE, Barnes Street, 2¾ m. SW. The big T-shaped house is probably late, see the spindly timbers. Yet the three-light windows on the W side have arched lights, unlikely after the middle of the C16. Vast chimneybreast here, stone below, brick higher up.

EAST SUTTON

ST PETER AND ST PAUL. The church lies beside and slightly below the road, presenting the unrestored N windows in close-up. Perp three-lighters in the N aisle. The N chapel has a steep roof, higher than the aisle, and Dec tracery of remarkable elaboration. N window and E window, each of three cusped and subcusped lights. The former is segment-headed, and the core of the complex design is three hollow-sided lozenges with long points springing from the lights. The other has a two-centred head in which daggers and quatrefoils are evenly distributed round five-pointed stars. Chancel E window designed in 1897 and in seventy years surprisingly decayed. Externally, there was much remodelling in the C15 and C16. S chapel with Late Perp windows. Early Perp S aisle windows. S porch. Perp W tower built in one with the N aisle wall. It has diagonal but-tresses and an octagonal S turret. But the arcades affirm that the church essentially belongs to the early C14. Octagonal piers. Arches doubly hollow-chamfered. No chancel arch, but W arches to the chapels. The two-bay arcade from N chapel to chancel more refined than the rest, the S chapel arcades crudely remodelled. The aisle arcades not quite a match. Crown-post roof trusses on pierced spandrels. Inside, the restorer in 1897 stopped just too soon. The scraped, unplastered walls confuse the eye. – FONT. Hexagonal bowl on seven shafts. A trefoiled arch sunk on each face. A late C13 piece, presumably. – TOWER SCREEN. Perp pieces re-used. – PULPIT. Early C17. A panel of birds in branches repeats each side. – STAINED GLASS. Hotch-potch of C14 and C15 bits and some armorial glass in the S chapel. – PLATE. Cup, 1562 by *I.S.*; Flagon, 1630 by *W.C.*; Pair of Almsdishes, 1766 by *Parker & Wakelin*; Cup inscribed 1817. – MONUMENTS. Robert Filmer † 1585. Plain tomb-chest with Ionic columns flanking the back plate. Skull below the inscription, obelisks above the columns. – Argall family, c.1605. Tablet. – Edmund Randolph † 1609. Hanging monument. Kneeling figures in the usual alabaster architectural frame. Above their heads, clasping hands reach out from clouds. – Sir Edward Filmer † 1629.

Brass plate nearly 7 ft long. On it are engraved, with considerable finesse, the figures of Sir Edward and his wife, and in the panel at the bottom their nine sons and nine daughters. Is *Edward Marshall*, who signs the brass, the well-known sculptor? It is not otherwise recorded that he worked as an engraver. – Sir Robert Filmer † 1720. Lively cartouche. – Sir Edward Filmer † 1755. Tablet, and upon it a bust of a togaed man. – Beversham Filmer † 1763. Baroque tablet. – Dorothea Filmer † 1793. Large, refined tablet with urns, signed by *John Golden*. – Sir John Filmer † 1797. Large, refined tablet, with an urn and an obelisk. – Rev. Sir John Filmer † 1834. Grecian hanging wall-monument, with figures of Faith, Hope, and Charity in high relief. Signed by *Ternouth*. – Sir Edward Filmer † 1857. Hanging monument with a relief. Draped Grecian figures like Ternouth's, but significantly the symbolism has become Christian, with hovering angels and rays of light falling on an open Bible.

EAST SUTTON PARK. Rambling red-brick mansion, added to at various times by successive generations of Filmers. What Sir Edward found when he bought the estate in 1610 was an H-shaped brick house, two-storeyed with gables. The hall screen bears the inlaid date 1570. The S front is of this date. Original gables on the wings, with moulded brick finials. The tight-packed centre, one bay either side of a projecting, two-storeyed porch, has C19 gables and a C19 Tudor-style doorway. Deep, moulded string-course. Early C17 rainwater-heads. Are the windows, with a transom and one or two mullions, a C19 restoration? The NW corner of the W wing appears beyond an C18 bay, but this is all, for in the mid C19 *C.J. Richardson* extended the house northwards,* and threw out a long service wing to the E. He remodelled the interior drastically too. Apart from the screen, with giant pilasters, only the hall overmantel is old.

A brick block, six bays by one, runs S from the SE corner of the old house. It is clearly contemporary with the house of 1570, and has three W gables with moulded finials, and intermediate gablets. Windows sashed in the C18. Was a similar wing intended, answering this to the W? The U-plan that would then have resulted would not have been the normal Elizabethan plan, e.g. of Wimbledon, for the ranges would touch only corner to corner.

---

* His designs, undated, are in the R.I.B.A.

Further s, a ragstone OFFICE BLOCK of similar proportions. No original window. Plainer gables. But again it belongs to the late C16. *Richardson*'s service courtyard incorporated both buildings on its w side. At the SE corner of the courtyard a Prospect Tower by Richardson, commanding a splendid view of the Weald.

Crazy LODGE, ¼ m. w of the church, doubtless *Richardson*'s too.

51 CHARLTON COURT, ⅓ m. SE. An interesting fragment of a house dated 1612 in the E gable.* Brick laid in English bond, with rendered dressings. Two-storeyed, with shaped gables, three on the s front, and one returning round the corner at each end. These are the most elaborate, rising by two waves separated by a step. Under each gable a bay projects, alternately triangular and polygonal. The unusual plan this produces closely resembles one of *John Thorpe*'s designs (as Sir John Summerson has pointed out) for a roughly square house. One must imagine, then, a second and third gable intended on the w and E fronts. Peculiar nook-shafts at the angles of the bays. Deep moulded string-courses. Windows of one, two, or three lights, with a transom, placed to conform to the symmetry of the s front. Rendered strapwork round the w gable. C19 NW porch. Various recent additions. Internally, the ground-floor plan consists of a w room and an E room with a C19 staircase occupying the centre third. Each room has an arcaded frieze, and plaster strapwork on the ceiling of the window-bay. Doors carved with typical early C17 figures of Faith, Hope, and Charity.

Contemporary brick STABLES, NE of the house. Modern gabled dormers.

4070

EAST WICKHAM

ST MICHAEL. Nave and chancel without any structural division. The two N lancets are genuine evidence, those on the s are not. Traces of the three E lancets inside. The w end was rebuilt in the early C19. w spirelet on the roof-ridge, 1897. – FONT. Dec. Hexagonal. Two ogee-ended quatrefoils on each face. – PULPIT. Jacobean. – WALL PAINTINGS. At the s end

* Hasted ascribed it to the period before 1585, but the style of the building makes this improbable. Sir Edward Filmer, on buying East Sutton Park, kept Charlton, which he already owned. Presumably he had begun his house before 1610, and hesitated for a year or two before deciding to abandon the new work and make East Sutton, on its loftier site, his main seat.

of the E wall, two large figures under arcading, C13. – A large figure of St Michael (N wall). This looks cruder work. – TILES. Three with patterns set in the altar step. – BRASSES. John de Bladigdone, c.1325. Charming and unusual, two tiny prim half-effigies in a frame of eight ogee lobes with finials. On the shaft his name in large letters. The date 1325 on the base is modern. The Arabic, not Roman, numerals show that. Total length: 44½ in. – William Payn † 1568. He wears the uniform of a Yeoman of the Guard. 12½ in. figures.

ECCLES *see* AYLESFORD

EDENBRIDGE 4040

ST PETER AND ST PAUL. Sandstone. The W tower is E.E., as the trefoiled lancets to N and S suggest, propped up later with vast diagonal buttresses. C13 evidence elsewhere – several renewed lancets, on the S side a quatrefoil over two trefoiled lights (i.e. embryonic tracery of the late C13), and fragments in the porch including one bit with stiff-leaf and another with small upright leaves. The interior does not immediately make the history plain either. Nave and chancel with a wide S aisle continued as a S chapel. The half-round arcade responds are C13, and probably early in the century. But the three piers of the arcade are octagonal, and their mouldings and the hollow-chamfered arches date them in the C14. Furthermore the piers have been heightened, and so has the S wall of the aisle. The chancel is clearly of the C14 – see the chancel arch and the N windows. (The bizarre E window was done in 1908. The architect misunderstood an old drawing.) In 1499 the S chapel was rebuilt to house the tomb of Richard Martyn. The piers again octagonal but characteristically Perp, and handsome too. C15 roof corbels in the nave and S aisle carved as angels, dragons, and so on. – PILLAR PISCINA, in the S chapel. With square Dec leaves, so later than most pillar piscinas. – FONT. Stone, but the Purbeck marble type. Square arcaded bowl on five shafts. C13. – FONT COVER. Ogee-shaped, with crockets up the ribs. – PULPIT. Eared panels in two tiers. Fanciful tapering balusters at the angles. Such motifs suggest it was made c.1630–40. – STAINED GLASS. Fragments in a chancel N window. – PLATE. Cup, 1670; Paten Cover, 1670 by *I.W.* – MONUMENTS. Of Richard Martyn's tomb (*see* above) only one end remains. – John Selyard † 1558. Small brass of a civilian. – William Seilyard † 1595. Small hanging monument, with typical kneeling figure before a prayer desk. – Nicholas Seyliard † 1625. Tablet decorated with alabaster knobs and an obelisk on top.

The church lies back E of the long main street, just at its narrowest and most rewarding point. Everything worth mention comes between the overhead sign of the Crown Hotel and the bridge over the river Eden. Beginning at the N, opposite the Crown Hotel, TAYLOR HOUSE, timber-framed, much pulled about. On the door the arms in the spandrel are of Sir William Taylour, Lord Mayor of London in 1469. An upper room has unusually much wall-painting. On one wall big scrolly arabesques of foliage, on another the arms of James I and part of the scene of Judith and Holofernes. Datable c.1610–20, and in the same sort of spirit as Thomas Toft's pottery. Staircase early C17 also, with flat shaped balusters. Three more houses with exposed timbers beyond on the w side: Nos 86–90 HIGH STREET has two early C17 gables; the TANYARD HOUSE and the house beyond are no later than the C15; a gabled cross-wing to the former, a weatherboarded cross-wing to the latter. The uprights on both houses still quite widely spaced. Behind Tanyard House a late C19 tanning shed, open below on brick piers. The walls of the drying rooms above are weatherboarded, with movable louvres: a good piece of industrial design. And so to the BRIDGE, dated 1836. Sandstone, of one wide arch. Rounded corner piers.

Much housing to the w of the High Street, all of it suburban in character except the L.C.C.'s STANGROVE PARK ESTATE, 1959–61 by the *L.C.C. Architect's Department*, under *Hubert Bennett*, where the long rows of two-storey cottages, wholly weatherboarded or wholly tile-hung, perfectly catch the Home Counties small-town feel.

GABRIELS MANOR, 1 m. W of S. A splendid C16 house. Three symmetrical gables to the E. Strongly asymmetrical S side, a big brick chimneybreast played off against a big timbered gable-end. Reconstruction after a fire in the 1930s was fairly faithful but made the most of the piquant contrasts.

DELAWARE, 1 m. E. Tall, tile-hung front. The door has a late C17 shell hood on richly carved brackets.

EGERTON

ST JAMES. The church was completely rebuilt in Dec times, chancel and nave, N chapel in one with the N aisle. Ragstone, unsympathetically handled by *Clarke* in 1854. Two-light N and s windows. Reticulated E window in the chapel, chancel E window wholly renewed. Outside they stand on a sharp string-course, within they are shafted. A lancet reset high in the s nave wall, over a lowside window, is the only intruder. Arcade of standard form, the chapel arch coarser than those to the aisle. Chancel arch of two hollow chamfers dying into the imposts. The massive W tower was building in the 1460s and 70s. Bequest to the 'new steeple' 1468, and for glazing and paving 1476. It is on the usual Kentish pattern, of three stages, with a NE turret. The buttresses however reach unusually high, via many set-offs, so that the tower looks unhappily cramped at the top. Fine four-light W window, the tracery with a transom, identical with the tower window at Charing near by. Tall and wide tower arch, set on steps, and with a stone bench N and S. Thus the present arrangement as a baptistery is the original one. PISCINA and triple SEDILIA, contemporary features of the chancel. Crown-post nave roof. – FONT. c.1476. Buttressed stem. Bowl on four demi-angels. On the eight sides, the Symbols of the Evangelists and roses alternately. Not well carved. – CHANDELIER. Early C18. Brass. Three tiers of branches. – ALTAR RAILS. 1958, by *Arthur Ayres*. Supported on kneeling figures of saints, successfully stylized. – PLATE. Cup and Paten Cover, 1562; Almsdish, 1683 by *E.M.*; Spoon, 1781 (?).

THE BEDEWELL, ⅝ m. W. C15 half-timbered house, with bold, curved braces. Mutilated two-centred doorway.

LINK FARM, ¾ m. SW. Finely preserved Wealden half-timbered house. The original arrangement of two-bay hall between two-storeyed jettied wings, with a doorway r. of the hall into the screens passage, disturbed only by the two-storeyed window, put in when the hall was halved in height late in the C16.

OLD HARROW FARM, 1 m. SW. Half-timbered, with an overhang all along the E front. Oriel windows on brackets above; bay windows on brick footings below. They are arranged to balance each other – in the way favoured after 1600 rather than before.

ELMERS END *see* BECKENHAM, p. 142

ERITH

ST JOHN THE BAPTIST. Largish, lowish, and not very attractive inside or out. In a heavy and silly restoration of 1877 by

Habershon & Pite, the s porch and N chapel and aisle were added, with a blocked N doorway and a lancet among Perp windows to deceive the unwary. Flint and stone walling reshuffled, all windows renewed, w tower largely rebuilt. The s doorway is C13, with a Purbeck marble shaft each side with narrow leaves up the waterleafy capitals. Trefoiled leaves on the stops of the hood-mould. Old, perhaps contemporary, s door, with two fine hinges. The doorway goes with the C13 s arcade, of three short round piers and double-chamfered arches. The SE quoin of an aisleless Norman nave has been incorporated in the jamb of an arch in the s chapel. The chancel itself shows quite a lot of its Norman features inside. It was unusually long and arcaded low down on the E wall (part of the s arch remains), and this arcading continued with one arch each on the N and s walls. One and a bit Norman windows to N and s. Traces of a doorway in the NW corner. Wide C13 arches into N and s chapels. Blocked clerestory windows on the N side. Loose scalloped capital in the s chapel. The w tower has clasping buttresses, which suggests a C13 date at the latest. It is not bonded into the nave w wall. – SUNDIAL. Outside, on a s buttress. Only interesting as being the gift of a certain Nicholas Stone in 1643. There is no real reason to suppose that this was Nicholas Stone the sculptor. – STAINED GLASS. E window of the s chapel by *Kempe*, 1905. – PLATE. Flagon, inscribed 1737. – BRASSES. Roger Sencler † 1425. 15 in. figure of a civilian. – John Ailemer † 1435. Civilian and his wife. Fine 33½ in. figures. – Emma Wode † 1471. Tall, thin figure in a peaked headdress. 26½ in. long. – John Mylner † 1511. 16 in. brasses. – Edward Hawte † 1537. Armoured 14½ in. figure. – Inscription to Anne Harman † 1574, palimpsest on a fragment of a Flemish brass of *c*.1500. – MONUMENTS. Elizabeth, Countess of Shrewsbury, † 1568. Recumbent effigy, still on a tomb-chest. Her head pillow lies on a half-rolled-up straw mat – a Netherlandish motif. The details of the tomb however are classical: Doric columns at the four corners and strapwork-enframed heraldic lozenges set in fine deep egg-and-dart borders. Well carved altogether. It might almost be in Westminster Abbey. – Francis Vanacker † 1686. In two parts. The inscription is on a small but lively cartouche. Below it a tomb-chest, with a plain black marble slab on top. The sides of the tomb are exceptionally finely carved with a laurel-wreath, bold drops of flowers and fruit, and, on the short end, the heads of three putti among clouds. – Lord Eardley and brother. By

the Norman stones re-used in the chamfered imposts. Two blocked N arches to the chancel, with C13 mouldings, and the shafted lancets from the demolished chapel reset in them. Trefoiled double PISCINA on shafts. C14 chancel arch. Arch to the transept of c.1200. The imposts have keeled angleshafts, the arch a slight chamfer. The N aisle is a very crude piece of work. Original arched brace roofs on enjoyable head corbels. – FONT. Perp. – ROYAL ARMS of George III. Recently restored.

Across the road from the church, a pretty stone BRIDGE, over the river Darent, believed by Jervoise to be no older than the C17. Beyond it, a favourite picture-postcard group, the white PLOUGH INN, the half-timbering exposed at the near end, to show C16 close-studding, with one concave-sided lozenge in the gable and a frilly bargeboard. Beyond again is a nice continuous-jetty house.

CASTLE, ¼ m. E of N. The high, featureless wall, built of flints, unknapped but laid carefully in courses, that faces the visitor approaching from the SW, continues, complete almost to the top, round an irregular polygon, c.200 ft across its longest dimension. Only a piece on the NW side has tumbled. It is the defensive boundary wall of an unusually wide, low, and flat motte, built c.1100. Mr Rigold's recent excavation showed that a timber watch-tower stood in the centre of the motte. Against the W stretch of wall marks of lean-to timber buildings. Evidence that these were not outbuildings, but for living, is the three garderobes in the SW corner, one of them the present entrance. These are dressed with tufa, a characteristic Early Norman building material. The bailey lay E of the motte. Nowhere in England is there a more complete example of a pre-keep castle.

In the first half of the C12 a characteristic stone HALL-HOUSE was built on the NE half of the motte. The undercroft of hall and solar remain, the former carried on two square piers. Four windows in a row lit the hall from its S end. Forebuilding on the W side and the beginning of the long flight of steps to it. Again the material is flint, but the quoins and arches are of re-used Roman tiles. Also in the C12 the curtain wall was raised in the NE corner and thickened to take an upper room; the main entrance, on the S side, improved with a bridge and an inner gate-tower, survives only in its foundations. Foundations only too of the large kitchen against the NW corner of the curtain wall.

FAIRFIELD

St Thomas a Becket. The diminutive, dumpy church set down pat on the marshes is a sweet sight. Red and blue brick walls, steep red-tiled roofs beautifully lichened. Low chancel, short nave with a shingled w bellcote. Square casement windows. Inside, the massive crown-post roofs are overwhelming, the chancel tiebeams only 7 ft from the ground. The church was entirely timber-framed, later cased in brick. It is not easy to feel confident of the date of the building. The proportions are Norman rather than anything else, the structure typically late medieval. A timber church existed in 1294, when it was reported to be in poor condition. In 1913 *W.D.Caröe* completely reconstructed the church and renewed most of the timbers.* But although he spoilt the texture of the interior, he preserved the FITTINGS. – PULPIT. A plain c18 three-decker, with BOX PEWS *en suite*. – FONT. Plain, heptagonal. Possibly Perp, or possibly of the 1660s.

FAIRLAWNE
¾ m. N of Shipbourne

A plain, and rather puzzling house. From the road the main block of ragstone, two-storeyed, nine windows wide, with windows in thick white surrounds and a porte-cochère of pairs of Tuscan columns, looks like work of the 1840s rather than anything else. But the three-storeyed extension on the l. is clearly c18, and so is the big off-centre belfry and cupola. Furthermore, the main front is obviously the same as Kip engraved in 1719, with a new stone cornice. The cornice carries on round the s and e fronts, which are both of brick. The s front has a centre pediment resting on the cornice. (The interior is all altered, but the plan, of rooms round a staircase well, suggests that originally there was a courtyard house. The GREAT ROOM however, to the e, was designed by *Gibbs*. The painted ceiling‡ is gone, but not the carved woodwork, pedimented doorcases on Ionic half-columns, with Gibbonsian swags above, and wall panels of small-scale, flat relief carving more French in style than English.)

FAIRSEAT *see* STANSTED

---

* Revealing photographs of work in progress are at the back of the church.
‡ For which the design survives in the Gibbs Collection at the Ashmolean Museum.

FALCONHURST *see* MARKBEECH

FARNBOROUGH
4060

The village is almost submerged by oncoming suburbia. But the church to the S on the hill among larches is still at the edge of open country.

ST GILES THE ABBOT. In 1641 a brief was granted for rebuilding the church after a storm. The nave, flint with big, square two-light windows with red-brick mullions, is of that date. W tower 1838: flint and yellow brick. Chancel 1886 by *Joseph Clarke*: flint and Bath stone. Polygonal NW vestry. The odd N projection must be a bit of the pre-storm church. The nave roof, of 1641, still has the traditional crown-posts, only slightly modified. – FONT. Octagonal. Simple geometrical designs and panelling on the bowl. Probably C14. – ORGAN CASE. *c.*1960. Pretty. High among the rafters above the W gallery. – BRONZE PLAQUE. Christ and the Apostles. Sombre Epsteinish faces. By *Elsie March*, 1939. – MONUMENT. Thomas Brome † 1673. Large architectural tablet signed by *Jasper Latham*.

HIGH ELMS, ½ m. SE. Built in 1840 for Sir J. W. Lubbock.* Not a small house, and the service wing extending to the E, of a size considered desirable in the 1840s, by no means small either. Yet it is a stuccoed villa, still treated with Regency precision. Three storeys under a shallow slate roof. The ground floor of the five-bay entrance (N) front projects, and across it are placed eight unfluted Greek Doric columns in antis, in a rhythm 1–1–2–2–1–1. Paterae over the columns in a deep, plain frieze. On the W front the centre three bays come forward in a one-storey bow. (The service wing stuccoed too.) Splendid trees in the park.

The stables are ¼ m. to the SW, in High Elms Road, and now called THE CLOCK HOUSE, because of the domed clock set high above the roofs on white posts. A pretty, informal group. The octagonal, white-weatherboarded garden building behind was built *c.*1850 to house a donkey-pump with a water-tank above.

FARNINGHAM
5060

ST PETER AND ST PAUL. Flint. C13 chancel and nave, C15 W tower. The tower a well-proportioned example of the Kentish type. Three stages. Diagonal buttresses. Octagonal NE turret.

---

* As Mr Eric Lubbock M.P. kindly informs me. Since this was written the house has been burnt down.

Four-centred tower arch with colossal mouldings. The rest is largely renewed outside: brick buttresses of 1790; E window of 1830 by *John Shaw*; all other windows, SE chapel, and N porch, 1868–71 by *Christian*. The C13 work then is best appreciated inside, especially the unusual E end of the nave, where the chancel arch has a blank arch each side, and a little lancet set within. Slight chamfers the only mouldings. In the chancel, three N lancets and one S, on a string-course. C13 keeled roll round the E window. Double PISCINA, shafted. RECESS in the SE corner of the nave, late C13, with big, plain, pierced cusps. At the W end of the same wall pieces of Norman voussoirs and a fragment of a COFFIN SLAB with a fine C13 foliated cross. – FONT. Perp. Octagonal. The faces of the bowl carved with the seven sacraments, as on many East Anglian fonts but hardly on any others. In Marriage the bride wears a headdress typical of the third quarter of the C15. – STAINED GLASS. NE nave window 1832, composed, partly of old pieces, by *Charles Winston*, son of the incumbent, and the man who first revived interest in medieval stained glass in C19 England. – Nave E window a C15-style archbishop by *Winston* copied from his exquisite drawing of Simon de Mepham, then in the E window of Meopham church. – E window 1843 by *Thomas Ward*. Far less scholarly and discriminating in its allegiance to a medieval style. – PLATE. Cup, 1595; Paten Cover, 1702; Paten, 1706. – MONUMENTS. William Gysborne † 1451. Brass, 12 in. long, demi-figure of a priest. – Alys Taillor † 1514. Very poor 13 in. brass. – William Petham † 1517. Brass of a kneeling civilian. 14 in. – Thomas Sibill † 1519. 17½ in. brass. – Anthony Rooper. The usual hanging monument of *c*.1600, with kneeling figures under arches, side columns, entablature and three cartouches of arms at the top. – William Hanger † 1751. Handsome hanging monument, with an urn, a broad obelisk, and nice trails of oak-leaves round the coat of arms. Signed by *Joseph Pickford*.

In the churchyard, SE of the church, MAUSOLEUM of Thomas Nash † 1778, begun before and completed after his death. Portland ashlar. A cube with side pieces, and an obelisk on the low stone dome. Rusticated quoins and frostwork on the lintel of the door. The other decoration is very sparing and exquisite. Nash's nephew and legatee was John Nash the architect. Stylistically it is quite possible that *John Nash* designed the mausoleum.

Farningham was in the C18 a stopping-place on the main Lon-

don to Dover road. The present A20 bypasses it. The result
is a handsome, almost entirely C18 village with a number of
grand houses. The church stands about half-way down the
street, with a long stone barn opposite. Further SE nothing to
look for specially, as only FARNINGHAM HOUSE, early C18,
has not been tampered with. To the NW a high wall on the l.,
hiding an C18 house with a nice forecourt and stables, and a
pasture on the r. as far as the river Darent. The best things
are over the river, and the Lion Hotel holds the centre of the
stage. Modest BRIDGE, of three low, yellow-brick arches,
1773 by *Edward Grey*, widened by *Whichcord* in 1833. N of
it a curious ornamental screen like a second bridge. Three
segmental arches, red brick with flint rustication, the heavy
humour of an C18 local mason, cf. cottages in Shoreham,
further down the valley. The LION HOTEL is a superb late
C18 coaching inn, with a red-brick front to the river, five
windows wide, three storeys high, the top one above the cornice. Balcony across the centre three bays, and under it windows in round-headed surrounds either side of the doorway.
Metal canopy to this like a croquet-hoop. The l. bay breaks
the scheme with a big upper bow-window under a Chinesey
metal hood. Close up to the road on the other side, an early
C19 Gothic cottage and a plastered half-timbered house with
a big curved corner upright. These flank the entrance to the
yard of the delightful MILL, a three-bay C18 house at its r.
end.* Beyond the Lion Hotel, WHITE HOUSE, built 'some few
years' before Hasted's edition of 1797. White picked out with
plenty of black. Square, three-storeyed, with a heavy top cornice and made as grand as possible by window-bays up the full
height of the W front, and nothing but Venetian windows on
the N and S. Simple-minded but successful. Thereafter cottages climb up on both sides of the little street, until SPARE-
PENNY LANE turns off to the l. Here THE MOUNT, *c.*1820,
yellow brick of course, and MOUNT PLEASANT, *c.*1720, red
brick of course; both perfect in their modest ways.

FAWKHAM

ST MARY. Small and pretty among trees, especially pretty
now that the walls are rendered grey and the stonework of the
windows whitewashed.‡ W spike on a white bellcote perched

---

* Mr Gravett notes that the chimneystacks are of grey brick towards the
road, red brick at the sides; a neat proof that grey were the expensive ones.
‡ Nave restored in 1959 by *Pamela Cunnington*.

on the roof ridge. Timber s porch. Norman windows, or traces of them, in the chancel N wall and in nave N and s walls. Various Dec insertions, but no additions to the Norman church. The interior is equally neat and humble, the walls and roofs whitewashed. C14 cusped arch in the s wall of the nave; another earlier one in the chancel N wall. The chancel arch has gone. The W bellcote supports are just four posts braced at the top, with pierced spandrels within the braces. – DOUBLE PISCINA. C14. Treated like a two-light window, with cusped Y-tracery. – WALL PAINTING. Figure of Christ in Majesty, in an almond-shaped frame, C13 and originally of high quality though faded now to a haunting pinkish blur. – STAINED GLASS. Several medieval fragments in the chancel (s window), including a C14 piece with St Anne teaching the Virgin to read. – MONUMENT. John Walter † 1625. Hanging monument. The usual kneeling figures, quite well carved.

SCUDDERS, ¾ m. SW. Timber-framed. The long plastered front to the road is decorated with sunk geometrical patterns; an embellishment probably of the C17.

FIELD GREEN HOUSE see SANDHURST

FILSTON HALL see SHOREHAM

7030

FINCHCOCKS
1¾ m. SW of Goudhurst

Edward Bathurst came into his inheritance in 1718. The house that was built for him, dated 1725 on the rainwater-heads, is the most notable Baroque house in the county; which is a way of saying that no Baroque house of the first rank can be found in Kent. For Finchcocks represents the moment when the country-house style of Vanbrugh and Archer was slipping down the scale into the hands of local master builders. One admires the bold conception almost interpreted with success, the panache with which a relatively small house is made to look grand, but one does not find intellectual subtlety or real drama. The house is executed in red brick, with brighter red dressings and darker red chimneys and parapets, a background enlivened with telling touches of white.

The entrance front faces E, a three-storeyed main block, seven windows wide, the third storey above a cornice, with two-storeyed wings which descend yet lower at the sides to curved pieces of wall. The crescendo towards the centre is the essence of the composition, but one which is hard to appreciate when, following the present drive, one approaches the façade obliquely. The centre block has the three middle bays differentiated from the rest. They break forward a little, with round-headed, not segmental windows, a peculiarly illogical pediment resting on the cornice and filled with martial trophies, and, in the wall above it, two round windows. The main chimneystacks continue the verticals. Plain, broad Tuscan doorcase on half-columns. Above it, a rubbed brick niche, intended originally to be decoration enough in itself, but now filled with a mutilated statue of Queen Anne from the Royal Exchange. The angles of the main block have stubby Tuscan pilasters, with pieces of white triglyph entablature upon them, continued above the cornice as pilaster strips and so to the deeply modelled brick parapet. The pilasters are the linking motif with the wings, standing forward of the main block and attached by convex quadrants of wall. The pilasters, entablature-chunks, and continuous cornice repeat in the wings, but lower, so that the cornice reaches only to the capitals of the main block pilasters, and the wing parapets are as high as the main block entablature. This is ingenious, but leaves the levels of the brick string-courses lower down unresolved. From N, W, and S the main block is revealed as to all intents the whole house. It is three bays deep and has end chimneystacks arched in a rather timid version of a Vanbrughian motif. The W front, of chequered brick, is basically the same as the E, minus the pediment and pilasters, and with a more emphatic parapet, which increases the cliff-like effect. The doorcase is a slightly simplified version of that on the E front, reflecting the fact that the hall runs the depth of the house. In the hall an exceedingly large fireplace (a C16 one incorporated in the new house?), with as an overmantel a large painting of Bathurst and his family by *James Maubart*. The staircase, with three turned balusters per tread, runs up from the NW corner of the hall and leads to a spacious upper landing with a fireplace.

C18 STABLES, NW of the house, of red brick, with lunette windows in the upper storey, the central one incorporated in the carriage-entrance.

FINCHDEN MANOR *see* TENTERDEN

FOOTS CRAY

4070

ALL SAINTS. By itself and oddly lonely among the unkempt meadows, considering that the factories of the Sidcup by-pass are a short half-mile away. The church is virtually a new building by *Hakewill c.*1863, though in lengthening the nave he went out of his way to keep the W spirelet, so that it now appears as a flèche. The timber W porch copies what was there before. One lancet in the chancel is old evidence, and two Perp windows in the nave are old. Also medieval the single exceedingly wide arch to the N aisle. – FONT. Purbeck marble, a good example of a common type. Square arcaded bowl, the sides slightly tapering. Four corner shafts with waterleaf capitals. Waterleaf is a motif of *c.*1190. – GATE to the rood-loft stairs, dated 1638. Made up from the altar rails, no doubt. – PAINTINGS. Two large, round-headed panels of Moses and Aaron, done with a good deal of panache. They will have been part of an altarpiece of *c.*1700. – PLATE. Paten and Flagon dated 1705. – MONUMENT. Reclining effigy of a lady under a brick arch in the N aisle. Her costume is of the mid C14. Much worn down, but the carving must originally have been of good quality. Long folds falling unbroken to her feet. Headless angel to support her pillows. The loose head of a chain-mailed knight thrown in to keep her company.

FOOTS CRAY PLACE was burnt down in 1950. It was the latest of the four English Villa Rotondas, built *c.*1756 for Bourchier Cleeve, not so much in imitation of Palladio as to outdo his friend, Lord Westmorland, at Mereworth.

CHURCH ROAD leads S from the church. At the S end, by the crossroads, the remains of the village: THE OLD HOUSE, early C19; and Nos 4–8, an upstanding row of early C18 cottages. Three storeys. Red brick. Moulded wood cornice, the sort banned by the Act of 1709.

5040

FORDCOMBE

ST PETER. 1847. Architect unknown. This is a pity, for outside there is, for that date, a lavish show of shafted lancets and dogtooth, e.g. all round the E triplet. Fine sandstone ashlar. Nave and chancel almost in one. Bell-gable standing in the chancel arch. Tall, stone-vaulted S porch, and an odd shallow N recess facing it. The interior is high, but wide as well, and in view of the exterior, rather plain. High, single-framed roof in six cants. 'A nobleman's very decent chapel. Lord Hardinge paid for most of it' (GR).

Lord Hardinge's seat was South Park, Penshurst, and it was no doubt through his concern that the separate village of Fordcombe grew up in the S of the parish. The agreeable group round a sloping green above the church is entirely of the C19. Sandstone, brick, tile-hanging, half-timbered gables.

SPRINGHILL, ⅓ m. NW, down the hill. To the l. a two-storey range, wholly tile-hung on a sandstone basement but timber-framed underneath. To the r., deliberately rising much higher, a gabled bay, projecting forward twice. Under each projection an oriel on carved brackets, one plus five plus one lights with a transom. On the upper one the date 1622. The bargeboard carved but not shaped. This is the sort of thing that inspired Norman Shaw's early style.

FORD PLACE see WROTHAM

FOUR ELMS

4040

ST PAUL. 1880 by *E. T. Hall* (GR). Sandstone treated crazy-paving-wise. Lancets. Apsidal w baptistery. – REREDOS. A noble white marble relief of the Adoration of the Magi, designed by *Lethaby* and executed by *Stirling Lee* and *Henry Pegram*.* – CHANCEL SCREEN and CHOIR STALLS. 1915 by *Lethaby*. – ORGAN CASE by *F. C. Eden*, 1923.

FOUR THROWS see HAWKHURST

FOUR WENTS see HAWKHURST

FRANKS see HORTON KIRBY

FRENCH HOUSE see LYMPNE

THE FRIARS see AYLESFORD

FRINDSBURY

7060

ALL SAINTS. Quite a sizeable Norman chancel, of flint. Original chancel arch, with renewed abaci. C14 w tower, of flint banded a little in stone at the bottom. No buttresses. Recessed shingled spire. Bold tower arch on octagonal

* The Rev. A. R. Penn kindly supplied these facts.

responds. Nave s arcade of three bays, piers octagonal, arches moulded with two hollow chamfers, by the details later than the tower. All the window tracery went in a restoration of 1824, so *Pearson*'s re-restoration of 1883 had no guidance. He added the N aisle, characteristically making the arcade an improved version of its fellow. The E wheel-window is by Pearson too, and the squints beside the chancel arch. – FONT. Perp. – CHANDELIER. Brass. Dated 1747. – WALL PAINTINGS. The figures on the splays of the Norman windows, found in 1883 and dated by Hope to *c.*1260, have now almost totally vanished. – ROYAL ARMS. Wood relief carved with ham-fisted gusto. – MONUMENTS. Thomas Butler † 1621. Plain tomb-chest with grotesque, un-classical angle shafts, and an inscription frame of wood like an overmantel. – William Watson, 1673. Alabaster tablet, with a scrolly pediment. – George Gunning † 1821. Signed by *J. Bacon Jun.* Hanging monument with a prostrate woman before a sepulchre. – Sarah Lady Staines † 1832. Signed by *S. Manning.* Hanging monument, with a prostrate woman, and a willow weeping over a monument. How tedious these hackneyed lamentations do become!

MANOR HOUSE, ¼ m. NE. Three-storeyed, red-brick C18 house, with lower wings. Behind it, an aisled BARN of spectacular length, over 210 ft, longer than any other entirely roofed barn in England. Twelve crown-post and tiebeam trusses. The walls retain their original upright weatherboarding. Mr Rigold dates the barn for constructional reasons no later than the early C14.

8040

FRITTENDEN

ST MARY. Rebuilt by *R.C. Hussey c.*1846–8, of dull brown sandstone dressed with Caen stone. Pale tiles. Nave and chancel, both with a s aisle. N aisle to the nave. s porch. w tower with an old Perp w window and a recessed stone spire with fancy lucarnes. Otherwise the church is very authentic-looking. Dec tracery of various local patterns. It seems that Hussey began in 1846 with the intention of repairing the old building; so when it came to rebuilding he honourably tried to make good what was lost without giving interest. The texture of course reveals the date unmistakably. N aisle added 1861. Interesting black and white chancel PAVEMENT. – STAINED GLASS. E window 1891 by *W. Bucknall & J. N. Comper.*

The two Gothic HOUSES, of sandstone, beside the road, one with ecclesiastical tool-shed, are no doubt by *Hussey* too.

PRIMARY SCHOOL, E of the church. 1845. Like an overgrown cottage orné. Red brick below, white weatherboarding above. Heavy black bargeboards. Symmetrical W front. Symmetrical E front, pinching the master's house tight till the gables scream.

POND'S FARM, ½ m. E. C16 timber-framed farmhouse, the uprights close-set, the overhang unbroken across the front.

FROGHOLE see CROCKHAM HILL

GABRIELS MANOR see EDENBRIDGE

GADSHILL see HIGHAM

GALLANTS MANOR see EAST FARLEIGH

GALLEY HILL see SWANSCOMBE

GILLINGHAM

7060

ST MARY THE VIRGIN. Here was the original village. The church alone now witnesses to it. Outside it looks a Perp church with a flint clerestoried nave and aisles, battlements at both levels, and a battlemented W tower of squared ragstone blocks now greatly decayed. SE circular stair-turret. Angle buttresses dying away very low down – their function being to thrust against the tierceron rib-vault on corner shafts inside. The E end however suggests that there will be earlier work within the church. Tall N and S chapels under their own gables. Ogee-headed low-side window half hidden by the S one. The Early Dec E window however is not evidence; it is *A.W.Blomfield*'s design – he restored the church in 1868–9. The story starts in fact *c.*1200, with the arches from the chancel to the chapels. There are two each side now, on a Dec pier. The responds however have scallops and upright leaves on the capitals, and there is a keeled roll round each W arch. This suggests that the E responds were moved eastwards when the chancel chapels were lengthened. The only other possibly E.E. work is the rogue square pier (with Perp chamfers) in the N and S nave arcades, and the abaci of the E responds. Dec SEDILIA with cusped ogee hood-moulds and new stiffleaf(!) finials. C15 nave arcades, circular piers with octagonal caps. C15 chancel arch. No tower arch, only a doorway. Three-sided W gallery. – FONT. Norman. Deep circular stone bowl round which run sixteen arches on shafts. Interlocked zeds round the top, zigzag at the bottom. – STAINED GLASS. E window, 1869. – PLATE. Cup, 1571; Almsdish, 1699. – MONUMENTS. Several nice tablets in the nave.

89 ST AUGUSTINE, Rainham Road. A striking and in many ways surprising work of *Temple Moore*'s last years. Built in 1916. Externally the nave and chancel show plain ragstone walling for a long way up. Coupled nave windows, single chancel windows, all of the same Dec design. It turns out that these are clerestory windows above a non-existent aisle hinted at inside. Exceedingly lofty arcade to a big N aisle. Quite a majestic chancel. Careful, even rather mannered, detailing.

ST BARNABAS, Nelson Road. 1889–90 by *J.E.K. & J.P.Cutts*. E.E. Red brick and stone. Nave and chancel of equal height. Lean-to aisles. S chancel chapel added 1914. Broad, solid interior. At £2,550 (G.S.) the Cuttses gave value for money. – REREDOS. 1902.

ST LUKE, Virginia Road. 1908 by *J.E.K. & J.P.Cutts*. The recipe as at St Barnabas, but Perp, as they wanted belatedly to get up-to-date. Extended at the W in 1925 by *Caröe*.

ST MARK, Canterbury Street. By *St Aubyn*, 1864–6. E.E. Nave and lean-to aisles, lower broad apsidal chancel. Stock brick, exposed inside, with unemphatic red-brick patterns. Short, round Bath stone piers. A tower was intended. Goodhart-Rendel saw it as an early and good example of a type Sir A.W. Blomfield would make his own.

BOWATER'S PAPER FACTORY, 1¼ m. S, beside A2. By *Farmer & Dark*, 1960–1. All sorts of paper and plastic bags are made within the single huge block, under its saw-toothed skyline of top-lights. The sky-blue punchball in front is a water tower.

Gillingham's aimless expansion to E and S needs no comment. The sub-centres it has created appear below.

BROMPTON

Brompton means the barracks, a self-contained community on the hill above Chatham Dockyard. The chalk escarpment to the S was built up with bastions and ravelins in 1756 by the engineer *Hugh Debbieg*. It is still known as CHATHAM LINES.

Brompton is a grid of narrow streets lying s of the main road from Gillingham to Chatham, at this point called Wood Street. The earliest housing, looking even earlier than the 1750s, is MANSION ROW, a continuous three-storeyed terrace, of red brick. Further SW, PROSPECT ROW, facing W, also continuous Georgian terrace housing, much less uniform, with a considerable variety of columned porches. No prospect however, at least from ground level, of anything but a rubbish dump.

BROMPTON BARRACKS, N of Wood Street, headquarters of the Royal School of Military Engineering. The oldest part, masked from the road by recent three-storeyed blocks by *W. S. Atkins & Partners*, is best approached from Pasley Road. This runs at r. angles to the axis of the spacious, symmetrical layout. To the l. *Matthew Digby Wyatt*'s tripartite ARCH, of 1856, in commemoration of those who fell in the Crimean War, closing the fourth side of a vast square. Round the other sides, three identical blocks, two-storeyed, of stock brick, made handsome by two giant Tuscan columns *in antis* in the centre of each, and angle turrets à la Holkham. 1804–6 was the date of their erection, Lt.-Colonel *R. D'Arcy* the designer. On the axis, E of Pasley Road, an OBELISK in memory of Lord Kitchener, a Boer War TRIUMPHAL ARCH, of 1902, and *Sir Frederick Ommanney*'s Italo-Frenchy INSTITUTE BUILDING of 1872–4, built of grey brick and pale terracotta. N of all this, where the ground slopes towards the river, much new building, many blocks of various sizes, by *W. S. Atkins & Partners*, in yellow brick, the windows in broad vertical strips. They seem disconcertingly unmonumental, by comparison with the rest, and surely here would have been a place for a symmetrical layout framing the view of the river, rather than this fashionably informal grouping.

Off PRINCE ARTHUR ROAD, the RAVELIN BUILDING, *c.*1904–7, largely designed by Major *E. C. S. Moore*. Big, square block, round an inner courtyard. Red-brick, the angle and entrance towers relieved with vertical stone strips. On each tower, behind a parapet that curves up at the corners, a brilliantly white globular dome. Quite a successful attempt to be monumental but light-hearted at the same time, in the way the Edwardians so enjoyed. It housed the Electrical School, and the domes hid searchlight projectors.*

* Lt.-Colonel F. T. Stear, secretary of the Royal Engineers Historical Society, was good enough to supply most of the above facts.

GRANGE

GRENCH MANOR, ¾ m. E of the parish church, in Grange Road.
The shells of two medieval buildings stand in the garden. Both
are of ragstone, with window reveals of pale yellow brick, so
consistently used that it must surely be an original feature.
The range by the road, with two pointed doorways in the s
wall, several small rectangular windows, and traces of an
upper storey, clearly had a secular purpose. The other, however, NW of the house, was the CHAPEL, built by Sir John
Philipott before 1389. (The Little Guide and Kelly both give
a definite date, 1378.) N, S, and W walls of a simple rectangular
building. N and S doorways, with two-centred arches and a
small chamfer (as on the other building). The windows are
segmental or trefoiled lancets, except the w, which has a drop-
shaped aperture over two lancets. Various irregularities in the
walls. Have they been tampered with?

TWYDALL

1½ m. SE

HOLY TRINITY, Twydall Green. 1963–4. The architects were
Ansell & Bailey. Square in plan, the altar set on one of the
diagonals, so that the congregation can participate in the services as closely as possible. This simple, honest function has
been clothed with the craziest display of modish Brutalism.
One half of the big pyramidal steel-framed roof structure rises
high into a prow above the other, to form two wedges of window lighting the altar from above. So far so good, in spite of
a certain exaggeration. But what is one to make of the low
walls from which the roof rises? Malformed stock bricks are
rudely laid (were the bricklayers blindfolded?) in chunks and
bastions and buttresses, but never in a straight bit of wall. The
PARISH HALL, linked to the S, is a little more self-controlled.

WIGMORE

ST MATTHEW, Drewery Drive. 1963–5, by *Peter Bosanquet &
Partners*. An informal, even incoherent, group of church, hall,
and parson's house, built of buff brick. Only the cross on the
cross-shaped campanile of darker brick makes it explicit from
outside that a church is here at all. There is certainly no pre-

paration for the moving interior. In plan the church is a blunt
T, with the raised altar standing free where the two bars join.*
Light floods on to the altar from the roof hovering low above
it and from a window that replaces the N wall. On the other
three sides square arms house the congregation. They are tall
and each is lit by a horizontal slit window at the top of the back
wall. A baptismal pool comes between the altar and the N
window, a hollow in a huge block of brilliantly white stone
half hidden by a rough rock and next to a lower pool, where an
inscription reads: 'Come unto Him our living stone.' Beyond
the window a small walled Garden of Rest, with more water.
So light, water, and stone are linked by complex symbolism
with baptism and death.‡

GLASSENBURY see CRANBROOK

GODDARD'S GREEN see CRANBROOK

GODINTON
2 m. NW of Ashford

9040

The noble amplitude of the park raises expectations of a house
more circumstantial than the rambling, mellow russet-brick
house finally revealed in a dell among clipped hedges, like a
miniature Compton Wynyates. The hedges belong to *Sir
Reginald Blomfield*'s formal garden of *c.*1902, and so do the
ramblings on the W side of the house. That leaves a squarish
two-storeyed block, bedizened with shaped gables. It is the E
front, built for Captain Nicholas Toke and dated 1628 on
rainwater-heads, which must be considered first. Shaped
gables, formed of a semicircle separated from the quadrants
below by a step, were up-to-date then, having first appeared
in Kent at Knole, in 1605. All the other features belong to a
local vernacular of a half-century's standing, untouched by
Renaissance fancies, except for the stone string-courses which
have grown into the full mouldings of an entablature. Symmetrical façade of shallow projecting wings and a centre of
four wide bays, the window-bays that come below the two
central gables an afterthought of 1631–2 – see how they cut
into the upper entablature. Three-light mullioned windows

* The Rev. W.B. Muller points out that the plan is intended to be felt
as a spiral from the entrance to the altar at the church's 'life centre'.

‡ Cheap finishes and lettering in a few places, that would be easy to
improve.

throughout, except for those in the bays. They have two plus four plus two lights, and the upper ones extend upwards with a third tier of lights. As we shall see, they belong to the most important C17 room. English bonding of the brick, which extends round the corner briefly to N and S. The N front, however, was built some time between 1791 and 1837; here the present entrance cleverly pastiches the C17 style, not at all a common thing at that date. It is a pity that no closer date can be provided. The S front, W of the C17 gable, has five C18 bays, with segment-headed windows, and C19 shaped gables.

All this quite masks the fact that Godinton was at first half-timbered, and is built round a tiny central courtyard, where some of the timbering still shows. The HALL in the centre of the N range keeps its big crown-post on a canted tiebeam, and the stop-chamfered wall plate on the S side. Trussed rafter roof, now hidden, smoke-blackened from the days when there was an open central hearth. They suggest that the hall-house was built in the C14. Canted ceiling of the 1620s. All the rest apparently Jacobean, but, it seems, made up entirely of pieces brought in by Nicholas Roundell Toke in the early C19. Panelling, some linenfold, some with profile heads, of the 1520s or 30s. Bethersden marble chimneypiece, its profile Gothic, decorated in a way datable c.1600.* Overmantel constituted from various C16 pieces, notably two splendid strap-work panels dated 1574, made to enclose intarsia ovals with the arms of Fermor quartering Browne, made c.1520. More panelling with profile heads in the E annexe to the hall, and in the so-called Chapel Room above, which is the solar of the C14, and has a crown-post hidden above the present ceiling.

Captain Toke's interiors were confined to the E range and the staircase which he built S of the hall, in space taken from the courtyard. The STAIRCASE, dated 1628, has pretensions to grandeur, with heraldic beasts on the newels, carved on their sides, and long-haired female figures on the upper balcony. Friezes of foliage and dragons. It is barbarously carved. Turned balusters. Some Continental C16 STAINED GLASS set in the staircase gallery windows. The LIBRARY downstairs has contemporary panelling, and an overmantel dated 1631 and carved only a little less crudely than the staircase. Quite a lively display of naked females symbolizing Faith and

---

* Another in the DINING ROOM, W of the hall.

Hope, the Pelican of Charity, and reliefs emblematic of two of the Continents (the r. one Africa, see the elephants). Marble* lintel patterned in low relief with stylized but savage dolphins.

The outstanding room is the GREAT CHAMBER, that occupies the whole centre of the upper floor of the E range. Panelled and given a sumptuous chimneypiece between 1632 and 1638, it represents as well as anything in the county the wild vigour of Jacobean decoration, that was going out of fashion by the 1630s. Panelling made restless by a lozenge in each panel. Pilasters of two patterns, both tapering, one fluted, one covered in arabesques. Frieze with many little figures in high relief, most of them soldiers illustrating the movements of pike drill, musket drill, and caliver drill. Overmantel with field sports in the frieze, Adam and Eve, and a stag by a tree under arcading, colonnettes, and no surface left unworked with some strapwork pattern or other. Deep, grey-marble lintel, just as busily carved, but most delightfully, in low relief, with flying, running, and creeping creatures, the grasshopper as big as the camel, among loopy branches and tendrils.

KITCHEN BLOCK, W of the house, with a C17 shaped gable. Much extended in the C19.

GOODS HILL see TENTERDEN

GORE COURT see OTHAM

GOUDHURST   7030

ST MARY. Sandstone. Aisled nave, chancel with chapels. W tower of 1638–40. *Edmund Kinsman*, *James Holmes* and *John Young* agreed to build it for £750. It is short and thick, with just the mixture of classical and Gothic to be found elsewhere in the 1630s, e.g. in the City of London at St Katherine Cree (1628–31), and at the Universities. Gothic battlements and belfry windows, classical W doorway, with niches l. and r. The large tripartite W window (identical with those at St Katherine Cree) is a bit of both, and so are the clasping buttresses, with a plinth moulding of classical profile. The exterior of the church looks Perp, but widened aisles hide the fact that there is earlier work within. The tracery in all but two of the windows was lost before *Slater & Carpenter* restored the church c.1865–70,

---

* Not Bethersden marble, Mr Hussey notes, for there are no fossilized shells in it.

but no doubt their reconstruction is roughly right. Theirs is the sw vestry. c13 evidence however in the chancel, two blocked e lancets and part of a n one. Five-bay arcades, not as even as they look at first sight. Two and a half bays of the n arcade are c13. Round piers, slightly double-chamfered arches. Then a c14 pier, and another, octagonal with concave sides. The e arch widened for the rood loft. The s arcade is all of the c14, the piers alternately round and octagonal, the e one a Perp replacement of a more complex shape, made necessary, as so often, by the rood loft. c14 chancel arch. c14 arches to the n chapel, with mouldings of two sunk quadrants. s chapel a standard c14 and c15 design. – FONT. Modern bowl on a Perp base, with symbols of the Evangelists squashed into the panels. – SCREEN, to the s chapel. Old base. – CHANDELIER. Brass. c18. – ARMOUR. Helm over the Colepeper monument in the s aisle. – STAINED GLASS. Fragments, mostly of the c15, gathered together in the s aisle w window. – PLATE. Cup, 1617; Paten, 1617 by *P.C.*; Flagon, 1722 by *Li.*, gilt; Alms-dish, 1732. – MONUMENTS. John Bedgebury † 1424. 39½ in. brass of an armoured man, under a canopy. – Late c15 tomb-chest, with a 25½ in. brass, probably for Sir John Culpeper † 1480. Segmental canopy with a pierced attic, on big, hollow-sided shafts. The canopy decorated with charming blank arcading on a miniature scale. – Brass of a man in fantastical plate armour, *c.*1520, a 25 in. figure. – Sir Alexander Cul-peper, 1537. Reclining effigies, of wood, the details in gesso, coloured, and placed in a bay window with arched lights. On the e jamb a two-tiered relief dated 1537, with tiny kneeling figures, God in Majesty, the Virgin and Child, and St George slaying the dragon in an inept Italianate pose. – Sir Alexander Colepeper † 1599. Erected 1608. In size the most ambitious monument in the church, but not well carved. Stereotyped design, with kneeling figures between columns, and sixteen small children below. But at the top, in an aedicule, a half-figure of an old man in armour holding a skull. – William Campion † 1615. Fine large hanging monument. Two crisply carved figures kneel within the usual architectural framework, with five tiny sons on the pedestal to the l. and four tiny daughters to the r. Open segmental pediment enclosing C-scrolls and bearing tiny, contorted, allegorical figures derived at heaven knows how many removes from Michelangelo's in the Medici Chapel. – John Bathurst † 1697. Ledger slab raised on four panelled shafts and a cartouche. – William Campion

† 1702. Large, plain hanging monument. On it a lively, turn-ing bust with arms, exceptionally well conceived and carved. 'Surely by *Bird*', is Dr Whinney's reaction. – Elizabeth Bathurst † 1715. Large marble tablet.

Goudhurst is splendidly situated on a hilltop. The church in its spacious churchyard occupies the flat summit, and the village is concentrated on the steep slope to the W. The houses, mostly tile-hung, some weatherboarded, some with the timbering ex-posed, fall into picturesque groups, from above and from be-low, but only CHURCH HOUSE demands a look for its own sake. This, at the top of the N side, is a C16 house with an over-hang, re-roofed *c.*1700 to incorporate an addition to the E, under an all-embracing hip. At the lower end the street breaks up rather indecisively, with a pond on the l. and a War Memorial on the r. The PARISH HALL, behind the former, *c.*1905, keeps successfully in the Goudhurst idiom, because that is an idiom natural to its architect. The silly little brick-nogged WESTMINSTER BANK, on the other hand, trying so hard to merge in, manages only to be conspicuously wrong.

PATTENDEN, 1 m. W of S. Restored C16 half-timbered house with continuous overhang and close-set uprights. A dozen other houses in the parish would look like this if the tiles were taken off them.

TWYSSENDEN, 2 m. W of S. Half-timbered in front. Nothing special. So the back is a great surprise, a late C16 sandstone façade with a classical centrepiece of exceeding gaucheness. Ionic pilasters divide the wide entrance bay from the narrow bays to l. and r. In the latter, niches and broken pediments perched on brackets above the heads of the niches. The pilaster capitals are of unbelievable crudity and carry not an entabla-ture but each its little rectangular scroll-topped block, like a hat. Semicircular doorway in a square frame. Cross-mullioned window above, with a hood-mould.

GRAIN 8070

At the furthest end of the Isle of Grain, looking down the Thames estuary; but the real remoteness of the place has been lost since the oil refinery arrived *c.*1954. No doubt it was the very remote-ness that let the refiners think that they had no duty to design and group their buildings decently. As a cheap substitute, large brick gatepiers and a flower bed or two beside the road. Yet the gleaming metal storage drums are splendid objects in themselves.

St JAMES. It is at once obvious that the church has been shorn of its aisles. This happened in 1815, the date recorded on the s porch. Dwarf sw tower of 1903–5, and NE sacristy. The nave windows all of this date. Outside one recognizes that the chancel is E.E. – one N and one s lancet, and a fraudulent-looking E triplet. Perp s doorway, and above it a gargoyle poking his tongue out and parting his beard. The interior, however, establishes that the nave is Norman in its walling. The heads of two original rere-arches in the s wall. The aisles were added shortly before 1200. Pointed arches on square piers. The sw respond, however, scalloped in a purely C12 way. The chancel arch has C12 imposts, with a zigzag roll at the w angle each side, ending in a scalloped capital. For the sharply pointed arch, with a slight chamfer, one would prefer to accept an early C13 date. C13 recesses each side of the chancel arch, dotted with red five-petal flowers. The interior of the chancel remarkable for its numerous recesses. s SEDILE and PISCINA, E AUMBRY, N PISCINA and AUMBRY. The E windows turn out to be genuine, with fine, long shafts, moulded caps and bases and multiple arch mouldings. – ALTAR RAILS. Plain C17. – PLATE. Cup and Paten Cover, 1569, the latter marked *I.P.* – BRASS. William Hykkes. A poor brass of *c.*1520, 18½ in. long.

GRANGE see GILLINGHAM

6070

GRAVESEND

In the present town the riverside port of Gravesend and the village of Milton run together. Gravesend's importance lay in its being the first main stop down the Thames from London. John Evelyn, when he went abroad, regularly 'took oares for Gravesend'. A fire in 1727 made a clean sweep of the old town, but the population began to increase only a century later. The 1830s were the period of Gravesend's greatest civic pride, with a new town hall, new piers, and a planned development joining up Milton with Gravesend. In 1821 there were 6,583 inhabitants. Twenty years later the population had more than doubled.

CHURCHES

St GEORGE. The old church fell a casualty to the fire. Rebuilding took place in 1731–3, with money provided under the 1711

Act, which had imposed a tax on coal to pay for fifty new churches in the London suburbs. The suburban churches had been costly and slow to build, which accounts, perhaps, for the sanctioning of this misuse of the tax. The new church cost £3,824; so it was fairly cheap, and the architect was a local man, *Charles Sloane*, carpenter, of Milton. He was no Hawksmoor or Archer, and the result is undistinguished. Brown brick. Nave and apsidal chancel. (The chancel rebuilt in 1892, re-using the Venetian window on the curve.) Big quoined w tower suddenly diminishing into a small square stage and an obelisk-like spire. Hideous N aisle of 1897, by *W. & C.A. Basset-Smith*. – ORGAN. 1764.

St ANDREW, Royal Pier Road. Built originally as a mission chapel for seamen. 1870–2 by *Street*. Just a rectangle jutting into the river, with low S (ritually w) vestibule and a big bell-gable for three bells. E.E. Ragstone and ashlar dressings. Yet Street takes nothing for granted. – STAINED GLASS. The complete set of *c.*1872 remains.

CHRIST CHURCH, Old Road East. 1854–6 by *R.C.Carpenter*, completed after his death by *Slater*. Taken down and faithfully rebuilt in 1934, but for the addition of a clerestory and two w bays to the nave. Long and low, a design of the greatest simplicity and clarity. Low aisles sweeping along past the central tower. The tower very low and, with its three set-offs to N and S, original and effective. Reticulated tracery in segment-headed windows. Inside, the tower space is included in the nave. Octagonal arcade piers. 'All detail intensely Kentish and local', says Goodhart-Rendel. That is true; the church is, as it were, Northfleet and Southfleet amalgamated and purified.

St JOHN THE EVANGELIST (R.C.), Milton Road. Built as an Anglican church in 1834 and bought for the Catholics in 1851.* Presbytery of 1859. The prominent NE (ritually NW) tower, one of the boldest accents in the town, was added in 1872–3 by *Goldie & Child*, with a Frenchy saddleback roof. Stock-brick church with the shallowest canted apse. Plaster rib-vaults to apse and vestibule. Etiolated cast-iron columns. Tall aisle corridors. The effect, now the galleries have gone, is airy and rather pleasant. The Geometrical tracery an addition, probably by *J.A.Hansom*, 1851.

St MARY (R.C. chapel), Rochester Road. Originally the parish church of Denton. Rescued from ruin and much rebuilt in

* I owe this information to Mr D. Evinson.

1901. Nave and chancel, basically c12. (Arcade of a blocked
s aisle visible inside.) e window original.

St Peter and St Paul, Milton Road, Milton. Perp w tower,
with diagonal buttresses. The rest of the church is a fragment,
looking most peculiar under its roof of 1790–2 (by *Thomas
Hall* of Dartford), crammed on it like a too-large hat. Aisleless
nave; no structural chancel. Traces in the e wall look like the
remains of the chancel arch. One unrestored s window, two
lights with an encircled octofoil above, the same as the tower
w window. Galleries inside, a w and a n gallery running slap
up to the e wall. Head corbels of the original roof below the
flat plaster ceiling. – SEDILIA. Three, rib-vaulted. One composition with the PISCINA. Dec. They must have been saved
from the demolished chancel. – FONT. 1852.

Methodist Church, Milton Road. Red brick and stone. se
tower and spire. 1906 by *Derek Buckler & Partners*.

Cemetery, Old Road West. 1838–41, by *Amon Henry Wilds* of
Brighton. The entrance lodges are gathered into a splendidly
inappropriate triumphal-arch composition. Brick rendered
pink. Four pairs of attached Greek Doric columns carrying
chunks of entablature. Entrance arch in the centre. Grecian
cemetery chapel, also rendered pink, set axially behind it.

PUBLIC BUILDINGS

Town Hall, High Street. The sandstone front of 1836 is by
Amon Henry Wilds, whose noble Greek Doric tetrastyle portico makes no concessions at all to the narrowness of the
street.* An archway under the portico leads past mean brick
back parts of 1895 to a covered MARKET (which replaces
Charles Fowler's colonnaded market of 1818–22).

Civic Centre. On a triangular site between Wrotham Road
and Windmill Street, 1964–8, by *H. T. Cadbury-Brown &
Partners*. To the n a paved square, the buildings grouped in a
deliberately broken-up way. Grey aggregate facing.

North West Kent College of Technology, Darnley
Road. 1892–3 by Lt.-Col. *C. T. Plunkett*, R.E. Red brick. Tall,
symmetrical front in Norman Shaw's brand of Queen Anne.
Further s in Pelham Road, new communal block by *Elie
Mayorcas* and *E. T. Ashley-Smith*, the County Architect.

National Sea Training School, on the marshes e of the
town, reached down Mark Lane. By *Lyons, Israel, Ellis &*

* PLATE. Silver-gilt mace, 1709 by *Benjamin Pyne*.

placed with brick on the ground floor. Half-H plan. The main front faces NW, with two-storeyed end bays, a two-storeyed timber porch, and original hall windows in the centre, a row high up to the l. of the big brick chimneybreast, and a large window r. of it, with four mullions and three transoms. The hall is exceptionally large and has a fine late C16 plaster ceiling, flat, with many moulded ribs making patterns of interlocked circles and small rosette bosses. High-relief plaster frieze. Fireplace arch of flattened four-centred shape. Six carved relief profile heads, *c.* 1530–40, companions to those at Godinton and Court Lodge.

YARDHURST, 1½ m. SW. Good half-timbered Wealden house. Close-studded, the hall two bays wide. The one out-of-the-usual feature is the tracery in the square-headed window lights of the jettied-out end bays. It is rarely that the original woodwork of such windows survives.

GREAT FISH HALL see TONBRIDGE

GREAT MAYTHAM see ROLVENDEN

GREATNESS see SEVENOAKS, p. 497

GREATSTONE-ON-SEA see LITTLESTONE-ON-SEA

GREENHITHE

ST MARY. By *George Vulliamy* and *J. Johnson*, 1855–6. 'Extremely cleverly detailed, like all of Johnson's work; – whether you like it or not is a different matter.' This is Goodhart-Rendel's verdict. The trouble is that Johnson bothered so much more about detailing than about the architecture. Ragstone. Rather ordinary clerestoried nave and aisles. Low chancel. w bell-gable. Dec. The ensemble of the w front however, with a gabled doorway rising into the window above, and a super-arch balancing on buttresses, is a little tour-de-force. But the clerestory windows are sheer perversity, blinded by internal shafts carrying useless archlets. Also much lively foliage inside, on the capitals and round the chancel arch. The chancel looks plain after the nave, now that *Hardman*'s polychrome decoration has gone. – FONT and PULPIT, no doubt also by *Johnson*, with lashings of foliage.

The church stands by the A226, with at the back COBHAM TERRACE, a series of tall Italianate villas to two patterns, built in 1845, in an attempt to give Greenhithe a residential district on the hill.

RESEARCH LABORATORIES of Associated Portland Cement, ¼ m. SW, in Stone parish. By *Westwood, Sons & Harrison*, *c.*1953.

Of course it is the cement works that have prevented Greenhithe from ever becoming residential. They are down near the Thames, W of the High Street. The cement dust is everywhere. The HIGH STREET is still just worth walking along, though now bitty as well as dour. At the W end, by itself across the road from the wharves, the WESTMINSTER BANK, late C18. Stock brick. Five bays, the centre three coming forward a little under a pediment. Porch on paired Doric columns. The street starts in earnest with cottages at first. The parapet of No. 47 curves up to make a third storey in the centre, a typical Early Georgian device. Opposite, the horrible ROMAN CATHOLIC CHURCH and PRIEST'S HOUSE, built as a friary by Italian Capuchins right on the shore in 1874. Further along on the r. Nos 17–21, three early C19 flint cottages as a symmetrical group. A crude, gabled Gothick affair. All the windows pointed, with raised surrounds of knobbly flint or brick. Ogeed side doorways. Beyond again, another stock-brick HOUSE, of three wide bays, the lower windows round-headed under sunk arches. The Greek Doric columns to the porch suggest a date *c.*1820.

INGRESS ABBEY. Large, square, and symmetrical, in a Tudor style. By *Charles Moreing*, 1832–3. The surprising thing is that the house is entirely of Portland ashlar; traditionally explained by the fact that stone from Old London Bridge was re-used. Vivacious skyline, of many gables and octagonal buttresses rising up with ogee caps. A big heraldic beast above the W front; the main front facing the river with a battlemented central tower and a two-storeyed oriel to it. The windows have mullions, transoms, and arched lights, all of wood.

IRON AGE SETTLEMENT. *See* Stone.

GRENCH MANOR *see* GILLINGHAM

5030

GROOMBRIDGE *

55 ST JOHN THE EVANGELIST. 'That worthy Patriot', John Packer of Groombridge Place, erected a private chapel beside

---

* For the rest of Groombridge, *see* The Buildings of England: Sussex.

the road in 1625. The tablet on the porch gives his reason: OB FOELICISSIMUM CAROLI PRINCIPIS EX HISPANIIS REDITUM – because Prince Charles had returned from Spain happily unmarried to the Infanta.* The chapel is still Gothic, with a few slightly wayward classical trimmings. The arch to the porch is classically semicircular, but rests on semi-octagonal responds. The beginnings of a pediment above. Brick, all laid as headers, and orange, iron-stained sandstone. Original s door with many small panels. There are diagonal buttresses, striped with sandstone bands as a sort of rustication. The Perp windows however must all be early C19. They are made of pallid sandstone,‡ and their rebuilding involved new gables to E and W, two new W buttresses, and tampering with the brickwork above all the side windows. Money was granted for 'enlargement' of the chapel in 1818; the weathervane on the W gable is dated 1825. Another restoration, after a fire at the E end, came in 1895.

The interior has no structural division of chancel from nave. The leggy timber roof appears to be wholly modern. – Of the original fittings there survive the FONT (fluted octagonal bowl, stem with a large jewelled waist-band) and the small PULPIT, keeping its sounding-board. – CHANCEL RAIL. Mostly modern, but the pattern, arches on Tuscan colonnettes, is probably all right. – STAINED GLASS. In the E window on the s side, a fine panel of heraldic glass of 1625, flanked by deceptive C19 imitations by *Clayton & Bell*. – The rest, except one other s window, is all by *Kempe*, 1894 (E window), 1896, and 1899. – MONUMENTS. Philip Packer † 1686. This must be by *Bushnell*, one of his most peculiar inventions. He is shown as a semi-naked figure seated in a niche, his head lolling pathetically on one side and an open book resting on his knee, i.e. at the moment of his death. – John Packer. A large tablet, erected in 1697, and detailed with unusual restraint and refinement.

GROOMBRIDGE PLACE. Groombridge, long owned by the Wallers, was bought by John Packer in 1618. His son, Philip, rebuilt the Waller house some time between John Evelyn's two visits of 1652 and 1674. His new brick house has with the

* Hasted calls the inscription 'now Obliterated'. In its present state it also bears the name William Camfield and the date 1757, i.e. it was in fact recut a little before Hasted's day.

‡ But two orangey stones re-used in the SW window may be evidence that the moulding of the mullions of 1625 was faithfully copied. Petrie's early C19 drawing proves that the tracery-pattern was not changed.

passing of time become one of the loveliest and mellowest in the southern counties, standing within a square moat a good deal too large for it; for Packer did not do the fashionable thing and seek a prospect from a new site on the hillside, but rebuilt inside what must have been the courtyard of the medieval house. Since then, by some miracle, no alteration, except sashing the windows, has ever been made. Groombridge belongs to the group of mid-c17 brick hipped-roofed houses in West Kent that begins with Chevening. The H-plan, the two storeys over an inconspicuous basement, the large brick quoins, the tall sunk panels in the chimneystacks, all connect it most closely with Yotes Court, Mereworth, of 1654–6. Yet compared with Yotes Groombridge is on the old-fashioned side. The centre bar of the H is but one room thick and contains only a hall and a chamber above; the front door leads into a lobby, the last vestige of the screens passage. The chimneybreasts project, and the windows only manage regularity on the entrance front. Such things were solecisms by the years that Coleshill was being built, let alone by 1674. So Packer probably rebuilt his house not long after Evelyn's first visit. The bonding of the brickwork is mainly Flemish. What gives the front distinction and even a *gusto italiano* such as Evelyn himself would have applauded, is the sandstone loggia of Ionic columns masking the two front doors, coming forward in the middle like a deep porch. It contains steps up to the loggia and has a crowning pediment. The forecourt gate-piers with pineapples and shell-headed niches are in the same classical taste. Inside, many re-used fittings from the old house. Linenfold panelling in a downstairs room with heads in the frieze and arabesques ending in dragons' heads.* The panelling in the chamber over the hall is also c16, painted to resemble inlay. New work only the staircase, and the drawing-room panelling and plaster ceiling, which has a large oval wreath of luscious fruit and flowers, boldly undercut – expertise of the 1670s this, rather than the 1650s. Contemporary brick STABLES to the S, also within the moat but on its very brink. Pretty lantern.

The village, on two sides of a triangular green, is part of the Groombridge Place estate, which accounts for its delightful trimness. On the W side, at the bottom, the DOWER HOUSE, brick, two-storeyed, with a big hipped roof. c17, and perhaps

* More like it is at the Old Parsonage, Brenchley, dated 1573. This was another Waller house.

by the same builder as Groombridge Place, for here, too, something has gone wrong with the design of the centre. Across the top of the green behind pollarded limes, THE WALKS, a long, nearly but not quite uniform, row of C18 cottages, red and blue brick below and tile-hung above. ASHURST HILL continues up to the l. of them with more continuous cottages. A little further up is COURT LODGE, two long, low, half-timbered ranges at r. angles. The tile-hung wing on the r. is the Court Lodge of Udimore, in Sussex, rebuilt here in 1912. The l. range modern, and the whole thing as self-conscious and nostalgic as a late Baillie Scott house.

HILLSIDE, on the main road at the top of the hill, is a smallish but excellent house by *Norman Shaw*, 1871. He is still playing with the motifs he had used at Glen Andred, his first Groombridge commission (over the border in Sussex). Brick and tile-hanging, and half-timbered gables high up over the garden. On the entrance side the asymmetry is most carefully studied, with a vast chimneybreast soaring above the gables, and a polygonal bay at the corner.

BURRSWOOD, ¾ m. NW. By *Decimus Burton*, 1831–8. He chose a Tudor style. The garden front is straightforward enough, four gables with tall chimneys between them. But on the entrance side the gallimaufry of motifs thrown together without any sense of scale or placing is almost unbelievable. Sham gables, lancets and eyebrow pediments jostle more authentically Tudor motifs. How could the architect of the Hyde Park Screen and Holwood handle another style so ineptly? Large recent additions in a milder Tudor by *Charles Beauchamp*. Chapel 1959, by the same. In the chapel the fittings are undistinguished, but all, it is worth noting, Baroque in style.

THE GROVE *see* PENSHURST

GROVEHURST *see* HORSMONDEN

HADLOW

6040

ST MARY. W doorway and NW quoin of a Saxo-Norman church, recognized by the large blocks of stone laid with a hint of long-and-short technique. C13 W tower – see one N and one S lancet – buttressed later; C13 chancel arch of unusual width and simplicity; chancel 1847; N aisle 1853. – DOOR to the tower, dated 1637. – CHAIR. Chairs are not usually mentioned in *The Buildings of England*. An exception must be made for this one. It is said to have come from Exeter Cathedral, and to be associated with Coverdale. But a close look shows that it was made up in the C19 from old bits: late C16 panels of allegorical figures low down at the side and a relief of the Expulsion which is probably C17 Flemish. – MONUMENT. Sir John Rivers † 1583. Hanging monument with the usual kneeling figures under arches between well-proportioned Corinthian columns. The inscription has been lost. – In the SW corner of the churchyard, the MAUSOLEUM of Walter Barton May, † 1855, introduces the wayward gothicism of that gentleman.

HADLOW CASTLE. Not that May's house is so inconspicuous that it needs an introduction. The TOWER shoots up 170 ft high, just to the S of the churchyard wall. It was part of the 'costly appendages and additions' made c.1838–40 by *Walter Barton May* to Hadlow Court Castle, which he had built a few years before. May seems to have designed the tower himself, inspired by that colossal folly, William Beckford's Fonthill. Indeed, May followed his model pretty closely, so the tower is octagonal, with gabled projections on the four cardinal sides of the lowest stage, and a four-storeyed main stage with pinnacles. With the slim crowning octagon he went one better than Fonthill. Beckford's tower had already collapsed in 1825, only eighteen years after it was finished. May however employed *George Ledwell Taylor*, engineer and architect to the Navy, to ensure that his should last better. It is of brick, rendered with Roman cement. The castle itself has been largely demolished. There remain the ENTRANCE GATEWAY and LODGES in the village street, and the STABLE COURT with two square angle-turreted pavilions, all in a bald and uninteresting castellated Gothic, far less convincing in detail than the tower. *J. B. Bunning* exhibited a design for the S front in 1821. He was nineteen at the time.

KENT FARM AND HORTICULTURAL INSTITUTE. By *E. T. Ashley-Smith*, the County Architect. Completed in 1967. Low-lying, informally grouped.

HADLOW PLACE, I m. W of S. Late C17 brick S front, of four irregular bays, with a two-storeyed porch and a hipped roof. Later additions behind and on the r. Inside, however, the SW room on the ground floor is wholly lined with linenfold panelling, a splendid, if composite, display. C16 stone fireplace, with a straight-sided arch, and a frieze of six small wood reliefs above, including three very Germanic heads of c.1530–40.

HADMAN BRIDGE *see* SMARDEN

HALE FARM *see* HORSMONDEN

HALE STREET *see* EAST PECKHAM

HALLING

7060

ST JOHN THE BAPTIST. Drastically restored on the outside by *H. Bensted* in 1889. His the naughty N porch and the fanciful Dec windows. His the S organ chamber and vestry. The building probably started as a simple Norman nave and chancel (like e.g. Paddlesworth or Dode), and the W quoins of the nave in part remain. The chancel is a C13 enlargement – see three N and two S lancets. Early C13 tower, as the tower arch shows, later buttressed and dressed with brick. Wide, separately gabled aisles added to the nave in the C14. They produce an interior of curiously unpleasant proportions, with puny three-bay arcades, a simple rendering of the standard type. The N arcade earlier than the S. The pre-arcade thickness of the wall remains at the W end and above the N arcade. Wide chancel arch dying into the imposts. C15 PISCINA on a shaft. – WALL PAINTINGS. Above the chancel arch. Last Supper and Passion scenes, in two tiers. Late C13. – STAINED GLASS. By*Kempe* the E window, 1892, a chancel S lancet, and the N aisle W, 1900. – BRASS. Silvester Lambarde † 1587, wife of the historian of Kent. Crudely engraved plate of a woman sitting up in a four-poster bed. 'Gemelliparae positum' says the inscription, and there are the twins in a cradle beside her.

The ragstone wall in the NE corner of the churchyard is what is left of the BISHOP'S PALACE. Three blocked trefoil-headed lancets with segmental rere-arches, made of an unusual reddy-brown sandstone. Return wall at the N end, not bonded in. Bishop Hamo de Hethe repaired and enlarged the palace between 1322 and 1337.

HALL PLACE *see* BEXLEY

HALSTEAD

4060

ST MARGARET. 1880 by *W. M. Teulon* (GR). In what way *St Aubyn* enlarged it in 1897 is not clear. Flint, with red-brick dressings everywhere but in the chancel. Aisles treated differently outside. Geometrical tracery. Deeply moulded brick arches to the arcades. The interior obscured by much STAINED GLASS, all of it poor. For the record, the Annunciation in a chancel S window is by *Kempe*, 1899, St Martin and St George, in the N aisle, by *Morris and Co.*, 1909; both, of course, instantly recognizable. – E window 1867 by *Powell's*, designed by *Casolani*. – ORGAN, probably by *Teulon*. Canted front. – MONUMENTS. Brasses to William Burys † 1444, in armour, 26 in. high, and to William Petley † 1528 and wife, also small. – James Ashe † 1733. White marble tablet. Cherubs at the top and cherubs' heads at the bottom. Signed by *Jonathan Barker*, his only known work.

HALSTEAD PLACE, across the road from the church, has been pulled down. In its grounds a SCHOOL by *Pite, Son & Fairweather*, 1954–6.

HAMDEN see SMARDEN

HAMMERFIELD see PENSHURST

HARBOURNE HOUSE see HIGH HALDEN

HARTLEY

ALL SAINTS. The only memorable thing about the church is the hinge-work of the S door, seven strong horizontal bars and crescent-shaped braces; an ordered arrangement, quite unlike the Staplehurst door. It is probably C12 like the nave – there is one small Norman S window and its twin in the N wall – for though the doorway is pointed, the door itself is round-headed. Accurate dating is not possible. Lower C13 chancel, and a plain C13 chancel arch. Cusped lancets in couples. Barred low-side windows formed in a N and S lancet. E wall and vestry 1860. W wall and bell-turret 1892, the turret based on Petrie's drawing of 1806. S porch 1899. – FONT. Purbeck marble base and eight small shafts. Encircled quatrefoils on the eight faces of the bowl. A marriage of the C13 and the C15, it seems. – PULPIT. Simplest Jacobean, the arcading merely incised. – MONUMENT. James Burrow † 1728. A good tablet, with two cherub heads at the bottom.

HARTS HEATH FARM see STAPLEHURST

HAWKENBURY see HEADCORN

HAWKHURST

St Laurence. At first sight the church appears entirely Perp, long, bold, and battlemented, with an undersized w tower, also battlemented. Masonry of squared ragstone blocks. The aisles run the full length of nave and chancel, and there are two-storeyed N and S porches, the latter with an octopartite rib-vault, and a polygonal N turret. E of the turret, however, three segment-headed Dec windows, rougher, and so earlier, walling, and the battlements clearly an addition. Furthermore the earlier walling omits the plinth, and the Dec windows have been raised bodily. And so round to the E side, where the chancel window is gloriously Late-Dec, c.1370 say. Very tall, of five lights grouped two, one, two. The centre light blossoms out into a bulb-like form enclosing a star of six many-cusped lozenges. Cusped encircled cinquefoil in the very tip of the gable above. Low E sacristy, formed in 1849 by *R.C.Carpenter* out of ruined walls, the remains of a low medieval E annex, originally linked by a doorway to the church. By now we are prepared to find that the interior is in fact Dec, masked outside by Perp rebuilding of the aisle walls, not by the usual widening, for the Dec E bay of the N aisle is already the full width. The mid-c14 work all of a piece: nave arcades, five bays, short octagonal piers; tremendously tall and wide chancel arch; equally tall and wide E window.* Are the arcades to the chancel chapels a crude Perp remodelling of earlier ones? Finally, take note of the restoration: *Carpenter* and then *Slater* between c.1853 and c.1859 renewed the w window of the tower and rebuilt the S aisle. All other windows were faithfully renewed c.1955. – font. Perp of the common octagonal type, with buttressed stem and roses and shields alternating on the bowl. – reredos. C17 panelling with two fluted Ionic pilasters. – relief. Of wood. A crudely executed Last Supper in a C17 frame. – painting. Copy of *Sarto*'s Medici Holy Family in the Palazzo Pitti, Florence. – plate. Two Cups and two Paten Covers of 1630. – brass. John Roberts † 1499, wife, six sons, and six daughters: very worn 18 in. civilians.

All Saints, Highgate. By *Sir G.G.Scott*, 1861. A fine landmark from the S, with its SE spire. Less attractive near at hand, of pale, bloodless sandstone, and an unadventurous nave-and-

---

* The internal shafts to the E window have a complex profile like that found in C14 work at Sandhurst and Rolvenden. It seems the trademark of a local mason with a gift for contriving broad internal spaces.

aisles design. Plate-traceried windows, those in the chancel gathered into a scheme of external arcading. Much foliage of a French type. The interior wholly faced with ashlar. – FONT. Like a Buckinghamshire Norman font, but with Frenchy foliage. – STAINED GLASS in the chancel, *c.*1861, very decayed. By *Clayton & Bell*.

Two Hawkhurst churches, because two villages. The old one consists mainly of cottages on the W and N sides of THE MOOR, a big mown green N of the church. Beside the church CHURCH COURT, L-shaped, brick below and half-timbered above, faces across to WETHERINGHOPE, an C18 red-brick house with a wooden Venetian window on the E front, which gives tone to the top end of The Moor. Prominent at the bottom end of The Moor *Joseph Clarke*'s SCHOOL of 1863, characteristically loud with its polychrome brick bands and peculiarly buttressed bell-turret. Nothing else deserves comment except perhaps two houses E of the church, neither with any special architectural merit, but neatly making the contrast of late C18 and early C19: demure COLLINGWOOD HOUSE, red brick, three bays and three storeys, and lower later wings; and immediately N of it, ELFORDS, a shambling, overgrown *cottage orné* with Tudor windows and bargeboarded gables.

HIGHGATE is modern Hawkhurst, grown up along the A268. First in date are DUNK'S SCHOOL AND ALMSHOUSES, 'Given by Sir Thomas Dunk Kt. 1723', opposite Scott's church. Red brick. The almshouses are humble wings on either side of the school, a square pavilion under a pyramid roof and clock-turret. The school is in better, plummier brick. W from the church on the l., the deftly handled VICTORIA HALL, also red brick, up-to-the-minute in 1875, the date it bears, with its crisp bargeboarded gables, porch composed with a bold polygonal window bay, and the soaring arcaded chimneystack at one end. The architect seems not to be recorded, which is tantalizing. Shaw and Devey, who might either have done it, both worked at Hawkhurst (*see* below). On the r. an early C19 shopping arcade, weatherboarded houses with big shop windows under a colonnade of thin cast-iron columns. The MHLG notes that one shop was 'Established 1830'. Then, a short way past the crossroads, OAKFIELD, a buff-coloured early C19 mansion, notable for a porch of fine coupled Ionic columns.

The few remaining houses that deserve seeking out are all in the N half of the parish, and so are best located from Highgate church.

MARLBOROUGH HOUSE SCHOOL, ½ m. w. Handsome red-brick house of 1723, two storeys under a parapet. N front of seven bays, E front of nine. They are versions of the same design, with the centre three bays slightly brought forward under a pinched pediment. The E front grows canted bays to l. and r., a rare growth as early as this. The pedimented doorcase is not original, but inside, hall and staircase have pretty C18 plasterwork ceilings in a vernacular Rococo style. Tiny sporting vignettes on the hall ceiling. The staircase window, which seems to be contemporary with the structure, is pointed.

At the back *George Devey* added an L-shaped wing in 1879–80 for Edward Hardcastle. The arm that joins the old house stays Georgian, the arm that reaches out to the W takes on Devey's typical late tile-hung style, Norman-Shaw-inspired. This part too is sensitively related to the C18 STABLES, to the N.

Across the road *Devey* enlarged two cottages at the same time. CHITTENDEN is quite big, just like one of his estate cottages at Nonington (E). CHITTENDEN LODGE is little and less imposed upon.*

LIMES GROVE, 1½ m. NW, on the main road. C18 vernacular at its most lovable. Brickwork of two reds, wide white doorcase, big white dormers, colossal chimneystack plumb over the middle; all done with tremendous care, yet careless of fashion.

At FOUR WENTS, 1¾ m. N, two almost equally lovable farmhouses, FOUR WENTS COTTAGES, timber-framed and with 1681 on the porch, and further E ATTWATERS, another long red-brick house.

HAWKHURST PLACE, ½ m. E, on the A268. C16 half-timbering. The front has an unbroken overhang for its full width, three symmetrical gables and oriels under them. The two round-headed doorways are not original.

THE OLD FORGE, another ½ m. E, at Four Throws, is a cottage by *Norman Shaw*, dated 1874. Tile-hung overhang on big white brackets; towering chimneystack.

HAYES

4060

ST MARY THE VIRGIN. Flint. A crushing restoration by *Sir G. G. Scott* c.1856–62, including a new N aisle, and a S aisle and transept of 1878 by *J. Oldrid Scott*, have left old walling in

* The Rev. J. A. Loyd Hardcastle is the generous source of information for this entry.

the chancel and one lancet in the nave w wall.* Inside the w
tower, however, blocked original c13 arches in the N and S
walls suggest it may have had an open ground storey. The
aisle windows are instructive – Scott *père* provides striking
plate tracery of his own invention; his son, twenty years later,
sets up replicas of the Late Perp windows he is displacing. The
workmanship equally mechanical in both. – REREDOS. 1905.
Probably designed by *Sir T. G. Jackson*. Expensive. – STAINED
GLASS. The N aisle is a good place to watch the progressive
dulling of colour in Victorian glass: NE window, 1850; centre,
1866 and 1870; NW, 1880. – MONUMENTS. Brasses of priests:
John Osteler, *c*.1460, demi-figure, 7 in. in length; John Andrew † 1479, 14 in.; John Heygge † 1523, 1 ft. – The only
other monument worth a glance is the cartouche to Ann
Cleaver † 1737.

HAYES GROVE, Prestons Road. The first view, of a fine Georgian front, is misleading. The centre five bays are genuinely of,
say, *c*.1730. Two storeys. Pilaster strips at the corners, the
centre window in a raised surround. Big doorcase with a segmental pediment. The wings however are a pastiche, and a
very clever one. The rainwater-heads dated 1899. Additions
on the E front too, doubling the canted bay to approximate to
symmetry. Original staircase, with three twisted balusters per
tread.

OAST HOUSE, Croydon Road, ¾ m. E of S. Built in the middle of
Hayes Common in 1873–4 by *Philip Webb* for the eccentric
Lord Sackville Cecil. Not a large house, but as independent-
minded as any by Webb and composed with a good deal more
finesse than Red House, as one would expect fourteen years
after that pioneering effort. Long and low, with a deep barn-
like roof and the chimneystacks in four massive slabs. The
materials squared ragstone blocks and red-brick dressings, not
always where expected. White window-frames and a little
white weatherboarding in the gables. The entrance (w) front
rather like an enlarged school (Webb's interest in Butterfield's
schools in the 1850s is documented), ending in gabled wings
of equal width but unequal projection. The windows are wide
and have his favourite segmental heads. (One or two window
sills lowered slightly in recent years.) In the centre three
evenly-spaced dormers of Queen Anne proportions. Low,
square porch running out the full depth of the r. wing. The E

* Old PISCINA and doorway reset in the vestry, so Mr John Armstrong
kindly tells me.

HEAVERHAM *see* KEMSING

HERONDEN *see* TENTERDEN

HERSTFIELD BRIDGE *see* BOUGHTON MONCHELSEA

HEVER

4040

ST PETER. Nave and chancel of Norman proportions, but one as wide as the other. The chancel has a plinth-moulding and must be a Perp rebuilding. Arcade to the narrow N aisle, on piers with two slight chamfers on the arches, i.e. C13 work. Unbuttressed W tower, with a lofty shingled spire. Here too the plinth-moulding suggests a Perp date, in spite of renewed lancets in the top stage. Early C16 N chapel with an original fireplace and chimneybreast. – PULPIT. C17. With a tester dated 1621. – LECTERN. 1894. A colossal piece of vernacular wrought-iron work.* – STAINED GLASS. Chancel S window 1877 by *Hardman*; E window 1898 by *Burlison & Grylls*, much less good. – PLATE. Cup and Paten Cover, 1576; Paten, *c.*1702. – BRASSES. Margaret Cheyne † 1419. Figure of a lady, 37 in. long. Angels hold a damask cushion for her head. – Sir Thomas Bullen, Earl of Wiltshire and Ormond and the father of Henry VIII's second Queen, † 1538. The once splendid tomb-chest, with canopied niches, desperately eaten away, is unlikely ever to have had Renaissance detail on it. The brass, 59 in. long, is intact, and one of the finest C16 brasses anywhere. He lies armoured, in his Garter robes, his feet on a wyvern, his head on a heavily mantled helmet. A close look disappoints, for the engraving has none of the refined subtlety of early brasses. – William Todde † 1585. Kneeling figure, a foot long.

CASTLE. Licence to crenellate was granted to Sir John de Cobham in 1384. His square, sandstone house stands within its moat, externally very little altered from its original condition, barring new windows and some C16 gables and chimney-stacks. In 1462 it was bought by Sir Geoffrey Bullen (or Boleyn), mercer and Lord Mayor of London. The Boleyns were on the way up, and by 1533 had produced a Queen of England; yet oddly enough they did nothing to transform their house into a worthy expression of their ambitions. That

---

* Designed, the Rev. J. B. Collins kindly tells me, by the then Rector, the Rev. *R.C.Lathom-Browne*, and made by the local blacksmith.

HERE·LIETH·S⸱THOMAS·BULLEN
KNIGHT·OF·THE·ORDER·OF·THE·GARTER
ERLE·OF·WILSCHER·AND·ERLE·OF·ORM
VNDE·WICHE·DECESSED·THE·12
DAI·OF·MARCHE·IN·THE·IERE
OF·OVR·LORDE·1538·

Hever, brass to Sir Thomas Bullen † 1538

was left to W. W. Astor, who had come over from America in 1890 to settle in England and who bought Hever in 1903. Nowhere is Edwardian craftsmanship displayed with more extravagant panache, yet without damaging the medieval exterior.

Hever is a semi-fortified house *par excellence*. The centre of 36 the s front is occupied by a massive, rectangular gatehouse, three storeys high. Square angle-turrets to this front, with arrow-loops at four levels, but no windows. The battlements carry on from this front all round the building, but there are no more turrets, and on the w side two chimneybreasts project, one square and one triangular. Another on the N side. No certainly original window; but the entrance arch is not only reinforced by buttresses, portcullis, and deep machicolations at the top, but embellished with a row of quatrefoils and trefoil-headed panels, doubled on the face of the buttresses. Windows with trefoiled lights; c15. Mostly however the windows are c16, square-headed, of one, two, or three arched lights, with a hood-mould. The hall window, near the NW corner, of two tall arched lights with a transom. Beside it an octagonal turret, with a projecting bay to the r. This has three storeys of four-light windows, with a row of quatrefoils under the upper two, and the date 1584 in the top row. That dates the stone and brick gables at the N end, with kneelers and short finials. Tall brick c16 chimneystacks, in pairs, and a two-storeyed brick bay on the E side.

The entrance arch is rib-vaulted, with two-centred intermediate arches. Yet the outer and inner arches are four-centred. This leads into the courtyard, so small that the gate-tower fills the whole s side. The other three ranges are timber-framed, with three bargeboarded gables on the N side, where the hall is. All the timbers renewed as part of the 1903–7 campaign, but the wooden doorway to the screens passage is in place, i.e. in line with the gateway. The only other old feature inside is the panelling of the long gallery that runs above the hall and the whole length of the N front, contrived no doubt *c.*1584, when the gables were put in to light it. The panelling is punctuated by pilasters.

Otherwise the interior is a display of virtuoso woodwork of 1903–7. The architect in charge was *Frank L. Pearson* (son of J.L.), the carver a Mr *Frith*. The style favoured is mostly Early Renaissance, i.e. *temp.* Anne Boleyn. Among the few genuine pieces the moulded beams in Henry VIII's room, the

stone chimneypiece with frontal caryatids in the morning
room and the overmantel above it, dated 1603, the latter from
Sparrowe's House at Ipswich, a coarse overmantel in the with-
drawing room, from a house in Devon, and in Viscount Roch-
ford's room in the E range, the foreign-looking wood reliefs
with Genesis scenes over the fireplace. The tiny oratory off
this room has especially exquisite woodwork and STAINED
GLASS of the Trinity, the Virgin, and St John, C13 French.

On the N side, linked by a bridge over the moat, *Pearson*
built a cluster of stone and half-timbered OFFICES and
GUEST COTTAGES, linked into a single complex round a system of courtyards, but visually so broken up as to seem like a
village huddled close to the protecting walls of the castle. It is
a most ingenious idea. How otherwise could one have created
an extra hundred or so rooms without endangering the
dominance of the castle? Was it Pearson's or Mr Astor's
idea?

In the GARDENS however feudalism is abandoned. They
lie E of the house. First comes a semicircular *bagnio*, backed
by a yew hedge with porphyry columns standing in niches cut
in the greenery. Beyond that the Italian Garden, with a rustic
loggia on the r. and a series of alcoves on the l. At the end a
stone classical loggia, designed by *Pearson* in 1908, and a 45-
acre lake.

The Italian Garden is a display case for Roman and Italian
Renaissance pieces in profusion. Much is of the highest
quality. The sarcophagi alone would deserve an honoured
position in the British Museum.

See
p.
643
HOW GREEN, 1 m. N. 1905–6 by *Weir Schultz*. The plan is
interesting, like three sides of a polygon. The elevations
gabled to emphasize this. Brick and tile-hanging. (PLASTER-
WORK by *Gimson* in the dining room.)

7070

HIGHAM

ST MARY. At the end of the road, on the edge of the marshes,
accompanied by a cottage or two. It is a church of much charm
and eccentricity, with its stripy walls of ragstone and knapped
flint, and its hunchbacked outline. Pleasant, whitewashed interior. Nave and slightly lower chancel, with a gabled S aisle
from E to W, as high as the nave. Shingled W spirelet on the
nave ridge. Two early windows – a single-splayed one high
up at the W end of the nave N wall, and the head of a small

window visible in the N wall of the aisle. The latter must be part of a double-splayed window in the S wall of the original Saxo-Norman chancel. C13 arch from the chancel to the aisle, on round responds. C13 lancet in the nave N wall, oddly low down. The church was remodelled in the C14. In 1357 a papal indulgence was granted to contributors to the repairs. S arcade of three arches on octagonal piers. The walls were completely recased, and almost completely rewindowed. The windows unfortunately all renewed in 1863 by *Robert Speechley*, and the patterns of flowing tracery are so fanciful, especially the E window of the aisle, reticulated with split cusps, that one is doubtful whether to believe that the renewal copied what was there, in spite of a writer in 1877 asserting that it did.* The present arrangement of the church is misleading, using the S aisle as nave and chancel. It is however a plausible arrangement, because the original chancel arch has gone, but the aisle has an arch, which may be a C13 division between aisle and chapel, or may be modern. PISCINA too in the present chancel, but only an AUMBRY (with its original door) in the old chancel.

A gratifying number of medieval FITTINGS. – FONT. Square bowl with chamfered corners, on five circular shafts. Probably no earlier than the C13. – PULPIT. C14. Wood. Six-sided. Buttresses set back from the angles. Long panels with traceried heads, and squares half-way down enclosing tracery patterns. – DOOR. C14, no doubt by the same carpenter as the pulpit. Treated like a four-light window with a transom. Delicate little mouchettes packed into the heads of the lights. The framing members enriched with four-petal flowers and a few small heads. – ROOD SCREEN. Still *in situ* between the original nave and chancel. Complete except for the loft and its coving. Perp. Five bays, with central doors. Each bay a four-light window with panel tracery in two tiers. Shafts, on which the coving rested on the W side. – STAINED GLASS. E window *c.*1855. Quite good for its date, with characteristically acid colouring. – PLATE. Cup, early C17; Almsdish, 1634 by *R.M.*; Paten, 1725 by *Thomas Tearle*. – MONUMENTS. C14 recess in the S wall. Big cusps, every other one ogeed. Hood-mould on crowned heads, the l. one a woman wearing a wimple. – Tomb-chest with wavily cusped panels, probably C15. – Elizabeth Botcher † 1615. Tomb-chest, with the

* Petrie's early C19 drawing of the church from the SW also shows elaborate Dec tracery.

most elementary pattern of squares within squares on the sides.

ST JOHN, Mid-Higham. 1860, by an unknown architect. Yet it is an expensive building, very deliberately architected. Short, high, clerestoried nave, short chancel nearly as high. SW porch-tower and spire. Subtle polychromy of ragstone and Bath stone. Dec tracery, employing an angular motif, a pointed quatrefoil set diagonally in a circle. Very angular arcades, with an emphatically awkward transition from square base to octagonal pier and the roll on the arch swallowed up by a colossal unmoulded block above the capital.

(ABBEY FARM, 100 yds E of St Mary's church, is built on the site of Higham Priory, a Benedictine foundation of 1148 for nuns. Excavation in 1966–7 suggested that the priory buildings were quite humble, a cruciform church without a crossing tower, and cloister, small chapter house, and warming house on the S side.)

HIGHAM HALL, ¾ m. N of St John. An C18 rarity, a genteel house quite unaware of symmetry. Red-brick S front of three dates, the doorway in a canted piece rising higher than the rest. Nicely enclosed by high brick walls and high yew hedges. C16 red brick barn SW of the walls (with an unusual crown-post roof, diagonally braced; MHLG).

GADSHILL, ½ m. S. Beside the A226. Famous for being the home of Charles Dickens. Built, however, in 1779 (MHLG). Red-brick N front, of three wide bays. Two storeys with frieze, parapet, mansard roof, and delicate open cupola. The central window of debased Venetian form. The side windows in two-storey bays.

RAILWAY TUNNEL, between Higham and Frindsbury. 3,909 yards long. It was built to take, not a railway, but a canal, between 1819 and 1824. The engineer was *William Tierney Clark*, best known for his iron bridge over the Danube at Budapest. The arch, 35 ft from the canal-bed to the top, far exceeded all other canal arches in size.

MONUMENT, Telegraph Hill, ¼ m. SE. Tall cemented obelisk to Charles Larkin, auctioneer of Rochester, to record his 'zealous exertions in promoting the Ever Memorable Measure of Parliamentary Reform, A.D. 1832'.

HIGH ELMS see FARNBOROUGH

HIGHGATE see HAWKHURST

HIGH HALDEN

ST MARY. The remarkable feature of the church is the belfry tower attached to the w end. It is entirely of timber, and its construction is similar to the better-known timber belfries in Essex. Low, octagonal ground stage, then a square storey, and finally an octagonal broach-spire. The bracing system is by scissor trusses, the upper stage carried independently on six posts. Some of the vertical boards cladding the ground stage cut away to make narrow traceried two-light windows. Timber w porch, C14, originally deeper. This leads into a 30 ft passage through the belfry, lined with Perp panelling. Perp tower screen integral with it. The tower arch itself appears late C14, and is of stone.

Now for the church. One N lancet in the chancel, which is otherwise Dec. The E window, with its suspicious combination of encircled cinquefoils and ogees, may be *Street*'s invention, part of his restoration of 1868. Chancel arch also of the C14. One-bay nave N aisle, like a *porticus*, though Perp in date. Perp S additions to chancel and nave, forming a continuous aisle, of two parts not aligned with one another. Idiosyncratic aisle arcade. It rests on round stumps, the remains perhaps of a C13 arcade. The piers are rectangular in plan, deepest from N to S and with attached shafts to E and W. Hollow-chamfered corners to the rectangle produce a blunt arrow-head profile. In 1501 money was left to the 'new aisle to be new built'. Crown-post nave roof. In the gable of the nave five trefoiled lancets, a C15 device, maybe, to light the rood. Timber S porch, the two-centred entrance arch of two colossal baulks. C15 cusped bargeboards. – FONT. Plain, probably of the C13, but still standing on its original plinth, which is an integral part of the pre-Perp arcade's w pier. – STAINED GLASS. Old pieces, including an armorial shield, in the quatrefoil of one chancel window. C15 angels in the tracery lights of a window in the S aisle.* – PLATE. Cup of 1562. – In the churchyard, S W of the church, a tomb-chest to which adheres a forlorn fragment of a brass, dated *c.*1600 by Mill Stephenson.

Street's activities included building the SCHOOL, opposite the church. 1868. Nothing special.

HARBOURNE HOUSE, ¾ m. S W. 1875 by *C.G.Wray*. Very red brick. It is meant to be Italianate, but is more like an Early

---

* Mr Councer mentions, in the E window of the S chapel, an Annunciation with censing angels.

Georgian box, with a weak s w tower. It is really of no interest except that big Victorian houses are rare in this part of Kent.

HIGH HALSTOW

ST MARGARET. Well placed on the hill, with a distant view over orchards to the s. Ragstone. At first sight entirely a Perp church. Clerestoried nave, with s porch and a lean-to s aisle continued as a chapel nearly to the E end. Two large windows with panel tracery on this side. Wills of 1472 and 1474 refer to new work on a chapel. The chancel of the same period, but the E window renewed. Similar N aisle, but one reset Dec window. Closer examination produces more evidence that the church was remodelled, not rebuilt, in the late C15. A quoin in the W wall shows that the nave once had no N aisle. The proportions of the chancel roof too look C13, not C15. Sure enough, the arches from the chancel to the N and s chapel of c.1200. s arch pointed but unchamfered. SE respond with angle-shafts and upright leaves on their capitals drooping over in a Romanesque way. N arch just chamfered, and the angle-shafts with moulded bases and capitals, i.e. a little later than its fellow. C15 chancel arch. C15 niche N of it. Good E.E. nave arcades, three bays, with round piers, two hollow chamfers on the arches, and finely moulded undercut caps and bases, and corbels E and W. That leaves the W tower arch. The tower arch is also Perp, but the tower itself seems to have been entirely rebuilt late in the C18.* Short and stocky, ragstone with red-brick plinth, buttresses, quoins, and parapet. Hood-moulded lancets. – FONT. Plain square bowl on corner shafts linked to the central stem. By the shaft-mouldings early C13 rather than C12. – PLATE. Cup and Paten Cover, 1664. – BRASSES. William Groby † 1398. 12½ in. demi-figure of a priest. – William Palke † 1618. 15½ in. figures.

HILDENBOROUGH

ST JOHN. 1843–4. The first in the long, long line of *Ewan Christian*'s churches, and one that shows him already knowing what he wants to do and, inside at any rate, doing it with considerable artistry. The exterior is nothing special, except perhaps for the SE tower with its slightly tapering sides and shingled spire (shingled lucarnes too). Lancets and prominent

* The comparison to make is with Shoreham, of 1775.

corbel-tables in harshly cut local sandstone. But inside, the[87] wide, low nave, wide transepts, wide, shallow apsidal chancel with no chancel arch, are all dominated by the tremendous arched-braced roofs, springing from corbels set down almost as low as the window sills. The arched braces are deeply moulded and break free from the roof timbers. A big pendant poises itself over the crossing. Christian's intention is clear – he has rethought the problem of the preaching church, to create a broad central space, which makes the galleries of the Commissioners' churches no longer necessary. E. B. Lamb's is the name especially connected with this type of church, yet Hildenborough is at least as early as any of his. Nave lengthened by one bay in 1896. – STAINED GLASS. The transept w windows have *Morris* glass. N, Joy, 1876; s, St John the Evangelist, 1881 by *Burne-Jones*.*

FOXBUSH (Our Lady's Convent), opposite the church. 1866 by *Somers Clarke*. Gothic mansion of dark red brick, with Bath stone dressings. The entrance (N) front, two-storeyed, with semi-dormers stabbing up through the eaves, toughly lets you take it or leave it. Broad, low, pyramid-roofed tower to the l., and a smaller, lower one to the r. On reflection one agrees to take it. *Somers Clarke*'s LODGE on the road, with its deep coved eaves, is firmly controlled too, but, unlike the house, not a bit acid.

Hildenborough is hideously overgrown. Post-war sprawl allowed by the county planners reaches nearly to Tonbridge.

HOLBOROUGH see SNODLAND

HOLMEWOOD see LANGTON GREEN

HOLWOOD

4060

3¾ m. SW of Bromley

Holwood was the suburban estate (at that time suburban in the Roman sense) of the younger William Pitt, who as Prime Minister found his recreation in the enlargement of his house and the improving of its grounds. For the former he employed *Soane* and for the latter *Repton*. Some of Repton's planting remains to the s of the house, gloriously framing a view into Kent. Soane's house, however, was short-lived. Burnt down, it was rebuilt by *Decimus Burton*, in 1823–6, for John Ward. The new house is large (larger than Pitt's), built of expensive

* As Mr A. C. Sewter kindly tells me.

white brick and Portland stone, and confidently and correctly Grecian: an impressive performance for an architect in his mid twenties. Entrance (N) front fifteen bays long, the centre seven two-storeyed with lower wings ending in pedimented pavilions. (That on the r. was originally a greenhouse.) Three-bay pediment over the centre. Columns only by the doorway. The heightening of part of the wings has blurred the clarity of this arrangement. The same rhythm on the garden front, but more emphatically stressed. Four giant Ionic columns against a wide bow in the centre; low Doric columns recessed in the wings.

Inside, a small, low, square hall with Ionic half-columns and a coffered ceiling leads into the large vestibule in the centre of the house. This has now been halved in height, but was originally lit by clerestory windows above the Corinthian columns of an upper gallery. The staircase plain, but also top-lit.

HILLFORT. In Holwood Park are the fragmentary remains of a hillfort of multivallate construction on the W and univallate on the N side. An inturned and presumably original entrance exists on the W.

HOMEWOOD see TENTERDEN

HOO

St WERBURGH. Quite a large church. Ragstone. Tall shingled spire. C13, enlarged in the C14 and the C15. The story starts with the nave arcades, three bays, with round piers and the arch moulding a double chamfer. C14 chancel arch. C14 widening of the aisles, and refenestration with cusped intersecting tracery. A blocked E arch in each aisle, but no further trace of chancel chapels. The Perp campaign involved widening the aisles yet further (without discarding the Dec windows), rebuilding the chancel, and adding a clerestory to the nave, N and S porches, and a W tower. The tower battlemented and with a NW turret, but clasped by the aisles. Nave roofs on wooden shafts coarsely carved with demi-angels instead of capitals. The shafts on plain stone corbels. PISCINA and three SEDILIA, with multi-cusped arches on long thick shafts of Bethersden marble – interesting as a Perp version of the standard E.E. composition. The rood screen spanned the full width of the church, see the doorways in the N aisle. – STAINED GLASS. The C15 glass of the chancel tracery-heads intact. Small angels. – A few more C15 pieces collected in the top of the s aisle w window. – As a contrast, Transfiguration, in the s aisle, signed by *Gibbs*. 1885. The usual childishly bright colours. – A good representative collection of BRASSES. John Brown † 1406. 15 in. demi-figure of a priest. – Richard Bayly, after 1406. 44 in. figure of a priest. Of the finest quality, but, alas, missing the head. – Nice effigy of a civilian. 18 in. Datable *c*.1430. – Stephen and Richard Charlis † 1446 (nave). Two identical civilians. Again 18 in. long. – Thomas Cobham † 1465 (s aisle), 37 in. figures. He wears elaborate plate armour. – Dorothye Plumley † 1615. 22½ in. long. The inevitable drop in skill and depth in the engraving. – James Plumley † 1640. 23½ in. figures. – MONUMENT. Edward Lake † 1845. Tomb-chest with an ogee canopy and pinnacles. The early C15 correctly evoked.

KINGSNORTH POWER STATION, 1¾ m. N E. 1963 by *R. Maggs*, architect on the staff of the consulting engineers, *L. G. Mouchel & Partners*. The thumping great chimney ruins the scale of the marshes and their intricate pattern of lagoons. Good evidence that Farmer & Dark are not an unnecessary luxury for the Central Electricity Generating Board. *See* p. 644

HOOK GREEN *see* MEOPHAM

HOPE ALL SAINTS

0020

1¼ m. N W of New Romney

The church is very ruined, six chunks of masonry standing on a mound in the marshes. No details left, but the extremities of nave and chancel still discernible. The process of detrition gently continues, and it seems right that it should: the action of time has become more interesting than the building it works on.

THE HOPFIELD *see* PLATT

HORNE'S PLACE *see* APPLEDORE

HORSMONDEN

7040

ST MARGARET. A church without a village, attended only by a lodge, a cottage, and a fine group of oasts. Sandstone, with a handsome C15 w tower. Four stages, with diagonal buttresses, SE turret, and battlements. Shafted w doorway in a square surround, with a hood on half-angels. Big window above it. The body of the church is early C14 in date. One exceptionally large lancet N and S in the chancel, and one two-light reticulated N window. Timber N porch. Arcades with three arches. One round pier, one octagonal, in each. The S arcade the earlier, with bolder moulded capitals, two plain chamfers on the arches, and a bunch of naturalistic leaves sketchily carved on the W respond. C15 clerestory. Modern chancel arch. The finest piece of carving in the church is the fragment of an arch over the tomb recess in the S side of the chancel. Just a row of four-petalled flowers with rippling petals and a bulgy stop. Datable c.1340, as the Grofhurst brass (see below) was originally set under it. Mid-C15 S chapel, built in one with a new S wall to the aisle, with, most unusually, two rood-loft staircase turrets, identical outside, but differing in internal mouldings. One comes in the usual position, the other one bay W of that. Restoration in 1867 by *T.H.Wyatt* (PF). Most of the N wall was rebuilt. – SCREEN. In the S chapel. C15, prettily crested. Bold inscription: [Or]ate pro bono statu Alecie Campson. – FONT. C15. Octagonal, with concave sides, roses and shields.* – CHANDELIER. Brass. Small. 1703. – STAINED GLASS. E window 1946; W window 1948, by *Rosemary Everett.* Typical hot colours and hectic shapes. – MONUMENTS. Henry de Grofhurst, after 1338. 46 in. brass of a priest under a slightly ogee-sided canopy. His stubbly beard and small pursed mouth suggest that the face is a portrait, yet other C14 brasses of priests, and the alabaster monument of Archbishop Stratford († 1348) in Canterbury Cathedral, portray closely similar faces. – Joan Austen † 1604. 18½ in. brass. – John Read, the inventor of the stomach pump, † 1847. A bust on a tablet.

ALL SAINTS, 2¼ m. N. 1869 by *R.Wheeler* of Brenchley. Small. Yellow brick, banded with red and black, typically for that date. Typical too the siting, the rotund E apse towards the road. The modern village, 1½ m. N, can be ignored by the seeker for worthwhile houses. Several of these however scattered about the parish.

OLD RECTORY, ½ m. N. Unbeautiful, almost symmetrical, S front contrived in the early C19 by stretching a battlemented white brick centre between the pre-existing red-brick gables to l. and r. The gables got droopy bargeboards at the same time. C18 E front, red brick, with a pair of canted bays. The

* Mr A. Cronk tells one that the front is a C17 copy.

1. *Countryside*: Romney Marsh

2. (above left) *Country Townscape*: Tenterden, High Street
3. (left) *Villagescape*: Lenham, Court Lodge Farm and church tower
4. (above) *Prehistory*: Aylesford, Countless Stones

5. (left) Rochester Castle, keep, 1127–39

6. (right) West Malling, St Leonard's Tower, c.1100

7. (below right) Rochester Cathedral, nave, mid twelfth century

8. (left) New Romney church, nave, mid twelfth century

9. (below left) Newenden church, font, Late Norman

10. (right) Swanscombe church, capital, late twelfth century

11. (below right) Rochester Cathedral, west doorway, mid to late twelfth century

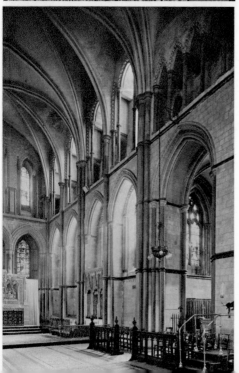

12. (left) Staplehurst church, south door, eleventh century (?)

13. (below left) Rochester Cathedral, presbytery, vaulted by 1214

14. (right) West Malling, Malling Abbey, cloister, thirteenth century

15. (below right) Stone church, late thirteenth century, chancel, arcading

16. (above) Woodchurch church, Early English
17. (above right) Barming church, bench end, probably German, *c.*1300
18. (right) Rochester Cathedral, monument to Bishop John de Bradfield †1283

19. (top) Penshurst church, coffin slab, thirteenth century
20. (above) Rochester Cathedral, monument to Bishop de St Martin
†1274
21. (above right) New Romney church, east end, early fourteenth
century
22. (right) Cliffe church, chancel, early fourteenth century

23. (above left) Nettlestead Place, undercroft, c.1250–60 (*Copyright Country Life*)
24. (left) Tonbridge Castle, gatehouse, c.1300
25. (top) Penshurst Place, licensed 1341
26. (above) Penshurst Place, licensed 1341, great hall, screen 1552 or later

27. (top) Nurstead Court, hall roof, c.1320
28. (above) Mersham, Court Lodge, c.1350
29. (right) Leeds, Battel Hall, laver, early fourteenth century

30. (above) Cobham church, sedilia and piscina, late fourteenth century
31. (above right) Maidstone, All Saints, begun 1395
32. (right) Mersham church, west window of north aisle, soon after 1396

33. (left) Tenterden church, tower, *c.*1449–*c.*1495

34. (below left) Brookland church, belfry, lowest stage thirteenth century, the rest fifteenth century

35. (right) Cooling Castle, licensed 1381, gatehouse

36. (below right) Hever Castle, licensed 1384

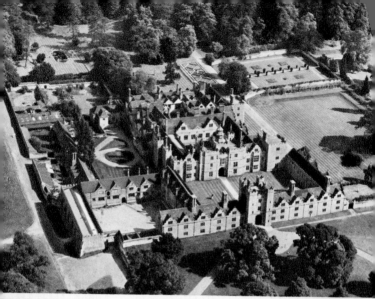

37. (top) Knole, mid fifteenth–early seventeenth century
38. (above) Teston Bridge, fourteenth century
39. (above right) Maidstone, tithe barn, fifteenth century
40. (right) Ightham Mote, chapel, early sixteenth century

41. (top) Lullingstone church, monument to Sir John Peche †1522
42. (above) Headcorn Manor, after 1516
43. (above right) Smallhythe church, 1516–17, and Priest's House,
early sixteenth century
44. (right) Boughton Malherbe, Boughton Place, c.1520–30 (*left*) and
1553 (*right*)

45. (left) Sissinghurst Castle, gatehouse, probably after 1558
(*Copyright Country Life*)
46. (top) Cobham church, monument to Sir George Brooke, 9th Lord
Cobham, 1561 (*Copyright Country Life*)
47. (above) Cobham Hall, south wing, 1580s

48. (left) Cobham Hall, porch in the north wing, 1591–4

49. (below left) Knole, Great Staircase, c. 1605

50. (right) Knole, Ballroom, c. 1605, chimneypiece (*Copyright Country Life*)

51. (above left) East Sutton, Charlton Court, dated 1612
52. (left) Somerhill, 1611 (*Copyright Country Life*)
53. (above) Maidstone, No. 78 Bank Street, pargetting, 1611

54. (above left) Rochester, St Nicholas, arcades rebuilt in 1624
55. (left) Groombridge church, 1625
56. (above) Chevening Park. Drawing on estate map of 1679

57. (above) Chevening Park, dining room panelling, by John Webb, *c*.1655 (*Copyright Country Life*)
58. (above right) Bexley, Hall Place, *c*.1649–53 remodelling
59. (right) Tunbridge Wells, King Charles the Martyr, ceiling, by John Wetherel, executed by Henry Doogood, 1690

60. (left) Maidstone, All Saints, monument to Sir John Astley †1639, by Edward Marshall

61. (above) Brenchley church, monument to Walter Roberts †1652

62. (left) Aylesford church, monument to Sir John Banks †1699, by John Nost(?)

63. (above) Chatham Dockyard, Main Gate, 1720

64. (below) Larkfield, Bradbourne, completed 1713–15 (*Copyright Country Life*)

65. (left) West Farleigh Hall, 1719, hall (*Copyright Country Life*)
66. (above) Mereworth Castle, long gallery, decorated *c.*1730

67. (top) Mereworth Castle, by Colen Campbell, roofed in 1723
68. (above) Sundridge, Combe Bank, by Roger Morris, c.1726(?)
69. (right) Mereworth church, 1744–6

In Memory of
PERCYVALL HART Esq.

The munificent Repairer and Beautifier
of this Church,
Himself a true Lover of the Church of England
And Representative of this County
In the two last Parliaments of her most Pious Majesty
QUEEN ANNE
During which time the Church and Clergy received
greater tokens of Royal Favour,
than from the Reformation to her time,
or since to this day.
M.r HART's steady Attachment to the
OLD ENGLISH CONSTITUTION
Disqualified him from sitting any more
in Parliament;
Abhorring all Venality,
And resenting as much to buy the Peoples Voices,
As to sell his own.
Conscious of having always performed
the interest of Great Britain
to that of any Foreign State.
He passed the remainder of his Life
in Honorable Retirement,
with as much Tranquility as possible,
Under the Declenssion, both of his own Health,
And that of his Native Country,
which when he could not serve,
He Could not but deplore.

He married SARAH,
Youngest daughter of
EDWARD DIXON Esq.r of Tunbridge,
by whom he had one Daughter,
ANNE.

Married to Sir THOMAS DYKE BARONETT,
of Horeham in Sussex.
He dyed on the 15.th day of October in y.e year 1738,
Aged 70.
M.rs HART dyed on the 8.th day of November 1720
Aged 53.
The Curious inspector of these Monuments
Will see a short Account of
An Ancient Family,
For more than four Centuries;
Continued with a moderate Estate,
Not wasted by Luxury,
Nor increased by Avarice

May their Posterity,
Emulating their Virtues,
Long enjoy their Possessions.
PERCYVALL HART Esq.r was Baptised 2.d of May 1666,
And Buryed November 6.th 1738.
M.rs SARAH HART Wife of PERCYVALL HART Esq.r
Was Buryed November 14.th 1720

70. (above) Lullingstone church, monument to Percyvall Hart †1738
71. (right) Trottiscliffe church, detail of pulpit, by Henry Keene,
1775

72. (above)
Shadoxhurst
church, detail of
monument to Sir
Charles Molloy
†1760, by Sir Henry
Cheere(?)

73. (right)
Rochester
Cathedral,
monument to Lady
Anne Henniker
†1792, figure of
Time by Thomas
Banks

74. (right)
Tunbridge Wells,
Holy Trinity,
monument to Maria
Thomas †1833, by
William Behnes

75. (below) Linton
church, monument
to Viscount Brome
†1835, by E. H.
Baily

SACRED TO THE MEMORY OF
MARIA,
WIFE OF JAMES THOMAS, ESQ.ᴿᴱ OF THE MADRAS CIVIL SERVICE
AND THIRD DAUGHTER OF W.F. WOODGATE, ESQ.ᴿᴱ
WHO DIED AT SEA THE 25ᵀᴴ OF MAY 1833, ON HER VOYAGE FROM INDIA TO ENGLAND,
ÆTAT 30 YEARS AND 4 MONTHS.

FOR TO ME TO LIVE IS CHRIST, AND TO DIE IS GAIN : PHIL. I W CHAP. 21 V.

DEAR AS THOU WERT, AND JUSTLY DEAR,
I WILL NOT WEEP FOR THEE;
ONE THOUGHT SHALL CHECK THE STARTING TEAR,
IT IS THAT THOU ART FREE.

GENTLY THE PASSING SPIRIT FLED,
SUSTAINED BY GRACE DIVINE;
OH MAY SUCH GRACE ON ME BE SHED,
AND MAKE MY END LIKE THINE.

CHARLES JAMES MANN, VISCOUNT BROME,
ONLY SON OF JAMES, FIFTH EARL CORNWALLIS;
DIED 27ᵀᴴ OF DECEMBER 1835, AGED 22.

HE IS NOT DEAD, BUT SLEEPETH.
MARK V. 39. LUKE VIII. 52. JOHN XI. 11.

76. (above) Brasted Place, by Robert Adam, 1784–5
77. (right) Cobham Hall, Gilt Hall (Music Room), ceiling 1672, galleries 1779(?), wall decoration by James Wyatt, 1791–3

78. (above) Cobham Hall, Mausoleum, by James Wyatt, 1783
79. (above right) Bromley, Sundridge Park, by Humphry Repton and John Nash, c.1796–9
80. (right) Holwood, by Decimus Burton, 1823–6

81. (above left) Tunbridge Wells, Calverley Park, by Decimus Burton, laid out in 1828
82. (left) Rochester, Fort Clarence, 1812
83. (above) Maidstone, County Hall, Shire Hall (Sessions House), by Sir Robert Smirke, 1824

84. (left)
Sissinghurst,
interior of oast,
early nineteenth
century

85. (below left)
Penshurst,
Leicester Square,
cottages by George
Devey, 1850

86. (right) Hadlow
Castle, tower, by
Walter Barton May
and George Ledwell
Taylor, *c.* 1838–40

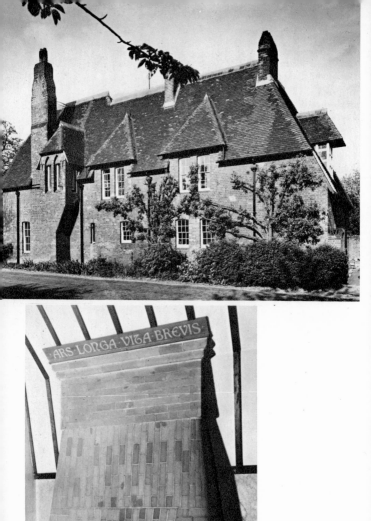

ARS·LONGA·VITA·BREVIS·

90. (above left) Bexleyheath, Red House, by Philip Webb, 1859–60
91. (left) Bexleyheath, Red House, by Philip Webb, 1859–60,
chimneypiece in the drawing room
92. (above) Sundridge, Combe Bank, Saloon, by Walter Crane,
c.1879–80

93. (above) Sevenoaks, Lime Tree Walk, by Sir T. G. Jackson, 1878–9
94. (above right) Chislehurst, Copley Dene, The Wilderness, by
Ernest Newton, *c.*1909
95. (right) Erith, oil works, by Christiani & Nielsen and S. Rowland
Pierce, 1913–17, interior of silos

96. (top) Shipbourne, The Wood House, by Walter Gropius and
Maxwell Fry, 1937 (*Copyright Country Life*)
97. (above) Dene Park, School for Spastics, by the Architects'
Co-partnership, 1961–3

98. (right)
Dungeness,
lighthouse, by
Ronald Ward &
Partners, 1959–60

99. (below right)
Tudeley church,
stained glass, by
Marc Chagall, 1967

100. New Ash Green, by Eric Lyons & Partners, begun 1966, Over Minnis

original house forms the present W part, timber-framing encased in brick. An overhang survives on the W front. The roof structure is probably of the early C15. It has moulded arched-brace trusses and curved windbraces, not a common Kentish structure.

SPELMONDEN, ½ m. S. Long, two-storeyed N front, the ground floor of sandstone. Late C15 details, such as the stone porch arch, and two two-light windows, one l., one r. of the porch. A straight vertical joint l. of the r. window. The upper parts of the house timber-framed and tile-hung.

HALE FARM, 1½ m. NW. C16 half-timbered farmhouse. The overhang unbroken round two fronts, as usual. Closely-spaced uprights, again as usual. Ochre-coloured plaster infill. Happily grouped in a valley bottom with black weather-boarded barns.

SPRIVERS, 1½ m. W of N. In 1756 Alexander Courthope encased his timber-framed house in brick and new-fronted it with a brick block to the E. The addition is nice but simple, five bays by one, two-storeyed. String-course and cornice of moulded brick. Hipped roof and three pedimented dormers. Plain pedimented doorcase. Small entrance hall, the walls decorated with plaster cartouches of arms, alternately large and small, in excellent Rococo plaster surrounds, without asymmetry.

BROAD FORD, 1 m. NE. The main front, facing N, attractively combines mid-C17 vernacular and late C18 Gothick, the timber-framing hidden by grey roughcast. An overhang, however, and three overhanging gables. Bulls-eye windows in the gables, and window bays reaching through both storeys below. Characteristic C17 window frames, the transoms arching up in the middle. Porch with an ogee arch and ogee windows on either side. Round the corner, on the E, more ogee windows in a big bay. Exposed half-timbering S of that. The r. bay of the N front, however, is the earliest part, and belonged at first probably to a Wealden house facing E. Mid-C16 hall fireplace with profile roundels and caryatids. Similar work in an upstairs room made up in the C18 into a chimneypiece. C18 staircase.

Delightful late C17 STABLES to the W. Chequered brick, with sandstone quoins and window lintels. One and a half storeys. Nine bays, the centre one advanced a little under a steep pediment. Low hipped roof. Casement windows. Across the road, a LODGE of Capel Manor.

CAPEL MANOR, 1½ m. NE, has itself been largely demolished.

11—W.K.W.

It was built in 1859–62 by *T.H.Wyatt*, in an Italian Gothic style, exploiting cream, green, and brown sandstone for polychromatic effects. A second LODGE and the SERVICE COURT remain, and the classical garden terraces on the hillside.

GROVEHURST, 2 m. NE. A lovely timber-framed house, rendered white, the gables effectively hung with red tiles. In plan a T, the cross-wing at the r. gabled front and back. The l. two-thirds a symmetrical composition of two gables projecting at two levels, with a two-storeyed porch (now blocked) between them. On one of these gables the date 1641. Two curious pent-porches upset the rhythm of the front. Long sweeping roof at the back. (Carved overmantel in one room, and Elizabethan panelling. Crown-post roof. MHLG)

WESTERNHANGER, 2¼ m. N. Two-thirds of a Wealden hall-house, facing N, the recessed centre blocked in the C16 with a close-studded wall. At the same date the S extension, with a continuous overhang, was added.

HORTON KIRBY

ST MARY. A cruciform E.E. building, of flint, impressive only within. Most impressive of all are the tight-pinched, soaring crossing arches. They are sharply pointed, and their enrichment is confined to slight stop-chamfers in pairs, and a deep moulded abacus. That suggests a date at the latest early in the C13. The fact that the half-blocked arches to the demolished aisles are round makes a date before 1200 preferable, and so do the shafts that grace the lancets of the chancel. They are of stone, not marble, there are numerous shaft-rings, and, most tellingly of all, the capitals are of the Canterbury type with a trumpet-shaped bowl, square abacus, and in one or two places unmistakable acanthus foliage. Say *c.*1190 and all requirements are satisfied. At that date the emphasis on height combined with narrowness at the crossing deserves to be remembered. Arcading, not shafted, low down round the transept walls, and the E lancets here in deep, double-chamfered recesses. External revision of the chancel lancets in the C14, C15, and C19. In fact, so much has happened to the exterior that the primary date is quite obscured. First, in the C14, the nave was rebuilt, except for the lower half of the W wall; and thereby the aisles were abolished. Equally drastically, in 1816–17 *George Smith* lopped off the E half of the chancel (re-using the old windows) and rebuilt the tower in brick. Finally, *Christian* gave all the stonework a heavy going-over, in 1862–3.

Several carved Norman stones, and a worn C13 head, reset in the S porch and over the W doorway. – CURIOSUM. Art Nouveau electrolier in the N transept. – PLATE. Cup, 1599; Flagon, 1620. – MONUMENTS. Alice Drayton † 1468. 4 ft brass of a lady in a horned head-dress. – John Browne † 1595. 23 in. brasses. – Several cartouches in the chancel, to members of the Bathurst family, the earliest to one who died in 1688.

FRANKS, ¾ m. SW. The house was built by Lancelot Bathurst, a London alderman, is dated 1591 on two plaster ceilings, and survives as one of the completest Elizabethan houses in the county. The plan is not the expansive half-H of Cobham, but a square, four ranges round a small central courtyard, i.e. the plan introduced to Kent a century earlier at Wickham Court, West Wickham. Built of warm red brick, in English bond, with flint footings and stone quoins and dressings, Franks has just one architectural fancy, the entrance doorway, which is classical, a round arch, with a Tuscan column to l. and r., bearing a triglyph frieze, segmental pediment, and finials. Otherwise, the straight-sided gables and the tall octagonal chimneystacks are as innocent of Renaissance forms as they would have been seventy years earlier. The windows, conspicuously large, with two or three mullions and a transom, the lights not arched, are the feature which tells most clearly the late Elizabethan date. Two-storeyed elevations, with attic windows in the gables. The S, E, and W fronts all strive for symmetry. The S front with the hall in the recessed centre, the entrance bay to the l., the dais window in the bay to the r., and a further gable and two-storey bay window to complete the façade each side. Projecting chimneybreasts give rhythm to the E front, and a roof-line that goes: gable, stacks, gable, stacks, stacks, gable. The W front, with only two chimneybreasts, managed symmetry in all but the central fenestration. C19 bay-window and adjustments to the parapet. The fancy ridge-tiles everywhere are of course C19 too, added when R. L. Roumieu remodelled the house in 1860–1, and added the polygonal turret in the centre of the N side.

(Internally Roumieu filled the courtyard with a spacious staircase, to produce the top-lit staircase hall in the centre of the house, a Victorian favourite. In other respects the interior was little altered. The porch still opens into the screens passage, but not the gallery over the passage illustrated in Nash's *Mansions*, 1839. The gallery screen does survive, half-timbered, the timbers making rectangles in rectangles, linked by bars, with plaster coats of arms, and a lattice grille at the top, to allow a view from gallery to hall. Plaster ceiling in the hall, with thin ribs. Fireplace arch still of Gothic outline. Simple wood overmantel. The dining room, E of the hall, has a similar plaster ceiling with the date 1591, coats of arms, and a deep strapwork frieze. Overmantel on caryatids. The original saloon, over the hall, has a cove to the ribbed plaster ceiling, and the most elaborate fireplace and overmantel in the house, which is not saying much. Wood doorcase with open pediment. Bedroom over the dining room, with the date 1591 in the ceiling again, and a later plaster frieze of swags.)

REYNOLDS PLACE, ½ m. S. The Elizabethan house, says Hasted, was like Franks but larger. What is left, after the greater part was pulled down in 1703, shows an E wall of brick in English bonding.

₉₀₄₀   HOTHFIELD

ST MARGARET. The church seems to hug the ground, long for its height, the length not countered by the squat W tower with its thick, shingled spike. The tower is Dec, see the W doorway and the tower arch with three chamfers dying into the imposts. The S aisle, with a plinth continued from the tower stair-turret, must be a little later. Square-headed, two-light windows with many cusped lights under a round arch, a delicately moulded design. Perp E window. The chancel projects by only one bay, and the features are C18 (rusticated ashlar buttresses) and C19 (E window). N aisle proportioned as the S, but with Perp two-light windows. Stone S porch. The lowness of the bright, broad interior is even more arresting. Arcades of only four, enormously wide, arches, mostly double-chamfered, on the shortest of piers. In 1598 the nave was gutted by lightning, so only the W responds are medieval. Hence too the pinkened stonework. Mostly the piers are of 1876, but the E pier each side is part of Sir John Tufton's restoration in 1603. Round, with a bowl-shaped capital cut, hardly carved, with very simplified upright leaves. Spindly contemporary roof. No chancel arch. Chancel N window, Dec, blocked by the vestry. PISCINA in the S aisle, multi-cusped like the windows there. – FONT. C17. Quite plain. Enclosed by a balustrade with tall twisted balusters. – PLATE. Cup, 1562; Paten, 1703, Flagon, 1707, both by *Francis Garthorne*. – MONUMENT. Sir John Tufton † 1624. High alabaster tomb-chest, with effigies of Sir John and his wife reclining on top, their eldest son kneeling in little at their heads, at their feet emblems, hers a colossal paw. Shallow arcading on the sides, and Ionic colonnettes, pink and black, with kneeling figures of children between them. Alabaster arch above, with bossy flowers. A restrainedly classical monument, not flying out in any Jacobean fancies.

HOTHFIELD PLACE, the severe stone mansion for the Earl of Thanet, designed, it seems, by *Samuel Wyatt*, was pulled down in 1954. The original farm buildings of *c*.1793, with octagonal dovecote, sw of the church, plus a few Neo-Georgian additions, have taken over the name. Lord Thanet's memory is kept green by the now rather overblown parkland and the stretches of massive buttressed park wall along the roads.

HOW GREEN *see* HEVER

HUNTON

7040

ST MARY. c13 chancel, see one N and one s lancet, the latter masked by the chapel added in 1866; c13 tower, with the w lancet shafted and a pyramid spire. Between them a nave rebuilt *c*.1300, notably lofty for its constricted length. The evidence for the date is in the design of the two N windows, of two uncusped lights with an unencircled quatrefoil poised on the point of each and a similarly naked sexfoil in the apex. Big Perp window between them. Of the chancel arch one can only say that the respond capitals have c14 mouldings. Three-bay s aisle, handsomely high, with octagonal piers and two hollow chamfers on the arches. Probably the arcade is no earlier than the square-headed Perp windows. Modest early c16 stone porch: bequest for building it, 1513, and another for roofing it, 1532. PISCINA-cum-AUMBRY in harness with the double SEDILIA, a delightful design, even if much renewed.* The piscina straddles the SE corner of the chancel, upheld on a wide-spreading frond of luxuriant stiff-leaf foliage. That makes for a date *c*.1280 or so. Bethersden marble shafts. The crockets and finials renewed in a too advanced style. Was the piscina gable originally as bare as it is now? Characteristic Dec arch, ogee with cusping, to the tomb recess in the N wall. – STAINED GLASS. Some old shields and

* No doubt in 1876 as part of *Christian*'s unkind refurbishing of the interior.

quarries, worth examining closely, among the mock-c13 roundels in the large N window. The latter were no doubt done by *George Austin*, of Canterbury Cathedral.* – PLATE. Cup and Paten Cover, 1654; Cup and Paten, 1714, the paten by *Humphrey Payne*; Flagon, inscribed 1715, by *Alice Sheene*; Almsdishes, a pair of 1716, by *Fa.* – MONUMENTS. (Brass – under the tower – of a civilian, for William Head † 1513.) – Sir Thomas Fane † 1606. Large alabaster standing monument. Reclining life-size figures, with a small kneeling daughter and a still-born child below. Corinthian pilasters and coffered arch supporting the crest (and a HELM), plus rather well designed and carved embellishments of a standardized kind. – Anne Fane † 1663. Tall base with drops of boldly simplified husks. On it a curvy two-handled urn. (Cf. the monument of the selfsame year at Tonbridge.) – Thomas Fane † 1692. Exceedingly large hanging monument, erected in 1711 and placed with disconcerting prominence over the preacher's head. More disconcerting still, the waist-length figure, his arm poised, his head cocked, seems in mid-sermon himself. Splendidly carved apparatus of mourning putti, side pilasters, and top cornice curving up in the middle. Fine large-scale leafage round the arms at the bottom. The monument looks like *Edward Stanton*'s work. – Henry Hatley † 1716. Tablet and a crisply carved bust. The convention whereby the hair is short, the clothing a semi-Roman *negligé* makes a date before *c.*1730 impossible. – Thomas Punnett † 1812. By *Regnart*. Meagre Grecian.

HUNTON COURT. Plain c18 house, built of ragstone, not a material in favour at the time. Entrance (w) front with a central three-bay pediment. Additions and embellishments of *c.*1848. The MHLG mentions the staircase and chimneypieces (brought in).

BUSTON, 1 m. NW. L-shaped house. The medieval origin of the N wing is vouched for by a four-centred stone doorway with a typical Perp moulding. The other half plain and rendered. Round the corner, however, a four-bay s front, in red and blue chequer brick, of the late c17. Hipped roof on a strong bracketed cornice. The same for four bays of the E front, with blocked cross-windows. Nothing remains of the early c16 work of Alderman Head, who, Philipot noted, 'added much both of Building and Magnificence to this Fabrick'. Nothing,

* The Rev. Douglas McLeod tells me that the glass is said to have come from Canterbury Cathedral.

that is, except the small ragstone BARN to the SE, with stepped gables in brick.

STONEWALL FARM, ½ m. SE. Half-H shaped house, timber-framed above, brick below. There is a date 1634 on a timber of the S side.

HUSHHEATH MANOR see STAPLEHURST

IDE HILL   *4050*

ST MARY. 1865–6 by *C. H. Cooke*. Ragstone galletted, that is, with stone chippings pushed into the mortar, a local tradition. Otherwise the church is both personal and true to its date, and in its way rather endearing. Tall N tower dwindling away to a shingled spirelet. Transeptlets. Canted end to the S vestry. Nave and chancel with plate tracery turning Geometrical for the E and W windows. Inside, the arch-braced roof rests on corbels carved with the leaves of hop, horse-chestnut, mulberry, and much else. – STAINED GLASS. Chancel N and S and all the nave windows by *A. Gibbs*, *c.*1863–9. Garish, but gay, unlike the E window of 1947, with its lumpish figures and muddy colours.

Modest houses round a big sloping green. Off its NW corner the SCHOOL of 1852 (Kelly) by *Street*. Symmetrical. Stone, with the characteristic window tympana tiled. Brick trim for the girls, stone trim for the boys. (Or is it the other way round ?)

IFIELD   *6070*

ST MARGARET. Roughcast nave and lower chancel, with a little white weatherboarded W spirelet, 're-edified' 1596, re-paired in 1638, and again in 1838 with square-headed windows of Perp form but with the typical deep external splays of pre-archaeological Gothic. The S low-side window a survivor from earlier days.

IFIELD COURT. Tall, austere, late C18 house, of brown brick, the ground-floor windows in two wide bows. Attached at the S a rectangular flint building greatly renewed, but with one C15 upper window on the E side, square-headed, of three cinquefoiled lights. Before 1909 there was more medieval work.

IGHTHAM   *5050*

ST PETER. Attractively coloured, with red brick on the tower, and rusty brown ironstone. But the church is really memorable only for the monuments it contains. The chancel may in origin be early, if the two tiny blocked windows high in the E gable are anything to go by. But the remarkable square-headed window on the N side, with a multi-cusped cinquefoil and curious ends to the cusps, like corks, was inserted under the will of Sir Thomas Cawne, 1373–4. It stands above his monument (*see* below). C14 nave arcades of three wide bays on octagonal piers. Narrow C15 S aisle, and S porch. Original wagon roof in the porch. Debased tower arch. The tower itself is Perp – see the diagonal buttresses and the plinth. Arched-braced roof of the nave, and, very cramped, of the S aisle. Brick N aisle of *c.*1639, the windows of two pointed lights, with a convex quadrant moulding – no hint of classical forms. – SCREEN (S aisle). The W part has a late C14 pattern, the N part a C15 one. Both are simple. – BOX PEWS. Early C17. – Similar PANELLING on the E wall. – CHANDELIER. Brass. 1759. – PLATE. Cup and Paten, 1616; two Flagons, 1690; Alms-dish, by *A.*, 1690; Paten, 1727 by *T.L.*; Cup, 1734. – MONU-MENTS. Sir Thomas Cawne, *c.*1373–4. Fine, well preserved figure of a knight in plate armour and mail, tilted slightly outwards under a cusped and subcusped arch with a square hood. His rigid pose, legs stiff and straight, one hand on his pigeon chest, the face inscrutable under the colossal helmet, is in complete contrast with the uneasy tossings and turnings of knightly effigies early in the C14. No incompetent sculptor carved it. The little lion at his feet is enough to prove that. The stiffness is rather another manifestation of the changed taste that forced the sinuous meanderings of Dec tracery into Perp rigidity. – Sir Richard Clement † 1528. Half a typical C16 brass, $10\frac{1}{2}$ in. of it. – Jane Lambard † 1573. Tombstone, by the font, with crude little brasses set in it. – Jane Dirkin † 1626. 24 in. brass. – Sir William Selby † 1611 and his nephew, also Sir William, † 1638. Large standing wall-monu-ment, with two reclining effigies, one above the other. Corinth-ian side columns and a coffered arch with a top achievement. The monument must be an amalgamation of two, or rather a half-finished monument was adapted to take the second figure. The armour of the two figures should be contrasted, and their poses, both semi-reclining on one elbow, but the later one so much more relaxed. – Dorothy Selby † 1641. By *Edward Marshall*. Large hanging monument. The finely conceived bust of the old lady is set within an oval recess, with as a back-ground reliefs of two of the scenes she had embroidered. At the sides large, elegantly swaying angels hold back curtains. Little mourning figures in shawls low down, little reclining angels high up, on the topmost of a complicated pile of broken pediments. Dame Dorothy's needlework was famous, and counted the chief of her virtues in the inscription:

> She was a Dorcas
> Whose curious Needle turned th' abused Stage
> Of this leud World into the golden Age:
> Whose Pen of Steel and silken Inck enrolled
> The Acts of Jonah in Records of Gold;
> Whose Arte disclosd that Plot, which had it taken;
> Rome had tryumph'd & Britans walls had shaken;
> She was
> In heart, a Lydia; and in tongue, a Hanna,
> In Zeale a Ruth; in Wedlock, a Susanna.
> Prudently Simple, providently Wary;
> To th' world a Martha: and to Heaven a Mary.

The heart of the village is a triangular widening of the road in a dip s of the church. The restored half-timbering, the inn-sign on a post in mid-tarmac, and the prominent petrol pumps make an uneasy mixture, too eagerly catering for all the needs of the sightseer. TOWN HOUSE, at the NW corner, is late C15, with overhanging gables at both ends and a modern porch. The r. gable is the higher. Opposite, a simple half-timbered front with an overhanging upper storey. The l. part was built in 1555. Thomas Skynner was fined for building his house encroaching on the highway. One can see why.

IGHTHAM MOTE. See p. 330.

IGHTHAM COURT, ⅓ m. N. The *pièce de résistance* is the naive classical frontispiece dated 1575, in the centre of the W front. Short, thin, widely-spaced columns climb laboriously, order by order, up four storeys to a flattened pediment. An early C19 porch, the datestone fixed to it, partly masks the ground-floor arcading. The frontispiece is of brick, like the rest of the building, with rendered details, but it is probably slightly younger than the house itself. All the windows are renewed, but Kip's engraving shows that the square-headed form with arched lights and hood-mould is a faithful copy, except in the frontispiece. There the windows have mullions and a transom. So when first built in the mid C16 the house had an H-plan. The W front three-storeyed, the rest of two storeys over a ragstone basement. The battlements and the bay-windows added c.1800. Stone quoins, and on the N side a two-storeyed stone bay for a side door. On the E side one original gable, and, in the recessed centre, the staircase tower. Kip shows the tower rising, as it still does, higher than the rest, with a window at the top. Was there then a belvedere room above the staircase after the fashion of the time ? (Cf. Melbury, Dorset, and Bisham Abbey.) The clock in the turret is dated 1801. Tall brick chimneystacks in rows, C20 copies of what Kip showed. Nothing inside goes back to the C16, except the back staircase. Early C19 staircase, perhaps by *Samuel Wyatt*, who did work at the house.

RASPIT HILL, 1½ m. SW. A large, late house by *Baillie Scott & Beresford*.

OLDBURY CAMP, 1 m. SW. This is a large univallate fort enclosing 123 acres with inturned entrances on the NE and S sides. Excavations revealed two periods of construction. The first, at the end of the C2 BC, consisted of a V-shaped ditch and dump rampart. In the C1 the site was remodelled by the Belgae, who recut the original ditch giving it a broad, flat-bottomed profile. At this period too the present elaborate entrances were constructed. On the E side of the hill are a series of ROCK SHELTERS which have produced evidence of occupation by Palaeolithic hunters.

IGHTHAM MOTE
½ m. S of Ivy Hatch

Ightham Mote is the most complete small medieval manor house in the county. The setting is perfect too. As the visitor descends through the woods from the N he passes a big tree-fringed lake on the l., and then at once there is the low, square, unassertive house within its moat. One ought to approach from the W, through the centre of the row of cottages beside the road, but that way is blocked now; though the inner side of this entrance range remains remarkably unaltered, half-timbered, the ends returned to join stone walls that run down to frame the W front of the house.

The earliest known owner of the Mote is Sir Thomas Cawne, in the third quarter of the C14. As we shall see, the kernel of the house is older than that. In the C15 it belonged to the Hauts. Richard Haut was Sheriff of Kent in 1478 and 1483, but forfeited his estates at the death of Edward IV. His son got them back, lost them again, and the grandson, as soon as he came of age, *c*.1506, sold Ightham Mote to Sir Richard Clement. Late in the C16 it passed to the Selbys.

The w front could be Haut's work and it could be Clement's. It is built wholly of ragstone, two-storeyed, rising in the centre to an entrance tower one storey higher, with a C16 or C17 brick parapet.* The fenestration makes a determined attempt to be regular (some windows in the l. half have been blocked), but the l. half is higher than the r. Arched lights in twos or threes, under square lintels, those in the tower cinque-cusped and with hood-moulds. The entrance arch, on the other hand, has an early C14 form, with a depressed, almost straight-sided arch and two orders, the inner rounded, the outer chamfered. C16 door, as the linenfold in the top panels tells. Round to the s now, to find that after the gable-end of the entrance range the upper storey turns to half-timbering, overhanging the lower walls. At the r. end a half-timbered gable. All the up-rights in the centre are new. More windows of *c*.1500 in the stone part of the walls, of various sizes and patterns. One sharply pointed, cinquefoiled lancet, the second piece of evi-dence from the C14. The E side looks what it is, the backside. At the SE end, however, a stack of seven brick chimneys in a row. So that is where the kitchen was. The windows r. of it are no earlier than the mid C16. Most of the rest of the E front is timber-framed with closely set uprights, over a stone ground floor. At one place, however, the stone walling ascends to a gable, with windows at three levels, the lowest C14, of two cinquefoiled lights. To the l. of this a simple stone back door-way, of medieval date. Finally the N side; visually the most attractive. The upper part of the l. two-thirds half-timbered again, of two heights and dates. The centre of the front pro-jects very far, and has four large rectangular windows with moulded frames, clearly to light an important room. Stone gable-end at the r., with a handsome but quite unexpected C18 Venetian window, superimposed on a large Jacobean window.

As soon as one enters the courtyard a great deal becomes clearer. One is facing the hall of the early C14 house, its r. ex-tremity marked by a straight joint in the wall, its l. by a break forward. Characteristic doorway, with a filleted roll on shafts with Bethersden marble caps, and a hood-mould on heads. The hall window however *c*.1500, square-headed, of five long cinque-cusped lights. The solar wing, to the l., is half-tim-

* The stone panel with an achievement, on the tower, bears the Selby arms.

bered above, externally at least, and, with the two gables and
pretty pierced bargeboards, of the c16. Turning back again
to the entrance range, the doorway and single-light windows
r. of the gateway again may, but need not, be c14. Some sort
of outbuildings, and a gatehouse, within the moat on this side
in the c14 are likely enough. Four-centred gateway arch on
this side, so the tower was without doubt begun from the
ground c.1500. Chimneybreast for the upper room in the gatehouse, flattening the proportions of the lower window and
pushing the upper to one side. Otherwise the w and s ranges
were re-windowed c.1800 with pointed windows and intersecting glazing-bars. The N range, however, which has already
been noted as a c16 rebuilding of consequence, rests on a
wooden loggia, except for the generous half-timbered projection at the l. end, with windows in two rows, lighting a staircase.

Architecturally the interior of the HALL is the finest thing
at Ightham Mote. The doorway leads straight into it, not into
a screens passage. This must always have been the arrangement, for there is no answering doorway in the E wall. Doorways however to kitchen and (smaller and blocked) to buttery.
The original layout of the service end is not clear. The hall is
spanned by a single pointed stone arch, with wooden arches
of equal size at each end. They rest on little caryatid figures,
the stone ones much the better carved. Arch moulding of
major and minor sunk quadrants. Large two-light c14 E window with a transom, the heads cinquefoiled into ogee shapes,
an octofoil at the head. Note the internal rebates for shutters.
c16 fireplace (1583 on the fireback). Overmantel and panelling
1872 by *Norman Shaw*. From the NE corner of the hall, a c14
doorway leads to a probably early c17 STAIRCASE. The staircase projects into a tiny courtyard between the hall and E
range, and must replace an original stairway. At the foot of it
a stone doorway into the room beyond the hall dais, and
another into the UNDERCROFT of the c14 chapel. It is the E
window of this undercroft that is visible outside. Two bays,
with quadripartite rib-vaults. No original feature in the first-
floor CHAPEL itself except the w doorway and beside it a
squint with a depressed ogee arch giving a view from the solar.
A piece of string-course in the SE corner. The SOLAR appears
wholly c16, and has a roof with the curious feature of tiebeams
in both directions and a crown-post on the intersection. Timber oriel window. N of the solar is the priest's room, lying E of

not really possible to distinguish between the two designers. – FONT. Peculiar prismatic shape. What is its date? – FONT COVER. Early C17. – CHANDELIER. Brass. C18. – LAMP HOLDER. In the N aisle. Copper and wrought iron; c.1893. An interesting piece, copied, it is said, from a Venetian model. – RELIEF. By the font. Bronze half-length Virgin and Child by *Henry Wilson*, who lived near by at Platt. Of about 1922. Intended for a monument. – STAINED GLASS. C13 roundel of the Virgin and Child in a s window of the nave. – A jumble of C14 and C15 glass in a nave N window. – Large, fragmentary figure of St Anne in a chancel s window, a quite exceptionally beautiful piece of C15 glass, the colours paled away to a near monochrome, but the drawing done with great tenderness. – Kemsing also has an unusually varied collection of early C20 glass. Alas, it does little to raise one's enthusiasm for the glass-painting of the period: E (1902) and w windows by *Comper*. All in primary colours with lots of white glass. – Transfiguration, in the nave, c.1905, designed by *Wilson*, made by *Whall*. – Crucifixion, in the chancel, c.1880. Germanic C16 gruesomeness softened for English tastes. The most worthwhile of the windows at a close look. Whom is it by? – N aisle w window 1935 by *Douglas Strachan*. No less sentimental than the rest, for all its acid colours.* – PLATE. Cup and Paten Cover, 1564. – COFFIN SLAB. One with a very decisive cross on it. Early C13? – MONUMENTS. Thomas de Hop † 1347. Good brass of a priest, a half-figure, 21 in. long. – The Bunce family. 1778. Large marble tablet.

The VILLAGE, SW of the church, is no more than a rather self-conscious group of tile-hung timber houses round a little triangle of green with a spring rising in it. THE BOX HOUSE, on the W side, has a long, complex front with a cusped, barge-boarded gable in the centre, plastered to look as if it were rusticated stone. The most noticeable building however is ST EDITH HALL at the E end, 1911 by *Godfrey Pinkerton*, typical of its date in striving to be pretty and circumstantial at the same time. In front is a hopscotch court. Architect and donor wanted to serve all age-groups in the village.

At the W end of HEAVERHAM, a charming hamlet 1 m. E, CROWDLEHAM, a yellow-brick house of c.1820, with telling touches of white and the interesting arrangement whereby the three-bay front has low, one-bay wings and is itself framed in

* Most of these facts are drawn from Mr V. E. Bowden's excellent guide to the church; others he has been kind enough to supply at my request.

a raised band of plain brickwork. The centre bay comes forward and rises to a lunette window and a rectangular top with steep, pedimental sides. Mid-c19 porch and alteration of the l. wing.

St Clere, 1⅜ m. N of E. 'Sir John Sedley in the time of Charles I erected a mansion for his residence which is now remaining.' So wrote Hasted in 1782. Sedley, the hottest Parliamentarian in the county, had a chapel in his 'dwelling house called St Cleres' consecrated by Bishop Bancroft in 1633. That must mark the date of his removal from the old house to the new. But is this new house the one we see today? At a distant view of the entrance (N) front one might imagine that this plain, two-and-a-half-storey mansion, five bays by two, was rebuilt after Hasted wrote. But no late c18 house ever had a row of tall chimneys on its roof-ridge, lozenge-shaped in plan and with a continuous capping; or octagonal turrets rising the full height of the corners of the entrance front; or was built in red brick laid in English bond. 1633 makes much better sense. Think of the chimneystacks at Kew Palace (1631), or the turrets which were part of the Elizabethan and Jacobean vocabulary. Raised brick window-surrounds with ears, raised brick quoins, both now cemented. These too are mid-c17, not c18, details. The present parapet however is of the c18; 1767 on a rainwater-head. Behind the parapet a hipped roof with pedimented dormers, and a nearly flat part N and S of the chimneystacks. Before the alterations the roof must have come down to a cornice. Was there a balustrade round the flat? If so, St Clere would, except for the turrets, have been almost identical with Chevening as we know it from the 1679 map. Chevening is 5½ m. from St Clere. No original interiors, but on all floors a double-pile plan, the ground floor symmetrical about the N–S axis. So, to sum up, we seem to have a rectangular, double-pile brick house dated to the early 1630s, related to Chevening, which in view of the controversial dating of that house and its link with the name of Inigo Jones, gives St Clere a national importance as one of the earliest examples of the house-type that Coleshill expressed most perfectly but which only became standardized after 1660, and has thus come to be known, quite wrongly, as the Wren type of house. Here, in its earliest manifestation, it is natural that the turrets, a freakish Jacobeanism, should not have yet been eliminated in the new rationalistic plan.

Spacious c18 staircase in the hall, with three turned balusters per tread. In the sw room a fireplace by *Soane* from the

Governor's Room in the Bank of England. Additions of 1882;
entrance porch, a bow and a bay on the w side, long extensions
to the E.

KENARDINGTON

9030

ST MARY. Church and vicarage lie by themselves on a knoll.
At the first view, as one approaches through the vicarage garden, the church seems normal enough: short E.E. tower, with
a circular N turret and the gable of a S aisle. But the nave and
chancel one expects beyond the tower are not there. After the
church had been struck by lightning in 1559, they were pulled
down, and the S aisle patched up as a church. The N wall that
was built then has buttresses and two-light windows that are
still whole-heartedly Perp. This is a fact worth remembering.
Marks on the tower suggest the nave had a narrow N aisle.
Also C13 are the base of a shaft built into the E wall and the
present S doorway with two continuous stopped chamfers.
Tall Dec windows in the S wall, now blocked or mutilated,
except one of c.1300 with a trefoil in a spherical triangle
joined by bars to its angles. Such linking bars are found at
Chartham c.1294. The interior is unattractively barren,
though, like so many churches round here, it escaped a heavy
C19 restoration. No worthwhile fittings, only a crude FONT,
probably C18 (see the tooling and the oval bowl), the VESTRY
SCREEN, 1717, with a crest of wooden spikes, and two white
oval TEXT BOARDS.

KENCH HILL see TENTERDEN

KENT HATCH see CROCKHAM HILL

KENWARD see PEMBURY and YALDING

KESTON

4060

Keston has no recognizable centre, and the church lies alone on
a lane below the road to Biggin Hill.

CHURCH. Nave and chancel. E.E., extended at the w in 1878 by
H.Blackwell and given a funny little bell-gable. Trefoiled N
and S lancets in the chancel. In the nave blocked S doorway
and blocked arch to a SE tower. (Cudham near by has a tower
in the same position.)* – STAINED GLASS. Love, by *Morris*

* In 1950 the tower was excavated and traces of an earlier rectangular
church found under the present one.

and Co., 1909 (A. C. Sewter). – PLATE. Cup, 1709 by *R.G.* ? – MONUMENT. George Kirkpatrick † 1838. Unsigned Grecian tablet. A bald pilgrim kneels holding a large cross, while a young woman in classical draperies holds the Bible for him to read. Confused and rather silly.

WINDMILL, ¾ m. NW. A post-mill in a splendid windy position, facing out over Surrey. Black and weatherboarded, on a brick roundhouse. Only the stumps of the sweeps are left. Inside is the date 1716, which makes it the oldest dated windmill to survive in Kent.

HILLFORT, on Keston Common. This a promontory site defended artificially on the S by a univallate earthwork (which now survives to a height of about 3 ft) and naturally on the E and W by boggy ground. A single, simple entrance occurs in the middle of the defences.

HILLFORT, in Holwood Park. *See* Holwood.

Remains of ROMAN BUILDINGS were found ⅓ m. NW of Keston Court Farm. Parts of two buildings were examined, a small corridor house 60 by 33 ft, and another house 100 ft to the N. Close by, a tomb or mausoleum was found consisting of a circular building 30 ft in diameter externally, with six radiating platforms of masonry which may originally have supported free-standing or engaged columns.

KEVINGTON *see* ST MARY CRAY

7030

KILNDOWN

CHRIST CHURCH. Viscount Beresford began the church in 1839, employing *Salvin* as architect. It is a sandstone box, with lancets and shallow buttresses, and a W tower and short stone broach spire.* Stringy hammerbeam roof spanning a prodigious width. How could such a thing begin to satisfy his twenty-year-old stepson, Alexander Beresford Hope, even in the same year a founder member of the Cambridge Camden Society, and later to finance the building of All Saints, Margaret Street, the Ecclesiologists' dream church? By March 1840 Beresford Hope appears to have taken charge of alterations. Externally, he had the spire enriched with lucarnes, and the embarrassingly low pitch of the roof masked with a

---

* Professor Hitchcock asserts that there was at first no architect. The row of morose head corbels at the root of the spire are own brothers of those on *Decimus Burton*'s Holy Trinity, Tunbridge Wells.

pierced parapet. But it was the interior that mattered, and between 1840 and 1845 Beresford Hope transformed the E end into a chancel, which *The Ecclesiologist* in 1845 acclaimed as 'A *whole* of colour . . . sucn as is to be seen, in no other English church at the present time'. Such it remains, with a few minor losses. Salvin had made no structural division between nave and chancel, and Beresford Hope's screen marks off a surprisingly short E portion. The shortness and the width make this, the first Camdenian chancel, very unlike the norm. Within it, and spilling out of it, an astonishingly full array of fittings. Stone ALTAR by *Salvin*, up three steps. – ROOD SCREEN and STALLS designed by *R.C.Carpenter* and carved by a Mr *Thomas*. – Large PULPIT, high in the wall, modelled on the famous Beaulieu Abbey refectory pulpit. – Brass LECTERN and two CROWNS for tapers by *Butterfield*. – Red and yellow encaustic tiles; the walls painted up to the window sills with stencilled patterns in red, gold and blue. The screen and pulpit painted too. This was the work of *Roos* and *Willement*. – STAINED GLASS in the E window by *Franz Eggert* of the Royal Works, Munich. More glass by the same in the nave.* No adequate glass could yet be procured from English firms. – OFFICE BOOKS, 1843, bound in red morocco with brass mounts. – Above the font a curious RELIEF of St George and the Dragon. Is this a genuine German piece of the C16? – The ORGAN came later, in 1860, and the REREDOS only in 1869, designed by *Slater* and executed by *Redfern*.

To sum up the 1840–5 fittings, they aim to reproduce medieval prototypes authentically with the minimum of self-expression on the designers' part. For the rich and vivid colouring there was adequate evidence. This was also Pugin's aim. Like Pugin's too, Beresford Hope's decoration is full of texts. Only the glass misses the mark, with its orangey-golds, its turquoises and purples, and its heavily modelled forms.

MONUMENTS in the churchyard. Viscount Beresford † 1854. – Alexander J. B. Beresford Hope † 1887. Designed in 1882 by *Carpenter & Ingelow*. They and the other Beresford tombs have little to recommend them aesthetically.

* The subjects were suggested by Beresford Hope: 'In the centre division of the E window, the representation of the Blessed Virgin with our Saviour in her arms, and two other divisions, St Peter and St Paul, the Apostles of the Jews and the Gentiles. On one side of the church, British Saints, and on the other, Fathers of the Western Church, taking care to prevent any imputation of Popery, to have none but Saints commemorated in the Calendar prefixed to the Church Prayer Book; to this none could object.'

LYCHGATE. 1860, presumably by *Slater*. Sandstone, vaulted.

SCHOOL, NW of the churchyard. 1846 by *Roos*. In a Tudor style, not well handled.

PARSONAGE, ¼ m. N. 1855 by *Carpenter*. Quite large. Sandstone ashlar. Trefoiled lancets in various groupings, with a transom. Some windows with Dec tracery, notably in the low passage-porch.

BEDGEBURY PARK, 1½ m. SE. Large classical mansion of sandstone, with a French pavilion roof high enough for dormers in two tiers. Its centre, two plus three plus two bays, encases a two-storeyed brick house said to have been built in 1688. Marshal Viscount Beresford, reformer of the Portuguese army, bought the house in 1836 and at once set about casing it in stone, raised it a storey higher, added three-bay wings to make an H plan, and crowned it all with a parapet. The stone is finely worked (on e.g. the pedimented window surrounds), but the stubby Ionic pilasters on the entrance vestibule, and the Venetian windows stretched across the canted ends of the wings on the garden side, give the late date away. The pavilion roof that took the place of the parapet in 1854–5 was added by Alexander Beresford Hope. The date seems improbably early for such a roof, but it is documented, and so is the fact that *R.C. Carpenter* was the architect. Even the tower, and lofty, somehow Alpine-looking, spire, added at the same time to the N side of the C18 stable court, are not what one expects of Carpenter, whose speciality was English Gothic.

The interior confirms one's suspicion that Beresford Hope's taste was ill defined. The neo-classical reliefs (by *Flaxman*?) in the vestibule and hall must be set down to the taste of his father, the Grecophile Thomas Hope; but not the white-marble hall chimneypiece, in a sort of Victorian Rococo, with heads of Victoria and Albert, nor the marquetry ceiling in the hall. The gaunt stone staircase belongs to 1855, and so do the plaster ceilings above it and in the great drawing room, Adamesque, but with strapwork. Mid-C18 decoration in one room, good panelling and pedimented doorcases, an oversized Kentian overmantel, and a plaster ceiling with crossed swords in the centre.*

---

* The scheme that occurred to Beresford Hope in 1851, as a memorial to his mother, was never realized, but it illustrates so well the strange muddle-headedness of his paternalistic philanthropy that it is worth quoting from the letter in which he described it to his friend Benjamin Webb. A memorial

COMBWELL, 1 m. E of S. An Augustinian abbey was founded here in Henry II's reign, and c.1220 reduced to the status of a priory. Nothing remains of the buildings, or of a large C17 house, that took the priory's place. The present house is modern (but the MHLG notes a chimneybreast at the back with a medieval figure blowing a horn, and a niche in the W wall).

RISEDEN, ½ m. NE, is a very pretty hamlet, its half-timbered houses, oasts, and minute early C19 cottages scattered about the sides of a valley. GATEHOUSE FARM, at the far end, with closely set uprights, is the chief building.

KINGSFORD STREET see MERSHAM

KINGSNORTH

ST MICHAEL AND ALL ANGELS. Built late in the C14, and the style may be called Late Dec or Early Perp according to taste. Just chancel,* nave plus stone S porch, and a plain un-battlemented W tower with angle buttresses. The details how-ever are telling. Take the window tracery – in the W window the quatrefoil has vertical bars clamped on either side of it; the N and S windows, square-headed and with hood-moulds, repeat a pattern of intersecting semicircles, which the cusping turns into two lights with a little quatrefoil above. The very Dec E window is modern. Notable tower arch, the responds with side pieces embraced by the deeply moulded capitals. Plain chancel arch. Very low S doorways in nave and chancel, the former with a Perp niche over it. – PULPIT. Plain C18. – STAINED GLASS. C15 heads in the tops of most of the nave windows. More noteworthy, the complete figure of St Michael, together with numerous contemporary quarries, early C15. The only colour used is yellow stain, except for the ruby dragon. It is difficult to praise the designer's artistry. – PLATE. Cup of 1568; Paten, 1723 by B.A. – MONUMENT. Humphrey Clarke † 1579. Plain Bethersden marble tomb-

chapel, with a hospice for clergy attached, almshouses and a reformatory school, were to be built in the woods as the centre of 'a model village for the labourers of the estate under the eye of the hospice and its Head, with a good cheap shop'. The boys in the reformatory were to 'create a fresh farm in the heart of the woods while reclaiming the moor and bog, an ideal training for future emigrants'. The hospice, on the other hand, was to be 'a temporary retreat for clergy who need retirement for their own devotions or studies, or change of air and rest. A Christian watering-place so to speak'.

* A N chancel chapel collapsed c.1768, hence the present windowless N wall. Hence too the indent of a brass now exposed in the churchyard.

chest, with 21 in. brasses on it. His HELM hangs on the wall above the tomb.

KIPPINGTON see SEVENOAKS, p. 497

KNOCK FARM see TENTERDEN

4050

KNOCKHOLT

ST KATHERINE. At a first view bizarre and not very attractive: a plain rectangle, long and narrow, of flint rendered yellow. Lancets of the early C19 type. Flint s tower with brick buttresses. A N aisle was added in 1881. Yet in the E wall, high up, are two Early Norman windows, widely spaced as if they originally flanked another. Inside, the arrangement turns out to be more complex – the windows are deeply splayed, and immediately below each is a wide round-headed recess. What sort of a church does all this imply? How much, if any, of the s wall is part of it?

5050

KNOLE

½ m. E of Sevenoaks

Thomas Bourchier, Archbishop of Canterbury from 1454 to 1486, bought the manor of Knole in 1456, and, after patching up the old manor house, set about to build himself a new great palace. Already in 1464 he was able to stay in it for a lengthy period. Bourchier's successors in the see, Morton (1486–1500) and Warham (1503–32), both spent considerable sums on Knole, but on the latter's death the manor was seized by Henry VIII. The King in his turn put substantial works in hand, costing £872 in 1543, £80 in 1546, and £770 in 1548. In 1566 Elizabeth I granted the estate to Sir Thomas Sackville, later Lord Buckhurst, who at first leased it. In 1603 the lease ran out, and Sackville, who became Earl of Dorset in 1604, undertook a major remodelling. This consisted of renewing the roofs, as the rainwater-heads show, embossed with his initials T.D. and the date 1605, and the sumptuous decoration of the suite of state rooms. The finishing touches were being put to the interior in 1608, the year of Dorset's death.

These are the scanty facts which need to be rehearsed as one enters the deer park and, dipping down into a small valley and up the other side, sees the great grey mansion brooding among the trees. The sombre colour of the ragstone walls, the low, spreading form of the vast house, deprive it of grandeur and beauty. Knole is neither sublime nor picturesque. It is, however, especially in the distant view, authentic, looking almost exactly now as it did in the year Thomas Sackville died. Here the ragstone has crumbled a little, there it has been sharply renewed, but otherwise no English house but Haddon has managed to remain motionless like this since the early C17, balanced between growth and decay.

Knole is built round three main courtyards. From front to back the total depth is about 400 ft. The visitor approaching from Sevenoaks, i.e. from the W, sees nothing but the range round the Green Court. One must however at once pass under the gate-tower and into the Green Court, for, as one sees straight away, this courtyard is loosely tacked on in front of the earlier house. The date of this great addition will be discussed below.

Archbishop Bourchier's mansion may be palatial in scale, but it makes very little architectural display. All is sober, unemphatic, even a trifle dull. Battlements externally and towards the courts. The characteristic moulding for windows and doorways a bold wave and a hollow. Windows almost always of two lights, their heads four-centred arches. The ranges are two-storeyed except on the S side. In the centre of his W front, Bourchier's Tower, broad, low, and unintimidating, of three storeys only, with wide rectangular turrets projecting barely a foot on the outer side, with subsidiary (garderobe?) turrets and undersized polygonal ones set far apart towards the court – a residence, not a piece of fortification, as the oriel window emphasizes, inserted to foul the machicolations. Four-centred entrance arch, and a wide four-centred super-arch dying into the turrets. Worn demi-angels in the spandrels, bearing shields. Two-bay octopartite vault on plain corbels. The oriel, canted, with four lights altogether, arched below the transom, cinquefoiled above it, and the enriched battlements above the machicolations complete the meagre total of decoration. The oriel is shafted internally. It lights a room with Bourchier's emblem, a Stafford knot carved on a corbel. The low, set-back central turret was built in the mid C18 (before 1778) to take the lantern removed from the hall. Typically incorrect C18 window tracery. Bourchier's Tower is the centre of an almost symmetrical front. How much of it is of the 1460s? The canted window-bays have

Elizabethan windows with straight-headed lights. In fact only one original window with a Bourchier moulding is now left, the topmost one in the l. turret of the gate-tower. Angle towers, that on the r., the King's Tower, much larger than that on the l., and with string-courses at different levels from the rest of the front. This suggests but does not prove – for string-courses change level often at Knole for no particular reason – that the tower was an addition.

It will be best to complete the description of the exterior taking the N, E, and S fronts in turn, though visitors are not generally allowed to see them close-to.

The N elevation is the least touched part of Bourchier's work. It is quite irregular, with two deep battlemented garde-robe turrets towards the W end and a chimneybreast between them; then the wall is returned to a gable higher than the battlements, the continuation of the hall roof. A meaningless corbel at the return and another below the gable. Low gabled service buildings in front,* and above and behind the N range of the back court, partly reconstructed in C18 brick.

The E front, facing the garden, is only stone on the ground floor. Windows of two types (wave plus hollow moulding, chamfer plus cavetto), which by their placing suggest to Mr Faulkner that Bourchier had on this façade a gatehouse, later obliterated. The upper storey, half-timbered and rendered, is clearly C17 work (after a fire in 1623?), with eight identical gables and eight identical oriel windows under pedimental gablets.

Bourchier's chapel lies at the SE corner, set back considerably from the E front. Lofty five-light E window with panel tracery in two tiers. Three S windows, segment-headed with three cinquefoiled lights and the typical, bold wave-moulding. So round to the S side itself which, omitting the chapel, is almost symmetrical and a characteristic Jacobean composition with its flat, gabled front and deep three-storeyed wings at the ends. Angle projections. Basically, however, the composition is C15, not C17. The SE tower, or Duke's Tower, is later than the chapel, because its E wall has been scooped away to leave room for the last of the chapel windows. Balancing SW wing, i.e. King's Tower, which has already been noted as a possible addition. New towers were to be built as early as 1467, and in the 1480s more accommodation had to be provided. Dorset's state rooms lie on the first floor behind this front,

* Mr P.A. Faulkner has found that they incorporate a truncated GATE-HOUSE of the Bourchier period.

and the near-regularity of the façade is due to him. Lofty windows lighting the state rooms, with three mullions and two transoms, and of course no arching of the lights. Big shaped gables, going up in a quadrant and a big step to an ogee top, on which a Sackville leopard crouches. Small obelisks on the steps and on the parapet between the gables. The stonework all recently renewed. The centre of the ground floor was opened up with a low but startlingly multicoloured arcade on stumpy Tuscan columns. Black touch; white, grey, and a vivid mottled marble.

So much for the exterior of Bourchier's house and its extent. To understand his planning one must return to Bourchier's Tower and enter his front courtyard, the STONE COURT. The hall lies in the usual position on the far side. This too was re-modelled externally c.1605. Shaped gables.* Bath stone colonnade masking its lower half, of well-proportioned Tuscan columns on high bases. Triglyph frieze, detailed with typical early C17 sparseness. Wooden balustrade dated 1748. Under the colonnade two Jacobean doorcases with pilasters and leopards in the spandrels. The r. is a dummy, the l. leads into the SCREENS PASSAGE. Here the immediately remarkable feature is that there are only two service doorways. This is however not because of Bourchier's meagre service arrangements, but because of their spaciousness. To reach the kitchen one leaves the screens passage at the far (E) end via a two-storeyed porch-like projection. A doorway (not original) on the l. opens on to a large vestibule,‡ E of which lies the huge KITCHEN, occupying the N side of the back court. It has an open arch-braced roof and three fireplaces, one S and two N. The back court itself is divided into three by a half-timbered gallery on four-centred arches, originally probably open, which takes a dog-legged course from the hall to the chapel in the SE corner. The courts are the WATER COURT on the N, the PHEASANT COURT on the S (timber-framed on all four sides – with a bay-window on the W side blocked by the ballroom panelling, proof that the half-timbered work is pre-1605), and a slit in the SE angle known as the MEN'S COURT. Wide four-centred arch in the SE corner of the Water Court, hidden by a lean-to, aligned with the back doorway in the E front. Another similar arch further N was originally a second

* The stone cartouche with flower garlands, between the gables, is dated 1701. It came from Copt Hall and has the arms of Cranfield.

‡ Identified by Mr P. A. Faulkner as the servery, with the Master Cook's gallery over. The disposition of the windows shows that it was originally two-storeyed.

major fireplace. Two straight joints in the E front roughly opposite it mask some tampering in this corner. Bourchier's state rooms must have extended down the s range of the back court, leading ultimately to the chapel.

To complete the description of the exterior one should return to the very beginning and consider the GREEN COURT. Its outer face is what first confronts the visitor, an even, two-storeyed front with a plain, not very high gate-tower in the centre. It returns at the N and s to enclose the Green Court. Square, battlemented angle turrets to the tower, a four-centred entrance arch with a hollow and a double-wave, i.e. not a Bourchier moulding. The Dorset arms inserted in the spandrels. (The spandrels on the inner side are in their original state.) Over the arch a two-light window with arched lights, and another at a higher level. A late C15 or an early C16 date would fit this equally well. Who then would have had a better motive for adding a new court considerably larger than either of the existing ones? The King surely rather than an Archbishop; so the date for it is the 1540s, and that makes the conservatism notable. Furthermore, the symmetry of the entrance front is probably misleading. Six three-light windows at each level either side of the tower, five shaped gables either side, just like those of the state room front, aligned over the windows and enclosing a similar attic window. The gables are clearly part of the 1605 re-roofing campaign. The windows are of sandstone (not of ragstone, as all genuine C15 and C16 windows are) and of unknown date, at any rate no earlier than the C17. The chimneystacks, however, which are part of the C16 building, do not come at regular intervals. Six octagonal brick shafts per stack, with star tops. The other original feature is also not consistent across the front. This is the plinth, which continues unbroken along the r. half and round the tower, but then, following the original ground level, disappears after three bays of the l. half. In the Green Court were lodgings just as in the Base Court at Hampton Court. Hence the many four-centred doorways, one N, two s, and six w. The s range hides the ORANGERY of 1823, which lies behind and has its Gothic façade to the s.

STABLE COURT, N of Green Court, probably c.1605. The small straight-sided gables and mullioned windows with cornices over them in the E range typical of the years before and after 1600. Exceedingly strong buttresses where the ground falls away to the N.

Thomas Sackville's alterations to the exterior of Knole crop up, as has been seen, in numerous places, but his major purpose was to create in the s range of Bourchier's house a series of state rooms that would for sumptuousness give place to none in England. Description of the INTERIOR can now follow the route taken by the guided tour.

GREAT HALL. This was of course Bourchier's hall, and the two doorways l. and r. of the dais end are of his time. The C17 work is quite modest, a flat plaster ceiling with small pendants and thin ribs (another in the screens passage), arcaded plaster frieze, and maybe the still Gothic fireplace (its sharply incised mouldings are quite unlike the 1460s style). Modest, that is, except for the SCREEN, a gargantuan edifice, carved with barbaric vitality. Caryatid couples on both levels.

The C15 s doorway opens onto the GREAT STAIRCASE. The 49 staircase rises beyond a Tuscan arcade round a spacious rectangular well to a first-floor landing with an Ionic arcade. Leopards with shields on the newels. The openness, the lightness, indeed the desire to make a grand architectural display of the staircase, were something new in 1605, and were eagerly taken up first at Hatfield, then in the 1620s at Blickling, Aston Hall, etc. The entire staircase is decorated with semigrisaille paintings, yellowish-green and grey, coarsely overpainted in the early C20, but even yet of a strange, haunting attraction. Under the lower arcade, the Four Ages of Man, based on engraved designs by *Marten de Vos*; on the staircase itself, pairs of mythical and allegorical figures; under the upper arcade, six Virtues above panels of Floris-like strapwork. Plaster ceiling with thin moulded ribs.

The s doorway on the staircase landing leads at once into the first of the state rooms, the ballroom, but first one must enter the E door to pass through a sequence of simple panelled early C17 rooms, the larger ones with giant pilasters and wood overmantels with caryatids. The sequence starts with the BROWN GALLERY, and continues in the E range with, on the r., LADY BETTY'S BEDROOM and LADY BETTY'S DRESSING ROOM, and on the l., the SPANGLE BEDROOM and SPANGLE DRESSING ROOM, NW of which the T-shaped LEICESTER GALLERY develops. In the Leicester Gallery a C15 stone fireplace. The room W of this is the VENETIAN AMBASSADOR'S BEDROOM, with, appropriately, a fine Venetian window and a mid-C18 fireplace.

The CHAPEL, in the SE corner, is not shown to the

public.* It has Jacobean woodwork, PULPIT and PEWS arranged as in a college chapel, carved with arches in perspective; FAMILY PEW in a gallery at the w end. – Contemporary ORGAN. – FONT *c*.1770. A bowl with a lid on a large marble stem. – PAINTINGS. Triptych. 1526. Very Germanic in style, but with an English inscription, and painted for Dr Avyngton to go in Winchester Cathedral. Signed by *T.G.* – Two large early C16 paintings in the style of *Quentin Massys*.

So back to the landing of the Great Staircase and at last into the STATE ROOMS. The BALLROOM, the first of them, is the most sumptuous ensemble of all, wholly a greyish white, for the panelling itself is whitened. Panelling of small fields between pilasters with well-carved composite capitals. Winged horses prancing out where the volutes should be. Plaster ceiling with broad, flat bands instead of thin ribs and embossed flowers – the pattern for all the state rooms. Broad bands are on the whole a sign of the C17, thin ribs of the C16. Oak frieze of unusual depth, carved in the highest relief with mermaids and other grotesque creatures. The *pièce de résistance*, however, as usual in Jacobean interiors, is the fireplace and overmantel reaching to the ceiling. Black, white, and grey marble. Engraved Bethersden marble lintel. On the overmantel exquisite drops of flowers and musical instruments, their urbane delicacy an odd contrast to the exaggerations all around. The unparalleled riches of C17 furniture, including the famous Carolean silver furniture and sconces in the ballroom and others of the state rooms, are beyond the terms of reference of *The Buildings of England*.

The state rooms continue in the s range of the Stone Court, w of the back staircase. The stairs lead down to the COLONNADE ROOM (not open to the public), and both were decorated with mural paintings in the late C17 – trophies on the staircase, urns in feigned niches in the Colonnade Room, continuing the pattern of Sackville's arcade, which is now glazed, but seems originally to have been intended to be open as a loggia, cf. Hatfield. Yet a plaster ceiling of *c*.1605. Beyond the staircase landing (through a C15 doorway) the REYNOLDS ROOM. Chimneypiece on bronze caryatids. Pink marble as well as the usual colours. The overmantel carved with sphinxes collapsing under the weight of putti who hold up trophies of arms. Plaster ceiling. Next, the CARTOON GALLERY. Almost monochrome

50

* It stands on an undercroft of Bourchier date with a ribbed barrel-vault, intended as a lower chapel (P.A. Faulkner).

chimneypiece of grey veined marble. Coupled Ionic columns and coupled caryatids. Plaster ceiling with ribs in a sinuous netlike pattern continued the whole length of the gallery. Vines trailing along the ribs, and sprigs of identifiable wild flowers between the ribs. The walls beside the chimneypiece and the whole s wall, including a big window bay, enriched with carved and painted pilasters, their capitals of an almost neo-classical refinement, the relief carving the usual pattern-book strapwork. The painting was executed by *Paul Isaacson*, who in 1608 received £100 for it.

The last room of the suite is the KING'S BEDROOM, in the King's Tower. The ceiling plasterwork here has the more disciplined pattern of raised ribs making squares, with a wreath in the centre of each. It is a pattern decidedly bolder in scale than the others, a pattern from which the characteristic mid-C17 ceiling could have developed even without the authority of Inigo Jones. (Blocked C15 doorways to garderobes at two levels.)

A ragstone wall of prodigious extent surrounds the GARDENS s of the house. Stone gatepiers of the late C17 with the Cranfield arms immediately r. of the entrance front. Wrought-iron gates and clairvoies on the W and s sides (one with the Cranfield cipher).

In the park, a little way beyond the SE corner of the walls, the BIRDHOUSE, an octagonal folly built *c.*1761, with crude Gothic windows and turrets carrying spirelets. The doorway and two windows, set into a wall l. of the Birdhouse, perhaps genuinely medieval.

KNOWLE HILL *see* ULCOMBE

LAMBERHURST   6030

Church and COURT LODGE, a plain C18 mansion, three-storeyed and sandstone-fronted, stand together above a landscaped valley, E of the village.

ST MARY. Dec nave and chancel, with s aisle to both and s porch, all rubble sandstone. Perp SW tower of coursed sandstone, battlemented, with a recessed shingled spire, and, a second abnormality, minus any W doorway. Perp also the five-light W window of the nave, a design of some individuality. Arcades of the standard form, octagonal piers and double-chamfered arches, the nave arcade the earlier; compare the chancel arcade capitals with those of the porch. Incorporated in the chancel arcade is a PISCINA and the simplest SEDILIA, just a stone bench pierced in the back with two quatrefoils.

See p. 644

At the E end a lower arch, also C14 but more vigorously pro-filed. Another PISCINA set into its E impost. Is this odd arrangement original? In the N wall opposite, a single large lancet also puzzles. Need it be evidence of an earlier church? C14 lancets however were usually trefoiled. Crown-post roof in the nave. – PULPIT dated 1630, and still keeping its small sounding-board. The arcading is standard, but the panels with heads on scrolled saltire crosses are not. The READING DESK below clearly made up in the C19. – TILES. Some with C14 patterns in the S chapel. – The Royal Arms of Queen Anne over the S door are really the top of an C18 REREDOS, with two big urns showing and putto-heads among clouds. – PLATE. Cup, 1633; Paten inscribed 1670. – MONUMENT. Richard Thomas † 1657. Black and white marble tablet typical of that date.

The village street is unusually complete and consistent, with two strong C19 accents to liven it up. At the N end the Jacobean SCHOOL of the 1850s and 1877, red brick, with shaped gables and a perky turret; and STAIR HOUSE down at the bottom, 1889 by *Christopher & White*, Norman-Shawish and picturesque as one views it obliquely. Opposite the latter, COGGERS HALL, the best old house, a long, close-studded front, much restored, jettied the whole way across, i.e. built in the C16 when a hall open to the roof had become obsolete.

LAMORBEY *see* SIDCUP, pp. 505, 506

8050

LANGLEY

ST MARY. Built in 1853–5 by *Butterfield*, for Dr Pusey's brother. The material is ragstone in squared blocks, the style late C13. A straightforward plan – chancel, nave, N aisle and vestry, W tower with a spire. (The church is said to be rebuilt on old foundations.) But Butterfield shows his hand in e.g. the sharpness of the gables, the thick tracery, the swelling broaches of the spire, and in a dry-eyed clarity and force in the whole design. Spare interior. Arcade on circular piers. Multiple-chamfered tower arch and chancel arch. The floor and lower part of the sanctuary walls tiled in rectangular

patterns of red, yellow, grey, and black. – Contemporary
STAINED GLASS, mostly destroyed. The tower window remains to show that it was very good. C13 style. It was made
by *Hardman* to *Butterfield*'s design. – FONT. This is a genuine
Late Perp piece. The usual thing: octagonal, concave-sided
bowl, with fleurs-de-lys, Tudor roses, and a flower.

SCHOOL and MASTER'S HOUSE, N of the church. Also by
Butterfield, 1853.* L-shaped ragstone group, the two parts
distinguished in a characteristic way. One-storeyed school on
the r. with a traceried end-window, the house higher but quite
informal, with a pointed porch-arch and a corbelled-out corner, rectangular windows and a tiny half-timbered gable.

CORNER FARM, ¼ m. NE, at the corner of Heath Road and
Horseshoes Lane. Fine restored half-timbered house now in
its original late C15 state. It is the standard Wealden formula
with a two-storeyed hall window of four-plus-four arched
lights with a transom, and a four-centred doorway.

RUMWOOD COURT, ½ m. NW. Apparently all modern phoney
half-timbering. All of the W front, however, except for the l.
bays, is in fact old and bears the date 1599. The tall, gabled
porch comes near the l. end, then, surprisingly close to it, a
projecting rectangular bay, also gabled, with a six-light dais
window, with two transoms. The cross wing to the r. is boldly
jettied out twice. Oriels under the overhangs here and in the
porch. Close-spaced uprights everywhere, and many horizontal beams too.

LANGTON GREEN

5030

ALL SAINTS. 1862–4 by *Sir George Gilbert Scott*. E.E. Sandstone. Nave, narrow N aisle and wide S aisle. Wide chancel.
The exterior undistinguished except for the N side, where the
roof sweeps down low over nave and aisle, so low that the
paired lancets break up into it under bargeboarded gables.
Dormer windows too. This arrangement, which is unusually
domestic, is apparently nevertheless part of the original design, though Goodhart-Rendel mentions enlargements of 1889
and 1902. The E end of the chancel is treated as a sanctuary inside and enriched with shafts accordingly. – PULPIT.
Sandstone. Covered with four-petalled flowers. – REREDOS.
Alabaster. Richest Dec style. In the centre the Supper at
Emmaus in coloured marbles and mosaic. – TROWEL and

* As Dr Paul Thompson confirms.

MALLET, in the s chapel, used for laying the foundation stone
in 1862. Worth noticing as examples of Tunbridge Ware, the
main product of C19 Tunbridge Wells. – STAINED GLASS.
Vestry E window, c.1862. St Mary Magdalen by *William
Morris*. – In the chancel, St Alban and St Stephen, 1865 by
Burne-Jones. – w window of 1865–6 by *Morris*. – s aisle w
window, 1865–6, St Mark by *Burne-Jones*, St Luke by *Morris*,
St John and St Matthew by *Ford Madox Brown*.* – But it
cannot be denied that *C.E. Kempe*'s E window of 1904 steals
the show. It is a Jesse Tree spread across five lancets. Unusually deep colours, and a positively Baroque vine-stem with
its many big leaves and luscious bunches of grapes.

The green is large and mown. On the w side the church, a tile-
hung C19 cottage, and LANGTON HOUSE, dated 1810, a
brick box painted white. Plenty of large trees between and
behind.

HOLMEWOOD, ½ m. SE. Built by *Decimus Burton* in 1827 and
originally called Mitchells. Sandstone, two storeys. Seven
bays by five. Porte-cochère with pairs of stumpy Greek Doric
columns. Otherwise the detail is no longer Greek. The top
parapet for example has sunk panels cut back in two layers.
Similar panels below the upper windows, and a string-course
on small shallow brackets. On the s front the three centre bays
are contained in a bow. Light reaches the narrow central hall
from an oval skylight via an oval oculus, a pinched version of
the arrangement Burton had used at Holwood. Dainty detailing of the doorcases, again not really Greek.

LARKFIELD

7050

HOLY TRINITY. 1854 by *R.P.Pope*. Not small. Ragstone. E.E.
style. Clerestoried nave with a s aisle and N arcade. Chancel.
Gargoyles. Pope had some fun at the w end, with a wheel
window, complex triple bell-gable, and big-bottomed buttresses. Arcades of short, round piers. Stiff-leaf capitals. FONT
and PULPIT to match. – STAINED GLASS. E and W windows
1858 by *Gibbs* (TK).

LYCHGATE also to match.

Larkfield is really no more than a main-road hamlet, on the A20.
It is at the moment being enveloped in new housing, estate
after estate of it. The pearl in the oyster is a group of COT-
TAGES on the A20, whitewashed brick but otherwise of all

* I owe these facts to Mr A. C. Sewter.

shapes and dates, the centrepiece a rather grand early C15
Wealden hall-house. The ends project on curved corner-
pieces, the framing widely spaced with curved braces.
Traceried window in the solar end.

BRADBOURNE, ¼ m. s of A20. Splendid and very delightful, 64
splendid because of the varied colour and texture of the brickwork, delightful because the three fronts contrast so surprisingly with one another. It was built for Sir Thomas Twisden
and completed in 1713–15. The approach from the NW,
through a park now given up to the experimental growing of
fruit-trees, shows the grandest front of the house, among big
park trees, planes and beeches, with a sickle-shaped lake to the
r. and behind. But the present entrance front is the N one,
modest by comparison, but establishing the themes which
the W and S fronts take up and elaborate. It is built of fine
red brick of two bright shades. Two-storeyed centre, not high,
of seven bays, framed between boldly projecting, windowless
wings, the r. one higher than its partner. Two window spaces in
each, and a tall rectangular chimneystack over the centre, with
a long rectangular sunk panel to stress the height. The only
other decoration is sunk panels over all the windows. Deep
porch, like a covered bridge, probably of the 1770s. The W
front, as we have had warning, is decisively higher, but still
only two-storeyed, for the lower windows have grown to an
exceeding tallness. Panelled parapet over a strong white cornice. Pedimented dormers. The system is kept simple:
3 plus 3 plus 3 bays, the central triplet pedimented and brought
forward a little, the corners stressed by coupled pilasters, the
centre bay by a grand doorcase plus an elliptical-headed window and an oval one in the pediment. No distraction then
from the exquisite colouring of the brickwork. Brown with
red dressings, the centre bays and the pilasters pinky-buff and
vermilion. Many subtle variations of colour besides. The s
front, like the N, has a centre and projecting wings. The centre
however only single-storeyed, with long windows. The wings
both tall and three windows wide, with central chimneystacks. Here the brickwork abandons colour variety for textural variety. Oval windows in the wings either side of a flat
rubbed brick panel laid as a *trompe l'œil* niche. In 1774 a robust
bow was added in the centre. It pulled the whole front into a
bizarre but rather successful composition.

  This disagreement between the three main façades raises
the question, is Bradbourne a pre-C18 house recased? The

interior answers that it must be. The N doorway leads into a small vestibule, into which is crammed a most sumptuous staircase. Three twisted balusters to the tread, the tread-ends carved, and their scrolly profile continued across the underside of the free-flying upper flight. Yet it leads only to three bedrooms. The original entrance in the W front gave into a two-storeyed hall, with a coved ceiling, simple panelling, but no decoration to match its scale. The main living rooms are on the S side. In the bow room and the room N of it marble fireplaces and simple plaster ceilings of c.1774, in the Adam manner, then the latest fashion. The stone-flagged hall on the E side of the house and its staircase are the heart of circulation in the house. Such a maladroit plan can only have resulted if old walls were kept. (Cellar on the N side with blocked windows and a C16 doorway.)

N of the house, delightful STABLES, one-storeyed, red and blue chequer brick, with a big hipped roof and a cupola in the centre of the S side. The W side is symmetrical too. Both fronts with the middle five bays as a pavilion, and doorcases in the wings.

LASHENDEN see BIDDENDEN

LEACON HALL see WAREHORNE

LEEDS

St NICHOLAS. '1137, Fundatio Ecclesie de Ledes', wrote William Thorn in the C14. That at any rate must be about the date of the massive ragstone W tower, with a large unmoulded window N and S, and shallow NE and SE pilaster buttresses, quoined in tufa. C13 shafted W doorway, of sandstone. The most impressive Norman piece is the tower arch, of three unmoulded orders, the innermost one flanked by fat rolls. Triply shafted responds, with single- and twin-scallop capitals. The N aisle has two tiny blocked tufa N windows, rebated externally for shutters, and one in the W wall. So the original church had aisles. But, alas, that is the end of the Norman work.[*] The present building has nave and aisles, chancel and chapels, the S gabled, the N battlemented, neither reaching to the E end. The chancel windows are cuspless, which suggests C16 rebuilding of the chancel. Three-bay

---

[*] But Mr P. J. Tester draws my attention to the fact that high up above the N arcade of the nave are two Saxon windows, originally splayed externally.

nave arcades. Octagonal piers with concave sides and two hollow chamfers on the arches. Perp chancel arch and w arches to the chapels. The s chapel, however, is c14. Ogee-headed PISCINA. The ogee hood-moulds to the s aisle windows and the s chapel E window have no warrant in pre-restoration drawings. Squints from both chapels, that to the N of three lights like a domestic window, that to the s through the triple SEDILIA, which have cuspless arched heads, reinforcing the evidence of the chancel windows. Boarded chancel roof with arched braces. Crown-post roof in the nave, and traceried wall-braces. – ROOD SCREEN. Perp. It stretches the full width of the church, with four-light windows, the tracery describing delicate ogees between the mullions. Shafts w and E for coves; but the present top is of 1892 by *W.B. Sanders.* – Jacobean PEW in the N chapel. – CHANDELIER. Brass; *c.*1778. – PLATE. Paten, 1681 by *L.S.*; Paten, 1738 by *R. Gurney & T. Cooke*(?); Cup, Flagon, and Almsdish, 1750 by *Gurney & Cooke.* – MONUMENTS. William Merden † 1509. Brass with 12½ in. figures. – Katherine Lambe † 1514. Brass, 8 in. long, of a lady with flowing hair. – Jane Countess of Carbery † 1643 and Sir William Meredith † 1675. Large standing wall-monument of black and white marble, erected after the latter's death. Recessed Ionic columns at the sides, and an open pediment starting from scrolls. – Sir Roger Meredith † 1738. Handsome architectural tablet, erected after 1742. Signed by *William Palmer.* – Henry Meredith. After 1758. The design, with cherubs reclining on the curved top of the inscription, and an urn between them, in a recess, and a broken pediment at the top, follows closely a design in Gibbs's *Book of Architecture* (1728), p. 123. The bloated cherubs are enough to show that it was interpreted by no master hand.

LEEDS PRIORY. The site of the priory, ¼ m. sw, founded in 1119 by Robert de Crevecœur for Augustinian Canons, is quite revealing. Hardly one stone stands on another above ground.* Less still of the interesting early c17 brick house of the Merediths, built on the site (see Badeslade's print of 1720).

LEEDS CASTLE. It is a case of distance lending enchantment. As it is glimpsed through the pines from the A20 Leeds seems enchanted, the perfect fairy-tale castle, rising sheer, grey, and battlemented from the reed-fringed lake. But as one drives through the park and passes above the w edge of the lake, the compact group falls apart into four separate buildings, the D-

* Excavation in 1846 established that the church had an apse and a crypt.

shaped gloriette at the N, linked only by a bridge to the main
building of 1822 at the N end of the main island, the Maiden's
Tower, on the E side of the main island, and the gatehouse at
its S extremity.

The building history is just as disjointed, and not without
its puzzles. Hugh de Crevecoeur held the manor *c*.1120, and it
remained in Crevecoeur hands until 1268. There must have
been a motte-and-bailey castle, corresponding to the gloriette
and main island, not necessarily moated, for the present lake
is created artificially in the marshy bottom. The 'stagnum' is
mentioned in 1272 however; and in that year Leeds came into
royal possession. It was a favourite castle of Edward I, who
made it over to Eleanor, his queen, and for the next two centuries it formed part of the Queen's dower. Much building
took place in the early C16, while the castle was still in royal
ownership, but in 1552 it was granted to Sir Anthony St
Leger. In 1632 Sir Thomas Colepeper bought it, and thereafter it descended, sometimes through the female line, until
in 1821 Fiennes Wykeham-Martin inherited and at once set
to rebuild the main building. It is this, with its turrets and
battlements, and the battlements he added to the gloriette
and Maiden's Tower, that makes Leeds look so medieval from
the N.

The entrance, over the S end of the lake, was guarded by an
unusually complex barbican, with a mill attached to the outer
side of it, to employ the water of the outflow stream. The
MILL, of ragstone, like the whole of the rest of the castle,
remains reasonably intact, a square building straddling the
stream, with small windows on two levels, their dressings now
gone. Repairs to the mill are recorded in 1298–9. The BAR-
BICAN was originally a triple one, to cover the roads to
Maidstone (W), Leeds (S), and Lenham (E). Only the first has
much left. The road, raised on a grassy causeway, passes
through a depressed-pointed arch, with a continuous chamfer,
a rounded inner order, and a portcullis groove. It then turns
at r. angles to pass under a second arch similarly fortified, and
set in a wall with two arrow-loops, and at its r. end, the jamb
of the S barbican's inner arch. Nothing at all of the E barbican.
Stone bridge of two arches over the moat.

After this the GATEHOUSE is remarkably modest, a low,
square block, barely a tower, with ranges running back
obliquely to l. and r. Blocked arrow-slits in the latter, and
Tudor windows. Over the entrance arch a projection with

machicoulis and a recess for the raised drawbridge: a C14 addition, perhaps. Within the entrance arch, which has the same mouldings as the barbican arches, passages lead to l. and r. and an inner arch to the passage that goes through to the bailey. The arrangement suggests that at some time the gatehouse was brought forward of its previous position. That will have been *c.*1296–9, when work was paid for on the 'great chamber above the gate' and on the bridge. No old windows in the gatehouse range which would have confirmed the date. Stumps of return walls at the E and W ends of the N wall – clearly a range ran N from the NW corner.

The remodelling of the gatehouse was part of Edward I's reinforcement of the main island's defences. A new WALL was built up from the bed of the moat, enclosing the whole island, and provided with D-shaped turrets, two on the W side and three on the E. In 1298–9 lead was bought for use 'super ij novis turellis'. Walls and turrets are now shaved down to the level of the lawn, and visually no longer serve to enclose the island. The single exception is the NE turret, which is intact, with a steep tiled roof, and garderobe and chimneybreast for an upper room. Timber-framed wall towards the island. Tunnel-vaulted WATER GATE near the SE corner.*

The MAIN BUILDING, which melts so perfectly into the ensemble from the N, as seen from the S, across an oval croquet lawn, seems a characteristically naive piece of early C19 medievalism, a blandly symmetrical, rectangular block, two-storeyed, with battlements, octagonal angle-turrets, and a boldly scaled tower in the centre. Large Tudor-style windows. *W. Twopeny* is recorded as the designer of a staircase, but not apparently of the building itself. A long pointed-tunnel-vaulted cellar running N–S under the house is the only remains of the important medieval building that occupied the site.

The isolated block E of the croquet lawn is the so-called MAIDEN'S TOWER. This is genuinely Tudor, with Wykeham-Martin battlements, and other tamperings by him, e.g. on both the doorways. Two storeys, with a third at a lower level on the E side. Projection here, with a chimneybreast starting at first-floor level. Otherwise the building is rectangular. Windows of two and three arched lights under straight hood-moulds.

---

* An earlier stone enceinte wall within the line of the present wall was discovered and its course plotted by Fiennes Wykeham-Martin. See his excellent monograph on Leeds Castle, published in 1869.

To reach the GLORIETTE one has to pass through the main building and across the two-storeyed bridge, redone in stone by Wykeham-Martin, instead of the two-storeyed wooden bridge that was there before. At the N end of the bridge there is a thin turret (with a BELL dated 1435) also called 'Glorietta' in documents. The King seems to have had a chamber in it. The gloriette is in plan a stretched D, of two storeys above a battered plinth that runs down into the water. Almost all the windows are Tudor, except for a few at the lower level, with two-centred arches and renewed Y-tracery. They cannot be studied close to except from a boat. On the W side a two-storeyed canted window bay, and garderobe projections at the NW and NE angles. The evidence then seems to say that the gloriette was built by Edward I, but that the upper storey is wholly Tudor.

Internally the rooms are in ranges E, W, and S of a narrow central courtyard. The original timber-framed walls were re-built in stone in the C19, except at the S end, and the interiors remodelled c.1927 by *Owen Little*. No informative original feature is left except the lower windows in the W half of the S wall. They are a long trefoiled lancet with a transom, a small trefoiled opening, and a pair of windows with Y-tracery. Inside, the long lancet has a hood on bunches of naturalistic vine-leaves, and the pair are enriched with clustered shafts and an arch-moulding of two sunk quadrants. Best-quality work of the 1290s, evidently.* In the literature the room they light is called a chapel, but there is no piscina; so its use must remain doubtful.

A final word is needed on the fittings brought in since 1927. Linenfold panelling lines the walls of the newel staircase in the SE corner of the gloriette. The rest, all classical, are now in the main building. Mid-C18 chimneypiece, doorcases, and panelling in the dining room, chimneypiece of the same period in the music room. The most important is the splendid stone chimneypiece of c.1570, from Woodlands Manor, Mere, in what is now the kitchen.

BATTEL HALL, ¼ m. E. Remarkable early C14 stone house. The plan is a half-H, the wings coming forward to the N. Hall and screens passage occupied the whole distance between them.

---

* The Y-tracery is misleading. The photograph in Wykeham-Martin's book shows split-cusped tracery, but pre-1821 drawings in the British Museum give the original pattern, a much-cusped quatrefoil over two cusped and subcusped lights.

On the N side the two tall windows that lit the hall, square-headed, of two lights under a hood-mould. The tracery has gone, but not the cinquefoiled cusping under the transom. At the r. end, doorway with a continuous hollow and a round. This has an inner hood-mould on heads, and beside it, spectacular surprise, a gigantic contemporary LAVER. Ogee arch on shafts, with leaf crockets and split cusps. Within it, a double-barrelled stone cistern, shaped like the battlemented towers of a castle. Lion's head spouts. Nothing like it survives anywhere else in England. The hall, no longer open to the roof, keeps a stone transverse roof arch with a sunk quadrant moulding, on crouching corbel figures.

s front with the original C14 doorway, and later windows and doorways, one with what looks like a slot for a door to be raised in.*

BATTEL HALL COTTAGES. Early C17. Timber-framed with brick-nogging. Five even gables on an overhang. Surely a row of cottages from the first.

In Lower Street, nothing but the MANOR HOUSE, two-thirds of a big Wealden half-timbered house, close-studded.

In Upper Street, VINEYS, a curious half-timbered group, bent back at an angle half-way along. BURGESS HALL, the grey rendered house opposite, contains, says the MHLG, four decorative paintings of *c.*1700, set in panelling.

LEIGH

ST MARY. Of the C13 building the s arcade of the nave, the tower arch, and the chancel arch survive. Circular piers and arches with two chamfers. All but the E bay of a N aisle of the same date was pulled down in the C15. One pier of the arcade has been revealed half buried in the wall, still with its original red stencilling, spiral lines up the pier, and stylized trails of foliage on the arches. C14 arcade to a s chancel chapel. A w tower with deep diagonal buttresses was begun early in the C16 – a bequest of money in 1525 was to be used 'when work is taken in hand'. Work was not however again taken in hand until 1862, when *Charles Bailey* completed the tower and rebuilt most of the walls. His battlements and polygonal turrets

* On the staircase a rare REREDOS PAINTING, early C14 and evidently from a Dominican house. The only ones in Kent were at Canterbury, and after 1346 at Dartford. Seven figures, the Virgin and Child in the middle, two Dominican Saints at the ends (as at Thornham Parva). The soft, rounded drapery folds are characteristic of the date (NP).

show that he had an eye for composing a picture. – FONT. Perp. Octagonal panelled bowl. – PULPIT. C17, with a wrought-iron HOURGLASS STAND dated 15–7 (the 9 is a modern insertion). – LECTERN. Incorporating a C17 Flemish relief in wood of the Journey to Emmaus. – STAINED GLASS. Exquisite C14 quatrefoil of the Virgin in the head of the N aisle window. – PLATE. Cup and Paten Cover, 1618 by *A.C.* – MONUMENTS. Brass rectangle of *c.*1580, crudely engraved with a shrouded corpse in an open tomb, and, behind, a woman rising up fully dressed, as an angel blows the last trump on a trombone. Such emphasis on the resurrection of the body was to be typical rather of the C17. – Abraham Harrison † 1717. Good cartouche with drapery and the head of a putto pouting at the bottom.

From the E the church groups charmingly with the GATEWAY and LODGE to Hall Place and, on the r., a heavily half-timbered HOUSE. The former are by *Devey*, the latter may be by *Sir Ernest George*. Both architects can be studied further in the village. First of all, the house immediately W of these is a typical *Devey* ESTATE COTTAGE, big as he liked them, and excellent of its kind. On the N side of the green-cum-cricket-pitch the group of almshouse-like COTTAGES forming three sides of a tiny square are of 1886 by *George & Peto*. More houses by *George*, recognizable by the inevitable half-timbering, along the Penshurst Road. Most conspicuous another group arranged almshouse-wise. Beyond this, PARK VIEW COTTAGES, a symmetrical Tudor-Gothic front of *c.*1820, interesting to compare with the heftier attempts of sixty years later at reaching the same effect. Then the EVANGELICAL FREE CHAPEL, and hall behind, 1871 by *Devey*, with red and blue diapered brickwork. Perp is the style, one not favoured by many at that date. Finally, on the r. another endearing *Devey* LODGE, just the thing for pixies.

HALL PLACE. *Devey* built the mansion in 1871–2 for Samuel Morley M.P., and it was his most expensive job. After the lodges it is, one must admit, somewhat stodgy, and intensely High Victorian in the sonorous pomposity with which the W front unrolls. The details on the other hand, as always with Devey, are taken from vernacular English sources; the style is basically Tudor. On the l. two gables, then a porch-tower and a complex polygonal bay, then four more gables with a step forward in the middle. To their r. rises a tall and thin circular turret, and the front is rounded off with a gabled bay

answering the one at the l., but set askew. Red brick with
bursts of blue diapering, and sandstone dressings. Mullioned-
and-transomed windows with arched lights. Various battlements and balustrades. Raised brick quoins however and, over
the bay-windows, bulgy brick friezes which are certainly not
Tudor. The same elements on the garden (E) side. This front
is in two halves, the N coming forward, the S lying back, with
another tower at the l. end. The N half has been gutted.

PAUL'S FARM, ½ m. SW. C16 timber-framed house with continuous overhang and a two-storeyed porch that has settled at
a rakish angle. All weatherboarded.

GREAT BARNETTS, ½ m. E. c.1600. Internal features of that
date are a fireplace with a convex stone surround embellished
with raised arabesques of foliage; and a wooden frieze above
it, of realistic bunches of grapes.

RAMHURST MANOR, 1 m. E. Said to have been built in 1729.
The S front has wings, that on the r. projecting much further
than the other. On the E side a splendid wooden shell-hood
over the doorway, on exceedingly deep carved brackets. Presumably not *in situ*.

LEIGH GREEN see TENTERDEN

LENHAM

ST MARY. A complicated building, finished off at the W with a
big and typically uncomplicated Perp W tower. Angle but- 3
tresses. NE turret, battlemented, like the tower. The plan of
the church is: nave with a N aisle and porch, chancel with a N
chapel divided by a passage from the NE vestry. Apparently
the earliest evidence is the head of a round-topped window
high in the E gable of the N chapel. The SE quoin of the nave
has tufa at the top, tile at the bottom, both early materials.
We are on surer ground in the chancel, which has two, and
had three, S lancets. The S wall shows by a vertical joint that
in the C13 the chancel was tripled in length. The E wall however was all rebuilt in 1857. The S wall of the nave, of flint like
the chancel and N chapel, may be early, but now has large
Perp windows. The aisle was added early in the C14. Reticulated windows. Octagonal arcade piers. Puny arches, with a
chamfer and a hollow chamfer. The E bay however was remodelled in the C15, probably in connexion with the rood
screen. Knapped flint N wall. The chancel arch is of this late

date – compare the impost bases with those in the E bay of the arcade. In this bay the arch has two hollow chamfers. Arcade to the chapel on a Late Perp pier of unbelievable crudeness, four shafts attached to a square core. Again the arch is much too small for it, which suggests that both arcades are late rebuildings. Yet if that is so, why are the arch mouldings not consistent? The interior of the chancel is greatly restored, but there is still a C13 PISCINA, very wide, almost like a seat with a drain; also an almost free-standing SEDILE, with arms and a cinquefoiled arch; and a stone ALTAR. – FONT. Perp panelled stem. – STALLS. Six on the S, five on the N, both returned at the W. Moulded MISERICORDS. Simple poppyheads. – LECTERN. Also medieval, of wood. Completely plain, on crude feet. Modern cresting on the standard. – PULPIT. Dated 1622 on the tester. Well above the average in elaboration for the period. The main motif is of vines growing from vases, with a pair of birds in their topmost branches. Dr J. C. Cox quoted a date 1574, and the question arises whether the pulpit is older than the tester. It is true that the feathers of the birds on the former are more schematized than on the backboard and tester. Yet the *tout ensemble* rouses no suspicions. – CHANDELIER. Brass. C18. Rococo decoration on the pendant. – WALL PAINTINGS. Bishop on the W splay of the SE chancel window. – On the S wall of the nave a large figure of St Michael weighing souls. Now greatly faded but once a fine thing. Dated *c.*1350 by Professor Tristram. – PLATE. Cup, 1562, one of the finest pieces of Elizabethan plate in the county. – MONUMENTS. Effigy of a priest, said to represent a rector who died in 1327. Now set in the wall, but giving as it were a view into an open coffin, of a fully robed figure, his head propped on a pile of cushions, his hands joined in prayer. Traces of colour. – Perp tomb-chest in the N chapel. – Henry Thompson † 1649. Tablet with a skull and cartouche between the ends of the open pediment.

Many early headstones in the CHURCHYARD, and a big monument with an urn (*c.*1777) by the N porch.

Lenham is a village to be savoured, and having cast a glance at the tombs, one must cast further glances round the churchyard in all directions to appreciate the fact that open country 3 begins at once to the S, beyond a farmyard with a nicely isolated aisled BARN in it; and to take in the houses peeping over the churchyard wall, a close-studded house to the E with a continuous jetty, a group of tile-hung cottages to the W, beside the LYCHGATE, which is a simple affair, basically medieval.

This W exit from the churchyard is the way to the village centre, a series of interlocked squares. The first, CHURCH SQUARE, is not even paved, and very small. From its NW corner the main SQUARE develops. The houses round it are largely of brick, many whitewashed, but none of special interest, except the partly disguised Wealden hall-house on the E side, a huge example of the type. STANFIELD HOUSE, on the W side, however, dominates by sheer size. It is early C19, and quite plain, except for a Soanian line incised in the smooth white wall above each window. The N side is masked by a row of pollarded lime trees, but the W half here is taken up by a spaciously proportioned Wealden half-timbered house. Just past this, up the Faversham Road, the old LOCKUP, with an ashlar front and a rusticated arch, the termination of a short, cobbled, and grassy street of C18 red-brick cottages. At the SW corner of the Square, a half-timbered range, with a big window with mullion, transom, and subsidiary mullions in threes, partly original. Here the HIGH STREET begins, with chequer-brick cottages on both sides, the W side above a raised pavement. Nothing to stop for however until the street turns a corner, past the one-storeyed brick HONYWOOD ALMS-HOUSES. Then at once HONYWOOD, a handsome half-timbered house dated 1621, and embossed with Anthony Honywood's initials. Symmetrical front, with two overhanging gables and a first-floor overhang. Oriel windows, all of five lights with a transom, under both overhangs, and grotesque bracket-figures. Central brick chimneystack, deprived of its tall, octagonal stacks. Yet it is odd that something so consciously architectural, and in its way sumptuous, should be so small and compact, just two rooms front and two back at each level. At this point it is best to stop, for the big recent housing estate further on is a joyless place. More new housing to the NW, and yet more beginning E of the church. They ram home the lesson once again that to get anything in the mid C20 as felicitous as the accidental growths of earlier centuries it is necessary to employ an architect sensitive but humble, and determined to sacrifice nothing that he finds. The two new school buildings, SW of the High Street, if not perhaps their surroundings, set a standard which the houses do not begin to emulate. The COUNTY PRIMARY SCHOOL, by *R.M.V. Messenger*, completed in 1957, is typical of the nice, quiet style of post-war schools. The new buildings at SWADELANDS SECONDARY SCHOOL, a decade later, by *Howell, Killick, Partridge & Amis* are more tensely cubic, and so more alien.

CHAPEL FARM, 1¼ m. E of S. Half-H house, of various dates, pulled into a roughly symmetrical shape in the C18. Inside, a Jacobean overmantel in the hall, and a contemporary plaster ceiling in the SE room, with thin ribs forming patterns of stars. Of Royton chapel, on the bank E of the house, no trace is now visible. (For panelling from the chapel, *see* Chilston Park, Boughton Malherbe, p. 169.)

LESNES ABBEY *see* BELVEDERE

LEWINS *see* CROCKHAM HILL

6050

LEYBOURNE

ST PETER AND ST PAUL. Nave and separate chancel, and a W tower (casing an old one) as part of *Sir A. Blomfield*'s restoration of 1873–7. N aisle and chapel, perhaps as late as *c.*1533. The original building Norman, with one S nave window to show it. A second rere-arch can be seen inside, and pretty C13 trails painted on the splays of the intact window. N arcade still the C14 standard, octagonal piers and double-chamfered arches. Large pointed recess at the SE corner of the nave; *c.*1200, suggests a much battered leaf corbel. SW lancet in the chancel set in a shafted blank arch, partly masked by the chancel arch, which came with the N arcade. – CURIOSA. Two wrought-iron crowns. – PLATE. Cup and Paten Cover, 1691 by *T.B.* – HEART SHRINE. Second half of the C13, reset in the N chapel. Like a double piscina, with two little free-standing caskets, gabled and decorated with simple geometrical patterns. Traditionally connected with Sir Roger de Leybourne who died in 1271. – MONUMENT. Louisa Brockman † 1837, but not made until 1866; by *J. S. Westmacott.* He used a Flaxman formula, a tablet flanked by relief figures.

LEYBOURNE CASTLE. From the road one sees only *Walter Godfrey*'s sophisticated essay of 1930 in a free Cotswold vernacular. Why he chose this far from obvious style is explained on the N side, by the lower half of a fortified stone gatehouse. Two broad semicircular turrets, and a triple-chamfered, depressed arch between them. Arrow-slits in the turrets, and widish, square windows above. Portcullis groove and the beginning of an upper arch over the entrance. The entrance

LOOSE

7050

The village is strewn about the sides of a little combe, interlaced by numerous rivulets. The BRIDGE of 1829 carrying the A229 over the valley reinforces the toylike scale. No special buildings, but a nice variety about those that catch the eye: the gabled and twice-projecting front of the CHEQUERS INN, and VALE HOUSE, a red-brick C18 box, opposite one another in the valley bottom. THE OLD WOOL HOUSE, Well Street, a close-timbered rectangle, lies high up the hill to the SW, and a rectangular stone building (a mill?) above it. The church, crouching beside a great yew, is no more than another incident.

ALL SAINTS. John Wotton, first master of Maidstone College (c.1400–17), restored the chapel of Loose 'quasi de novo'. Enlarged 1820. Nave severely damaged by fire in 1878, and reconstructed at once. The nave arcades and all windows are new.* Nave and aisles, chancel and chapels, tower W of the S aisle, shingled spire. S porch entered by its E side. As far as the history goes, one can only note the clasping buttresses at the E end of the chancel, and the odd position of the almost windowless tower, linked to the church only by a small Perp doorway. Perp chancel arch, with continuous mouldings, a hollow chamfer and a double wave. Simple Perp PISCINA. Dec and Perp window tracery. – STAINED GLASS. Two windows in the N aisle, 1892 by *Kempe*. – PLATE. Cup, inscribed 1590; Paten, 1704 by *John Sutton*; Flagon, 1715 by *Ro.*; Almsdish, 1716. – MONUMENT. Richard Beale † 1702. Tablet with two cherub heads at the bottom.

LOSSENHAM see NEWENDEN

LUDDESDOWN

6060

ST PETER AND ST PAUL. Chancel, nave and S aisle, S porch, W tower, virtually all rebuilt in 1866 by *R.P. Pope*. He lengthened the chancel, shifted the arcade a few feet to the S, and heightened the tower. The only original features, apart from the heads of a Perp window or two, are the angle buttresses of the tower, with quoins of tufa – a rare use of the material in post-Norman work – the S doorway, the chancel arch, the simplest of C13 designs, and the late C14 arcade of

---

* A Mr *Buck* was employed as architect, so the Rev. J. C. Priestman tells me.

two bays. Low plain doorway from the church to the tower.* –
REREDOS. By *Earp* to *Christian*'s design. – WALL PAINTINGS.
1894 by *Heaton, Butler & Bayne*. – (BRASS. Man in armour,
*c.*1450. 17 in. figure.)

LUDDESDOWN COURT, immediately W of the church. Two-
storeyed L-shaped building of flint, with Caen stone dressings.
Brick addition at the E. Many original openings in the old part,
almost all of them remarkably small. This is why an exceedingly early date, *c.*1100 or earlier, has been assumed for the
house. Mrs Wood dates it more prudently to the C13. The
plan is a normal one for that century, a first-floor hall, with a
solar wing extending to the N. The solar wing narrows in its
N half, and ends in a ruined dovecote. W doorway to the hall
undercroft. Windows with segmental or round-headed rere-
arches. The memorable feature however is a perfectly preserved fireplace on the N side of the hall. The lintel is straight
and made up of joggled stones, not voussoirs. Chamfered
imposts curve forward as corbels to support it. Plain pyramidal hood repaired in C16 brick. The wall is corbelled out in
the undercroft to take the weight. Entrance to the hall was up
an outside staircase and through a door immediately r. of the
fireplace.

In a remote valley 1½ m. S, the disused church of DODE. Norman nave and straight-ended chancel, of coursed flints, greatly
restored in 1905–6. In fact not a single dressed stone had remained.

LULLINGSTONE

5060

House, church and gatehouse stand on three sides of a vast lawn,
with a lovely long lake stretching away to the S.

ST BOTOLPH. The little flint building, nave and lower chancel,
looks Norman in shape. The earliest evidence is on the con-
trary of the early C14. All windows Dec, two- and three-light,
the E window reticulated, one on the S side with a pre-ogee
pattern of encircled trefoils over cinquefoiled lights. Early C16
N chapel, of brick and stone dressings. Large early C18 S
porch, early C18 roofs on white cornices, and W bell-turret.
The 'munificent repairer and beautifier' of the church was
Percyvall Hart, who died in 1738. The particular beauty is the
plaster ceilings. Plaster window-surrounds and chancel arch,
decorated with alternate mitres and crowns. Hart was a fervent

* I owe the details of Pope's activities to Canon Bernard Wigan, who
tells me that further fanciful ideas were vetoed after a report by Joseph Clarke.

admirer of Queen Anne, and a Non-Juror. Simple contemporary fittings: PULPIT, BENCHES, and black and white marble PAVEMENT. – ROOD SCREEN. A delightful Late Perp piece, made between the years 1502 and 1522, for on the panelling appear the pomegranate of Aragon and the rebus of Sir John Peche (*see* below), an E on a peach.* No Renaissance detail yet, but the tracery has, typically, lost its Perp uprightness and grown thorn-like cusps and roses flower among them. Above the entrance a canopy projecting in two concave steps to a point. Inside, a vault with pendants. C18 balustrade, a happy blend of opposites, bursting forward in the centre to a hollow-sided point. – STAINED GLASS. An unusual and interesting collection. Early C16 figures in the E window and scenes in the nave S window. The latter includes the gruesome martyrdom of St Erasmus, his entrails extracted with a winch. – There is some armorial glass in the E window of the chapel. – Also in the chapel three small panels dated 1563, and, far finer, three early C14 figures. – The two N nave windows have glass of 1754, signed by *W. Peckitt* of York. Figures of saints, coarsely drawn, the thick black folds coming out like tadpoles, the dominant colours deep yellow and purple. – PLATE. Cup, 1646 by *A.F.*; Paten, 1743. – BRASSES. Sir William Peche † 1487. 38½ in. long. Armoured figure, his head on a helm with flowing mantling. Long Latin inscription, but the date, remarkably, in Arabic numerals. – Alice Baldwin † 1533. 15½ in. figure. – Elizabeth Brooke † 1544. 23½ in. figure. – MONUMENTS. Sir John Peche † 1522. Very grand, and set in 41 the most honourable position, on the N side of the chancel, open to the chapel as well. No doubt the monument caused the chapel to be built. Plain slab, with, below, behind rows of nearly round-headed arches, where one would expect a gisant, the reclining figure of Sir John in a tabard, his head on a helmet with splendidly undercut mantling. Canopy to the roof, panelled on the underside, blank tracery, cresting, and more bravura mantling on the sides. As with the screen, no Renaissance details yet. – Sir Percyvall Hart † 1581. Standing wall-monument, very large and grand, but a sad drop in quality. Reclining effigies on a sarcophagus, under an overwhelmingly heavy top storey. Painted putti up here. Early C19 Gothic iron bracing arches. – Sir George Hart † 1587. Erected after 1603. No canopy. Just a tomb-chest and reclining figures

* Mr C. R. Councer tells me that Peche's will of 1522 describes the works in the church as complete and orders the completion of his monument.

clasping hands, and at the corners small standing figures of Labor, Quies, Mors, and Resurrectio. – Percyvall Hart † 1738. The non-juring church-beautifier's monument encrusts the whole w wall of the chapel with Rococo-Gothick arcading. Shafts like bamboos. Palm fronds and olive shoots instead of crockets. – Anne Dyke † 1763. Excellent hanging monument in various marbles, yellow as well as grey and white. Sarcophagus with urns and a scrolly top. Above this an obelisk, against which dancing putti hang a profile medallion of a formidable old lady. One would like to know who the sculptor was – whether he was Sir Henry Cheere.

GATEHOUSE. Of the C16. Red brick, with traces of a diaper pattern, much restored. Three-storeyed. The plan is a rectangle, with polygonal turrets attached to the outer face, and polygonal projections from the inner. Moulded brick entrance arch on both sides, four-centred. Wooden mullioned-and-transomed windows, the lights not arched; so a date before the middle of the century is unlikely. Doorways to the projections. Terracotta panels on the turrets, with quatrefoil loops, for decoration not defence. Battlements, on a corbel frieze of cut brick. Contemporary one-storey range to the s, and traces of the same to the N.

Until the mid C18 there was a second, inner, gatehouse, and a moat round the house. Buck's print records them, and so does a large painting in the house. That is why there seems such a wide gap now between gatehouse and house. The house itself, LULLINGSTONE CASTLE, as it is misleadingly called, looks early C18, but the very shape of the w front, facing the lawn, is enough to show that it is applied to something older. Three-bay centre of two storeys, then symmetrical three-bay blocks a storey higher and projecting a good way. These continue, after a slight step back, for another two bays to l. and r., not quite evenly. It is plain work, with no more enrichment than a roll-moulding round the windows, moulded brick string-courses, and a wood cornice, enriched with carved brackets in the centre. Early C20 one-storeyed vestibule across the recessed centre, and a pedimented porch. On the N side at once C16 evidence, two three-storeyed canted bays, with moulded brick plinths, but no original windows. Further l. and lying back some way, a two-storeyed C16 range, part flint, part brick, with two chimneybreasts and a blocked four-centred brick doorway at the l. end. Round the corner the house is still two-storeyed, with an C18 canted porch-bay, and two more C16 chimneybreasts, one with a crowstepped top. C18 pavilion at the SE corner, with a big Venetian window. S front again of flint and brick, with sash windows, and the jambs of an upper mullioned window. There is an irregular internal courtyard, inaccessible except through the house. This has rendered walls, but mullioned windows, mostly of five un-arched lights, with a transom, three storeys of them in the N range, two storeys in the E, and an original doorway here too.

The interior is largely C18, but again perplexing in plan. The two-storeyed centre of the W front is wholly occupied by the hall. In its NE corner a rusticated arch leads to the stair-case, with slim turned balusters, vertically symmetrical, grouped in fours at the newels. The State Drawing Room oc-cupies the upper two floors in the W front N of the hall. It lies end-on to the façade, and has a late C16 plaster barrel-vault with thick enriched ribs in a pattern of intersecting pointed quatrefoils, three big pendants, and roundels of Roman Emperors, one curious design repeated again and again, except for Nero, over the fireplace, who is recognizably Nero, jowls and all. Early C18 panelling with fluted Corinthian pilasters.

IRON AGE SETTLEMENT, overlooking Lullingstone Castle. On the hill a series of Iron Age storage pits have been discovered containing Iron Age A and wheel-turned Belgic wares. There may originally have been a hillfort on this eminence, but intensive cultivation has obliterated all traces of it.

The ROMAN VILLA at Lullingstone is one of the few villas in the county to have been scientifically excavated and attractively exposed for public inspection (by the Ministry of Public Building and Works). It lies on the side of the Darent valley, less than half a mile from Eynsford Station.

The first masonry house, built about 80–90, was a simple affair consisting of a range of rooms linked by a front veranda and a back corridor. At the N end lay a cellar reached by a flight of wooden stairs. Later, towards the end of the C2, the building was aggrandized by the addition of a modest, but comfortable, suite of heated baths attached to the S end. But more important changes took place at the N end, where an entirely new 'cult room' was constructed surrounded by an ambulatory in a method similar to Romano–Celtic temples. Together with the cellar, which was modified at this time, the room was evidently used for religious activities – presum-ably at this stage pagan. Among the alterations made to the cellar was the construction of a niche ornamented with a magnificent painting originally depicting three water nymphs (two survive). Spring water was contained within a masonry tank in the floor in front of the niche, emphasizing the connection of these religious rooms with water deities. The cellar and cult rooms were linked by a flight of steps to the rest of the villa.

It seems that after 200 the residence was not kept in repair, but part of it was modified to serve as a tannery. By the end of the c3, however, a series of repairs and modifications were undertaken at the N end. The final alterations took place in the c4. In the main part of the villa a large apsidal dining room was built, adorned with a fine mosaic depicting Europa abducted by Jupiter in the guise of a white bull. The dining room opened into a large reception room floored at this stage with a mosaic incorporating a picture of Bellerophon astride Pegasus slaying the Chimaera. These two chambers would have formed the central functional unit of the villa. Significant alterations were also undertaken at the N end of the building, when a Christian chapel was built over the old cellar, which by now served as a sealed off repository for the busts of two ancestors. The chapel, unique in Britain, was adorned with painted wall plaster showing Christians with arms outstretched in a position of prayer. One of its walls also bore a *Chi Rho* monogram enclosed in a wreath. In the outer chamber was another *Chi Rho*. This remarkable villa was eventually destroyed by fire in the c5.

Close to the house itself were three other buildings: a simple circular temple of c2 date, a temple mausoleum built in the c4 in normal Romano–Celtic style with a central cella surrounded by an ambulatory, and a large granary of the late c3.

The quality of the excavation and the imaginative presentation, together with the delightful setting, make the site one of the most interesting Roman show-pieces in the country.

LYDD

The visitor approaches Lydd over the level marsh for many miles and from far away the church tower stands up from a clump of bosky trees. Yet Lydd is mentioned in documents of the c8, still possesses part of a Saxon church, and was incorporated as a town by charter of Edward I. Its present isolation began in 1287, when a storm shifted the mouth of the river Rother from New Romney to Rye.

ALL SAINTS. The church is archaeologically of the highest interest and architecturally on a grand scale. Chancel with chapels stopping well short of the E end. Nave and aisles under three equal gables. The total length of the church is 199 ft and the w tower is 132 ft high. The tower was built in 1442–6 by *Thomas Stanley*, one of the senior masons at Canterbury Cathedral. It cost £280. As, out of the scores of Perp towers in Kent, it is among the tiny handful of unstandardized ones, it deserves detailed description. Ragstone. Three tall stages. What enrichment there is concentrates on the w entrance. Twin doorways combined into one composition with a tall Perp window of two twin lights under a super-arch. Tiny quatrefoil bell-openings to N and s barely punctuate the plain masonry. Angle buttresses becoming diagonal via squinches high up, and supporting plain (rebuilt?) pinnacles. Low, plain battlements. The octagonal sw stair-turret is also provided with angle buttresses dying away near the top, an apparently simple arrangement that creates a surprising complexity of inclined planes. Above, a thick crocketed pinnacle. Inside, the exceedingly pretty lierne-vault, with many small bosses, proclaims the Canterbury connexion.

The long, low church that goes with this tower and matches its proportions so well is, in spite of its Dec and Perp windows, a uniform E.E. building, as one sees as soon as one enters. It has suffered various vicissitudes, notably the bombing and complete rebuilding of the chancel (in 1958, by *Anthony Swaine*, who had in 1951–3 done a good restoration of the other parts), but they have not spoiled the sober, serious design, unenriched but not austere, of the C13 builder. The proportions are everything, the details nothing; though the architectural historian will have to describe the details. Chancel lancets under trefoiled rere-arches. Wide nave and wide aisles (not widened later, as the C13 string-course in the aisles shows. See too the N doorway with many delicate mouldings). Seven-bay arcades of short circular piers with circular capitals and abaci. Developments in the pier details have to be recorded. The two E piers each side have waterholding bases, followed by one with two flattened rolls on the base. The three w piers are slimmer, their bases and caps a different, coarser design. They must be a later reconstruction. Canon Livett pointed out that these piers are of ragstone laid in deep courses, while Caen or Reigate stone in shallow courses was used in the C13 work. Wide and high arches of two orders, plainly chamfered. All responds, of the arcades, chancel arch, and arches to N and S chapels, tripartite under semi-octagonal abaci. Several responds have tiny stiffleaf sprigs on the capitals.

Finally, the archaeology. The rough rubble walling of the NW corner is not an inspiring sight. Yet it is the remains of a Saxon church. The picture is clearer inside. Three blocked N arches, with round heads irregularly turned with thin stones, stepped abaci, and rectangular piers. A deeply splayed clerestory window above. A wider blocked arch in the W wall, and the stump of one wall of the W *porticus* into which it opened. These must have belonged to an unusually small basilican, that is aisled, nave. The set-off on which the aisle roof rested is clearly visible outside. A W annex and an apsidal chancel can also be assumed. The date of this church is disputed, but Sir Eric Fletcher and Mr Jackson note as very early features the arches set back on their jambs and the single-splay window (altered to double-splay later). In fact the nearest parallel in size and plan is the C5 Romano-British church excavated at Silchester. The masonry shows none of the knowledge of Roman building techniques so evident in the early C7 churches at Canterbury. Indeed Lydd stands quite apart from Augustinian importations.

FURNISHINGS. FONT. Mid-C18. Gadrooned on bowl and stem. – PULPIT. Plain late C18. – Fragments of a SCREEN. Panels displayed on a board like so many butterflies. Perhaps this is the best way to enjoy the tracery pattern of staggered battlemented transoms, a delicately wayward Perp idea. – CHANDELIERS. Brass. A double branch in the chancel, dated 1753, a single branch in each chapel. – PLATE. Cup, 1562; Almsdish, 1680 by *T.K.*; Paten, dated 1705; Paten, 1719 by *Ma.*; Set given by Dr Tenison, Flagon 1737, Cup and Paten 1740. – Numerous BRASSES, mostly in various parts of the nave. As usual, the earliest are the most rewarding, both for variety and for quality. – John Motesfont † 1420 (chancel). A serene 37 in. priest. – John Thomas † 1429. Tiny. – Thomas Godefray † 1430 and wife. Two 4 ft figures under canopies. – Civilian identified as Robert Cokyram † 1508. – Man, *c.*1520. – Thomas Harte † 1557 and wife. – Peter Godfrye † 1566 and wife. – Thomas Bate † 1578 (chancel). – Man, *c.*1590, Lady, *c.*1590. – Clement Stuppeny † 1608 (chancel). All these are civilians. – MONUMENTS. Cross-legged knight under an early C14 arch in the N chapel. Indifferent quality. – Thomas

Godfrey † 1623. A well characterized frontal bust in a plain roundel. – Anne Russell and her infant son † 1781. Signed *Flaxman*, 1814. An angel carries up the baby to his mother standing on a cloud which two angels struggle to support. The pictorialism of the billowy clouds and their happy-go-lucky disregard for the enclosing frame are sure signs that the monument was carved at the earlier, not the later, date. This makes it Flaxman's earliest monument.

The church is of course visually the centre of Lydd. From it short walks may be made to W and S.

The HIGH STREET runs W from the churchyard on a gently curving course, quite urban at first, the houses continuous on both sides. Nothing higher than two storeys, and a nice variety of brick and stucco. Only the TOWN HALL, half-way down on the l., needs comment – unassertive late C18 blue-brick front, the lower windows set under six irregular blank arches turned in red rubbed brick. Further on the houses gradually become sparser (though the spaces are fast being filled in with bungalows), until at the very end on the r. TOURNEY HALL is reached, the most ambitious private house on Romney Marsh. Early C18, five bays, two storeys. Grey brick, headers only, and red-brick dressings. Giant pilasters at the angles. Doorway with brick pilasters and entablature, and on it an upper pair of pilasters framing the central window. The other windows vertically linked by bands of red brick. The roof has been victorianized.

S of the church there is even less architecture to see, but a nice series of spaces to walk through. First into CORONATION SQUARE, not a square at all, but a small triangle. SKINNER STREET leads off the SW angle, and here is the RECTORY, dated 1695 over the door. Two storeys with a big hipped roof, five bays, widely spaced in the centre. Painted white, with bold black quoins and a bold black cornice. Skinner Street leads at once into THE RIPE, which is also triangular, but vast and grassy, and bordered on all sides by houses very much too small for it. It is an oddly exhilarating end to the town, a sharp reminder of the marsh beyond.

LYMPNE   *1030*

ST STEPHEN. Ragstone. Norman central tower, but no transepts, just a N aisle built in the C13 and extended past the tower. Clasping buttresses and four stages to the tower. Nave and aisle. Windows all put back to lancets in *St Aubyn*'s pedantic restoration of 1878–80. The chancel is E.E., sizeable but quite plain and needing no more said than that there are along the N and S walls continuous stone benches. The question to be asked is: what was the original shape of the Norman church? One assumes that the tower was built to separate nave and chancel, as it does now. Its E and W arches are Norman. Enriched abaci. W arch rebuilt pointed. Why then has the W wall of the tower blank arcading of three sunk arches, like that on the S wall? Because, as Canon Livett pointed out, it was built, in the late C11, as a W tower. The stumps of walling at its NE and SE corners belonged to the Early Norman nave, not to the chancel. The original E end was excavated by Livett beyond the present E wall. In the C12 the tower became central when a nave was built W of it. – FONT. Norman. Square bowl, much polished up, on modern shafts. – STAINED GLASS. E window 1950 by *J. E. Nuttgens*. – PLATE. Cup, by *William Andrewes*, and Paten Cover of 1698. – MONUMENT. C14 cusped recess in the N aisle, a rare example of Dec work without any finesse.

LYMPNE CASTLE. Built of ragstone, only a few feet SW of the church, on the edge of the escarpment above Romney Marsh. 'Castle' is a courtesy title; Leland described it, more accurately, as 'lyke a castelet embatelyd'. It represents the typical late medieval manor-house plan, of an open hall, entered on the N side through a two-storeyed porch, with kitchen and buttery in the two-storeyed E end, and solar at the W end, which is also of two storeys. Purely decorative battlements, but beyond the solar a low tower, also battlemented and bowed to the W. Church and manor had belonged to the Archdeacons of Canterbury since the C11. The present building seems wholly C15, unless the thick walls at the E end belonged to a free-standing square tower earlier than the rest. Most openings restored. There was evidence for the design of the hall windows, of two lights with a transom, the lights below trefoiled, the lights above it cinquefoiled, a pointed quatrefoil in the head. Two-centred doorways, chamfered or moulded with a double wave. Archway through a buttress against the hall S wall, and the springing of an arch at a higher level W of it. Crown-post in the upper room at the solar end.

The gabled, stone buildings grouped with such conscious charm to the NW, and the range of cottages beside the road, were executed by *Sir Robert Lorimer* in 1906–12 for F. J. Tennant, who found the place in ruins, and left it somehow anaesthetized and stripped of its history.

The Roman fort of LEMANIS, hanging on a clay slope below the village of Lympne, is one of the few ruins still to retain a Victorian flavour – heaps of rubble framed with wild flowers, browsing cattle, and the hazy marsh in the background. Springs, cutting into the clay, have caused serious subsidence and slipping of the Roman walls, giving a confusing impression, but originally the walls enclosed a semi-rectangular fort 10–11 acres in extent. They were 12–14 ft thick and 20 ft high, built of coursed rubble with limestone facings and bonding courses at intervals. Externally a number of semicircular bastions projected from the wall, with which they were bonded. The main gate lay in the centre of the E wall; not much can be seen, but Victorian excavations showed it to be a simple 11 ft wide opening flanked by two solid bastions, the whole structure being based on two courses of large stone blocks. A narrow postern was found in the W wall. Two masonry buildings have been excavated inside, the *principia*, or headquarters, and a small bath suite. The fort was probably built in the 280s under Carausius, but judging from quantities of earlier material there must have been a naval base here in the C2. Coin evidence suggests abandonment about 370, possibly because of the land-slipping.

(FRENCH HOUSE, ½ m. w. This timber-framed house, of the Wealden type, was carried bodily down the hill by a landslip in 1734. It was unscathed; which says something for having a timber frame. Mr K. Gravett).

PORT LYMPNE, 1 m. w. Large red-brick house in a fine position on the escarpment above Romney Marsh, built by *Sir Herbert Baker* in his Cape Dutch manner *c.*1912 for Sir Philip Sassoon. It lacked verve, but what it was given after the First World War was an overdose of magnificence, by *Philip Tilden*, with a Moorish patio, colonnaded quadrant wings, a flight of marble steps down the hill, and a swimming pool as the centrepiece of the neo-Roman garden layout. The interior was made into an interesting expression of the taste of the Paris Exhibition of 1925. Ironwork by *Bainbridge Reynolds*. Dining room frieze by *Glyn Philpot*. Drawing room murals by Monsieur *Sert*. Garden Room decorated with architectural views *c.*1933 by *Rex Whistler*.

ASHDEN HOUSE, 1½ m. w. Similar escarpment site, with a view

over Romney Marsh, for a low, white, informal house, with black-eaved monopitch roofs, built in 1964 by *Sir Hugh Casson*. All windows towards the view.

Remains of a CHAPEL at COURT AT STREET, 1½ m. w, below the brow of the hill. Late Perp, as the w doorway shows. Ragstone. It was here that visions were seen by Elizabeth Barton, the Holy Maid of Kent, beheaded in 1534 for rousing opposition to Henry VIII's marriage with Anne Boleyn.

MABLEDON

5040

1½ m. sw of Tonbridge

Built for James Burton, himself an architect, builder and developer of St Leonards. He employed *J. J. Parkinson* to design it, and got an elegant imitation of a castellated mansion with battlements, Tudor chimneystacks, and shafted windowlights. Sandstone. In 1810 the house was about five years old. Enlarged *c.*1829 by James's son, *Decimus Burton*. The plan is interesting. The two main fronts face s and e, with at the junction a large polygonal bay and a turret behind, making a central feature at which the long drive aims. Decimus Burton stressed this unusual arrangement further by adding thin round towers at the far ends of the s and e fronts. His additions no more grammatical than what he was adding to. Still, in the last Georgian year, the distant picturesque castellated outline mattered, and close-up consistency did not.

MAIDSTONE

7050

INTRODUCTION

As a county town Maidstone was a late starter.* The principal medieval ornaments, College, Archbishop's Palace, and Corpus Christi Fraternity, were only what any moderately prosperous town could have chanced to acquire. The town was not incorporated until 1549, but the county administration gradually came to be consolidated in it, because of its central position in the

* As for Roman Maidstone, remains of a ROMAN VILLA were discovered at the Mount. Another building, unearthed in Loose Road, was a CORRIDOR VILLA with an elongated apsidal-ended room to the s. Close by was an unusual octagonal room with external buttresses and a hypocaust, possibly part of the baths.

county. The shire court had met at Penenden Heath, 1½ m. NE of the town, since the time of Domesday. In the C17 and C18 the market prospered. In 1697 Celia Fiennes noted that the 'very pretty houses about the town look like the habitations of rich men'. In the C19 the staple industry changed from making linen thread to brewing beer, and in the 1820s and 30s Maidstone first took its county-town status seriously. It has been left to the mid C20 to destroy the close texture of the 'neate market towne'. No coherent C20 redevelopment yet, though enough has gone at the S end to make that possible. The population in 1801 was 8,027, in 1851 had risen to 20,801, by 1901 to 33,572, and to 59,790 in 1961. Since then the population has jumped up a good deal further.

CHURCHES

ALL SAINTS. In 1395 Archbishop Courtenay received the [31] authority of Pope Boniface IX to make the parish church of Maidstone collegiate. Not only was a college erected to house the master and clerks (for which *see* below), but the church itself was completely rebuilt. And so Kent came to possess its grandest Perp church. As will later be noted, it was intended to have been even grander; and one must admit that judged against national standards, against Louth or Lavenham, against St Mary Redcliffe or Holy Trinity, Hull, this spreading, plainly battlemented, ragstone building with its under-sized SW tower cannot be called spectacular. The best view is from the N, of the whole length, 227 ft in all, and an even display of large four-light windows, practically filling the wall-space from buttress to buttress. They rest on a string-course. Tracery of cusped panelling, occasionally double-tiered, the lower tier cusped at the foot too. One N window does not conform, an Early Perp one, from the demolished church? Chancel E window enlarged 1871. What then is the plan? The chancel has aisles, and so has the nave, of much greater width. Vestry with a parvis off the S chancel aisle. The tower stands over the porch, which was to have been vaulted. Impressive nave arcades of six bays, the arches high and not very wide, proportions like the nave of Canterbury Cathedral. Continuous mouldings, wave, hollow, wave, with capitals only to the E and W shafts. Nothing is made of the clerestory, which is too low to be visible at all outside. Chancel arcades as high, but the arches wider. As the aisles are here so much narrower, the chancel feels quite different from the nave. Wall shafts in the s chancel aisle, evidence of an intention to vault. This must have been where building started. The roofs are all by *Pearson*, whose restoration of 1886, costing £12,000 (PF), seems to have done little other damage. – SEDILIA. Exceedingly sumptuous, incorporating at the back the monument of the first master of the college. (For this *see* below.) Four seats and a credence (not a piscina), vaulted, with canopies projecting as three sides of an octagon, with gables and vaults inside. Openwork spires over the centre three, a very graceful composition. – STALLS. The full medieval complement in the chancel. Most have MISERICORDS, with shields, leaves, heads, and one with a half-length cook brandishing a spoon. – FONT. Early C17. Octagonal, still with crude Perp mouldings, and shields and foliage on the faces. The date is arrived at by comparison with the Queenborough (E) font of 1610. – SCREENS. One bay of the N parclose screen is old. – Rood screen 1886 by *Pearson*. – REREDOS. 1896 by *Pearson*. Stone, of a height and sumptuousness to outshine the sedilia. – STAINED GLASS. A full set of Victorian glass, not of the best. *Capronnier*'s E window of 1872, which cost £1,000, is luckily a total loss behind the reredos. – s window by *Powell & Co.*, 1855 (TK). – The other s windows, and the chancel aisle E and NW windows, by *Wailes*, c.1855–61. – The rest much later, by *Lavers & Westlake* (N aisle) and *Clayton & Bell* (w window and NE chancel window). – PLATE. Pair of Cups and Covers, 1637 by *P.B.*; Flagon, 1641 by *R.S.*; Paten, 1680 by *F.S.*, a large one; Paten by *I.Y.*, 1685; Almsdish of 1719 by *St.*; Flagon, 1733 by *Richard Gurney & Thomas Cooke*; Almsdish given in 1734; two Patens of 1747 by *Jacob Marshe*(?). – MONUMENTS. Indent only of the brass to Archbishop Courtenay † 1396. – John Wotton † 1417. The monument, in the back of the sedilia, may have been erected in his life-time. Tomb-chest with quatrefoils, and the indent of a brass. Canopy with four gables and cresting, double gables at the sides. The back has PAINTING: Wotton presented to the Virgin by Saints, the figures tall, boneless, and unimaginatively grouped. – Thomas Beale † 1593 (s chancel aisle). Hanging, with a brass. It shows six generations of the Beale family kneeling on shelves. – Thomas Washington † 1619 (s aisle). Black and white pedimented tablet of *c.* 1650. – Thomas Carkaredg † 1639 (N chancel aisle). Hanging monument with kneeling figures in an architectural frame. – Sir John Astley † 1639 (w end). By

Edward Marshall. One of the most fabulous examples of that short-lived fashion begun in 1631 by Dr Donne for monuments with lifesize standing figures in their shrouds. Here there are four, a man and woman in niches at the top, a man and woman at the bottom standing on brackets carved into lively little lions. Inscriptions on slabs like open doors. The figures make enigmatic gestures with their arms. – Humphrey Tufton (s aisle). Erected in 1642, with a typical frontal bust in an oval. Black and white marble. – John Davy † 1631 (s chancel chapel). Monument erected in 1651. A good example of the more animated mid-C17 type, with half-length man and wife clasping hands. Relief busts of the children in roundels at the bottom. – Jacob, Lord Astley, 1653 (w end). Just a white coat of arms on a black slab on four bulbous white balusters. Set up by *John & Henry Stone*. – Thomas Knatchbull, 1653 (w end). Black and white architectural standing monument. Not good. – Eliza Callant † 1715 (N chancel aisle). Tablet hung with drapery. – William Dixon † 1725. Handsome tablet of the late C17 type, with side-scrolls, swags, and curvaceous open pediment. – Edward Hunter † 1757 (w end). Tablet with a fine putto on a pedestal. He looks down at a horn, a book, and a skull. – Anna Wilson † 1775 (s aisle). Large tablet with a draped urn in relief. Tightly controlled detail, neo-classical in spirit. – Sir Charles Booth † 1795 (s aisle). By *Nollekens*. Tablet with a mourning putto. – Lt-Col. William Havelock and other officers † 1848 (w end). By *R. Westmacott Jun*. Relief of a soldier by a palm tree pointing out the inscription to a boy in a tunic.

ST FAITH, Station Road. 1872 by *E.W. Stephens*, a local architect, who made a worthy effort to live up to the important site. Ragstone. Clerestoried nave, lower chancel. Tall, plain SW porch tower. The E aspect the liveliest. Polygonal, gableted apse, and matching N vestry. Sandstone arcade piers.

ST FRANCIS (R.C.), Week Street. A funny little building by *C.G. Wray*, 1880. Nearly detached 'SW' spire. Flowing tracery. Enlarged brick aisles, and a low W addition of 1959.

ST JOHN THE EVANGELIST, Mote Park. By *Blandford*, another local architect. 1861. A village church for the parkland situation. Nave and lower chancel. Ragstone and ashlar, nicely textured. Trefoiled lancets.

ST LUKE, St Luke's Road. 1896–7 by *W.H. Seth-Smith*, an all-out Art Nouveau affair, expensive, designed with the intensest care for details, but absolutely no delicacy of feeling.

Ragstone and ashlar. Nave, with a transeptal E bay, and a chancel as high. Narrow aisles, not expressed outside. Low, broad proportions as favoured in the nineties. Colossal windows with writhing Dec tracery. Arcades of three elliptical arches on couples of stout columns, that would do splendidly for a music hall. Carving on capitals and round the arches, by *Aumonier* and *Gilbert Seale*, worth a look. – ORGAN CASE. 1899 by *Seth-Smith*. – REREDOS no doubt by him too. – PULPIT. 1911 by *Seth-Smith & Monro*. All with aggressive scrolls. – ALTAR RAILS by *Bainbridge Reynolds*. – WALL PAINTING, on the chancel S wall, *c.*1918, by *Ivon Hitchens*. Harts by the waterbrook, among stylized trees. The manner of the Douanier Rousseau, and the feeling of Mabel Lucy Attwell. – GLASS. Not stained, but tinted. The leads describe sinuous, tulip-like shapes.

ST MICHAEL AND ALL ANGELS, Tonbridge Road. 1876 by *Sir Arthur Blomfield*. Large and tired. Give me E. W. Stephens any day. Pretty apsidal NE chapel, 1902 by *Nicholson & Corlette*.

ST PAUL, Randall Street. By *Peck & Stephens*, 1859–61. Gutted in 1963 (but to be restored?). Ragstone. Dec. Cross-gabled aisles. Showy NW spire over the porch.

ST PETER, St Peter's Street. The mid-C13 chapel of the hospital founded W of the Medway by Archbishop Boniface after 1244, and enlarged into a parish church in 1836–7 by *Whichcord Sen.*, who added W transepts and reset the W wall beyond them. Ragstone. Long lancets, a triplet E and W. They are shafted internally, rest on a string-course, and have a continuous hood-mould. PISCINA and triple trefoiled SEDILIA. The classic C13 proportions of the building are compromised by Whichcord's mean roof.

ST PHILIP, Waterloo Street. 1856–8 by *Whichcord & Whichcord*. N aisle 1869, chancel and porch-steeple 1878, all by *Stephens*. Ragstone. Dec. Typical Stephens, one would say. – PLATE. Cup, 1799 by *John Emes*.

ST STEPHEN, Tovil. 1839–41, by *Whichcord Sen.* Ragstone. Undivided nave and chancel ending in a polygonal apse. W tower and shingled spire. Lancets. It is clear inside that Whichcord learnt little about C13 scale and mouldings during his work at St Peter.

Pleasant ragstone SCHOOL of 1840 across the road.

HOLY TRINITY, Church Street. Now disused. 1826–8 by *Whichcord*. Classical. Ragstone. Rather a grand W front, pedimented with Tuscan pilasters, and a spire behind. Nothing remarkable really, but competent.

CONGREGATIONAL CHURCH, King Street. 1860–2 by *Peck & Stephens*. Tall and short, with their favourite cross-gables and their favourite porch-spire, with angels. But the thrilling thing about the church is the STAINED GLASS of the E window, a panel of the Good Shepherd which is *Burne-Jones's* first known stained glass design, made by *Powell's c.*1857. How it comes to be here, goodness knows. The shepherd is a romantic figure with his heavy brown locks and his piebald breeches, and a big red sun makes him a halo. Vivid emerald greens, blues, and purples. But Burne-Jones has already grasped the essentials of the art, uses no shading, and makes the leads do most of the drawing.

CONGREGATIONAL CHURCH, Tonbridge Road. 1875 by *C. Pertwee*. Ragstone with thin red-brick bands. Big rounded apse into the corner. Tall, straight SW tower. Plate tracery. More forceful than most of Maidstone's churches.

METHODIST CHAPEL, Union Street. 1823. In the lancet style of the time, with a later porch.

UNITARIAN CHAPEL. *See* p. 393.

CEMETERY, Sutton Road. Gate lodge, and the usual spireleted chapel, 1858 by *Peck & Stephens* (GS).

PUBLIC BUILDINGS

COUNTY HALL, at the junction of County Road and Lower Boxley Road. 1915 by *F.W.Ruck*. On a corner site close up to the road. Typical, but not good, neo-Baroque building, with a broken pediment on pairs of Ionic columns over the entrance arch. Ashlar, and a rusticated granite basement. Constricted extensions of the front on each side. Long and very feeble additions of 1937 (Lower Boxley Road) and 1939 (County Road). It was impossible to deepen them because of the prison walls behind (*see* below). Through the central arch, across a small courtyard, the recently restored front of *Sir R. Smirke's* SHIRE HALL (now Sessions House) of 1824. A small but 83 perfect example of his 'rectangular' style. Two-storeyed ashlar block, with a centre containing the doorway and a trio of arched upper windows, and Schinkelesque flanking towers. The wings to l. and r. hidden by later additions. Original entrance hall with a staircase sweeping up at the far end.

COUNTY ADMINISTRATIVE HEADQUARTERS, Springfield. A

13—W.K.W.

recent development round *Waterhouse*'s red-brick and yellow-terracotta mansion dated 1891, now the Education Department. The new buildings, all good and all designed by *E.T. Ashley-Smith*, the County Architect, stand between the mansion and the road. At the S end a long WAREHOUSE BLOCK, three-storeyed, the upper two steel-framed and projecting in all directions. W of this, lower down the hill, a five-storey slab, the windows in continuous bands. The most conspicuous group is the COUNTY LIBRARY, beside the road. The reference library, a low, octagonal, weatherboarded block, with shallow gables in each direction, is connected by offices to the book stack, a twelve-storey point block. Down the hill from this a low L-shaped range, tile-hung below the windows.

TOWN HALL, High Street. 1762–3. Portland-ashlar ground floor of blank arcading. Red-brick upper storey, dressed with stone. N and S fronts of five bays, the centre brought forward slightly. The E end projects emphatically towards the wider top part of the street, as three sides of an octagon. Pedimented upper windows here and on the N front, the pediments alternately triangular and segmental. This forthright, no-nonsense exterior makes the charming painted decoration of the Council Chamber doubly delightful by the contrast. Drops of musical instruments on the walls. Sparing, but good, Rococo plasterwork on the ceiling, and painted decoration as well. – CORPORATION PLATE. Two maces, gilt, one probably of 1549, the other probably of 1649. – Loving Cup, 1799.

MUSEUM, St Faith's Street. The core is Chillington Manor, an Early Elizabethan house, built by Nicholas Barham, who bought the manor in 1561. Heavily restored in 1875. Deep red brick, with stone dressings all new. The S front, facing the street, is E-shaped in plan. Two storeys, the rectangular projections going a storey higher to gables with kneelers, and finials added at the restoration. The hall, in the r. half of the front, has its original screen, solid but for a frieze pierced with a lattice of tiny quatrefoils. Main staircase 1877–8.

The additions to l. and r., which so rudely push the C16 house into the background, trumping its gables with pairs of large shaped ones, are the COLLEGE OF ART, 1897, and ART GALLERY, 1890 by *H.Bensted*. Further addition to the r. of 1923.

At the back the story is even more complicated. NE staircase projection of the original house. Then a half-timbered piece, running N, to a brick tower, old at the bottom but characteristically Victorian in its corbelled-out half-timbered top. This wing ends in a stone CHAPEL of 1874. The W side of this wing is the re-erected COURT LODGE of East Farleigh, a spectacular, but greatly renewed piece of half-timbering. Closely spaced uprights and a continuous band of windows at the top of the whole overhanging upper storey. Gabled porch. The back of Chillington Manor itself is largely of 1875, but r. of this is a fine red-brick front (or back) of seven bays (the first and seventh narrow ones). Sunk panels below the windows. Hipped roof and pedimented dormers. Loose in the courtyard here, two columns from St Faith's Chapel, which stood up the hill to the N, and one from Boxley Abbey.*

CENTRAL LIBRARY, St Faith's Street. 1964, by the Borough Engineer's Department (Borough Engineer: *R. Orrell*).

TECHNICAL HIGH SCHOOL FOR BOYS, Oakwood Park. 1958–9 by *John W. Poltock*.

SENACRE SECONDARY SCHOOL, Shepway. Perhaps the best of the recent Maidstone schools. The first part designed by *Denis Darbison* and completed in 1957. Extensions by *Denis Clapson*, 1963.

WEST KENT GENERAL HOSPITAL, Marsham Street. By *John Whichcord Sen*. Italianate. Red brick and stone. Symmetrical, with additions. Kelly's date is 1832, but that seems too early. Could even *Blandford*'s alterations of 1862 (GS) have produced this ?

OAKWOOD HOSPITAL, St Andrew's Road. 1830, the *magnum opus* of *John Whichcord Sen*. Grandiloquent entrance past LODGES high on a plinth of rockily banded rustication, and gateposts with great iron lamps on them. This and the avenue of Wellingtonias might be the prelude to a hotel in Cannes or Monte Carlo, rather than to a hospital. But the hospital lives up to it. Ragstone. Four-storey centre of five bays, with a pediment and a double-decker porch, arcaded under paired Tuscan columns. The rest is only of three storeys, breaking back and then coming forward again. Isolated blocks further back to l. and r.

OPHTHALMIC HOSPITAL, Church Street. 1852 by *Whichcord & Ashpitel*. Weakly Jacobean. Ragstone.

PUBLIC BATHS, Fair Meadow. 1851–2 by *Whichcord & Ashpitel*. Italianate. Equally timid, but much more acceptable.

* As Mr Grove kindly tells me.

GAOL, Lower Boxley Road. 1810–17 by *D. A. Alexander*. Massive ragstone perimeter wall. Within it, in the centre, a round tower, which originally housed the governor below the prison chapel. The layout of the chapel was such that the prisoners could all see the chaplain, without being able to see one another. This inhuman arrangement was used elsewhere, e.g. at Lincoln, and was typical of early C19 'improvements' in prison design.

INVICTA PARK BARRACKS, Chatham Road. 1962–5, in two phases, the first by the *Directorate of Works War Office*, Senior Architect *Ralph Iredale*, the second after the War Office Directorate had been merged with the Ministry of Works, under *Sir D.E.E. Gibson*. The former used the CLASP method of construction, the latter the NENK method, developed by Iredale. But the architects were also concerned to create an environment as unbarracklike as possible, and they had for their site the splendid park of PARK HOUSE, a square early C19 ragstone mansion, with a three-bay bow to the W and a mansard roof, now the officers' mess. The new buildings have been excellently sited, grouped easily and not too tightly among the trees. They are all rectangular and low, nothing higher than three storeys, brick, or tile-hung and weatherboarded, different in colour and shape according to their use. ADMINISTRATIVE OFFICES and WORKSHOPS, l. of the entrance, weatherboarded black and white; NAAFI and RESIDENTIAL BLOCKS, r. of the entrance, hung with red tiles with white weatherboarding. Further E, over the brow of the hill, SERGEANTS' MESS, and MARRIED QUARTERS, stepped terraces, yellow brick and brown tile-hanging.

PERAMBULATION

The church is the centre of an unusually large and varied conglomeration of medieval buildings, college, palace, and tithe barn. They are all of grey, crumbly ragstone, and look best from across the river. Close to, C19 ragstone buildings to the S and E intrude, and the recent inner by-pass, Bishop's Way, pushes it away into a corner, cutting off the visual link with the centre of the town.

Archbishop Courtenay's COLLEGE, for a master and twenty-four chaplains, lies S of the church. Permission from the King to impress masons to build it was granted in 1396. When Courtenay died two years later his executors testified that the college was up. Impressive GATE TOWER, rectangular, of three storeys, with battlements. Major and minor entrance arches, but only a single inner arch. Tierceron star vault. A room occupies the entire top floor of the tower. Three N windows, of two lights, transomed, with cinquecusped and cusped lights. Fireplace in the E wall. Below this, on the l. of the entrance arch, a two-storeyed room with a large oven, no doubt for baking bread to be distributed as alms at the gate. Two-storeyed range joined to the W of the gate tower, with two-light windows of equal importance on each floor, three each side of a chimneybreast on the N side. Refectory and kitchen on the ground floor, and the chaplain's rooms above. At the W end, the River Tower, with rooms on three storeys and a drainage system in the basement. So that completes the accommodation needed by the college. Yet on the S side a return wing runs from the W end of the refectory range. This joins another two-storeyed stone building, the so-called MASTER'S HOUSE (now Music Centre), which must be earlier than the rest, by its rougher masonry and by the pairs of ogee-headed lights low in the E wall. Gable with an upper ogeed lancet at the S end. The other upper windows are of the C18, the W side largely modern. Inside, various Perp doorways and fireplaces that do nothing to make the original layout clear. Blocked doorway at the first-floor level in the N wall, so the linking range has been lowered by a storey. Free-standing to the SE the MASTER'S TOWER, of the 1396–8 campaign, but really another gateway, with blocked E and W arches, an upper room, and a polygonal N staircase-turret. It must have been the main entrance to the college from the river, and the perimeter wall must have stepped back sharply from the river bank at this point. The wall went a long way further S, for the original S GATEWAY remains in ruins.

There is nothing else to see S of this, so the ARCHBISHOP'S PALACE, close to the NW corner of the church, naturally comes next. The main front, facing E, however, is Elizabethan, a symmetrical façade added by the Astley family to their once-episcopal home. Notably low two-storeyed centre, with a notably steep and high tiled roof. Two-storeyed porch, with a round-headed entrance arch, and a classically moulded string-course (renewed).* The typical E-plan is achieved by, most unusually, two-storeyed porches l. and r. of the centre one (which is blind and has a surreptitious door to the ground

* The main window of the porch is modern.

floor to the r. of it). These have flights of steps up to first-floor
doorways on their inner sides, and set back above them a gable
over a full-scale third-storey window. The gables on kneelers
and trimmed with spiralling finials with balls on them. Rectangular windows with two mullions and a transom, the lights
not arched. Beyond the façade, to l. and r., half-timbered extensions, balanced but not symmetrical, which is something
of a comedown. They hide the fact that the earlier stone house
extended as far as they, but set back considerably. The N front
was rebuilt in 1909. On the river side the palace rises almost
from the water. It is much taller here, but still only two-
storeyed. The windows are all of 1909, and only the two-
lighter in line below the gable is based on adequate evidence.
This gable is roughly in the centre of the front, but over the r.
of three bays, marked out by straight joints to l. and r. and a
sloping plinth. At the S end the wall runs back from the brink,
but there is no pre-Courtenay evidence.* First a part with
two buttresses, then a half-timbered tile-hung overhang,
then lower service quarters. Internally the palace has a
C16 staircase inside the r. porch, which also leads to a
barrel-vaulted room lit by the oriel, and S of this, the hall,
centred on the Elizabethan front and filling the depth of the
building.

Stone OUTBUILDING to the SE, with C14 undercroft, and
two parallel stone walls E of it (the E one the churchyard W
wall) which Canon Livett believed to be Early Norman. What
did they belong to?

E of the Palace, by Mill Street, the GATEHOUSE (now
Department of Weights and Measures), a small rectangular
building without any archway, but with various C14 single-
light windows in its S wall and a C13 doorway. In fact it was
never a gatehouse, but a small C13 house, of the type with an
upper hall.‡ On the N side it drops a long way down to a
stream. Garderobe projection here. Below the road at this
point part of a medieval BRIDGE can be seen.

But the finest evidence of the Archbishops' activities at Maidstone is the grand TITHE BARN, E of the church. It has stone
walls, buttresses dividing it into six bays, a depressed-headed
arch into each bay. The roof, constructed with crown-posts
and raking struts, was treated as an upper floor from the first –

* Lambarde attributes the palace to mid-C14 Archbishops, using materials
from Wrotham Palace.
‡ Mr E. W. Parkin kindly told me of his analysis.

the original outer staircase remains, l. of the porch. The upper storey of the porch is timber-framed with modern brick-nogging, a chestnutty red, much needed among all these grey walls. The barn now contains a collection of splendid coaches.

So at last we are ready to move away into the town; not yet N to the High Street, but into KNIGHTRIDER STREET at the s end of the tithe barn. Here, on the l., the four remaining bays of the BLUECOAT SCHOOL, erected 1720. The BAPTIST CHURCH, 1906, replaced the rest. Then, standing back more grandly, KNIGHTRIDER HOUSE, a plain yellow-and-red-brick box, three storeys, five windows by four, once the home of William Shipley, founder of the Royal Society of Arts, now the bus station offices. At the corner into LOWER STONE STREET, one of the few Maidstone houses to display its half-timbering. The l. side of Lower Stone Street has an almost continuous first-floor overhang but the half-timbering is hidden behind rendered fronts of the C18. No. 28, of 1716, however, is a complete rebuilding, a handsome façade and the last complete survivor of an early C18 type once common in Maidstone's streets. Three storeys, five bays, spaced 2, 1, 2, but not quite regular. Rendered. The first floor treated as a *piano nobile*, with window architraves, and for the centre window a triangular pediment, cutting into a broad string-course. Cornice with richly carved consoles. Big doorcase on fluted Corinthian pilasters, with a broken segmental pediment filled with lavishly carved foliage, blunted by generations of paint; cartouche with the date. The cornice carries on across No. 26, a poor relation clearly done at the same time. On the r. side mostly C19 commercial buildings, until No. 11, near the street's end, early C18, with a carved bracket cornice, rusticated basement, and quoins, all rendered. At once the narrow street is broken open by the GRANADA CINEMA on the r., *Cecil Massey*'s belated Edwardianism of 1933, with a giant upper Corinthian portico, and to the l. by the bus station and the wide spaces of PALACE AVENUE. Here, on the l., the shockingly *retardataire* MAGISTRATES COURT, of 1934–5 by *Ruck & Smith*. Tudor. Ragstone. Governed by being only two streets away from church, palace, and college, genuine medieval ragstone buildings. But on the r., across the mill pond, the vast cream ROOTES SHOWROOMS, built in 1938, making no concessions to anything, least of all to the scale of the town. Large horizontal sweeps of window, weak central and end stresses, but modernistic details reserved for the entrance at the w end, in Mill Street.

Back now into GABRIEL'S HILL the continuation of Lower Stone Street. Again the l. side preserves its pre-C19 character better, but only the STONE STREET CLUB is anything special, stuccoed white, with a three-bay centre and lower, slightly set back, balustraded wings where the doorways are. Probably of the 1830s, but no coarsening yet of the classical details. The upper part of Gabriel's Hill is narrow and dominated by the sign of RANDALL'S SHOE SHOP, a gloriously large gilt top-boot on a vast, scrolly iron bracket. The shop itself dates from c.1860. Further up on the r. another good early C18 console cornice.

And so to the crossroads at the top of the High Street. Two directions have to be pursued, N into Week Street and the streets that run off it down to the river, and w down the High Street itself and over the Medway bridge to pick up a few outlying items.

First then into WEEK STREET, narrow and busy with shoppers. An eye kept above the shop-line will be rewarded first on the r. by another enriched cornice, to Nos 34–6, above Early Georgian brickwork on No. 34, the brickwork of No. 36 wiped out by Freeman, Hardy and Willis's shop. Next door, however, a completely new shop, for DAVID GREIG, outstandingly well done. By *Robert Paine & Partners* of Canterbury (partner in charge, *M. R. Crux*). Completed 1966. Entirely glazed façade, steel-framed, with the entrance at the r., and over it, inside, but visible through the glass, a huge steel pendant, a spiralling conical shape, and further back the name 'David Greig' in large letters, where the height of the interior is halved. By these simple means the street-line is preserved, the depth within defined, and shoppers enticed inside. It looks so easy, yet how often is it done? Before going down Earl Street, on the l., one should continue for a short way in Week Street, to see, on the l., No. 55, with its two upper storeys pargetted and dated 1680. An ambitious scheme of swags between vases on the lower level and ovals above, separated by pilasters, carried out very crudely and without much vigour. Even so, it does not deserve its present fate. The plaster should be strengthened before any more falls off. Opposite, UNION STREET, where on the r. *E. W. Stephens*'s CHURCH INSTITUTE, of 1882, cuts a dash. Plenty of vigour here. Red brick and stone. Shafted geometrical tracery at all levels.

See p. 644

Now back and down EARL STREET, which is now the most consistent street in the town, mostly two-storeyed half-timbered houses rendered. On the l. however, Nos 13–15 rises to three storeys, red brick, five windows wide. C18. The doorcase, a broken pediment on attached Tuscan columns, and the raised window-frame above it are the only embellishments, and they don't make the date more precise. No. 20, on the same side, is a warehouse over a shop, with a two-storey hoist in use. Then, in MARKET BUILDINGS, ugly mid-C19 arcading, and facing it the UNITARIAN CHAPEL of 1736, perfectly preserved, small and square, of dark red brick, with a pyramidal slate roof, and angle pilaster strips so pronounced that they look more like barely-projecting bastions. (Original layout inside, with the original pulpit and gallery. The E wall, behind the former, however, set back a few feet.)

Back in Earl Street, on the N side, No. 38, another C18 brick front, red and yellow with segment-headed windows and white key-blocks. Double porch. Then back to the S side for Nos 31–3, a tall half-H shaped house, built it is said early in the C17 for Andrew Broughton. The plan suggests such a date; so do the canted bays at the ends of the wings. Divided into two in the C18 and given dress of that date, roughcast walls, raised quoins, and sash windows, running in bands round the bays. Next door to this the NORWICH UNION, in a mid-C20 style, but somehow reminiscent of a bank of the 1860s. At the bottom end of the street the big FREMLIN'S BREWERY, of 1870, looms behind the N side, with its big-scale brick arcading and pilasters. On the S, first No. 45, a tall timber-framed front, the centre symmetrical, with two gables above two canted window-bays, the window-frames with the simplest C17 relief patterns. Restored in 1892.

Then CORPUS CHRISTI HALL. The range towards the road, ragstone and half-timbered, is greatly restored and in part modern, but, behind the E end of it, lying N–S, is the original hall of the Fraternity. A charter was granted in 1441, but the Fraternity existed at least from 1422, when John Hyssenden enfeoffed twenty-five inhabitants of Maidstone, elderly and discreet men, in 'a certain edifice, to be called the Brethren Halle' with its cloisters and outbuildings. The HALL, 66 ft by 26 ft 6 in., must, as Hyssenden's words imply, have been in existence already in 1422. The two original E and W windows, two lights with a transom, have an ogee quatrefoil at the head, flanked by horizontal bars, a typically Early Perp shape. At the N end, a doorway each side into the screens passage. They are two-centred, with a continuous moulding, a hollow, a roll, and a hollow. Three doors from the passage into the service wing to the N. Chimneybreast on the W side of the service wing. The hall has a crown-post roof, and a moulded beam across the N bay, at a height of c.8 ft from the ground. What was its purpose ? After the Reformation the buildings housed the Grammar School. The cloisters remained at least until 1740. Today the hall is unglazed and used as a storeroom. It deserves a better fate.

With that Earl Street ends and we should, leaving the Public Baths (*see* p. 387) away to the l., turn r. into WATERSIDE past more intimidating breweries. Then at the corner of St Faith's Street comes a good mixed row, starting above a raised walk with a white rendered house with an overhang, two gables to the W and four to the S, and descending to an c18 red-brick terrace. Happily they have been recently restored, and not, like so much in Maidstone, demolished. But there is no need to pursue that further. ST FAITH'S STREET itself needs to be explored. Nothing at the bottom end, until, on the l., the Borough Library and Museum (*see* p. 386), with cars parked opposite the site of more demolished houses. Then, on the r., SIR JOHN BANKS'S ALMSHOUSES, built in 1700. Six of them, in a two-storey block twelve windows wide, the centre two in a slight projection under a pediment. They are built of a dusky red brick. The brief remaining stretch of Week Street contains nothing until at the very end on the r., behind St Francis's R.C. church, GROVE HOUSE, quite a swagger Early Georgian front, of dark brown and plum brick, three-storeyed, five bays, the centre one wider and coming forward a little. Rich console cornice for the low roof. All the windows except on the top level have round heads and white keystones. The centre one goes one better, with a rusticated brick surround. Heavy Tuscan porch. It is worth going round into County Road, to see how the building dies away behind its imposing façade. Good contemporary staircase with twisted balusters.

See p. 644

The continuation of Week Street beyond the roundabout and County Hall calls itself Sandling Road at first. Nothing here, but when the name changes to CHATHAM ROAD, Springfield (*see* p. 385) comes on the l., Invicta Barracks (p. 388) on the r. Opposite the latter, on the RINGLESTONE ESTATE, quite good recent housing by the Borough Engineer's Department .

(Borough Engineer: *R. Orrell*). Also some stepped terraces, by *John Voelcker*, due to be built in 1968.* A short way further N in Chatham Road, OLD FARM HOUSE, a restored Wealden house, recessed centre between wings projecting in their upper halves, the closely set uprights exposed.

That completes the N half of the town, E of the river, and a fresh start must be made again at the top of the HIGH STREET. At the crossroads itself a tall three- or four-storeyed building on each corner, C16 with a double overhang at the SW corner.‡ C18, rounded at the angle, at the SE corner, c.1860 at the NW, the end of a long Italianate block, but at the NE, on quite a new scale, an eleven-storey OFFICE BLOCK, 1968 by *Bader & Miller*, set back, luckily, from the corner. In the centre of the High Street a DRINKING FOUNTAIN, c.1862, with a statue of Queen Victoria by *John Thomas*, set up by *Blandford* after Thomas's death under a shrine-like canopy, gabled and crocketed, with angels at the four corners. There is plenty of room for it, for the High Street has the short, wide shape characteristic of a street that has grown up on either side of a market place. The Town Hall stands, again characteristically, at the end of an island site. Narrow Bank Street S of it originally belonged to the market place.

The S side of the High Street begins, appropriately, with several half-timbered houses, which do not unfortunately stand up to close scrutiny. The timbers that are not restorations are phoney. So the first shop to dwell on is BLAKE & SON, something in every way unexpected. This iron-framed front, with infilling of green tiles, dates from c.1855, by *Ashpitel & Whichcord*. The framing, only exposed on the first floor, has, inevitably, shafted arcading with a frilly pendant frieze. The ground floor altered. The N side of the street meanwhile is dominated by two Portland stone palazzo fronts, the WESTMINSTER BANK, 1909 by *W. Campbell-Jones* in an Edwardian Baroque style, and the ROYAL INSURANCE OFFICES, 1827 by *Whichcord Sen.*, a fine, restrained façade of seven bays, of rusticated blank arcading on the ground floor, with engaged fluted Ionic columns above, running through two floors and

* Why, architectural qualities apart, is such ingenuity allowed its head on this tiny site, while whole fields on the edge of the town, e.g. near Allington and E of Mote Park, are squandered by development companies under a wasteful layout of 'chalet-bungalows'?

‡ (Medieval undercroft under this building; NMR. And another, says Mr Gravett, under a house opposite.)

carrying a completely plain entablature. This rises slightly in the centre to support a shield of arms.

BANK STREET should now be investigated. On the l. side an almost continuous overhang, of C16 and C17 timber-framed houses, but the façades practically all altered and restored. No. 78 however is something special, four-storeyed with two overhangs, the upper supported on Ionic and Corinthian colonnettes. Behind them splendid pargetting, with the Royal Arms, Prince of Wales's feathers, and the date 1611. Modern colouring, recently redone, in vulgar pink, yellow, and green, vulgarly shaded – an excellent match for the vulgarity of the plasterwork. Central projecting window with a transom and four mullions, the centre two carved into caryatids and linked in an arch, a form related to the famous windows at Sparrowe's House, Ipswich, of 1670, where the transom itself arches up. This example, so many years earlier, needs to be set against them.

And now finally we come to BARCLAYS BANK, which lies at the bottom end of the island, fronting on to Bank Street and High Street and prominently situated at the head of the slope down to the Medway Bridge; 1958 by *Sir William Holford & Partners*. Four storeys. Black brick and Portland stone, with decorative bands of flint low down and bronze-framed bay windows to the banking room. As the recital suggests, it is a matter of trying too hard. The building tries to be worthy of its site, and that deserves praise. But the materials uneasily echo the colours of half-timbering, with fussy patterns, and to the w an oriel and a recessed attic. But at any rate it is fussing towards an end, which cannot be said of the jazzy PRICERITE SUPERMARKET opposite. In PUDDING LANE, a turning to the r. at this point, STAR HOUSE by *Robert Sharp*, 1935, five-storeyed cement-faced block, with windows in horizontal bands, and a vertical central window set back in a hollow – a typical piece of overstatement.

Nothing in the lower part of the High Street, and nothing over the bridge until the road forks. The r. fork, LONDON ROAD, has, almost at once on the l., a big OFFICE BLOCK by *Paul Manousso*, 1964–6, characterful but without fashionable tricks. Thereafter, on the l., prosperous housing of the 1820s and 30s, a terrace and semi-detached pairs, pedimented pavilions with low additions at the sides; and then, when these have given way to Victorian houses, FANUM HOUSE (Automobile Association Headquarters), late C18, red brick, three storeys.

Elaborate lead down-pipes, with the date. Doorcase, up five steps, on fluted Doric pilasters. The hall reaches through the depth of the house, and out of it rises an ample staircase, richly endowed with fluted Corinthian colonnettes as newels, three balusters per tread, one tightly twisted, one fluted, and one loosely twisted, and all with Ionic capitals tilted to the angle of the handrail. Carved tread-ends.

Large but self-effacing wing of 1884 at the back. Contemporary garden walls enclosing a forecourt, with railings and fine wrought-iron gates and *clair-voie*.

The STABLES lie back on the r. They are plainly of the same date as the house, in spite of 1779 on the weathervane. Charming clock turret, very much too large. 'Mind the Time', it says under the clock. The clock face in a surround curving up to a point in the middle, a typical shape of the 1720s. Further E a lower BARN to match.

Finally, beside the road, a short row of COTTAGES, red and blue brick below, tile-hung above, and keeping all their original fitments, even down to the window-catches. Long may they stay like that!

MEOPHAM

6060

ST JOHN THE BAPTIST. From the road the church is an impressive sight, with its stately W tower, matching the proportions of the clerestoried nave and chancel. The church is a complete rebuilding of the early C14, and for once we have a documented date to help us: the dedication took place in 1325. As Meopham fits comfortably into the sequence of Dec churches in north-west Kent, it is especially worthwhile to ponder its details and see whether this date surprises. First the chancel windows, all more or less renewed, but, according to early C19 drawings, accurately so. The S windows have uncusped lancet lights with a large circle over and a quatrefoil in it, i.e. pure Geometrical; and still with the major and minor mouldings distinguished. The three-light E window is a little more advanced, cusped intersecting tracery, with encircled quatrefoils of two sizes. The E window of the N chapel (reset) goes to the extent of trefoiling the heads of the lights. So in the early 1320s, it seems, ogees were unknown in Meopham.* Proceeding westwards, the chancel arch, the five-bay arcades,

* The chancel has been busily victorianized inside. Restoration 1859. REREDOS of 1874.

and the tower arch are identical, with double-chamfered arches and octagonal piers. So much was inevitable. But the base-mouldings and the convex, not undercut, abaci are what we should expect in the early C14. The chancel arch is built off centre, to give the rood loft staircase room, which shows that a rood loft was intended from the start. Quatrefoil clerestory windows. The aisles themselves are a Perp rebuilding: Hasted says Archbishop Courtenay (1381–96) was responsible. The arch to the N chapel from the aisle also Perp – see its mouldings. The tower's W doorway is Victorian, and the top stage was added in the C19 in place of a spire, but below, all windows are trefoiled lancets – again, had one not known, one would have dated it too early. Shallow angle buttresses. – FONT. Perp. Octagonal bowl, its gently concave sides carved with shallow patterns, each one different. – PULPIT. A superb late C17 piece, with the quality and the apparatus of putti heads, drops of flowers, and marquetry panels one expects to find in the City churches. In fact it has strayed from St Margaret Westminster and carries the date 1682. – STAINED GLASS. An *omnium gatherum* of C15 bits in the S aisle. At the top a Bishop and St Catherine. – PLATE. Cup and Paten Cover, 1679, the former engraved with masks and swags, the latter bearing the mark *A.R.*; Flagon, 1756 by *T.W.*; Paten given in 1825. – MONUMENTS. Katherine Masters † 1750. Large architectural tablet by *Thomas Beard*, old-fashioned for that date. – Elizabeth Bayley † 1838. Grecian, with a crouching woman looking yearningly up. By *R.J. Wyatt* of Rome. – Sir John Bayley † 1841. By *E.B. Stephens*. Also Grecian, with small figures of Virtues. On top, however, a bust.

Meopham must be one of the longest villages in the county, desperately strung out along the main road. The church is by itself near the N end. Further S, the best bit is the Green, with the WINDMILL, of the smock variety, and built in 1801. Black weatherboarding and white sails, boat-shaped cap. It is almost identical with the West Kingsdown mill.

THE HAVEN, Hook Green. 1936 by *Marjorie Tall*. An early attempt to soften the white box of the International style of the thirties, without going modernistic. Brick painted white. Flat roof with eaves. Curious narrow central bow containing the staircase. These Regency reminiscences do not really work.

CAMER COURT, ½ m. NE. The five-bay centre is dated 1716 at the back. Blue and red brick. Off-centre porch with Tuscan columns. Bow-ended addition to the r. (The MHLG mentions the staircase.)

MEREWORTH

6050

MEREWORTH CASTLE . The first salvo in the war in which the Baroque style practised by Wren and developed by Hawksmoor and Vanbrugh fell before the authority of Palladio was fired at the publication of Volume I of Colen Campbell's *Vitruvius Britannicus* in 1715. True, Campbell's purpose was partly jingoistic, to prove that architecturally 'in most we equal, and in some Things we surpass, our Neighbours', and he summed up his introduction with the words: 'It is then with the Renowned Palladio we enter the Lists, to whom we oppose the Famous Inigo Jones.' True, too, William Benson's Wilbury House of 1710 had already taken Jones, or rather his pupil John Webb, for a model. Yet, by the time Lord Burlington had joined in, as enthusiast, patron, and practitioner, had visited Italy a second time expressly to see Palladio's works at Vicenza and Venice, and had acquired large numbers of the master's drawings, the protagonists had shifted their ground and become Palladians *tout court*. In 1723 Burlington designed a town house for General Wade that was nothing more than a Palladio design executed in London instead of Vicenza. But, once again, *Colen Campbell* was first, for in 1723 the shell of Mereworth Castle was completed, and Mereworth is a straight copy of Palladio's famous villa overlooking Vicenza, the Villa Rotonda.

Campbell's client was John Fane, who in 1736 inherited the Earldom of Westmorland. In the 1720s however he did not have to support the state appropriate to a peer, and could indulge his fancy. Palladio's villa had been a scholar's retreat from the heat of the town, and Fane can hardly have intended Mereworth to have been more than an occasional residence. Yet it was not a belvedere, set on a hilltop, as Palladio's villa was, with a portico each way to catch the view, but a castle (Campbell calls it that) surrounded by a moat. The moat has been filled in, but as approached from the N over a lake, the house is splendidly framed by its free-standing pavilions l. and r. and by two giant cedars. Behind the house a landscaped valley sweeps up to the horizon.

Campbell's building is larger than its model in all dimensions, a square of 90 ft, 55 ft high, surmounted by a dome 67 much more than hemispherical, thrusting upwards with strong ribs to a heavy, blind lantern in a way that has a decidedly Baroque emphasis. The lantern is blind because it hides the twenty-four chimney flues, carried up between the internal and external skins of the dome. The walls are stuccoed an ochre colour, in the Italian manner, but the four hexastyle Ionic porticoes, the entablatures, and the window surrounds are of Portland stone 'as much inriched as the Rules of our Art can admit'. Pedimented and balconied *piano nobile* windows, one each side of each portico. Grand, easy flights of steps to the N and S porticoes, and the basement carried on underneath them all. Thus, and this is the most important departure from Palladio, the plan is not symmetrical about both axes. Internally Palladio and logic are abandoned to the extent that there is only a N vestibule; the E and W ones give place to enlarged rooms, and the S one completely vanishes, as a long gallery occupies the full width of the S front. Bedrooms in the attic storey and servants' room contrived in a mezzanine under the E and W porticoes where the main rooms are lower.

The decoration internally is in quality the equal of the exterior, and in sumptuousness far surpasses it. In the vaulted VESTIBULE a foretaste of the plasterwork, heads before big shells over the side doors, and a pair of life-size female allegories over the arched doorway to the central rotunda. The rotunda, or SALON, to give it Campbell's name, is domed, and subdued but adequate light enters via four oculi in the dome. It has plaster coffering. Round the upper part of the walls runs a deep balustraded gallery on carved brackets, an adaptation of Jones's at the Queen's House to another shape. More plasterwork on the soffit here. The plaster enrichment, by Bagutti, is somewhat elaborated from the design in *Vitruvius Britannicus*, Vol. III, of 1725, but the basic arrangement of four major and four minor doorways (two of the latter to the staircases, little circular ones), at ground level and balcony level, is the same. Pairs of female figures with emblems of arts and sciences, pairs of putti and busts before shells above the doorways. On the dull orange walls more white plaster decoration, spaced out item by item, with no visual link from one part to the next. This treatment is characteristic of Campbell's classicism, not at all like the typical Palladian interior as conceived by William Kent. Oblong relief panels, portrait busts, and foliage drops enclosing portrait medallions, no doubt of Fane's forebears, an archaeological reference to the ancestral portraits in ancient Roman houses.

The glory of the LONG GALLERY is the ceiling, the central part containing illusionistic paintings in a series of round and oval compartments defined by enriched ribs. The deep cove, a cove *à la* Wilton, signed by the Venetian *Francesco Sleter* and dated 1732 is a very beautiful design in grey, pink, and gold on several levels of illusion.* The doorcases and chimney-pieces again splendid but isolated features on the N wall, helping to reduce the sense of length in the room.

In the E and W rooms similar painted ceilings and chimney-pieces, on a smaller scale. The ceilings of the NE and NW rooms incomplete, but a fine frieze of swags and bucrania in the former, and a noble white marble fireplace in the latter, with wreaths of vines, as the room was originally the dining room.

The two PAVILIONS match the house perfectly, each a central cube, with a low pyramid roof and blind lantern, and attached to it three deep pedimented porticoes, one Tuscan, the others arcaded. Rendered walls, Portland stone dressings. Triglyph frieze round all the parts, with, in the metopes, the Nevill bull for Fane's ancestors, and the Cavendish knot for his wife. Were they built at the same time as the house ? They are not attached to it – indeed the moat made that impossible. Campbell makes no mention of them in *Vitruvius Britannicus*. Perhaps Fane needed more accommodation after 1736, when he inherited the peerage. The W pavilion nearly, but not quite, encroaches on the site of the medieval church, rebuilt only in 1744 (*see* below). Yet recently-discovered drawings by Campbell include two for service pavilions, not admittedly for the executed design, but dated 1722 and 1723. That seems to prove that they were at any rate intended from the first. (In the E pavilion an upper room has the ceiling and chimney-wall decorated with c18 shellwork of fantastic virtuosity, especially the almost free-standing cranes and dolphins by grottoes.)

LODGES. Plain and large, stuccoed. Mid-Georgian. Now on the wrong side of the road, which has been moved.

TRIUMPHAL ARCH, ⅝ m. S. At the head of the valley, but no longer visible from the house, as of course it was built to be. Brick faced with sandstone ashlar. Central arch flanked by coupled composite half-columns.

---

* The ceiling, as Mr Francis Watson has pointed out, is typical of early c18 work in the Veneto.

ST LAWRENCE. Rebuilt by the Earl of Westmorland in 1744–6, ⅝ m. NW of its old position. It is the outstanding C18 church in the county, in scale and ambition and in architectural interest. It is a thousand pities that the architect's name is unknown. The materials are ragstone blocks with dressings of sandstone ashlar. The exterior is a goulash of famous London churches, the steeple copied almost directly from Gibbs's St Martin-in-the-Fields, set over the W end of a low rectangular body, with end pediments and colossally deep eaves, after the manner of Inigo Jones at St Paul, Covent Garden, and a semi-circular Tuscan W porch, nearer Archer's at St Paul Deptford than St Mary-le-Strand. Plain windows with key-blocks, the E three with an arched centre one, which makes a sort of Venetian window, and a grandiose Roman Baths window (i.e. a tripartite lunette) in the pediment.

69   The interior is quite another thing. One enters through a circular vestibule which is below the tower. The spaces l. and r. of the vestibule are filled with monuments saved from the old church, but the main vessel takes the form of a wide, barrel-vaulted nave, and narrow, flat-roofed aisles, with close-set, unfluted Doric columns carrying not arches but a heavy entablature. Attached half-columns against all four walls. The nave is three times the width of each aisle, and the aisles consist of a series of square bays. The effect is of an austere neo-classicism unprecedented in Georgian England.* Lord Burlington's York Assembly Rooms of 1730, recreating Palladio's 'Egyptian Hall', has aisles as narrow, but is Corinthian. And surely this is significant. The interior seems to express the learning and ruthless fervour of the first generation of Palladians, Burlington above all, expressed outside as a 'Tuscan barn'. Is it possible then that Lord Westmorland got a design for the church even in the twenties, and when he came to execute it twenty years later its meaning was forgotten and the spire and portico introduced as fashionable extras? The interior is painted, the columns to look like marble, the ceilings with coffering, not very convincingly. – FONT. Marble; c.1746. – STAINED GLASS. The upper E window is filled with C16, C17, and C18 heraldic glass, in uniform cartouches, some dated 1562. More in a SW window dated 1562 and 1567. – PLATE. Elizabethan Cup without a stem; gilt Cup, 1624 by

---

* But the columns have no bases not because they are Greek Doric forty years before their time but because there was panelling originally up the lowest third of the columns.

T.F.; Almsdish, 1680 by *F.S.*; Paten, 1698 by *Robert Cooper*(?). – MONUMENTS. Sir John de Mereworth † 1366. Fine brass of a knight under a canopy 33 in. to the top of his legs. Very close in style to the contemporary brasses at Cobham. – William Shosmyth † 1479. Brass of 18 in. civilians. – Fine large C15 alabaster reclining effigy of a knight. – Sir Thomas Nevell. Early C16 standing monument with a quatrefoiled tomb-chest and a poor 18 in. brass. On the plain surround two angels in high relief and a half-length angel with emblems of the Passion, a conceit reminiscent of the Beauchamp Chapel of *c.*1450–60 in St Mary, Warwick. – Small Late Perp wall-tomb, with a panelled base and shallow vaulted canopy, set at the SW corner of the church. On the flat surface two hands in relief holding a heart. – Sir Thomas Fane † 1589. Grandiose standing monument. His widow died in 1626, but the monument's erection was delayed until 1639. Reclining effigies, and two kneeling sons below. Pairs of large Corinthian columns, and an entablature bulging forward in the centre. This makes an oval space on the soffit, carved with clouds, below which two gilt putti hover bearing a crown and palms. Big top achievement. – James Master † 1689. Marble cartouche. – Attached to the exterior of the S wall, a TABLET to Francesco Sleter, the decorative painter (*see* above), † 1775.

YOTES COURT, ¾ m. S of W. A valuable mid-C17 red-brick house, built for James Master, valuable because it is dated 1656 and 1658 on the chimneystacks. The plan is an H, a five-bay centre, two rooms deep, and wings, projecting not far, two windows wide. Two storeys, except to the E, where the ground drops, and there are three. There too irregularities occur in the fenestration, forced by the back stairs. Hipped roof on a deep coved cornice, except at the back, where there are three gables, not the remains of an earlier house, but to roof the deep centre – evidence in fact that by the 1650s a hipped roof was thought more handsome than gables. Tall, rectangular chimneystacks with sunk, arched panels. No other enrichment but raised quoins and raised flat window surrounds with ears, all cemented and painted white. The windows seem very white because C18 sashes have been slipped inside the frames of the original casements. Original staircase with stout turned balusters of Jonesian shape. The walls and ceiling painted in the mid C18, with two grisaille figures in feigned niches on the former, and the latter charmingly made to seem like the sky, beyond a balustrade with putti flying about with garlands.*

MERSHAM

32 ST JOHN THE BAPTIST. The w window is unforgettable, wide enough to take all twelve Apostles in glass. Row of shields below. Row of quatrefoils above. Extraordinarily gauchely organized upper part, where it seems that two-light windows are incorporated on their sides. Heraldry dates it soon after 1396. The N windows in nave and chancel, part of the same remodelling, are segment-headed, Perp not Dec. But the walls are Norman. The reset s doorway suggests that. The enlargement that put on a s chapel, s aisle, and a short, thick tower w of it, belongs to the late C13. One aisle lancet. Lancets in the tower. Arcade of five bays in all, the w three the earlier, so the pier bases imply. Round piers. Double-chamfered arches. The chancel E window may be no later, with cusped intersecting tracery. Perp NE vestry rebuilt in the C19. – FONT. Square bowl. Quatrefoils in circles on two sides. Cusped ogee arches on the other two. – ALTAR RAILS. Strapwork panels. Balls on foliage finials. Early C17. – SCREEN. To the s chapel. Early C18. Twisted balusters. Iron spikes on top. – STAINED GLASS. A small amount in the w window, two and a half of the Apostles, sleeping soldiers from a Resurrection, and two Evangelists' symbols. The subject matter must have been as complex as the layout. – C15 figures in a chancel N window, St George, a small St Christopher, and St Edmund Rich. – Borders in the head of a nave window. – ARMOUR. Helm in the chancel. – MONUMENTS. Brass of a priest, c.1420, a refined half-figure, 14½ in. long. – 17 in. brasses, figures of civilians, very crude; c.1520. – Richard Knatchbull † 1590. Hanging monument with figures kneeling in prayer. – Margaret Collyns † 1595. Tiny tablet signed by *Evesham*. Small beginnings. – Lady Bridget Knatchbull. Carved by *Nicholas Stone* in 1626 for £30, a surprisingly small sum, even for this modest wall-monument. Kneeling figure under an entablature that bows forward in the middle. Angels l. and r. draw back curtains. – Sir Norton Knatchbull † 1636. Low, standing monument framed in pairs of undersized Ionic columns. Up-to-date in being austerely black and white, less so in having a

* Mr Cornforth dates the ceiling c.1740 and argues for *Francis Hayman* as the painter.

big armoured effigy propped stiffly on one elbow. The incompetent sculptor could not form it in the round. Original railings. – Sir Norton Knatchbull † 1684. Tablet with side scrolls. – Sir John Knatchbull † 1696. Big tablet with the full paraphernalia of putto heads, flowers, trumpets, scrolls at the side, and on top two putti lifting a baldacchino from before a pyramid. – Sir Wyndham Knatchbull † 1763. Designed by *Adam*, carved by *Tyler*. Just an elegant small tablet.

COURT LODGE. Dec stone house W of the church; in plan a 28 plain rectangle. Big hipped roof. On the E side a doorway with a hollow and a roll, a big renewed two-light window with a transom and a concave-sided hexagon at the top, and an upper window of two ogee-trefoiled lights. They indicate that the solar and kitchen did not flank the open hall, but lay one over the other, both at the S end. Small C19 N addition. Contemporary aisled BARN to the W.

STONEGREEN HALL, ¾ m. SW. Like two early C18 five-bay houses set together to make an L. Two-storeyed, of two different heights. Pedimented central doorcase to each half. Half-timbered no doubt inside, refaced (says Igglesden) in 1712.

NEW HOUSE, Kingsford Street, ⅜ m. N. Early C18 again, very similar to Stonegreen Hall but presenting a uniform seven-bay front to the NE. Chequer brick.

GLEBE HOUSE, almost opposite, is also C18. Brick. Threestoreyed. Parapet with sunk panels.

MERSHAM-LE-HATCH, ¾ m. NE. The first completely new house built by *Robert Adam* after returning, spiritually reborn, from four years in Rome. His patron was the young Sir Wyndham Knatchbull, who died in 1763, a year after laying the first stone. His uncle, Sir Edward, carried on the building 'according to the first design'. The roof went on in 1765, the interiors were fitted up in 1766. Accounts and letters show that Sir Edward, though he carried through the decoration to the end, was tight with his money. Yet the plan and elevation were fixed by Sir Wyndham, and they are not only austere, but unadventurous into the bargain. For all Adam's fine talk of 'movement', for all his examination of the Roman Baths and Diocletian's palace at Spalato, the entrance front at Mersham almost duplicates Dumfries House, designed in 1754, before he ever left Scotland. Red brick with the minimum of Portland stone dressings. Main block of two storeys on a basement, four bays deep, seven wide; the centre three bays standing slightly forward under a pediment. Low hipped roof. Pedimented Tuscan doorcase, and a broad flight of steps up to it. Architraves only for the windows l. and r. of the doorcase. Square pavilions flank the main block, lying forward and linked to it by straight balustraded corridors. The pavilions are lower by half a storey, and have pyramid roofs. The N front, facing down a slope to the lake, is less of a Palladian cliché. The main block is a full three storeys, and stands well forward from the wings, the centre three bays in a bold bow. Pedimented central window, the rest quite plain. Stone loggia of paired Tuscan columns round the bow, a wholly appropriate addition of 1872 by *St Aubyn*, to make the N the entrance side.

The plan again is a standard mid-C18 one, a double pile three rooms wide, the central third, being deeper, taking the top-lit staircase in the centre. It was in the decoration of the rooms of course that Adam's novel ideas found expression: not so much in the staircase, rising in a square well from basement to oval skylight, simply balustraded, and with Ionic loggias on the upper landing, but in the delicate restraint of the doorcases, marble chimneypieces (carved by *Thomas Carter*), and plaster ceilings (by *Joseph Rose*). The lofty hall has recently lost most of its plasterwork. Chimneypiece overmantels a reinterpretation of Gibbs, with grisaille paintings of a Roman marriage and a Roman sacrifice, by *Zucchi*. In the dining room, E of the hall, a ceiling with sparse geometrical panels. Only the ceiling of the bow-ended drawing room has the full characteristic Adam flavour. It was not designed until 1772.

4070

MOTTINGHAM

ELTHAM COLLEGE, Grove Park Road. Rendered house of 1856, nine bays and two storeys with a one-storey porch on four Tuscan columns. Italianate tower behind at one corner. The chapel of 1903, towards the road, is as sprightly as the house is limp.

IRONMONGERS' ALMSHOUSES. Moved from Shoreditch in 1912* into these neo-Wren ranges by *George Hubbard*. Morden College, Blackheath, was very obviously his model. The statue of the founder, Sir Robert Geffrye, by *John Nost, 1723,* is set up on the garden side of the new buildings. Geffrye died in 1703. His monument has also migrated here, a fine Baroque cartouche with a mourning putto each side and a relief of the Lord Mayor's regalia below.

Towards Chislehurst, to the S of Mottingham Road, a large L.C.C. ESTATE of the 1930s (architect to the Council *G. Topham Forrest*; N. Taylor).

NEPICAR HOUSE *see* WROTHAM

NETTLESTEAD

6050

ST MARY. The church's apparent isolation above the Medway is illusory. Over the wall to the S was, and in part still is, the medieval manor house of the Pympes, and church and manor are intimately related. It was Reginald Pympe († 1438) who put the glass in the nave, and a glance at the church shows that the nave was built to take the glass. Nettlestead is, indeed, in its relatively humble way, conceived like the Sainte-Chapelle as a receptacle, a neutral framework for beautiful objects. The wall space on the N and S is almost wholly occupied by four tall three-light windows, set between deep gabled buttresses that reach up to the very eaves. The windows segment-headed, with panel tracery under ogees in each light, still an Early Perp feeling. The low chancel was not built with the nave, see the straight joint between them. The moulded strings on the E wall of the nave suggest that something wider and higher had been intended. Canon Livett noted that the proportions of nave and chancel are much like those of a simple Norman church. He thought old foundations might have been re-used. The tower survives of the pre-Pympe church, with one or two lancets. Its W doorway, however, and the window looking into the church were inserted by *Joseph Clarke* in 1858. (They came, it is said, from Teston

* The original almshouses are now the Geffrye Museum.

church, pulled down *c*.1736.) Tower arch heightened 1841. S porch *c*.1496, the year John Pympe left money to build it. – STAINED GLASS. A bitter disappointment; very little old glass is left, and that not of high quality. A storm in 1763 destroyed all on the S side. Most of the original glass in the tracery however is there, canopy-work and angels holding shields. The central N window of the nave is all of *c*.1438 except two heads – figures of St Thomas, St Bartholomew, and St Matthew, part of a series of the twelve Apostles (cf. Fairford, etc.). – In the NW window small scenes from the life of Thomas Becket. – NE window 1894, a very deceptive 'forgery' by *T.F.Curtis* of *Ward & Hughes*. – SE window 1911, not nearly so clever. – In the chancel the glass was originally of the 1460s. E window, Crucifixion, by *Curtis*. The Virgin and St John are said to be largely old, though they don't look it. – The NW window is old, St Stephen and St Lawrence, like identical twins. – PLATE. Cup and Paten Cover, 1599(?).

NETTLESTEAD PLACE. From the road one approaches the medieval manor house down a long drive under a stone gatehouse with a timber-framed upper room, and tiny shouldered doorway to a porter's lodge on the l. One's hopes rise; but the first view of the house, L-shaped and Tudor, dashes them again – there is nothing to be seen but *Morley Horder* of 1922. Round the back, however, facing S, there is medieval work: a two-storeyed ragstone range with small square windows below and irregularly spaced two-light Perp windows above, two square-headed and three four-centred. At intervals three rectangular projections, not bonded into the wall, but governing the arrangement of the upper windows. They seem to be nothing but unusually large and conspicuous garderobes. But even this does not prepare the visitor for what is inside. The lower floor of this building, masked by the new work on the N side, is a splendid C13 vaulted undercroft, of four bays and two aisles divided by short round piers. Quadripartite vaults with chamfered ribs that meet the walls on simple corbels. Mrs Wood dates it *c*.1250–60. A simple C13 doorway in the E wall leads straight into the new work, for the short C15 E addition is somewhat narrower than the undercroft. No trace of C13 work in the upper storey.

MILBAY CAMP. The site is set on a slight slope in marshy woodland. The earthworks are preserved only on the S and W, where they are traceable for some 1500 ft.

NEW ASH GREEN

6060

2½ m. s of Longfield

The biggest venture of Span and their architects, *Eric Lyons &*
Partners, developers of many excellent small suburban estates. New Ash Green is to be a self-sufficient town, with
houses for 8,000 people, a pedestrian shopping centre, church,
school, playing fields, a little light industry; in fact a complete
little world, in upland country on the North Downs. The site
runs to 430 acres, but buildings will cover only 190 of them;
thus the town's self-containment will be ensured. Planning
permission was granted in 1965, on condition that 450 houses
should be set aside for G.L.C. overspill, to leaven the lump of
owner-occupieds. At the time of writing the first neighbourhood is complete, the second approaching completion. The
short, two-storeyed terraces of houses, brick below, the upper
floor hung with black tiles or vertically boarded, and the
blocks of garages, are sited to create the maximum of variety
in the tightly textured environment with the minimum of
architectural striving. It is as it should be: the proof of the
architect's success will be in the living, not the looking. But in
terms of messing up the countryside New Ash Green must
inevitably be less destructive than the easy-going, unforeseen,
do-it-yourself sprawls which is all that Hartley, Longfield,
and New Barn to the N have become, or Meopham to the E,
or West Kingsdown to the SW. If the planners make New
Ash Green their model, there may still be some country left
in North-West Kent in twenty years' time. There will be very
little otherwise.

NEWCHURCH

0030

ST PETER AND ST PAUL. Quite large, of ragstone, but one of
the few over-restored churches on Romney Marsh. The restorer of *c.*1845 renewed all the tracery and invented the E
window. E.E. chancel, Perp W tower, otherwise Dec. Four-
bay nave arcade with the usual octagonal piers and double-
chamfered arches. Wide S aisle, yet wider N aisle, both
continued eastwards as one-bay chapels. These have arches
to the chancel showing that chapels already existed in the C13.
The windows at Newchurch form a good anthology of Dec
tracery patterns favoured in Kent. Y-tracery in the S aisle. In

the N aisle the N windows are reticulated, and the E has cusped intersecting tracery. Only in the S chapel is something less run-of-the-mill attempted. The E window has a large cusped encircled sexfoil with concave sides. In the apex of the S window a similar sexfoil above three ogee-headed lights balancing trefoils on their heads. So not even here are there any flowing patterns; and indeed the mouchette, the basic ingredient of the characteristic flame-like designs of the Midlands, appears rarely in Kent. S (rebuilt) and N porches. – FONT. Perp. Buttressed stem. Octagonal concave-sided bowl bearing roses and shields on alternate faces. On two shields the keys of St Peter and the sword of St Paul. – STALLS. The traceried fronts to three in the chancel seem to be old. – SCREENS to N and S chapels. Simple Perp, much renewed. – CHEST. c14; chip-carved with geometric patterns and a row of ogees. – PLATE. Cup, 1568; Paten cover, 1727 by *Timothy Ley*.

RUINS OF EASTBRIDGE CHURCH, 1¼ m. NE, in Burmarsh parish. Fragments of the tower and the nave W wall survive to quite a height. Excavation in 1933 revealed the very irregular plan of the chancel, probably of the c14.

NEWENDEN

ST PETER. A funny little building above a bend in the road, a fragment of a much larger church. Demolition in 1700 left only the nave and N aisle, with its c14 arcade on octagonal piers. Traces of a S aisle. Midget SW tower and spire of 1859, by *G. M. Hills*. Midget neo-Norman chancel of 1930–1. – FONT. A grand Late Norman piece. The square bowl stands on a thick circular stem and four attached shafts with big leaf capitals. Three faces of the bowl are carved – E, leaves and pomegranates in a geometrical frame; S, four roundels, three with grotesque creatures in them; W, a big wyvern and a big lion licking a leaf. – SCREEN. Perp, on the S side. – PULPIT. Jacobean. Perp cresting from a screen tacked on round the top. – PLATE. Elizabethan Cup; Paten dated 1576; Paten Cover dated 1577.

LOSSENHAM was founded c.1242 for Carmelite Friars. No trace of medieval buildings has been found. It was one of the very earliest Carmelite houses in England: Aylesford and Hulne, the first, were founded in 1241.

(CASTLE TOLL, 1½ m. NE. Motte and bailey within a very large earlier earthwork, covering 18½ acres.)

NEW ROMNEY

ST NICHOLAS. For a Norman church to be enlarged eastwards
in the C14 is not an unusual procedure, but when the work of
both periods is as splendid as it is here, and the junction made
thus boldly, the result is magnificent indeed. An ambitious
Norman church was built *c.*1160–70, aisled and richly arcaded
on the w front. Of this four bays of the nave remain, retaining
in the two w bays the original narrow aisles and two clerestory
windows visible outside to the N. Traces too of a N doorway.
Short, strong piers, alternately round and octagonal, as was 8
very rare before the choir of Canterbury Cathedral popularized such alternation. Square capitals with many small
scallops. Further alternation on the arches, between plain and
decorated with embattling. Each clerestory window sits
directly on the summit of the arch below. Immediately after,
a proud tower was added to the w, blocking the arcading of
the previous front, two tiers of which partly survive high up
inside. They are lavishly but monotonously decorated with
zigzag. The repertoire of the new work is a good deal wider,
though as a design the tower is less coherent than those of
St Clement, Sandwich, for instance, or New Shoreham, in
Sussex. The tower is of five stages, with the stump of a stone
spire. Broad clasping buttresses, especially broad at the NW,
where a staircase-turret goes up, turning octagonal towards
the top. Big octagonal pinnacles, the w two shafted at the
angles. In each stage windows in varying numbers, all shafted,
but in their details chronicling the development of the Transitional style. The lavish w doorway has triple shafts, but the
motifs of the arch are confined to zigzag and a roll overlapped
by a series of shapes each, as it were, like the club on a playing-
card but with only one lobe. They must be interpreted as the
last abstract vestiges of beakheads (and were used by William
of Sens in the upper aisle windows at Canterbury). On the
next stage some waterleaf capitals appear, and above that the
windows gain pointed arches. The most curious feature of the
tower, however, is that it is clasped by narrow aisles, producing three tower arches, which show that the aisles were
not later additions. These arches too are much enriched.
Jamb shafts with volute capitals and deeply moulded abaci.
The E arch has crocket capitals which presuppose the 1175–80
work at Canterbury, and a steeply pointed arch. (The scallop

caps on the E side of this arch must be part of the mid-C12 work.)

In the early C14 four new bays were added to the E, to make a chancel as wide as the nave, and much wider aisles. These aisles were carried westwards to embrace two of the remaining bays of the Norman nave.* At the E the three coterminous gables crown a splendid display of reticulated tracery, three then five then three lights. Slim octagonal piers, double-chamfered arches. The chancel arch and its fellows to N and S have only one chamfer, plus the stumps of a second. Low walls across the E bay of each arcade accommodate a simple PISCINA and triple SEDILIA in the chancel and both aisles. Early C14 RECESS in the N chapel with a depressed arch with big cusping and a frieze of large four-petalled flowers.

The S.P.A.B., which had been founded in 1878, with William Morris as its first Secretary, won one of its early victories at New Romney. In 1880 restoration was in progress under *J. O. Scott*, who began by pulling down and renewing the two Norman bays of the N aisle. The Society protested. The vicar was hostile, the architect silent. The Society published the whole correspondence in the local newspapers, and no more of this restoration by rebuilding was done; so the 'grave and satisfying simplicity' of the interior remains. The roofs are still plastered, the floors still keep their old tiles and many LEDGER STONES (worth looking at as a first-rate anthology of lettering over a century from 1683). – BOX PEWS. A complete set, low and townish. – A few TILES in the N aisle with C14 patterns. – CHANDELIER, dated 1745. Brass. – ALTAR RAILS. Early C18. Strong but elegant turned balusters. – TOWER SCREENS. Dated 1602. Strong but rustic turned balusters. – PLATE. All gilt. A set by *Fawdery*, 1698; Almsdish, 1701, by *Fawdery*; Flagon, inscribed 1715, by *David Williams*; Almsdish, 1728. – BRASSES. Thomas Lambard † 1510. – Thomas Smyth † 1610.

The scale of the church matched New Romney's importance as one of the Cinque Ports. Domesday Book records three parish churches, a priory, and a hospital. At that time the river Rother flowed out into the sea at New Romney and the sea itself came up close to the town. The Rother was diverted

---

* But the responds of the half-arches into the Norman aisles seem by their mouldings to be C13, so there must have been a previous attempt at enlargement.

to Rye after the storm of 1287, the sea gradually receded, and New Romney was stranded. Of the churches only St Nicholas survived beyond 1550. Today the town is more than a village, but not much more. The church lies on its s edge and the long, straight High Street is the spine of an unusually regular grid of streets. New Romney is reputedly a planned town of the Saxon period.

CHURCH APPROACH leads from the church to the High Street. In it, the ASSEMBLY ROOMS, a fine early C18 front in blue and red brick. Three bays marked by giant pilasters. Deep dentilled cornice. The centre pilasters take in the ample door surround on the way up. A big, flat pedimental gable curtly caps it all. Adjoining, on the l., the SCHOOLROOM, dated 1676, yet still built of the local small yellow bricks. The improvement in brickwork over those, it may be, forty years is startling and impressive. (The back of the Assembly Rooms displays its medieval origin.)

At once into the HIGH STREET, where, immediately opposite, the PRIORY HOUSE is the highest accent of the street. Red brick, seven bays, only two storeys. On the ground floor two wide, slightly bowed, shop windows. Behind this C18 front, in ASHFORD ROAD, ST JOHN'S PRIORY, a medieval building, two storeys high, continued by a long stone wall. On both a picturesque array of medieval fragments, all very worn, heads, doorways, etc. The windows with Y-tracery look no older than C19, which leaves nothing as evidence of the building's original character.

Back in the High Street, the adjoining house has a nice C18 porch with a broken pediment on Tuscan columns. Across the street, the TOWN HALL is effectively of 1884. (PLATE. A pair of silver-gilt maces, 1724.) Nothing more on either side until at the far w end West Street, where some WALLING, laid in flint and stone bands, is said to be all that remains of the church of St Lawrence. The almshouses of New Romney are of the humblest. In West Street SOUTHLAND'S ALMSHOUSES, 1734, has its windows arranged in quincunx fashion. Further on and round the corner, in St John's Road, the DERING ALMSHOUSES, a one-storeyed row of six, bearing the date 1770. See p. 644

So much for the w half of the town. At the E end nothing at all to report, except a recent addition to the SCHOOL, an attractive vertically-boarded block towards the street. 1958 by *Willan Stewart & Waite*.

14—W.K.W.

NORHEADS FARM *see* BIGGIN HILL

NORTH CRAY

4070

ST JAMES. Rebuilt by *Edwin Nash*. Nave 1850-2, chancel 1871.
Rock-faced ragstone. NW tower of 1857; shingled spire. Dec,
with one or two mild surprises; e.g. the lights of the E window
alternately wide and narrow, and the pretty arch to the organ
recess, cusped many many times. – PULPIT. A good C17
piece. Pilasters and a bold convex cornice covered with small-
scale arabesques. It has a date 1637. – CHANCEL WOOD-
WORK, all brought in and much of it foreign, but made up
into a unified whole of some splendour. The climax is the
REREDOS, large panels in very high relief of the Adoration of
the Magi and the Flight into Egypt. The STALLS incorporate
Düreresque reliefs of the Adoration of the Magi and of the
Shepherds (S) and the Visitation and Circumcision (N). Behind
the stalls on the N side, a C15 RELIEF of the Seven Acts of
Mercy. The end panels, with Renaissance shell-hoods, must
be later. Also several pierced panels of foliage. – PAINTING.
A large and damaged Crucifixion. By *Gessi*, says Kelly. –
PLATE. Flagon, 1674 by *T.L.*; Cup and two Patens, 1708 by
Gabriel Sleath. – MONUMENTS. Elizabeth Buggin † 1650.
Large black-and-white-marble architectural tablet. – William
Wiffin, *c*.1652. Small tablet with an oversized open pediment.
– Octavia, Lady Ellenborough, † 1819. By *Chantrey*, 1821.
Kneeling woman looking up, a wreath of flowers at her feet.
Chantrey used the design again at Weybridge, Surrey. – Alice
Morris † 1894, signed by *J. Nelson MacBean*. Relief of an air-
borne woman in Grecian draperies, her upraised arms fully in
the round. Such allegorical females were becoming old-
fashioned in Chantrey's day.

North Cray is the most rural of the Crays. The churchyard fits
into a corner of the park of NORTH CRAY PLACE, beside the
colossal kitchen-garden walls. The walls run along the road
for quite a way, though houses hide behind them now instead
of vegetables. At the W end of the churchyard a handsome
early C18 wrought-iron GATE leads into the park.

6070

NORTHFLEET

ST BOTOLPH. Of the churches on the Thameside chalk cliffs
none is more dramatically sited than Northfleet. From the W

end of the churchyard the view over the boskage of a vast disused quarry is the sort to delight the picturesque traveller. Turning back to the church, one finds a virtually complete structure of the early C14, on an impressively large scale. It must have been more impressive still before the W tower collapsed. In 1717 a perfectly adequate tower was built within the walls of the old one, and the N wall converted into a grand long flight of steps. Six-bay nave. Battlemented aisles and s porch. Octagonal NW stair-turret. Chancel of four bays. The windows offer a wide variety of tracery patterns, all of them renewed (accurately, except for the second window from the E in the N aisle?) in 1852 by *Brandon & Ritchie*. (They fortunately did not touch the flintwork of the walls, which is attractively random.) The combination of geometrical motifs, such as spherical triangles, and ogees is characteristic of Kent, and the split cusps in the s aisle E window are the hallmark of so-called 'Kentish tracery'. The interior is extraordinarily spacious, although too thoroughly restored and tidied up. Standard arcades of double-chamfered arches on octagonal piers. Clerestory windows in the shape of barbed trefoils. The W half of the s arcade however survives from an earlier building. The piers, alternating round and octagonal, and the two plain square orders of the arches are clearly C13. Taking this hint, a second look outside shows, not more C13 evidence, but the SW corner of an aisleless Saxon church, long-and-short quoins for the full height. In the s aisle, Dec PISCINA and fine triple SEDILIA. The aggressive chancel SEDILIA are by *E.W. Godwin*, part of his restoration of 1862. The chancel arch also his. – CHANCEL SCREEN. Of the date of the church, i.e. very early C14. Central arch with naturalistic foliage on the capitals and in the spandrels. Otherwise single lights between slender ringed shafts. Each light with a trefoiled head balancing a pointed trefoil on it. A pointed trefoil also in each spandrel. How pleasant that such a charming piece should have survived! – CHANDELIER. Brass. Dated 1732. – STAINED GLASS. E window 1861. Unusually good, with its pinks, lavenders, and greens. – MONUMENTS. Brass to Peter de Lacy † 1375. Large, i.e. 4½ ft, full-length, priest, the lines emphatically incised. Abrupt modern border; originally there was a canopy. – William Lye † 1391, another very similar brass, but only half-length (18 in.). – Brass to William Rickhill † 1433. Armoured man, 2 ft in length, and his elongated wife. – Richard Crich † 1709. Standing wall-monument under a big broken segmental pediment. Crich and his wife kneel side by side, facing outwards, their heads turned to the r., their clasped hands raised to the l. One can only interpret this curious pose as a hesitant English attempt to show Italian Baroque ecstasy. (They look towards the altar.) The monument is not signed, but it looks like the work of *Edward Stanton*.* – Several good architectural tablets, e.g. James Fortrye † 1674. The others all early C18. One to James Fortrye, † 1737, is signed by *William Palmer*. – Ursula Fortrye † 1740. With a bust. By *P. Scheemakers* (Gunnis).

See
p.
644ALL SAINTS, Perry Street. 1868–71, by *James Brooks*. Not an especially large church but an extremely powerful one. Ragstone with ashlar dressings. Straight-ended chancel and severely Romanesque nave with small grouped clerestory windows and low aisles. The interior is equally austere, lit from the ends by tall w lancets with a plate-traceried rose over, and a Geometrical e window. Large expanses of exposed ragstone. Trussed rafter roofs. Low circular piers with startling square stiff-leaf capitals, of an idiosyncratic design based on the capitals at Rodmell or St Anne, Lewes. The foliage is ever so slightly different on each capital.

ST MARK, Rosherville. By *H. & E. Rose*, 1851–3. Rock-faced ragstone. w tower and spire. Gabled aisles. Low, short chancel. Fancy plate tracery. Cost £7,000 (GS). A good deal of that must have gone on the sculpture inside, leaf corbels and so forth. – STAINED GLASS. e window 1853, by *Wailes*.

OUR LADY OF THE ASSUMPTION (R.C.), The Hill. 1914 by *Sir Giles Scott*. Built of warm brown brick. A little self-consciously dramatic, but for its date remarkably independent. It is still unmistakably a Gothic church, but little bursts of busy tracery and the low pointed arcade arches are the only period details in it. Bare, soaring w tower, dissolving into small forms at the very top, the outline that Scott used again in the central tower of Liverpool Cathedral. In plan the church is nearly a rectangle. Bold channelled podium. Low aisles and bands of clerestory windows tell against tall gabled w chapels and e transepts. Inside, the sanctuary arch is rectangular, and the sanctuary a flood of light from the transept windows.

HUGGENS COLLEGE, High Street, at the corner of Stonebridge Road. Almshouses for fifty inmates, so on an impressively large scale. Tudor style. Stock brick. By *W. Chadwick*, c.1844. Four two-storeyed ranges round a quadrangle. Chapel

* As Dr Margaret Whinney convinces me.

crocket capital datable to the last, post-William-of-Sens years
of the C12. – STAINED GLASS. Chancel windows by *Holiday*,
1893 and 1898. Unpleasant emphasis on the bodies of the saints.
COURT LODGE. T-shaped house. Half-timbered N range, towards the church, with close uprights and an overhang in all
directions. Vast C16 chimneybreast – diapered brickwork, but
only the stumps of the stacks.

ORPINGTON   *4060*

Orpington spreads and spreads, middle-class commuterland, a
land of serpentine, tree-lined residential roads. The first estates
for commuters were built in the 1920s. Between 1931 and 1939
the population of the Urban District nearly doubled. By 1961
the population was 80,277.

ALL SAINTS. The medieval church is small and now relegated
to be the ante-chapel to a new building three times its size,
thrown out to the S. The new building of 1957–8, by *Geddes
Hyslop*, uses brick and flint, i.e. local materials, but the minimal Gothic design is flimsy and unconvincing. Wide, light
interior, though here too the aisle vaults, for instance, look
disturbingly like cardboard. The walls of the old nave are
unusually tall for its width. They suggest Saxon work, and
indeed a Saxon SUNDIAL has come to light in the S wall. The
sundial is inscribed in runes, one of only three Anglo-Saxon
runic inscriptions so far found in South-East England, with
the Roman letters OR . . . VM (i.e. orologium viatorum, perhaps, to show what it is); and with an Old English sentence,
parts of which Mr R. I. Page has translated: '. . . to count
and to hold' and 'for him who knows how to seek out how'
(referring presumably to users of the sundial). At present it
is upside down. N tower, W doorway, and chancel arch are all
part of a remodelling of *c*.1200. Evidence of lancets in the
chancel. The tower has a rib-vaulted ground stage, once used
as a chapel, see the PISCINA. (The tower rebuilt externally in
the late C18 in flint and brick.) On the chancel arch keeled
angle rolls and keeled shafts with little crocket capitals. Lavish
W doorway of two orders of shafts with leaves on the capitals
much damaged but apparently undecided whether to be waterleaf or crockets. Richly moulded pointed arch including a row
of small dogtooth and big undercut zigzag. W porch built by
rector Nicholas, who died in 1370 and desired to be buried
there. His tomb is beneath a big but delicately carved ogee

arch with crockets and a finial and a very depressed and cuspy sub-arch. Perp N chancel chapel, which carries the Rufford arms in many places. – FONT COVER. C15. Plain ribs and a finial. – SCREEN. With a rood loft. 1916, designed by *W.D. Caröe.* – REREDOS. Large triptych by *Brian Thomas, c.*1959. The C20 might never have been. – PLATE. Cup and Cover, 1634; Paten, 1681(?) by *M.S.* – MONUMENTS. Thomas Wilkynson † 1511. Coarse brass of a priest, 37 in. long, which is bigger than usual at that date. – William Gee † 1815, Richard Carew † 1816, Richard Gee † 1817, three Grecian tablets whose only mark of distinction is that they are by *Chantrey.*

ST ANDREW, South Cray. 1892–3 by *Hide & Newberry.* Oddly like a Commissioners' church outside. Romanesque interior. Recent matching W extension.

ST PAUL, Crofton. By *A.B. Knapp-Fisher,* 1958. The church of 1887 is now the parish hall. Don't miss its lychgate.

THE PRIORY. Built in 1393 and 'greatly improved' in 1471 by Prior Selling. It seems to have been both the clergy-house for the rector of Orpington and his numerous chaplains,* and a stopping place for the priors of Canterbury Cathedral. The medieval buildings are all of flint, but have been so renewed that they inspire little confidence. However, the E wing, at the back, is clearly the earliest part. There are traces in it of three single-light windows. In front of this, the main range consists of an open hall, with a simple Perp entrance doorway behind the porch at the S end, and one original doorway to the service wing. Bay-window at the dais end. The solar wing at the N has been enlarged. In it one ground-floor room with Elizabethan plasterwork, foliage trails on the frieze and the roof-beams. Attached to the S, PUBLIC LIBRARY, by *Lord Mottistone,* opened 1961. A spirited attempt to be modern and drop historicist hints at the same time.

A long range of timber-framed OUTBUILDINGS fronts on to Church Hill. Weatherboarding above flint and brick towards the road, but the original framing exposed on the priory side. High central entrance for carts, with a room over it. All now dilapidated, but it would be a real loss to this, the only characterful part of Orpington, if they went.

Orpington Station is the site of a ROMAN VILLA of flint and chalk – altered several times.

* Until modern times St Mary Cray, Hayes, Downe, and Knockholt were all chapelries of Orpington.

OTFORD

ST BARTHOLOMEW. Picturesque, not historical, considerations make the church stick in the mind. Short, fat, rendered w tower, with a stumpy shingled spire and a timber w porch dated 1637. Nave built of unsplit flints set wide apart in the mortar. The N and w walls must be as early as the C11. See too the nave quoins here. The N windows however are Dec. C14 chancel. NE vestry with two small Tudor windows.* On the s side a Late Perp aisle, called 'the newe ile' in a will of 1532 (says Mr Stoyel), gabled and continuing eastwards as a chapel. Fine Dec E window, renewed c.1845. In 1863 *Street* restored the church. This meant a new chancel arch and new arcade to replace a wooden one. The tower is Transitional. The two tiny tower windows have round heads internally and deep splays; the tower doorway and arch, however, are pointed. – FONT COVER. Early C17, greatly renewed. – PULPIT. Stone. Presumably *Street*'s. – CHANDELIERS. Brass. All C20 except the large one in the chancel, which is notable in having a faceted bulb and reflectors shaped as flowers. – ARMOUR. C16 helm, of Greenwich make. – STAINED GLASS. Small C17 Continental painted panels in the E window. – Two s aisle windows by *Hardman*, c.1868. – PLATE. Cup and Paten Cover, 1666, the latter by *C. T.*

MONUMENTS. Late Perp wall-tomb set as an Easter Sepulchre. There are shields in cusped quatrefoils at the bottom. Panelling on the back and the sloping reveals. Top cresting. No sign that there was an effigy, or even a brass. – David Polhill † 1754. By *Cheere*, and very characteristic of the sculptor. The first-rate bust stands on a scrolly, scaly pedestal. Grey obelisk at the back, yellow mottled marble on the side scrolls and at the bottom, a background for three putto heads. All the details, e.g. the brackets, carved with great bravura. – Charles Polhill † 1755. This is also by *Cheere*, and one of his major monuments. Full-length standing figure wearing a voluminous toga and leaning on a large urn in the pose of Guelfi's Craggs monument in Westminster Abbey. Charles Polhill stands on a sarcophagus, l. and r. of which female allegorical figures are seated. Relief medallion at the top with his wife's profile. The various parts of the composition do not make a coherent whole, and Cheere cannot begin to compare

* And an internal recess in the w wall, identified by Mr A. D. Stoyel as a wafer oven.

with Roubiliac in inventiveness, but the crisp carving of the small curling shapes is truly Rococo, and the way the busy folds of the toga tell against the plain yellow marble urn is highly effective. – Charles Polhill † 1805. By *J. Bacon Jun.* Hanging monument, hackneyed in its symbolism, a willow weeping over a draped urn and so on, but with an engagingly direct profile of the toothless old gentleman.

ARCHBISHOPS' PALACE. Considering that Thomas Bourchier, Archbishop of Canterbury, had bequeathed his vast palace of Knole to his successors, one is astonished at the extravagance of Archbishop Warham in transforming a manor house only three miles away into another palace hardly less vast. Lambarde, looking sourly back from the other side of the Reformation, assumed that Warham wished 'to leave to posteritie some glorious monument of his worldly wealth and misbegotten treasure'. Warham himself called it his 'power house'. He succeeded to the see in 1503 and by 1518 Otford Palace was in use.

The palace was built round two courtyards, and the fragment that survives formed the w half of the entrance range of the outer court, which would thus in its entirety have been *c.*220 ft wide. The material is brick consistently diapered and dressed with stone. At the w end a tower-like structure standing at the angle, almost detached from the main range, remains up to the second storey. Within it, octagonal rooms on all three levels can be traced, each with a fireplace on the NW side, a doorway at the SE corner, and a garderobe tower to the SW – see the partitions inside the tower to keep the three shoots separate. The stream that trickles past on the S side will in the C16 have been subterranean. The doorways open on to a stair-turret, which oddly apparently gave no access to the main entrance range. Of this range only the lowest storey survives, incorporated in a row of cottages. On the S side it was originally pierced, it seems, by a series of square openings with depressed-arched heads of moulded brick, i.e. it was treated as a cloister. Later chimneybreast built across two of the openings. The range ends at the E in a polygonal bay, one of a pair flanking the main gateway, with a staircase-turret on the inner (S) side. Nothing is left of the gateway, except the base of the W jamb, moulded in a complex way on the outer face, and with two big chamfers inside. All the windows are square-headed of one or two lights, their heads four-centred arches, and the surrounds are moulded with a wave identical to the window mouldings of Knole of forty years earlier. Nothing more inventive in the other surviving features. 100 yds to the s, in the back gardens of houses in Bubblestone Road, ragstone footings of a wall with four polygonal projections and two buttresses. These must also have belonged to the palace, in some way or other, and stress its great scale.

There is something very attractive about the nonchalance that allows the palace ruins to be part cottages, part a funny, familiar old thing in a field. What a pity that the rest of the village cannot be as much at ease. Roads have encroached on THE GREEN, and left the village pond in the middle of a roundabout. The church hangs back unassumingly on the e side, and COLLITS WELL, the big house of c.1790 that was meant to dominate, has been rendered, with debased classical trimmings of the 1850s. That leaves, at the s end, HOLMSDALE VILLA and HOLMSDALE HOUSE, two two-storeyed red-brick houses with five-bay fronts, Early Georgian and built as a semi-detached pair, a remarkable thing at that date.

The HIGH STREET, which runs w from the NW corner of the roundabout, also leaves a nice taste as one dashes through in a car, but will not bear savouring. The BULL INN, a short way down on the l., is largely c20, but contains a mid-c16 stone fireplace; it is Gothic in outline, but the relief patterns on the lintel include simple strapwork and acanthus foliage. Above it, two carved profile heads in roundels, the woodwork of the 1530s and 40s so often met with in Kent. The tradition that they came from the Archbishop's Palace may well be wrong; for surveys of 1547 and 1573 show that after the Reformation the palace quickly deteriorated, and it is not likely that new fittings were put in. Just beyond, *T. G. Jackson's* SCHOOL of 1872. It is quite a surprise that any architect had a hand in it. The CHURCH HALL, opposite, is a much better example of a simple building designed so that it does not hector its simple companions, but managing to get the proportions just right too. No wonder; for *Lutyens* himself designed it, in 1909. His brother was the vicar of Otford. The last house on the l., BROUGHTON MANOR, has a genuine c17 gable at the back, half-timbered and with a shaped bargeboard. (Inside, the medieval hall, now divided, and a solar added in the later c16. Mr K. Gravett)

Evidence of a ROMAN BUILDING was found e of the railway station.

OTHAM

ST NICHOLAS. Ragstone. Nave with a N aisle starting some way from the W end. Chancel. S tower, boarded at the top with a shingled spire, a spike on a truncated pyramid. That produces a pretty and individual distant outline; but *R. Wheeler*'s drastic restoration of 1864–5 has ruined close-up charm and authenticity. Two external features need a word. First, the tower is by the crudeness of its rubble walling and indecisive quoins, as well as by its position, early. Traces of a blocked E doorway. Small tufa windows, the S one altered into a lancet. Secondly, the N doorway is in its original state and clearly C14. A row of four ogee trefoil-headed panels within the square outer moulding. C14 chancel arch. C14 arch from nave to aisle. Spindly crown-post nave roof; but the atmosphere of the interior pleases. – FONT. Only the bowl is old, but four of its eight sides have delightful early C14 carvings on their sloping undersides, a frowning face, two calf's heads, and a leaf. – PLATE. Cup of 1562 and Elizabethan Paten; Paten, 1717 by *John Bathe*; Flagon, 1737 by *Joseph Smith*. – MONUMENTS. Lavinus Buffkin † 1620. By *Maximilian Colt*, whose design is at the College of Arms. It is a design of the highest interest, an architectural tablet, with busts in sunk roundels between Corinthian columns that carry not a pediment but a curvy gable with achievement. Alabaster and touch, producing white and black contrasts. Both design and colouring were to have lively careers through the C17. – Thomas Hendley. Dated 1678. Fine architectural tablet with a scrolly open pediment. White marble and black marble. – Elizabeth Hendley. Dated 1721. Curvaceous cartouche, excessively badly carved.

Otham is famous for its timber-framed houses. The three to which the fame attaches stand apart from one another, but all overlooking a small valley SE of the church.

WARDES is archaeologically the important one. The N front, the oldest part, of the C14, seems to be constructed in the normal Wealden way, with an open hall between two-storeyed jettied ends. The hipped roof however only covers the E two-thirds, and the W part belongs to a C16 wing. Wardes, in fact, represents an earlier, more compact type of house, in which the solar sat on top of the service rooms at one end of the hall. Entrance doorways however facing one another at the far end from the solar–service wing. Widely spaced uprights and bold

S-curved braces. The hall truss has a tall crown-post on a tie-beam supported on curved braces, which form a two-centred arch. Mr J. T. Smith sees this as the last vestige of aisled hall construction. Restored and the hall reopened to the roof c.1912 for Sir Louis Mallet.

SYNYARDS. Straightforward, very regular and handsome early C16 Wealden house, with a gable added in 1663. Four-centred doorway into the screens passage. Service wing r. of it. Wider solar wing, at the l. end, with the upper floor projecting on the floor beams to the side as well as to the front. (Early Tudor tempera paintings in a bedroom.) Restored in 1905 by *P. M. Johnston*.

STONEACRE. C16, an enlargement of the Wealden house, in that the wings are gabled. (Open hall with a crown-post of four clustered shafts.) *Aymer Vallance* in 1920 however restored and enlarged the building into a museum piece. The s gable is all new, the N wing, with its diamond bracing and dates 1546 and 1629, is the reconstructed N end of North Bore Place, Chiddingstone. (Stone fireplace from the George Inn, Sitting-bourne.)

GORE COURT, ½ m. s. Large, many-gabled, with a gabled porch. Rendered white, with windows all sashed or early C19 pointed, i.e. a half-timbered house that nobody got round to restoring, and perhaps a salutary antidote to the glamorized condition of Otham's other houses. (Gable dated 1577. *J.B.A.A.*, 1895, p. 183)

OXEN HOATH *see* WEST PECKHAM

OWLETTS *see* COBHAM

PADDLESWORTH *see* SNODLAND

PADDOCK WOOD

6040

ST ANDREW. 1953 by *Cecil Burns* of Tunbridge Wells. Red brick. Gothic tracery without historical precedent. Chancel, aisled nave, and a thick, short octagonal tower between them, which produces an ungainly outline. Better inside, round-arched throughout, with deep internal aisle buttresses pierced for passages, as it might have been done fifty years earlier. White walls, pale blue tunnel-vaults, shallow gilt dome under the tower.

N of the station, two buildings which sum up the *raison d'être* of Paddock Wood. S.C.A.T.S. GRAIN-DRYING STORE was

built in 1944 for the Ministry of Works, under the supervision
of *C. Bristow*. No attempt was made to make it seem smaller
than it is. Alongside it, the HOPS MARKETING BOARD
WAREHOUSE, concrete, a second unshrinking giant. Completed in 1954, by *A. C. Fairtlough & D. R. Morris*.
The less said about the rest of the town, and its mindless sprawl,
the better.

PAGEHURST *see* STAPLEHURST

PARIS HOUSE *see* EAST MALLING

PATTENDEN *see* GOUDHURST

PAUL'S FARM *see* LEIGH

6040
PEMBURY

ST PETER. By itself, 1½ m. N of the present village. The short
nave, of small, very dark brown sandstone blocks, looks immediately the earliest part. One tiny Norman window in its S
wall confirms the impression, as does the arch of the S doorway. The C14 added a short broad W tower, with a shingled
spire, and lengthened and remodelled the chancel. S porch.
Coats of arms on the chancel buttresses (renewed on the N
side) include Hardreshull and Colepeper. John Colepeper in
1355 obtained a licence to build a perpetual chantry in the
churchyard. Good crown-post roof in the nave, moulded tiebeams on pierced spandrels. Otherwise the interior is unattractive, over-restored by *R. Wheeler* of Brenchley in 1867
(PF). Did he supply the alien REREDOS, SEDILIA, and
FONT? – BRASS. Elizabeth Rowe † 1607, aged 'eight years
wanting three months'. Yet she looks a grown woman.
A new church, also ST PETER, was built on the main road in
1846–7 at the expense of the Marquess Camden, by *E. W.
Stephens*. Sandstone, in a mechanical Perp. SW tower and recessed spire. It is not, however, a preaching house any more.
ALMSHOUSES. A two-storeyed range facing the new church.
1716 repaired in 1802, says the inscription. So the brick is
rendered, the windows are given labels, and the central pediment has been made a gable with pendulous bargeboards.
BAYHALL, 1 m. S, an interesting house of the 1650s, with giant
pilasters, that advanced mid-C17 motif, was demolished after
1908. A red-brick BARN with sandstone quoins remains.

LITTLE HAWKWELL, 1¾ m. NE. The house contains a reset staircase of the mid C17. Bulbous turned balusters. Sparingly carved, e.g. with a dog coursing among foliage scrolls.

DOWER HOUSE (Territorial Army Headquarters), ½ m. W. 1904–5 by *Mallows & Grocock*, i.e. C. E. Mallows, better known for his glamorous drawings of other men's buildings. Quite an impressive exercise in the Voysey manner. Asymmetrical entrance (E) front, garden front nearly symmetrical, with projecting wings. Roughcast, and a bit of red brick low down by the porch. The composition as a whole strikes one as a little arch and self-conscious, especially the windows muddling up the levels in the gable at the r. end of the E front. LODGE beside the road, also by *Mallows & Grocock*.

See
p.
645

PENGE

3070

CHRIST CHURCH, Croydon Road. By *W. Bassett-Smith*. Begun in 1884. Rock-faced ragstone. Dec. A W tower was intended.

ST JOHN THE EVANGELIST, Beckenham Road. 1850. By *Edwin Nash & J. N. Round*. Nash added the gabled aisles in 1861, and the transepts in 1866. Rock-faced ragstone. W tower and stone broach spire. Geometrical tracery, treated in Nash's quirky way. The best thing inside is the open timber roofs, those in the transepts especially provocative, with beams from all four directions meeting in mid air.

CONGREGATIONAL CHURCH, Beckenham Road. 1912 by *P. Morley Horder*. Passage aisles and clerestory. Shafts on large, excellently carved corbels.

FREE WATERMEN AND LIGHTERMEN'S ALMSHOUSES, Beckenham Road. The most prominent building in Penge, two-storeyed ranges round three sides of a quadrangle reaching a climax in a gate-tower at the back, with battlemented turrets and ogee lead caps. Built by *George Porter* in 1840–1, when Tudor was the inevitable style for almshouses.*

KING WILLIAM NAVAL ASYLUM, St John's Road. Founded in 1847, designed by *Philip Hardwick* and paid for by Queen Adelaide. More Tudor almshouses round an open-ended square. Red brick and stone, with black diaper patterns. Quite humble, but not only more correct than Porter could manage to be, but much more sensitively designed. Hardwick was rare

---

* Some curious details, e.g. the porter's lodge growing out of the wall, can be attributed to the fact that the young *S. S. Teulon* was Porter's assistant (N. Taylor).

in his generation, an architect who handled all styles with equal distinction.

Penge is for most people a joke, an epitome of the dreary suburban non-place. It is a reputation not quite deserved, and a journey from the Crystal Palace down the hill to the High Street and beyond yields several buildings worth a look.

CRYSTAL PALACE PARK ROAD is lined for its full length down the r. side with tall red mansions of the 1880s. (1882 is the date on Nos. 57 and 61.) The most self-indulgent are towards the top end. Half way down on the l., the CHULSA ESTATE is an especially good example of the gentle, craftsmanly style of the 1950s. By *James & Bywater*. Yellow brick very sparingly patterned. Shallow-pitched roofs. Five-storey Y-shaped blocks with lower terraces further down the hill. Near the bottom of the hill PARK COURT is a pre-war estate typical of its time and carefully done. Brick painted white. Flat roofs with projecting eaves. The blocks only three storeys high, and, one notices, still carefully symmetrical. 1936 by *Frederick Gibberd*.

Nothing in the High Street, but at the far end, next to the Congregational church, KENILWORTH COURT, by *Royce, Stephenson & Tasker*, 1961–2. Shops and a filling station, nicely grouped and designed with excellent restraint and firmness. Slate-hung between the windows.

5040

PENSHURST

ST JOHN THE BAPTIST. Sandstone, appearing wholly of the C19 from outside, except for a Perp w tower decidedly more curious than beautiful. It has deep, diagonal buttresses with too many set-offs near the top, battlements, and, rising from within them, battlemented corner turrets with bald pinnacles. Nave and gabled aisles, chancel and gabled chapels, not enlarged in the C19. S (Sidney) chapel however rebuilt in 1820 by *J. B. Rebecca* in a gawky style that perfectly, but probably unintentionally, answers that of the tower. Bold, thistly foliage bosses and spandrels on the s porch and E doorway, unusually convincing for the date. N aisle and chancel E wall rebuilt in 1864–5 by *Sir G. G. Scott*. s windows all new too. The interior takes us back to the C13. E.E. N arcade of three bays on round piers, the capital of the w one particularly primitive; early C14 s arcade continued with the same octagonal piers and bold capitals in the two bays to the s chapel. Similar w arch in the chapel, with a big leaf-head corbel. This is set in a wall dividing chapel from aisle. Here too is a lancet rebated towards the w, evidence of a C13 s chapel or vestry. The chancel arch must be *Scott*'s, timber, with pierced spandrels, resting on big stone angels. Two unequal arches to the N chapel, one with a hood-mould on typical mid-C14 heads. Perp clerestory in nave and chancel. Finally, the interior of the Sidney Chapel. *Rebecca*'s pointed tunnel-vault is charming, panelled, with cusped heads to the panels and bumpy foliage bosses, but springing from rows of moulded corbels, incongruously E.E. in style. The vault is painted, with Sidney shields of arms hung on sinuous trees. – FONT. Perp. Panelled stem. Shields in quatrefoils on the bowl. – CHANCEL SCREEN. 1895 by *Bodley & Garner* (BW). Extremely ornate and pretty. – STAINED GLASS. Heraldic, in the tower window, with a date 1627. – Chancel s clerestory windows 1884 by *Holiday*. – ALTAR FRONTALS. By *Beatrice Bendelow*, 1966. – MONUMENTS. Sir Stephen de Penchester † 1299 (Sidney Chapel). Purbeck marble effigy of a knight in chain mail, drawing his sword, broken off below the waist. – Two C13 coffin slabs (under the tower) with foliated crosses. On one the cross is superimposed on an anguished-looking woman, her hands raised in prayer. As the bottom half of the slab is missing, interpretation is not easy. For instance, is she shown about to rise from an open tomb? At any rate it is a highly remarkable and expressive piece of sculpture. – Pawle Yden † 1514. Brass. 19 in. figures. – Sir William Sydney † 1553 (Sidney Chapel). Characteristic Late Perp design, untouched by any hint of the Renaissance, except for the acanthus scrolls round the brass inscription plate. Tomb-chest. Back-plate framed by twisted shafts that carry a deep, panelled cresting. – William Coventry † 1686 (s aisle). Massive architectural tablet of extremely fine quality. White and black marble. Putti hold aloft an urn at the top.* – Robert, 4th Earl of Leicester, 1704 (Sidney Chapel). The last work of *William Stanton*, completed after Stanton's death by *William Woodman*. Standing wall-monument, a design of great charm but little dignity. On a tall pedestal two dancing angels with big wings hold out their hands to balance a big urn. Infant heads in the clouds above, titled with the

---

* *William Kidwell* must have been the sculptor. Employed elsewhere by the Coventrys, he signs an almost identical monument at Finglass, Co. Dublin. Date of death 1700.

names of the Earl's children. – Gilbert Spencer, 1730 (chancel). Large architectural tablet. – Philip, 5th Earl of Leicester, and others (Sidney Chapel). 1743. Marble tomb-chest and grey obelisk behind with a splendid coat of arms and supporters. – Sophia, Lady De L'Isle, † 1837 (Sidney Chapel). Signed by *W. Theed*. Life-size figure of a lady in Grecian draperies on a pedestal. She holds a Bible and raises her eyes aloft. Cold. – 1st Viscount Hardinge † 1856 (N aisle). Heavy Gothic tablet, with a profile medallion, designed by *Salvin* and carved by *Pfyffers* (PF). – War Memorial (nave N). 1947. Designed by *Sir Giles Scott*.

25 PENSHURST PLACE. There is no finer or more complete C14 manor house than Penshurst Place. The first distant view from the W, however, of the house across a broad expanse of meadow, tells nothing of that. The vastly extended front, *c*. 280 ft from the massive tower at the N end to the tower that answers it at the S, is predominantly Tudor and Elizabethan and early C19, the l. part set back a long way from the towers, with ranges running back to it. The route taken by the public from the S leads through the gardens, and now the character of the original house begins to be more easily perceived; and it is time to give some facts about the man who built it. Sir John de Pulteney, draper and merchant of London, Lord Mayor four times between 1331 and 1337, founder of a chantry for three priests in St Paul's Cathedral, of a college for a master, thirteen priests, and four choristers in the City church of St Laurence Pountney, and of a Carmelite friary in Coventry, and the possessor of immense wealth, built a house in London that at his death became the residence of the Black Prince. Pulteney's country house was princely too. Licence to crenellate Penshurst was granted in 1341. It is a measure of Pulteney's self-confidence that the house he built was without fortification of any kind.

To reach it the way lies through the detached GARDEN TOWER, which seems a sort of isolated gatehouse. But the rough stumps of high walls in its W and E sides suggest that it was once linked with the SW corner tower, and with a similar tower further E, fragmentarily preserved. The NW tower, and the King's Tower in the N range, placed, like the Garden Tower, in line with the porch of the C14 house, are further parts of a complete system of fortified walls that enclosed Pulteney's unfortified manor house. Part of the wall N of the SW tower survives, running unbroken into the end wall of the

square, extended to the road by further cottages l. and r. 85 dated 1850. These are by *Devey*, ragstone below, half-timbered above, jettied out and rendered. During a century they have mellowed to match the rest perfectly. E of the group the wall of Penshurst Place begins, continued at r. angles via a Tudor-style GATEWAY and LODGE, by *Devey* but incorporating old work and a datestone of 1662. The road runs down from there to a BRIDGE, also by *Devey*. It is worth going down to the bridge and looking back, at the complex, asymmetrical, and intensely picturesque group that clusters around the church tower. Analyse what a large part of it did not exist before 1850, and it is evident that Devey's early studies under John Sell Cotman developed more than his exquisite watercolour style: it developed a painter's eye for composition.

The W half of the village is dominated by the L-shaped VIL-LAGE HALL of 1898. Red brick over sandstone, which creeps up irregularly into the brick area. Dutch gables. Half-timbered gable-end. These are Deveyisms, but it was the rector's son, *Maxwell Maberlay Smith*, who was responsible for them. E of it a street runs S. In this, the best building is COLQUHOUN HOUSE. C18. Red brick once whitewashed. Three bays, the centre bay wider and brought forward a little. It rises from the second storey to a third, with a pediment. The sides of the pediment continue down over the outer bays. A cottage (BOUTIQUE) with a gable projecting, with an oriel under, dated 161.. Then further S, THE BIRCHES, an early C19, townish, rendered box, with a white wooden loggia of Tuscan piers: the sort of thing that Devey was rebelling against.

SOUTH PARK, ⅞ m. SW. *Salvin*'s house for Lord Hardinge has been largely demolished. A small part, with an octagonal S turret, plus a white-brick addition of 1960 by *Lord Cumlisse*, with modish vertical slit windows, make up the present house. Colossal bronze equestrian STATUE in front of it, signed by *J. H. Foley*, 1858.

THE GROVE, ⅞ m. SW. Sandstone *cottage orné* by *Decimus Burton*, 1831–2.

THE YEWS, ¼ m. SE. Built *c*.1820. Sandstone façade of three bays, the outer windows in the shallowest of bows.

The COTTAGE on Rogue Hill, dated 1867, a scherzo on a Wealden half-timbered house, is doubtless by *Devey* too.

SWAYLANDS, ⅝ m. SE. The early C19 house, rendered, sym-metrical, gabled, and in a minimal Tudor style, received extensive additions by *Devey*. These are also Tudor, in part gabled, in part battlemented, of plum brick with Devey's favourite diapering. E front of prodigious length, returned at the S, where the front door is, and at the N for a service wing. Two storeys below the gables. Various towers with polygonal turrets, mostly low, one rising above the rest with an extra tall, thick-topped turret. Mullioned-and-transomed windows, those in the N half with arched lights. The garden front is more organized, repeating the three equal gables of the earlier house, first in line with it, then in a plane further forwards. In 1890 *Macartney* made additions, probably the arched loggia at the N end, and the low, pilastered block W of Devey's stable court.

At POUNDSBRIDGE, 1½ m. SE, an uneventful CHAPEL by *Macartney*, 1888, and THE PICTURE HOUSE, half-timbered, two-storeyed, H-shaped, bearing the gargantuan date 1593. The r. wing has an oriel and a bargeboarded gable.

HAMMERFIELD, ½ m. W of N. Early C19 house remodelled and enlarged in the early 1850s by *Devey*, once again in his diapered Tudor style. Spindly octagonal N turret with an ogee lead cap. (The garden front, with five gables all different in size and materials, shows that at this early stage Devey did not design happily on a large scale.) The grounds are said to have been laid out by *Paxton*. The COTTAGE immediately S looks to be by *Devey*, an especially nice example of his style on a small scale.

REDLEAF, I m. W of N. The house has been demolished and the grounds laid out by William Wells early in the C19 partly built on. Still however numerous conifers, as typically proto-Victorian in their luxuriance as the rockery and crazy paving, which Wells is said to have introduced here for the first time in England. By the road two COTTAGES, dated 1825 and 1826, half-timbered over sandstone, with heavy chimneystacks. Thick, ugly, and unconvincing, they make an interesting comparison with Devey's cottages.*

PERRY STREET *see* NORTHFLEET

4060

PETTS WOOD

ST FRANCIS, Willett Way. 1934–5, by *Geoffrey Mullins* of Chislehurst. Brick. Fashionably jagged treatment of the win-

* Loudon illustrated them in the *Gardener's Magazine* in 1839. Can they be early essays of his collaborator, *E. B. Lamb*?

dows. – STAINED GLASS. E window by *James Hogan*, 1946. Above average for its date, one is ashamed to say.

PIX'S FARM *see* ROLVENDEN

PLAISTOW *see* BROMLEY, p. 178

PLATT 6050

ST MARY. 1841–2 by *Whichcord & Walker*. Quite large and well sited above the road, with a Perp-looking tower that does justice to the site. Yet it has lancets. Cruciform church also with lancets, and simple geometrical tracery in the transepts. The surprise is the timber roof: hammerbeams of prodigious projection, big circles in the spandrels, and a welter of flying arches over the crossing. Nothing but the skinny timbers distinguishes it from the fiercest production of Lamb or Teulon.

THE HOPFIELD, ¼ m. SE. Designed by *Colin Lucas* as a weekend cottage for himself and completed in 1933, just before he joined Connell & Ward in the leading partnership in Britain to champion the International Modern Style in the pre-war years. Lucas was plainly as committed as the others, and his own house is an almost absurdly extreme statement, even with the later weak addition to the N. Small, white, rendered concrete box with one large horizontal upper window towards the road. From an upper balcony at the SW corner a staircase juts out, first at r. angles, then sharply descending like a chute. It was to have led to a swimming pool which never got built.

PLAXTOL 6050

CHURCH. Built* in 1649, as the inscription over the S doorway records. That hardly seems a probable date, at first sight of the ragstone church. W tower, nave with short transepts, and chancel. More information on the E wall: enlarged 1852, chancel erected 1885, enlarged 1894. But that is wrong, as photos of 1889 in the church show. At that date it was a wide, long, but simple rectangle. In fact chancel and transepts are all of 1894, by *Robert Pearsall*. In assessing the C17 church one has got to take into account two things: first that all windows but the tower W window were renewed in 1852; and secondly the possibility that parts of a pre-existing chapel were

* On the initiative of Nicholas Miller of Oxen Hoath (Alan Everitt).

salvaged. Surely for instance the s doorway is c15. Yet the plinth moulding round the whole building looks no less Perp. The window tracery however looks c17 in the patterns, but c19 in the mouldings. No cusping, but in the N transept N window (original E window) ogeed intersecting tracery, and the nave windows have upside-down drops over two plain pointed lights. That is the sort of minimally Gothic design one expects.* The interior is equally perplexing. The tower arch, pointed but with raised bands for abaci, is obviously of 1649. But what about the hammerbeam roof, as gaunt as one of the 1830s? Yet the trusses rest on stone wall-shafts with moulded capitals that would pass for c15 ones. On the other hand, the very idea of such wall shafts cannot have been a Perp one; so on balance one accepts the whole nave interior as 1649, a gratifying conclusion. – REREDOS. An excessively unsympathetic frame for the little wooden reliefs of Passion scenes. The reliefs must be c15 Flemish. The voluminous, crinkly draperies very characteristic. Note too the stylized rocks. Another carved PANEL (c17?), of the Crossing of the Red Sea, as a reredos in the s transept. – PULPIT. c17. Not English? The relief figures obviously don't belong. – CHANDELIERS. A pair dated 1785. Brass. Unusually refined and elaborate, the arms with uncommon Rococo details. – PLATE. Cup and Paten, 1711 by *Anthony Nelme*(?). – MONUMENT. Thomas Dalyson † 1741. Pretty, busy cartouche, still in the late c17 manner.

The church is the centre of the tiny village. CHURCH ROW, curving away to the w, is particularly pleasing, but may be no older than the 1850s. One should refrain from taking the road that dips sharply down to the E. That will only spoil one's enjoyment – in spite of SPOUT HOUSE, at the very foot of the hill, an early timber-framed house, jettied only at one of the short ends, i.e. pre-Wealden. A little way NE of the church, on the other hand, NUT TREE HALL, an impressive-looking half-timbered house that may be entirely from the hand of *Harrison Townsend*, 1905. Next door to that, THE GRANGE, with an eccentric early c18 front. Brown brick with plum-brick dressings, and white keystones. Three-storeyed centre and lower, not quite identical, wings set back a bit. Central doorcase with carved brackets. The windows cluster round it, a semicircular-headed one each side, an oval

* Yet Petrie's early c19 drawing shows only Late Perp windows of three cusped lights, just like the windows at Groombridge.

one above. The other windows all rectangular, making four in all at the lowest level, then three, and only one at the top. Contemporary hall with the staircase going up at the l. to reach a balcony – a very simple version of what happens at West Farleigh Hall.

BROADFIELD, 1 m. E. Chequer-brick cottage, dated 1700 in deliciously big digits.

OLD SOAR, 1¼ m. N of E. The complete solar end of a stone house of c.1290. An C18 red-brick house stands where the hall stood. The building is two-storeyed, of irregular but carefully laid ragstone blocks. The solar itself, on a pointed-tunnel-vaulted undercroft, lies SE–NW, and the rectangular projection running out towards the road from its E corner is the chapel, the barely smaller, square block at its N corner a garderobe, both for use at first-floor level. Solar end windows, chapel E window, with Y-tracery not original. All other windows and doorways depressed-pointed, with a big chamfer, except for one NE window in the solar, with a shouldered lintel and stop-chamfered jambs. Cross-loops for the garderobe. Internally not much more. Newel staircase to the solar from the W corner of the undercroft. One jamb of the solar fireplace in the NW wall. Original crown-post roof, with, one notes, straight braces. Blocked arch towards the hall, and a blocked opening l. of it and two cupboards. In the chapel a foliage corbel, and cinquefoiled PISCINA, which looks post-1300, with its crook-backed leaves up the gable. No ogees though. What survives of the HALL is not visible to the public. This is a corbel, with trefoil foliage on the capital and oakleaves below the shaft, supporting a beam. It is evidence of a gallery over the dais. (Traces of the dais too.) Doorway l. of the corbel into the solar undercroft. So the hall was at ground level.

A ROMAN VILLA, including a bath house, was found 1 m. SE of the village.

PLUCKLEY   9040

ST NICHOLAS. Ragstone. The extent of the C13 church is defined by the traces of E lancets in the chancel, and by the W tower, originally unbuttressed, with lancets at two levels to N, W, and S. Recessed shingled spire. Early in the C14 the nave was rebuilt with a S aisle, but keeping the W arch of the previous aisle (pointed, just chamfered, arch on imposts). Standard arcade with big jutting capitals and the two arch-chamfers hollowed. s chapel, added by Richard Dering in 1475. At the same time the aisle was re-windowed and the rood screen erected, see the turret. Chancel arch gone. Crownpost roof in the nave. Perp s porch, Perp N vestry. – FONT. Perp. – PARCLOSE SCREENS to the Dering Chapel. One is Late Perp, with pretty tracery in the square-headed lights, a frieze of foliage, and cresting, almost a pair with the screen at Ulcombe. Is *c.*1475 too early a date for it? – The other, erected in 1635, has fat Ionic colonnettes in two tiers, with Gothic-looking arcading between the upper ones, and crude foliage spandrels below, a typical piece of Gothic-classical compromise. – STAINED GLASS. E window and Annunciation in a N window. 1954 by *Francis Stephens & John Haywood.* Like coloured woodcuts, but more tautly designed than many in this post-war twilight of the art. – PLATE. All gilt. C17 Cup; C17 Paten Cover by *R.H.*; Cup, 1629 by *R.S.*; Paten, 1697 by *B.A.*; Flagon, 1791 by *John Robins*(?); Almsdish, 1794 by the same. – BRASSES. Richard Malemayns † 1440. 30 in. armoured figure. – The other seven brasses, three in the nave, four in the s chapel, to members of the Dering family, with dates between 1425 and 1610, are ingenious forgeries of *c.*1628–35 by Sir Edward Dering, whose passionate antiquarian studies were, characteristically, bound up with pride in his own family. Close inspection gives most of them away, in spite of the antiquary's attention to details of costume and armour.

Pluckley village, red-brick cottages at all angles round a tiny square, if one can give the forecourt of the Black Horse Inn so formal a title, is largely of the C19. SCHOOL of 1849 on the w side, the church peeping over the rooftops from the s. All the exits are masked, so that the village seems cosily self-sufficient. The windows of all the cottages are of two arched lights, usually under a depressed relieving arch. The explanation of this peculiarity is that Sir Edward Cholmeley Dering (1807–96), fancying that they brought luck, had them fitted in his own house, Surrenden Dering (*see* below), and in all buildings on his estate.

SURRENDEN DERING, ¾ m. E. Sir Edward Dering's H-shaped red-brick house of the 1630s, with a skyline of shaped gables like neighbouring Godinton's, was burnt down in 1952. The N wing, which escaped, is largely C18 outside, but built to match the C17 work, and tricked out with Sir Edward Cholmeley Dering's lucky windows. – Late C18 STABLES at

r. angles, to the N. Red brick. Very high central arch under a pedimental gable.

ROOTING, 1¼ m. E. Only the cross-wing of a late C14 timber-framed house survives. It has in its E end very bold and surprising bracing that forms patterns from S-curves, quadrants, and half-circles, clearly meant always to be exposed to view. Crown-post roof inside.

At DOWLE STREET, 1¼ m. SE, an early half-timbered house, the upper storey projecting at the short ends, but not to the front. That is to say, the typical Wealden arrangement has not yet been quite evolved. Compare it with GORE COURT, also at Dowle Street, the normal C15 Wealden thing; with a later gabled bay in the hall, also a normal thing.

POND'S FARM see FRITTENDEN

PORT LYMPNE see LYMPNE

THE POSTERN see TUDELEY

POUNDSBRIDGE see PENSHURST

PRESTON HALL see AYLESFORD

RABBIT'S CROSS FARM see BOUGHTON MONCHELSEA

RAINHAM

ST MARGARET. A fine plain Perp W tower. Ragstone. Diagonal buttresses up two of the three stages. Battlements to tower and octagonal NE turret. Renewed W window. Nave with a N aisle almost as wide. No S aisle now, though from without there appears to be one. The arcade must have been removed in medieval times. Chancel and gabled N chapel of equal length. Walls and windows all meticulously reworked, a restoration of 1869–71 by *Joseph Clarke*. Only the Early Perp E window of the chancel is old, and the others cannot be trusted, especially those with split-cusped Kentish tracery. Old S porch, modern N porch. Inside, the church is revealed as a C14 remodelling of an early C13 building. Part of the chancel wall-arcading remains from the earlier date, four bays on the S, only the E bay on the N (now pierced, and with a later arch). Keeled shafts, square abaci with chamfered corners. Chamfered arches. Lancets were set within the arches; cf. the chancels

of Stockbury, Lower Halstow, and Ash (near Wrotham). –
SEDILIA, with three cinquefoiled arches under straight-
sided gables. Are they C14? Later C13 two-bay arcade to the
N chapel. No chancel arch. Early C14 N arcade of five bays.
Octagonal piers and arches with two hollow chamfers. The
large lancet near the W end of the aisle may well be contemporary. Crown-post roofs everywhere. 'Celure', i.e. enriched
ceiling over the rood, painted with roses 'en soleil', the emblem of Edward IV. – PARCLOSE SCREEN. Perp. Single
square-headed lights with animals, heads, and leaves carved
in the spandrels of the lights. Alternate shafts have been cut
away. – CHEST. Oak. C14. Carved with two tiers of tracery
within deep cusped panels. A fine piece, to be compared with
chests at Faversham and St John's Hospital, Canterbury. –
WALL PAINTINGS, nave S wall. Three painted areas remain,
and one can just work out that the E one is an Annunciation, of
c.1340, the centre a Last Judgement, and the W a C15 St
Christopher, painted on top of a C14 St Christopher. –
STAINED GLASS. Nave SE window by *Hardman*, 1871. –
BRASSES. William Aucher † 1514. A knight. 18½ in. figure.
– William Bloor † 1529. Civilian. Large (34 in.) and bad. – A
foot-long wife and four children, the survivors of a larger
family, c.1530. – John Norden † 158–, 21 in., and one of his
three wives. – MONUMENTS. Late Perp tomb-chest with
square flowers in square cusped panels on the sides. Indent
of a brass. – Thomas Norreys † 1624. Small hanging monument
with kneeling effigies. The sleeping child below, in a sort of
predella, is John Norreys † 1627. – George Tufton, 2nd Earl
of Thanet, † 1670 from wounds sustained at Neustadt four
years before. Seated figure on a tall pedestal. He is in Roman
armour and wears a heavy helmet on his flowing locks. This is
the pattern of *Nicholas Stone*'s fifty-years-older monument to
Francis Holles in Westminster Abbey. – Nicholas Tufton, 3rd
Earl of Thanet, † 1679. Also a life-size figure on a tall base,
but decidedly up-to-date in that he stands, in contemporary
dress, i.e. in his peer's robes, arrogantly posed. Mrs Esdaile
thought both statues might be by *Sir William Wilson*. They
are both rather clumsily handled.

BERENGROVE PARK, Berengrave Lane. Red brick, Georgian.
Four bays, two storeys, and a parapet. Porch on fluted Doric
columns.

RAMHURST MANOR *see* LEIGH

RASPIT HILL *see* IGHTHAM

READING STREET

St Mary. The church of Ebony, on the landlocked Isle of Oxney, was demolished in 1858, and rebuilt with the old stones a little further N. The work took three months and cost £270, and surprisingly the architect in charge of the operation was *S. S. Teulon*. Surprisingly, because the simple Perp chapel was not pepped up at all in the process. Even the little bell-turret he provided is quite in a vernacular spirit. Otherwise the building remains the chapel built at the cost of John Raynold shortly before 1525. – PULPIT. C18. Quite plain, between a boldly projecting cornice and a yet more boldly projecting base moulding.

REDLEAF *see* PENSHURST

REYNOLDS PLACE *see* HORTON KIRBY

RIDLEY

St Peter. Norman nave – see one tiny N window high up. Blocked arch to a C13 chancel chapel. Chancel renewed in the C19. Does the curious Dec E window represent its original form? The weatherboarded spirelet on the roof-ridge was put up not long before 1797; no doubt the nave was lengthened and the S porch built at the same time. – FONT. C19. A handsome Dec-cum-Perp piece, absurdly too large for this church. – LECTERN. Wood. Probably C18; like a music stand. – PLATE. Cup of 1635.

Court Farm House lines up beside the church, a nice hipped-roofed house of the early C18, red brick chequered with blue headers. The heads of the centre ground-floor windows are cut into frills.

RISEDEN *see* KILNDOWN

RIVERHEAD

St Mary. A naive little building by *Decimus Burton*, 1831, in a lancet style. The view of the W front from the road down below is indeed rather sweet, a short tower pinched between steep roofs. Recessed spire. The plaster rib-vault of the nave equally sweet. As an archaeological touch, leaf bosses there and leaf capitals to the three internal w arches and the w doorway, half inaccurately observed stiffleaf, half Dec. Tactful chancel of 1882 by *Sir A. W. Blomfield*. – REREDOS. Mosaic panel of Christ in Majesty, by *Salviati*, 1894. The rest of the somewhat Morrisite decoration of the sanctuary as late as 1910–17, by *Powell*'s. – STATUE. Virgin and Child. Wood. C18. Italian.

COUNTY PRIMARY SCHOOL, Witches Lane. 1965 by *E. T. Ashley-Smith*, the County Architect. Low. Yellow brick finished off with a deep white band of weatherboarding.

In WORSHIPS HILL, opposite the church, pleasantly jumbled C18 houses. RIVERHEAD HOUSE, on the l., alone needs individual mention. It has an early C18 façade of nine bays, minus its central doorway, but plus a big addition to the w, dated 1765 on a rainwater-head. C19 Amherst estate housing across the road.

The Amherst house, MONTREAL, has been demolished. General Amherst built it in 1764–75 after his North American campaigns, which led by the surrender of Montreal to all Canada's falling into British power. On an OBELISK, $\frac{3}{4}$ m. SW, is the full list of his victories – ten in four years. Yet further SW, a dilapidated SUMMER HOUSE, with a stone arch facing w. In it a quotation from Ambrosius's *De Officiis* beginning 'Bona quidem est agricultura', to show that at home the General could settle down happily too.

ROMAN ROCHESTER

Not much survives of the Roman town of DUROBRIVAE, but traces of its walls are known, defined roughly by the Medway, the Common, Free School Lane, and the s side of the castle – enclosing altogether about 23 acres. Recent excavation has shown that the town wall, of masonry, was inserted into the front of an earlier defensive rampart some time in the early c3. Odd fragments of building have turned up in the town from time to time.

THE CATHEDRAL

INTRODUCTION

In any distant view of Rochester it is the castle that dominates. The cathedral lies lower, and its stocky tower and short, thick spire cannot match the masterful keep. From the w and N, from the railway, from the hills behind Strood and Frindsbury, the two grey shapes, the one upright, the other crouching, appear above the river, now one in front, now the other, but always so that the cathedral seems to shelter under the castle. And so it was at the beginning. Rochester is the second oldest see in England. In 604 St Augustine ordained Justus, one of the missionary band who had settled with him in Canterbury, as first bishop. King Ethelbert, says Bede, built a church, dedicated to St Andrew, and Justus placed it in the hands of secular canons. In 670 the bishop was referred to as the Bishop of the Castle of West Kent.

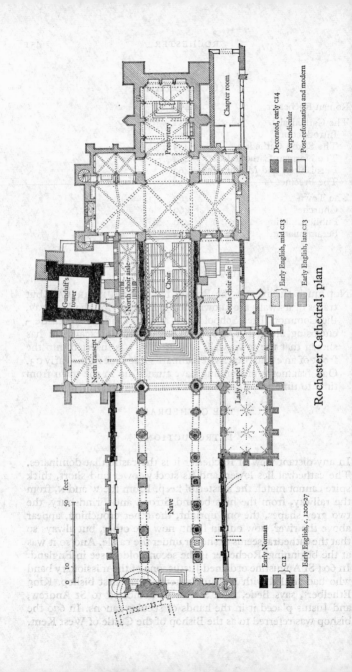

Rochester Cathedral, plan

The present buildings belong largely to the C12. In 1076 Lanfranc, Archbishop of Canterbury, appointed a reforming bishop, Gundulf, a monk of Bec, who had been his chamberlain. Benedictine monks replaced the secular canons. Gundulf made a great reputation as a builder, and by his death in 1108 had built a completely new cathedral church. Nothing of this can now be seen except the detached N tower, and part of the crypt. A consecration took place in 1130, it is said. Gervase records devastating fires in 1137 and 1179, but the latter at any rate cannot have been as serious as he makes out, for the present nave and W front are of the mid C12.

Early in the C13, Rochester, like so many other cathedrals and abbeys, was reconstructed in its E parts, up to and including the transepts, and greatly enlarged, with a second pair of transepts between presbytery and choir. The work was done in several stages. The money for it came from the offerings at the shrine of St William of Perth, a baker murdered at Rochester in 1201 when on a pilgrimage to the Holy Land. Buried in the cathedral, miracles conveniently began to occur at his tomb, and Rochester, like Canterbury, had a money-making martyr. William of Hoo when sacrist built 'totum chorum' with these funds. The presbytery must have been vaulted by 1214, for Bishop de Glanvill, who died that year, was buried there. 1227: 'introitus in novum chorum'. No consecration however took place until 1240. After the C13 no addition to the structure was made except the Lady Chapel W of the S transept, the occasional doorway here and there, a few larger windows, and a Perp W window and clerestory in the nave; and the minimum even of repair work was done, until by the C19 drastic restoration was necessary, to the exterior at any rate. The major C19 campaigns were *Cottingham*'s in 1825 (central tower rebuilt), *Sir G. G. Scott*'s *c.*1870 (much new stonework; E gables built up), and *Pearson*'s in 1888 (W front largely refaced and turrets reconstructed). Finally in 1904–5 the central tower was again rebuilt, in accordance with C17 prints, by *C. Hodgson Fowler*. The total length of the cathedral is 305 ft 6 in., of the choir and presbytery 147 ft 6 in. The main transept is 120 ft across, the E transept 88 ft.

THE SAXON CATHEDRAL

Justus's church of St Andrew, built *c.*604, was, naturally enough, similar to the earliest churches of Canterbury (St Pancras, St Mary). Part of the stilted apse and the SE corner of the rectangular nave of a small stone building were found during excavation in 1889, under the N half of the W front of the present building. The outline of the apse is marked in the pavement. In 1876, under the outer wall of the S aisle, remains had already been found, with a floor of red *opus signinum*, just like the flooring of the other C7 churches. Hope interpreted the walling beside it as an apse with a wall to the W. Was that part of a second early church? St Augustine Canterbury had as many as four together, aligned along one axis. Did Rochester follow suit, in a less organized way? When the site was re-excavated in 1927 no trace of the apse was to be seen, so no certain answer can be given to these questions. As for the later, larger Saxon cathedral which superseded the C7 building, the SW angle of its N transept has in 1968 been identified by Dr Ralegh Radford below floor level in the present N transept.*

THE NORMAN CATHEDRAL

Gundulf (1077–1108), encouraged and aided by Lanfranc at Canterbury, built a completely new church, and finished it 'in a few years'. GUNDULF'S TOWER, in the angle between N transept and N choir aisle, belongs by its construction as well as by its name to the earliest Norman period. It was built to stand free, almost square, with heavy clasping buttresses. Before c.1779, when the top third was taken down, it rose about as high as the transept, and was crowned with a ring of machicoulis. These must have been an addition, of the C14 perhaps, but the question remains whether defence was the primary purpose of its building. Original windows, small and deeply splayed, at three levels, and an arch at the S end of the W wall at the highest level, a doorway it may be, to a bridge by which the tower could be in private communication with the N transept.

In the church itself Gundulf must be supposed to have followed the general medieval practice and built from E to W. Nothing that he did remains above ground, so the CRYPT is the place to start. Mostly it is C13, but the two W bays remain of the Norman one, below the E, not the W end of the present choir. Short, slender round shafts and responds, groin-vaults without the normal transverse and longitudinal arches. The

* Information from Mr Emil Godfrey. Loose in the crypt, a small fragment of Saxon carved stone, with interlace and the haunches of a four-legged beast.

capitals are very simple, shallow without abaci, and making the transition from square to round by means of keeled corners, i.e. not yet with the block shape almost universal by c.1100. Bases of two rude rolls. Unmoulded tufa arches N and S lead into the crypt aisles, also groin-vaulted, below the choir aisles. Hope established that two bays further to the E were demolished, and that originally the crypt and its aisles ended in a straight line, with an immensely thick wall, and a one-bay square E projection in the centre. Such a termination is Saxon rather than Norman (before the Cistercians popularized the square-ended plan); so Lanfranc and his followers did not sweep away all earlier ecclesiastical traditions, it seems.*

The interior of the NAVE must be considered next, or rather 7 the six bays, three-quarters of the whole, which were left untouched when the enthusiasm for rebuilding, which had been sustained throughout the C13, finally gave out. Inspection should begin in the S aisle. The outer wall is largely that of Gundulf's church. A small piece of stonework, exposed near the W end, shows the characteristic Early Norman herringbone lay of the rubble stone. Internal pilaster buttresses, quite plain, with a plain string-course carried round them at the level of the arcade capitals. At the level of the gallery they are cut off suddenly, where the top of the wall has been rebuilt. But at least one can say that no aisle vaults were intended. Similar, somewhat shallower, buttresses in the N aisle. They are however a C17 rebuilding.‡ The three E bays of the N aisle wall, not touched in the C13, are Norman, but no longer in the early undecorated style. The pilaster buttresses have nookshafts; the string-course is enriched with a succulent pattern of lozenges. Similar buttresses and string-course here outside, the sole surviving Norman features of the N and S nave walls. This mid-C12 piece of wall, as Dr Fairweather has emphasized, is aligned, not with the rest of the nave, but with the crypt, the cloisters, and the whole E end. So the conclusion is that Gundulf's nave, not just the S aisle wall, exists encased in the present arcades. The change of axis was effected by Ernulf's new cloisters after 1114.

The nave is strikingly broad and low and, it must be admitted, not a distinguished piece of architecture. The eleva-

---

* It has recently been established that the E end of Malling Abbey was similar (see p. 576).

‡ Hope reported that he had excavated the footings of the four E bays of Gundulf's N wall.

tion is the normal for major Anglo-Norman churches: arcade –
gallery – clerestory, though the clerestory is a Perp rebuilding.
This mutilation apart, the Rochester treatment is a curiously
unresolved and bitty one. In the first place the piers within
each arcade are, all six of them, different, though answering
one another N–S. Only the westernmost piers, in the form of an
octagon stretched on the E–W axis, have a simple shape. The
rest consist of shafts and fat half-columns attached to a
basically square core. The gallery is subdivided, with shafts
doubled in depth because there is a passage in the thickness of
the wall. (Pointed tunnel-vault to the passage.) The wall-
passage gives some circulation at the upper level, which is
restricted by the very curious fact that the gallery has no floor.
Some explanation of this peculiarity is needed, and yet what
can it be ? String-courses divide the three storeys horizontally;
but the vertical division, by shafts, descends no lower than the
arcade capitals. Upwards the shafts have been cut away at gallery level. The string-courses continue across the W end, the
upper one dropping a fraction, dividing into tiers the tight
arcading with which the nave W wall was originally covered.
Most of the upper part of the wall went when the immense
eight-light Perp window took the place of the original one.
Just enough is left to show that the proportions of the arches
there bore no relation to the openings of gallery and clerestory.
   The enrichment of the nave is, by contrast, pretty consistent. All capitals are scalloped, except for those in the two W
bays of the gallery where the scallops turn into embryonic
leaves. Round all the arches a simple row of zigzag runs, with
nailhead on the arcade hood-moulds, and half-pellets on the
hood-moulds of the gallery arches. The gallery tympana form
the focus of the decoration, filled with busy patterns of square
stylized flowers. The W end again dissents, with billet on the
hood-moulds, and a rope moulding round the inner arch of
the central doorway. Embattling on the doorway to the SW
turret. The other variations are trifling. The most important
is the fact that the N arcade is given zigzag towards the aisle,
but the S arcade is not. The four W bays of the N arcade have
leaf spurs on the pier bases. On the S side, on the other hand,
a start was made above the westernmost pier – giving the two
arcade spandrels a pair of sunk roundels.
   The WEST FRONT is logical, balanced, and well-proportioned, which can be said of very few Norman façades in
England. The logic of it is that the nave and aisles are ex-

pressed by turrets at their outer angles.* Between them, the aisle end walls are slightly recessed, but the nave is not. The outer turrets – the N square, the S octagonal in the top two stages – of five stages are stout enough to take stair-turrets, the slenderer inner ones, of seven shallower stages, just overtop them. Thick conical caps to them all. Each stage above the lowest is arcaded, with tiny arches on long shafts, the former decorated with stylized leaves, the capitals of the latter far more varied than those inside. On the inner turrets lintels appear at one level, and intersecting arches at the next. Variegation of the wall texture by laying the ashlar blocks lozenge-fashion in places. Even so at a distant view, the impression is of all-over homogeneity. The taste for this sort of façade treatment must have been learnt by English masons from West France and Poitou. Even the great Perp window does not upset the rhythm of closely spaced uprights – the many mullions carry on where the colonnettes leave off. NW doorway of 1327. *Pearson* in 1888–9 restored the turrets in accordance with King's engraving of 1655. He had to rebuild the whole of the N one, and the inner N and outer S turrets above the roof-line. He refaced much of the rest, but did not touch the sculpture; and that is what remains to be considered.

The SCULPTURE is concentrated on the central doorway,[11] and decorates the jamb-shafts, tympanum, and five orders of radiating voussoirs. On the tympanum is Christ in Majesty, supported by angels, flanked by the symbols of the Evangelists, with the twelve Apostles on the lintel, i.e. basically the scheme of the W portal at Chartres. The mere mention of it brings home how modest in ambition and attainment is the Rochester tympanum. The voussoirs are carved into violently curling leaves, transmogrified as often as not into beasts viciously biting their tails or their backs. The jamb-shafts, five each side, are plain, with carved capitals and bosses, except that the second shaft each side is developed into a column figure, Solomon on the l., the Queen of Sheba on the r. They are more worn even than the rest of the carving, but such figures were an invention of the Île de France, and first appeared at Saint Denis in the 1140s. They and the tympanum

---

* This simple solution was apparently not hit on at once. Hope discovered foundations for two W towers, and the W piers of the arcades are enlarged as if to receive them. During Pearson's underpinning of the façade footings of an earlier front were found, in the shape of a straight wall exactly below the present one, and as wide.

make this doorway the most French piece of C12 sculpture in England. What is disconcerting is that elements should appear here in a combination that is unknown to France itself.

PRESBYTERY, CHOIR, AND TRANSEPTS. Here the EX-TERIOR deserves to be examined first. Straight-ended presbytery. E transepts with E chapels projecting. From the E one is at once struck by the massiveness of the architecture, especially the colossal buttressing angle-turrets.* There is far more sheer unrelieved wall than in the Norman parts. Above a blank storey, two levels of generously proportioned lancets in threes, with two rows of dogtooth on the reveals. The elevation, counting the crypt, reads as four-storeyed, with string-courses carried round everything and over the heads of the lancets, to separate each level from the one above. The upper two string-courses were introduced by *Scott*, who also replaced a Perp window by the upper trio of lancets. His treatment of the gable too is not authorized by early illustrations, and no reflection of the low-pitched roof behind it either. His alterations give the elevation a coherence it may not originally have had. Angle turrets gabled at the top in all directions, with an absurdly small pinnacle set where the gables cross. There was evidence for the restoration like that.

The scheme established at the E end is carried on round the side walls of the presbytery, and in the NE transept, with the modifications necessitated by the transept E chapel. The presbytery is divided into two plus two bays by a far-projecting polygonal buttress with angles cut in to take shafts originally. Dec tracery inserted in the lower lancets here. The SE transept, however, operated a different system, as it was interfered with by the cloisters. But complete refacing in the C19 leaves its original treatment in doubt. One or two Dec windows are inserted, with flowing tracery.

The exterior of the choir aisles is uninformative, but the MAIN TRANSEPTS introduce new motifs. Taking the N again first, one at once notices a decisive lightening of effect. The lancets are brought into a scheme of arcading, alternately wide and narrow, on both the N and W sides. Restrained use of Purbeck marble shafts. The buttressing is reduced to angle buttresses with regular set-offs. Early illustrations show three large foiled circles in the gable. All heavily restored by Scott again, faithfully this time, it seems. The S transept has bar

* Which are solid, up almost to the top. The identical ones on the NE transept, on the other hand, contain stair-turrets.

The SOUTH CHOIR AISLE, on the other hand, is most awkwardly managed. It is not in fact truly an aisle, for at the E end it opens into the transept by a mere door, and it is widened to occupy the whole space up to the N wall of the cloister. Various wall shafts and buttressing for the choir vault, but no coherent system is established. E.E. doorway to the crypt.*

The choir was taken into use in 1227, but the remodelling of crossing and main transepts seems not to have been proceeded with at once. The E arch of the crossing, and the arches to the choir aisles, must have been built in one with the choir; further W there are substantial changes in design. Purbeck marble is abandoned except on the W piers of the crossing, and the arches into the nave aisles, and although dogtooth and billet mouldings survive, the shaft bases are no longer waterholding. Piers with multiple shafting at the crossing. On the W piers further development in detail, such as the profiles of caps and shaft-rings. Sexpartite rib-vault, with additional ridge-ribs running N–S, to the NORTH TRANSEPT, with foliage bosses. Plenty of marble shafting round the lancets. On the W wall, blank arcading at the lowest level, on fine big head corbels; on the E side, a shallow chapel with a shafted PISCINA in the E wall, and stiffleaf on the capitals of the N window. The most important innovation however is that the N wall at last introduces the normal three-storeyed cathedral elevation. The SOUTH TRANSEPT is clearly later, for the lower windows are Y-traceried. The vault was never fully constructed. The present vault is of wood. The E and W elevation is again two-storeyed. Within the blank arch on the E wall, part of an earlier arch not easy to account for.‡

A start was made with remodelling the nave too. The lancet at the SW corner of the N transept suggests that aisles narrower than the Norman ones were envisaged. All that was in the end done, was to rebuild the first two bays of the nave arcades on each side. Structurally, it was necessary to do this at the same time as the crossing was rebuilt, to provide buttressing. Extra buttressing mass left on the N side. The gallery openings were blocked, and the nave arcades raised in height. Had the whole

---

* NP notes the two puzzling E.E. arches in the E wall of the S choir aisle, and points out that the masonry of the S wall seems Norman.

‡ NP draws my attention to the blocked doorway in the choir aisle, which, together with the partly preserved lancet, can only mean that the large arch in the transept was built as part of a plan not carried on with and so left filled in against a future knocking out.

nave been remodelled, the heightened arches still with the close C12 spacing, the piers, in fact little reduced in bulk, would have produced an uncomfortably claustrophobic effect. The piers were built up into a lozenge-shaped core, and sparse black shafts set against it. Arch mouldings with sunk quadrants; so the building programme was dragging on into the last decade or two of the C13. The second pier each side was left half altered, the respond capital on the S side carved into fine naturalistic leaves. At the crossing the shafts spring from a height of 14 ft from the ground, i.e. above the level of the pulpitum.

That was the last structural alteration to the cathedral during the Middle Ages, except for the LADY CHAPEL, tucked into the angle between S aisle and S transept. It is Late Perp, possibly in course of completion in 1512–13. It is open to the aisle by three arches, replying to the windows, with stone screens across their lower parts, and open to the transept by a single arch double the size and considerably coarser in the mouldings. Was the S transept then intended to be the choir of the Lady Chapel, and the new work the nave of it? Windows set in reveals taken down almost to the floor, with a wave and hollow moulding. Slim clustered wall shafts for vaulting, never carried out.

FURNISHINGS AND MONUMENTS

by position from E to W

PRESBYTERY. REREDOS. By *Sir G. G. Scott*, *c.*1875. – MONUMENTS. First those on the N side, from E to W, then the S side similarly. Purbeck marble effigy of a bishop, identified as that of Bishop de St Martin † 1274, who was buried 'iuxta maius altare a parte boriali'. The effigy, with arms raised, is badly worn, and was originally flanked by slender shafts to support the exceedingly heavy gabled canopy. Plenty of delightful detail survives here, with bar tracery and even naturalistic leaves, decidedly advanced for the 1270s. – Gabled tomb-chest, traditionally that of Bishop de Glanvill † 1214. Purbeck marble. The front arcaded with seven pointed arches, and big upright leaves under them. The sloping lid almost broken, but keeping two sunk quatrefoils that frame half-length figures. Still Romanesque in feeling. It should be compared with the contemporary monument (Archbishop Walter's?)

at Canterbury. – Bishop John de Sheppey † 1360. The effigy was found in the wall in 1825; hence the original colouring is remarkably well preserved,* so that it should be an object of pilgrimage to find what medieval freestone effigies were intended to look like. There is great insistence on correct depiction of the details of his robes. C16 iron railings. C19 canopy palely copied from the superb pieces of the original canopy now kept in the crypt.

S side: Bishop Ingoldsthorpe † 1291, who was buried 'juxta magnum altare ex parte australi'. Purbeck marble. Reclining effigy under a gabled canopy. Ivy-leaf capitals of the side shafts. The pattern then is the same as the St Martin monument, and is no advance on it. Simplified canopy; heavier, coarser drapery folds. – Late C13 gabled tomb-slab of Purbeck marble, carved with two croziers along the ridge, from which sprout oak and other simple leaves.

NORTH-EAST TRANSEPT. TILES. A few old patches, some with patterns. – STATUE. Figure of a bishop, removed in 1888 from the N turret of the W front. As the turret was an C18 rebuild, the original position of the statue cannot now be discovered. Possibly the wider arches, now filled with modern statues, above the W portal, were meant to take statues from the first. The back of the figure proves that it has been cut from a wall, not lifted from a tomb. In style the figure belongs to the very end of the C12, see the V-shaped folds of his cope, cut with a beginning of weighty plasticity, and the four-petalled flowers at the sides of his robe, in advance of anything on the W front. – PAINTING. St Sebastian and St Roch. Venetian, c.1500. – MONUMENTS. Purbeck marble tomb-chest. Earliest C13. Four quatrefoils on the sides, enclosing leaf crosses. Romanesque leaves in the spandrels. Foliated cross on top. It stands under a somewhat later arch, pointed, outlined with a keeled roll and set on fine, big, undercut corbels of trefoil leaves. Remains of WALL PAINTING by it, c.1300, of trails of maple and vine leaves. – Bishop Walter de Merton † 1277. Vaulted double canopy on clustered marble shafts. Naturalistic leaf crockets and fine panels of oakleaves in quatrefoils on the gables. Once again, bang up to date.

---

* Mr Gerald Cobb draws my attention to a letter of Cottingham's, in which he mentions a 'drunken artist' who, misunderstanding his orders, started retouching the effigy. Cottingham had the repaint taken off and reports the figure 'now brought so nearly back to the state in which we found it that the most fastidious antiquary could find but little fault with us'.

Much restored. The alabaster effigy is wholly new, designed in 1852 by *R.C.Hussey* (Kelly). – Bishop John Lowe † 1467. Plain tomb-chest, with inscriptions and shields in quatrefoils on the side. – Bishop John Warner † 1666. Standing monument signed by *Joshua Marshall*. Segmental pediment on Corinthian columns. Black and white marble. A typical piece. – Archdeacon Lee Warner † 1679. Standing monument with scrolls and columns set back beside the large inscription. Urn between the ends of an open pediment. By *John Shorthose*. – Lee Warner † 1698. Similar standing monument, with putti at the top drawing back the curtains of a baldacchino.

CHOIR. SCREEN of stone; *Scott*, in 1876, placed the ORGAN on it. Niches with statues, designed by *Pearson* and carved by Mr *Hitch*. Original C13 shafted W doorway. The E face retains original C13 woodwork of the PULPITUM, with arcading on octagonal shafts, and the S doorpost, carved with the wing of an angel and trefoil leaves, part presumably of the canopy of the Bishop's stall. – The back STALLS incorporate trefoiled arches on octagonal shafts, more of the original choir fittings of *c.*1227, the earliest to survive in England. *Scott*'s stalls are quite simple. They incorporate Early Renaissance panelling. Hope mentions desks made in 1541. – WALL PAINTINGS. The W end and the N and S walls below the first string-course are completely painted, mostly in 1876, following traces that remained of a medieval design. The English lion and French fleur-de-lys, repeated again and again, i.e. the arms adopted by Edward III in 1340. – C13 Wheel of Fortune, or rather half of it, on the NE pier. Very well preserved, and of quite high quality. The tall figure of Fortune stands within the wheel, while two figures scramble upwards among the spokes, and a king at the top is about to topple from his perch.

NORTH CHOIR AISLE. MONUMENTS. C14 tomb-chest under a canopy, assumed to commemorate Bishop Hamo de Hethe † 1352. The tomb-chest is panelled, the canopy cusped so that spiritedly carved heads among leaves come in the spandrels. Slightly concave-sided gable, and idiosyncratic crockets with square lobes growing from it. Compare and contrast with the Chapter-Room doorway. – William Streaton † 1609. Small hanging monument, with small figures kneeling in prayer, as usual.

SOUTH CHOIR AISLE. WALL PAINTINGS. High in a niche on a buttress of the choir wall, a late C13 Crucifix. – Very faded St Christopher on the W wall. – MONUMENT. Headless

Purbeck marble effigy of a bishop, flatter and so earlier than [18] the St Martin and Ingoldsthorpe effigies, i.e. not later than the first half of the C13. It is set under a later arch, with cusps split back, and a trefoil at the apex also with split cusps. At the back, tiny naturalistic vine leaves. The cusping is exactly like the tracery at Chartham of c.1294, especially in the way the points are turned over as if made of plasticine. It is datable a decade earlier, for it must cover the tomb of Bishop John de Bradfield † 1283, who was buried 'iuxta ostium crubitorum' (i.e. by the steps to the crypt).

NORTH TRANSEPT. STAINED GLASS. Lower triplet of lancets 1859 by *Clayton & Bell* (TK). – MONUMENTS. Augustine Caesar † 1677. Large tablet with side-columns, and an inscription in Latin and Greek, worthy of his name. Very restrained. – John Parr † 1792. Hanging monument in yellow, white, and grey marble. Sarcophagus, urns, and pedimented obelisk.

SOUTH TRANSEPT. STAINED GLASS. E clerestory windows 1898 by *Kempe*. – MONUMENTS. Sir Richard Head † 1689. Attributed to *Gibbons* since the mid C18 and a favourite design of his: a three-quarter-face relief portrait in an oval medallion, with a gadrooned projection below and a swag of flowers looped above it. – Richard Watts, 1736. The C16 benefactor is commemorated by a frontal bearded bust, a copy of a C16 original, set in a Gibbsian hanging frame. *Charles Easton* was paid £50 for making both. – Sir Edmund Head, 1798 by *Flaxman*. Just a Grecian tablet. – Sir William Franklin † 1833. Fine aristocratic bust on a pedestal, by *Samuel Joseph*, 1837. – James Forbes † 1836. Heavy Grecian tablet, with a profile medallion. – Dean Hole, 1905 by *F. W. Pomeroy*. Marble recumbent effigy.

NAVE. FONT. Dedicated 1893, carved by *Earp*. – CHANDELIERS. 1957. Small cup-shaped shades, hanging at many different levels from a brass ring. They are by *Emil Godfrey*, the cathedral architect, and the sole addition to the furnishings that the C20 has yet made. – STAINED GLASS. N aisle W window by *Kempe*, 1901. – MONUMENTS. NORTH AISLE. Francis Barrell † 1679. Elegant draped cartouche. – Francis Barrell † 1724. Large architectural tablet signed by *Robert Taylor*. – Ann Spice † 1795. Tablet with an urn on a yellow marble ground. – SOUTH AISLE. Richard Somer † 1682. Tablet with a scrolly open pediment. – Lady Ann Henniker † 1792. Grand [73] standing monument under a Gothick arch. White sarcophagus in front of a black pyramid. A figure of Truth stands to the l., Time is seated to the r. These figures, of *Coade* stone, were designed by *Banks*. Time is an especially vivid creation, the complex pose and succulent detailing still wholly Baroque in feeling. – John Lord Henniker. By *J. Bacon Jun.*, 1806, and a pompous affair. A pair to the last in scale, but altogether of marble. The symbolism however is Christian. A girl, holding a nest with a pelican in her piety, leans on a sarcophagus and is about to be wreathed with olive by a substantial crowned female. At the top rays and 'Sic itur ad astra'. Lord Henniker's medallion portrait at the bottom l. corner. – PLATE. All gilt. Two Patens or Tazzas, 1530 and 1531; Cover, 1532; double Set, made in 1653 for the Duke of Lennox for use at Cobham Hall.

THE PRECINCT

The cathedral occupied the SW quarter of the Roman town (*see* above, p. 451), so that, although the monks managed to expand their precinct little by little towards the S, its dimensions were never large, and the SW corner of the Roman wall still stands, tightly hemming in the old Bishop's Palace. Today it is the perfect antithesis to the High Street, small-scale, waywardly irregular, and almost free of traffic.

From the High Street the entry is via COLLEGE GATE. This is banded with stone and flint, with four-centred inner and outer arches. Blocked openings N and S. Timber-framed upper storey, gabled and overhanging twice. Within the gateway, a row of houses starts on the l. at once, the first one with a richly carved bressumer, the rest a late C18 stock-brick terrace. St Nicholas church (*see* p. 469) continues the row, immediately N of the cathedral, just in the same relationship as St Margaret's church has to Westminster Abbey. The informality of it all is disarming. Tombstones between church and cathedral, and a big monument on the grassy triangle to the W, under a prostrate mulberry tree. Beyond that the dipping greensward of the castle ditch, and the grey keep looming above it.

Across the street from the SW corner of the cathedral stands the funny little C18 brick CHAPTER CLERK'S OFFICE, one-storeyed, under a big pediment to the E. Pedimented doorcase on the same side. Beyond it a long range, three storeys high, incorporating as its W half the OLD BISHOP'S PALACE, presumably the New Palace referred to in 1459. Rubble stone.

No datable feature, except a small C15 window high in the S wall. The rest is C18, of red brick, matching the medieval height. (Inside, a C17 staircase, with heraldic beasts on the newels.)

The road, curving past the site of the cloisters (*see* below), comes abruptly to MINOR CANON ROW, a three-storeyed brick terrace of seven houses built in 1736. Plain but substantial. Fourteen hipped gables at the back. And so to the Prior's Gate and the S extremity of the precinct.

The PRIOR'S GATE is C15, two-storeyed and built of stone. Four-centred entrance arches, and an octopartite rib-vault. C19 Dec N window. SE of Minor Canon Row, another plain but characterful C18 brick house, ORIEL HOUSE. Three bays and three storeys. The centre one is distinguished in the usual way by coming forward under a pediment. Lunette top window, with a sort of dissected Venetian window repeated twice below it. Doorway in a raised brick surround in the r. bay, and a balancing surround to a window in the l. bay.

Finally, a few yards need to be retraced, to the S side of the choir of the cathedral, to study the MONASTIC BUILDINGS.

CLOISTERS. It is most unusual for the cloister to adjoin the chancel rather than the nave. Gundulf, says the Textus Roffensis, 'constructed all the necessary offices for the monks'. Nothing of that is left, for the cloister remains, as we shall see, are no earlier than Ernulf's time. Did Ernulf then begin a second cloister, E of Gundulf's? That is the generally accepted explanation, though no trace of earlier cloisters has ever been found. Single-storeyed Perp GATEWAY at the SW corner, and beyond it, down a few steps, a square chamber with Norman shafts in trios at the angles. Springers of vaulting were found in 1938. It must have formed an undercroft to the cellarer's lodging.

From here a length of the Roman town wall runs eastwards. The refectory was built against its S side, over 124 ft long. Nothing of that except the entrance doorway, with a two-bay vaulted LAVATORY and a towel-recess on the r. behind a big trefoiled arch, built by Prior Helias during the first twenty years of the C13.

The real rewards are on the E side, where the whole outer wall of the E cloister walk remains. Ernulf, bishop from 1114 to 1124, 'fecit dormitorium, capitulum, refectorium'. The cloister wall, behind which the first two of these lie, is decorated with intersecting blank arcading, a constant motif of the early C12 work at Canterbury, executed when Ernulf was

prior there. Even more tellingly Ernulfian is the treatment of
the ashlar wall over the triple entrance arches to the CHAPTER
HOUSE, with a diaper pattern, in which the diagonal bands
are incised so that they seem double, one half overlapping at
an intersection, while the other half underlaps, so to speak, a
subtlety that occurs identically on the walls of the N passage to
the crypt at Canterbury. The chapter house façade is two-
storeyed, with three shafted upper windows with zigzag, and
three doorways below, the outer ones blocked, the inner
richly sculptured. The problem is whether such sculpture is
possible as early as before 1125. The doorway to the dormitory
stairs, to the r., with a tympanum carved with a terribly decayed relief of the Sacrifice of Isaac,* must be considered
with it. There are Saxon overtones in the tympanum, such as
the hand of God shooting out of a stylized puff of cloud; but
everything else, much of it very peculiar and hard to parallel
in England, suggests a date not before the mid C12 – in particular the black shafts (of Tournai marble), the greatest rarity
in England before Canterbury Cathedral made such shafting
popular. A capital of c.1160 excavated at Faversham and the
shafts at Iffley of c.1170 are just about the only other examples.
Prowling beasts in panels on the abaci, and, once, in roundels
on the voussoirs. Birds in foliage on the capitals. Bases with
claw-like spurs. The strangest motif is the heads, some with
horns, that project fully in the round from the imposts. Such
heads however do turn up in the Prior's Doorway at Ely, where
they are datable c.1140. These doorways then seem to be insertions, probably after the fire of 1137, which is recorded to
have damaged the chapter house. Very clever insertions for
the diapered walling show no signs of disturbance.‡

The CHAPTER HOUSE is rectangular. The E wall, inside
the Deanery, has more intersecting arcading, on shafts, with
sub-arches from shaft to shaft. The N and S walls show evidence of a Perp remodelling, demi-angel corbels for a timber
roof, and a jamb of a vaulted vestibule underneath a W gallery,
over which a passage will have led from the dormitory to the
choir of the cathedral, when at long last the monks could no
longer endure descending into the night air of the cloisters in
order to say their offices.

* The fragment of inscription 'ARIES PER CORNUA' is the confirmatory
clue to the subject.

‡ Miss K. Galbraith, who discussed the sculpture with me, assures me
that a competent stonemason could make an insertion like this and leave no
trace that he had done so.

The DORMITORY UNDERCROFT, excavated by St John Hope, was 91 ft by 41 ft. Two of the short round responds are exposed, with simple scallop capitals.

E of the cathedral, the DEANERY (now Theological College), through the SEXTRY GATE. E front of three storeys, seven bays in all, the centre three projecting. These are a refacing by the Dean in office in 1767–75; the wings are his predecessor's (c.1765). Both parts faced with ragstone blocks, with red-brick dressings. C19 additions.

THE TOWN

CHURCHES

ST MARGARET, St Margaret's Street. High up, with a view across the Medway to industrial Strood. Perp W tower of ragstone, the battlements chequered with flint. NE turret. Diagonal buttresses disappearing below the third stage. Bequest of 1457 'ad facturam unius novi campanilis'. The church, rebuilt in 1823–4, is just what one would expect at that date, a big rendered box, with a short chancel ending in an E pediment continued by N porch and S vestry. But the chancel is an addition, made in 1839–40 by R.C.Hussey, even then a full-blooded Goth, but here unexpectedly conforming with what he found. Nave tunnel-vault on preposterously elongated Ionic columns springing from galleries on skinny Greek Doric columns. Dec E window of 1872. No doubt further improvements were intended at that time. – PLATE. All gilt. Paten, 1695 by I.C.; Paten and Flagon, 1700, the latter by Anne Sheen; Cup, 1754 by T.W. – MONUMENTS. Thomas Cod † 1465. 15½ in. brass of a half-length priest, palimpsest on another just like it. Rhyming Latin inscription, which tells how, as vicar, 'campanili succurrit tempore vili'. – Many tablets, the earliest one to Thomas Manly † 1690, in a moulded black marble frame, and, outside that, an alabaster one with luscious fruit and flowers.

ST NICHOLAS. Built in the cathedral churchyard and dedicated in 1423. Before that the parishioners had worshipped in the nave of the cathedral. Ragstone. Low NW tower, originally detached, it seems. Aisled nave and chancel. After a fire there was a re-dedication in 1624. Externally one would not guess that, for the Dec windows are of 1860–2. Yet the C17 tracery, astonishingly, was Geometrical too. Five-bay arcades and 54 chancel arch remarkably monumental for the early C17, stone, making, as so often, a point-blank compromise between Gothic and classical: Tuscan columns, pointed arches moulded with a wave and a thick roll. Nave roof and chancel c.1800, done by a deft hand. The w end and aisles have recently been screened off to form diocesan offices. – FONT. Perp. Concave-sided bowl. – PLATE. Cup and Paten Cover, 1602; Cup and Paten Cover, 1609, by *T.F.*; Paten and a pair of Flagons, 1701 by *John Cory*; Almsdish, 1701 by *Seth Lofthouse*; Almsdish, 1726 by *Fi.* – MONUMENTS. George Wilson † 1629. Tiny tablet with tiny kneeling figures. – Thomas Rocke, 1635. Not much larger, also with kneeling figures. Signed by *John & Matthias Christmas*. – Philip Bartholomew † 1696 (N aisle). Fine hanging monument, flanked by drops of flowers, and crowned with a pair of putti. – Robert Conny † 1723 (S aisle). Tablet with side scrolls. – George Gordon † 1759 (S aisle). Pedimented hanging monument framing a putto astride a pedestal. He looks down on a heap of bones, a skull, and a book. Background of brown veined marble. A fine conception, *Sir Robert Taylor*'s.*

ST PETER, King Street. 1858–60. An unusually meaty and well-thought-out building, one of *Christian*'s best. On a sloping site, so that from the E one looks down on it, and sees a polygonal apse under a tall, sharp roof, and the much lower S aisle, gabled to the E, and with three cross-gables. SW porch-tower, not high, and given a saddleback roof, like a fourth gable at a higher level. Ragstone and polychrome brickwork. Huge three-light aisle windows with red-brick tympana and red and yellow brick surrounds. Rose window high in the skewed w wall. Equally idiosyncratic interior, wide but not long, as full as possible of light and uninterrupted space. Arcade on strong, lofty circular piers. Naturalistic leaf capitals.

SYNAGOGUE, High Street, nearly in Chatham. 1869 by *H.H. Collins*. In an unbelievably ugly Romanesque style.

CEMETERY, Maidstone Road. Chapels by *M.Bulmer*, 1865 (GS), a pair, with a steeple on the ground between them.

PUBLIC BUILDINGS

CASTLE. The Medway crossing was the most vulnerable part of Watling Street, so it is no wonder that a mighty keep was built here above the main road from London to Dover and the

* The monument is not signed, but Taylor's design is at the Taylorian Institute, Oxford.

Continent. The tallest of the tower keeps of England, 125 ft to the top of the corner-turrets, it dominates river, town, and cathedral.

In 1127 Henry II granted the castle to William of Corbeuil, Archbishop of Canterbury, and it was he who, according to Gervase, during the next twelve years, erected 'egregiam turrim'. This is the present KEEP, built of ragstone rubble, with dressings of Caen stone, 70 ft square in plan. A rectangular forebuilding reaches up two-thirds of the height of the N wall. The way into the keep was through this, up a now ruined flight of steps that begins round the NW corner. Angle turrets, firmly but not excessively projecting, with set-back corners. SE turret rebuilt circular after it had been undermined by King John's engineers in 1215, the fate to which square-cornered towers were vulnerable. Repairs to the keep in 1226–32 cost £530. Pilaster buttress up the centre of each wall. Windows at five levels, and a sixth in the turrets. Large upper windows, of the hall, at an unassailable height.

The FOREBUILDING has a tunnel-vaulted basement, originally a dungeon no doubt. Upper room with paired lights, and at the top a CHAPEL, the chancel arch carried on a tunnel-vault. Unlike the later keep at Dover, the chapel is more austere than the rest, having merely unmoulded rere-arches to the windows. The doorway at the head of the steps leads into the first floor of the forebuilding. A second immediately, at r. angles, into the keep proper, with a portcullis slot. Both have angle shafts with scalloped capitals, and outward-pointing zigzag round the arch, the standard method of enriching the doorways and windows of the keep. A cross-wall divides the KEEP E–W into two equal halves. Well-shaft in the middle of it, with openings at each floor-level. Newel staircase, groin-vaulted, in the NE turret. Wall-passages at several levels, a tunnel-vaulted one opening to the upper level of the hall as a gallery, and a groin-vaulted one at the highest level. The HALL occupies the third and fourth storeys, and here the cross-wall becomes an arcade, of two plus two bays on massive round piers with square, scalloped capitals. A permanent screen ran across the lower part of the arcade, represented now by the enriched doorway in the W bay. Hall main doorway on the N side. Fireplaces N and S with flues running obliquely through the wall. Above the hall, two solars.

The keep stands at the S end of the sloping, roughly oval, bailey. A curtain wall runs round the greater part of it, varying in height, and clearly of various dates. Against the W side evidence of an upper hall on an undercroft. The river side of this piece of walling has the ragstone laid in herringbone courses, which suggests that it is Early Norman in date. It must be part of the stone castle which Bishop Gundulf built in 1087–9, one of the earliest masonry castles in the kingdom.

The S stretch, with a circular SE bastion, is clearly post-assault, the mending of the curtain wall recorded in 1221–2. On the E side there are two square wall-turrets, with cinque-foiled windows, and projections on their E sides. They are built of larger blocks of stone, and belong to a later strengthening of the walls. The blank pointed arches here on the outer side seem to be no more than a means of strengthening the wall.

GUILDHALL. 1687. It must have looked very swagger when it stood free, without the wings joining it to the street-line. Open below on pairs of Tuscan columns. Red brick above, with quoins and raised panels below the windows. Hipped roof on a cornice of richly carved brackets. Four windows, the centre two in a shallow projection crowned with a segmental pediment. They have moulded brick frames, keystones, and rustication, not an original feature, it seems; see Badeslade's engraving. STAIRCASE with short, fat, turned balusters. Œil-de-bœuf windows light it from the top. Plaster swags round them, and a rich plaster ceiling, with a free-flying putto in the centre. Similar, less good, plaster ceiling in the HALL, dated 1695. The original layout of the hall is intact, with wall-panelling and a balustrade with strong, turned balusters. – INSIGNIA. Mace, 1661 by *I.K.*; Sergeants' Maces, a pair, 1767 by *Fuller White*; Oar, parcel gilt, 1748 by *Edward Aldridge*; Water Bailiff's Oar, 1723 by *E.L.*; Tankard, 1631(?) by *M.G.*

POLICE STATION, King Street. By *Jempson & Cairnduff*, in association with the County Architect's Department. Completed 1966. Well sited on a slope, though it has broken up the tight texture of streets around it, which is a pity. Five-storey block, the windows in continuous bands, well supported by low, red-brick outliers on all sides. Visually, the block needs a few more storeys.

MEDWAY COLLEGE OF ART, Corporation Street. 1905 by *R.V. Russell & Cooper*. Quite an impressive building, red brick with plenty of ashlar dressings, in a neo-English-Baroque style.

KING'S SCHOOL. Main school 1842 by *Vulliamy*, enlarged in

1911. Tudoresque. – SCHOOL HOUSE, in Maidstone Road, of 1878 is by *Butterfield*, determinedly cranky. Three storeys with gables. Triangular S porch with a colossal pinnacle. Red brick with bumpy bands of ragstone, carrying on relentlessly across the windows.

SIR JOSEPH WILLIAMSON'S MATHEMATICAL SCHOOL, High Street. 1892 by *G.E.Bond*. Tall and very red, in Sir Ernest George's Queen Anne style.

WATTS'S CHARITY, High Street. *See* Perambulation, p. 475. See p. 645

WATTS ALMSHOUSES, Maidstone Road. 1858 by *Charles Foord* (GS). Jacobean style with knobs on. Long, symmetrical, multifariously diversified block for eighteen residents. The cost was £3,449, so Mr Foord made the money work hard.

FOORD ALMSHOUSES, Priestfields. 1926–7, enlarged in 1931, so that sixty-three residents can be housed. An honourable Rochester tradition is thus continued in a magnificent manner; but as architecture *Sir Guy Dawber*'s Carobethan quadrangles are pure escapism. Open-ended front court 80 yds square. One-storeyed ranges rising to two in the centre. Indoor sanitation, but two pumps. That sums it up. What fun it must have been to fetch water by pail! What fun to peer out of a mullioned window! In its way, of course, it is very charming: Dawber knew his craft.

In the hall, flashy WALL PAINTINGS by *Gerald Moira* with scenes from the history of Rochester. – Huge, Chinesey gilt and painted LANTERN by *Bainbridge Reynolds*. – STAINED GLASS by *Anning Bell*. Very poor. It was a period when the decorative arts in England were at a desperately low ebb.

ST BARTHOLOMEW'S HOSPITAL, New Road. Above the Norman St Bartholomew's Hospital (*see* Chatham). Red-brick cliff by *R.P.Pope*, 1862 (GS). An absurd, early C19, castellated and stuccoed LODGE at the foot of the hill is now part of the hospital buildings.

PERAMBULATION

The High Street is the spine of Rochester, the successor of the E–W road bisecting the Roman town, which means that it continues in a straight line all the way from the crossing over the Medway. Let us assume that cathedral and castle have been visited first. The way out of the castle bailey then is down the steps in the NW corner, to the Esplanade. At once on the r. the ragstone BRIDGE CHAPEL, rescued from ruin and re-win-

dowed in 1937. It stood opposite the end of the great stone
bridge built at the expense of Sir Robert Knolles and Sir John
de Cobham from 1387. In scale the bridge vied with London
Bridge, with eleven arches and a total length of 570 ft. It was
demolished in 1857 and replaced by *Cubitt*'s bridge on the
downstream side. The present bridge dates from 1914. Beside
the chapel, CASTLE CLUB, three-bay Grecian stuccoed front,
with recessed Ionic columns above the ground-floor level.

And so r., and into the straight, funnel-like HIGH STREET. It
is narrow and full of traffic, and is not immediately attractive to the eye. But it has enough character to make one regret
the mean insertions of the C20 staggering back a pace from the
street-line, reducing the tension again and again. The only
way really to make the confined space less oppressive without
losing the virtues of confinement is by opening up deep pockets
of space, as La Providence (*see* below) demonstrates. Pieces of
wider pavement are just not enough. Still, there are plenty of
things to comment on, intriguing and memorable in themselves.

The Guildhall (*see* above) is very near the beginning on the N
side, just beyond the jolly Jacobean-style MEDWAY CON-
SERVANCY OFFICES, of 1909 by *G.E.Bond*, ashlar, bowing
out over the pavement with a big central window. Brick angle
tower at the back. They face the plain, flat, nine-bay front of
the VICTORIA AND BULL HOTEL, in stock brick, typical of
the late C18, with the wide central opening necessary in
coaching days. Under the GEORGE INN, a little further along
on the N side, a four-bay undercroft, *c.*1320. Quadripartite
rib-vault. Foliage boss and corbels.

The S side continues with high stock-brick frontages. No. 42
takes its place among them, of dull red brick, three bays and
three storeys, dated 1778 by the MHLG. It is simply and successfully distinguished by a long, looping stucco ribbon over
the first-floor windows, with Adamesque wreaths twining
down from it. Beyond it, at the time of writing, an ominous
gap, and a new MARTINS BANK across the way to show how
it should not be filled. But from far away a colossal clock has
appeared jutting out over the street. It belongs to the CORN
EXCHANGE, the gift in 1706 of Sir Cloudesley Shovel, who
was M.P. for Rochester besides being a distinguished admiral.
Only the façade remains, but it is in itself the most delightful
contribution to the street. Red brick. Narrow, under a big
pediment with carved brackets. Slim windows, the upper with

frilled lintels, the lower with keystones growing into fantastic, moulded brick brackets. Colossal doorcase with a colossal, open, swan-neck pediment on richly carved spandrels and brackets. Early C18 red and grey brick frontage next door.

The next stretch begins beyond the crossroads with Boley Hill and Northgate. The former leads into the precinct and beyond. In due course it must be pursued, but not yet. Beside it, College Gate (see p. 466), but as the street continues one has no further hint of the presence of the cathedral close at hand. Varied run of C18 houses on the N side. On the S side, nothing but the petite and pretty neo-Wren MIDLAND BANK, of c.1929. Big central arched window, with square windows above and below, in the channelled walling. Well-placed pieces of carving. Ashlar of artificial stone. Then suddenly the houses are cut away to reveal dramatically the whole E end of the cathedral, behind a neat Memorial Garden. Behind the first house on the S after this, a curious C17 PAVILION, with a window with the typical arched centre to the transom, on mullions carved with caryatids. Then for a time the N side again becomes more interesting, with the early C18 GORDON HOTEL, three-storeyed, four windows wide. Red brick and grey headers. Contemporary staircase, and dog-gate at the foot of it, with a pierced panel of foliage at the top. Beyond it the GAS BOARD SHOWROOMS, a 1930s effort, fatuously pretending to be a second Guildhall; and the restored ashlar front of WATTS'S CHARITY, founded in 1579, for a night's lodging 'for six poor travellers, not being rogues or proctors', and rebuilt in 1771 on the old lines with three even gables, small mullioned windows, but classical mouldings. *Isaac Dent* was master-mason.

The next unexpected interruption, still on the N side, is LA PROVIDENCE, heralded by red-brick and stucco Italianate lodges, three-storeyed, of c.1840. Wrought-iron balconies, with heavy palmettes. They guard the entrance to a humble quadrangle, with two-storeyed brick ranges of the same date, practically rebuilt in 1957–9 by *Grellier & Sons*. Again these are, or were, almshouses; founded in 1718, says an inscription, for poor French Protestants and their descendants. Nothing more, until at last the street curves, at the point where the East Gate of the town stood. On the site, the red cliff of the Mathematical School (see Public Buildings), and, opposite, a big gap made by the start of Maidstone Road. A stretch of the medieval TOWN WALLS to the N in FREE SCHOOL LANE. Battlements and a round angle turret.

Up MAIDSTONE ROAD the most important town-house historically in Rochester, RESTORATION HOUSE. Basically of the C16, the plan is U-shaped, but the wings are not built in one with the centre, or at least don't look as if they are. That is because the centre was refaced in the mid C17. It is a most interesting display of cut and moulded brickwork, confused a good deal by pits and pock-marks where bricks have decayed. Five bays. Bays 1, 3, and 5 break boldly forward, which makes for a certain cramping. Rustication low down. Rusticated surrounds to the lower windows. Quoins wherever possible. Round porch arch, and beside it the high bases of pilasters that stretch up to the eaves. They frame a window with a raised surround lobed in the middle. Similar surrounds to other windows. It is all highly peculiar and undisciplined, and hard to date. About 1640 is possible, and so also is c.1670. (Internally the medieval plan of hall, solar, and service wing is easily made out. Strapwork on the parlour chimneypiece and frieze. Late C17 staircase.)

Back in the High Street, at once l. and r. two early C17 houses, notably expansive, as they are beyond the constricted confines of the medieval town. Nos 150–4 overhangs the street, a triple-gabled timber-framed house, the lowest of the three storeys now shops. Two overhangs and overhanging gables. Symmetrical oriel windows on brackets. All the uprights carved with geometrical patterns. Enriched brick chimneystack. EASTGATE HOUSE, opposite, stands end-on to the road, presenting a gable-end with three overhangs over a brick ground storey. Oriels on brackets. The E front is greatly restored. Towards the street, a four-storeyed polygonal brick turret. The rest is symmetrical, timber-framed with bricknogging. Two-storeyed brick porch with a four-centred stone doorway under a brick pediment on pilasters. Polygonal bays l. and r. Continuous bands of window at two levels. Three equal gables on the w side. Hall chimneypiece with caryatids on the overmantel, made up from old pieces. Plaster ceiling with plants in a geometrical pattern of ribs, and the arms of Sir Peter Buck, Clerk of the Acts in the Navy Board. The date on the chimneypiece here is 1590. The house is now a museum. Small public garden behind. In it the CHALET brought from Switzerland for Charles Dickens at his home at Gadshill, Higham. The only reason for pursuing the High Street any further is BERKELEY HOUSE, at the far end on the r. Handsome stuccoed composition of the end of the C18. Three-bay front with lower wings projecting l. and r. Tripartite lower windows under sunk lunettes. Porch up curved flights of steps, with fine Corinthian columns and a pediment. It is astonishing how close to the roadway a gentleman's genteel villa could be built.

The High Street continues at a low level towards Chatham, and in it are several more C18 houses, now rather jaded, behind a raised walk on the r.; but STAR HILL branches r. up the hill. Star Hill was laid out c.1790 with tall, stock-brick terraces, uniform on the l., more broken on the r., and really in DELCE ROAD. TROY TOWN, built up on the slopes SW, around KING STREET and UNION STREET, with similar terraces, c.1786–90, has been chopped up by recent demolition and redevelopment.

BOLEY HILL and the development of the town S of the precincts needs to be perambulated with a fresh start from the castle. S of the castle a cluster of houses, none particularly gratifying to the eye externally. Inside the OLD HALL however some remarkable late C16 painted panelling. A ground-floor room at the back keeps a complete display, and so does an upper room in the E bay. Small panels, with a repeated pattern of arabesques in the centre of each. No strapwork. Gilding in the upper room. Two contemporary painted figures, of Faith and Justice, very crude, in the lower. In the room behind the E gable, walls and canted ceiling vault were originally covered with a geometrical pattern in primary colours. Monochrome wall paintings, of the C17, on the stairs to it. In the garden of SATIS HOUSE a mound which by tradition is the motte of the pre-Gundulf castle, outside the Roman town walls.

Further S, ST MARGARET'S STREET climbs the hill. Half-way up, a happily varied group of C18 and early C19 houses, varied especially in height. It starts with Nos 12 to 20, built in 1724. Two-storeyed, nine bays under a hipped roof. Red brick. Aprons to all the windows. S of St Margaret's church, THE GLEANINGS, a circumstantial house of c.1800, rendered an ugly buff. Fashionably two-faced exterior, Grecian towards the road, castellated towards the river. Castle Goring, Sussex, of c.1790 is the *locus classicus* of that particular piece of stage management. The centre of the road front breaks forward a bit under a pediment. One bay each side. Windows in wide surrounds, cut back in layers.

32 Finally, at the highest point, the truly Vanbrughian FORT CLARENCE, built in 1812 as a belated piece of anti-Napoleonic defence. Massive stock-brick tower with round angle turrets, and immense, stylized machicoulis of stone over the gateway to the N.

ROGUE HILL see PENSHURST

ROLVENDEN

8030

ST MARY THE VIRGIN. Rubble sandstone, the W tower piquantly different from the rest, of chocolate-coloured ironstone with white rag quoins. The earliest evidence is of the C13 – two N lancets in the chancel, and parts of two more in the S wall. Moulded rere-arches with hoods and shafts. Big gaunt Perp E window, five lights with a transom (bequest to make it, 1472). Early C14 nave. Arcades of five arches. Lofty, graceful piers, alternately round and octagonal. The S arcade earlier by its mouldings. The N aisle windows are Dec. The tower was probably added next, with its Dec W windows, the upper with the tracery cusps split. Shallow angle buttresses rising high up. Holy-water stoup inside. At the same time perhaps the chancel arch was inserted and chapels were added, each opening into the chancel by two arches, one wide, one narrow. Odd, wilful profile to the arches, produced by running the sunk quadrant moulding through arch, capital, and respond. – FITTINGS. Of the decadent fittings deplored by *The Ecclesiologist* nothing remains except the WEST GALLERY, seeming to cave in under the weight of the organ, and the FAMILY PEW of the Gybbon-Monypennys. It is a first-floor pew, furnished with a carpet, ten chairs, and a table. Good view of the altar, but no view of the pulpit, one notes. Gallery and pew both 1825. The other plentiful woodwork, with coarse Perp cusping, was carved by the Vicar *c*.1900. – FONT. Hexagonal. On the bowl shields, encircled quatrefoils, and one mouchette wheel. Peculiar fins at the base. – STAINED GLASS. E window 1848. Still painterly, with typical deep rich reds, blues, and yellows. – PLATE. Set by *L.E.*, 1706(?). – MONUMENTS. Robert Gybbon † 1719. Standing monument with putto heads and an urn. – James Monypenny † 1719. Standing monument with putti and a garlanded urn. – Henry Tennant. Designed by *Lutyens*, 1936. Much more personal, and dramatically placed in the head of an arch to the N chapel.

The church, on a mound, is the climax of the village street, though, coming from the N, one does not see it at once. At the N end especially much white weatherboarding, even on a big Wealden hall-house. At the s end the houses at last fall back to reveal the church and another white house at the corner of the churchyard. It is a square, early C19 house, with weatherboarding grooved in imitation of stone, a bowed shop window looking down the street, and a prim house-front towards the churchyard. On the l. the HOUSING ESTATE of 1947 keeps tactfully back behind hawthorns. The symmetrical siting of the houses however is surely not appropriate here.

(Timber-framed houses in Maytham Road include WESLEY HOUSE, with an originally open hall and longitudinal overhang – a pre-Wealden type. Mr K. Gravett)

WINDMILL, ½ m. NW. Tarred post-mill on a brick base. Gloriously big white sweeps.

PIX'S FARM, ½ m. E. Tile-hung except for three bargeboarded gables, the outer ones coming forward a bit. Originally it must have been an impressive C16 front.

FRENSHAM, Rolvenden Layne. A fragment of a C17 brick house, much pulled about. The two-storeyed porch is still largely trustworthy; over the doorway a many-moulded brick cornice on pilasters, and above, a shaped gable, the shapes punctuated by obelisks. Hasted says the house was built after 1660, and that is not impossible.

GREAT MAYTHAM, ½ m. SE. 1909 by *Sir Edwin Lutyens*. Neo-Georgian. Formal, handsome, and extremely large. The centre block incorporates a house of 1721. Lutyens encased it, added a third storey and a high hipped roof with dormers, and extended it to l. and r. with three-bay wings and two-bay pavilions, making a house 168 ft long. For vertical emphasis, bare walls and strong chimneystacks suffice. Blue-grey brick with sparing red dressings.

The drive leads through a LODGE up a straight avenue to the house – a suitably formal approach. The lodge is distinctly more energetically designed than the house.

ROMDEN CASTLE see SMARDEN

ROOTING see PLUCKLEY

ROSHERVILLE see NORTHFLEET

ROYDON HALL see EAST PECKHAM

RUCKINGE

ST MARY MAGDALENE. Beside the road, above the expanses of the marsh. Dec chancel, N chapel and nave with narrow aisles, Norman W tower. Timber N porch with a pretty but mutilated bargeboard. The tower is massive, with a C13 top stage and an egregious steeple consisting of a lead-covered spike on a squat pyramid. The W doorway is a characteristic Norman piece, the arch decorated with a roll, zigzag on a roll, and a double roll, on two orders of shafts with diapered cushion capitals. A Perp doorway is set within it. S doorway, reset, Norman and similar. Consistent Dec work: windows with cusped intersecting tracery, the usual octagonal piers and arches with two chamfers. The pier supporting the chancel arch is a Perp replacement. All the stonework inside dismally scaled after a fire long ago. – PISCINA in the E wall of the chancel with a trefoiled head. – STALLS. L-shaped on the S, with elementary poppyheads. The N stalls preserve four old traceried panels. – REREDOS (under the tower). C18. Ten Commandments etc. under a central broken pediment. The usual robust but sophisticated script. – STAINED GLASS. A little C14 grisaille in the N aisle E window, borders and an angel. – PLATE. Cup, 1582, by *W. Horn* (?); Paten Cover, 1585 by *B.N.*

RUFFIN'S HILL *see* ALDINGTON

RUMWOOD COURT *see* LANGLEY

RUSTHALL

ST PAUL. 1849–50 by *H.J. Stevens* of Derby, with *N.E. Stevens*, a local man (GR). Local material, sandstone slightly rock-tooled. Cruciform, with a substantial central tower and a long nave. Lancets, trefoiled in the chancel, shafted at the E and in the tower. N aisle, nearly as wide as the nave, added in 1864–5 by *Stevens & Robinson*. W porch 1918. Large, 'interesting' Dec W window – of the same date. It is inside that the fun starts. The walls are a smooth, sandstone ashlar, a neutral background against which surprising things happen. Colossal splays to the lancets reach down to the ground, but stop under a hood-mould making a trefoiled head. Arcade of sharply pointed arches on thick, fat, black veined marble piers of quatrefoil section. Aggressive foliage capitals, all different.

The crossing arches however, all but the E, with two continuous chamfers. Strong timber roofs throughout, that in the tower with diagonal arches crossed by a lozenge of four arches joining the centre of each side to its neighbours, like Moorish roofs. – FONT. 1850. A copy of the E.E. font at Weston, Lincolnshire. – REREDOS. Designed c.1869 by J. Norton.

The CHURCHYARD is chock-a-block with expensive tombstones and memorials, commemorating the rich who had retired to Tunbridge Wells.

RUST HALL, ¼ m. W. Early C19 *cottage orné* recently enlarged in an approximately similar style.

RUXLEY

The one-time church of ST BOTOLPH seems to be at the end of its useful life, even as a barn. It was never more than a chapel, a simple rectangle. The flint and rubble stone walls intact. Surviving details, e.g. the window rere-arches, and the simple PISCINA and SEDILIA, are early C14. Above the A20 on a hummock with, one is surprised to find, far-extending views in all directions.*

RYARSH

ST MARTIN. Reached through a cherry orchard. Perp W tower, very like those at Addington and Birling near by. Early Perp W window. Diagonal buttresses. SE turret, conspicuous with its pyramidal tiled cap. Early Norman nave and chancel, as one tiny N window in each testifies. The chancel E quoins, and part of the nave W ones as well, of tufa; also herringbone N walling. Perp S aisle, with a brick and timber gable. Stone S porch. The two-bay S arcade, however, looks C14. Wide chancel arch with similar details. Perhaps the aisle was widened a little in the C15 – see a string which suggests there was once a lean-to aisle roof. Chalk rere-arches to the three Norman E windows. Also, a much rarer survival, a Norman PISCINA. Scalloped bowl, moulded rim.

ST CLERE see KEMSING

ST JOHN'S JERUSALEM see SUTTON-AT-HONE

* Excavation in 1968 has revealed footings of an earlier church under the present building (P. J. Tester).

ST LEONARDS TOWER *see* WEST MALLING

ST MARY CRAY

The post-war expansion in the Cray Valley has been terrific. Many small factories in the valley w of the river, housing on the slopes behind and also on the E side. Renewal of the old High Street is only beginning now. So it is an indictment of the planners that St Mary Cray is no place to linger in, and an indictment of the architects, and also it must be admitted of post-war austerity, that there is hardly anything worthy to be mentioned in *The Buildings of England*; not a factory, not a school, not a housing estate, just one undistinguished church.

ST MARY. Below the intimidating arches of the railway viaduct. Flint. Outside all one sees is of the restorations of 1861–3 (*E. Nash*), 1876, and 1895. The characteristic SE vestry is Nash's, with needle-sharp lancets and a fantastic chimney. But the Dec and Perp tracery was faithfully copied. Three windows have 'Kentish' tracery, that is trefoils or quatrefoils with split-back cusps, a device favoured in the first third of the C14. But in essence the church is early C13. W tower and shingled spire. Nave and aisles of three bays. Sturdy round piers, pointed arches with a small chamfer and a keeled roll. The arches only of the s arcade C14. The evidence at the E end is later. C14 chancel arch. Shallow chapel at the end of the s aisle, with a long squint. The N chapel virtually all rebuilt. – SCREENS. Perp. Simple s chapel screen. Tower screen with pretty intersecting tracery. – PLATE. Cup and Paten Cover, 1576; Almsdish, 1640; Paten, 1720 by *Joseph Ward*(?). – BRASSES. Richard Abery † 1508 and wives. He seems to have married identical triplets. 11 in. figures. – Richard Manning † 1604 and wife. Civilian. 22 in. long. – Philadelphia († 1747) and Benjamin Greenwood † 1773. The last pre-Oxford-Movement brasses, says Mrs Esdaile. The little figures scratched rather than engraved. He wears a wig, frock-coat, and flowered waistcoat. – Small hanging MONUMENT to Margaret Crewes † 1602. Kneeling figures.

ST JOSEPH (R.C.), High Street. Conspicuous brick tower with a red and white metal construction on top, like an agricultural exhibit. By *D. Plaskett Marshall*. Completed 1959.

The long, narrow High Street has lost a good many of its houses. Of those that are left the only one of consequence is THE ROOKERY, half-way along (now the offices of the Ministry of

Social Security). Late C18. Red brick. Three storeys and five bays. Everything happens in the centre bay. It projects a little; porch on Greek Doric columns, Venetian window over, semicircular lunette window at the top.

KEVINGTON COUNTY PRIMARY SCHOOL, ¾ m. SE. Big, square, red-brick house, five bays by six. Three storeys. Wide bow the full height of the s front. Generous white window surrounds. About 1830 seems the most likely date. Red-brick and flint STABLES.

ST MARY IN THE MARSH

0020

ST MARY. Very much in the marsh. Church, pub, and a few council houses at a bend in the road. The church is a delight, almost unrestored, yet fresh and neat within and without. Chancel, nave, and separately gabled aisles, s porch, w tower. The tower is Norman for its full height, see the windows in all three stages of the N wall. Tower arch on big round responds with many-scalloped capitals. Otherwise the fabric is Late E.E. Wide chancel of two bays with large lancets. PISCINA (a double drain) and two stepped SEDILIA as a group, all with trefoiled arches. The four-light E window has Geometrical tracery without ogees (a quatrefoil set diagonally over three pointed quatrefoils) and a hollow-chamfered rere-arch on circular shafts. If it is contemporary with the rest of the chancel, as it seems to be, the 'E.E.' work must be c.1300.* Nave arcades of three bays, circular piers with deeply moulded capitals, arches with two hollow-chamfered orders. The N arcade ends at the w on a fine head wearing the mouldings like a tremendous hat. N aisle windows square-headed Perp, those of the s aisle of c.1800, with low-slung labels. Crown-post roofs on straight tiebeams. A few patterned TILES in the chancel. – ROYAL ARMS of George III, dated 1775. – PLATE. Cup of 1578, the bowl fluted below and engraved above with an eagle, a snail, and a grasshopper. – (BRASSES. Maud Jamys † 1499 and William Gregory † 1502, at the w end of the nave.)

ST MARY'S HOO

8070

ST MARY. Ragstone. Dec nave. The unrestored SW window vouches for the tracery pattern, a stretched quatrefoil with wide barbs over two ogee lights. Undersized chancel, com-

* Big recess at the w end of the chancel s wall. A blocked low-side window?

pletely rebuilt, probably *c*.1881, to the design of *E. W. Stephens*
(BW). Modern N porch, Dec N doorway. The W tower, also too
small for the nave, seems by its unbuttressed outline to be
C13. But that cannot be so – for the plinth moulding is undoubtedly Perp. Small Perp windows in the top stage, the
other windows mere rectangular slits. A doorway with a hollow chamfer does duty for the tower arch. W wall of the nave
built in one with the tower. Nave roof supported on straight
tiebeams with pierced spandrels. The peculiar crown-posts
are not old. – PLATE. Cup and Paten Cover, 1573, the former
with the maker's mark, *I.C.*; Paten, 1705(?) by *E.A.*

4060   ST PAUL'S CRAY

ST PAULINUS. Church, school, and a row of early C19 cottages
look across a loop of the river Cray (limpidly purling over
sludge), to a shaggy water-meadow: memorably different from
the shopping-parades and light industry around. The church
has quite an interesting history. The N chapel to the chancel is
separately gabled and has a NE quoin of Roman tiles. In its N
wall an early lancet, in its W wall a blocked round arch with a
slight chamfer. Traces of a round-headed E window (one of a
triplet?) as well. High up the N wall of the nave, a blocked
early window, its rere-arch visible inside, turned a little
irregularly in tiles. So we seem to have evidence of a Saxon
nave, a Saxon N porticus, and an early C12 N aisle made to
communicate with the porticus, but later demolished.* The
later parts are notable too, dating from *c*.1200 or a very little
later. W tower and shingled spire. (The convincing doorway and
the unconvincing window above it are alike inventions of
c.1860.) Nave with blocked N arcade and S aisle. Chancel. The
work is characterized by circular piers, pointed arches, and upright leaves and heads on some of the capitals. The fascinating
thing is that in spite of the crude carving they are unmistakably
acanthus leaves. The source for such a motif must be Canterbury Cathedral of 1175–80. The SE respond and pier have
them, on the latter arranged with laborious symmetry, and the
W respond of the arch to the N chapel, where some trefoil and
spade-shaped leaves occur as well. In the chancel the outer
jambs of a trio of E windows, and a curious large recess in the
N wall. That it was never an arch to a chapel is shown by the
string-course running across the back wall. There was heavy

* Mr P. J. Tester has suggested to me that this is what the evidence means.

restoration in 1856–61, and the S chapel was added in 1863. Typically the Victorian restorer had to go one better and provide professional leaves and heads on the capitals of his S chapel arches. Any tampering he may have done to the original work is now obscured by whitewash. He is not above suspicion. Boarded sanctuary roof, prettily stencilled green, grey, and gold.* – FONT. Octagonal. Elementary panelling of the bowl, a sunk panel and two sunk hyphens. More likely to be C17 than C15. – LECTERN. Charming and highly unusual. Wood, carved as a pelican in her piety, on a twisted stem. It must be foreign, C18. – PLATE. Cup of 1718. – MONUMENTS. (C13 coffin lid in the S chapel, with a very odd cross and floriated stem.) – Earl Sydney † 1890. A tablet done to look like a late C17 one. Rather well done.

ST BARNABAS, Rushet Road. 1962–4 by *E. F. Starling*. Greek-cross plan with the angles between the arms partly filled up. Big copper tent roof and flèche. Internal galleries on three sides and light directed on to the chancel.

BRONZE AGE ENCLOSURE, on the site of the modern church on Broomwood Hill. It consisted of a rectangular embanked enclosure 120 ft by 60 ft with entrances in the middle of the E and W sides. Within were the foundations of at least two circular timber-built huts and a general scatter of flint-knapping debris and artefacts of Early Bronze Age character.

SANDHURST   7020

The village is big, straggling, and not very attractive, but the church stands apart from it all to the S, looking over Kent Ditch into Sussex.

ST NICHOLAS. Sandstone; sizeable. Heavily restored and the chancel largely rebuilt by *R. H. Carpenter* in 1875. The W tower is C14, with its reticulated W window (renewed) and tall, shallow angle buttresses. It has lost its top. Internally the tower is impressively spacious, opening by arches to N and S into lean-to aisles. Very personal detailing of the responds – semi-octagonal with a sunk quadrant giving the capitals a wiggle – by the mason who worked at Rolvenden. Short, stocky nave arcades, with octagonal piers C14 of two dates. They must have replaced earlier arcades, if the clerestory lancets, not centred above the arches, are C13. The proportions of the arcades suggest Norman predecessors. C14 evidence in

* Damaged by fire in September 1968.

the chancel (see the aumbry) and N chapel. Traces of a S
porch. Timber N porch of 1875. – FONT. Sandstone. Octagonal, with a Dec tracery pattern repeated on each face. –
STAINED GLASS. C15 glass in the S aisle E window: St Michael
weighing souls. S window: St George, a priest, and an abbess.
Poor quality, as C15 glass often is. – PLATE. Gilt Cup, 1562;
Paten, 1722.

FIELD GREEN HOUSE, 1½ m. N. Mid-C18 house of five bays
and two storeys. Plum and blue brick and scarlet dressings.
The cornice kinks up over the centre window. The brick
gablet above with an elementary Venetian window must be
later.

₆₀₃₀   SCOTNEY CASTLE

                    1 m. SE of Lamberhurst

Scotney consists of the fragment of a C14 moated castle in the
valley with a C17 house attached, and a new house built on
the hill for Edward Hussey in 1837–44. Hussey had advice on
the siting of his house from William Sawrey Gilpin, nephew
of the Rev. William Gilpin, that arbiter on the appreciation
of picturesque scenery. The old castle had to become an
incident in the picturesque view from the hill, and to achieve
this the bold decision was taken to quarry stone for the house
from the hillside below. It is this quarry, filled with shrubs
and framed by trees, that forms the foreground of the idyllic
view of the castle from the house. The castle is equally enchanting when seen at close quarters: Hussey pulled down
part of the C17 house to make it so. Artistically this is the great
achievement at Scotney, one of the last and one of the loveliest
landscapes in the C18 pictorial tradition.

The buildings themselves, however, are not at all without
interest. Roger Ashburnham fortified his house late in the
C14, probably as a result of the French sack of Rye and
Winchelsea in 1377. The moat was made to encircle two
islands, the eastern one strengthened with curtain walls and
four circular corner towers. Of these, that at the S corner
stands to its full height, minus the battlements. It is low and
fat, with a ring of deep machicolations round the top. The
pretty C17 conical roof and lantern quite deprive it of whatever menacing aspect it may once have had. The base of the
gatehouse, with strong diagonal buttresses, remains in the
centre of the SW side, approached over a stone bridge in place

of the wooden drawbridge. Ashburnham's manor house stood within the curtain walls, with the entrance to his hall opposite the gatehouse. Nothing of it is left except the jamb of the entrance doorway (at the N end of the C17 building) and the springing of the arch at the far end of the screens passage.

In the C16 the living quarters were reconstructed – see one brick gable high up with a two-light window in it. But in the mid C17 a much more thoroughgoing attempt was made to turn the old castle into an up-to-date mansion, by refacing it in ashlar on both sides to make a three-storey range, fifteen bays wide. It was a most ambitious project – in scale and proportions like the unexecuted design for Wilton and John Webb's grandiose façade designs. Too ambitious, indeed, for barely half the block materialized and the W entrance front was cobbled up in brick. Edward Hussey dismantled a good deal, but enough survives to show the character of the work. The windows are classically proportioned, with broad, flat, eared surrounds. Those on the W front have radiating voussoirs, those on the E break through the string-courses. On the E the central feature, slightly projecting, stands almost to the very top. It has big crude quoins, and from the string-course hang big oblong blocks. The window over the doorway has instead of a pediment an Ionic capital barbarously stretched to reach across it.* All this suggests a date c.1635, and but for a certain coarseness is worthy of Nicholas Stone. On the W front a large boss, c.1300, from Bayham Abbey. Inside the cottage, a Jacobean staircase with turned balusters and enriched newels. The pargetted oriel windows were added in 1849, replacing equally attractive Gothick ones.

The architect of Edward Hussey's new house was *Anthony Salvin*. He made his first designs in 1835, and building went on from 1837 to 1844. Salvin had made his name designing in the Tudor style, and he keeps to it here. The entrance front groups loosely about a battlemented tower, with the house extending to the r. and the slightly lower service wing coming forward on the l. Salvin's detail is telling if not yet always archaeologically correct, e.g. the battlements stepping up from tower to higher turret, or the subtle contrast between the gables on the house and on the service wing. The garden front more nearly symmetrical and a little tame. In plan, the house is interesting, a double pile, as compact and rational as an C18 house; but the front door leads into the l. end of the hall,

* A barbarism Serlio is authority for, on a chimneypiece in Book IV.

which has a bay-window at the 'dais' end – a medieval quotation, as it were. Salvin's interiors however are Jacobean, with strapwork on the plaster ceilings, and panelling which in the dining room may incorporate early C17 Continental pieces. Above the panelling flock wallpaper in red, blue, and gold, designed by *Willement*.* In an upstairs room, a fine mid-C18 chimneypiece, with undercut rocaille-work.

SCUDDERS *see* FAWKHAM

5050

SEAL

ST PETER. The fine W tower was under construction *c.*1520–9. It is the usual Kentish kind, battlemented, of three stages, with angle buttresses and a strong octagonal SE stair-turret. Four-light W window in a deep reveal, and shafted W doorway under a square hood, the standard piece of swagger. Nave and chancel with S aisle, S porch, S chapel, and SE vestry. N aisle of 1855, lengthened eastwards in 1879. Throughout, the material is a pale, greenish sandstone. The earliest evidence appears in the S aisle, one blocked lancet and the three-bay arcade, with one round, one octagonal pier, the mouldings deep and undercut, i.e. of the C13. Two hollow-chamfered arch mouldings. Late Perp S chapel, continuing the aisle. Chancel E window also Perp, but not so late, for the arched lights are cusped. – PULPIT. Of *c.*1630. Perspective arches on the faces and tapering angle pilasters. – LECTERN. 1920. Wood. Angel holding a wreath. – SCREEN. 1931, by *C.R.Ashbee*. Gothic and quite uneventful. – CHANDELIER. Dated 1725. Brass. – CUPBOARD. C18. Reliefs on the doors. – STAINED GLASS. E windows of the chancel and S chapel signed by *F.W.Oliphant*, 1856 and 1858. – PLATE. Cup and Paten Cover, inscribed 1674, by *W.B.* – MONUMENTS. Sir William de Bryene † 1395. Excellent, straightforward brass of a knight, 54 in. long. – John Theobauld † 1577. 11½ in. brass palimpsest on a very crude brass of a lady of *c.*1500. – John Theobald. Tablet with Ionic side pilasters, set up after 1605. – Steven Theobald † 1619. Similar to the last but more elaborate. – John Chichester. Large cartouche, dated 1680, of the highest sculptural quality. – Camden family. Five heavy Grecian tablets made in 1832 by *Chantrey*. That of the 1st Marquess Camden has a profile medallion bust among his Lord Chancellor's regalia. –

* So Mr Christopher Hussey kindly tells me.

1st Lord Hillingdon † 1898. White marble portrait relief. – Elizabeth Mills † 1908. Bronze sleeping child on a pedestal. The little figure cocooned in big wings is conceived with much tenderness, and for originality is far and away the most interesting object in the church.

DORTON HOUSE (Wildernesse), ½ m. s. Irregular, three-storeyed stone mansion in extremely plain classical dress. At the s end is a mid-C18 house, of two storeys, heightened to three by *George Dance Jun.*, who remodelled the house *c.*1800 for the Marquess Camden. Nothing of his is left inside, except perhaps the screen of Ionic columns in a room in the sw corner. All the rest belongs to the 1880s.

STONEPITTS, 1¼ m. E. Elizabethan H-shaped house, considerably altered and improved, as they say, after 1928 by *G. L. Kennedy*. The entrance front faces N, and is of red brick on stone footings. Two-storeyed. The wings have a large outer and a small inner gable, making a symmetrical outline; the recessed centre is almost all altered. Porch under the smaller of the l. gables, with a straight-sided arch and a hood-mould. Such original windows as remain are also of stone, with one transom and three, four, or five mullions, the placing of them not quite symmetrical. w side of ragstone, with mullioned windows and a big chimneybreast. Half-timbered, tile-hung addition to the E side.

SEAL HOLLOW *see* SEVENOAKS, p. 497

SELLINDGE

0030

ST MARY. Norman windows in the w tower. Tower arch pointed however; and the head of the w doorway segmental, not semicircular. The nave may pre-date it; the SE quoin is built without dressed stones, a Saxo-Norman feature. Yet the general impression is of an E.E. church. The N aisle and chapel came in the C13, and so did remodelling of the chancel, with an external string-course. The string-course on the N wall, and the lancet over it, now inside the church, show that the chancel was dealt with first, the chapel added later. Crown-post nave roof, made when a timber nave arcade was substituted for the stone one. – STAINED GLASS. N chapel E window, Transfiguration, by *Gibbs*. Dazzling colours, dizzying stars and flowers; in its way completely successful. Date of death 1863. – PLATE. Paten, 1708 by *John Ruslen*. – MONUMENTS.

Sir Peter Heyman. Early C17 tomb-chest under a lofty Late Perp arch. At its foot kneels the hefty alabaster figure of a man.* – Thomas Godfrey † 1664. Large architectural tablet, the pediments two deep.

SOMERFIELD COURT. Handsome brick house of c.1700, spoilt by a heavy brick porch and the blocking of half the windows. Seven bays by three. Two storeys. Hipped roofs. The raised quoins are of brick, and so are the moulded frames of the niches that come between the windows on the short sides.

SEVENOAKS

CHURCHES

ST NICHOLAS. Characteristically a town church, and, unlike many town churches, lying close up to the High Street. Ragstone and sandstone. At first sight all is Perp, and all carved stonework renewed. Battlemented aisles stopping one bay from the E end. Tall W tower, of three stages, with angle buttresses. Bulbous cap to its NE turret. Two-storeyed S porch, also with a polygonal turret. Only the four W bays of the N aisle show earlier evidence – they have two-light Dec windows. The battlements and clerestory, however authentic they may look, were only added in 1812, when S.P.Cockerell restored the church. He sent in a bill for over £6,930, and the restoration cost altogether about £10,000, a fantastic sum for that date. It included rebuilding the top stage of the tower. Another restoration, by Christian in 1878, left no old windows. Vestry of 1909 by Sir T.G.Jackson. Cockerell's plaster vault in the nave was replaced in 1954–8. Inside, one finds that the church's bones are not Perp at all. The nave arcades, of five bays, on tall octagonal piers with two hollow chamfers on the arches, must be C13 by the deeply undercut mouldings of bases and capitals. Chancel arch responds, flanked by round shafts, of the same date. Before 1812 the lower part of a tower on clustered piers is reported to have stood over the N aisle. The chancel itself and the chancel chapels are a Perp rebuilding. Two-bay arcades to N and S, with piers of the four-shaft-and-four-hollow variety. – PISCINA with a shelf. – FONT. Perp. – PULPIT. Hexagonal. Ionic pilasters bent across the angles. Small-scale strapwork enrichment. Perspective arches

* The Rev. P.M. Jaquet tells me that the figure of Heyman and that of his wife originally knelt upon the tomb-chest.

on each side. Made in 1635 for £8 10s., by 'the joyner of Sevenoaks'. – STAINED GLASS. Sanctuary s window 1858, and typically bright with pinks and purples. – Tower window 1887 by *Dixon*. – Most of the s aisle windows are filled with *Kempe* glass – dates between 1882 and 1909. – w window 1927 by *Kempe & Tower*. – Windows in a similar style by *Heaton, Butler & Bayne*, 1886 (Resurrection), and *Powell*'s, 1910 (archbishops). – One N aisle window by *Powell*'s, 1879, two by *Kempe & Tower*, 1907. – PLATE. Cup and Paten Cover, 1617, the latter marked *T.F.*; Cup and Paten Cover, 1633 by *W.C.*; Flagon, 1638 by *R.S.*; Paten, 1683. – MONUMENTS. William Lambarde † 1601 and Moulton Lambarde † 1634. The former was the author of *A Perambulation of Kent*, but the latter's death prompted this tablet, with its broken segmental pediment and bold side scrolls hung with plump swags. The half capitals from which the scrolls begin are a typical motif of the 1630s. – Lady Margaret Boswell. The monument was erected in 1692, but it looks more like 1632 in its pattern, a kneeling figure half turning outwards, under a canopy with curtains held by two large angels in long robes. The sculptural quality is not high. – Sir John Fermor † 1722. Signed by *Andrew Carpenter*. Large hanging monument. Two putti lament at the bottom; a curved cornice on fluted pilasters encloses the top. In the centre an extremely demonstrative scrolly cartouche with the inscription. – Admiral Amherst and Lieutenant-General Amherst, 1781. Hanging monument with a trophy of armour. – Jeffery, Lord Amherst, † 1797. A pair to the last. Both monuments are by *W. Tyler*. – Charles, 1st Earl Whitworth, † 1825. By *J.E.Carew*. Unusual for this date in being classical but not Grecian. Very heavy tablet flanked by pilasters on consoles. Bust at the top. – (Sir Thomas Graham Jackson, the architect (*see* above), † 1924. Small tablet, w of the N doorway.)

ST JOHN, St John's Hill. A cheap church. Nave with a big gable-end to the road, 1858–9 by *Morphew & Green*. N aisle 1878. Unfinished E parts of 1901, attempting to rebuild completely on a larger scale.

ST LUKE, Eardley Road. 1903–4 by *J. T. Lee*, completed in reduced circumstances by *F. R. Pite*, 1957–8. – PULPIT. Simple Jacobean, originally at Lynsted. – PAINTING. Last Supper, by *Albani*.

ST MARY, Kippington Road. An expensive church. 1878–80 by *J. M. Hooker*. Cost, £12,500. This gave a spacious building, with a big tower over the SW porch, plenty of shafting, e.g. on the clerestory inside, and plenty of sculpture. Rock-faced ragstone. E.E. – FONT. Marble. Said to have been copied from one in Florence Cathedral. – STAINED GLASS, in every single window. Chancel glass by *Heaton, Butler & Bayne*; w rose window by *Clayton & Bell*.

ST THOMAS OF CANTERBURY (R.C.), Granville Road. 1896 by *F. A. Walters*. Romanesque. Rendered. The sanctuary rises high outside, and bears a spirelet. No drama however inside. w front and tower added by *Walters* in 1925.

CONGREGATIONAL CHURCH, St John's Hill. Conspicuously situated on an angle site. The thin tower clasped by steep roofs does not make the most of it. Peculiar cross-gables along the side with an alternation of windows between normal eaves and round ones with a fancy flowing pattern. The gables also are alternately tall and short. Ragstone. The architect was *J. Tarring*, the date 1865.

PUBLIC BUILDINGS

SEVENOAKS SCHOOL. A school for the free education of poor children was founded in 1432, by Sir William Sennocke, himself a foundling and Lord Mayor of London. When the school and the almshouses that went with them were rebuilt in 1724–32, designs were provided by no less a personage and no less an architect than *Lord Burlington*. The designs, published in 1727 by William Kent, do not correspond in detail with the present buildings. Naturally Burlington would not supervise a job like this, and it was no doubt the local masons who introduced modifications as work went on. What suggests that local men were in charge is the building material, roughly squared ragstone blocks with stone chippings in the cracks (i.e. galletted). The architect would surely have insisted on a more urbane texture than results from this local technique. The buildings are grouped with the almshouses in two long blocks beside the road, and the school as a tall pavilion set back in the centre of the composition. The almshouses are kept plain, as if they were the farm buildings of a Palladio villa, two-storeyed except in the centre, where, over a rusticated archway, there is a blind third storey and a pedimental gable. Six bays either side of the archway, with superimposed niches between the third and fourth bays. Blank Venetian windows on the short ends. The school has the centre three bays of four storeys under a low pyramidal roof with a white octagonal lantern at the apex. The wings are of only two bays, and a storey lower than the centre. Here are the doorways, round-headed and rusticated. The windows on the two main floors of the centre have the same form, the top windows raised surrounds with ears and prominent keystones. The r. wing has been heightened, and upsets the symmetry. Visually it would be well worth while to take it down to its original height. Modern buildings, none of them noteworthy, behind.

LADY BOSWELL'S SCHOOL, London Road. Dated 1818, and *C. R. Cockerell*'s first building. It is almost vernacular in style,* a three-bay block under a pediment, with the lower windows set in sunk arches. The doorways in one-bay extensions each side, originally low, but later heightened. The only evidence that the architect was a man of sensitivity is in the careful interplay of smooth ashlar and rougher ragstone.

WALTHAMSTOW HALL SCHOOL, Holly Bush Lane. Built in 1878–82 by *E. C. Robins*, to educate the daughters of Christian missionaries of all denominations. Red brick, tile-hung at the top. Arched chimneystacks. Gables. Large, and, in spite of these Norman-Shavian ingredients, institutional in appearance.

WILDERNESSE SECONDARY SCHOOL, Seal Hollow Road. Very low and spreading, nowhere more than one storey high. By *S. H. Loweth*, the County Architect, and completed in 1950, as a primary school. Second stage completed in 1962.

HOSPITAL, OUTPATIENTS AND MATERNITY BLOCK, Hospital Road. 1964–5 by *Gollins, Melvin, Ward & Partners* in association with *C. F. Scott*, Architect to the Regional Hospital Board. An independent block, across the road from the main hospital buildings, so nothing blurs its admirable crispness. Grey structure. White spandrel panels. The joints emphasized in black. The upper storey of the rectangular block is carried out past the lower on all sides, on steel supports of I section. It is to form the nucleus of a whole new hospital.

PERAMBULATION

The High Street begins at the very s end of the town, with a view at the start across Knole Park. (For Knole, *see* p. 342.)

* Mr Eugene Dodd on the other hand calls it a 'neat little essay in Laugierian fundamentalism'. There was only £500 to spend; so Cockerell could not have the cast-iron principals he wanted inside.

In the relatively short stretch before it divides and descends into the valley, there are more worthwhile buildings than in almost any other street in the county. OAK END starts the r. side, C18, dark brown brick, with a three-storeyed projecting porch. Cosmetic work by *Baillie Scott & Beresford* has made it properly unassertive. The first loud chord is struck by the ROYAL OAK HOTEL, a plain, strong, highly effective front of *c.*1820. Three tall storeys; five bays, the centre three recessed a little. Ragstone walling, with red-brick quoins and red-brick rustication up the sides of the windows. Wide but shallow porch on squat coupled Tuscan columns, not fluted. Scrolly ironwork balcony above. It faces the restrained ranges of Burlington's school. This side continues more humbly, with attractive tile-hung cottages, including the POST OFFICE; timber-framed of course underneath. Just by the entrance to Knole Park and just before the church, each side has a worthwhile house. On the r. MANOR HOUSE, lying back and not part of the street, a square ragstone house of *c.*1800, of five bays in a 2–1–2 rhythm marked by giant pilasters, with Portland stone slabs as capitals. The austerity is lightened by the pretty fanlight of the front door. On the other side of the road an equally idiosyncratic late C17 red-brick house, THE CHANTRY. It stands right on the street, with a centre of five bays and short one-bay wings touching the pavement. Blank ovals of rubbed brick in the blind windows on the sides of the wings. Over the plain doorcase the centre window has a raised brick surround (now painted white), crowned by the stabbing sides of a little open pediment. White string-course and white dentilled cornice. The casement windows are modern, but just right. Staircase with charming turned balusters. Addition of 1905 to the S, reticent on the street side, but all-out William-and-Mary towards the garden. C17 garden walls, one brick of which is dated 1686. That might date the house, or it might be just a shade early.

Beyond the church the late C18 OLD VICARAGE, with a rusticated doorcase that is worth a glance. As the road bends and narrows, OLD HOUSE, another fine front of *c.*1700, very awkwardly placed on the corner. Red brick flecked with blue vitrified bricks. It has seven bays altogether, and two storeys with a hipped slate roof. The centre bay is wide and breaks forward with brick ovals flanking window and doorway. It is indeed just wide enough to accommodate a steep pediment. White dentilled cornice. White doorcase, a broad segmental pediment on fluted Doric pilasters. Thereafter cottages on both sides, broken only by TEMPLE HOUSE, tall, gabled, and of very red brick, a typically insensitive insertion of 1884, insensitively plonked on a grass mound. The street's valedictory gesture on the l. is THE WHITE HOUSE, stuccoed, of three-plus-three-plus-three bays, the centre rising up with a pediment. Across the upper half a row of stunted Corinthian pilasters, the debased classicism of c.1840. THE RED HOUSE, opposite, is the finest house in the street, built in 1686 for John Couchman of Tooting. It represents the late C17 ideal. Red brick. Seven bays (bays one and seven are narrow ones) with lower one-bay wings set back at the sides. Two storeys. Big hipped roof with a deep cornice on richly carved brackets. Bold, plain chimneystacks. The doorcase is the only false note, a late C18 insertion with elongated attached columns. Staircase with two twisted balusters per tread, not yet as elegantly carpentered as early C18 staircases usually are. The C18 STABLES stand to the r., end-on to the road. Blocked doorway with a vermiculated surround.

So ends the really worthwhile part of the town. The perambulation may however be prolonged considerably to take in a few minor items. As the road divides, the High Street continues as the r. fork. At once a gaggle of neo-Georgian banks signalizes the beginning of the modern shopping centre. At the very junction the MIDLAND BANK of 1922–3 by *Whinney Son & Austen Hall*, who could think of nothing more exciting to do than have a bowed end and stone for brick on the corner. No more comment is needed until, at the corner of DORSET STREET, the amusing MARKET HOUSE of 1843, originally open on an arcade and with a top pediment. Rendered, but given a fillip by the terracotta panels between the windows and a terracotta frieze of swags. If they were not inserted later, that is a very early date in the C19 for terracotta. BLIGH'S HOTEL was an isolated Tudor farmhouse, now much restored. Further down, when the shops have ended, THE VINE, a triangular cricket ground, with an interesting early C19 weatherboarded CRICKET PAVILION at the S end. VINE HOUSE faces the lower end of The Vine. It is late C18, square, red brick, and of unsatisfactory proportions. Doorcase with vermiculated rustication and a head on the keystone, like the doorcases in Bedford Square, but meanly proportioned.

If one returns to the dividing of the roads again and takes the l. fork, there is a little more to see. A short way down on the r. is

Lady Boswell's School. On the l., in SOUTH PARK, the offices of MARLEY TILES, a modern block of brick, with windows in long bands. 1965 by *J. H. Alleyn*. The next road to the N is LIME TREE WALK, where a row of twenty-four cottages on the r. and a hall, originally a COFFEE HOUSE, are early works of *Sir T. G. Jackson*. The latter is dated 1882.* Architecturally the cottages are especially successful, exploiting the slight slope to add variety to an already varied array of gables, dormers, and oriel windows. Red brick and rendering. Complex Dutch gables on the Coffee House. Socially the scheme was even more enterprising, and gives one a good deal of respect for Jackson and his father, who together bought the land and developed it for working men, in the middle of an area earmarked for 'high-class development', in an attempt to break down class localization. The sort of environment, cosy and cleverly designed, with plenty of visual variety, which Norman Shaw and his collaborators had produced for their middle-class suburb at Bedford Park in the 1870s, the Jacksons were ready to offer to those whom only a few like Ruskin and William Morris would have credited with the aesthetic sensibility to appreciate it. 1878-9 is the date of the cottages.

Lower down the hill, first, EARDLEY ROAD, off which is the drive to the EMILY JACKSON WING HOSPITAL, built in 1901 by *Sir T. G. Jackson* as a hospital, in a full-blooded William-and-Mary style. Not many architects were then reproducing it with such archaeological correctness. Canted wings, however, and his favourite materials, rendered walls and red-brick dressings. Tremendous grey slate hipped roof. In CLARENDON ROAD, the continuation of Eardley Road, LYNCH HOUSE, 1899 by *Niven & Wigglesworth*, neatly epitomizes the ideals of the opposite camp. Red brick and shaped gables are the themes, on which witty variations are played without recourse to symmetry. TUBS HILL HOUSE, near the foot of the hill, with two nine-storey slabs at r. angles to the road, is on a scale new to Sevenoaks. Alas, it is thuddingly dull architecture. Just before the railway, on the r., ST BOTOLPH'S AVENUE, co-operative housing of 1906 by *Unwin*. More co-operative housing of 1903-6 in HOLYOAKE TERRACE, immediately across the railway. Finally, a short way further along the London Road, BOSPHORUS HOUSE in KIPPINGTON ROAD. This, by *Leslie Gooday*, c.1961-2, though quite small, shows a more radical approach to de-

* And has a staircase made from the altar rails of the church, of 1732.

signing a house than anything else in the town. In plan the ground floor consists of two interlocked Ls, and the cedar-clad bedroom block rides above them, supported independently on six piers of its own. The house is nice to look at, too.

KIPPINGTON HOUSE, much further up Kippington Road. The house was almost rebuilt after 1760 by Sir Charles Farnaby. Seven bays, the centre three under a pediment, and projecting slightly. The brickwork has been rendered and is now painted a pale green. Early c19 porch and big additions behind. The chaste marble chimneypieces in hall etc. are by *Adam* himself, 1764.

COTTAGES in Mill Lane, Greatness, 1½ m. N. Ten two-storeyed cottages, built of local ragstone, and made into a composition by the pediment over the centre. They were built by the Nouaille family *c.*1765 to house the workers in their lace factory at Greatness. The black-boarded MILL higher up the lane has been rebuilt since lace-making days. Another, plainer, row of COTTAGES round the corner.

BRADBOURNE FARM, Bradbourne Vale Road, near Riverhead. A delightful example of a common type; *c.*1700. Red brick chequered with blue headers. Five bays. Two storeys. Hipped roof; dormers. Deep white cornice and white stringcourse. Late c18 doorcase. The farm buildings make a fine group.

SEAL HOLLOW HOUSE, Bayham Road. 1908 by *Baillie Scott.* It is sad to report that, at the time of writing, ten houses are being built in the garden, and that the house has lost the garage (a very early garage) from the E end and the billiard-room from the W. Still, the rest is safe, a small but good example of Baillie Scott's early manner. Roughcast, L-shaped, the porch on the N side characteristically sunk within the building. Half-timbered gable l. of it. The centre of the S front is taken up with a gable and a polygonal bay under a candle-snuffer cap. Because of the gently sloping site there is much play with changes of room-level inside. The main rooms all face S. Two excellent fireplaces, one with a copper hood, the other tiled.

SEVENOAKS WEALD

ST GEORGE. Nave and W tower of 1820, chancel of 1872 by *T. G. Jackson.* Outside and in, the contrast between the two parts could not be more telling. Compare e.g. the bare, under-cusped Dec tracery of the nave windows (in Portland stone) with Jackson's line-for-line sandstone copies of the windows at Chartham. The interior of the chancel glows with stencilling – there are even rosettes on the window-mullions. Awkward conflict between stylized foliage patterns and hyperrealistic figure scenes. – The STAINED GLASS, also by *Jackson*, shows especially painfully what a flabby designer he really was. E window 1872, N window 1874, both made by *Powell & Sons*. – REREDOS. Mosaic. By *T. Gambier-Parry*.

WICKHURST MANOR, ¾ m. w. Embedded in the C19 house is a large medieval hall, with an open crown-post roof. The masonry of the centre of the S front belongs to it. C15 moulded stone doorway at the l. Two-centred arch, but of the large square-headed windows only one hood-mould is original.

SEVINGTON

0040

ST MARY. Lonely and a little forlorn, as it will always have been. The nave must be Norman in its walling, as the E arch to the narrow, windowless S aisle has a round head. A second, pointed arch, with a slight chamfer, shows that the aisle was extended towards the w *c.*1200. E.E. chancel. The two E lancets originally shafted inside. Arch from chancel to aisle too low to pass through without stooping. The broad, originally unbuttressed w tower also E.E. Tower arch on crude C14 head corbels. Tall, shingled broach-spire. Perp window high in the N wall, to light the rood. What was the pointed recess below it for? Medieval timber S porch, as simple as can be. – STAINED GLASS. The jumble in a nave N window includes a dainty little C14 Virgin and Child. – Indents of seven large BRASSES. What a show they must once have made!

SHADOXHURST

9030

ST PETER AND ST PAUL. A humble, pretty church, thoroughly but sympathetically restored in 1868–9. The peculiar part is the w end, where a tiny pyramidal bellcote sits on an arch formed by the merging of two buttresses. E.E. chancel. One large N lancet, and another on the s.* Otherwise the building is of the Dec period. Ogee quatrefoils in the nave windows. Standard C14 chancel arch. AUMBRY, PISCINA, and SEDILE, formed on the dropped sill of a lancet, and reticulated E window comprise the remodelling of the chancel. Crown-post

* The w lancet in the nave is modern.

nave roof. Large stone brackets in the E jambs of the NE and SE windows of the nave must have supported the rood loft. The floor level will necessarily have been lower then. C18 brick S porch. – ARMOUR. Helm, sword, and gauntlets in the chancel. – STAINED GLASS. C14 fragments in two N quatrefoils. More pieces in the W lancet. – PLATE. Cup of 1562. – MONUMENT. Admiral Sir Charles Molloy † 1760. A splendid72 hanging monument, of white and yellow marble, totally unexpected in these surroundings.* It must be by *Cheere*. A mourning putto holds a medallion with an excellently characterized relief bust of the Admiral. On either side sprout out cannons, compasses, and other nautical paraphernalia. Handsome inscription in a handsome Baroque surround.

At the W gate of the churchyard is what seems to be a stone cottage with shaped gables. It is in fact the SCHOOL, dated 1846 e.g. on its comical lead down-pipe. The gables are the trademark of C19 estate building by the Tokes of Godinton (cf. Great Chart).

C20 bungalows trail along most of the roads in the parish.

SHIPBOURNE

ST GILES. Rebuilt in 1721–2 by *James Gibbs* and once again in 1880–1 by *Mann & Saunders*, at the expense of Edward Cazalet of Fairlawne.‡ Not large, E.E., but making a show, in the way estate churches tend to do. Cruciform, the central tower vaulted in stone within. Stiff leaf carving and wall stencilling in plenty inside, and a vulgar PULPIT. – PLATE. Cup and Paten Cover, 1624, the latter by *R.B.* – MONUMENT. 1st Lord Barnard † 1723. The monument, erected in his lifetime, was designed by *Gibbs*, and the character of the carving makes it almost certain that the young *Rysbrack* was the sculptor. It is on a grand scale: Lord and Lady Barnard sit pensively one each side of a large urn on a gadrooned base, and in front of it their daughter reclines. Corinthian pilasters and top pediment with putti on the sloping sides. Rather meagre flowers framing the inscription.

Estate housing near the church, notably a jolly pub of c.1881 to the S, and a double cottage answering it on the N. Lower

---

* Molloy was Lord of the Manor, and did not live in this desolate forested area.

‡ Part of an arch of the medieval church remains in the N wall of the vestry, so the Ven. E. E. Maples Earle reports.

down, across the road, first LADY VANE CLOSE, more estate housing, as recent as 1955, flats in two-storeyed blocks making three sides of a square. The architect was *Kenneth G. Miller*. s again, the PRIMARY SCHOOL, 1852, of galletted ragstone, with red-brick dressings, mid-C19 vernacular characteristic of these villages between Tonbridge and the Downs.

The village lies on the w side of a big undulating green. On its
96   s side one house of national interest, THE WOOD HOUSE, 1937 by *Walter Gropius* himself, completed by *Maxwell Fry* after Gropius had left for the United States. The successors to The Wood House are across the Atlantic. The name is significant: at a time when the whiteness of reinforced concrete seemed the inevitable idiom to express the modernism of the thirties Gropius turned back to natural materials. The facing material is creosoted weatherboarding, the eaves, painted white, project boldly on the ends of the roof timbers. Two-storeyed s block, with a low wing running back at both ends, the w one part of the house, and ending with the garage, the e one merely sheds. Vertically proportioned windows grouped in long rows. The roofs all tilted slightly, and with many variations in level.

SHIRLEY FARM *see* WOODCHURCH

5060   ## SHOREHAM

St PETER AND St PAUL. Largely Late Perp. Nave and chancel in one. s aisle stretching the full length, with a continuous arcade on piers of four shafts and four hollows. Timber s porch. This must be Late Perp too, though the corner posts are vast, so vast that the doorway spandrels are carved out of the solid. E.E. tower arch and, inside the tower, parts of two windows and the w doorway. Early Dec N wall: see the RECESS with an arch on stops of naturalistic foliage, vine, and buttercup. The short N chapel Early Perp.* Large w tower, an enjoyably self-confident hybrid of *c.*1775, of flint with lavish red-brick trimmings. The church was drastically restored in 1864 by *Woodyer*, who rebuilt the chancel and added the NE vestry. But the long, evenly-lit interior pleases, for its fittings, for its monuments, and for the old flagstones, salvaged from the demolished Shoreham Place and laid here in 1957. – ROOD SCREEN. A unique survival for Kent in that it extends the full

---

* In 1956–7 the foundations of the Norman chancel (*c.*12 ft square) were found under the nave.

width of the church and keeps its loft, coved both to W and E. Of the Devon type, though plain by Devon standards. Just one band of vine trail and cresting. The tracery is almost all modern. – ORGAN CASE. 1730, from Westminster Abbey. It encased the organ given by George II for his Coronation. – PULPIT. Wood, also from Westminster Abbey. Designed in 1827 by *Blore*. The Geometrical tracery under crocketed gables is unexpectedly convincing for its date. Cut down.* – STAINED GLASS. Joy, Creation, and Love, 1903 by *Morris & Co.* to *Burne-Jones*'s design (A. C. Sewter). Large Botticellian figures. – MONUMENTS. Four to various members of the Borrett family, all incorporating busts. Two are signed by *Sir Henry Cheere* and the others must be by him too. – Anne Borrett † 1725. – John Borrett † 1739 and wife. Black sarcophagus between busts on low pedestals. Tall obelisk behind. – Sir Abraham Shard † 1746 and wife (née Borrett). White sarcophagus between busts on high pedestals. Obelisk behind. – Susannah Borrett † 1751. Superb architectural parts, but the busts are disturbingly cold and aloof.

The sweeping hills of the Shoreham Valley have not changed much since Samuel Palmer's day. The village is large and varied. From the church at the E end the street runs gently down to the river Darent. Beside the lychgate is a funny flint COTTAGE, banded vertically with red brick, the bricks projecting occasionally. At once the road squeezes between a row of cottages on the r. and the jettied corner of the OLD GEORGE INN. Thereafter houses on the N side only. At the bottom, where the road meets the stream, RIVERSIDE HOUSE, dated 1774. Red brick and grey headers. Doorcase on Tuscan half-columns. The road now turns l. over the river, but a lane continues on the E side. In the lane FLINT COTTAGE, another, even more hectic variant on the local flint and brick vernacular. Colossal warty flints. Over the door a roundel in a niche apparently made of clinkers. Then WATER HOUSE, stuccoed, where Samuel Palmer used to stay but looking a little later than 1830. A little further down the lane is a good modern HOUSE by *J. M. Austin-Smith & Partners*, c.1959.

Over the river nothing to notice individually, though there are many pleasant cottages.

DUNSTALL PRIORY, ½ m. NE. Originally called Gold-hill. Described as 'new building' in 1806, when *Robert Lugar* exhibited his design. He had published a similar one in *Architec-*

* Mr Laurence Tanner kindly provided these details.

tural Sketches the year before. It is an Italianate villa, one of the very first. Nash's Cronkhill is only four years older. Two-storeyed throughout, but of two different heights. At the s end, to look down the valley, a round tower rises above the roof-line. (Cronkhill also has such a tower.) What Lugar misses is Nash's feeling for picturesque grouping.

By the main road two large Grecian URNS in the hedge.

FILSTON HALL, ¾ m. SW. A delightful but puzzling C17 moated house. Brick. Two storeys on a basement. Three gables to N and S. The fronts are not symmetrical, though they make some attempt to be. A date in the second quarter of the century seems to be indicated, though the house must have been tampered with later. The datestone of 1690 could even refer to reconstruction of the walls, for the bonding is all Flemish (English bonding however in the cellars and the attics). The s wall recased in the C20. Staircase with strong turned balusters. Big internal doorcase and panelling, late C17.

SHOREHAM CASTLE, 1 m. N. The farmhouse displays to the E a twice-projecting gable-end with closely set uprights. Its s wall is built into a chunk of flint walling 6 ft thick which narrows and curves round to the E.

SHORNE

ST PETER AND ST PAUL. Quite a jigsaw puzzle. Every century from the C11 to the C15 has contributed. The earliest evidence externally is the lancet in the W wall of the N aisle. Its opposite number in the s aisle is early C14, with cusped intersecting tracery. Dec windows in the N aisle and N chapel. Perp N porch, of stone. Five-light Perp E window. The s aisle banded with flint and stone, a C14 mannerism in this part of Kent (cf. e.g. Cliffe, Higham). Otherwise the s side all renewed in 1874–5 by *T. H. Wyatt*, who was entirely responsible for the aggressive plate tracery of the s chapel. It is hard now to understand the frame of mind of a restorer who in 1873 could publish details of the original windows in a book on Gothic Architecture (by Raphael Brandon, Wyatt's partner), then two years later completely renew many of them and overtrump them all with new ones of his own design. Perp W tower. Flint. Diagonal buttresses. Disorganized octagonal NE turret. The growth of the church can be unravelled only inside. The first thread is Saxon, the wall through which the N arcade is pierced. Over the centre arch a double-splayed window. The w bay of the N arcade in the chancel also has walling of Saxon thinness. Possibly the E arch of the nave arcade opened originally into a N *porticus*. The arch is round-headed, with a single square order on chamfered imposts. Square jambs. The next bay of the N aisle was opened up late in the C12. Pointed arch on round responds. Also the respond of an arch across the N aisle, and a small Late Norman capital reset beside it, carved with two grotesque heads. The C13 saw great enlargements: a W bay to the N aisle, a N chancel chapel, and a new chancel arch, of which only a stretch of filleted angle roll half-hiding dogtooth remains low down on each side. Later in the century the Saxon chancel was tripled in length, with chapels the full distance. The arches here are doubly hollow-chamfered and have hood-moulds. Octagonal E respond each side, a circular pier, and, on the N, a tall, slender shaft acting as a W respond. The S side altered in the C14. Three-bay C14 S aisle of standard design. The chancel arch remodelled, and almost certainly widened, in the same century. Tall C15 tower arch. – FONT. Perp. Seven of the eight faces of the bowl are carved. Working clockwise from the E the subjects are: Chalice with a rayed host, Baptism of Christ, St Michael weighing souls, IHS on a shield, blank, Lamb and Flag, St Peter as a bishop holding a church, the Resurrection. By East Anglian standards not especially impressive, but in Kent only Southfleet can compare with it – the comparison is a close one. – CHAN-DELIERS. A pair of small brass ones in the sanctuary. – ORGAN CASE. Given in 1817. Gothick. – PLATE. Cup, 1597; Paten, 1734. – MONUMENTS. Cross-legged Knight. Stone. Late C13. Very worn, but it must have originally been an effigy of high quality. He turns half to his right and lethargically makes to draw his sword. – John Smyth † 1457. Brass demi-figures only 6 in. high. – The lower half of a brass of a lady, c.1470. – Elynor Allen † 1583. 18 in. brass. – George Page † 1611. Four large kneeling figures, two and two, under coffered arches. Bad.

Until the last year or two the village was nothing but a short street running up the hillside N of the church. Now there are patches of new housing all over the place. Something good could have been made of expansion even on this scale, especially in the dell down from the E end of the church, but not by dotting the houses about one by one, careless of the contours and of one another.

ST KATHERINE'S CHAPEL, ¼ m. N. C14 flint chapel, banded

with stone on the N side. Single-light windows with ogee heads. PISCINA and shafted SEDILE. Nearly doubled in length in the C15. Suppressed in 1545. Restored as the chapel of a R.C. convent shortly before 1898. New E window.

SHORTLANDS

4060

ST MARY. 1953–5 by *Ansell & Bailey*. – SCULPTURE. On the W front. The Flight into Egypt by *John Skeaping*.

KINGSWOOD HOUSE, Valley Road. A comfortably designed Old People's Home, on a sloping site, by *Clifford Culpin & Partners*, completed 1963.

SIDCUP

4070

ST ANDREW, Maylands Drive. 1964 by *D.F.Martin-Smith*. Ingenious, fashionable, and slightly absurd. In plan an octagon, set on a slope so that the church proper, reached from the road by a glazed bridge, occupies only the roof. The walls, of charcoal brick with a band of windows above, are the walls of the parish room. The roof swoops down on four sides, and on the other four comes forward as sharp gables glazed at the ends. It makes of course a centralized building, and a very small one.

CHRIST CHURCH, Main Road. 1900–1 by *A.R.Barker & Son*. Ragstone banded with ashlar. Plate tracery in the tall clerestory. Lancets in triplets in the low pent aisles. Chancel with a canted apse. It reads like the description of a church of the 1870s. SE tower never begun.

ST JOHN, Church Road. 1882–99 by *Fellowes-Prynne*. Impressively big in scale, E.E., of stock brick, the dressings in red brick and stone, an artificial red stone in the chancel. The stump of a SW tower. Very long clerestoried nave, with clustered piers, the inevitable stone screen, and tiers of saints on the slant each side of it. Nobility is what Fellowes-Prynne aimed at, the nobility Pearson achieved so effortlessly. He does not achieve it for two reasons: first, there is not enough tension in the proportions, the nave especially seeming broad and spreading; and secondly, the details are largely left to look after themselves. See, e.g., the way the vaulting-shafts reach aimlessly down the wall, unrelated to the arcades; or the useless transepts, twelve inches deeper than the aisles, their sole function to create a mild diversion outside. – PULPIT. Oak.

Inscribed: Antwerp 1651. Twisted columns at the angles, relief busts of the four Evangelists on the sides.

St Lawrence (R.C.), Main Road. 1906 by *Edward Goldie*.* Stock brick. Round-arched style. Cruciform, with a shallow central dome, expressed outside by a low octagon gabled in the four main directions.

Holy Trinity, Lamorbey. Built by *Christian* in 1879 and restored in 1949 after bomb damage. The ragstone laid crazy-paving style gives it a c19 texture; but the planning, nave and gabled aisles somewhat subordinated, chancel with short gabled chapels, is medievalizing, and the effect inside is really remarkably like a medieval church. Dec tracery with no Victorian fancies.

Congregational Church. 1887–8 by *G. Baines*. Plate tracery with foiled openings like a series of explosions all over the building.

Cray Valley Technical School, Sidcup Bypass. 1938 by *Christiani & Nielsen*. A design that has worn extremely well. Deep red brick and extensive glazing. The se front is symmetrical, three-storeyed, the bands of windows turning the corners at the ends. Set back at each end two glazed staircase towers with bowed ends, *à la* Gropius. The entrance however comes at the extreme r. end, and starts the highly asymmetrical NE front, dominated by the glazed bow, and gradually dying away into the slope via a completely glazed hall block. The higher part behind is a later addition.

Queen Mary's Hospital. *See* Frognal House, below.

Sidcup is Chislehurst *ultra montes*, or at any rate Chislehurst N of the A20. Its classiness was diminished in the building boom between the wars, and several recent office blocks are changing its character again. Yet even now the c18 flavour of mansions in their parks is not completely lost. It will be best to deal with these survivors first.

Frognal House, Frognal Avenue. Large, roughly square house, early c18 in appearance, but certainly not in origin. The E front is the grandest, two-storeyed like the rest, but eleven bays wide, and the windows segment-headed and tall in their proportions. Yellow and red brick. Top parapet. Central doorcase with richly carved brackets. But the windows cluster together in one place, their regularity disturbed by the pre-existing work behind. Badeslade's print of 1719 shows the

---

* Information from Mr D. Evinson.

front as it is now. Not so the s front, which in 1719 had a row of shaped gables instead of the present parapet curving up at the ends. The shorter windows, rougher brickwork, and moulded brick cornice on this side all go with the mid-c17 date that such gables imply. Eleven bays again, nine windows and two blank spaces at the r. The N and W fronts quite irregular. The kernel is probably a courtyard house, but Philipot mentions 'additional Building annexed to the ancient Structure' early in the c17. Fine early c18 STAIRCASE, with the usual carved tread-ends, one twisted and one fluted baluster per step, issuing from bulbs of foliage, and, to make it extra grand, fluted Corinthian columns as newels.

Early c18 wrought-iron GATES in the long wall that follows the road.

The house is now part of Queen Mary's Hospital, and a promising programme of reconstruction of the hospital has begun N and W of it. So far, as follows: the MATERNITY DEPARTMENT, off Chislehurst Road. 1966 by *C. F. Scott*, Regional Architect (*E. J. Wilson*, project architect). Two-storey square block, formed on the entrance (N) side into a symmetrical group, which recedes from a grey-brick fore-building, to the shiny white main block with, again recessed, a black cube of water-tanks and other essentials frankly revealed at the top. The NURSES' HOUSING, N of Frognal House, steps gently down the hill, in series of linked pavilions, and at the N end in flat-roofed blocks. Completed 1965, by *W. H. Watkins*, *Gray & Partners*. Both architects are to collaborate in further new buildings in 1968–9.

LAMORBEY PARK, Burnt Oak Lane. Built *c.*1744–8 for William Steele, but altered in 1784 (the date on a rainwater-head). To judge from a plan made after this date, it was then, as now, a three-storeyed house of eight not-quite-regular bays by five, with low wings to the W. Some time after 1812 *John Shaw Sen.* regularized the rectangular external outlines, making it nine bays by three, with porch-bays to the E in bays three and seven. It is now faced with stock brick, with Jacobean trimmings, panels of strapwork in the parapet, and strapwork cresting to the projections. The bay-window to the S which already existed got mullions and transoms, and curious three-dimensional strapwork finials. What was the date of all this? Jacobeanisms as early as the second decade of the c19 would be highly remarkable.

Visually the centre of Sidcup, in so far as it can be said to have a centre at all, is THE GREEN. And the *clou* of The Green is the MANOR HOUSE (now Council Offices). Late c18,* of pinky brick laid with, for that date, remarkable roughness. Three-storeyed, the façade to The Green of five bays, extended on each side by the profiles of the full-grown bows on the side façades. The three middle bays are as it were a frontispiece pedimented, with white string-courses and the centre windows under a giant sunk arch. The porch is four very thin Tuscan columns; the window above it vestigial Venetian. Seven windows on the N side, all but the central one in two full-scale bows.

SIDCUP PLACE, S of The Green, has an c18 core. This had the remarkable plan of a square of three bays, with rectangular projections diagonally at the corners. Only the E one stands free now, from additions of 1853, c.1896, and the 1920s. The tradition is that it was built in imitation of a fort, in 1743.‡ (Splendid late c18 marble chimneypiece with large nymphs in relief at the sides, and small nymphs dancing in the frieze. NMR)

N of The Green, in STATION ROAD, two new six-storey office blocks, not large, but as emphatic as the mid 1960s can be. SIDCUP HOUSE, 1965 by *Bernard Engle & Partners*, has an open ground storey on thumping great V-shaped piers, and the OFFICES N of it grow in two directions from a tower-like structure of exposed concrete housing the staircases. By the *Owen Luder Partnership*, 1966. N again, by the station, a long, thin, sixteen-storey slab of OFFICES, completed in 1966. The architects were *Douglas Marriott & Partners*, and precious little of architectural qualities they managed to infuse into it.

Further N and E, in Blackfen Road, CHAPEL HOUSE, built c.1760 as an eyecatcher at the S end of Danson Park. It is nothing but a roughcast cottage, with a lead spire at its N end, and a low flattened turret towards the road. The traceried windows must be part of a c19 remodelling.

A postscript is needed on the FACTORIES beside the Sidcup Bypass, at the far SE corner of Sidcup. KLINGERIT, 1935–6 by *Wallis Gilbert & Partners*, shows knowledge of Dutch Expressionist brickwork. Symmetrical block. Brown brick of two shades, the paler laid in the usual way, the reddy bricks

* 1790, says Mr B. N. Nunns.

‡ But Mr Nunns notes that the house is not marked on Andrews, Dury, and Herbert's map of 1769. *Joseph Trought* exhibited a design of a house with this plan in 1767.

mostly laid on end. They add emphasis to the horizontal strips of window and the verticals of the centrepiece. Also little windows across angles, with projecting frames to draw attention to this feat. The swoopy italic lettering goes a good way to cancel out the jaggedness. Other modernistic details. SCHWEPPES, by the roundabout, is of 1961–2, a big-boned piece by *Tripe & Wakeham*.

SINGLETON MANOR *see* GREAT CHART

7030
SISSINGHURST

HOLY TRINITY. 1837–8 by *J. Jennings* of Hawkhurst. Well built of squared sandstone blocks, but otherwise a poor thing, with a lean W tower and the usual wide nave and stunted chancel. Lancets. The E triplet with its hood-mould on demi-angels is the only personal flicker.

SISSINGHURST CASTLE. The soaring brick tower rises improbably above the wooded hillocks of the Weald. It is all that remains of a great Elizabethan courtyard-house, built apparently by Sir Richard Baker, who inherited in 1558, entertained Queen Elizabeth at Sissinghurst in 1573, and died in 1594. The entrance range that confronts the visitor is not part of that house, but of an earlier one. It is of red brick with a wide four-centred entrance archway in the middle, the hood-mould and shields in the spandrels renewed. Three-storeyed gabled bays flank it. The windows here are brick, four-centred, sunk within surrounds and with weak hood-moulds above. The brick tracery is modern. At ground level, in each projecting bay, a wide, deep, blank arch, like a fireplace opening. What were they for? The r. bay has a moulded string-course at the sides, continued for some way along the adjoining wall, but the l. does not. On the inner side the gable is over the archway and there are two tall chimneystacks beside it.[*] Contemporary two-storey brick ranges each side, the r. one extended further probably in the C17. The Elizabethan mansion was built on the axis of the entrance arch, but not parallel with the entrance range. Ranges of rooms were built only round three sides of the courtyard, and on the fourth (W) had been the gate-tower stood in the centre of a simple wall. This had been a normal French château plan since Bury (begun 1511), but

---

[*] The coat of arms over the archway, dated 1548, is irrelevant; it was brought from Carnock, Stirlingshire.

was not usual in England. The four-storeyed gate-tower is[45] wholly built of brick, with quoins, windows, string-courses, etc., rendered to imitate stone. In plan it is a rectangle with an octagon attached to the middle of the short sides. These octagonal side-turrets are carried up a little higher than the main part and originally ended in bulbous cupolas, for which shingled caps have been substituted, with big weather-vanes, dated 1839. The outer arch is four-centred, but the large four-light windows in each storey above have a transom but no arched heads, and, instead of hood-moulds, pieces of entablature above them. On the inner side there is more emphatic classical detail, a round arch, and two superimposed orders of Tuscan pilasters framing the arch and the window above. Such classical motifs – and there were more in the demolished ranges, including the hall porch with coupled columns in two tiers – presuppose the classicism of Old Somerset House (1547–52), though such exaggeratedly high gate-towers had already developed to the climax of say Layer Marney in the early 1520s. Of the two COTTAGES embowered in the enchanting gardens the NE one, square, with a gable in each direction, was always isolated from the main ranges but may also be C16. The SE cottage, however, was the SE corner of the courtyard house, though it now has no feature of interest.

SLADE GREEN see ERITH

SMALLHYTHE

8030

By the roadside, a tiny group of great charm, just two humble tile-hung cottages on the W, but on the E not only the church,[43] but also PRIEST'S HOUSE and SMALLHYTHE PLACE, two splendid early C16 half-timbered houses, both close-studded and with the upper storey overhanging right across the front. Both restored, but the oak untreated and the infill buff, leaving them more mellow than most 'black and white' houses. Ellen Terry lived at Smallhythe Place.

ST JOHN THE BAPTIST. The church was rebuilt in 1516–17. It is of red brick, merely a chapel without a structural chancel. The E and W gables stepped; low W porch also with a partly stepped gable and a minute image-niche above. The windows all have brick tracery (renewed), that in the N and S windows a simplified pattern of mouchettes. E window of stone, 1884.

ASHENDEN, ¾ m. N. 'Lately built' in 1798, i.e. with a new red-brick E front, to put a mask of near-symmetry over the jumble behind. The mask has five bays, two storeys, a hipped roof, and dormers. Big doorcase with attached columns (fluted Ionic) and a bulgy frieze and pediment. The house has a wonderful view over a private valley.

SMARDEN

ST MICHAEL. Chancel, and nave much higher and wider (nicknamed 'the barn of Kent'), built of stone, at one go, in the second quarter of the C14. Original fenestration, of uniform two-light windows, and an E three-lighter, with three ogee-lobed quatrefoils over cinquefoiled lights. Late Perp supplements in the nave. The rere-arches are odd, splayed so wide as to lose touch with the windows, and carried down to the floor as shallow recesses. A big corbel head and two colonnettes, of Bethersden marble, are arranged to take a widening of the NE rere-arch. Plain chancel arch, its head supplied at *Clarke*'s self-effacing restoration of 1869. To the l. and r. of it contemporary altar REREDOSES (the painted parts limply supplied in the C20); two rows of little trefoiled arches on corbels, those on the N side crisply carved with leaves and a head or two. At the E end of the chancel not only embattled SEDILIA and a PISCINA, the only features without ogees, but also a low-side window in the SE corner, a curious position, and near it another PISCINA and AUMBRY. Inordinately wide E recess, and small N recess, without dressed stones. Scissor-beam roofs, the nave being too wide for the usual tiebeams. Fine big Perp W tower, better thought out than most. Three stages, divided by strings that lock logically into the set-offs of the diagonal buttresses. Bold battlements. Polygonal NE turret. – FONT. Bethersden marble, desperately worn. Octagonal bowl on nine shafts. Ogee arches on the bowl, so it is of the date of the church. – ALTAR RAILS. Early C18. Slender twisted balusters. – (ALMS BOX. Nailed to the top is an enamelled plate of the Baptism of Christ(?). Limoges? C13?) – STAINED GLASS. *Omnium gatherum* of old bits in the chancel s window. – PLATE. Cup made by *Anthony Nelme*, Paten by *P.E.*, both in 1713.

Smarden, like Tenterden and Cranbrook, was one of the Wealden market towns, licensed by Edward III in 1332. But, unlike them, it never grew bigger than a village. Today it is just one short street, with the church at the W end (cf. Biddenden, Bethersden), a plan made especially charming by the

CHURCH GATE, a tiny quadrangle, open-ended towards the street, with the way into the churchyard through the corner of a house. The village is excellently cared for, but without any of the chi-chi trifles that overlay with a suburban air so many of the best villages in South-East England. The HIGH STREET itself is all modest cottages, continuous on both sides, the half-timbering mostly exposed on the N side, the S cottages almost all weatherboarded. Beyond these DRAGON HOUSE, L-shaped, half-timbered, with a gable twice overhanging towards the road. The dragons come in a frieze on the upper overhang, a C17 embellishment no doubt. Then the street breaks up, with cottages at random, and, on the r., the rendered ZION CHAPEL of 1841, with a pediment. Then another big half-timbered house, CHESSENDEN, the best example in Smarden of the typical Wealden arrangement of an open hall between two-storeyed wings, overhanging but kept within the simple hipped roof. When the hall had a floor put across it, then came the two-storeyed canted bay, and the gable over it. Close studding in the centre. Curved braces in the wings. Blocked four-centred doorway. Finally, on the l. the stone SCHOOL, of 1864.

Two more fine half-timbered houses N of the church, in Water Lane. First HARTNUP HOUSE. The date 1671 refers only to the gable and the window-bay below it. The rest is a century or more older. T-shaped, the N wing overhanging three ways, the S wing brick-nogged. THE CLOTH HALL, close-studded, seems to be a small C16 Wealden-type house, extended at the S end, but not hipped-roofed as usual. Instead a N gable, with a hoist and two loft doors. THATCHED HOUSE, 100 yds SW of the church, is large and early half-timbered. No overhang. Widely spaced uprights. Two-centred doorway of two giant baulks.

Plenty of worthwhile farmhouses in the parish, usually happily grouped with barns and outbuildings. Only a few can be mentioned by name here.

ROMDEN CASTLE, 1 m. E. Externally all C18, with a square four-storeyed tower. Red brick. Before 1866 the three-bay bow had a fellow, and they marked the ends of a symmetrical façade.

HAMDEN, 1¼ m. SE. An almost complete C14 hall-house of a rare type is hidden here, by stone behind and C19 brick (there is a date 1839) in front. Outside, only the entrance to the porch, a two-centred arch made from two baulks of wood, suggests that the house has timber framing; and only the very long sweep of tiled roof on the r. half suggests the construction of the hall, with vestigial aisles. Within, there is the whole of the hall-truss, which manages to span the full width by means of base crucks and arched braces carrying a steeply cambered tiebeam and a short crown-post. The upper part of the construction resembles the main truss at Nurstead Court, but by means of the crucks the aisle posts of Nurstead can here be done away with. Exactly similar solutions have been found in Sussex (Chennells Brook Farm, Horsham; Homewood Farm, Bolney). Aisle posts were used at Hamden only in the screens partition. (One post survives.) The separately roofed cross-wing, at the lower end of the hall, was later doubled in width.

WESTHOY FARM, 1¼ m. w. Small, but unrestored, Wealden house, with closely set timbers exposed and painted black.

WATCH HOUSE, 1¼ m. NW. C16, half-timbered. Continuous overhang – that is to say, there was never a hall open to the roof.

HADMAN BRIDGE, ⅞ m. w. Medieval. Two pointed stone arches.

9020

SNARGATE

ST DUNSTAN. Quite large. Nave and chancel with continuous aisles, reaching to the E wall of the chancel.* N aisle with a separate gable, s aisle lean-to. C15 W tower of the usual Kentish kind. s porch. Most windows are Perp or of the restoration of 1870–2 (by C. T. Whitley of Dover). Nave arcades of four bays. Circular piers with moulded capitals and bases, E.E. of two dates, s earlier than N. The s arcade rests on corbels at E and W, the latter with crocket foliage, the crockets broken off. Chancel of two bays, C14 arcades, thin octagonal piers, this time the N earlier than the s. Between nave and chancel arcades pieces of blank wall, but no trace that there was ever a chancel arch. Crown-post roofs and tiebeams on pierced spandrels. In the N aisle tiebeams with square carved bosses. – TILES. A few by the font with patterns, much worn. – TEXT BOARDS. Seven of the black ovals found again and again round here. – LEAD PLATE, from the

* In the E wall of the s aisle a small doorway and a stump of walling are remains of an E vestry or an anchorite's cell.

roof. The embossed inscription reads 'J. Bourne, C. Warden – Warrington Romney plumber T. Apps carpenter and all his jolly men, 1780'. – MONUMENT. Tomb-chest with pointed quatrefoils on the sides. On it the indent of a brass.

SNAVE 0020

ST AUGUSTINE. Down a grassy avenue and closely surrounded by trees. C15 W tower, nave, chancel, and N chapel. The external detail suspect. *C. T. Whitley* of Dover restored the church in 1873. Inside, tower arch, chancel arch, arch to the N chapel, all of the simplest, but establishing a C13 date for the whole structure. The aisleless nave unusually wide, opening into both chancel and chapel. Perp PISCINA and embattled SEDILE. The nave roof has tall, lean crown-posts on straight tiebeams, signs of an early date. In the chancel the tiebeam is cambered and the timbers more healthily proportioned. – PULPIT. Made up with tracery from a Perp screen. – PLATE. Cup, 1554(?). Local make ?

SNODLAND 7060

ALL SAINTS. A large ragstone church beside the Medway, across a loop in the river from Burham old church.* From the W it looks most eccentric, a low gable of a peculiarly obtuse pitch and a full-scale Perp SW porch tower. The W end also shows that narrow aisles were added to an aisleless nave. Low W porch, *c.*1461. Dec W and S windows. Early Perp N windows, between deep buttresses. In the E gable of the nave two encircled quatrefoils. Quite a long chancel with two N lancets (part of a third inside), and a Dec window at the W end. Is the Perp E window in its original state ? C19 S vestry, blocking the E window of the S aisle. *Blomfield* restored the church in 1870. The tower opens into the church with a full-scale arch. This has been converted to a doorway by re-using the DOORS of the Perp rood screen. C15 leaf BOSSES reset under the tower. Four-bay arcades of round piers. Two hollow chamfers on the arches. Fairly deep mouldings, but early C14, not C13. Weedy C14 chancel arch. A string-course, in the form of a fat roll, runs round the chancel, and up and over the SEDILIA, three under a single arch trimmed with gargantuan free-standing

* Halling and Wouldham, a mile or so upstream, are a second pair of riverbank churches. Is there any significance in their being sited like this ?

cusps. The early C14 N window interferes with the string-course. Rood-loft doorways on the S side, fixing the site of the rood loft one bay W of the chancel arch. – WALL PAINTING. Early C14 Crucifixion on a S pier, devastatingly retouched. The original outlines incised, presumably from a cartoon. – STAINED GLASS. A few muddled fragments in one N lancet. – BRASSES (all of civilians). John Brigge † 1441. Headless, originally c.12 in. long. – Roger Perot † 1486. 20 in. figure. – Edward Bischoptre † 1487 and wife. 18 in. figures, thin and boneless. – Man and two wives, c.1530. 15 in. long. – MONUMENT. Martha Manley † 1682. Cartouche of well carved pulpy scrollwork.

Snodland is an industrial village, dominated by the CEMENT WORKS at Holborough. The High Street, aligned on the tower of the parish church, is enlivened only by MULBERRY COTTAGE, a Wealden half-timbered house much too heavy-handedly done up, and, across the road, VELES GARDEN, an attractive row of cottages, of 1932.

PADDLESWORTH, a hamlet on the open hillside below the Downs, $1\frac{1}{2}$ m. W, makes a very nice group. Humble C18 red-brick farmhouse with various barns, and across the road, the disused CHURCH. This is Norman, nave and straight-ended chancel, the sort of thing most of the churches around here started off as. No original window. (C13 chancel arch.)

SOLE STREET see COBHAM

SOMERFIELD COURT see SELLINDGE

6040

SOMERHILL
$1\frac{1}{2}$ m. SE of Tonbridge

52 An ambitious Jacobean mansion, sited as proudly on its hilltop as Wollaton or Hardwick. It was built for the fourth Earl of Clanricarde, who by marrying the Earl of Essex's widow c.1603 came to possess the South Frith estate, part of the demesne of Tonbridge Castle. Apparently work on the house did not start at once – rainwater-heads bear the dates 1611 and 1613. The exterior, of local sandstone ashlar, remains almost untouched; inside, nothing survives from the C17 except two chimneypieces and the essentials of the plan.

The plan was, it seems, provided by *John Thorpe*, among whose drawings one entitled 'Lo: Clanrickard' agrees with

Somerhill as built in all but the forms of some of the window-bays. The house is H-shaped, and the plan advanced for its date in having the hall axially across the depth of the centre bar of the H. That is, the main door leads into the middle of one of its short sides. Charlton House, Greenwich, of just the same date, has the same arrangement, but it occurs at Hardwick already in the 1590s. By it the medieval position of the hall off-centre and entered through a screens passage was finally abandoned, and the symmetry of the exterior penetrates inside the house. Sir John Summerson has pointed out that the Somerhill plan is one of several Thorpe based on a plan of Palladio's.* The Italian impetus for the change is worth noting.

By contrast the elevations, though symmetrical on all four sides, are almost vernacular in their sequence of straight-sided gables with inconspicuous finials, and tall brick chimney-stacks. Shallow, battlemented window-bays on the wings and in the centre. Otherwise cross-windows of one mullion and one transom (largely renewed). Shallow battlemented porch with a round-headed doorway between Doric pilasters. Triglyph frieze. These are the only classical features to break the house's unadorned restraint, and they themselves are restrained enough. Fine original rainwater-heads, similar to the ones at Knole. A one-storey service courtyard to the N, with tall gabled dormers. Kneelers and ball-finials to the gables. Doorways with four-centred arches. A stable court, extending yet further N down the hill, was added in 1877, together with a prominent clock tower.

SOUTH ASH MANOR see ASH

SOUTHBOROUGH

ST PETER. 1830–1 by *Decimus Burton.* Yellow brick and sandstone, and only interesting for the additions made in 1883 by *Christian,* a W tower and spire supported by two-storeyed projections (porches and staircases) N and S, a clerestoried chancel, buttresses, and geometrical tracery cleverly transforming Burton's wide lancets. – MONUMENT. John Wilson † 1835. By *S. Manning.* Hanging monument, with a relief of an open book resting by a monument, a confusing idea.

CHRIST CHURCH, Prospect Road. 1870–1 by *T. K. Green* of

* For the Villa Valmarana at Lisiera.

Archer & Green, completed to the original design in 1889. Sandstone with darker sandstone bands. Cruciform, all four arms wide and low. Lean-to nave aisles. The chancel lies towards the road, and the porch leads into the E side of the S transept. Quite effective fenestration, especially the geometrical-cum-plate tracery. Cast-iron nave columns. Bold and ugly boarded roofs, arched braces everywhere, except in the chancel, where scissor trusses disappear into a flat top part. Altogether a meaty church. Too strong meat for today's taste, for the red brick exposed inside and banded with black has been whitewashed – and the capitals gilded!

ST THOMAS, Pennington Road. 1860–1 by *H.Pownall*. S transept by *R.H.Garling*, 1888.

RIDGEWAYE SCHOOL, off Yew Tree Road. Completed in 1956. By *Gollins, Melvin, Ward & Partners*, in collaboration with the County Architect. Not one of their best works.

The sloping common, with St Peter's church at the N end, is still happily informal, with cottages and circumstantial mid-C19 Italianate terraces haphazardly on the E and S sides, masking it from the main road. It runs away to woods at the W, and here at the bottom of the slope, in Holden Road, is one really substantial house, HOLDEN HOUSE. Red brick, but perhaps as late as *c.*1800. Two and a half storeys. Five bays by three. The roof behind a parapet, the porch on paired Doric columns. One-storeyed addition at the l., with a conservatory behind. The house stands in a perfectly preserved Victorian garden, dotted with specimen conifers.

In LONDON ROAD, beyond the N end of the common, LITTLE BOUNDES, C18, brick painted white, tile-hung at the sides. Two storeys, five windows, spaced 2, 1, 2, big hipped roof with dormers, symmetrical chimneystacks. Pretty porch, half a hexagon, with thin fluted columns, *c.*1780. Further on, a sandstone LODGE of the 1830s catches the eye. Great Bounds, to which it belonged, has been demolished.

BENTHAM HILL, ⅝ m. SW. A mansion of considerable size, built in 1832–3 by *Decimus Burton*, as if it were an overgrown *cottage orné* in sandstone. Bargeboarded gables. Mullioned-and-transomed windows with hood-moulds to the lower ones, but the odd lancet as well. Rendered Tudor chimneystacks. In plan the house is a compact L, with a canted bay projecting southwestwards from the inner angle. Stone porch of three four-centred arches set against this. This convenient and potentially picturesque plan is visually quite wasted, for Burton seems to have been unable to group effectively any but the simplest, most stereotyped motifs. The N front works best, with its one big and three small gables, and a projecting rough-hewn basement. The E front is more developed than the others, but also more amorphous. The wing projecting at the l., however, ends in a composition which is certainly original, a chimneybreast growing out of a sort of plinth, with a window punched in its middle. This sort of thing is prophetic of the way High Victorian architects like Teulon would design; and indeed is like E. B. Lamb's designs published already in the 30s.

DAVID SALOMONS' HOUSE (Convalescent Home), $\frac{7}{8}$ m. SW. *Burton* built a house called Broomhill here for Sir David Salomons, the pioneer campaigner for the rights of Jews to hold public office, and himself Lord Mayor of London. It cannot now be found behind additions of 1854, 1863, 1908, 1910, and 1913. The additions are of sandstone, Italianate, and doubtless the original building was too.

NE of the house a tremendously tall round WATER TOWER with a taller round turret, both battlemented. Yellow brick with a few red-brick bands and tiny window-surrounds. Low castellated walls with arrow-slits masking the S side. An additional function of this monster was as a mounting for a telescope. The tower was designed by *Sir David Lionel Salomons*, the second baronet, a pioneer electrical engineer and inventor.

Further NE, the fantastic STABLES, built in 1890–4 in red brick with copious Portland stone dressings to look like a French *hôtel*, apparently modelled on one of the more licentious engravings of du Cerceau. Corps-de-logis with a steep pavilion roof and stone cupola, side wings coming forward to enclose a courtyard, and a screen wall across the S end, punctuated with an arch and a pair of colossal Ionic columns. Chimneystacks like Ionic columns. Numerous Venetian windows in the wings. *Sir David Lionel Salomons* designed the stables too.

SOUTH CRAY see ORPINGTON

SOUTHFLEET

6070

ST NICHOLAS. A complete Dec church. The W tower is unusually austere, unbuttressed, of three stages, each set back a little from the one below. Octagonal higher NE stair-turret. Flint and ragstone, attempting a chequer pattern. The rest of the church is of flint, and over-restored outside. Chancel, nave and aisles with three equal gables, the aisles stopping one bay short of the W end of the nave. Tracery in the limited range usual in Kent; but the chancel windows alternate with two designs, one purely Geometrical, the other with ogees throughout, an interesting overlap, similar to what occurs later with Dec and Perp patterns. Characteristic spacious C14 interior, with standard piers and arches. The chancel arch so wide that it makes no pause before the chancel. PISCINA and three tall SEDILIA under depressed ogee arches, the shafts and many details renewed. Under a cinquefoiled crocketed arch in the s aisle some fragments of SCULPTURE, especially a small and exquisite mid-C14 figure of God, in a nodding ogee niche. – FONT. Perp. The eight faces of the bowl carved with a miscellany of subjects: a bishop, a chalice with rayed host, the Resurrection, the Baptism of Christ, an archangel, the Sacred Name, the Lamb and flag, heraldic beast. The standard of carving is low. – STALLS. Five in the chancel with plain MISERICORDS and poppyheads, one in the shape of a great drooping leaf. – BENCHES. Plain, square-ended, in the N aisle, attached to embattled wall-panelling, the latter an unusual survival. – TILES. A few near the sedilia; C14. – PULPIT. Spacious. Probably made up of Jacobean panels. – CHANDELIER. Brass; 1768. – WALL PAINTINGS. Portrait roundels of Latimer and Ridley on the N and S walls of the chancel, set in wide borders of a red and blue repeating pattern. Not easy to date; could they be part of the beautification of the chancel in 1768, noted by Hasted? – PLATE. Cup and Cover, 1617; Flagon, 1633. – MONUMENTS. Brasses, in chancel or s aisle: Joan Urban † 1414, 21 in. lady on a bracket, a lively doggie at her feet. – John Urban † 1420 and wife. Good 3 ft figures. – John Tubney. Half-length priest. He died in 1456. – Thomas Cowell, c.1520. Minute (6 in.) shrouded corpse. – John Sedley, wife, three sons, and two daughters, c.1520. Small figures on a small tomb-chest. Otherwise the only monuments to note are: John Sedley † 1605. Large alabaster wall-monument. He reclines, armoured, under a coffered arch between Corinthian columns. – Joseph Brooke † 1796. Chaste tablet signed by *John Golden*, of No. 97, High Holborn.

The church and the irregular gabled and plastered COURT LODGE are up a short lane from the crossroads. CHURCH

COTTAGES, a picturesque row, represent one complete hall-house of the Wealden type, with an unusually long service end at the s. The timbers all new, except the braces across the recessed centre. At the corner opposite, the SCHOOL incorporates the front of the school founded in 1637 by Sir John Sedley, three symmetrical red-brick bays, with a porch in the centre. Semicircular porch arch. Mullioned windows, four lights with a transom.

OLD RECTORY, ¼ m. s. A stone, that is to say flint, house of the C14 probably built by Thomas of Alkham, rector from 1323. The usual arrangement of open hall and cross wings is easy to make out, the hipped s wing containing the solar, though georgianization and subsequent gothicking leave few original features outside – the head of a small window high in the w wall of the s wing, trefoiled with split cusps, and at the back one hall window, with a mullion and a transom and sexfoiled ogees in the square head. (In the E wall of this wing a single-light window, and the doorway to the solar at first-floor level.) Mutilated crown-post roof in the s wing.

SOUTH PARK see PENSHURST

SPELDHURST

As one approaches from the s the village groups itself round the church tower in a way that is highly picturesque. It is entirely a C19 picture. On the l. the sandstone SCHOOL of 1859 (Kelly) and MASTER'S HOUSE, both gabled and with characteristic pointed tympana over several of the windows. Beyond, the houses cluster by the crossroads, THE OLD RECTORY on the r. brick and tile-hung, stepping forward three times to get round the corner. Timber porch on the skew and big diagonal chimneystacks behind. The vista ends with the LYCHGATE and, beyond it, the big-boned tower of the church.

ST MARY THE VIRGIN. The medieval church was destroyed by lightning in 1791 and of it nothing now remains visible except part of the N wall of the tower and some fragments built into the NE vestry. A second church, of c.1797, was entirely replaced in 1870–1 by a third, to the designs of *J. Oldrid Scott*. He provided a big, strong, straightforward building with rich, mainly late C13 details. Quatrefoil piers with fillets in the angles. The roof structure is unusual, trefoiled in section, with collar-beams and windbraces. But the most enjoyable items of *Scott*'s work are the SOUTH DOOR, with curly, C13-style hingework, and the FONT, octagonal with excellently designed stiffleaf panels under arcading. – BRASS CANDEL-ABRA. Large, by *J. O. Scott*, 1889 (Kelly). – TILES. Sparingly patterned; in the chancel.

But the glory of Speldhurst is the STAINED GLASS, by *Morris & Co.* The NE and SE windows of the chancel are by *Clayton & Bell*, c.1871, characteristic, and they can be used as a control against which to judge the rest. – The W window is an early work of *C. E. Kempe*, 1878. – Now for the Morris glass.* That in the N aisle came first. W window 1873. Six angels, by *William Morris*, Christ in Glory in the vesica above, by *Burne-Jones*. – NW window 1873, saints by *Burne-Jones*. – NE window 1873, St Gregory by *Burne-Jones*, St Augustine by *Morris*. – The centre window of the N aisle also designed by *Burne-Jones*, but not until 1898. – The nave S windows are all by *Burne-Jones*, and in each light a small grisaille scene comes below the main figure: SW windows, 1874; S central and SE windows, 1875, the four Evangelists, Michelangelesque fig-ures quite unlike the rest. – Chancel SW window 1875 by *Burne-Jones*, again different: the Cleansing of Naaman and the Baptism of Christ, with many small figures in brown, blue, and blue-green. – N aisle E window 1876, six saints by *Burne-Jones*. How inventive and versatile Burne-Jones was in his early maturity! The E bay of the aisle is the organ chamber. The organ in two parts, N and S, fills most of it, so that the window is seen, as it were, at the end of a tunnel. – The E window, alas, is not, as it should be, the climax of the scheme, but disastrously alien. Crucifixion, 1905, a *Burne-Jones* design used after Burne-Jones's death. Conventional and the flesh a repulsive pink.

MONUMENTS. Among the rows of tablets under the tower only the following are noteworthy. John Yorke † 1798 and Martin Yorke † 1805, both made in the latter year by *John Bacon Jun*. Both have urns on pedestals and military trophies. John Yorke was drowned off Brazil, so on his also a relief of a sailing ship. – William Raymond † 1836, by *Thomas Denman*, copied from *Flaxman*'s monument to Agnes Cromwell in Chichester Cathedral. Denman was Flaxman's brother-in-law, and this was not the only occasion on which he filched Flaxman's designs.

* All details kindly provided by Mr A. C. Sewter.

In the CHURCHYARD, NE of the church, Coade-stone monument to William Nesbitt † 1807, signed by *Coade's*, with a large flaming lamp on top. – SW of the church two headstones, worth a look: Richard Cossum † 1721, with a relief of the Good Samaritan, and Sophia, wife of *Charles Cripps*, mason, † 1821, who no doubt carved this rustic paraphrase of Roubiliac's vision of the Last Judgement on the Hargrave monument in Westminster Abbey.

BROOMHILL BANK. A dreary sandstone villa, with large additions in yellow brick for the school now occupying the house by *Pite, Son & Fairweather*, 1951–8. One-storey classrooms to the SE, three-storey dormitory blocks to the W.

Opposite the gate a funny little CHAPEL, dated 1878 in the porch gable. Rock-faced sandstone. Symmetrical front to the road about a big porch carrying a spirelet. Large Perp square-headed windows. Who could have done such a thing at such a date?

SPELMONDEN see HORSMONDEN

SPRINGHILL see FORDCOMBE

SPRIVERS see HORSMONDEN

STANDEN see BIDDENDEN

STANSTED

ST MARY. Externally the details do not inspire confidence, owing to various campaigns of restoration in the last century. Inside however chancel arch, tower arch, and the arcade of the N aisle are all of a piece, and all Early Perp. Standard octagonal piers. Two hollow chamfers on the arches. Complete rebuildings *c.*1400 are not common in Kent. – CHANCEL SCREEN. The row of ogee quatrefoils at the top appears to be old, and such a pattern would be older than the church. – PLATE. Cup and Paten of 1694 by *Fawdery*.

There is no proper village of Stansted, but the WAR MEMORIAL (down the hill from the church) would do credit to any London suburb. A nearly naked man holds out a large palm branch.

FAIRSEAT, I m. SE, is a hamlet of handsome houses, especially FAIRSEAT MANOR, which was built for John Cox, who died in 1736. The doorcase, with its cornice curving up to a point in the middle, is characteristically Early Georgian, and so are the narrow windows beside it. Five bays, two storeys, and a plain top parapet. Pilaster strips carrying vases. Blue brick, laid as headers only, and much red-brick relief.

STAPLEHURST

12 ALL SAINTS. One will not easily forget the hingework of the s DOOR, one of the strangest examples of the universal urge to imagine life in inanimate objects. These seemingly random fragments of iron nailed to the door are unmistakably shaped into the semblance of sea creatures. There is a long, beaked thing – a sort of flying-fish – and an eel, a two-headed serpent, and a shoal of small fishes. Also a boat and a cross in a circle. The outline at the top shows that it once fitted a round-headed doorway; so it cannot be later than the C12.

The church itself, of sandstone rubble, is large, and inside rather bare. Well proportioned W tower, the C15 standard in Kent, with angle buttresses and a SE turret. Worn coats of arms on the W doorway, one tentatively identified in 1872 as that of a vicar who died in 1417, which seems rather too early. Gabled S aisle, with renewed Dec windows on a string-course, continued as a S chapel, as wide but with Perp windows and a plinth. Stone S porch with a crown-post. The chancel E window renewed, but two pretty, early C14 N windows, with the same tracery design in two-light and one-light versions. The round squint low in this wall was for the use of an anchorite. The foundations of his cell have been excavated. Renewed Dec N windows in the nave, and the jamb of an earlier one. NW organ chamber, 1876. Nave arcade partly late C12. The W respond has a square abacus and spurs on the base. Spurs on a round pier further E. The two W piers, one round, one octagonal, have mouldings too bold to be pre-C13. Arches with two slight chamfers. The E arch was rebuilt in ragstone when the rood loft was installed. Chancel arch and W arch to the chapel, 1853. Two-bay arcade to the chapel, again of the C13. – PANELLING. Sixteen panels set in the tower roof, carved with the rose and the Aragon pomegranate, which gives an early C16 date. Also clothworking emblems, e.g. a pair of shears. – CHANDELIER. Brass. 1808. – STAINED GLASS. A panel of medieval fragments. – E window with many angels, 1882. – One N window 1952 by *Owen Jennings*. Like a woodcut. –

PLATE. Cup and Paten Cover, 1619, by *A.I. & W.I.*; Paten, 1720 by *Anthony Nelme*; Flagon, 1760 by *C.B.*; Cup, 1774 by *E. Romer*(?). – BRASS of a Lady, *c.*1580. 34 in. figure, better than many of that late date.

PRIMARY SCHOOL. 1873 by Professor *T. Hayter Lewis* (Kelly). Ragstone. Large and pretentious, as Victorian village schools rarely are.

The church stands, tower-on to the road, almost at the summit of the village street. Opposite, a varied row, plastered and with exposed timbering, raised above the roadway. Further N, over the brow, one or two buildings catch the eye. On the r. the early C18 POST OFFICE, the usual two-storeyed, hipped-roofed house, five windows wide, in red and yellow brick; and the long, restored row of timber-framed CROWN COTTAGES, continuously projecting at first-floor level. On the l. only the austere, rectangular VINE HOUSE; C18. Yellow brick. Beyond the end of the street proper, LODDENDEN MANOR, a typical C16 half-timbered house, the upper floor projecting, the uprights close-set, the manorial surroundings, with ancient elms and wrought-iron gates, incongruous enough considering the house's original modest status. Recent housing estates opposite.

In the other direction, s of the church, after a little, a row of ESTATE COTTAGES, and FULLER HOUSE, half-timbered with gothicizing windows, not, it seems, a C16 house romanticized *c.*1800, but an unusually convincing piece of Tudor vernacular revival of *c.*1830.

Several large farmhouses, worth noting for one reason or another, are scattered about the parish.

HUSHHEATH MANOR, 2¼ m. SW. C16 half-timbered house, greatly restored, but handsome, for besides the continuous overhang, there are two gables, one large, one small, with oriels under them. But HARTS HEATH FARM, ¼ m. further N, is more lovable; two-thirds of a Wealden hall house, by itself in a meadow with a tarred barn.

GREAT PAGEHURST and LITTLE PAGEHURST, 1 m. N of w, make one of the happiest vernacular groups in the Weald. Great Pagehurst has a group of outsize chimneystacks.

STARKEY CASTLE FARM *see* WOULDHAM

STOCKS *see* WITTERSHAM

STOKE

ST PETER AND ST PAUL. A quaint combination of sweeping red-tiled roofs and the stump of a grey ragstone tower. A steady stream of bequests from 1506 to 1541 failed to raise the tower above the second stage. Low diagonal buttresses. Simple W doorway, and nothing grander than a square-headed window over it. There was an earlier tower which needed repair in 1479. The tower arch is C14. The nave is Transitional, say c.1190. Three-bay arcades, with narrow aisles. In the N aisle one lancet with a round-headed rere-arch, and part of a second. The arcades may be of the same date. They both have pointed arches with the plainest square profile. Also, both have scallop capitals. The scallops on the S side normal and well-formed. Those on the N side no more than pathetic grooves, but trying to be scallops all the same. (See Allhallows for similar capitals.) The S piers circular, the N piers octagonal. W of both arcades part of another C12 arch, on a simple impost, cut short by the tower. One N and one S lancet in the chancel. C19 E lancets and chancel arch. The latter aggressively Transitional, in the Victorian way, going two or three better than the genuine work. Nave roof consisting of crown-posts with two-way struts, on straight tiebeams. – FONT. Plain tub, as at Allhallows. C13, judging by the base moulding. – PLATE. Cup of 1741. – MONUMENTS. Brass to William Cardyf † 1415. Fragment only. – Foliated COFFIN SLAB in the chancel.

STONE

2 m. E of Dartford

ST MARY THE VIRGIN. The church is unforgettable, and its dingily dramatic surroundings are in their way equally so. The churchyard, on a promontory of the chalk cliffs above the Thames estuary, stands at the brink of a quarry, where two tremendous chimneys endlessly spew forth cement dust. From the outside the church is more curious than beautiful. Flint, patched in places with brick. Short, clumsy tower within the W bay of the nave. Lean-to aisles, their windows plate-traceried, better preserved on the N than the S side. The chancel however rising much higher than the nave, its tall, deep buttresses and especially the gloriously large Geometrical windows, reveal unusual ambition on the part of the C13 builders. There are few facts to explain this ambition. The Bishops of Rochester had a manor house at Stone, and the church was in their patronage. Yet the links of style are not with Rochester but with Westminster Abbey. To see this one must go inside.

Noble and uniform late C13 interior; three-bay nave, tall and elegantly proportioned, and rib-vaulted chancel of two bays and a half, enriched with exquisite wall arcading. All above the arcading in the chancel is the work of *G. E. Street*, who restored the church *c*.1859–60. He had adequate evidence for what he did. The chancel was originally vaulted (its 'stone roofe' was taken down *c*.1640), and the design of his three big bar-traceried windows was based on the tracery of the E window of the N aisle, which remained intact but for the foiling of the circles. They are a sexfoil over two quatrefoils. Street's side windows have a quatrefoil over two cinquefoils, the E window a quatrefoil over two sexfoils. While these details may be Street's, the sculpture lower down was mercifully left untouched.

Now for the details of the original work. Caen and Gatton stone. Liberal Purbeck marble shafts. The detailing should begin in the chancel. The chancel arch is narrowed to withhold a full view of the chancel until one enters it, a most effective stroke. The vault has two bays plus a W bay half as long and not quite so wide. The W bay has a pointed tunnel-vault, the ribs of the other bays are carried down on Purbeck shafts to the ground. Waterholding bases. The three-light windows fully occupy the wall-space of the centre bays each side down to a dado-moulding, below which there is trefoiled blank arcading on shafts right round the two E bays. It is the spandrels of this arcading that are given rich sculptural treatment with magnificent panels of trefoil-leaf foliage in relief, the tendrils and leaves arranged with masterly lucidity, a lucidity exactly in harmony with the tone of the architecture. These panels are identical in character with those in similar arcading at Westminster Abbey, particularly in the choir chapels. This puts the date of Stone *c*.1260, and means that the Westminster masons themselves must have been responsible for building the church. The bar tracery, too, is just as at Westminster. The spandrels were no doubt carved in the Abbey yards, and not *in situ*; the fact that the half-panels at the end of each bay are in all cases too small suggests that the wrong measurements were sent up to Westminster.

Stiffleaf capitals to the w responds. The chancel arch has a trio of shafts, with Purbeck shaftlets in the angles, stiffleaf, not just trefoil leaves, on the capitals here, and shaft-rings. On the w side there is a row of dogtooth reinterpreted on a grand scale in terms of foliage and sunk quatrefoils filled with carved leafage, a delicious display.

If the chancel seems broad and spacious, the three-bay nave is by contrast narrow and lofty in appearance, although, not being vaulted, its roof-ridge is externally considerably lower than the chancel's. The arcade piers are quatrefoil in plan, with Purbeck shafts in the diagonals. Stiffleaf capitals *en suite* with the chancel arch. Much-moulded arches, the e one each side with dogtooth between the two soffit ribs. In the centre bay the dogtooth is left out, and in the w bay the pair of ribs is reduced to one. The aisles have an e window each, and these and the NE and SE windows are treated more richly than the rest, with internal shafting. Development in the rere-arch moulding too, to make a second consistent crescendo of enrichment from w to e. The plate tracery in the aisle windows is no evidence that building began with the nave, but rather that the newfangled bar tracery could not yet be manipulated in any but the largest windows. The w responds indeed abandon the waterholding bases, so they were the last part to be erected in the C13. In the s aisle a fragment of further wall-arcading, this time with small dogtooth round plain pointed arches, and part of a spandrel not so mutilated that a figure rising from a tomb can't be made out. A Last Judgement must have been intended. There are similar figural spandrels in the N transept at Westminster.

Early in the C14 the church was lengthened by a bay, and a tower placed within it. Without doubt there was an attempt to match what already existed. The C13 w and N doorways were reset. Dec windows, however, and no longer the expensive internal walling with ashlar blocks. The most instructive part, however, is the tower arches. The three main arches copy the complicated mouldings of the w bay of the nave arcade, and the responds are clearly modelled on the C13 ones, but the capitals are not of stiffleaf but have knobbly oak and maple leaves trailing over them, a most telling departure from E.E. standards of logic, so that the leaves no longer look as if they support anything. The inconspicuous half-arches across the aisles have Dec mouldings, with double waves. Small Perp N chapel, built *c.*1527 off the chancel. – PULPIT carved by

Earp, *c*.1860. Coarse by comparison with the medieval work. – PAINTINGS. Excellent late C13 wall paintings in the N aisle, also, it seems, from the royal workshops. Between the first and the second window E of the N doorway the Virgin and Child under a pointed-trefoiled canopy with buttress-shafts l. and r. Between the second and the third window the Murder of Thomas Becket. The Knights in armour are on the l. E of the third window Virgin and Child under a gabled pointed-trefoiled arch. Also other traces. – STAINED GLASS. N aisle E window by *Wailes*, *c*.1860. As Street remarked at the time, 'it is only to be regretted that in brilliancy of colour and nervousness of drawing he does not yet by any means equal the old school of painters in glass'. This criticism also applies to the other more literally medievalizing glass in the church. – MONUMENTS. John Lumbarde † 1408. Brass with an exquisite small figure of a priest in an octofoil on a long foliated stem. Round the lobes of the octofoil in Latin the text from the Book of Job, 'I know that my Redeemer liveth . . .'. – Sir John Wiltshire, in the chapel built in accordance with his will, 1526–7. Small tomb-chest with quatrefoils and a panelled back. (The brasses on the back have gone.) Straight top with vine-trail and cresting of stylized leaves. Well carved. No sign yet of the coming Renaissance. – Robert Chapman † 1574, also in the N chapel. Small hanging monument with small kneeling figures. About as inspired as the doggerel verses below.

Street's rectory has been replaced, but the simple flint and red-brick SCHOOL next door could be by him.

STONE HOUSE HOSPITAL and THE HOLLIES, 1 m. SW. Two hospitals, built as a single lunatic asylum in 1862, by *J. B. Bunning*. Cost £37,784 (GS). Brown stock brick and stone. Tudor. The centrepiece a tall thin campanile madly corbelled out near the top. At the N end, CHAPEL by *Andrew Murray*, 1898. Dec. Blackest knapped flints. SW spirelet.

STONE CASTLE, ½ m. S. Mostly drearily Tudoresque, made drearier by the materials, flint and stock brick. *Henry Hakewill* († 1830) made alterations and Greenwood in 1838 calls it 'considerably improved and enlarged within these few years'. But the house incorporates at the SE corner a square medieval fortified tower about forty feet high. Entirely built of flint, there are no features by which it can be dated, just two arrow-slits in the N wall. The MHLG suggests that it is late C12.

IRON AGE SETTLEMENT, in Stone Castle quarry. Excavations

in 1960 revealed a hut circle with associated circular enclosure, hearths, and grain storage pits containing Iron Age B pottery.

STONEGREEN HALL see MERSHAM

STONE-IN-OXNEY

St Mary. A complete Perp church, rebuilt after a fire of 1464. W tower. Nave and aisles, chancel with short chapels. But the design is limp and unimaginative, still even keeping faith in octagonal piers, and a thorough going-over by *Ewan Christian* in 1874 has not helped. – SCREENS. N chapel Perp. – Tower screen dated 1705. Rustic. – ROMAN ALTAR to Mithras. Under the tower. It is of ragstone and very weathered, but a relief of a bull can still just be made out. – PLATE. Paten, 1707 by *F.A.*

Just W of the church, TILMENDEN is timber-framed, in the usual Wealden arrangement, but made especially pretty by the little oriel window tucked into the set-back centre.

STONEPITTS see SEAL

STONEWALL FARM see HUNTON

STROOD

St Nicholas. A medieval tower and a church of 1812 by *Sir Robert Smirke*. They make a very bad match; the tower tall, thin, and banded with flint and ragstone; the church a wide, lumbering thing in ragstone only, with a pedimented S appendage that is the porch and an identical E appendage that is the chancel. Round-headed windows with the oddest mullion-and-transom plate tracery, inserted later. Interior bereft of its galleries. What date is the tower? The round-headed W doorway and blocked window over are not Norman evidence – the window has a Perp rere-arch. C19 lancets. The tower arch is Perp, and so may the whole tower be, in spite of the lack of buttresses. Vestiges of the medieval church can be seen underneath the nave floor – they include the base of an early C12 respond. (The incised SLAB to Mariote Creye, *c.*1300, is not readily visible there.)

ENGLISH MARTYRS (R.C.), Frindsbury Road. 1963–4 by *Eduardo Dodds*. A modishly contorted silhouette, of trios of windows pushing up elliptically, and a roof that looks buckled by some colossal force. The interior much better, a rhomboid in plan, lit from the W by large windows. The altar stands across one corner, and the boarded timber roof rises above it like the rays of the sun – symbolism which justifies the external peculiarities. Nothing inside however justifies those triplet windows.

ST FRANCIS OF ASSISI (R.C.), Galahad Avenue. By *D. Pamplin*, completed in 1960. Very tepid, under a tent roof.

ST MARY, Vicarage Road. 1868–9 by *Sir Arthur Blomfield*. A thoroughly convincing building, tautly designed and with an excellent use of materials. Ragstone outside, yellow brick inside, with lively but not strident red brick patterns. Stone arcades, and a telling use of carved foliage. Lofty clerestoried nave between low aisles. Spacious chancel, with N and S chapels treated differently. Plate tracery and Geometrical tracery. The most original part is the W end; original, e.g., in the way the transition from the aisles to the nave gable is accomplished by small but complex buttresses, and in the lively W spirelet, again with ingenious buttressing excrescences at its base. The W door leads into a low vestibule on which a gallery is contrived with a stone traceried screen. Only here is Blomfield not quite in control, failing to resolve the disparate scales of the screen and balcony shafts.* – REREDOS. The kernel of it is a large alabaster relief of the Supper at Emmaus, carved with rare feeling and sincerity.‡ Mosaics by *Salviati*, 1869.

METHODIST CHURCH, corner of Frindsbury Road and Cliffe Road. 1887 by *J. W. Nash*. Red brick, a little yellow brick, and a little stone. A funny tower and spire l. of the entrance front, and the start of another to the r. Probably not intended to be funny.

TEMPLE MANOR, Priory Road. Part of a C13 flint manor house of the Knights Templars, a most surprising thing to find in the middle of an industrial estate. It has been rescued from ruin and excellently restored by the Ministry of Public Building and Works, keeping the C16 red-brick additions to E and

---

* The contract price was only £6,083, compared with the £8,500 that Smirke's church cost (*The Times*, 9 February 1962).

‡ Carved by a certain *T. Bromfield*, according to information received from Mr H. J. Wright.

w and the giant chimneybreast at the heart of the building. The C13 work is a satisfyingly complete entity, a first-floor hall on an undercroft. A wall excavated running N from the NE corner is all that has been found of the rest of the manor house. The undercroft, of three bays, has quadripartite vaults with chamfered ribs resting on extremely short semicircular responds. The vault compartments filled with squared chalk blocks. The hall is reached up an outer staircase and via a rich doorway, with Purbeck marble shafts outlined with a keeled roll. Its side walls are arcaded internally, five arches to the s and three to the N, all originally on free-standing shafts with moulded caps and bases. The arches chamfered and large enough to have lancets set under some of them. A single lancet each side E of the arcading. The E wall all gone, but in the w wall one long central lancet chamfered and rebated externally, and a low blocked doorway at the s end. It appears to be work of c.1250 or a little earlier.

SUNDRIDGE

CHURCH.* Rubble sandstone building, well set on the leafy slope above the village, between the grounds of the sandstone MANOR HOUSE (to the s) and the park of the OLD RECTORY, a spreading early C19 stuccoed house. In its bones the church belongs to the early C13. Three-bay nave arcades of round piers, with double-chamfered arches. The s capitals more developed than the N. Similar arcades, of two bays, to the N and s chapels, not an exact match in details, and again the s later than the N. Of the E triplet of shafted lancets nothing but the outermost jambs remain. Double PISCINA on a central shaft. Aisles and chapels were never widened, only heightened very much. Quatrefoil clerestory windows of the nave visible internally, above the line of the C13 lean-to aisle roofs.‡ C15 chancel arch. Blocked s doorways high up, to the rood loft. All windows lofty three-light Perp, their jambs carried down to make seats – all, that is, except the chancel N and s lancets, of C19 origin. J. Carter remodelled the chancel c.1808 for Lord Frederick Campbell of Combe Bank. The short, thick w tower, which is what the traveller comes to first, is left until last be-

* The dedication is not known.

‡ The nave w wall and the w ends of the N and s walls are especially thick up to the level of the arcade arch-heads. So the w end of the aisleless pre-C13 building is not altogether lost.

cause it puzzles. It was clearly unbuttressed to start with. The proportions suggest the C13. Yet the tower arch is Perp, ham-fisted Perp. Windows and w doorway Perp or nothing special. Primitive-looking N stair-turret, dying by several set-offs into the tower low down. Yet it has a plinth – again, evidence of a Perp date. Shingled broach-spire.* – FONT. Perp. Octagonal and plain, except for eight crudely carved corbel heads. – SCREEN. Two Perp four-light 'windows' N and S of the chancel arch. – CHANDELIER. Brass. Dated 1726. Especially fine, a pair to the chandelier at Chiddingstone. – STAINED GLASS. E window after 1868. – s aisle s window, the Seven Acts of Mercy, nicely conceived in a C15 Netherlandish style. Date of death 1874. – Chancel lancets, 1878 by *Holiday*. – s aisle w window, Annunciation by *Kempe*, 1891. – PLATE. Cup and Paten Cover, 1663 by *I.C.* – MONUMENTS. Roger Isly † 1429. Brass of a man in armour, 35½ in. long. – 42½ in. brass of a Civilian, *c.*1460. – Thomas Isley † 1518. 20½ in. brasses, with ten sons and three daughters in little. A sad decline in quality. – Parts of a Perp tomb-chest, including a shield-bearing demi-angel, set into the chancel N wall. – John Isley † 1484. Tomb-chest with armorial shields in roundels. Above, frieze of encircled quatrefoils and cresting, on octagonal shafts. – John Hyde † 1677. Black and white marble tablet, with a segmental pediment on Ionic columns. – John Hyde † 1729. Veined marble tablet, with a scrolly open pediment on fluted composite half-columns. – Duchess of Argyll and Lady Caroline Conway. A pair of busts of Roman matrons, carved in 1808 by *Anne Seymour Damer*, the latter's daughter, and protégée of Horace Walpole.‡

Near the bottom of CHURCH ROAD, MOND FLATS, six in a pair of semi-detached cottages of 1910–13, conceived with hardly appropriate Baroque grandiloquence. Double flight of steps climbing up to clear the arched passageway in the centre. Said to have been designed by a Pole.

OLD HALL, ½ m. NE, on the A25. Not in itself a specially impressive early C16 half-timbered Wealden house, but interesting because *Beresford Pite* restored the complete original fenestration, and had good evidence for all of it. The hall

---

* *Street* restored the church in 1848–9, so Mr Stoyel tells me. He did it self-effacingly.

‡ At his death in 1797 he bequeathed her Strawberry Hill, to live in during her lifetime. In the churchyard, E of the church, the chaste neo-classical monument of Dr Beilby Porteus, Bishop of London, † 1809.

window of three plus three arched lights with a transom. Ground-floor window with wider arched lights, taken as evidence that this was a shop. The rest are less expansive, just square openings with close-set vertical timber bars of square section.

68 COMBE BANK, ⅝ m. NW. The best expression of second-generation Palladianism in the county, built by *Roger Morris* for Colonel John Campbell, who in 1761 became the fourth Duke of Argyll. The exact date of building is not known. An early C19 sketch by John Carter of the hall has the jotted date 1726 or 7. Square, two-storeyed block, three by three bays, with square angle turrets rising half a storey higher, pyramidally roofed. Low pyramidal main roof and an octagonal lantern. The whole composition is very closely based on Burlington's Tottenham Park, Wiltshire, of 1721; an excellent illustration of the way the Palladians succeeded in calling a halt to stylistic evolution. Rusticated quoins. Top balustrade. Gibbs surrounds and pediments to the ground-floor windows. Similar doorcase, but with Ionic columns trapped in the rustication. These features are executed in ashlar; the rest of the house is rendered white. Only the W front breaks the all-round symmetry, for here the main block pushes forward past the turrets, and has a pediment. This arrangement too is imitated from Tottenham Park. The entrance side is on the E, and the doorway has been brought forward to form a porch, linked by screens of two columns to the turrets l. and r., a happy notion. Large additions to the N, roughly in the same style, badly upset the relatively small scale of the original house. *D. A. Alexander* made alterations at some unspecified date. The N side of this was vamped up in 1907. DORMITORY BLOCK, linked to the N, for the convent which now occupies the house.

The plan of the house is not, as one would expect, symmetrical. One enters into the l. end of the hall. This leaves space for a room S of it. The staircase lies behind the hall, and the Saloon occupies the full width of the projecting centre of the W front. Mid-C18 decoration everywhere but in the Saloon, and coved ceilings in all the ground-floor rooms. The HALL has a plaster ceiling with enriched ribs in a geometrical pattern and a frieze. Pedimented doorcases. Niches and swags. Overmantel in the SW room. The STAIRCASE is exceptionally fine,*

* But not the original one, which was quite a small affair, in a tower attached to the N side of the house.

rising the full height of the house and top-lit. The stairs rise round three sides of a square well. First-floor balconies N and s with tripartite openings and groin-vaulted landings. Wrought-iron balustrade of close-set, upward-surging Ss.* The *tour-de-force* however is *Walter Crane*'s redecoration of the SALOON *c.*1879–80, for Dr William Spottiswoode, the printer mathematician, and newly elected President of the Royal Society. The 'fons et origo' of the whole scheme were some early C16 Florentine paintings of cart-drawing amorini, set by Crane in the frieze at the top of the walls. His own supplementary figures are easy to spot. The walls are otherwise covered with a stamped and gilded paper, the doors and window-shutters with more of Crane's bony, androgynous amorini. Chimneypiece with quattrocento details, a relief of the Fates, and a specially designed fireplace, grate, and fender. The ceiling reaches a climax of metallic splendour, with emblematic relief figures in gesso painted bronze and silver. The subjects are, in the centre, the sun, seasons, and signs of the zodiac, supported by large winged figures; in the side panels the hours and times of the day; and in the large panels in the two ends the Planets. How gratifying that the scheme, so unusually ambitious, should remain complete, and be now excellently restored.

Two rooms in the N addition need comment. They are both of *c.*1907, for Mond, by *Walter Cave*, in a very convincing Adam style.‡ The ceiling of the bow-ended room facing W would take in an expert. The ballroom (now CHAPEL), however, is a fine design in its own right. The long room is tunnel-vaulted, with penetrations. These give room for semi-circular lunettes over the windows (and the answering blank panels on the s wall) with fluted fans in them. Sunk columns either side of the windows carry an entablature continuous round the whole room.

SUNDRIDGE PARK *see* BROMLEY, p. 182

SURRENDEN DERING *see* PLUCKLEY

SUTTON-AT-HONE

St JOHN THE BAPTIST. An early C14 church, nave, chancel,

* The staircase is later than 1807. Mr Harold Kalman suggested to me that it may be C20.

‡ *Adam* himself made designs for greatly enlarging the house in 1775–7, but in the end nothing was done. Drawings in the Soane Museum.

and s aisle, with a tall, deep s porch of stone. w tower of Perp type, with diagonal buttresses and a round se turret. The tracery is completely renewed but interesting in its patterns; reticulated in the aisle, with mouchettes cascading outwards in the nave and chancel side windows. The e window is a rarity in Kent, a Dec window with a truly flowing design. Three lights only, and a flow of some confusion. *Christian* in 1862 rebuilt the arcade* in a disastrously aggressive and alien way. Chancel arch of two sunk quadrants passing without a capital into polygonal imposts, stopped on the e face high up with big, knobbly stops, a typical early c14 shape, but one that may have given Christian the excuse he was looking for. At any rate he repeats the shape on the bases of his piers. Early c14 PISCINA. – TOWER SCREEN. Big geometrical patterns. Of *c.*1615, the date when the building was gutted. – PULPIT and READING DESK. Of a similar date. – STAINED GLASS. In the N and S windows oval grisaille scenes like engravings. Continental and c17. – PLATE. Cup, 1621 by *H.B.*; Paten Cover, 1621; Paten, 1709; Flagon (or rather a Tankard), 1724 by *I.B.* – MONUMENTS. Sir Thomas Smith † 1625. Fine large standing monument, still Jacobean in that the effigy reclines, on a sarcophagus, under heavy architecture. But in deference to up-to-date fashion the alabaster and black touch is left uncoloured, and there is a monumentality in the Corinthian columns and the open pediment that is new. Behind the columns reliefs with sextant, barrel, etc., i.e. the full equipment of a merchantman. Smith's voyages took him from the Amazon to the Volga, and he gave his name to Smith's Sound. – Abraham Hill † 1721. Large architectural tablet signed by *Robert Taylor*, father of Sir Robert, the architect. – Francisca Hill † 1736. Incorporating a large three-quarter-length portrait in relief, dated 1726. She turns in a lively pose, hand to chin. Rupert Gunnis felt the relief was 'almost certainly' by *Taylor*.

ALMSHOUSES, ⅝ m. e of s, in the village street. Red brick. Two storeys. Dated 1597.

ST JOHN'S JERUSALEM, ½ m. se. Part of a commandery of the Knights Hospitaller, who were given the manor in 1199. Partly transformed in brick and stucco in the c18, when Edward Hasted, the county historian, lived here. It is now a place of great charm, locked between the arms of the river Darent, and overhung by a great cedar and a great copper

---

* There had been a serious fire in 1615.

beech. C13 chapel at the E end.* Flint and rubble walls. Three
E lancets, with the caps of internal shafts. (The colonnettes
are of plaster.) Two s lancets, a buttress, and a blocked doorway, where C17 brick refacing begins. Three N lancets and a
buttress further w. The w end of the chapel is lost in the remodelling. Plain double PISCINA inside. Mid-C18 S doorcase, pedimented, with a Gibbs surround. The rectangular
block at the w end, set back slightly from the s front, but projecting considerably to the N, looks like an C18 addition. Yet
it is C13 in its walling.‡ What was the layout of the domestic
parts of the commandery, however, cannot be said.

SUTTON PLACE, ½ m. N. Of the great house built c.1600 by
Sir Thomas Smith one wing remains, transformed after 1767
into a stuccoed two-storeyed block, eleven windows wide.
Uninhabited at the time of writing. The splendid red-brick
PARK WALLS that border the Darenth Road are the really See
p.
645
worthwhile Elizabethan survival.

SUTTON VALENCE

8040

ST MARY. Rebuilt in 1823–8 by *W. Ashenden & Sons*,§ in local
ragstone. w tower, nave with a shallow s porch, chancel with
chamfered E corners and N and S chapels. Dec E window 1866
by *Habershon*. The nave, built at first for galleries, was so
wide that in 1874 *G. M. Hills* could easily insert arcades. The
lofty octagonal piers, their sides slightly concave, copy the
chancel and chapel arches saved from the medieval church.
The Perp side windows must be of 1874. – FONT. Perp.
Octagonal. Four-petalled flowers on the sides of the bowl,
which again are slightly concave. – STAINED GLASS. E window 1866 by *Lavers & Barraud*. – MONUMENT. Priscilla
Crispe † 1823. Adamesque tablet signed by *D. Seares* of
Maidstone.

SCHOOL. Founded in 1578 by William Lambe, a London
clothworker. A complete new set of buildings came in 1910–14,
designed by *Adams, Holden & Pearson*, which probably means
by *Charles Holden*. They occupy three sides of a square open

* In 1234 Henry III ordered five oaks from Tonbridge forest for the roof.
So that dates the chapel.

‡ Recent photographs taken when the rendering was off show traces of
two upper lancets, not as long as the chapel ones, in the w wall, and a doorway on the s side. I am grateful to Mr Tallents for showing me these photographs.

§ So Goodhart-Rendel read the worn inscription.

to the s, classrooms in the two-storeyed centre and boarding houses in the wings, half a storey higher, with rather bald yet higher pieces where centre and wings meet. Red brick, the wings tile-hung on their s faces, where too the skyline breaks into asymmetrical gables and tall chimneystacks. The rest is rather formal, the neo-Georgianisms predominant. The centre three bays cant forward slightly, a lead-faced clock turret over. Austerely blocky staircase towers rise at the junctions of wings and centre. Assembly Hall, N of the centre block, lit from lunette clerestory windows, one N, one W, one E. Remarkably undecorated interior. The astringent Holden flavour is discernible everywhere.

The CHAPEL of 1928, to the NW, carries on the same style, much less assuredly. The SCIENCE BLOCK, E of the main buildings, is of 1956 by *Seely & Paget*. At the W end REFECTORY and BOARDING HOUSE, 1961–2 by *Laurence King & Partners*. None of this is anything special.

The ragstone OLD SCHOOL, of 1863, lies below the brow of the hill to the s.

PRIMARY SCHOOL. 1914. Gabled and roughcast.

CASTLE, ⅓ m. E. Remains of a small square Norman keep, only 22 ft across internally. It is built of ragstone, the walls *c*. 8 ft thick, with a tunnel-vaulted passage at first-floor level in the s wall. Sockets for floor joists there. The other walls now rise less high. Pronounced clasping buttresses. There seems to have been a forebuilding on the N side. The keep stands on the very brim of the ragstone escarpment, panoramically commanding the Weald. It is now much overgrown and surrounded by a hazel grove, so that nothing is to be seen of the curtain wall to the W and the tower to the E, which Harold Sands could still trace in 1902.

'Town Sutton' is a courtesy title, for Sutton Valence has barely outgrown the proportions of a village. It grew up beside the Maidstone–Tenterden road on the steep slope of the ragstone ridge, not along the road, but following the contours of the hillside. The church lies W of the road, the village E of it, stacked in four levels one below the other, the school at the top, streets on two levels, and post-war estates among orchard-trees lower down, each with an unimpeded prospect over the Weald. Turning off the A274 one is presented at once with a choice of upper and lower road. The latter, to the triangular GREEN with C18 and C19 cottages on its s side, ends at the rebuilt LAMBE'S ALMSHOUSES, a modest ragstone range of

1888 by *F. W. Porter*. The higher route however is the more
rewarding, beginning at HIGH STREET, where the original
C16 LAMBE'S ALMSHOUSES, a humble, one-storeyed row
of six, are overwhelmed by half-a-dozen mighty lime trees.
Pairs of arched lights for windows, and nearly round-headed
doorways. As the street changes its name to BROAD STREET,
it broadens, to be stopped at the far end by the CONGREGA-
TIONAL CHAPEL. The row of cottages that follows the upper
side of the street and turns away l. to avoid the chapel is a
charming example of unity in diversity. The materials con-
tinually vary between tile-hanging, white weatherboard, and
chequered brickwork, bay-windows encroach irregularly on
to the pavement of ragstone setts, and the only grander houses
are an early C18 five-bay house, with a frieze of quatrefoils in
the doorcase, and the plastered front of the SWAN INN, a
large, timber-framed building of Wealden construction.
The lower side of the street is patchier, which maintains the
open texture of the village. Near the E end, VALENCE HOUSE,
the best individual house. Half-timbered but rendered white.
Symmetrical N front, of two overhanging gables with a two-
storeyed gabled porch between, and a central brick chimneystack. All the windows have two mullions and a transom, the
transom arched in the centre light, a typical later C17 form.
The symmetry too suggests a C17 date; the date on a finial
however is 1598. Additions to the S, including a sheer chimneybreast, made in 1880, in a Norman Shaw style.

SWANLEY

ST PAUL, Swanley Village. A village church, by *Christian*,
1860–1 (tower 1862–5). Nave and small apsidal chancel. W
tower with a top-heavy shingled spire. Ragstone banded with
red and yellow brick. Dec tracery. All quite forcefully done,
not without one or two wickednesses: the overgrown chancel
lancet that needs a gablet to fit it in, and the S porch with a
profile like a witch's hat. The chancel arch, however, on
monstrous, malformed responds, makes one wonder just how
much control Christian had of his effects. Rich MOSAICS and
FRESCOES in the chancel; STAINED GLASS by *Schrigley &
Hunt* of Lancaster.
The church stands in a grove of pines. The SCHOOL, of 1862,
by the road, is also by *Christian*. So is the former VICARAGE.
ST MARY THE VIRGIN. On the A20, the church of the modern

town, if town it can be called. *Dudley Newman*, who designed it in 1901, certainly produced a town church. Tall, short, and sheer, incomplete to the s and w. Nave, chancel, and apse. Red brick. Spacious interior, like a Fellowes-Prynne church. The faults are in details, such as the clumsily big Dec tracery, and the pinched arches of the arcades.

KENT COUNTY COUNCIL OFFICES, Sycamore Road. Built by *Newman & Newman* as a County Council School Hospital and opened in 1903. Thirty cottages at the back for the children to live in, a plan intended to stamp out ophthalmia, 'the scourge of the Poor Law Schools'.

LONDON FIRE BRIGADE TRAINING COLLEGE, ¾ m. s of St Paul's church. Built in 1891–2 as a Convalescent Home, by *Woodd & Ainslie*. Of vast size and considerable pretensions, but hopeless as architecture. Sir Ernest George gone symmetrical, with a top dressing of meagre turrets, central pediment, and a sort of neo-Norman doorway.

FILLING STATION, at the w end of the town, on the A20. Of *c.*1957, by *J. Burkett, G. Sheere & R. W. Wilkinson.* Why aren't there more filling stations as carefully done and characterful as this ? The pumps in a ring round a sixteen-sided glass-clad drum, where the paper-work is dealt with.

New HOUSING s of the railway station, not notable in itself, but noteworthy in that an eight-storey OFFICE BLOCK stands in the middle of it, which puts work round the corner from home as it almost never is in Britain. The offices, completed in 1966, are by *Rodney J. Allen.*

SWANSCOMBE

ST PETER AND ST PAUL. Heavily restored in 1872–3 by *Jabez Bignell*, and repaired again by him after a fire in 1902. None of the Dec and Perp windows trustworthy, the flint walling too tidy. But an interesting history is there to be unravelled, and it starts early. The lower part of the w tower is Saxon, as the double-splayed N window shows, the external splay turned incompetently with Roman tiles. Then Norman work of two periods. The chancel, lengthened later, has a blocked Norman window to N and s, and in the nave are traces of round-headed recesses in the E wall, flanking the chancel arch. To the nave, late in the C12, narrow aisles and a clerestory were added. Three-bay arcades. Pointed arches with angle rolls. Short circular piers and square abaci with chamfered corners. On

the capitals of the E responds upright pointed leaves; on the E
pier of each arcade classic waterleaf. Later the narrow aisles
were heightened (so the clerestory windows now appear inside
the church), but not widened. Tower reconstructed in the
C13. Chancel arch C14. – FONT. Norman, tub-shaped. Terribly defaced, but one big beast can be made out, enough to
show that it was once a fine thing. – LECTERN. Oak. Perp.
Sparingly decorated, on each face just a large sunk roundel of
leafage. One of only two medieval lecterns in the county (cf.
Detling (E) for the other). – PULPIT. C18. – CHANDELIER.
Brass. Dated 1687, i.e. uncommonly early. Certainly it has
none of the characteristic swagger of C18 branches. – PLATE.
Cup, 1623; Gilt Paten and Flagon, given in 1730. – MONU-
MENTS. Sir Raphe Weldon † 1609. Large standing wall-
monument. He in armour lies turned on his elbow, above and
behind his recumbent wife. His pose convinces, and so does his
little wizened face. Eight small children kneel below. Two
obelisks on the front corners. – Anthony Weldon † 1613.
Hanging monument. Kneeling figure under a coffered arch.
Obelisks at the sides, cartouche at the top. – Dame Elinor
Weldon † 1622. Similar pattern but under a broken pediment.
– (Henry Roebuck † 1796. By *Sir R. Westmacott*. Draped urn
and below an elegantly reclining female figure, quite small.)
– Sir Erasmus Wilson † 1884. Tomb-chest of red-veined
alabaster. Much stiffleaf on top.

ALL SAINTS, Galley Hill. By *Norman Shaw* and begun in 1894.
Crisp and severe, the walls of very black knapped flints with
very white stone dressings. Dec and Perp windows. Slate
roofs coming down unbroken over nave and aisles, which clasp
the central tower. The chancel, as high as the nave, looks by
contrast tall and sheer. The tower is oddly low, bravely managing to heave itself above the roofs, the effect emphasized by
shallow battlements that hump up in the middle. After this
the interior is sweet and comforting. Octagonal sandstone
piers, tower supports set well back, not breaking up the space.
The S aisle is yet unbuilt. – FURNISHINGS. Excellent contemporary woodwork in an Arts and Crafts Perp, the *leitmotif*
a depressed ogee. The various fittings happily ring the changes
on richness and simplicity. – PULPIT and READING DESK
rich, PANELLING and REREDOS simple, made of exceedingly
wide vertical boards. The ORGAN CASE is part of the scheme
too. – LITANY DESK. Spanish. Brought from Seville in 1911.
Canted front with paintings. – CHANDELIER. Brass. Made in

Rotterdam in 1729. – PAINTINGS. Early C16 Flemish Deposition, in the reredos. – Virgin and Child, by *Albertinelli*. – Copy of *Titian*'s Entombment in the Louvre. – Message of the Angel to Joseph (a very rare subject); late C16. Venetian. – *See* Crucifixion, by *Annibale Carracci*. – STAINED GLASS. N aisle p. E window by *Christopher Whall*.
645

COUNCIL OFFICES, Manor House, immediately S of the medieval church. 1963–4 by *John Voelcker*. Grey brick and hot brown woodwork. All the forms deliberately jagged and broken up in the 1960s way.

SWAYLANDS *see* PENSHURST

TELEGRAPH HILL *see* HIGHAM

8030

TENTERDEN

33 ST MILDRED. The magnificent grey W tower, the finest of any parish church in Kent, dominates the little town. It is of four tall stages, with deep angle buttresses going up almost to the top, octagonal corner turrets, and bold crocketed pinnacles. As at Lydd, there is a double W doorway, square-headed, with a tall transomed four-light window immediately above it. Then only tiny windows until the twin two-lighters in the top stage. Correspondingly noble tower arch inside. Bequests chart the leisurely progress of its erection: 1449, 1461 bequest of twelve timbers, 1469, 1471, 1473 mentioning a 'glazyd' window in the W part, 1476 for a 'chyme', and 1495 for the stair-turret. Externally the church stands up well to the scale of the tower, unified by tall, deep buttresses though by no means uniform in detail. Rubble sandstone walling, with many pieces of a deep brown ironstone. All tracery lost, then replaced by *G. M. Hills* (or by *Christian*; PF) *c.*1864–6. Sadly the interior, partly devitalized by Hills's restoration, and partly because of narrow aisles and ill proportioned arcades, has less appeal than most of the big Wealden churches. The history of the building seems to be something like this. The chancel basically C13, with one N lancet. The responds of the S chapel also C13, linked now by a single colossal arch but originally no doubt with an intermediate pier and two arches. So the C13 chancel would have been quite long. Dec N chapel, with square-headed N windows and flowing tracery in the E one (N.B.: the mouchettes are packed in a keyhole-shaped motif, for which cf., on a much larger scale, Hawkhurst E window). The aisled

nave also C14, the S aisle with slender piers, alternating round and octagonal, on high bases. The mouldings differ.* Stone S porch. Genuine Dec S doorway. The N arcade, of fat ugly piers, has double-chamfered arches identical with the S arches. Could the piers have been encased later in the C14 to give them extra strength? The N responds, however, are detailed like the S arcade. Perp N aisle windows, with a blank bay where the porch is on the S side, and sure enough a STOUP in this bay shows there was once a N doorway too. Finally the S aisle was extended to the E as a rebuilt S chancel chapel, interfering with the E end of the nave arcade. SE vestry. The tower tacked on to the church by lengths of blank wall. C19 chancel arch, but note two trefoiled lancets high above it. Nave E windows are rare in this part of England. – FONT. Perp. Hexagonal, for a change. On a centre shaft and shafts at the angles, which is highly unusual in the C15. Two pointed quatrefoils on each face. – RELIEF (N chapel W wall). Resurrection. Alabaster, C15. Small and mutilated. – STAINED GLASS. Lots of it, and none of it good, though the bright E and W (1864) windows are much more acceptable than the anaemic S windows, 1865–80, signed by *H. Hughes*. – (SW window by *Ward & Hughes*.) – MONUMENT. Herbert Whitfeld † 1622. Standing monument, with large figures kneeling at a prayer-desk, i.e. the type more usual on a smaller scale. The arch over them encrusted with shields of arms. Nice iron railings, not contemporary it seems. – In the CHURCHYARD a number of fine C18 headstones, some with allegorical reliefs.

ST MICHAEL. 1862–3 by *Gordon M. Hills*. The church looks well on a slope above the red brick SCHOOL of 1861 and 1960–1. SE tower and spire. NE vestry chimney. Lancets to the S, otherwise plate tracery. Ragstone. – MONUMENT. Seaman Beale, the first vicar. White marble, with a relief of St Michael trampling Satan. Erected 1901.

PERAMBULATION. The church stands just N of the High Street, half-way along it. A walk in either direction is rewarding. If one first turns E the TOWN HALL, dated 1790, comes at once, plain and modest, its balcony reaching across the pavement.‡ The TUDOR ROSE CAFE faces it, the best of the few half-timbered houses in the High Street, close-studded and originally with a recessed centre, but jettied across the recess in

* One capital is evidently C13.

‡ PLATE. Three small Maces, the larger two 1660 and gilt. The smallest of a similar date and less than 6 in. long – literally a pocket mace.

the C16, when the open hall had a floor put across it. Nos 19–21, nearly next door, is a single late C18 front characteristic of the local style of the time, with russet mathematical tiles, white wood quoins, and shallow modillion cornice. Loft door and hoist in the l. bay. The street ends on the l. with EASTWELL HOUSE, of the early C18 but horribly mutilated. The original doorcase has been tacked on in front of the shopfronts. It has a triglyph frieze on Tuscan columns and a cartouche in the pediment. LLOYDS BANK, opposite, again C18, has a less ambitious doorcase. Where the road forks, the urban character continues on the l. in EAST CROSS, with Nos 8–11, a tall late C18 terrace, tile-hung and typical. As individual houses begin, the l. side remains the one to watch and remains C18. First YEW TREE HOUSE and MIRIAM HOUSE, not quite a pair, faced with mathematical tiles, not bricks. The former with a doorhood on carved brackets. Then THE WHITE HOUSE, with a good doorcase on Ionic columns and tripartite windows, the lower ones arched in the centre, i.e. simple Venetian. The UNITARIAN CHAPEL, beside it, the humblest of brick cottages. Inside however the original woodwork of 1746 is still there, galleries on three sides, the pulpit and fine chairs railed off on the fourth side.

Now back and down the r. fork, which is Oaks Road. Here the only thing to search out is HALES PLACE, to which belong the exceedingly interesting remains of an Elizabethan garden. Brick walls enclose a rectangle, with octagonal two-storeyed PAVILION at the E corners. They are of brick, and have blocked arched lights in pairs and, by the doorways, elongated Tuscan columns. Outside the rectangle, a little WELLHOUSE with crowstepped gables. The house has all gone except a wide and deep four-centred entrance arch, also in brick. C17 grotesque brackets on the front door of the present house.

The two best examples of C18 Tenterden vernacular are still to come. First EAST HILL HOUSE, where the road forks, three storeys and five bays, tile-hung, the front of pink mathematical tiles. The builder has displayed his repertoire up the middle of the façade, a wide doorway with a pediment decorated with little Gothic corbels, next a Venetian window with a moulded frieze and rusticated arch, and at the top a round window whirling round like a mouchette wheel. CRAYTHORNE HOUSE, up the l. fork, at the crossroads, has the same tall, square proportions but is more successfully composed. Hasted in 1790 calls it new built. Faced with wood blocks cut to look like rusticated ashlar, and painted white. Three very wide bays, to show off the walling. Doorcase on Doric columns, with a pedimented window and a lunette above.

The High Street W from the church at once broadens out with trees and grass slopes each side. It would be fine and spacious but for the lines of cars parked all day. A tall preliminary accent on each side, a long range of c.1800 on the l., with an overhang that hints that what one sees hides something older, and on the r. the Italianate WESTMINSTER BANK, of 1866, by *Frederick Chancellor* of Chelmsford. Thereafter nothing to note, except that the s side is mostly cottages behind their gardens. Among the cottages No. 91, PITTLESDEN GATE-HOUSE, a tiny half-timbered hipped-roofed house. No overhang; widely spaced timbers, suggesting an early, probably C14, date. (Complete solar-hall-service arrangement inside.) Mr E. W. Parkin calls it the sole survivor of three such gatehouses to a long-lost C14 mansion. Finally the road narrows and the stone GATEHOUSE of Heronden Hall closes the view. Beside it on the r. WESTFIELD HOUSE is a nice red-brick house of c.1700, with a characteristically bold hipped roof. Just beyond, past one of Tenterden's recent misguided neo-Georgian estates, is WESTWELL, the best house in the town, bearing the prominent date 1711. (Rainwater-heads on the E side dated 1718.) Seven bays by four, the basic system of two storeys and dormers in a hipped roof half hidden by the parapet gets distinction from the windows concentrated in the centre and the tall bold chimneystacks, and richness from the caramel-coloured sandstone mixing with the reds of the brickwork. But this is not all: there is an open pediment over the centre window, on tapering fluted pilasters, a deep moulded cornice, keystones to the windows and architraves to the lower ones. The builder then in a frenzy of enthusiasm gave piecrust edgings to all the raised panels in the parapet and between the windows. (Staircase with three twisted balusters to each tread.)

Now back to the crossroads and down Smallhythe Road, where, on the r., CHESTNUT HOUSE has a pleasant early C18 front. A little further along on the same side is THE CEDARS, Early Georgian, two storeys and five bays, plum-coloured brick, the roof hipped. The porch has Ionic columns and a broken pediment, but the remarkable thing is round the corner on the s side, a big contemporary brick bow the full height of the house, with battlements. May's work at Windsor in the 1670s was castellated, and with Vanbrugh's interest in castles such fancies gained a certain mild popularity. At this point the perambulator may feel he has footed it enough, so the remaining houses are better described individually.

HERONDEN HALL, ½ m. SW, in a small park. Stone, Tudor, with a symmetrical N front, the windows beside the porch exceedingly deep. The architect was *Donthorne*, and the date 1853.

HERONDEN, Smallhythe Road. 1818, according to Sir Charles Igglesden. A dull professional job in white brick, with a porch on pairs of stretched Greek Doric columns.

MORGHEW, I m. S. Nice late C18, with a Venetian window between two window-bays. Brick.

GOODS HILL COTTAGES, I½ m. NW. A tall, white, weatherboarded row of four cottages, alone and rather endearing for their pathetic attempt at Venetian windows.

HOMEWOOD, Ashford Road. Dated 1766 on the rusticated doorway. Three bays, five storeys. Low hipped roof. Red brick, and plain except for a string-course and the typical Tenterden cornice.

KNOCK FARM, I m. N. Half-timbered, restored but still madly sagging. Long front with widely spaced studs, and a continuous overhang.

At LEIGH GREEN, I m. E on the Appledore Road, BRUNGER FARM, more mid-C16 brickwork, with stepped E gable and stepped central porch.

FINCHDEN MANOR, beyond on the l., has been much added to and altered. The main front to the road is timber-framed, with overhanging gables and a two-storeyed porch. C17 geometrical decoration on the porch, and another bit to the l. with a date 1658. Good brick stables NE of the house, c.1670. The main part has a hipped roof on a cornice with big shaped brackets. English bonding.

KENCH HILL, I½ m. SE, must be c.1770, as it is almost a twin of Homewood (*see* above). It only differs in the doorcase, which has a segmental pediment on Tuscan pilasters.

TESTON

ST PETER AND ST PAUL. Rebuilt by Sir Philip Boteler, who obtained a faculty to do so in 1736. The church is cruciform, of galletted ragstone, and best seen from the W, where the greyness is relieved by the brick top to the tower and a tall recessed spire. Gothic tracery was put into transept and chancel windows in 1846. – REREDOS. Quite grand, and no doubt of *c.*1736. Fluted Corinthian columns in the centre and an open pediment. Pilasters at the sides, extending the woodwork right across the chancel. They frame, as usual, Ten Commandments, Lord's Prayer, and Creed. Also texts at the top. – PLATE. Paten, 1685 by *M.*; Flagon, 1696 by *C.T.*; Paten, 1757 by *Robert Rew*(?).

BRIDGE over the river Medway. Ragstone. Only the centre three arches are medieval, but the C19 extensions match exactly. The arches barely pointed, the cutwaters carried up to make refuge-recesses beside the roadway.

BARHAM COURT. 'Greatly improved' by Sir Philip Boteler, who died in 1772, and again before 1808. Hasted (1798) knew it as a white stuccoed house. Now large and grey, the columns all added in 1933 after a fire. W of the house, an elegant ORANGERY, all glazed between Ionic pilasters, that become columns in the three centre bays. Built, no doubt, *c.*1800.

Thatched LODGE by the church. Also a pair of square single-storeyed LODGES, white with big quoins, on the main road.

ROMAN VILLA, overlooking the Medway. Parts of two rooms with pillared hypocausts belonging to a bath suite were found; to one of the rooms was attached a buttressed apse.

THAMESMEAD *see* ERITH

TILDEN *see* HEADCORN

TONBRIDGE

ST PETER AND ST PAUL. The church, though not small, lies back invisible to the E of the High Street. Wholly built of local sandstone, but unattractive since wholesale renewal and enlargement by *Christian*, 1877–9, who added an outer S aisle to the existing one, built only in 1820. The battlemented W tower is early C14, with trefoiled lancets low down and angle buttresses. It now looks too small for the church. But the earliest part is the chancel, as the irregular rubble walling on the N side shows. There is one Norman N window, with traces of another W of it. The larger round-headed window to the E must be a fake, and set in what is no doubt a lengthening of the original chancel. C14 chancel arch, of two hollow chamfers dying into the wall. C13 five-bay N arcade in the nave, of tall piers with moulded caps. At the W an alternating rhythm of

18—W.K.W.

round and octagonal piers is set up, but both the two E piers and the E respond are round, nor is their stonework reddened (by fire?) like that of the W piers. But the arcade is too restored to make it safe to assume anything about the order in which the piers were built. Trefoiled double PISCINA in the N aisle. – FONT. 1766, of veined white marble, now disused. – PLATE. Paten and Almsdish, 1719 by *Pe.*; Cup, 1760; Salver, 1785 by *Hester Bateman.* – MONUMENTS. Sir Anthony Denton and wife (chancel). He died in 1615 and she put up the monument after his death. Only the effigies and inscription remain. Both effigies semi-reclining, his, of alabaster, an armoured figure stiffly lying on his side; hers, of stone, shrouded but in an easier pose, made perhaps ten or fifteen years after her husband's. – George Barker † 1663 (chancel). Rectangular tablet with a tight frame of gristly strapwork, very Mannerist in feeling. – Philadelphia Lyttelton † 1663 (tower). Standing monument. On a base of unusual purity for that date stands a two-handled vase of typically coarse bulginess.* – Ann Meyrick † 1731 (chancel). Oval tablet framed in a cartouche of a similarly gristly kind, but much freer and more relaxed in the design, as one would expect at this much later date. – Richard Children † 1753 (N aisle). Signed by *Roubiliac*, and a fine thing, though small-scale. A weeping putto draws drapery over an urn. Long verse inscription: its author uses convention and artifice to veil sentiment just as Roubiliac does. – James Alexander † 1848 (vestry). By *J. G. Lough.* Seated woman holding a cross, i.e. christianized Grecian.

CORPUS CHRISTI (R.C.), Lyons Crescent. Built *c.*1894 by *W. Barnsley Hughes* (GR). The interior is what one expects of that date, narrow aisles and shallow brick arches running into lozenge-shaped piers of stone. Room however for a gallery above the aisles, as well as a clerestory. Not done with any great conviction. – PRIEST'S HOUSE adjoining.

ST SAVIOUR, Dry Hill Park Crescent. 1876 by *Ewan Christian.* E.E. Nave and apsed chancel in one. Red brick. Really of no interest.

ST STEPHEN, Quarry Hill Road. Also by *Christian*, and to look at equally dull, of ragstone laid like crazy-paving, which is never a success. 1851–4. Typically broad and low, in plan a rectangle, with the tower and high stone spire standing in the SE corner. Nave and aisles under three equal gables. Short chancel. – STAINED GLASS. In all but the E window glass by

* Identical monument at Hunton.

Morris & Co., 1910–13, i.e. long after both Morris and Burne-Jones were dead. Goodhart-Rendel calls it 'as dreadful and melodramatic as usual'.

CASTLE. The town of Tonbridge grew up by a ford over the river Medway, and the function of the castle was to guard it. That it also dominated the town is hard to realize today, when it is almost hidden from the street by trees; but one can vividly appreciate its power if one traces out the medieval town defences: first, on the W side, the bank and ditch W of the Cattle Market, Bordyke (i.e. the Borough Ditch) to the N, and at the SE corner another steep bank S of East Street. The massively fortified gatehouse of the castle, built ominously on the townward and not the river side, could have overlooked every house in the town and was only a long stone's throw from the furthest one.

Tyrannizing the townspeople was not however the original purpose of the castle. The Norman MOTTE AND BAILEY stretch along the river, and it is the embanked E end of the bailey that faces the High Street. The motte itself, at the NW corner of the bailey, survives to its full height, an impressively sheer and regular cone. A circular sandstone SHELL KEEP crowned it, a strengthening of the fortifications datable probably to the C13. The walls are now only stumps about 3 ft high, but showing traces of buttresses and a battered base. The keep became obsolete *c.*1300, when the formidable gatehouse was built on the N side of the bailey and the latter enclosed with strong walls. Gatehouse and walls of finely laid sandstone ashlar that has weathered wonderfully well. (A rougher piece of walling immediately W of the inner front of the gatehouse shows that there were earlier stone bailey walls.) The wall on the S side, towards the river, rises still to a considerable height, but robbed of its facing stones. In it four garderobe shoots, discharging originally into the river, are the only features of the E half. Further W a postern gate, and beside it, on the inner side, the jambs of an internal doorway. These are of course all evidence for a range of living rooms on this side of the bailey, but a description of 1520 merely says that this side 'was intended to have been made for lodgings'. Another, higher, chunk of walling at the SE corner was presumably part of the Water Tower, also mentioned in 1520. No stone residential range was ever built because the GATEHOUSE had a great hall[24] on its top floor. This inconvenient arrangement occurs e.g. at Dunstanburgh in Northumberland *c.*1315, where it was soon superseded. At Tonbridge however it was tolerated, though such a fortified residential gatehouse was as awkward to live in as a Norman tower keep and had not even the advantage of standing at the farthest side from the enemy. Not that an aggressor would have had much hope of storming the gatehouse, so well is it provided with arrow-slits (on the inner side as well as the outer!), concealed machicolations, and grooves for two portcullises and two pairs of folding gates. It rises three-storeyed above a deep moat, now filled in on the E side. Putlog holes show it had a drawbridge. Guardrooms flank the entrance; the portcullis room is in the centre of the first floor, with living rooms on either side, with fireplaces and garderobes, and on the top floor a great hall, 55 ft by 29 ft, also with a fireplace. Three trefoiled lancets on the inner face, and two two-light windows with Geometrical tracery and hood-moulds on big head-stops, the latter lighting the hall. The front has broad semicircular projections, and at the back there are circular corner towers. On both sides the entrance arch is cut back by many chamfers revealing the vast thickness of the wall. Outside, a tall super-arch as well. Pointed tunnel-vault to the gateway, with transverse arches. Square holes for the boiling oil. Visually the effect is bold and intimidating. Inside however some carved decoration was allowed, a little foliage by a first-floor fireplace hood; and in the hall one window-hood rests on exquisitely classical female heads, and the fireplace hood has a fierce male head and side shafts disappearing into the mouths of ogres. Otherwise all internal features were hacked away when the castle was dismantled by order of Parliament in 1646.

IRON AGE HILLFORT, on Castle Hill. Only the E and NE stretches of the rampart of this fort survived. On the E there are two lines of banks and ditches; on the NE it is of univallate construction. An entrance on the E side has been excavated, although no finds were made.

TONBRIDGE SCHOOL. The history of the school follows the pattern familiar e.g. from Rugby, Uppingham, or Dulwich, the pattern of the small local school blossoming suddenly in the middle of the C19 through the dynamism of a single headmaster. Sir Andrew Judde founded a 'Free Grammar School' at Tonbridge in 1553.* So it remained until Dr Welldon be-

* Thus giving the town what it had refused thirty years before. In 1525 Wolsey had offered them a school if they would allow the priory to be suppressed. The townspeople voted to keep the latter and so lost both. The last remains of the PRIORY disappeared when the railway was laid out in 1840.

came headmaster and transformed it into a boarding school drawing pupils from far and wide. The C16 schoolhouse was pulled down in 1864. The present buildings of sandstone facing the High Street form an E-shaped group enclosing at the N end OLD JUDDE HOUSE, a red-brick C18 house much tampered with at various times. The centre bar of the E is the OLD CHAPEL, 1859 by *Wadmore & Baker*. At the S end is all that remains of the earlier school, a Tudoresque front, battlemented turrets framing a bay-window of many lights, built in 1827 to balance a genuine one. In 1863–4 *E.H.Burnell* placed the HEADMASTER'S HOUSE behind this front and stretched out SCHOOL HOUSE as a long tall range at the back, centred about a somewhat inconspicuous tower. *Burnell*'s SCIENCE BLOCK came at the other end in 1887. The façade was completed in 1894 by *W. Campbell-Jones*, who filled in the gap with classrooms and a larger tower, that shifts the focus of the group to the r. At the back the plan is an E again. The centre stroke is *Campbell-Jones*'s BIG SCHOOL of 1894.

To the N *Campbell-Jones* in 1900–2 built the red-brick and sandstone CHAPEL, the largest and best building in the school, if not perhaps especially full of character. In the chapel the WAR MEMORIAL in the form of a gateway from the ante-chapel to the chapel. 1918–25. Designed and partly executed by *Henry Wilson*, a late work of that ardent Arts and Crafts sculptor and decorator, using the sumptuous materials he loved. Bronze group of St George and three angels, well placed over the low entrance. Flanking panels of splendidly patterned alabaster. Relief of the Virgin and Child on a higher register, and at the very top a youthful Christ in bronze. Bronze gates with rows of small angels. – STAINED GLASS. Sanctuary windows *c*. 1902 and 1905 by *Christopher Whall*. – FRESCO of the Last Supper by *Luini*, first quarter of the C16, alleged to have been removed from the Oratorio of S. Ambrogio in Milan.

Balancing the chapel to the S the LIBRARY by *Sir William Holford*, 1960–2. The decision was taken to keep in keeping with the neo-Gothic of the rest by a steep pitched roof, bay-windows, and vestigially Perp openings in the cloister, yet to outdo everything else in substituting Clipsham ashlar for the rough-hewn local sandstone. When did expensive materials ever make up for timid design?

JUDD SCHOOL, Brook Street. 1895 by *Campbell-Jones*. Large utilitarian additions in 1930–1.

TECHNICAL HIGH SCHOOL FOR GIRLS, Tudeley Lane. A

good modern group, with windows in long bands. Mono-pitch roofs. Yellow brick and black brick. Completed in 1962 by *Charles Pike & Partners*.

PERAMBULATION. Tonbridge, like Sevenoaks and like scores of Wealden villages, grew along the main road. So a perambulation consists of little more than a walk up the N half of the High Street. The Medway bridge is the half-way mark, and there is nothing to note s of it. Up the hill from the bridge however there is first a view of the bailey wall of the castle, newly revealed by demolition of a group of half-timbered houses that ought never to have been allowed to go. The castle is historically no part of the High Street. Just not demolished are two fine and large C15 half-timbered houses. First THE CHEQUERS, with gables to l. and r., both with cusped bargeboards; the l. gable larger and richer. COBLEY'S, next door, is more obviously planned for a cramped site in a street. Two three-storeyed gables, with symmetrical curved braces at two levels. The roof arrangement is most unusual inside: tiebeams, carrying crown-posts, run the depth of each gable, and not across the width of them. In EAST STREET, almost opposite, the PORTREEVE'S HOUSE, a C16 half-timbered house, with oriel windows on brackets. Further up on the r., the ROSE AND CROWN HOTEL has a long C18 brick front, mellowed to the loveliest colours, chequered plum and blue with mottled orange rubbed-brick dressings. The porch comes right across the pavement and supports a splendidly large coat of arms of the Duchess of Kent. At the top of the High Street BORDYKE goes off to the r. It is the most attractive street in the town. No individual building however needs to be described except THE PRIORY, at r. angles to the road. Short sandstone elevation containing two four-light mullioned-and-transomed windows, with architraves, not hood-moulds – suggesting a date for it in the last quarter of the C16. Round the corner a vast sandstone chimneybreast with octagonal brick stacks. Nos 12 and 14 are a pair of narrow three-storeyed houses, a little like overgrown lodge-gates. Perhaps c.1830. Finally, back in the High Street, opposite Tonbridge School, FEROX HALL, a stately front, c.1740, victorianized behind. Red brick beautifully laid. Seven bays and two and a half storeys. Giant pilasters at the angles and marking off the centre bay. Porch on stone Tuscan columns with a triglyph frieze. Two-storeyed hall inside, out of which the staircase rises in a theatrical manner, at first in one flight, then dividing into two which lead up into balustraded balconies. The superstructure arched towards the hall and supported on square Doric piers.

GREAT FISH HALL, 1¾ m. NE. Late C18. Red brick with white string-courses, five bays by five. Three-storeyed.

TOVIL see MAIDSTONE, p. 384

TOYS HILL

2¼ m. SE of Westerham

4050

A view-catching colony, like Crockham Hill, but a C20 one. The TALLY-HO INN is its hub. Just E of the inn is an excellent small house by *Powell & Moya*, 1954, sunk into the hillside below the road. It can teach a lesson in humility e.g. to PIPPINS, next door.

TROTTISCLIFFE

6060

ST PETER AND ST PAUL. A complete, small Norman church. Original N and S windows in the chancel. The chancel is unusually long, the nave unusual in being only fractionally wider than the chancel. Typical materials, big flints as found, set in widely spaced courses, and tufa dressings. SW tower, of knapped flints, barely buttressed, but, as it hides a C13 doorway and blocks a C13 lancet, it cannot be early. All details, in fact, including the plinth, are Perp. A will of 1509 refers to work on it. W wall of the nave rebuilt in 1885 as an exercise in knapped flint technique. E window 1875. PISCINA built in one piece with an early C14 window. Nice interior, crowded out with a big ORGAN, BOX PEWS and fine C18 WOODWORK at the E end not made for the church. – REREDOS. Fluted Corinthian pilasters flanking two cartouches carved with reliefs of the Circumcision and the Flight into Egypt. – ALTAR RAILS. Twisted balusters, enriched newels, and leaf bosses. – PULPIT. Magnificent, reaching to the roof beams. It was designed, in 1775 by *Henry Keene*, for Westminster Abbey, and came to this humble resting-place in 1824. The most exotic feature is the palm tree that carries the sounding board. For the rest, the details are indiscriminately Gothic and classical. – READING DESK. Made up from Jacobean bits. From the old pulpit? – STAINED GLASS. (Medieval canopies and a small Trinity in the nave N window.) – E window 1875 by *Gibbs*. Insensitive. – W window 1885 by *Ward & Hughes*. Limply sentimental. – PLATE. Cup, 1576; Paten, 1699 (?); Almsdish, 1821. – BRASS. William Crofton † 1483. 18 in. figures.

The church is isolated from the village, among open fields below the North Downs. Its only companions are COURT LODGE, C18, with big rusticated brick gatepiers, and some stone COTTAGES (1758 on the datestones) of local rust-coloured sandstone. It is a characteristic, if not a particularly picturesque, group.

CHAMBERED TOMB, ½ m. E of the church. The surviving monument is a stone chamber 13 ft by 5 ft wide composed of four enormous sandstone slabs standing at the E end of a roughly rectangular mound 90 ft long revetted with boulders. The chamber contained twenty-two inhumation burials.

6040

TUDELEY

ALL SAINTS. Approached across a farmyard. Hasted calls the church 'lately rebuilt', and in 1765 an appeal had been made for £1,125 for the rebuilding. Plain W tower, red brick on a sandstone base, with a tiled spirelet. Sandstone footings in the nave, suggesting that the foundations of a medieval church were re-used. The walling in the chancel seems medieval. All windows and the N aisle of 1876 by *R. Medley Fulford* of Exeter, very well done. Aggressive chancel arch by *Wadmore & Baker*, 1885. Restored in 1967 by *Robert Potter* with a greenish marbled nave vault. – ALTAR RAILS. Late C17. – STAINED GLASS. E window 1967 by *Marc Chagall*, his only work in stained glass in the country. The window commemorates Sarah d'Avigdor-Goldsmid, who was drowned in a sailing accident. Below floats a girl in a trough of waves. This part is predominantly blue. Above appears a vision of the crucified Christ, with angels, and a rider on a scarlet horse at the foot of the cross. Yellows blaze out up here. Chagall has taken to designing for stained glass only late in life, and he uses the medium somewhat as if he were working in water-colours. Here it is moving to realize how the washy blues and the lozenge-shaped pieces of glass suggest the idle swell of the sea. – PLATE. Cup, 1569 by *T.E.* – MONUMENTS. Thomas Stydolf † 1457. Brass. Dainty 20 in. figures. – George Fane † 1571. Tomb-chest with a canopy that consists of an entablature on Ionic columns, both correctly detailed, a fact worth noting at this date. No effigy at all. – Sarah d'Avigdor-Goldsmid † 1963. Finely lettered tablet by *Will Carter*.

THE POSTERN, 1 m. NW. A charming and remote-seeming hamlet, though only a mile from Tonbridge. The handsome brick houses of the early C18 make it memorable. POSTERN FARM, of five bays and two storeys, has a capacious hipped roof on a dentilled cornice and the narrow windows beside the door that were a fashion of c.1700. Good group of OASTS.

POSTERN HOUSE is a brighter red, and grander for having three storeys and the roof behind a parapet. Early C18 W front with the centre bay of the five more generously spaced than the rest. The entrance was moved round to the N late in the C18, as the wide semicircular glazed fanlight shows.

TUNBRIDGE WELLS

INTRODUCTION

By tradition the wells were discovered by Dudley, Lord North. See p. 645 In 1606, dissipated and dyspeptic, and bored with a rest cure he had been taking at Eridge Castle, he started to ride back to London. Passing through a wood he noticed water 'which seemed to claim his attention, on account of the shining mineral scum that everywhere swam on its surface, as well as on account of the ochreous substance which subsided at the bottom'.* It tasted promising too, and the following year he returned for a full course of drinking, which, it is said, had an entirely beneficial effect. In 1608 seven springs were found and enclosed, and their fame increased so greatly that in 1630 Queen Henrietta Maria, after the birth of Prince Charles, spent six weeks in a tent, taking the waters. Generally however people stayed at Tonbridge, Southborough, or Rusthall, and the first public buildings near the wells came only in the 1660s. A chapel followed in 1676. The charm of the place for the C18 mind was characteristically summed up in 1766: 'At a little distance, it bears the appearance of a town in the midst of woods, and conveys to the imagination the soothing idea of a rural romantic retirement, while it actually affords all the conveniences of a city life.' In 1810 Tunbridge Wells was still a 'hamlet', an 'assemblage of buildings', 'erected . . . without a plan or semblance of regularity'. The 1830s were the great period of residential expansion, with Decimus Burton's Calverley scheme realized with remarkable completeness. The impetus given by Burton has never slackened since, but the architectural quality of the

* The waters are chalybeate, the iron in the form of ferrous carbonate.

houses after 1840 is almost without exception low, as the Perambulation will suggest. Sadly, no better report can be given of the rebuilding that goes on at the moment in many places around the town.

CHURCHES

KING CHARLES THE MARTYR. Stuart patronage of the wells has already been noted, but such a dedication in the 1670s deserves to be pondered on.* The original building, a simple rectangle oriented N–S, was erected in 1676–8, extended northwards c.1682, and an exact double was added to the W in 1688–90. This produced a building almost square in plan, though N–S was still the longer axis. *Christian*'s restoration came in 1882, and a short E chancel was added, to produce a normal orientation. The exterior is humble, red brick, chequered more or less regularly with blue headers. Two gables to N and S, a clock turret and cupola on the SE gable. Large round-headed windows, as many as six in the W wall.‡ The church's glory is its plaster ceilings, carried on two Ionic columns on high bases. They are built up of a series of shallow domes, and the pattern reflects the three stages of its growth. *John Wetherel* designed and executed the ceiling of 1678, a quincunx of low circular domes, outlined by wreaths of fruit or chains of husks, and with crossed palms and putto heads in the flat interspaces. The richer N addition, with an octagonal dome, was also designed by *Wetherel*, but *Henry Doogood* executed it. In 1690 *Doogood* repeated the whole scheme in the W half. It is worth going into the galleries to compare the two hands: Doogood interprets the pattern with greater bravura (see how he curls back the petals of the husks, which Wetherel left inert and stylized) and makes the motifs fill their spaces more completely. – CHANCEL WOODWORK. Pierced friezes and Creed and Lord's Prayer in elaborate frames. Brought from the demolished Wren church of St Antholin in the City. – FONT. 1906. Soapy white marble. Typical of its date. – STAINED GLASS. Most regrettable E window of 1901.

* The visitors to the wells were mostly Royalists, who wished to counter the local Puritan element, which had named the slopes E and W of the wells Mount Sion and Mount Ephraim.

‡ The contemporary lists of contributors and disbursements, framed in the church, comprise a complete building account. No architect claimed fees, and why should there have been one? Mr *Greene*, bricklayer, was paid £331 10s. for the 'skelliton' of the chapel, and *John Waghorne* was responsible for the two enlargements. The total expenditure for 1676–96 was £2278 1s. 7d.

ST AUGUSTINE (R.C.), Hanover Road. By *Joseph Ireland*. Opened in 1838. Classical rectangle, of rendered stone with pedimental gables, and rusticated quoins and window surrounds. Measly tower of 1889 by *Brett A. Elphicke* (D. Evinson). Internally the flat roofs finely coffered. Altarpiece framed by giant Corinthian columns.*

ST BARNABAS, Stanley Road. 1889–93 by *J. E. K. & J. P. Cutts*. A grandly proportioned church, of brick and sandstone. The chancel as high as the nave and both loftily clerestoried. Shingled flèche over the chancel arch. Lancets in threes and plate tracery. Unusual treatment of the E wall, canted internally on its lower part, with blank arcading that continues the rhythm of the chapel arcades. Fine solid timber roofs. Tower not built.

CHRIST CHURCH, High Street. By *R. Palmer Brown*, 1836–41 (GR). White brick and stone. Neo-Norman, and coarse as only that style could be. Deep, arcaded W portico-porch the full width of the building. – STAINED GLASS. *Morris* glass in the E window, designed by *Burne-Jones*, 1878.

ST JAMES, St James's Road. 1860–2 by *Christian*. The materials are Jackwood and Wadhurst sandstone. Dec style. Nave and gabled aisles. Short canted apsidal chancel. Tower and stone spire over the porch in the NW corner. Arcades of four bays, with round piers and foliage on the capitals. The most personal details are reserved for the tower, where one finds curious plate tracery to the belfry windows and lucarnes on colonettes. – FONT. Given in 1914. Near life-size marble angel holding a shell, a copy of *Thorwaldsen*'s famous font, of 1823.

Is CHURCH HOUSE, with its lean proportions, *Christian*'s too?

ST JOHN, St John's Road. *A. D. Gough*'s church of 1858 only survives in its E parts, the canted apse and transepts. His Dec style and the crazy-paving lay of the ragstone was faithfully followed in the numerous additions. N transept extended 1864, N aisle 1871 by *E. E. Cronk*, who in 1896 built the S aisle, W tower, and flanking porch-passages. New roofs then too. The original nave windows re-used in the aisles. Cronk's tracery is very swirly. Badly proportioned interior, the aisles excessively wide, and opening into the transepts by excruciatingly splayed arches. – STAINED GLASS. E window 1893 by *Kempe*.

* Progress has decreed that the church be demolished, to make way for a supermarket. It's hardly worth asking whether the substitute will be as good architecture as this was.

St Luke, St Luke's Road. 1910 by *Cronk*. Like a church of the 1870s.

St Mark, Broadwater Down. Built in 1864–6 at the expense of the Earl of Abergavenny. At a distant view quite a handsome church. Polygonal E end, transepts, clerestoried nave, NW tower and spire. Close to, however, one sees so many oddities of detailing that it is no surprise to find that the architect was *R. L. Roumieu*. Pale sandstone, the tracery of a darker, yellower, sandstone. The tracery is Dec, but freely introduces unwarranted forms. Steeply sloping window-sills; steeply sloping set-offs to the buttresses, which looks effective on the tower. On the spire strange lucarnes. They rest on buttress-like projections on the belfry stage of the tower, which in turn rest on colonnettes. On the N side a clock surround crashes through the colonnette. Arcades of four bays, the arches striped cream and yellow. Weird E piers, enlarged to take the transept arches as well. What an incredibly complex and ugly shape *Roumieu* achieved, and how gratuitously! (S extension 1968 by *J. J. Aylward*.)

St Peter, Bayhall Road. 1874–5 by *Cronk*. N aisle of 1889 by *Cronk & Cronk*. Sandstone. Dec. Nave and chancel. N aisle as long as both, with a NW tower and spire.

Holy Trinity, Church Road. 1827–9, by that unspeakable Goth, *Decimus Burton*. It cost £10,591 and looks worth every penny of that. Rather one complains at Burton's utter insensitivity to scale and his unreasoning approach to the Gothic style. His idea of a grand town church is a Commissioners' church inflated to twice the normal size and built of sandstone ashlar. So there are a short chancel, nave and aisles under one roof, and a W tower clasped by porches. Polygonal NE vestry. Emphatic buttresses and between them windows of two lights with cusped Y-tracery and hood-moulds on huge, staring head-corbels. Four-light E window with thick, but for its date quite enterprising, Dec tracery. Arcades of five bays, with polygonal piers that have peculiar rectangular back pieces to take the galleries. Moulded capitals, from which the arches are unable to spring truly. Most awkward of all, the piers continue upwards, undiminished, to run slap into a flat ceiling. Thin ribs start from the meeting point, and intersect at quite good foliage bosses. – Font. Marble. An C18 shape. Can it be of the date of the church? – Stained glass. E window *c.*1830. Typical, with its sepia modelling and patches of deep
74 colour. – Monuments. Maria Thomas † 1833. By *William*

Behnes. Fine Grecian hanging monument. Before a stele a boat bearing a draped coffin rides on stylized waves. – Lt Charles Newton † 1843. By *R. Westmacott Jun*. His sword and cap rest on the sill below the inscription. – Anne Burmester † 1848. By the *Marble Works, Westminster*. Large hanging monument with a kneeling female.

The PRIORY, in a Tudor style, and the battlemented entrance archway in Mount Pleasant Road, must be *Burton*'s too.

CONGREGATIONAL CHURCH, Mount Pleasant. Sandstone. The grand Tuscan temple portico was added in 1866 to a church of 1845–8 that seems designed to receive it. Tuscan pilasters, round-headed windows. The style is typically Non-conformist, strikingly more Roman than the Catholic church near by. – LECTURE HALL of 1866.

EMMANUEL (Countess of Huntingdon's Connexion), Mount Ephraim. 1867 by *Wimble & Taylor*. Ragstone. Dec style. With a spire.

PUBLIC BUILDINGS

TOWN HALL, Mount Pleasant Road. 1939 by *Percy Thomas & Ernest Prestwich*. Big and boring, with the entrance on a chamfered corner, a compromise between a neo-Georgian style and the tamest sort of Expressionism. Even the materials, brown brick and stone, seem washed out. PUBLIC LIBRARY next door, part of the same scheme.

CENTRE FOR EDUCATION AND ART, Monson Road. 1901–2 by *H. T. Hare*. Built as the Technical School. A lively façade, in red brick and stone, with three gigantic semi-dormers, and a deep stone frieze with Renaissance motifs, carried round three large mullioned-and-transomed oriels.

OPERA HOUSE, Mount Pleasant Road. Now a bingo hall and bank. 1897 by *John P. Briggs* (GS). Large enough to occupy a whole block. Baroque, and of a flamboyance already fully Edwardian.

SKINNERS' SCHOOL, St John's Road. By *E. H. Burnell*, 1886. Asymmetrical group, with a small porch-tower towards the l., plate-traceried windows lighting the schoolroom, and a gable with half-timbering at the r. Additions in 1899–1900 by *Campbell-Jones*; new DINING HALL, LABORATORIES, etc., by *R. N. Wakelin* of *Campbell-Jones & Sons*, completed 1960.

WEST KENT TECHNICAL COLLEGE, St John's Road. *Elie*

Mayorcas's one-storey workshop block, with its crinkly roof to give clerestory lighting, catches the eye. 1958–9.

KENT AND SUSSEX HOSPITAL, Mount Ephraim. By *Cecil Burns*, 1934. Symmetrical towards the road, of three storeys, descending to two, and then to colonnades on primitive columns. Two-storeyed central porch, with similar columns. The materials are brown brick and concrete, which is used as deep horizontal exposed bands, almost in the 1960s manner. Tall, narrow windows stretch from band to band. The inspiration is from Perret.

EYNSHAM HOUSE (HOSPITAL SERVICE PLAN), St John's Road. Also by *Burns*, and highly interesting for its use of an exposed concrete frame as early as 1931. This, and the whole form of the church, was for Britain a uniquely literal transcription of Perret's stripped Beaux-Arts planning and trabeated concrete detailing. It was originally a Christian Scientist church, but in 1959 was emasculated by *Burns & Guthrie* to adapt it for its present use as offices. The plan was a D, bowed towards the road. The further half of the circle now completed. Two storeys plus a third, recessed. Originally the ground floor was open on round concrete piers, and the tall segment-headed windows, breaking into the top storey, had concrete tracery. It is a great pity that such a rarity has lost its most remarkable features.

TUNBRIDGE WELLS AND COUNTIES CLUB, London Road. 1909. This too is by *Cecil Burns*, and shows that he began as a thoroughgoing neo-Georgian. The gauged brickwork shows considerable expertise.

PERAMBULATION

Naturally one should start from King Charles the Martyr church, immediately s of which a narrow opening leads to The Pantiles, the kernel of the town. To the w however, across LONDON ROAD, rises THE COMMON, criss-crossed by roads, but otherwise as rough as when Henrietta Maria camped on it. Outcrops of sandstone rocks.

HIGH ROCKS HILLFORT. This is a bivallate earthwork of some 20 acres which has been shown by excavation to be of two structural periods. The earlier is marked by the inner bank and ditch, of dump construction. In the CI B.C. the outer, stone-faced rampart with its broad flat-bottomed ditch was added. Both phases had an entrance on the E.

THE PANTILES is the perfect pedestrian precinct. Here are the springs of chalybeate water, bubbling into two basins in the NW corner. A promenade near the springs was first laid out in 1638, and the row of houses and shops on the W side was rebuilt in a regular manner after 1687, with a colonnade.* So it is today, with an upper walk at the level of the colonnade, nearly 200 yds long, curving gently towards the l. On its E edge a row of pollarded lime trees marks the drop to the lower walk, which is more irregular. First it grows out into a little square, then it narrows before rising to go the last part of the way at the upper level. From there steps lead down to a third level, which alone admits traffic. But to begin again in the NW corner, the BATH HOUSE, behind the springs, was built c.1804 by J. T. Groves. Stuccoed, with giant Tuscan pilasters, and a later canopy over the springs, on spindly iron columns. The colonnade is mostly of Tuscan columns, but has been patched in several places. The houses behind it, three- and four-storeyed, mostly C19, but quite varied and vernacular. The memorable bit of the E side is the projecting block, with the raised MUSICK GALLERY at the S end, with pretty, early C19 balustrading. The N part of this block is early C20, and the emphatic red brick makes a very successful accent. On STRAWSON'S, in between, a big board dated 1706, under a scrolly open pediment, carved with the trade-mark of Hughes of Maidstone, who had a general stores here. At the lowest level the CORN EXCHANGE, built in 1801–2 as a theatre. Three storeys, three wide bays. Stuccoed. Porch on Greek Doric columns. Next to it, the taller, wider, and grander ROYAL VICTORIA HOTEL, with the Assembly Rooms. Stuccoed white. Giant pilasters, over a rusticated ground floor painted black. Splendid coat of arms with supporters on the porch, which again has Greek Doric columns. They are the arms of Queen Victoria's parents, the Duke and Duchess of Kent.

Immediately S of The Pantiles, the site of the Pump Room awaits redevelopment (with an OFFICE BLOCK by *Michael Lyell & Associates*). There is no point in pursuing this direction further. Back to the church and now E of it, up CUMBERLAND WALK, a mere path. Here are three especially nice houses of c.1830. Nos 6 and 7 are a pair, insouciantly combining rusticated

* The Walks were first paved in 1700, but repaved with flagstones in 1793, and renamed The Parade. Fifteen of the original so-called pantiles are relaid on the W side, near the springs. Curiously, The Parade came to be known as The Pantiles only as recently as 1887.

walling with hood-moulds and Gothic glazing-bars in the windows. They both have porches with clustered shafts, but No. 7 is distinguished by giant pilasters with capitals in the form of ammonite shells, the perquisite of *Amon Wilds*, of Brighton. No. 8 is taller and more circumstantial, with a first-floor balcony on very long supports. But this too echoes Brighton, in its walling of big round pebbles. White-brick window dressings and quoins, round-headed doorway in a generous coved recess of red rubbed brickwork.

The main development of the town has been northwards, and at each stage houses have spread up the hillside to the E. So as one finally leaves the church towards the N the bottom of the High Street is reached. Nothing of note in it, except possibly the neo-Adam NATIONAL PROVINCIAL BANK of 1914 at the corner of Mount Sion. In MOUNT SION itself big houses of the 1830s, none of them needing to be singled out. At the top however IVY CHIMNEYS, which is C18. Red brick, with a bow towards the E. Here the road turns l. at the crown of the hill, and shortly leads into THE GROVE, four acres assigned as an open space by the Duke of Buckingham in 1707. Oaks were planted on it at first, but today their heirs are limes and beeches. From the far side several lanes lead on to GROVE HILL ROAD, where there is more, more regular, housing of the 1830s, mostly stuccoed pairs with pedimental gables. From Grove Hill Road one can reach Calverley Park, but to make the best sense of Burton's whole scheme it will be better to descend again, to the bottom of Mount Pleasant. Nothing in MOUNT PLEASANT itself, which was built up on its E side in the 1870s at a go, with at the foot the GREAT HALL (now Court School of Dancing) of 1870, excruciatingly ill-proportioned. Bulbous French roofs on the wings but not on the centre. At the top of the hill, by the town hall, Holy Trinity church appears on the l.

To the r., in CRESCENT ROAD, *Decimus Burton*'s Calverley scheme begins to unfold. The land belonged to John Ward, for whom Burton had built Holwood (*see* p. 317) in 1824, and the layout was established in 1828, i.e. in the same year as Burton began the St Leonards development at Hastings for his father. The inspiration of both is Nash at Regents Park. At Calverley, Burton planned a series of villas overlooking a private park, a row of shops, other individual houses, and a hotel.[*]

* Holy Trinity church, across Mount Pleasant Road, is of course meaningfully related to the estate.

In Crescent Road, on the l., Nos 9–10 CALVERLEY TERRACE, a semi-detached pair, built of sandstone, the material Burton used throughout. On the r. the CALVERLEY HOTEL, built by *Burton* as a private house, enlarged by him and opened as a hotel in 1840. As a result the large scale seems unhappily judged. CALVERLEY PARK CRESCENT comes next on the r., a slightly curved terrace of seventeen houses, three-storeyed, with a covered promenade in front on the thinnest cast-iron supports. Built soon after 1830, with shops in the ground floor, but almost at once converted into private houses. The architectural treatment is very simple, the centre five bays and one at each end emphasized by an extra cornice and tripartite windows. Immediately SE of this, VICTORIA LODGE, a high, thin, sandstone arch, with low, square side rooms, fronted with pairs of heavy Greek Doric attached columns. This marks the entrance to CALVERLEY PARK. 81 Nineteen villas, arranged in a rough semicircle, look down from behind garden hedges on to the Calverley Grounds, the landscaped slope of Mount Pleasant. It is suburbia's *beau idéal*, lavish with space, architecturally solid but not pretentious. Indeed Burton here shows up at his very best. The designs are varied, never repeating one another, but the idiom is spare, relaxed, and remarkably homogeneous, a good deal more so in fact than Nash had been at Park Village East. One accent is allowed per house, usually a bow or a canted bay, or a part raised higher than the rest, and the accent may be central or at one side. Great play is made with verandas; the roofs are low, on deep bracketed eaves. Only an occasional hood-mould breaks the simplified Italianate style. KESTON LODGE, NE of Calverley Park Crescent, and FARNBOROUGH LODGE, at the SE corner, are both one-storeyed sandstone cottages. The former has an octagonal part towards the road and a tall chimneystack.*

CAMDEN PARK was laid out further SE *c.*1853 in imitation of Calverley Park, but only five houses were built (by 1863).‡ In design they clearly depend on Burton too, but the Italianate details are coarser and more numerous, the materials typically white brick and stone, or a rendering of Roman cement. At

---

* Outlying houses in *Burton*'s Calverley Park manner are: THE HOLLIES, in Calverley Park Gardens, and THE WOODLANDS, in Pembury Road. The latter has a jumped-up broken pediment to crown it.

‡ But Colbran's *Handbook* for 1847 speaks of land already laid out by Marquess Camden for houses designed by *Decimus Burton*.

the E end, in FOREST ROAD, a new eight-storey block of government OFFICES, with a three-storey wing coming forward at r. angles. 1963 by *R.P. Mills*.

The return route to the centre of the town should be by CALVERLEY ROAD, where *Decimus Burton*'s OLD TOWN HALL, 1835, still remains, much altered. It was built as a market hall, the centrepiece of a group. On each side two pairs of semi-detached houses act as supporting pavilions. Sandstone. Classical, with central pediments but no columns. These too have been spoilt by modern shopfronts. Further down, at the corner of Camden Road, NATIONAL PROVIDENT BUILDING, a new shopping parade, neo-Georgian, forsooth, in 1966. The architects were *Green, Lloyd & Son*.

w of Mount Pleasant Road there is much less to note. The higher end of the Common is very picturesque, with a heavily barge-boarded cottage growing out of a big rock. In LONDON ROAD, No. 72 has a nice Chinesey balcony, but neither here nor in MOUNT EPHRAIM, on the top side of the Common, is there any other building worth comment. All the big hotels are distressingly ugly. In NEVILL PARK and HUNGERSHALL PARK, further W, more ugly Italianate houses of the 1850s and 60s, mostly done over with Roman cement.*

TWYDALL see GILLINGHAM

TWYSSENDEN see GOUDHURST

ULCOMBE

8040

ALL SAINTS. Ragstone church set on the ragstone hills with a grand view S over the Weald. The history of the building is complex. Two blocked Norman N windows tell of an aisleless nave. Early in the C13 one very wide bay of a N chapel and a whole S aisle were thrown out. Slightly-chamfered arches and jambs of the rectangular piers. Undercut abacus moulding. Similar, extraordinarily lofty, chancel arch, with simple abaci, chamfered on their undersides. The Norman chancel had however possessed a S chapel even earlier. Two-bay arcade on a round pier with a square, scallop capital and arches pointed but unmoulded. Chancel rebuilt with generously increased

* *John Billing* built a villa in the former in 1855. No. 11 Hungershall Park, so Mr Geoffrey Spain informs me, was designed by *H.H.Cronk* in 1862, and cost £2,132.

dimensions in a full-blown E.E. style.* Triplet of tall E
lancets, with Purbeck marble shafts internally, with stone caps,
bases, and shaft-rings, and a continuous hollow-chamfered
moulding dotted with stylized roses. N and S sanctuary windows under relieving arches. The windows however are early
C14, the S one an especially interesting one, first because it
is made of Bethersden marble, secondly for its tracery of
quatrefoils, split-cusped and linked by bars to the framework.
That is as at Chartham c.1294, but here they are above ogee-
headed lights. Various Dec and Perp windows in other places.
The S chapel e.g. has all reticulated tracery. Late Perp N chapel,
with straight-headed N windows and an arcade pier of the
four-shafts-and-four-hollows variety. Perp W tower. Diagonal
buttresses, SE turret, and Dec S annexe.

The interior has recently been whitewashed, which helps a lot
to give it unity. Well designed arrangement of the sanctuary,
1960–1 by *Colin Shewring*. – SCREENS. Dec in the S chapel,
with cuspless mouchette wheels. – STALLS integral with it, and
four old MISERICORDS, with a lion and double-ended dragons.
– Late Perp screen in the N chapel, of charming daintiness. –
STAINED GLASS. N chapel E window. Old quarries and
armorial glass. – WALL PAINTINGS. The soffit of the N aisle
arch has a bold contemporary pattern of chevrons. Small C13
Crucifixion on the E respond of the S chapel arcade. In the S
aisle, Dives and Lazarus and St Michael overcoming Satan;
and, on the soffit of one of the arches, drawn with far
greater skill, a crucified Christ, late C13. As in contemporary manuscript illuminations, the lines describing the contorted limbs
are beautifully sinuous but not in the least expressive. – PLATE.
Cup and Paten, 1697 by *William Gamble*. – MONUMENTS.
William Maydestone † 1419. 34 in. brass, of a knight, under a
canopy, standing on a flower-strewn mound. – Brass of a
knight † 1442. 38 in. figure. – Radulph Sentleger † 1470. Fine,
flamboyant brass. 43 in. figures, he in fantastic plate armour,
she with a butterfly headdress. – Sir Francis Clerke † 1685.
Big black and white architectural tablet of high quality. –
Francis Clerke † 1691. Elegant draped cartouche. – William
Belcher † 1709. Tablet, with two putto heads at the bottom.
– Samuel Belcher † 1760. Tablet, with one putto head. – Rev.
Stringer Belcher and others, c.1819. Draped urn on a Soanian
tablet with tapering sides. *Charles King* signs it. – Marquess of

* From the early C13 the incumbent of Ulcombe had the title Archpriest.
No other evidence that the church was ever collegiate.

Ormonde † 1820. By *J. Bacon Jun. & S. Manning.* Hanging monument with the standard mourning female by a sarcophagus. – Lady Sarah Wandesforde † 1838. By *T. & E. Gaffin.* Tablet with the standard woman borne by an angel heavenward.

ULCOMBE PLACE, beside the church. Ragstone façade with an early C19 veranda. (Blocked C14 arch inside. MHLG)

At Knowle Hill, ¾ m. SE, KNOWLE HILL HOUSE, refronted in 1736 in plum-coloured brick. Two storeys. Steep hipped roof behind a parapet. Segmental windows; pilaster strips marking the three bays. Also LOWER KNOWLE HILL FARMHOUSE, E-shaped half-timbered house, once the rectory, now tile-hung up to the gables.

Like most of the half-hill–half-Weald parishes, Ulcombe has plenty of half-timbered houses scattered through it, more or less disguised. It is perhaps worth singling out BOY COURT, 2¼ m. S, for its fanciful curved bracing, the demure, chequered brick front of the C18, and as a group with oast-houses behind.

5050

UNDERRIVER

ST MARGARET. 1870–5 by *Sir G. G. Scott* at the expense of the Hon. J. R. Davison. Nave and lower chancel. W bell-gable. Timber N porch. Late C13 style. – ORGAN CASE. Early Renaissance detail. 1934 by *Caröe.*

ST JULIAN'S, ¾ m. NW. Built in 1818–20 by *J. B. Papworth* for J. C. Herries (statesman and briefly Chancellor of the Exchequer), in a superb position on the S slope of the sandstone hills. Yellow brick. Symmetrical S front with three shaped gables, a very early instance of the C19 revival of Jacobean shapes, and three stone window-bays, rising the full two storeys and superabundantly glazed. Mullions and simple Perp tracery. The E and W fronts were originally triple-gabled too, with crisp, white bargeboards, hood-moulds to the windows, and a pinnacled entrance porch on the E side; but the N gable of each has disappeared in the enlargement of the service parts to a full three storeys. *Pennethorne* enlarged the house; but these adaptations are largely the work of the *Architects' Co-Partnership,* from 1951 onwards, converting the house into a group of co-operative flats. They have done it with engaging informality and tact – big windows, pale yellow brick – but without compromising themselves. No original interiors, apart from three upper rooms on the S side with groin-vaults.

UPNOR

ST JAMES. By *Ewan Christian*. Red brick. Cruciform, with an apsidal E end. Lancets. The church was paid for by Captain and Mrs Savage and completed in 1878.

CASTLE. Built on the bank of the Medway in 1559–67 to guard the new dockyards at Chatham across the water. The designer, *Sir Richard Lee*, abandoned the geometrical plans of Henry VIII's castles, for the defences needed to be directed only towards the E, and built a two-storeyed, rectangular main block, of ragstone broken forward in the centre with a polygonal bay to take a circular staircase, and at the ends of the E front with circular turrets, with garderobes. Bulls-eye windows with classical mouldings, a later insertion; doorways with four-centred heads. A start was also made on round-fronted turrets l. and r., with splayed openings for guns to cover the castle's flanks. The main gun platform however was the low, triangular bastion in front of the main building. In 1599–1601 landward defences were improved by *Arthur Gregory*. He linked the side turrets with the main block and continued the walls back to enclose a rectangular courtyard. In the centre of the w wall a gatehouse was constructed, with rectangular corner towers on the inner side, and a drawbridge. Brick heightening of the gatehouse and coping of all walls in 1653.

In 1667 the Dutch sailed up the Medway and put Upnor Castle to the very test it was built to withstand. It failed the test, and de Ruyter set fire to the English fleet. In 1669 *Sir Bernard de Gomme*'s blockhouses on both sides of the river reinforced the defences, and as late as *c.*1718 a three-storeyed block of BARRACKS was built (brown brick, rusticated quoins), s of the castle.

CASTLE HOUSE, 100 yds w. Early C19 five-bay E front, added to a late C17 building, with a complex system of gables to the w, the centre gable shaped.

A Dickensian STREET, of weatherboarded and stock-brick cottages, runs down the hill to the water's edge s of the castle enclosure. The finest view downstream however is to be had N of the castle, with the three-masted ARETHUSA training ship backed by the wooded slopes of the Grain peninsula.

UPPER BUSH *see* CUXTON

VANE COURT *see* BIDDENDEN

WALDERSLADE

A largely post-war extension of Chatham southwards into the chalk valleys. The waves of red-brick houses swirling along the contours have not yet wiped out entirely the beauty of the hills. Recently a village centre has grown up, one not without merit.

ST PHILIP AND ST JAMES, King George's Road. 1961–2 by *D.J.Pamplin*. Yellow brick. Rectangular plan. Monopitch roof, with a reverse slope to give hidden side-lighting to the sanctuary. Mannered arrangement of windows in the s wall. – PARISH HALL on the s side, enclosing a grassy quadrangle.

Good new PUBLIC LIBRARY of 1957 to the SE, in the same style. By *L.W.Russell*, of *Chatham Borough Engineer and Surveyor's Department*. Hall and pavilion added in 1964 by the same department.

Across the main road, off Bradfield's Avenue, WALDERSLADE SECONDARY SCHOOLS, an excellent pair of small, crisp schools by *Richard Sheppard, Robson & Partners*, completed in 1958.

S of the church, in Snodhurst Avenue, OLD PEOPLE'S COMMUNITY DWELLINGS, opened in 1967. Here too the design came from the *Chatham Borough Engineer and Surveyor's Department* (*W.L.Cooke* architect). Much less well detailed than the other recent buildings, but a commendable attempt to make use of the slope, instead of pretending it isn't there. Designers of housing please note.

WAREHORNE

ST MATTHEW. A nice village, nothing but a handful of houses scattered haphazard round a tiny green and the church behind trees to the s. The church itself is without and within most enjoyably unrestored. Big bleak red-brick W tower of 1773, and small red-brick N porch with a compass gable. Otherwise externally all is Dec. In the aisles cusped intersecting tracery and large windows to light aisle altars.* The side windows of the chancel, of two long square-headed lights (with segmental rere-arches), cannot be earlier than the middle of the C14. The E window is of course Perp. The interior is delightfully spacious, full of light from the tall windows. Lofty Perp tower arch. Arcades on slim and exceedingly elegant piers of local marble, the mouldings of the E pier of each clearly later than

* The E window of the N aisle must have been tampered with.

the w. The head that supports the mighty mouldings of the NW corbel is as boldly simplified as if Henry Moore had done it. In the chancel another unusual Dec arrangement of PISCINA and SEDILIA: the sill of the SE window is dropped and the piscina contrived in the canted angle. Along the back, a trail of foliage, exquisite but with many pieces broken off. Nice simple C19 BOX PEWS and FITTINGS, especially the moveable PULPIT. – Four TEXT BOARDS under the tower. – STAINED GLASS. In the tracery of a N aisle window, two roundels of a man with a sword and a man with a buckler. – In a S window a mythical monster, part lion, part man. – PLATE. Cup, late C17; Flagon, 1722; Paten, 1737 by *Thomas Tearle*.

LEACON HALL, ½ m. NW. An almost perfect Queen Anne house. Red brick with grey vitrified headers. Seven bays, two storeys. Hipped roof with dormers and big chimneystacks. Rubbed-brick window heads cut into fanciful frills. On the present glazed porch the original carved porch brackets are hung, upside-down. The house was built by Thomas Hodges, and there is a date 1708 inside.

WATCH HOUSE see SMARDEN

WATERINGBURY

ST JOHN THE BAPTIST. E.E. rendered W tower (shingled spire rebuilt in 1886), Perp chancel. Unpleasant C19 work in between, with grey slate roofs and yellow Bath stone tracery. *Joseph Clarke* was the culprit – he added the S aisle in 1856. N aisle 1883–4 by *W. O. Milne*. Originally the nave was Perp, with tall three-light windows, rather like Nettlestead. Two of the windows survive, as the W windows of the aisles. Old roof in the nave, tiebeams on stone demi-angel corbels. Clarke's S arcade is for 1856 an enterprising piece of simplification, with the arches dying into circular piers without any capitals.* – PLATE. Elizabethan Cup; Cup and Cover, *c.*1675, tall, gilt, with foliage and figures in high relief and a Vernicle held by cherubs; Paten and Flagon, 1737. – MONUMENTS. The church pales before the gorgeous tomb of Olyver Style, erected in 1628, by which time such ostentatious displays were going out of fashion. Standing monument with a recumbent man in aldermanic robes, and his wife behind on a slightly higher level.

* CURIOSUM. Dumb Borse Holder, a manorial not an ecclesiastical instrument, a sort of wooden truncheon with an iron spike at the top and an iron ring at the bottom, the former for breaking down doors with.

Coupled Ionic columns carry a deep coffered arch with three big armorial cartouches. Behind the columns on the l. an angel holding a crown, on the r. a skeleton in a shroud, both carved with considerable bravura. – Mendham Evans † 1853. Draped woman leaning on an urn. Weak and flaccid, especially by the contrast. Hopelessly out of date too, in the 1850s: Bacon was doing this sort of thing seventy years before. – In the CHURCHYARD the MONUMENT of Sir Oliver Style † 1702 stands right by the s porch, impossible to miss, with its flamboyant display of five fluted urns.

WATERINGBURY PLACE. Just W of the church, but entirely hidden from view. The house was built in 1707 by Thomas Style, of fine crimson, vermilion, and russet brick. Seven bays by five, of three storeys, the top one above a broad white frieze and cornice. Panelled top parapet. The E (original entrance) front has a three-bay centre breaking forward slightly. This and the angles are marked by giant Ionic pilasters, and the frieze is on this side embellished with brackets grouped in threes with a singleton between each group. Angle pilasters and a third storey above the entablature were the distinctive features of Captain Winde's Buckingham House (later Buckingham Palace) of 1703–5, and were taken up again enthusiastically in the 1720s by architects like Francis Smith of Warwick. Wateringbury is by comparison a little lean and leggy, an early but provincial version of the theme. Italianate additions of the 1850s to the N. The hall runs the full depth of the house (did it do so from the first ?), and out of it the staircase rises spaciously. Three slim twisted balusters to each tread. Several fine mid and late c18 chimneypieces have been brought in, especially a Rysbrackian one in stone with a relief of putti painting, sculpting, etc. The circular ceiling painting in the SW room originally formed the centrepiece of *Valdré*'s decoration of the Music Room at Stowe, 1777–80.

THATCHED HOUSE, nearly opposite the church. White early c19 box, with big extensions behind. The thatch comes down on three sides as two-storey gabled verandas, held up by wooden posts.

LEASDENE, E of Thatched House, is dangerously fashionable housing of 1966, by *Belcher & Clapson* (in association with *P. R. Beake*), each bungalow seeming its own little courtyard prison.

WAYSTRODE MANOR *see* COWDEN

WEAVER'S COURT see BIDDENDEN

WELLING 4070

ST JOHN, Roseacre Road. 1925 by *Evelyn Hellicar*. Brown brick, in the simplest Perp style; as if it were something shameful to be still building a Gothic church in the 1920s. It is indeed a shame that an architect should build in a style he no longer believes in.

ST MARY THE VIRGIN, Wickham Street. 1954–5 by *Thomas F. Ford*. The exterior is no more impressive than St John. Red brick, in a sort of Georgian–Early Christian style, with a thin Lombard s tower. Inside it is pure Soane revival, and not bad in its way. A building like this epitomizes all that mid-C20 architecture ought not to be, yet one at least feels that Mr Ford got a kick out of designing it. – WALL PAINTINGS. E wall, Ascension by *Hans Feibusch*. – The rest by *Clare Dawson*, Old and New Testament scenes arranged typologically, in accordance with common medieval practice.

Welling is almost wholly a creation of the 1920s and 30s, and its churches match the timidity of the faceless and seemingly endless housing around.

WELL STREET see EAST MALLING

WESTERHAM 4050

ST MARY. A characteristic outline from the valley, three equal E gables, with a sturdy shingled spire behind – which signifies continuous aisles to nave and chancel and a w tower. A nearer approach is disappointing, as every single window is harshly and pedantically renewed. *Teulon* made 'alterations' in 1854. Another restoration in 1882. Rubble sandstone walls. There is external evidence of the C13 – a blocked arch in the s wall of the tower, and the quoins of an aisleless chancel and traces of its E triplet. Perp arcades. No chancel arch. The piers all have four shafts and four hollows, and they carry depressed arches; but the enlargement was done piecemeal, and the N and S arcades do not make a pair either in the chancel or in the nave. The chancel s arcade is cut out of the thick C13 chancel wall. As for the curious arcading high in the s wall of the aisle, Canon Livett thought it was done to thicken the wall enough for the wall-plate of the roof. The roofs are mostly boarded with moulded principals and ridge-ribs. Crown-posts in the chancel aisles. – TOWER STAIRS. Spiralling up in an open octagonal cage. Much renewed, but basically medieval. – FONT. Standard Perp. Octagonal. Quatrefoils on the bowl. – ROYAL ARMS, of Edward VI. The only arms of this reign and so, but for Rushbrooke, Suffolk, the earliest of all to survive in England. Oil on panel. Much better done than most later Royal Arms, and with a few Early Renaissance details typical of the period (1547–53). – ORGAN CASE. 1871 by *J. F. Bentley*. Vivaciously Perp.* – STAINED GLASS. Two S windows by *Powell*'s, both with glowing turquoise and orange, but the SE window, designed by *Holiday* in 1864, much better than *Casolani*'s of 1866. Holiday had been looking at the Pre-Raphaelites. – Aisle E windows by *Kempe*, S 1888, N 1890. – PLATE. Cup and Paten Cover of 1566, the cup by *I.P.* – Covered Cup, 1600, made in Nuremberg, by *G. S.* Repoussé strapwork all over the cup. The finial of the cover is a man with a shield.‡ – Paten, 1616?; Paten, 1691; Flagon and pair of Almsdishes, 1719. – The BRASSES are all late and mostly small. A list can suffice. Richard Potter † 1511 and two wives. – Richard Hayward † 1529. – Thomas Potter † 1531. – John Stacey † 1533. – Wm. Myddilton † 1557 and two wives. – Wm. Stace † 1566 and two wives. – Wm. Dye † 1567. – MONUMENTS. Hanging monument to Thomas Potter † 1611, with the usual small kneeling figures. – Mary Hardy † 1716. Tablet with twisted columns, attributed by Rupert Gunnis to *James Hardy*. A number of other good tablets.

The main street curls sinuously up the hill and over and down again. The best houses are at the beginning and at the end, and in the middle the 'neat, handsome, well-built market town' that Defoe knew is being dangerously diluted by shopping parades and a block of flats in no relation to anything else.

QUEBEC HOUSE starts the town at the E end. Such a square brick block, three storeys high and with three gables a side, must be early C17. The brick hoods of the gable windows, ironed flat as it were, give the date away. The windows otherwise all altered a hundred years later. The gables to the road modern, but no doubt correct. Inside, re-used C16 fireplaces and a sturdy mid-C17 staircase; but there must have been a drastic re-arrangement of the plan. GROSVENOR HOUSE,

* Major J. R. O'B. Warde quotes correspondence that shows the organ cost £465, its case £25

‡ On permanent loan to the Victoria and Albert Museum.

across the road, is the handsomest house in Westerham, early
C18 and very urbane. Blue brick headers, trimmed with red
brick. Two storeys and five bays. Giant corner pilasters. Plain
parapet over a moulded brick cornice. Segmental heads to the
windows and brick keystones. The doorcase has Doric pilasters,
a triglyph frieze, and the panelled reveals splayed out.

Round THE GREEN there is nothing to comment on except
THE PHEASANTRY of *c.*1700, on the l., looking more than
ever like a doll's house now that it is painted salmon pink and
powder blue. At the top end of The Green *Derwent Wood*'s
STATUE of General Wolfe, 1910, the *clou* of the town. Lead _{See}
on a bulgy stone base. Wolfe, in a cocked hat, awkwardly _{p.}
brandishes his sword. Something slicker would not have ₆₄₅
fitted so well. Here LONDON ROAD goes down to the r. In it,
first the MORETON ALMSHOUSES, of 1874, heavily picturesque, half-timbered above, sandstone below. Pretty well-head
by the road. Then the low, grey-brick buildings of the
WESTERHAM PRESS. 1965–6 by *Stevens, Giddens & Partners*.
Nice and unassuming.

MARKET SQUARE, just the street broadening at the top of the
rise, is dominated by the early C19 KING'S ARMS, stuccoed
and nicely painted black, grey, and blue. At the far end of
LODGE LANE, which runs off to the l. a little further on,
SQUERRIES LODGE, a large, plain C18 house rendered an
ochreous colour. Incorporated in its SE corner however most
interesting fragments of a mid-C13 stone house. Outside one
sees, in the E wall of the main block, the head of a sizeable
plate-traceried window. A narrow two-storeyed stone block
runs further E, S of this window. No original external features,
except putlog-holes. The SW quoin remains, and a large
buttress cased in brick on the S side. Internally however the
picture fills out considerably. Rere-arch to the plate-traceried
window, and close by, at r. angles, a richly moulded C13 arch
at a slightly lower level. Have we then the N doorway and E
window of a first-floor hall? The SE projection has a small E
window with chamfered segmental rere-arch, a narrow doorway in the S wall, chamfered inside and rebated outside, with
a later window masking it from without, and W of and at r.
angles to it, another similar doorway. The medieval house
extended further W. The evidence here on the ground floor
consists of a pair of doorways on the N side, and a double
stone corbel at ceiling height in the S wall.

Thereafter the High Street narrows and twists down until houses

give way on the l. to meadows and on the r. to industry – the
BREWERY of 1899. Beyond it only GREAT MORETONS, early
C18 much added to, and FARLEY, c.1700, five by five bays
and a big hipped roof. The fields opposite are the park of
Squerries Court, and the entrance comes almost at once.

SQUERRIES COURT. A fine late C17 house without much individual character but unusually craftsmanly in the brickwork. Built before 1686. Two storeys, seven bays, the centre
three breaking forward a little under a pediment. Hipped
roof, dormers, and broad stacks. Rubbed-brick pilaster strips
round the angles. The garden front an exact duplicate. Later
entrance porch; stone, Tuscan columns *in antis*.

The house faces over a lake to a knoll, where stands a little
sandstone PAVILION, built in 1735, with a Venetian motif
opening in each side.*

WEST FARLEIGH

ALL SAINTS. A complete Early Norman church, nave and
straight-ended chancel. One tiny E window flanked by lancets,
and a N and a S window high in the nave. All the other original
features, i.e. E quoins, chancel arch, and W doorway (within
the tower), are of tufa, recognizable by the pitted surface, like
a petrified sponge. The depressed chancel arch has nothing
but two plain square orders, but a fat roll goes round the arch
of the W doorway, and of its shafts one cushion capital is left.
Thin Perp W tower, with NE turret, octagonal at the top. No
buttresses. Money was bequeathed in 1523 'to the makyng of
the Stiple'. Tower heightened in 1841. – PISCINAS, in chancel
and nave, both of chalk and both consisting of two plain
pointed arches at r. angles to each other. – RECESS in the nave,
richly cusped, as at East Farleigh, with a modern square hood.
– FONT COVER. Perp, of wood, just ogee in profile and with
crockets up the ribs and an octagonal finial. – FAMILY PEW,
now at the back of the church. C18. – PLATE. Paten and
Flagon of 1719. – MONUMENTS. Edward Lawrence † 1605.
Small hanging monument. He, his wife, six sons, and five
daughters, little kneeling figures, are crammed into the usual
architectural surround. – The rest are a fine group of purely
architectural tablets increasingly elaborate as the years go by.
Augustine Skynner † 1672. Black and white, with Ionic

* At Squerries Court Farm a good stone DOVECOTE (P. J. Tester).

columns recessed at the sides. – Jane Brewer † 1676. Similar, but with side scrolls and a scrolly pediment. – Jane Brewer † 1716, by *Robert Taylor*. Distinctly larger, and entirely of grey-veined marble. Fluted Doric pilasters on a bold gadrooned base. Cherub heads at the bottom, a vase and lamps at the top. – Edward Goulston † 1720. Similar, but with 'acanthus' capitals. Finely carved, crackly forms, especially the skull at the bottom.

SCHOOL, ¼ m. SW. Prominently dated 1845, and a fascinating contrast with the school at East Farleigh. Picturesque irregular front of yellow brick and red brick. Big segment-headed windows, gables with big bargeboards tweaked down at the corners. Obviously it is a descendant of the *cottage orné*, and equally obviously Street's schools develop from this sort of thing.*

COURT LODGE, beside the church and enclosing it in its park. Three-storeyed rendered front of *c*.1800. On a rusticated basement giant pilasters between the windows. They have anthemium capitals. Porch with unfluted Greek Doric columns.

WEST FARLEIGH HALL, ¾ m. SW. A splendid Early Georgian house, appearing behind a wall as the *clou* of the best hamlet in the parish. Long and low front, of nine bays divided by giant pilasters in a rhythm three-plus-three-plus-three. Two storeys, bold dentilled cornice and panelled parapet. The date 1719 appears on a rainwater-head: Badeslade's engraving of that year shows a third storey above the cornice, which would have given the front more normal proportions but not necessarily made it more successful. Dull brown brick enlivened by the vivid red of the rubbed-brick details. The windows all have segmental heads, key blocks, and sunk panels below them, double ones to the upper windows. All the brickwork beautifully executed. Later C18 porch, broken pediment on columns with anthemium capitals. In the two-storeyed hall a most unusual and spectacular arrangement of the staircase. It goes[65] up in the far r. corner, rising out of sight behind a first-floor balcony that stretches the full width of the hall, supported in the centre on a great square fluted Corinthian pier, and bellying forward at the sides, where it rises with a few more steps. Slim twisted balusters throughout. In a NE room a large relief bust of John Locke and part of the late C18 library decoration

---

* Miss A. E. Wakefield tells me that the builders were *Tassell & Bulman*, who sent in an estimate for £312. Did they design what they built?

from The Rookery, Bromley. An Adamesque marble fireplace with terms, in a SE room, comes from the same source.*

STABLES of 1790 SW of the house. Red brick. Wide central pediment. Side windows under sunk arches.

WESTHOY FARM see SMARDEN

WEST HYTHE

¾ m. SE of Lympne

ST MARY. The three walls of the nave, of coursed stone, and the pointed chancel arch of the ruined parish church yet stand. The arch of the blocked S doorway, with chip-carved diapering, guarantees the nave's Norman date.

WEST KINGSDOWN

A higgledy-piggledy scatter of bungalows along the A20, with no sense of place. At the S end there is a recently restored WINDMILL, a black weatherboarded smock, white sweeps and fantail, moved here from Farningham in 1880. The three churches of the parish all lie away from the houses.

ST EDMUND. Hidden in a wood, within sound of Brands Hatch. The nave and the tall lean tower at its SE corner are Saxo-Norman, showing one small S window in the nave, with jambs of flint and irregular voussoir stones. The tower is square, of flint, with flint quoins (which makes one think that the round flint towers of East Anglia and Sussex were a local fashion as much as a necessity). In the E wall of the tower a tall blocked arch. Did it open into an apse, as at Godmersham? I.e., was it used as a chapel, in the manner of tower-naves such as Barton-on-Humber? The chancel too may be contemporary, though its windows are Dec. Traces of a short Norman S aisle and of a later S chancel chapel. – WALL PAINTINGS on the splays of the early window. On the l. the Sacrifice of Cain and Abel, on the r. Cain killing Abel. Tristram dated them to the second half of the C12. – STAINED GLASS. Two C14 quatrefoils in the nave N windows: Christ in Majesty, and a crowned Virgin and Child. – A few more bits in a S window. – PLATE. Cup and Paten, 1713 by *Matthew Lofthouse*.

On the other side of the main road, 1¼ m. SW, is what remains of another Early Norman church, of MAPLESCOMBE. Origin-

* As Major-General C. W. Norman pointed out to me.

ally a nave and apsidal chancel in one with it; now just a chunk of flint wall among some elder bushes.

At the furthest end of Knatt's Valley, 2 m. W of West Kingsdown church, in a position that is still amazingly remote, *Talbot Bury* built in 1851–2 what was to be the nucleus of a new parish of WOODLANDS, i.e. CHURCH, SCHOOL, and VICAR-AGE, all three with bell-gables, the school mimicking the shape of the church. Major Vincent, a surgeon at Guy's Hospital, paid for the church.

WEST MALLING

6050

ST MARY. An uncommon history has produced the present pleasing building. Early Norman evidence in the chancel, one blocked tufa S window and part of another. Also a quoin in the N wall to mark a later lengthening. Renewed lancets, but a genuine C13 N doorway, with dogtooth on the outer mould-ing. Naturally, the lengthening was a C13 event. Early Nor-man evidence again at the W end, herringbone walling low in the N and S walls of the tower. Also a round-headed window high in the W wall. The tower is short and substantial. The needle spire that shoots up so high from it came only in 1837. Nave rebuilt in 1780–2 by *Gwilt*, and rebuilt again by *Mickle-thwaite*, 1900–1, leaving the C18 E end and half the W wall. N porch 1903. In every way Micklethwaite did a well-mannered, sensitive job. He used local ragstone, not the rubble of the rest of the church, but squared blocks chosen with great care to get subtle variations of colour. Nave and battlemented aisles. Clerestory. Square-headed windows and reticulated tracery, the aisle windows widely spaced. All the forms low. Arcades of standard local type, but with the vertical piece above the capital so much a favourite late in the C19. In the chancel more C13 details, original lancet rere-arches, those in the sanctuary shafted. Contemporary SEDILIA. Medieval SE vestry. One last remark needs making about the nave. There must of course originally have been a Norman one filling the gap between chancel and tower, 72 ft long, i.e. quite unusually long. In fact, as an excavation in 1901 revealed, the nave took up only the E two-thirds of the gap – the W part was an E annex to the tower.* Tower, annex, and nave were all the same width. – STAINED GLASS. E window 1865 by *Lavers & Bar-raud*. – ROYAL ARMS of James II. A remarkably lavish piece,

* A Saxon idea? asks NP.

with a deep relief border of flowers and fruit. – MONUMENTS. William Millys † 1497. 15½ in. brass of a civilian. – Elizabeth Perepoynt † 1543. Top half of a brass, originally *c.*38 in. long. – Sir Robert Brett † 1624. Large alabaster standing monument, with reclining effigies. Coupled black Ionic columns, carrying a deep coffered arch, with cartouches of arms at the top. Shrouded skeleton and a kneeling child behind the columns. So the design is very close to the Style monument at near-by Wateringbury (1628). This, commemorating the earlier death, even so looks like the derivative one. Latin verses in elegantly turned iambics. – Mary Sneeth † 1718. Fine big cartouche. – Peter Elliston † 1720. Architectural tablet. – Humphrey Bartholmew † 1764. Tablet with an open pediment.

MALLING ABBEY. Gundulf, the first Norman Bishop of Rochester, founded a Benedictine nunnery at Malling before 1090. The church was dedicated in 1106. In the C18 the abbey ruins became the sport of Frazer Honeywood, who built himself a house among and out of them. Since 1893 however Benedictine nuns have returned, and in 1916 an Anglican Benedictine community was established here. Unfortunately for *The Buildings of England* this means that Honeywood's house and the medieval cloisters are within the enclosure and the attempt at description below (set in brackets) is based on inadequate photographs and pre-enclosure descriptions.

The GATEHOUSE presents a C15 appearance outside, with the usual two arches, a large two-centred one for carts, and a small four-centred one r. of it for foot-passengers. The same bold mouldings for each. Shields with symbols of the Passion on the string-course above the latter. Two chimneybreasts to the l., one to the r., the only evidence on this side of habitation. On the inner side the upper storey projects, plastered and half-timbered behind. The chapel projecting at the NE corner however has a Dec s window, and a large E one completely renewed. Perp stoup by the doorway.

Turning now to look at the abbey buildings, one sees on the l. the w front of the Norman abbey, and linked to its s wall the w range of *Maguire & Murray*'s recent cloisters. The C15 GUEST HOUSE is in front of this, with a long wing added in the C20 to its w side. Nothing but the chimneystacks of the C18 house can be seen over the roof of the cloister.

THE NORMAN ABBEY. It is not clear whether the tower-like structure, which is the only surviving part of the abbey church with any architectural significance, was a w tower from the start or whether the w façade was in the C14 or C15 converted into one. Certainly that is the date of the octagonal top stage, and it rests internally on four pointed squinches no older than itself. The w front has angle turrets. The wall between, now flush with them, was brought forward in the C18. The turrets are arcaded, the lowest two tiers of tufa, with unmoulded outlines, clearly late C11. Above this the dressings turn to Caen stone, and the arches have zigzag, with curved not straight zigs, and shafts, a square and two octagonal stages, the top one making big free-standing pinnacles. A row of arcading across the whole front below the pinnacles, and here the shafts have waterleaf capitals. So this second campaign is no earlier than *c.*1190. In 1190, says Gervase, a fire destroyed much of the town and abbey. Rebuilding took place then at once, and the model of course was Rochester Cathedral, adapted to a church without aisles. Of this aisleless church, only the s wall of the nave and the s transept stand above ground. Herringbone laying of the former, in the latter two blocked Early Norman s windows, and later Norman ones to replace them. It has been suggested that the transept may have been turned into a dormitory in its upper half. In 1962 Mr Biddle excavated the chancel, and found that the original E end was square with a rectangular chapel projecting from the centre of the E wall. That is the plan, a most unusual plan, that Hope believed the Norman cathedral at Rochester to have had.

CONVENT CHURCH. By *Maguire & Murray*, completed in 1966. It stands on the site of the medieval crossing, beyond a serpentine rivulet. The church is the greatest possible contrast to this fanciful landscaping. The nuns wished for something simple and austere, and that is what they have been given, a rectangular, windowless block rounded at both ends, that grows out of the sloping roof of a rectangular ambulatory. A row of small lunette windows here, and roof-lighting of the main body. The materials are creamy-grey ballast blocks, and warm brown tiles. Humble NE annex for visitors; sw chapel, the link with the nuns' enclosure. Inside all the parts are one, evenly lit. The lowering, shuttered-concrete ambulatory ceiling hovers overhead like a thundercloud, broken by a flood of serene light from above in the centre. Mellow tiled floors, the nuns' choir sunk two steps, the altar free-standing on a plinth one step higher. Simple furnishings.

(The CLOISTERS, also by *Maguire & Murray*, are not visitable by the public. They lie sw of the church, and incorporate

14   in the s walk a length of c13 cloister arcading of outstanding
      quality. Quatrefoil shafts two deep, arches of trefoil shape.
      Trilobed leaves interlacing on the capitals, in a row round each
      arch, and sunk in spandrel roundels.

      Immediately s of this the c18 house. According to Hasted,
      it was built by Frazer Honeywood, who bought the estate in
      1740 and died in 1764. The fact then that he used medieval
      windows from the ruined abbey in his new residence, and,
      what is more, allowed them to dictate the Gothic character of
      the whole building, is of considerable historical importance.
      Ragstone ashlar. N and s fronts identical, two-storeyed, of
      seven bays in the rhythm 1,5,1, the end bays with sharp gables
      which even have cuspy bargeboards (an original feature ?).
      Parapet over the rest. Dormers peep over it, and a steep tiled
      roof. For the most part the windows are Perp, of two or three
      cinquefoiled lights. Geometrical tracery that must be a
      Honeywood invention only in the end windows. The doorway
      has buttresses, shafts, and an encircled quatrefoil under a
      pointed arch.)

      RESIDENTIAL BLOCK, SE of the house, 1935 by *Sir Charles
      Nicholson.*

Church and abbey lie at the two extremes of the little town. A
      walk from the one to the other, down the straight, gentle slope
      of the High Street, and then r. into Swan Street, is for the most
      part uneventful, yet a continuous pleasure, all c18 and early
      c19, orderly red and brown brick and white stucco fronts.
      The church, at the s end, lies away to the w, and it is the
      impassive, white BROME HOUSE, of *c.*1830, that has the view
      down the wide street.

The HIGH STREET starts formally, Early Georgianly, with
      STREET HOUSE on the l., and lying back, next door, the
      surprising ochre front of the VICARAGE, with Gothick blank
      arcading and interlacing window-bars. There is no point in
      remarking further until the street, which has been widening
      gradually, is abruptly pinched in on the l. Here ARUNDEL
      HOUSE, just before the pinch, rears up with one of those plain,
      handsome fronts the mid c18 were so good at, nothing but
      three storeys of brickwork five windows wide, with a smart
      doorcase. In the narrows the r. side makes a happy mixed group
      of c18 brick and plastered gables. Behind HARRINGTON'S
      shop is a two-storeyed rectangular stone building, end-on to
      the road. It has a great surprise inside. In the N and s walls are
      mid-c12 windows, shafted, with scallop capitals and zigzagged

arches. They lit an upper hall. Not so surprising after all that a Norman house should survive just here. It must have been connected with the abbey.

Nothing in the lower High Street except CONNAUGHT HOUSE, half-way down on the l., c.1800. The upper floor faced with wood blocks grooved to imitate masonry, but almost wholly occupied by a giant Venetian window. Contemporary shop-front. In SWAN STREET more happy groups on the l., again C18 and early C19. Then comes the abbey gatehouse on the r. and, on the l., CADE HOUSE, c.1800. Three storeys, three windows. Red brick. Pyramid slate roof. Again it's plain to the point of austerity, but there is more finesse in the proportions than one might suppose at first glance. The final house on the l. however is something much more special. WENT HOUSE, lying rather low and close to the road behind splendid wrought-iron gates, is the most sumptuous house in West Malling. The date is c.1720, the sumptuousness all a matter of brick detailing. Two storeys with a deep dentilled brick cornice and a parapet with sunk panels of a brighter red. Five bays with l. and r. one-bay projections, or rather pavilions, as they project at the sides too. No regularity however about the sides of the house, only an attempt on the w. Segment-headed windows, and early C19 shutters (and pretty metal hoods on the E side). Contemporary staircase with two twisted and one turned baluster per step. Opposite, a CASCADE, formed in 1810, under a Gothic arch.

MANOR HOUSE, 100 yds S of the church. Above the road, with on the other side a park and delightful lake, an ideal protection for the S end of the town. The house is in origin early C18, as the staircase testifies. So too the long low proportions. Eight bays by four, two storeys. What one sees now is all c.1840, grey rendered walls, top parapet, stone porch of coupled Tuscan columns. Screen walls run out from the back corners of the house, that on the r. with Ionic columns framing the windows of an orangery.

MALLING PLACE, ⅜ m. SW. The long, complex N front must be an early C20 scherzo on C17 and C18 themes, with three imported doorcases and three bays of genuine C18 brickwork in the middle.

ST LEONARDS TOWER, ½ m. SW. Yet another Norman edifice. 6 A small tower, remarkably preserved, perched on a sloping shelf of rock. Tufa dressings. Windows at two levels, those on the E and S set in rows of blank arches, as undecorated as the windows themselves. Shallow clasping buttresses, the NW one enlarged to take a stair-turret. Centre buttresses in the s wall. Evidence inside that there were upper and lower floors, the lower only *c*.5 ft above ground level. Curious deep, stepped window sills. It all points to a date *c*.1100 i.e. the date of the lowest stages of the abbey tower, and of Gundulf's tower at Rochester. In 1198 St Leonard's cemetery is mentioned, and there are later references to a chapel. Yet this is no church tower, but a free-standing keep tower.

WEST PECKHAM

6050

St Dunstan. The w tower is of two dates, but Saxon for its full height – which is not great. Ragstone rubble; no proper quoins. Windows at two levels, the upper single-splayed, the lower double-splayed. Irregular voussoir stones in them all. Nave and chancel in one, the latter with one s lancet (and the rere-arch of a second inside). Early C14 N aisle and chapel. Standard arcades. One Dec N window. The chapel was in the C17 charmingly fitted up as the Bartholomew family pew, on first-floor level, reached by stairs from an E doorway. Screens of two ill-proportioned composite columns to w and s. The doorway to the pew proper is a fine late C17 piece of joinery, worthy of a London carver. It has an open segmental pediment and drops of fruit falling over it from a cartouche of arms. Pierced side scrolls and panels. In the vestibule, in a cramped position, large marble MONUMENT to Leonard Bartholmew † 1721. He and his wife recline on a shelf, propped on an elbow shoulder to shoulder, and gesticulating tentatively with their free hands. Drapery above the inscription. Mrs Esdaile, quoting no evidence, gave *Richard Crutcher* as the sculptor's name. Original railings. Hatchments on the ceiling; various tablets on the walls, among them the pedimented one to Sir Nicholas Miller † 1658. – FONT. C12 or C13. Plain square bowl on five shafts. – STAINED GLASS. Old quarry with the lamb and flag in the chancel lancet. – PLATE. Cup and Paten Cover, 1630 by *M.C.*; Flagon, 1699 by *D.E.* – BRASS. Lady Elizabeth Culpepir † after 1457. 19 in. figure of a lady wearing a butterfly headdress, on a plain tomb-chest.

Duke's Place, ¼ m. E. Land at West Peckham was granted to the Knights Hospitaller in 1337, and Duke's Place is held by tradition to be their preceptory. This large, half-timbered, L-shaped house does not go back to the C14, quite. Mr Parkin dates the back range to 1408. Its broad studs and curved braces suggest of course a fairly early date. The service end was here. After a fire about 1500 the range towards the road, hall and solar, was rebuilt in splendid style, with cusped and traceried windows (greatly restored), and a hall window of six lights with a transom. (Traces of a pair to it at the back.) Crown-post hall roof, supported on a tiebeam and wall posts as well.

OXEN HOATH, ⅞ m. S of W. Late C18 or early C19 ragstone *See p. 645* house, five bays by seven. The W front three-storeyed, the centre brought forward a little. The S front no lower, but two-storeyed, with the three middle bays in a broad bow. Highly bizarre roof-line, added in 1878 by *Burn & McVicar Anderson*. There is a Frenchy dome over the bow, and a white cornice all round, into which pediments have jumped from the windows below. Low SE tower of the same date. Service wings run back to the N. In the W wing a blocked three-light window with a transom, all that remains of a big, square mid-C17 house, of brick with shaped gables. (See Badeslade's print.)

C17 brick COTTAGE W of the house, overshadowed by an avenue of superb cedars.

HAMPTONS, 1½ m. S of W. Designed by *R. W. Jearrad*, later to make his name at Cheltenham, and building in 1813. Yellow brick with stone dressings. Seven-bay S front, the centre bay wide enough for a porch with two pairs of Greek Ionic columns. Service wing to the r. not at all subordinated. The house was gutted in 1883.

STABLES, E of the house. Ragstone. Pedimented centre block, and one-storeyed wings. Arcaded.

WEST WICKHAM

3060

Sir Henry Heydon, who died in 1504, 'buildid', in the words of Leland, 'a right fair Manor Place, and a fair Chirche'. Church and Court, together on a gentle hillside, are yet isolated from the C20 suburb in the valley by a *cordon sanitaire* of playing fields. Real farmland to the W.

ST JOHN THE BAPTIST. Greatly restored and rebuilt. The late C15 windows of two cinquefoiled lights under a straight-sided arch occur in all parts of the church. In the W part however they are reset, for in 1847 nave, N aisle, and SW tower were rebuilt in flint, by *Whichcord & Whichcord*. Chancel and N chapel of ragstone rubble, the former rendered, the latter re-modelled in 1961 to take a first-floor vestry. S organ chamber by *Sedding*, 1889, chequered in a mannered way. Leland's 'buildid' exaggerates however, for the arches to the chapel are C14. Simpler, slightly later, chancel arch. The arcade of 1847 simpler still, but solid and quite convincing. WEST GALLERY. – PULPIT, SCREENS, ORGAN CASE, etc., by *Sedding*. – TILES. In the sanctuary, many with patterns. – STAINED GLASS. Figures of the earliest C16 in three windows of the N chapel, reset among modern quarries. – Kneeling skeleton in the E window, with the Heydon arms. The style and orangey colouring characteristic of the Flemish glass painters, who were working in London by the late C15. – Several *Kempe* windows: N aisle, 1896; S windows, 1899; E window, 1901. – MONUMENTS. William de Thorp † 1407. Brass of a priest, a foot and a half long. – John Stokton † 1515. Brass of a priest, a foot long. – Margaret Hobbes † 1608. Alabaster hanging monument. Small figure seated frontally, a stillborn child at her feet. Black backing to throw up the silhouette. – Samuel Lennard † 1618. Plain alabaster tomb-chest (used as an altar). The mottled pattern of the material appreciated for its own sake, something rare even among furniture-makers before the late C17. – Elizabeth Howell † 1838. Simple Baroque cartouche, a surprising throw-back. – Simple LYCHGATE, medieval, but greatly restored.

WICKHAM COURT. Sir Henry Heydon bought the manor in 1469. The house he built is of brick, with renewed stone dressings. It is not large, but even in its present mutilated state it makes a forceful architectural impact.* The almost square plan with octagonal corner turrets has an unmistakably fortified character. Quatrefoil loops low down in the turrets. Yet there is no sign that a moat ever surrounded the house, no trace of a gatehouse, i.e. no trace of any of the preliminaries that would make defence credible. Projecting chimneybreasts on the N and S sides. Later low W porch, and within it the four-centred entrance doorway with shields of arms in the spandrels, Sir Henry's and his wife's. The interior of the house has been greatly altered, but the arrangement of the rooms round the four sides of a tiny courtyard, no more than *c*.16 ft square, is original. The courtyard is now covered and takes a staircase. The C15 timber-framed courtyard walls however are intact, with the l. jamb of a sizeable mullioned window on the N side. Original fireplace in the large room it lights, which must have

* The mutilations are C19 mullioned windows throughout, a recessed top storey, and modern battlements and tops to the turrets.

been the hall – one-storeyed, one notes. The W end of this room can hardly be genuine, with an oriel under a timber recess, and steps coming up below it. Elaborate carved corbels. A considerable amount of armorial GLASS of the C16 and C17 here and in other rooms. Where then should one place Wickham Court in the history of house-planning? In the line of descent from the Bodiam type of castle certainly, for its squareness, its ranges of rooms round a central courtyard, and for the angle turrets. But what in the C14 could accommodate the garrison of a cattle, has by the end of the C15 become telescoped to house a single family, until the courtyard is not much more than a light-well. Yet, curiously, nothing like this recurs until White Hall, Shrewsbury, of 1578, without the turrets, and Barlborough, 1584, combined with a new interest in a spectacular and symmetrical exterior.

The modern suburb has its own High Street, 1 m. NW of the old church. Little comment is called for on the efforts of the C20.

ST FRANCIS OF ASSISI. 1935–6 by *Newberry & Fowler*. Neo-Perp. Buff brick. SE tower. Intended N aisle not built.

ST MARK (R.C.), at the junction of High Street and Manor Park Road. 1962–3 by *Bingham Towner Associates*. Stock brick. The plan is a distorted octagon, with a parish room at the E end pushing the altar into an almost central position. Timber tent roof and hefty canopy under a skylight to emphasize this position.

GLEBE HOUSE, Corkscrew Hill. Half-H plan, the wings ending in the simplest shaped gables. Rendered. Probably of the early C18.

WICKHURST MANOR see SEVENOAKS WEALD

WIGMORE see GILLINGHAM

WILLESBOROUGH

ST MARY. From the N all looks new, with the harsh Dec tracery of *Pearson*'s aisle of 1868, and a much restored W tower. The bipartite shingled spire, square below and octagonal above, was all rebuilt on the old lines in 1865. The tower has one S lancet and a fine shafted W doorway to establish the C13 date. A quick look outside shows a separately gabled Perp S aisle continued past half the chancel, and a Dec chancel. The E window is a memorable one, five lights grouped in a 2-1-2

rhythm and a large quatrefoil set on its side in the apex. Ogees
everywhere – every curve has its answering reverse curve.
Stone s porch. The earliest feature however is in the w gable
of the s aisle, a tiny window which is very high up and turned
crudely with small stones. It has all the signs of Saxon work.
This would imply that the present s aisle was originally the
nave and chancel of a Saxon church, but one looks in vain for
any more Saxon signs. Dr and Mrs Taylor however noted
that the sixteen westernmost feet of the s wall are only 2 ft
7 in. thick, i.e. of a characteristically Saxon thinness. The
plinth to the E bay of the aisle shows that it was added later,*
but that is too far E to affect the supposed Saxon part. Good
C13 s arcade, the two W piers round, the two E piers octagonal.
Uniform double-chamfered arches, wide and low. Chancel
arch on C14 head corbels. They are very damaged, but one
can make out that the s head is a woman's, wearing a wimple.
Dec PISCINA and triple SEDILIA, with straight embattled
top. The E sedile is higher and more grandly treated than the
other two, because the priest sat above and not between his
two acolytes. – STAINED GLASS. Good early C14 glass in two
chancel windows, the s one greatly reorganized and renewed
in 1868, the N more interesting, because it includes two saints,
typically elegant figures, standing under heavy tabernacles. –
MONUMENT. Charles Warton † 1863. Alabaster. Relief bust
with side whiskers, the central feature of a rich reredos-like
composition.

Two timber BARNS s of the church, the larger one aisled.

BOYS HALL, ¼ m. SW. Stone mansion built, according to
Hasted, in 1616. Considerably altered, but one bay on the SW
front has mullioned windows of one plus four plus one lights
with a transom. Straight-sided gables. Tall grouped chimneystacks.

WINDMILL, ½ m. N. The usual octagonal white boarded smock-
mill. Skeletal sweeps. Built in 1869 by *John Hill* of Ashford.

WILMINGTON

ST MICHAEL. *E. Cresy* rebuilt the N aisle in 1839, *Christian* rebuilt the chancel in 1884, *R. Marchant* rebuilt the nave and s
aisle in 1909–22 (with Arts and Crafts details). All that that
left of the medieval church was the W end of the nave, built up

* About 1471, the date of a will that refers to the new work on the s side
(Mr W.P. Garner's information).

into a low tower. The thin walls and a small single-splayed window on the s side make a pre-Conquest date possible. The window is remarkably low down. – FONT. An attempt to square the circle. Too plain to be datable. – PULPIT. Dated 1655, but still in the style of the 1630s (cf. Crayford, North Cray). – PLATE. Paten, 1712 by *B.A.* – MONUMENTS. Anne Bathurst, *c.*1727. Small lively cartouche. – William East † 1835. Pompous Grecian tablet.

WILMINGTON HOUSE. Only the façade of the early C18 house is left. Two storeys with a parapet. Seven bays, the first and seventh projecting as tiny wings, a characteristic arrangement that gives a pair of closets, not full-sized rooms. Brown brick enriched with a vivid red brick, used to good effect in the moulded cornice and a rusticated surround for the central window.

WILSLEY GREEN *see* CRANBROOK

WITTERSHAM

ST JOHN THE BAPTIST. From the N the church looks entirely Perp, with its handsome w tower, sandstone with ragstone quoins. Angle buttresses with many set-offs, battlements to tower and NW turret, and a tall transomed w window. Money was left 'to the new steeple' in 1501 and for glazing a window in it. But, as usual, the tower was added to an earlier church, in this case a Dec one. In the chancel the restorations of 1847, and of 1892 and 1898 (by *E.H.Parkes*), have left almost nothing one can rely on. The Geometrical E window, if correct, is to a pattern of *c.*1300. – PISCINA and SEDILIA united by their hood-mould, which is brought down into deep complex corbels between each sedile: another example of the Dec refusal to be content with stereotypes. The nave and aisles are continued in the usual way as short chancel chapels, and here the C14 work has a great deal of character. The octagonal piers are concave-sided, gouged out with such ferocity that capitals and bases take on a fearsome spikiness. As for tracery, the w window of the s aisle has the interesting motif of a cusped sexfoil in a circle, between pointed trefoils. Use was made of various bits of a C13 church, i.e. two arches and two piers in the N arcade, and one (later) pier in the s arcade. Also the E respond of the former has stiffleaf sprigs. (Its partner on the s respond is a modern match-up.) Chancel arch modern. Old

crown-post roofs remain in nave and s aisle. – BRASS. Stevyn
Audyan † 1523, a civilian 18 in. long.

WITTERSHAM HOUSE, opposite the church. One of *Lutyens*'s
most suavely neo-Georgian designs, 1906–9, for the Hon.
Alfred Lyttelton.* Nothing can be seen outside of the earlier
house Lutyens encased. Nine bays by nine, two storeys, long
and low under a low pantiled roof. A restrained design certainly, but not constrained, for plenty happens along the
façades. On the entrance front a wide central pediment and
under it a one-storey loggia with the front door characteristically set behind in a concave bow. On either side the windows
are syncopated, two above to three below. The same rhythm
reappears in the centre of the garden front.

STOCKS WINDMILL, 1 m. NE. A post-mill in excellent condition. White weatherboarding and a brick base painted black.
It bears the date 1781 on the centre post inside. The windmill
stands in the hamlet of THE STOCKS, which has several
characterful houses, especially one by the crossroads entirely
clothed in fish-scale tiles.

Further SW, BUDD'S FARM, a broad late C17 front of eight bays,
keeping its large casement windows.

9030

WOODCHURCH

ALL SAINTS. A large, robust, and complete E.E. church. Rubble
stone rendered. Externally the scale and period are apparent
in the three grand E lancets and in the tower, also with lancets,
but crowned by an unusually tall shingled spire and strengthened with angle buttresses of colossal projection. The original
design however is blurred outside by a Perp enlargement:
chancel chapels, battlemented on the N and with a tall separate
gable on the S, and widening of the aisles. Perp too the ambitious two-storeyed N porch. Note the small rectangular
windows in the W bay of the N aisle – what did they light? A
vestry? *Ferrey* at his restoration in 1858 tried to imply that
what was for the Victorians the best period of Gothic architecture was also represented, by putting a Dec window in the
tower and another in the S chapel. As usual in Kent, then, the
exterior does little to prepare one for the beauty of the interior.
For Woodchurch is without doubt beautiful inside, beautiful
in its pure and noble sanctuary, and, if one prefers a more

* Lyttelton recommended Lutyens as architect for the Hampstead Garden
Suburb.

masculine word, handsome in its nave arcades. The sanctuary
lancets unusually long and close-set with many deep arch-
mouldings and hood-moulds, and triplets of shafts between
the windows. Shaft-rings on the E shafts. Double PISCINA
with trefoiled heads and three SEDILIA with moulded arches
on shafts. The shafts throughout appear to be of local marble
(quarried at Bethersden, the next-door village), but a close
look shows that many of them are freestone waxed to turn
them grey. The rest of the chancel is quite plain – and must
have been so even before the chapel arches were pierced
through the walls. Nave arcades of four bays. Short thick
piers alternately round and octagonal, heavy moulded caps
and bases; arches of one huge chamfer. (Again, the piers are
freestone waxed.) The tower arch the same, the chancel arch
of the same date but less boldly conceived. The sanctuary
speaks exalted poetry, the nave forthright prose, a wonderfully
wide range for the simple vocabulary of the C13 to encom-

Woodchurch church, brass to Nichol de Gore † 1333

pass. The church belonged to the See of Canterbury. Inside
the tower, wide two-centred arches to N and S – what were they
for ? – FONT. Norman. Square arcaded bowl on five circular
shafts. Once more, waxed and not marble. – PULPIT. Incorporating linenfold panels of great delicacy and C16 traceried
heads. – STALLS. The fronts made up with more of the same
woodwork. – MISERICORDS. Two. Perp foliage. – STAINED
GLASS. C13 medallion, of the Entombment of the Virgin
(s aisle), badly preserved. – C15 fragment above it, with the
head of Christ. – Three C16 and C17 Flemish panels in the N
chapel; the largest and earliest a Vernicle held by three saints.
– Good E window by *Kempe*, 1895. – PLATE. Cup and Paten
Cover by *I.A.*, 1595, the cup on a C17 stem; Paten, 1707 by
John Bodington; Flagon, 1723 by *B.N.* – BRASSES. Nichol de
Gore † 1333. A priest in full vestments in an encircled quatre-
foil with four finials. Round the circle a rhyming inscription in
French. The figure is 13 in. high. – Thomas Harlakynden
† 1558. Foot-long kneeling figures.

The village is a large one, disposed round a roughly triangular
green, whose apex is somewhere near the church. No individual houses to mention except HENDON PLACE, late C15,
close-studded half-timbering, making what looks like two-
thirds of a Wealden hall-house. The l. end has its upper floor
jettied out, the eaves are carried on braces across the next two
bays, but where one expects the balancing jettied bay at the r.
end, the house stops. The big hipped roof suggests that there
never was another bay.

WINDMILL, ¼ m. N. Tall white boarded smock-mill. The sweeps
are lost except for the spines. The usual boat-shaped cap. The
mill was moved here in 1852.

(SHIRLEY FARM, 1½ m. SW. Isolated on a hump just above the
old sea level on Shirley Moor, a Wealden hall house with an
outside door at one end, said to be for the storage of wool.
Mr K. Gravett)

WOODLANDS *see* WEST KINGSDOWN

7 060   •   WOULDHAM

ALL SAINTS. The continuous and eccentric growth of the
church can be picked out stage by stage. In the beginning was
a Late Saxon church. Its chancel creates the narrowness of the
W half of the present chancel. One double-splayed window of

its nave above the S arcade. The W quoins, including tile and tufa, visible outside. A narrow one-bay C12 aisle at the NW end of the nave (an odd place) would explain the W respond with scallop capital made of small blocks of stone. This aisle *c*.1200 was lengthened to two bays – round pier and two slightly-chamfered arches. In the same campaign a two-bay S aisle. C13 lengthening of the S aisle to the W end, but by only one arch – with two slight chamfers. Also C13 the narrow N chancel chapel, and the lengthened chancel with various lancets, set in crude wall arcading. Two square AUMBRIES in the E wall. In the C14 the N aisle was completed and a S chancel chapel built, of flint, with one square-headed S window. Good three-light Dec E window of the chancel. Later the S aisle was widened to align with it. The last item was a tower, built, most unusually for the C15, NW of the N aisle. No buttresses. Wide polygonal E stair-turret. Several bequests towards its erection between 1460 and 1483. – REREDOS, in the S chapel. Perp, square-headed panels in two tiers. – MONUMENTS. Brass in the chancel N wall of Morley Monox † 1602. Kneeling figures and the following mottoes in Latin, Italian, French, and Spanish.

> Non quam diu sed quam bene
>
> La vita del huomo e come
> Un fiore vapore e fumo
>
> Ayes memoire de to createur
> Es iours de ta ieunesse
>
> En hora buena nace quien
> Con buena se y fama muere *

– William Bewly, *c*.1600. Insignificant hanging monument with kneeling figures.

STARKEY CASTLE FARM, ¾ m. N. Ragstone building, rectangular, with a hipped-roofed appendage at the SW corner, and a further annex SW of that. The main block rises higher at the S end under a transverse gable. Staircase projection on the W side, and a late C14 doorway l. of it. On the E front a second doorway in line with the first. Clearly they mark the ends of the screens passage. The high building then is the service wing, and the staircase leads to its upper floor. Hall of two bays, the buttresses carrying the weight of the main truss (a two-centred wooden arch on stone demi-angel corbels). The appendage is

* Mottoes which the Rev. M. B. Perkins was kind enough to transcribe.

a generous garderobe wing with privy pit (cf. Old Soar). The solar end demolished, together with Sir Humphrey Starkey's late c15 chapel etc. c15 windows however of two arched lights, except for the big windows on the E side, which early in the c19 replaced medieval ones of the same sort and size.

WROTHAM

ST GEORGE. A generously proportioned early c14 church, with a typical c15 W tower. The tower has angle buttresses and a NE turret, and, more remarkably, a passage through it with a three-bay rib-vault, to allow processions to encircle the church without descending on to the road. Two-storeyed S porch, also vaulted. The nave has gabled aisles, linked by a passage in the thickness of the wall above the chancel arch, a highly unusual feature of enigmatic purpose, reached by a staircase from the S aisle. Externally the church is not particularly attractive, the walling haphazard rubble, the windows all renewed: chancel restored c.1861 by *Newman & Billing*, tower restored 1876 by *R. Wheeler* (PF). The Perp E window, of Portland stone, was inserted in 1958, and started life as the W window of St Alban, Wood Street, in the City, Gothic survival of as late as 1633–4.

The internal system is of circular arcade piers and double-chamfered arches. The N arcade, of four arches, is simpler and more E.E. in character than the S. The latter has been respaced to produce three arches, including a very wide E one, no doubt needed for the rood loft. Perp W responds. Tall Perp tower arch. The chancel arch has mouldings identical with the S arcade and is married on to the string-course that passes round the entire chancel. The string-course is cut by the S priest's doorway and the NE doorway to the Late Perp vestry, but it rises over the PISCINA, which is the most telling original feature, with its cinquefoiled ogee arch and hood-mould on, not heads, but ballflowers, making one of their rare appearances in the South-East of England. Identical PISCINA (minus the hood-mould) in the S aisle. – FONT. c13. Octagonal, with two shallow sunk arches on each face. – ROOD SCREEN. Perp. Square-headed lights in threes. Very heavily renewed. – PULPIT. Of c.1861. Stone with marble shafts. Supported on a well carved group of large angels. Altogether most ambitious. – REREDOS in the S aisle. Designed by *Comper*, 1907. It frames a painting with the blue-robed, rose-chapleted angels of the Wilton Diptych. The 'English' source is typical of this phase of church furnishing. – BENEFACTIONS BOARDS under the tower. In a surround, with fern-leaves sprouting out at r. angles all round, that look late C17 but may date only from *c*.1800. – MONUMENTS. A number of brasses, all depressingly crude. Thomas Nysell † 1498. 18½ in. figures. – John Burgoyn, *c*.1500. 14 in. long. – Thomas Pekham † 1512. In armour, 23½ in. long. – Reynold Pekham † 1525. In armour, his wife in a heraldic mantle. 28 in. figures. – James Pekham † 1532. A figure 25 in. long, the inscription lost. – William Clerke † 1611. 26½ in. figures. – Elizabeth Crispe † 1615, 22 in. figure, in a modish costume. – Equally numerous wall monuments, but these too are unexciting. Not all need be listed. Robert Rychers † 1588. Black marble incised slab of the kneeling family, set in an alabaster architectural framework. – Nicholas Miller. Black tablet with a bust facing the front between the points of a white open pediment. Erected in 1661. – Lucretia Betenson † between 1756 and 1762. Considerably suaver, but also incorporating a bust – in relief on a draped roundel set on a slightly concave background with a crumply top. Rupert Gunnis tentatively suggested an attribution to *Nicholas Read*. – Harriot Moore † 1840 and George Moore † 1845. A pair of bulky standing monuments, marble reliefs of sarcophagi and draped urns under heavy crocketed gables – an unmitigated confrontation in the Battle of the Styles.

The church lies on the N side of THE SQUARE, with Wrotham Place (*see* below), its outbuildings, walls, and wrought-iron gateway, on the s side. From there the HIGH STREET runs to the w, compact but varied, ending on the r. with WEST HOUSE, a broad, plain, red-brick mid-Georgian front with a broad, plain doorcase. Beyond, out of sight round the corner, THE ELMS, Early Georgian, its doorcase of impressive dimensions. From the s side of the High Street ST MARY'S LANE drops gently downhill, with cottages behind raised walks. Here again only one building to comment on, the humble stone ALMSHOUSES of 1806. They are by *John Carter*, the pioneer recorder of medieval buildings. Pointed doorways and coupled lancets however are all that make them Gothic. The front breaks forward in the centre as if waiting to be crowned by a pediment.

WROTHAM PLACE. Two-thirds of an Elizabethan mansion, of red brick with stone dressings, much tampered with in the

C19: additions at the W end; mullioned-and-transomed windows all renewed, it seems, notwithstanding the decayed state of the upper ones. The building is basically a rectangle. The entrance front faces N, with a projecting porch at the r. end with a C17 cartouche of arms of Sir John Rayney, and two rectangular window-bays ending in blunt-topped gables. Round the corner a big chimneybreast, and on the S side another, with a diaper pattern, belonging to the hall. All other features on the S side suspect, except a stone doorway, of two-centred shape. This, and the porch doorway, which has a continuous hollow and a sunk quadrant, must be re-used C15 pieces. At the l. end of the S front a C19 projection, and an originally almost independent block of the C17, with a gable of the same blunted form as those on the N side. Few internal features. The porch leads into the NW corner of the hall, as the screens passage has gone. Big bare C18 chimneypiece with a fine inset marble relief. One would like to know who carved it. An original fireplace in the E room, with a straight-sided arch and schematized strapwork on the lintel. One panelled upper room with a simple overmantel of c.1600. The date 1621, boldly painted over the front door in the C19, must be too late.

Range of contemporary brick OUTBUILDINGS coming forward from the NW corner, ending in a big gable towards The Square with various brick finials.

ARCHBISHOP'S PALACE. Remains E of the church. The palace was said to have been largely pulled down in the C14 to build the new palace at Maidstone. The present building, of ragstone blocks, has no original feature. The ruined extension at the E end ran further N than the main part.

COURT LODGE, NW of the church. 1801–2 by *Samuel Wyatt*, built as the rectory. Rendered white. The entrance front faces N, with five windows on the upper floor, the centre three closely spaced. Below, windows in the end bays and a porch on four Greek columns, with slightly peculiar fluting. On the garden front the centre three bays are in a segmental bow, behind which appears one of Wyatt's favourite shallow lead domes. Low W addition, long E service wing.

YALDHAM MANOR, 1½ m. w. The kernel is a medieval open hall, with moulded arched-braced principals. Original doorways, not apparently *in situ*, at front and back. A mid-C17 casing in brick added or incorporated a wing to the SW. Geometrical brick patterns in its gables. The entrance (N)

from was given four small straight-sided gables (now tiled)
and windows sunk under segmental arches that step up in the
middle, a trick that gives the date away. Victorian additions
and a forest of Victorian chimneystacks.*

NEPICAR HOUSE, 1¼ m. SE. Fine block of *c*.1700 added in front
of an earlier house. Five bays, two storeys. Red brick with
regular blue headers. Big-hipped roof. The porch has an enriched shell-hood on carved brackets. The house faces the
A20 but is, happily, no longer derelict.

FORD PLACE, 1½ m. SE. An interesting fragment, one wing of a
large Elizabethan or Jacobean mansion. The plan must have
been a half-H of which the centre and N wing have disappeared.
Two-storeyed brick range, with a large stepped gable towards
the road, and on the N side three shaped gables, of the geometrical shape familiar from Knole etc. Mullioned-and-
transomed windows, of brick to resemble stone. On the S side
a medley of materials, rubble stone and rendering. Three
chimneybreasts, with modern stacks. On the stacks the dates,
in C20 numerals, 1582 and 1605. What is the warrant for them?
The plan of the house would suit the earlier date, the gables
can hardly be prior to the latter – the date of the Knole gables.
Inside, the wing incorporates the crown-post roof of an earlier
house, modified and jacked up to a greater height. Fine stone
chimneypiece in an upper room, the lintel incised with arabesques and squirrels.

YALDHAM MANOR *see* WROTHAM

YALDING   6050

ST PETER AND ST PAUL. Quite large, of ragstone, and unusually
regular in plan. Chancel, transepts, nave with aisles, W tower.
The N aisle continues along the side of the tower. The tower,
originally unbuttressed but of considerable size, is remembered
for its plain top, telling against the circular SE turret with
bulbous lead cap and vane dated 1734. Windows all red brick,
so the C13 date is only established internally, by rere-arches
on the S and W sides, and the tower arch, on round responds.
C13 chancel, see part of a blocked N lancet, two S lancets, and
a fragmentary third. The four-bay nave and transepts and the
chancel arch E of them a rebuilding of the C14, broad and
dignified. Octagonal piers and double-hollow-chamfered

* Photographs preserved in the house record its un-victorianized state. I
am grateful to Mr Lade for showing them to me.

arches. N and S porches also of that date, the outer arches of sandstone. The sandstone geometrical tracery in the transepts and a few aisle windows is all a restoration, but copying original evidence. No ogees here yet, but, remembering Meopham, one willingly reconciles that with a date as late as c.1325. PISCINA of C13 type in the S transept. One nagging question remains. How did there come to be so much room between tower and chancel for this spacious rebuilding of the nave, with transepts into the bargain? A possible answer would be that the C13 chancel originally extended further W, and was partly absorbed by the rebuilding. One would then explain the fact that the two SE lancets are enriched with internal rolls and linking strings, while the lancet W of them is not, by supposing a richer treatment of the original sanctuary. Blocked openings in chancel and N transept, to the rood-loft staircase. Perp priest's door and low-side window S of the chancel. Boarded nave roof enriched with a lattice of ribs with bosses, not as a celure over the rood-loft, but over the bay opposite the porches. Simple row of Xs in boxes however above the chancel arch. – PULPIT. Stone. 1860. – PLATE. Elizabethan Cup; Paten, Flagon, and Almsdish, 1700 by *G.A.* – MONUMENTS. Panelled tomb-chest in the S transept, under a cusped and subcusped arch. – Ambrose Warde † 1637. From the inscription one extracts the information that the monument was put up after 1656. This is important, for the design is a curious hybrid, a large hanging monument, the architectural parts of which are of black and white marble, but with alabaster swags, sundry cartouches, and, in particular, alabaster figures, kneeling, the man and his wife at a prayer-desk, the children in the predella, in a way that would have been out of fashion even by 1637. The main figures however turn outwards in a Baroque way, addressing themselves to the spectator and not to their prayers. – John Ousnam † 1703. Cartouche. Two putto heads and a skull among the drapery looped round it. – Jane Akers † 1804. Fragile neo-classical relief of an angel carrying a child.

The large village is divided into two by the river Beult. The N half is the better, a curving, gently sloping street with wide grass verges. Two handsome houses here, one on each side. On the E, below the church, HOLBOROUGH HOUSE, a demure little early C18 hipped-roofed house. Six bays, two storeys, dormers, and a central chimneystack. Orangey-red brick adornments, including cut heads to some of the windows and raised panels between the windows, two with pie-crust edges. Also a small blank tablet with colonnettes and scrolly open pediment, all in cut brick. The doorcase is in the l. bay, which suggests that the later additions to the l. in a conforming style really mask an older house. COURT LODGE, a little higher up, is not much earlier, say *c.*1690, and not much larger, but there is about it a striving after grandeur with minimal resources which gives it a good deal of charm. Seven bays, the centre three projecting a very little under a bare, rather steep pediment. Two storeys, roof with two dormers and gabled, not hipped, ends. Velvety red and blue chequered brickwork, enlivened by a more vivid rubbed brick, stone key-blocks, and outsize rusticated stone quoins. Garden front identically designed but carried out entirely in plum-coloured brick. From the road a glimpse of BARNS at the back and a whole battery of OASTS.

At the top of the street CLEAVES, a rambling group, the centre of which was the Grammar School founded in 1663. In front a tiny square C18 brick building, the LOCKUP, with iron-studded door and a judas that opens. The very last house in VICARAGE ROAD, which runs E from Cleaves, is WARDE'S MOAT on the r., a delightfully incongruous sight, a red-brick C18 box encircled by a brimming moat. Rebuilt as the vicarage after 1759. Five bays by five. The top storey above a moulded brick cornice. Pedimented doorcase on Doric pilasters. Brick STABLES, with a pedimented centre part. Almost opposite, CHEVENEY (really in Hunton parish), a large half-timbered house. Only the L-shaped s front is old.

To the s, the village street ends at the approach to the TOWN BRIDGE. The bridge is medieval, built of ragstone and, with seven arches and a length of 100 ft, enough to span the marshy ground on either side of the river as well as the river itself. A second medieval bridge, this one over the Medway, is TWYFORD BRIDGE, ½ m. s of w, with pointed cutwaters and brick refuges in the road on both sides. Four irregular pointed arches. LADDINGFORD BRIDGE, 1 m. sw, spans the third branch, the river Teise. The bridge has but two arches and the upper parts are all rebuilt in brick.

At BENOVER, a hamlet 1 m. s, several timber-framed houses. The most spectacular is NORMAN COTTAGES, lying back w of the road. The first floor projects with three oriel windows, which nestle under the three overhanging gables, one small and two large. Probably no earlier than the first half of the

C17. It is built, most unusually, round a small courtyard. Structurally, the greatest interest attaches to BURNT HOUSE; for its upper floor projects only at the short ends, not at all a common arrangement in Kent, and an early one. Mr Rigold notes that the construction is with upper crucks. GLASS HOUSE, a little way s, is the usual C16 type, with an overhang continuous across the front.

KENWARD, 1 m. NW. Two-storeyed C18 house, roughcast and rather unattractive outside. The main fronts face N and W. The former, nine bays long, has a plain pediment over the centre three, and a porch with paired Tuscan columns. The W front is later, with three windows on the l. in a shallow bow, and three windows on the right masked by a Tuscan colonnade, which continues round the corner on the s side. Characteristic mid-C18 interiors, hall and NE and SW rooms. All have cornices with carved brackets, finely carved chimney-pieces, and proud pedimented doorcases. Staircase with two slim twisted balusters per tread.*

BOW HILL HOUSE, 1½ m. W of N. Symmetrically fronted early C19 Gothick cottage, added to at the r. end and at the back. Roughcast. Canted bays, flanking the front door, each with three whopping lancets. Lancets higher up, in pairs under straight-topped hood-moulds. Two big gables, coming down to their lowest points, illogically enough, over the centre window. Spindly and rather funny.

YARDHURST see GREAT CHART

THE YEWS see PENSHURST

YOTES COURT see MEREWORTH

---

* The last Kenward died in 1749. His only daughter had married Sir John Shaw, who no doubt was the builder of the house. See the Kenward monument in the church. The MHLG narrows the date of erection to 1752.

GLOSSARY

ABACUS: flat slab on the top of a capital (q.v.).

ABUTMENT: solid masonry placed to resist the lateral pressure of a vault.

ACANTHUS: plant with thick fleshy and scalloped leaves used as part of the decoration of a Corinthian capital (q.v.) and in some types of leaf carving.

ACHIEVEMENT OF ARMS: in heraldry, a complete display of armorial bearings.

ACROTERION: foliage-carved block on the end or top of a classical pediment.

ADDORSED: two human figures, animals, or birds, etc., placed symmetrically so that they turn their backs to each other.

AEDICULE, AEDICULA: framing of a window or door by columns and a pediment (q.v.).

AFFRONTED: two human figures, animals, or birds, etc., placed symmetrically so that they face each other.

AGGER: Latin term for the built-up foundations of Roman roads; also sometimes applied to the banks of hill-forts or other earthworks.

AMBULATORY: semicircular or polygonal aisle enclosing an apse (q.v.).

ANNULET: *see* Shaft-ring.

ANSE DE PANIER: *see* Arch, Basket.

ANTEPENDIUM: covering of the front of an altar, usually by textiles or metalwork.

ANTIS, IN: *see* Portico.

APSE: vaulted semicircular or polygonal end of a chancel or a chapel.

ARABESQUE: light and fanciful surface decoration using combinations of flowing lines, tendrils, etc., interspersed with vases, animals, etc.

ARCADE: range of arches supported on piers or columns, free-standing: or, BLIND ARCADE, the same attached to a wall.

ARCH: round-headed, i.e. semicircular; pointed, i.e. consisting of two curves, each drawn from one centre, and meeting in a point at the top; segmental, i.e. in the form of a segment;

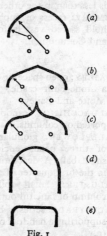

Fig. 1

pointed; four-centred (a Late Medieval form), *see* Fig. 1(a); Tudor (also a Late Medieval form), *see* Fig. 1(*b*); Ogee (introduced *c.* 1300 and specially popular in the C14), *see* Fig. 1(*c*); Stilted, *see* Fig. 1(*d*); Basket, with lintel connected to the jambs by concave quadrant curves, *see* Fig. 1(*e*).

ARCHITRAVE: lowest of the three main parts of the entablature (q.v.) of an order (q.v.) (*see* Fig. 12).

ARCHIVOLT: under-surface of an arch (also called Soffit).

ARRIS: sharp edge at the meeting of two surfaces.

ASHLAR: masonry of large blocks wrought to even faces and square edges.

ATLANTES: male counterparts of caryatids (q.v.).

ATRIUM: inner court of a Roman house, also open court in front of a church.

ATTACHED: *see* Engaged.

ATTIC: topmost storey of a house, if distance from floor to ceiling is less than in the others.

AUMBRY: recess or cupboard to hold sacred vessels for Mass and Communion.

B AILEY: open space or court of a stone-built castle; *see* also Motte-and-Bailey.

BALDACCHINO: canopy supported on columns.

BALLFLOWER: globular flower of three petals enclosing a small ball. A decoration used in the first quarter of the C14.

BALUSTER: small pillar or column of fanciful outline.

BALUSTRADE: series of balusters supporting a handrail or coping (q.v.).

BARBICAN: outwork defending the entrance to a castle.

BARGEBOARDS: projecting decorated boards placed against the incline of the gable of a building and hiding the horizontal roof timbers.

BARROW: *see* Bell, Bowl, Disc, Long, *and* Pond Barrow.

BASILICA: in medieval architecture an aisled church with a clerestory.

BASKET ARCH: *see* Arch (Fig. 1e).

BASTION: projection at the angle of a fortification.

BATTER: inclined face of a wall.

BATTLEMENT: parapet with a series of indentations or embrasures with raised portions or merlons between (also called Crenellation).

BAYS: internal compartments of a building; each divided from the other not by solid walls but by divisions only marked in the side walls (columns, pilasters, etc.) or the ceiling (beams, etc.). Also external divisions of a building by fenestration.

BAY-WINDOW: angular or curved projection of a house front with ample fenestration. If curved, also called bow-window; if on an upper floor only, also called oriel or oriel window.

BEAKER FOLK: Late New Stone Age warrior invaders from the Continent who buried their dead in round barrows and introduced the first metal tools and weapons to Britain.

BEAKHEAD: Norman ornamental motif consisting of a row of bird or beast heads with beaks biting usually into a roll moulding.

BELFRY: turret on a roof to hang bells in.

BELGAE: Aristocratic warrior bands who settled in Britain in two main waves in the C I B.C. In Britain their culture is termed Iron Age C.

BELL BARROW: Early Bronze Age round barrow in which the mound is separated from its encircling ditch by a flat platform or berm (q.v.).

BELLCOTE: framework on a roof to hang bells from.

BERM: level area separating ditch from bank on a hill-fort or barrow.

BILLET FRIEZE: Norman ornamental motif made up of short raised rectangles placed at regular intervals.

BIVALLATE: Of a hill-fort: defended by two concentric banks and ditches.

BLOCK CAPITAL: Romanesque capital cut from a cube by having the lower angles rounded off to the circular shaft below (also called Cushion Capital) (Fig. 2).

Fig. 2

BOND, ENGLISH Or FLEMISH: see Brickwork.

BOSS: knob or projection usually placed to cover the intersection of ribs in a vault.

BOWL BARROW: round barrow surrounded by a quarry ditch. Introduced in Late Neolithic times, the form continued until the Saxon period.

BOW-WINDOW: see Bay-Window.

BOX: A small country house, e.g. a shooting box. A convenient term to describe a compact minor dwelling, e.g. a rectory.

BOX PEW: pew with a high wooden enclosure.

BRACES: see Roof.

BRACKET: small supporting piece of stone, etc., to carry a projecting horizontal.

BRESSUMER: beam in a timber-framed building to support the, usually projecting, superstructure.

BRICKWORK: *Header:* brick laid so that the end only appears on the face of the wall. *Stretcher:* brick laid so that the side only appears on the face of the wall. *English Bond:* method of laying bricks so that alternate courses or layers on the face of the wall are composed of headers or stretchers only (Fig. 3*a*). *Flemish Bond:* method of laying bricks so that alternate headers and stretchers appear in each course on the face of the wall (Fig. 3*b*).

(*a*)

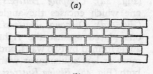

(*b*)

Fig. 3

BROACH: see Spire.

BROKEN PEDIMENT: see Pediment.

BRONZE AGE: In Britain, the period from c. 1600 to 600 B.C.

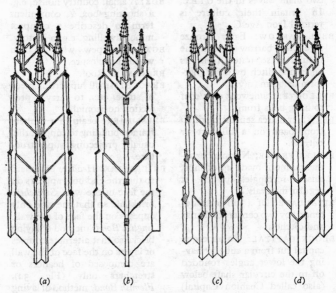

Fig. 4

BUCRANIUM: ox skull.

BUTTRESS: mass of brickwork or masonry projecting from or built against a wall to give additional strength. *Angle Buttresses:* two meeting at an angle of 90° at the angle of a building (Fig. 4*a*). *Clasping Buttress:* one which encases the angle (Fig. 4*d*). *Diagonal Buttress:* one placed against the right angle formed by two walls, and more or less equiangular with both (Fig. 4*b*). *Flying Buttress:* arch or half arch transmitting the thrust of a vault or roof from the upper part of a wall to an outer support or buttress. *Setback Buttress:* angle buttress set slightly back from the angle (Fig. 4*c*).

CABLE MOULDING: Norman moulding imitating a twisted cord.

CAIRN: a mound of stones usually covering a burial.

CAMBER: slight rise or upward curve of an otherwise horizontal structure.

CAMPANILE: isolated bell tower.

CANOPY: projection or hood over an altar, pulpit, niche, statue, etc.

CAP: in a windmill the crowning feature.

CAPITAL: head or top part of a column.

CARTOUCHE: tablet with an ornate frame, usually enclosing an inscription.

CARYATID: whole female figure

supporting an entablature or other similar member. *Termini Caryatids:* female busts or demi-figures or three-quarter figures supporting an entablature or other similar member and placed at the top of termini pilasters (q.v.). Cf. Atlantes.

CASTELLATED: decorated with battlements.

CELURE: panelled and adorned part of a wagon-roof above the rood or the altar.

CENSER: vessel for the burning of incense.

CENTERING: wooden framework used in arch and vault construction and removed when the mortar has set.

CHALICE: cup used in the Communion service or at Mass. *See also* Recusant Chalice.

CHAMBERED TOMB: burial mound of the New Stone Age having a stone-built chamber and entrance passage covered by an earthen barrow or stone cairn. The form was introduced to Britain from the Mediterranean.

CHAMFER: surface made by cutting across the square angle of a stone block, piece of wood, etc., at an angle of 45° to the other two surfaces.

CHANCEL: that part of the E end of a church in which the altar is placed, usually applied to the whole continuation of the nave E of the crossing.

CHANCEL ARCH: arch at the W end of the chancel.

CHANTRY CHAPEL: chapel attached to, or inside, a church, endowed for the saying of Masses for the soul of the founder or some other individual.

CHEVET: French term for the E end of a church (chancel, ambulatory, and radiating chapels).

CHEVRON: Norman moulding forming a zigzag.

CHOIR: that part of the church where divine service is sung.

CIBORIUM: a baldacchino.

CINQUEFOIL: *see* Foil.

CIST: stone-lined or slab-built grave. First appears in Late Neolithic times. It continued to be used in the Early Christian period.

CLAPPER BRIDGE: bridge made of large slabs of stone, some built up to make rough piers and other longer ones laid on top to make the roadway.

CLASSIC: here used to mean the moment of highest achievement of a style.

CLASSICAL: here used as the term for Greek and Roman architecture and any subsequent styles inspired by it.

CLERESTORY: upper storey of the nave walls of a church, pierced by windows.

COADE STONE: artificial (cast) stone made in the late C18 and the early C19 by Coade and Sealy in London.

COB: walling material made of mixed clay and straw.

COFFERING: decorating a ceiling with sunk square or polygonal ornamental panels.

COLLAR-BEAM: *see* Roof.

COLONNADE: range of columns.

COLONNETTE: small column.

COLUMNA ROSTRATA: column decorated with carved prows of ships to celebrate a naval victory.

COMPOSITE: *see* Order.

CONSOLE: bracket (q.v.) with a compound curved outline.

COPING: capping or covering to a wall.

CORBEL: block of stone projecting from a wall, supporting some horizontal feature.

CORBEL TABLE: series of corbels, occurring just below the roof eaves externally or internally, often seen in Norman buildings.

CORINTHIAN: see Order.

CORNICE: in classical architecture the top section of the entablature (q.v.). Also for a projecting decorative feature along the top of a wall, arch, etc.

CORRIDOR VILLA: see Villa.

COUNTERSCARP BANK: small bank on the down-hill or outer side of a hill-fort ditch.

COURTYARD VILLA: see Villa.

COVE, COVING: concave undersurface in the nature of a hollow moulding but on a larger scale.

COVER PATEN: cover to a Communion cup, suitable for use as a paten or plate for the consecrated bread.

CRADLE ROOF: see Wagon roof.

CRENELLATION: see Battlement.

CREST, CRESTING: ornamental finish along the top of a screen, etc.

CRINKLE-CRANKLE WALL: undulating wall.

CROCKET, CROCKETING: decorative features placed on the sloping sides of spires, pinnacles, gables, etc., in Gothic architecture, carved in various leaf shapes and placed at regular intervals.

CROCKET CAPITAL: see Fig. 5. An Early Gothic form.

CROMLECH: word of Celtic origin still occasionally used of single free-standing stones ascribed to the Neolithic or Bronze Age periods.

Fig. 5

CROSSING: space at the intersection of nave, chancel, and transepts.

CROSS-WINDOWS: windows with one mullion and one transom.

CRUCK: big curved beam supporting both walls and roof of a cottage.

CRYPT: underground room usually below the E end of a church.

CUPOLA: small polygonal or circular domed turret crowning a roof.

CURTAIN WALL: connecting wall between the towers of a castle.

CUSHION CAPITAL: see Block Capital.

CUSP: projecting point between the foils in a foiled Gothic arch.

DADO: decorative covering of the lower part of a wall.

DAGGER: tracery motif of the Dec style. It is a lancet shape rounded or pointed at the head, pointed at the foot, and cusped inside (see Fig. 6).

Fig. 6

DAIS: raised platform at one end of a room.

DEC ('DECORATED'): historical division of English Gothic architecture covering the period from c.1290 to c.1350.

DEMI-COLUMNS: columns half sunk into a wall.

DIAPER WORK: surface decoration composed of square or lozenge shapes.

DISC BARROW: Bronze Age round barrow with inconspicuous central mound surrounded by bank and ditch.

DOGTOOTH: typical E.E. ornament consisting of a series of four-cornered stars placed diagonally and raised pyramidally (Fig. 7).

Fig. 7

DOMICAL VAULT: see Vault.

DONJON: see Keep.

DORIC: see Order.

DORMER (WINDOW): window placed vertically in the sloping plane of a roof.

DRIPSTONE: see Hood-mould.

DRUM: circular or polygonal vertical wall of a dome or cupola.

E.E. ('EARLY ENGLISH'): historical division of English Gothic architecture roughly covering the C13.

EASTER SEPULCHRE: recess with tomb-chest usually in the wall of a chancel, the tomb-chest to receive an effigy of Christ for Easter celebrations.

EAVES: underpart of a sloping roof overhanging a wall.

EAVES CORNICE: cornice below the eaves of a roof.

ECHINUS: Convex or projecting moulding supporting the abacus of a Greek Doric capital, sometimes bearing an egg and dart pattern.

EMBATTLED: see Battlement.

EMBRASURE: small opening in the wall or parapet of a fortified building, usually splayed on the inside.

ENCAUSTIC TILES: earthenware glazed and decorated tiles used for paving.

ENGAGED COLUMNS: columns attached to, or partly sunk into, a wall.

ENGLISH BOND: see Brickwork.

ENTABLATURE: in classical architecture the whole of the horizontal members above a column (that is architrave, frieze, and cornice) (see Fig. 12).

ENTASIS: very slight convex deviation from a straight line; used on Greek columns and sometimes on spires to prevent an optical illusion of concavity.

ENTRESOL: see Mezzanine.

EPITAPH: hanging wall monument.

ESCUTCHEON: shield for armorial bearings.

EXEDRA: the apsidal end of a room. See Apse.

FAN-VAULT: see Vault.

FERETORY: place behind the high altar where the chief shrine of a church is kept.

FESTOON: carved garland of flowers and fruit suspended at both ends.

FILLET: narrow flat band running down a shaft or along a roll moulding.

FINIAL: top of a canopy, gable, pinnacle.

FLAGON: vessel for the wine used in the Communion service.

FLAMBOYANT: properly the latest phase of French Gothic architecture where the window tracery takes on wavy undulating lines.

FLÈCHE: slender wooden spire on the centre of a roof (also called Spirelet).

FLEMISH BOND: *see* Brickwork.

FLEURON: decorative carved flower or leaf.

FLUSHWORK: decorative use of flint in conjunction with dressed stone so as to form patterns: tracery, initials, etc.

FLUTING: vertical channelling in the shaft of a column.

FLYING BUTTRESS: *see* Buttress.

FOIL: lobe formed by the cusping (q.v.) of a circle or an arch. Trefoil, quatrefoil, cinquefoil, multifoil, express the number of leaf shapes to be seen.

FOLIATED: carved with leaf shapes.

FOSSE: ditch.

FOUR-CENTRED ARCH: *see* Arch.

FRATER: refectory or dining hall of a monastery.

FRESCO: wall painting on wet plaster.

FRIEZE: middle division of a classical entablature (q.v.) (*see* Fig. 12).

FRONTAL: covering for the front of an altar.

GABLE: *Dutch gable:* A gable with curved sides crowned by a pediment, characteristic of c.1630–50 (Fig. 8a). *Shaped gable:* A gable with multi-curved sides characteristic of c.1600–50 (Fig. 8b).

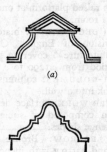

(a)

(b)

Fig. 8

GADROONED: enriched with a series of convex ridges, the opposite of fluting.

GALILEE: chapel or vestibule usually at the W end of a church enclosing the porch. Also called Narthex (q.v.).

GALLERY: in church architecture upper storey above an aisle, opened in arches to the nave. Also called Tribune and often erroneously Triforium (q.v.).

GALLERY GRAVE: chambered tomb (q.v.) in which there is little or no differentiation between the entrance passage and the actual burial chamber(s).

GARDEROBE: lavatory or privy in a medieval building.

GARGOYLE: water spout projecting from the parapet of a wall or tower; carved into a human or animal shape.

GAZEBO: lookout tower or raised summer house in a picturesque garden.

'GEOMETRICAL': *see* Tracery.

'GIBBS SURROUND': of a doorway or window. An c18 motif consisting of a surround with alternating larger and smaller blocks of stone, quoin-wise, or intermittent large blocks, sometimes with a narrow raised band connecting them up the verticals and along the face of the arch (Fig. 9).

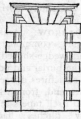

Fig. 9

GROIN: sharp edge at the meeting of two cells of a cross-vault.

GROIN-VAULT: *see* Vault.

GROTESQUE: fanciful ornamental decoration: *see also* Arabesque.

HAGIOSCOPE: *see* Squint.

HALF-TIMBERING: *see* Timber-Framing.

HALL CHURCH: church in which nave and aisles are of equal height or approximately so.

HAMMERBEAM: *see* Roof.

HANAP: large metal cup, generally made for domestic use, standing on an elaborate base and stem; with a very ornate cover frequently crowned with a little steeple.

HEADERS: *see* Brickwork.

HERRINGBONE WORK: brick, stone, or tile construction where the component blocks are laid diagonally instead of flat. Alternate courses lie in opposing directions to make a zigzag pattern up the face of the wall.

HEXASTYLE: having six detached columns.

HILL-FORT: Iron Age earthwork enclosed by a ditch and bank system; in the later part of the period the defences multiplied in size and complexity. They vary from about an acre to over 30 acres in area, and are usually built with careful regard to natural elevations or promontories.

HIPPED ROOF: *see* Roof.

HOOD-MOULD: projecting moulding above an arch or a lintel to throw off water (also called Dripstone or Label).

ICONOGRAPHY: the science of the subject matter of works of the visual arts.

IMPOST: bracket in a wall, usually formed of mouldings, on which the ends of an arch rest.

INDENT: shape chiselled out in a stone slab to receive a brass.

INGLENOOK: bench or seat built in beside a fireplace, sometimes covered by the chimneybreast, occasionally lit by small windows on each side of the fire.

INTERCOLUMNIATION: the space between columns.

IONIC: *see* Order (Fig. 12).

IRON AGE: in Britain the period from *c.* 600 B.C. to the coming of the Romans. The term is also used for those un-Romanized native communities which survived until the Saxon incursions.

JAMB: straight side of an archway, doorway, or window.

KEEL MOULDING: moulding whose outline is in section like that of the keel of a ship.

KEEP: massive tower of a Norman castle.

KEYSTONE: middle stone in an arch or a rib-vault.

KING-POST: see Roof (Fig. 14).

KNOP: a knob-like thickening in the stem of a chalice.

LABEL: see Hood-mould.

LABEL STOP: ornamental boss at the end of a hood-mould (q.v.).

LACED WINDOWS: windows pulled visually together by strips, usually in brick of a different colour, which continue vertically the lines of the vertical parts of the window surrounds. The motif is typical of c. 1720.

LANCET WINDOW: slender pointed-arched window.

LANTERN: in architecture, a small circular or polygonal turret with windows all round crowning a roof (see Cupola) or a dome.

LANTERN CROSS: churchyard cross with lantern-shaped top usually with sculptured representations on the sides of the top.

LEAN-TO ROOF: roof with one slope only, built against a higher wall.

LESENE or PILASTER STRIP: pilaster without base or capital.

LIERNE: see Vault (Fig. 21).

LINENFOLD: Tudor panelling ornamented with a conventional representation of a piece of linen laid in vertical folds. The piece is repeated in each panel.

LINTEL: horizontal beam or stone bridging an opening.

LOGGIA: recessed colonnade (q.v.).

LONG AND SHORT WORK: Saxon quoins (q.v.) consisting of stones placed with the long sides alternately upright and horizontal.

LONG BARROW: unchambered Neolithic communal burial mound, wedge-shaped in plan, with the burial and occasional other structures massed at the broader end, from which the mound itself tapers in height; quarry ditches flank the mound.

LOUVRE: opening, often with lantern (q.v.) over, in the roof of a room to let the smoke from a central hearth escape.

LOWER PALAEOLITHIC: see Palaeolithic.

LOZENGE: diamond shape.

LUCARNE: small opening to let light in.

LUNETTE: tympanum (q.v.) or semicircular opening.

LYCH GATE: wooden gate structure with a roof and open sides placed at the entrance to a churchyard to provide space for the reception of a coffin. The word lych is Saxon and means a corpse.

LYNCHET: long terraced strip of soil accumulating on the downward side of prehistoric and medieval fields due to soil creep from continuous ploughing along the contours.

MACHICOLATION: projecting gallery on brackets constructed on the outside of castle towers or walls. The gallery has holes the floor to drop missiles through.

MAJOLICA: ornamented glazed earthenware.

MANSARD: *see* Roof.

MATHEMATICAL TILES: Small facing tiles the size of brick headers, applied to timber-framed walls to make them appear brick-built.

MEGALITHIC TOMB: stone-built burial chamber of the New Stone Age covered by an earth or stone mound. The form was introduced to Britain from the Mediterranean area.

MERLON: *see* Battlement.

MESOLITHIC: 'Middle Stone' Age; the post-glacial period of hunting and fishing communities dating in Britain from *c.* 8000 B.C. to the arrival of Neolithic communities, with which they must have considerably overlapped.

METOPE: in classical architecture of the Doric order (q.v.) the space in the frieze between the triglyphs (Fig. 12).

MEZZANINE: low storey placed between two higher ones.

MISERERE: *see* Misericord.

MISERICORD: bracket placed on the underside of a hinged choir stall seat which, when turned up, provided the occupant of the seat with a support during long periods of standing (also called Miserere).

MODILLION: small bracket of which large numbers (modillion frieze) are often placed below a cornice (q.v.) in classical architecture.

MOTTE: steep mound forming the main feature of C11 and C12 castles.

MOTTE-AND-BAILEY: post-Roman and Norman defence system consisting of an earthen mound (the motte) topped with a wooden tower eccentrically placed within a bailey (q.v.), with enclosure ditch and palisade, and with the rare addition of an internal bank.

MOUCHETTE: tracery motif in curvilinear tracery, a curved dagger (q.v.), specially popular in the early C14 (Fig. 10).

Fig. 10

MULLION: vertical post or upright dividing a window into two or more 'lights'.

MULTIVALLATE: Of a hill-fort: defended by three or more concentric banks and ditches.

MUNTIN: post as a rule moulded and part of a screen.

NAIL-HEAD: E.E. ornamental motif, consisting of small pyramids regularly repeated (Fig. 11).

Fig. 11

NARTHEX: enclosed vestibule or covered porch at the main entrance to a church (*see* Galilee).

NEOLITHIC: 'New Stone' Age, dating in Britain from the appearance from the Continent of the first settled farming communities *c.* 3500 B.C. until the introduction of the Bronze Age.

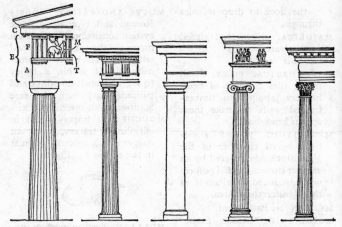

Fig. 12–Orders of Columns (Greek Doric, Roman Doric, Tuscan Doric, Ionic, Corinthian) E, Entablature; C, Cornice; F, Frieze; A, Architrave; M, Metope; T, Triglyph.

NEWEL: central post in a circular or winding staircase; also the principal post when a flight of stairs meets a landing.

NOOK-SHAFT: shaft set in the angle of a pier or respond or wall, or the angle of the jamb of a window or doorway.

OBELISK: lofty pillar of square section tapering at the top and ending pyramidally.

OGEE: see Arch (Fig. 1c).

ORATORY: small private chapel in a house.

ORDER: (1) of a doorway or window: series of concentric steps receding towards the opening; (2) in classical architecture: column with base, shaft, capital, and entablature (q.v.) according to one of the following styles: Greek Doric, Roman Doric, Tuscan Doric, Ionic, Corinthian, Composite. The established details are

very elaborate, and some specialist architectural work should be consulted for further guidance (see Fig. 12).

ORIEL: see Bay-Window.

OVERHANG: projection of the upper storey of a house.

OVERSAILING COURSES: series of stone or brick courses, each one projecting beyond the one below it.

PALAEOLITHIC: 'Old Stone' Age; the first period of human culture, commencing in the Ice Age and immediately prior to the Mesolithic; the Lower Palaeolithic is the older phase, the Upper Palaeolithic the later.

PALIMPSEST: (1) of a brass: where a metal plate has been re-used by turning over and engraving on the back; (2) of a wall painting: where one overlaps and partly obscures an earlier one.

PALLADIAN: architecture following the ideas and principles of Andrea Palladio, 1518–80.

PANTILE: tile of curved S-shaped section.

PARAPET: low wall placed to protect any spot where there is a sudden drop, for example on a bridge, quay, hillside, housetop, etc.

PARGETTING: plaster work with patterns and ornaments either in relief or engraved on it.

PARVIS: term wrongly applied to a room over a church porch. These rooms were often used as a schoolroom or as a store room.

PATEN: plate to hold the bread at Communion or Mass.

PATERA: small flat circular or oval ornament in classical architecture.

PEDIMENT: low-pitched gable used in classical, Renaissance, and neo-classical architecture above a portico and above doors, windows, etc. It may be straight-sided or curved segmentally. *Broken Pediment:* one where the centre portion of the base is left open. *Open Pediment:* one where the centre portion of the sloping sides is left out.

PENDANT: boss (q.v.) elongated so that it seems to hang down.

PENDENTIF: concave triangular spandrel used to lead from the angle of two walls to the base of a circular dome. It is constructed as part of the hemisphere over a diameter the size of the diagonal of the basic square (Fig. 13).

PERP (PERPENDICULAR): historical division of English Gothic architecture covering

20—W.K.W.

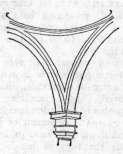

Fig. 13

the period from c.1335–50 to c.1530.

PIANO NOBILE: principal storey of a house with the reception rooms; usually the first floor.

PIAZZA: open space surrounded by buildings; in C17 and C18 England sometimes used to mean a long colonnade or loggia.

PIER: strong, solid support, frequently square in section or of composite section (compound pier).

PIETRA DURA: ornamental or scenic inlay by means of thin slabs of stone.

PILASTER: shallow pier attached to a wall. *Termini Pilasters:* pilasters with sides tapering downwards.

PILLAR PISCINA: free-standing piscina on a pillar.

PINNACLE: ornamental form crowning a spire, tower, buttress, etc., usually of steep pyramidal, conical, or some similar shape.

PISCINA: basin for washing the Communion or Mass vessels, provided with a drain. Generally set in or against the wall to the S of an altar.

PLAISANCE: summer-house, pleasure house near a mansion.

PLATE TRACERY: *see* Tracery.

PLINTH: projecting base of a wall or column, generally chamfered (q.v.) or moulded at the top.

POND BARROW: rare type of Bronze Age barrow consisting of a circular depression, usually paved, and containing a number of cremation burials.

POPPYHEAD: ornament of leaf and flower type used to decorate the tops of bench- or stall-ends.

PORTCULLIS: gate constructed to rise and fall in vertical grooves; used in gateways of castles.

PORTE COCHÈRE: porch large enough to admit wheeled vehicles.

PORTICO: centre-piece of a house or a church with classical detached or attached columns and a pediment. A portico is called *prostyle* or *in antis* according to whether it projects from or recedes into a building. In a portico *in antis* the columns range with the side walls.

POSTERN: small gateway at the back of a building.

PREDELLA: in an altarpiece the horizontal strip below the main representation, often used for a number of subsidiary representations in a row.

PRESBYTERY: the part of the church lying E of the choir. It is the part where the altar is placed.

PRINCIPAL: *see* Roof (Fig. 14).

PRIORY: monastic house whose head is a prior or prioress, not an abbot or abbess.

PROSTYLE: with free-standing columns in a row.

PULPITUM: stone screen in a major church provided to shut off the choir from the nave and also as a backing for the return choir stalls.

PULVINATED FRIEZE: frieze with a bold convex moulding.

PURLIN: *see* Roof (Figs. 14, 15).

PUTTO: small naked boy.

QUADRANGLE: inner courtyard in a large building.

QUARRY: in stained-glass work, a small diamond or square-shaped piece of glass set diagonally.

QUATREFOIL: *see* Foil.

QUEEN-POSTS: *see* Roof (Fig. 15).

QUOINS: dressed stones at the angles of a building. Sometimes all the stones are of the same size; more often they are alternately large and small.

RADIATING CHAPELS: chapels projecting radially from an ambulatory or an apse.

RAFTER: *see* Roof.

RAMPART: stone wall or wall of earth surrounding a castle, fortress, or fortified city.

RAMPART-WALK: path along the inner face of a rampart.

REBATE: continuous rectangular notch cut on an edge.

REBUS: pun, a play on words. The literal translation and illustration of a name for artistic and heraldic purposes (Belton = bell, tun).

RECUSANT CHALICE: chalice made after the Reformation and before Catholic Emancipation for Roman Catholic use.

REEDING: decoration with parallel convex mouldings touching one another.

REFECTORY: dining hall; *see* Frater.

RENDERING: plastering of an outer wall.

REPOUSSÉ: decoration of metal work by relief designs, formed by beating the metal from the back.

REREDOS: structure behind and above an altar.

RESPOND: half-pier bonded into a wall and carrying one end of an arch.

RETABLE: altarpiece, a picture or piece of carving, standing behind and attached to an altar.

RETICULATION: *see* Tracery (Fig. 20*e*).

REVEAL: that part of a jamb (q.v.) which lies between the glass or door and the outer surface of the wall.

RIB-VAULT: *see* Vault.

ROCOCO: latest phase of the Baroque style, current in most Continental countries between *c.* 1720 and *c.* 1760.

ROLL MOULDING: moulding of semicircular or more than semicircular section.

ROMANESQUE: that style in architecture which was current in the CII and CI2 and preceded the Gothic style (in England often called Norman). (Some scholars extend the use of the term Romanesque back to the CIO or C9.)

ROMANO-BRITISH: A somewhat vague term applied to the period and cultural features of Britain affected by the Roman occupation of the CI–5 A.D.

ROOD: cross or crucifix.

ROOD LOFT: singing gallery on the top of the rood screen, often supported by a coving.

ROOD SCREEN: *see* Screen.

ROOD STAIRS: stairs to give access to the rood loft.

ROOF: *Single-framed:* if consisting entirely of transverse members (such as rafters with or without braces, collars, tie-beams, king-posts or queen-posts, etc.) not tied together longitudinally. *Double-framed:* if longitudinal members (such as a ridge beam and purlins) are employed. As a rule in such cases the rafters are divided into stronger principals and weaker subsidiary rafters.

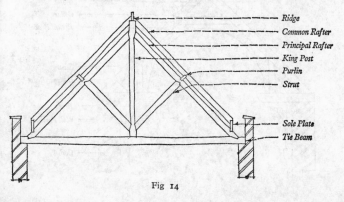

Fig 14

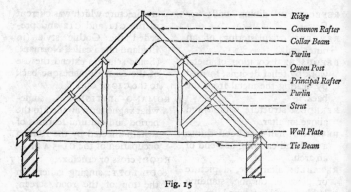

Fig. 15

Hipped: roof with sloped instead of vertical ends. Mansard: roof with a double slope, the lower slope being larger and steeper than the upper. Saddleback: tower roof shaped like an ordinary gabled timber roof. The following members have special names: Rafter: roof-timber sloping up from the wall plate to the ridge. Principal: principal rafter, usually corresponding to the main bay divisions of the nave or chancel below. Wall Plate: timber laid longitudinally on the top of a wall. Purlin: longitudinal member laid parallel with wall plate and ridge beam some way up the slope of the roof. Tie-beam: beam connecting the two slopes of a roof across at its foot, usually at the height of the wall plate, to prevent the roof from spreading. Collar-beam: tie-beam applied higher up the slope of the roof. Strut: upright timber connecting the

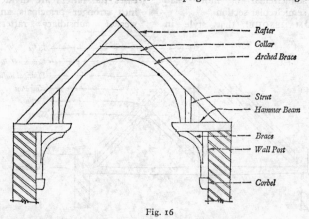

Fig. 16

tie-beam with the rafter above it. *King-post:* upright timber connecting a tie-beam and collar-beam with the ridge beam. *Queen-posts:* two struts placed symmetrically on a tie-beam or collar-beam. *Braces:* inclined timbers inserted to strengthen others. Usually braces connect a collar-beam with the rafters below or a tie-beam with the wall below. Braces can be straight or curved (also called arched). *Hammer-beam:* beam projecting at right angles, usually from the top of a wall, to carry arched braces or struts and arched braces. (*See* Figs. 14, 15, 16.)

ROSE WINDOW (or WHEEL WINDOW): circular window with patterned tracery arranged to radiate from the centre.

ROTUNDA: building circular in plan.

RUBBLE: building stones, not square or hewn, nor laid in regular courses.

RUSTICATION: *rock-faced* if the surfaces of large blocks of ashlar stone are left rough like rock; *smooth* if the ashlar blocks are smooth and separated by V-joints; *banded* if the separation by V-joints applies only to the horizontals.

Saddleback: *see* Roof.

SALTIRE CROSS: equal-limbed cross placed diagonally.

SANCTUARY: (1) area around the main altar of a church (*see* Presbytery); (2) sacred site consisting of wood or stone uprights enclosed by a circular bank and ditch. Beginning in the Neolithic, they were elaborated in the succeeding Bronze Age. The best known examples are Stonehenge and Avebury.

SARCOPHAGUS: elaborately carved coffin.

SCAGLIOLA: material composed of cement and colouring matter to imitate marble.

SCALLOPED CAPITAL: development of the block capital (q.v.) in which the single semi-circular surface is elaborated into a series of truncated cones (Fig. 17).

Fig. 17

SCARP: artificial cutting away of the ground to form a steep slope.

SCREEN: *Parclose screen:* screen separating a chapel from the rest of a church. *Rood screen:* screen below the rood (q.v.), usually at the w end of a chancel.

SCREENS PASSAGE: passage between the entrances to kitchen, buttery, etc., and the screen behind which lies the hall of a medieval house.

SEDILIA: seats for the priests (usually three) on the s side of the chancel of a church.

SEGMENTAL ARCH: *see* Arch.

SET-OFF: *see* Weathering.

SEXPARTITE: *see* Vault.

SGRAFFITO: pattern incised into plaster so as to expose a dark surface underneath.

SHAFT-RING: motif of the C12 and C13 consisting of a ring round a circular pier or a shaft attached to a pier.

SHEILA-NA-GIG: fertility figure, usually with legs wide open.

SILL: lower horizontal part of the frame of a window.

SLATEHANGING: the covering of walls by overlapping rows of slates, on a timber substructure.

SOFFIT: underside of an arch, lintel, etc.

SOLAR: upper living-room of a medieval house.

SOPRAPORTE: painting above the door of a room, usual in the C17 and C18.

SOUNDING BOARD: horizontal board or canopy over a pulpit. Also called Tester.

SPANDREL: triangular surface between one side of an arch, the horizontal drawn from its apex, and the vertical drawn from its springer; also the surface between two arches.

SPERE-TRUSS: roof truss on two free-standing posts to mask the division between screens passage and hall. The screen itself, where a spere-truss exists, was originally movable.

SPIRE: tall pyramidal or conical pointed erection often built on top of a tower, turret, etc. *Broach Spire:* spire which is generally octagonal in plan rising from the top or parapet of a square tower. A small inclined piece of masonry covers the vacant triangular space at each of the four angles of the square and is carried up to a point along the diagonal sides of the octagon. *Needle Spire:* thin spire rising from the centre of a tower roof, well inside the parapet.

SPIRELET: *see* Flèche.

SPLAY: chamfer, usually of the jamb of a window.

SPRINGING: level at which an arch rises from its supports.

SQUINCH: arch or system of concentric arches thrown across the angle between two walls to support a superstructure, for example a dome (Fig. 18).

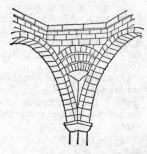

Fig. 18

SQUINT: hole cut in a wall or through a pier to allow a view of the main altar of a church from places whence it could not otherwise be seen (also called Hagioscope).

STALL: carved seat, one of a row, made of wood or stone.

STAUNCHION: upright iron or steel member.

STEEPLE: the tower of a church together with a spire, cupola, etc.

STIFF-LEAF: E.E. type of foliage of many-lobed shapes (Fig. 19).

STILTED: *see* Arch.

STOREY-POSTS: the principal posts of a timber-framed wall.

STOUP: vessel for the reception of holy water, usually placed near a door.

Fig. 19

STRAINER ARCH: arch inserted across a room to prevent the walls from leaning.

STRAPWORK: C16 decoration consisting of interlaced bands, and forms similar to fretwork or cut and bent leather.

STRETCHER: see Brickwork.

STRING COURSE: projecting horizontal band or moulding set in the surface of a wall.

STRUT: see Roof.

STUCCO: plaster work.

STUDS: the subsidiary vertical timber members of a timber-framed wall.

SWAG: festoon formed by a carved piece of cloth suspended from both ends.

TABERNACLE: richly ornamented niche or free-standing canopy. Usually contains the Holy Sacrament.

TARSIA: inlay in various woods.

TAZZA: shallow bowl on a foot.

TERMINAL FIGURES (TERMS, TERMINI): upper part of a human figure growing out of a pier, pilaster, etc., which tapers towards the base. See also Caryatid, Pilaster.

TERRACOTTA: burnt clay, unglazed.

TESSELLATED PAVEMENT: mosaic flooring, particularly Roman, consisting of small 'tesserae' or cubes of glass, stone, or brick.

TESSERAE: see Tessellated Pavement.

TESTER: see Sounding Board.

TETRASTYLE: having four detached columns.

THREE-DECKER PULPIT: pulpit with Clerk's Stall below and Reading Desk below the Clerk's Stall.

TIE-BEAM: see Roof (Figs. 14, 15).

TIERCERON: see Vault (Fig. 21).

TILEHANGING: see Slatehanging.

TIMBER-FRAMING: method of construction where walls are built of timber framework with the spaces filled in by plaster or brickwork. Sometimes the timber is covered over with plaster or boarding laid horizontally.

TOMB-CHEST: chest-shaped stone coffin, the most usual medieval form of funeral monument.

TOUCH: soft black marble quarried near Tournai.

TOURELLE: turret corbelled out from the wall.

TRACERY: intersecting ribwork in the upper part of a window, or used decoratively in blank arches, on vaults, etc. *Plate tracery: see* Fig. 20(*a*). Early form of tracery where decoratively shaped openings are cut through the solid stone infilling in a window head. *Bar tracery:* a form introduced into England *c.* 1250. Intersecting ribwork made up of slender shafts, continuing the lines of the mullions of windows up to a decorative mesh in the head of the window. *Geometrical tracery: see* Fig. 20(*b*). Tracery characteristic of *c.* 1250–1310 consisting chiefly of circles of foiled circles. *Y-tracery: see*

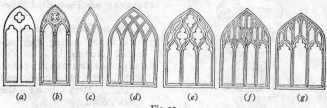

(a)   (b)   (c)   (d)   (e)   (f)   (g)

Fig. 20

Fig. 20(c). Tracery consisting of a mullion which branches into two forming a Y shape; typical of *c.* 1300. *Intersecting tracery: see* Fig. 20(d). Tracery in which each mullion of a window branches out into two curved bars in such a way that every one of them is drawn with the same radius from a different centre. The result is that every light of the window is a lancet and every two, three, four, etc., lights together form a pointed arch. This treatment also is typical of *c.* 1300. *Reticulated tracery: see* Fig. 20(e). Tracery typical of the early C14 consisting entirely of circles drawn at top and bottom into ogee shapes so that a net-like appearance results. *Panel tracery: see* Fig. 20(f) *and* (g). Perp tracery, which is formed of upright straight-sided panels above lights of a window.

TRANSEPT: transverse portion of a cross-shaped church.

TRANSOM: horizontal bar across the openings of a window.

TRANSVERSE ARCH: *see* Vault.

TRIBUNE: *see* Gallery.

TRICIPUT, SIGNUM TRICIPUT: sign of the Trinity expressed by three faces belonging to one head.

TRIFORIUM: arcaded wall pas-sage or blank arcading facing the nave at the height of the aisle roof and below the clere-story (q.v.) windows. (*See* Gallery.)

TRIGLYPHS: blocks with vertical grooves separating the metopes (q.v.) in the Doric frieze (Fig. 12).

TROPHY: sculptured group of arms or armour, used as a memorial of victory.

TRUMEAU: stone mullion (q.v.) supporting the tympanum (q.v.) of a wide doorway.

TUMULUS: *see* Barrow.

TURRET: very small tower, round or polygonal in plan.

TUSCAN: *see* Order.

TYMPANUM: space between the lintel of a doorway and the arch above it.

UNDERCROFT: vaulted room, sometimes underground, be-low a church or chapel.

UNIVALLATE: of a hill-fort: defended by a single bank and ditch.

UPPER PALAEOLITHIC: *see* Palaeolithic.

VAULT: *Barrel-vault: see* Tunnel-vault. *Cross-vault: see* Groin-vault. *Domical vault:* square or polygonal dome ris-

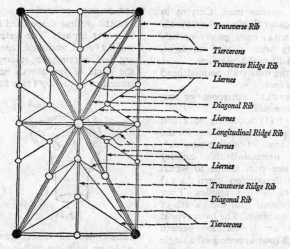

Transverse Rib

Tiercerons

Transverse Ridge Rib

Liernes

Diagonal Rib

Liernes

Longitudinal Ridge Rib

Liernes

Liernes

Transverse Ridge Rib

Diagonal Rib

Tiercerons

Fig. 21

ing direct on a square or polygonal bay, the curved surfaces separated by groins (q.v.). *Fan-vault:* Late Medieval vault where all ribs springing from one springer are of the same length, the same distance from the next, and the same curvature. *Groin-vault* or *Cross-vault:* vault of two tunnel-vaults of identical shape intersecting each other at r. angles. Chiefly Norman and Renaissance. *Lierne:* tertiary rib, that is, rib which does not spring either from one of the main springers or from the central boss. Introduced in the C14, continues to the C16. *Quadripartite vault:* one wherein one bay of vaulting is divided into four parts. *Rib-vault:* vault with diagonal ribs projecting along the groins. *Ridge-rib:* rib along the longitudinal

21—W.K.W.

or transverse ridge of a vault. Introduced in the early C13. *Sexpartite vault:* one wherein one bay of quadripartite vaulting is divided into two parts transversely so that each bay of vaulting has six parts. *Tierceron:* secondary rib, that is, rib which issues from one of the main springers or the central boss and leads to a place on a ridge-rib. Introduced in the early C13. *Transverse arch:* arch separating one bay of a vault from the next. *Tunnel-vault* or *Barrel-vault:* vault of semicircular or pointed section. Chiefly Norman and Renaissance. (*See* Fig. 21.)

VAULTING SHAFT: vertical member leading to the springer of a vault.

VENETIAN WINDOW: window with three openings, the central one arched and wider than the outside ones. Current in England chiefly in the C17–18.

VERANDA: open gallery or balcony with a roof on light, usually metal, supports.

VESICA: oval with pointed head and foot.

VESTIBULE: anteroom or entrance hall.

VILLA: (1) according to Gwilt (1842) 'a country house for the residence of opulent persons'; (2) Romano-British country houses cum farms, to which the description given in (1) more or less applies. They developed with the growth of urbanization. The basic type is the simple corridor pattern with rooms opening off a single passage; the next stage is the addition of wings. The courtyard villa fills a square plan with subsidiary buildings and an enclosure wall with a gate facing the main corridor block.

VITRIFIED: made similar to glass.

VITRUVIAN OPENING: A door or window which diminishes towards the top, as advocated by Vitruvius, bk. IV, chapter VI.

VOLUTE: spiral scroll, one of the component parts of an Ionic column (see Order).

VOUSSOIR: wedge-shaped stone used in arch construction.

WAGON ROOF: roof in which by closely set rafters with arched braces the appearance of the inside of a canvas tilt over a wagon is achieved. Wagon roofs can be panelled or plastered (ceiled) or left uncovered.

WAINSCOT: timber lining to walls.

WALL PLATE: see Roof.

WATERLEAF: leaf shape used in later C12 capitals. The waterleaf is a broad, unribbed, tapering leaf curving up towards the angle of the abacus and turned in at the top (Fig. 22).

Fig. 22

WEALDEN HOUSE: timber-framed house with the hall in the centre and wings projecting only slightly and only on the jutting upper floor. The roof, however, runs through without a break between wings and hall, and the eaves of the hall part are therefore exceptionally deep. They are supported by diagonal, usually curved, braces starting from the short inner sides of the overhanging wings and rising parallel with the front wall of the hall towards the centre of the eaves.

WEATHERBOARDING: overlapping horizontal boards, covering a timber-framed wall.

WEATHERING: sloped horizontal surface on sills, buttresses, etc., to throw off water.

WEEPERS: small figures placed in niches along the sides of some medieval tombs (also called Mourners).

WHEEL WINDOW: see Rose Window.

INDEX OF PLATES

INDEX OF ARTISTS

INDEX OF PLACES

ADDENDA

(JANUARY 1969)

p. 133 [Ashford.] ½ m. further w, between Brunswick Road and the railway, a new FACTORY, for Walter Jones & Co. by *Arup Associates*, illustrated in 1968.

p. 145 [Beckenham.] Further w in The Avenue some remarkably sculptural low-rise flats are going up, in white brick with far-projecting concrete staircase ramps. The architects are *Derek Sharp Associates*.

p. 155 [Bexleyheath, Danson Park.] Taylor certainly employed Casali elsewhere, e.g. at Asgill House, Richmond, with results similar to these. But a booklet on Danson Park published in 1924 asserts that the Dining Room paintings were done in 1766 by 'C. Pavillo'. Mrs Ruth Hutcherson makes the attractive suggestion that this may mean *Charles Pavillon*, a French painter who exhibited decorative pictures in the earliest years of the R.A. and died in Edinburgh in 1771. The Danson paintings are apparently unsigned, and the booklet does not reveal the source of its information.

p. 167 [Boughton Malherbe, St Nicholas.] Hasted's account of the pyramidal monument does not agree with Harris's in his *History of Kent*, as the Rev L. E. C. Evans kindly pointed out to me. The inscriptions on the faces of the pyramid are exceedingly worn, but with Mr Evans's help I have deciphered enough to say that Harris, not Hasted, is right: Katherine, Countess of Chesterfield, erected the monument to Daniel O'Neale, her third husband, 'as one of the last markes of her kindness to shew her Affection longer then her weake Breath could serve to expresse it'. Inscriptions on the other faces record her death, and that of her first husband, Henry, Lord Stanhope, † 1635.

p. 312 [Hever Castle.] The collection of Roman sculpture has been listed and briefly discussed by Dr Donald Strong in *Connoisseur* (April 1968), pp. 215ff. The choicest pieces to look out for are: the circular WELL HEAD with dancing Maenads, in the Chess Garden; the porphyry BATH SUPPORT, a rare survival of classical furniture, of the C2 A.D.; two especially fine Roman ALTARS of the C1 A.D., one in use as the base of a statute of Ganymede; and above all the SARCOPHAGI. There are fourteen of these altogether, some fragmentary. The earliest, mid C2 A.D., is carved with the Labours of Hercules. The other outstanding examples are one with putti holding swags and small narrative scenes (a Hadrianic type), and a round-ended one with Bacchanalian scenes and handles in the form of lion heads. This Dr Strong dates *c*. A.D. 300.

p. 319 [Hoo.] The HEAD OFFICE for Berry Wiggins & Co., by the *Austin Smith, Salmon, Lord Partnership*, has recently been illustrated, for its resourceful use of concrete.

p. 350 [Lamberhurst, St Mary.] Mrs Jill Allibone tells me of drawings by Edward Hussey which record work done in the 1870s. At that time two further lancets were exposed, low in the N and S walls of the S chapel. They suggest that the church originally extended (stepping down the hill?) further to the E.

p. 376 [Lydd.] The results of Mr Jackson's and Sir Eric Fletcher's recent excavations are reported in the 1968 number of the *Journal of the British Archaeological Association*. They establish as far as will ever be possible the form of the early basilica: that it probably had a semicircular apse of 8 ft radius, that the N aisle was 8 ft wide, that there was a grand W entrance to the nave and a W annex more extensive than had hitherto been assumed. Recent geological research has shown that a big area round Lydd was never inundated in Late Roman times like the rest of Romney Marsh.

p. 392 [Maidstone.] The CHURCH INSTITUTE was demolished in 1968. Probably few tears were shed; but this was a lively, characterful building, which Maidstone, of all places, could ill afford to lose.

p. 394 [Maidstone.] The sloping roof at the back of GROVE HOUSE having been built up, it is now no longer worth a look.

p. 417 [New Romney.] Also in the High Street, ELECTRIC HOUSE, which Mr S. E. Rigold reports to be at its heart a stone-built house of the C14, of single-aisled construction.

p. 420 [Northfleet.] The timber-framed house, ¼ m. N of the church, in SPRINGHEAD ROAD, though badly over-restored, is worth a note, because it was built as the Rectory. Wealden construction. Information from Mr P. J. Tester.

p. 433 [Pembury.] KENWARD, ½ m. NW. A typical medium-sized Victorian Gothic mansion, built by *R. H. Carpenter* in 1875 on the foundations of Decimus Burton's classical Spring Grove. It is instructive to see how Carpenter has conjured a varied and irregular outline from the rectangular plan.

p. 473 [Rochester.] WARREN WOOD SECONDARY SCHOOL FOR GIRLS, City Way. 1953 by *Yorke, Rosenberg & Mardall*. In the same high class as their school at Whitstable.

p. 535 [Sutton-at-Hone.] Since this was written Sutton Place has been pulled down.
At HAWLEY MANOR, 1 m. N, there is a fine Elizabethan brick DOVECOTE (P. J. Tester's information).

p. 540 [Swanscombe, All Saints.] Since the time of writing, the two Venetian paintings have been sold, and the others restored. Mr W. Mostyn-Owen considers the Virgin and Child 'closer to *Giuliano Bugiardini*', and the Crucifixion to be only 'Carracci style'. (Information kindly communicated by Mr Jeremy White.)

p. 553 [Tunbridge Wells.] The story seems in essence to be true. The steward at Eridge, however, recording his grandfather's eye-witness account, dates Lord North's discovery 1615 or 1616 and implies that he realized its commercial potential at once (*Camden Miscellany*, III (1855), pp. v-vi). Lord North himself claimed to have discovered Epsom waters as well, concluding enigmatically: 'Much more I could say, but I rather hint than handle, – rather open a door to a large prospect than give it' (Amsinck, *Tunbridge Wells*, 1810, p. 4).

p. 571 [Westerham.] A seated STATUE of Westerham's other local hero, Sir Winston Churchill, is due to be set up on The Green in 1969. The sculptor is *Oscar Nemon*.

p. 581 [West Peckham, Oxen Hoath.] Mrs Jill Allibone has recently identified a drawing by *Salvin* at the R.I.B.A. as a design for Oxen Hoath, datable *c.*1846-7. The surprising thing is that the Frenchy roof and dormers are all there, plus a separate steep, sharp, hipped roof over the entrance bay, now removed. One did not suspect Salvin of Francophilia, which at this early date is noteworthy. So what did Burn & McVicar Anderson do in 1878?